THE
UNIVERSITY ED
of the

Handbook of Evaluation Research

THE SOCIETY FOR THE PSYCHOLOGICAL STUDY OF SOCIAL ISSUES (SPSSI)

The Society for the Psychological Study of Social Issues was the sponsor of the original two-volume *Handbook of Evaluation Research*. This sponsorship was part of the Society's publication program, which is geared toward the encouragement of theoretically meaningful and empirically sound research on social issues. The *Handbook* has become a standard reference in evaluation. The present publication includes selected chapters from the original volumes, with updated bibliographies. SPSSI is pleased to sponsor this new edition in order to increase the availability of this important work for students and others involved in evaluation research.

—Lois Wladis Hoffman
SPSSI President

THE
UNIVERSITY EDITION
of the

Handbook of Evaluation Research

Edited by
ELMER L. STRUENING
New York State
Office of Mental Health
Psychiatric Institute
and *Columbia University*

and
MARILYNN B. BREWER
University of California, Los Angeles

Sponsored by the
SOCIETY FOR THE PSYCHOLOGICAL
STUDY OF SOCIAL ISSUES

 SAGE PUBLICATIONS   Beverly Hills / London / New Delhi

Copyright © 1983 by Sage Publications, Inc.

For information address:

SAGE Publications, Inc.
275 South Beverly Drive
Beverly Hills, California 90212

SAGE Publications India Pvt. Ltd.
C-236 Defence Colony
New Delhi 110 024, India

SAGE Publications Ltd
28 Banner Street
London EC1Y 8QE, England

Printed in the United States of America

Library of Congress Cataloging in Publication Data

Main entry under title:

The University edition of the Handbook of evaluation research.

    Includes bibliographies and index.
    1. Social sciences—Methodology—Addresses, essays,
lectures. 2. Evaluation research (Social action programs)
—Addresses, essays, lectures. I. Struening, Elmer L.
(Elmer Louis), 1924- . II. Brewer, Marilynn B.,
1942- . III. Handbook of evaluation research.
H62.U58   1983   300'.72   83-22899
ISBN 0-8039-2162-4 (pbk.)

FIRST PRINTING

CONTENTS

This
volume
is
dedicated
to
the memory
of

Marcia Guttentag
1932-1977

Good Friend and Esteemed Colleague
Co-editor
of the
Handbook of Evaluation Research
and
Former President
of
The Society for the Psychological Study
of
Social Issues

ACKNOWLEDGMENTS

The editors thank the contributors to the *Handbook* who agreed to reprint their articles in the present edition and to provide supplementary bibliographic materials. We appreciate the willingness of the following publishers to grant permission to reproduce previously published articles or selected portions of books: American Psychological Association, McGraw-Hill Book Company, Brunner/Mazel, Inc., Oxford University Press, and Baywood Publishing Co.

We also gratefully acknowledge the contribution of the following individuals who helped in the development of the present volume: Mattie L. Jones, Bruce G. Link, William D. Neigher, and Charles Windle.

PREFACE

The original two-volume *Handbook of Evaluation Research* was the product of the collective effort of an interdisciplinary team of social scientists, many of whom could be counted among the founders of evaluation research. Guidance for the development of the *Handbook* came from an editorial planning committee established by the Society for the Psychological Study of Social Issues, whose membership included Donald T. Campbell, Isidor Chein, Jacob Cohen, Howard Davis, Ward Edwards, Nathan Gage, Terence Hopkins, Hylan Lewis, Peter Rossi, M. Brewster Smith, and Lauren Wispé. The initial planning of the work was supported by a small grant from the Society for the Psychological Study of Social Issues and continued with the support of a contract from the Mental Health Services Branch of the National Institute of Mental Health.

The *Handbook* was intended to serve as both a sourcebook of expert opinion and a text for courses in evaluation at the graduate level. Over its eight-year history it has become a standard reference in the field and a source of text materials for a generation of applied social scientists. The production of this abridged "university edition" of the *Handbook* was prompted largely by a recognition of the role of the *Handbook* in graduate training and a desire to make the core contents available to new cohorts of students and practicing evaluators. Selected for inclusion in this edition were those contributions that have proven to be most utilized for instructional purposes because of their status as "classic" treatments of major issues in the field of evaluation research. In addition, these selections have been supplemented by an expanded bibliography appended to each article to update the student on developments that have taken place since the original publication. All told, the edition contains a listing of over 400 new references that have been compiled by the senior editor and/or the chapter authors, making this volume an important and useful resource. Thus this one volume provides both original contributions and a ready source of bibliographic materials representing the current state of the art in program evaluation methodology and philosophy.

—E.L.S. and M.B.B.

I

INTRODUCTION

EVALUATION: PAST AND PRESENT

MARILYNN B. BREWER

Institute for Social Science Research
University of California, Los Angeles

When the *Handbook* originally appeared in late 1975, it helped shape a newly emerging field of applied social science, which came to be known as "program evaluation research." Initially conceived as a field of applied methodology, program evaluation provided an opportunity for social scientists to work with policymakers in trying to assess the impact of governmental programs designed to cure social ills or promote social change. Early treatises on evaluation research design (for example, Cronbach, 1963; Campbell, 1969; Fairweather, 1967; Suchman, 1967) originated in the various social science disciplines—primarily psychology, education, and economics—and reflected the methodological predilections of the parent disciplines. Quite rapidly, however, the field evolved into a separate specialization, distinct from its diverse origins. By 1976, a number of textbooks and anthologies in the area had appeared (for example, in addition to the *Handbook,* Anderson, Ball, Murphy, et al., 1975; Bennett & Lumsdaine, 1975; Glass, 1976; Riecken & Boruch, 1974; Rossi & Williams, 1972; Weiss, 1972), journals devoted specifically to program evaluation were being developed (such as *Evaluation Quarterly,* subsequently *Evaluation Review; Evaluation and Program Planning;* and *Studies in Educational Evaluation*), and the Evaluation Research Society (ERS) was founded. (The Council for Applied Social Research was also founded in the same year and later merged with ERS.) Evaluation research soon became international in scope, with concomitant development occurring in Europe and elsewhere (Levine et al., 1981).

Impetus to the rapid development of program evaluation as a field of applied social research came from the Great Society programs of Lyndon Johnson's administration in the 1960s. Federal programs—many of them initiated by the Office of Economic Opportunity—were subjected to large-scale quantitative evaluation. Because of this association with federal agencies, single, nationwide evaluations of federally funded social programs became the modal or dominant form of evaluation research. Characteristic of this period were such massive national studies as the evaluation of Head Start (Cicirelli et al., 1969), Title I of the Elementary and Secondary Education Act (McLaughlin, 1975), the Manpower Development and Training Act (Main, 1968), the Educational Performance Contracting Experiments (Garfinkle & Gramlich, 1973), Follow-Through Planned Variations (Cline et al., 1975; Rivlin & Timpane, 1975), and the Negative Income Tax Experiment (Kershaw & Fair, 1976; Rossi & Lyall, 1976). During the same time period, the Veterans Administration was supporting some large-scale evaluations in the organization of mental health services (Fairweather et al., 1974). For 1970 alone, Bernstein and Freeman (1975) were able to identify 382 federally funded evaluation research studies of federal programs.

Through experience—both positive and negative—with this type of large-scale evaluation project, the field of evaluation research matured rapidly and visibly. Evaluation research itself underwent evaluation (for example, see Bernstein, & Freeman 1975; Cronbach et al., 1980; Wholey, 1979), and controversies developed around issues such as the proper role of evaluation research in political decision making, the most appropriate research approaches, and the organization of evaluation research efforts. Some of these controversies reflect fundamental differences among evaluation researchers and utilizers as to the nature and purpose of program evaluation studies, differences that reflect the diverse origins of the field. A number of such issues are discussed below in order to provide a contextual framework for the selected readings included in the present volume.

EVALUATION RESEARCH AND SOCIAL POLICY

Science Versus Policy

The original proponents of evaluation research clearly recognized that the purposes of such research were different from those of basic science. Yet the basic concept of the field was that of extending the scientific model into the domain of policymaking, and adherence to the traditions of scientific methodology was the hallmark of evaluation research, distinguishing it from other forms of political fact-finding. But science and politics do not always mix well, and some tension between scientific "respectability" and policy relevance of research has been intrinsic to the field from its inception (Weiss, 1981).

Some of the tension derives from confusion about the role of evaluation research in the political decision-making process. Evaluation research was intended to *inform* policymaking, not to *replace* political process. But the role of consultant is easily confused with that of advocate, and in many instances the results of evaluation studies were touted as *the* basis for administrative decision making, with the promise of providing a single, definite answer to whether a particular social program was worthwhile or not. Such a conception of the role of evaluation research is incompatible with both the scientific model and with realities of political decision making. First of all, science recognizes that the results of any single investigation are equivocal and should never be considered in isolation from other results and theory. In the second place, while decisions— such as to fund or not to fund—may be binary in nature, evidence about program outcomes comes in the form of *degrees* of effect that have to be interpreted subjectively as to whether they represent a meaningful or practically significant result. Finally, political decisions rest on many factors besides the demonstrated effectiveness of a program in meeting specific goals. As Berk and Rossi (1976, p. 344) put it: "While evaluation research is political, it is no substitute for politics. Social science can demystify, but it remains the task of politics to interpret the meaning of demystification for direction of political policy."

If the task of evaluation research is taken to be more modest than that of substituting for political process, then it is important to clarify at what points in the policymaking process research data might be informative, and what types of research would be most useful at those different points. The various functions that have been identified for empirical research in policymaking include the following:

Needs assessment. At early stages of policy formation there is a need for accurate information about the extent and distribution of a given social problem. At this point personal testimony and experience can be supplemented with quantitative data derived from survey or observational studies. In 1968, for instance, the Office of Economic Opportunity designed a Survey of Economic Opportunity to provide an assessment of the extent and distribution of poverty in urban areas, and the Coleman et al. (1966) report was mandated by Congress to assess how educational services and facilities were distributed among the poor. Such research is essentially descriptive and its quality depends primarily on the adequacy of measures and sampling techniques employed.

Policy-oriented research. One link between basic research, oriented toward understanding the processes underlying a given social phenomenon, and social policy is research designed explicitly to determine how policies and programs might affect the phenomenon in question. Such policy-oriented research is concerned not only with the causes of a particular social problem, but, more specifically, with those causes that might be amenable to changes in public policy. So, for instance, while a basic social science analysis of delinquent behavior might look at effects of family interaction patterns, policy research would be more interested in the effects of school environment, since in our system the latter are subject to policy intervention, while the former are not.

Program development. Pilot studies of programs at their initial conceptual- ization stage·provide a valuable research opportunity in which controlled experiments can be undertaken to test program concepts on a small scale. The purpose of evaluation research at this stage is not to assess the overall impact of the program but to provide feedback to program developers that can lead to changes or alterations in the program design. Research conducted in the service of program development is often referred to as "formative evaluation" (Scriven, 1967).

Feasibility studies. Once a social program or intervention has been designed, the next question is whether or how the program can be implemented on a large scale through existing agencies or institutions. Feasibility studies are designed to assess whether the program as planned can be delivered within various organizational contexts. The purpose of such field testing is not to assess the effectiveness of the program in meeting its ultimate goals but more simply to determine whether the program components can be implemented as intended and whether the services reach the target populations.

Evaluation of program effectiveness. Addressing the question of whether or not a specific social program has had an effect on the social problem it was designed to alleviate—"summative evaluation" (Scriven, 1967)—is what most regard as the essence of evaluation research. We place it here in the context of other evaluation-relevant activities in order to distinguish it from these other research purposes and to make clear that not all evaluation tasks call for effectiveness assessment. The effectiveness question is inevitably one of *causal* hypothesis testing—did the program have an impact above and beyond what would have happened in the absence of the program? Research directed toward answering such a question requires a number of prior conditions that make the program potentially evaluable in this sense. Among the requisite conditions for effectiveness evaluation are (1) that the goals or objectives of the program be sufficiently specified to allow for definable outcomes, (2) that the program be well enough defined to determine whether it is present or absent in a given setting, and (3) that some basis for observing or estimating the state of outcomes in the absence of the program be available for *comparison* to program outcomes. All of these conditions are not easily met, and many of the problems associated with program evaluation can be traced to instances in which evaluators or policy-makers have attempted to do effectiveness assessments in settings where feasibility or developmental evaluation efforts would have been more appropriate.

Cost-benefit analysis. The analysis of program benefits relative to program costs requires not only assessing *whether* that program has had an effect but also estimating the *size* of the effect associated with the program. Relatively few full-fledged cost-benefit evaluations have been done of social programs, in part because of the difficulties of obtaining good effectiveness estimates and in part because of the absence of a common "yardstick" for measuring both costs and effects in the social domain. Nonetheless, some models are available for research comparing the size of effects associated with alternative programs that share common goals but different dollar costs.

Evaluation Versus Accountability

Just as the goals of evaluation research need to be distinguished from those of basic science, it is important to distinguish between program evaluation and evaluation of program administrators. Evaluation research has been intimately associated with the so-called accountability movement in public administration, with attendant confusions of roles and purposes. Program monitoring requires that program administrators provide adequate records of funds expended and documentation that expenditures are associated with delivery of intended services. Accountability usually involves assessment of the fiscal records or management practices of specific administrators or particular program sites, relative to some performance standards or criteria. Program effectiveness evaluation, on the other hand, involves assessment of effects of the program in its generic sense, in comparison to alternative programs or program strategies. Unfortunately, good effectiveness research usually requires some information on program implementation in specific sites and hence almost invariably becomes confused with evaluation of program personnel. Such confusions create suspicion of and resistance to program evaluation efforts on the part of program administrators. In order to avoid such effects, some evaluators (for example, see Campbell, 1979) have recommended that decisions regarding administrative careers be made independent of program evaluation outcomes.

Another arena in which efforts at evaluation and accountability have become intertwined is in the development of "social indicators." Interest in assessing program impact has created a demand for quantitative indices of the status of social well-being of the nation that parallel indicators of economic status, such as gross national product. To this end, various record-keeping activities and information systems (such as crime statistics, mental hospital admissions and releases, and political opinion polls) are being utilized as "trace" measures of social welfare at given points in time. To the extent that such records monitor the social processes of interest, their regular aggregation into quantitative indices can be a boon to systematic program evaluation. There is a persistent danger, however, whenever the numerical values on such indices become a tool for administrative decision making. As Campbell (1979, p. 85) put it: "The more any quantitative social indicator is used for social decision-making, the more subject it will be to corruption pressures and the more apt it will be to distort and corrupt the social processes it is intended to monitor." In effect, once a record becomes a performance *criterion,* it may *replace* the social phenomenon as the object of change, thus introducing new sources of bias or invalidity that misrepresent actual change. The relative susceptibility of different indices to such biases and distortions is a critical factor in evaluation research.

Large-Scale Versus Small-Scale Efforts

Closely tied to the issues of policy relevance of program evaluation research is the question of whether evaluation efforts should be devoted primarily to broadly implemented federal programs on a nationwide scale or to smaller-scale, locally implemented programs. As was mentioned above, much of the impetus for program evaluation research came from assessment of federal programs with a single evaluation design applied nationally. The many technical and practical problems arising from such a research strategy have led a number of evaluators to recommend an alternative approach—that of multiple, independent, local evaluations of a given program concept (see Campbell, 1979; Cook, 1981; Cronbach et al., 1980). The potential advantages of discrete, small-scale evaluations include the opportunity for simultaneous replication of program effects under different administrative conditions, cross-validation of research findings, and the use of multiple measures and indicators. It is also possible that the lower cost associated with local evaluations would encourage testing bolder innovations on more radical programs than would be likely on a national scale. Thus not only the replicability of findings but the range of programs to be evaluated might be improved by moving to a smaller scale.

A change in recommendation from large- to small-scale evaluation studies marks a shift from the notion of a single, definitive evaluation of a program concept to that of *competing* evaluations at different project sites with different implementation strategies and different research designs. While the results of any one such study may be equivocal—because of local implementation problems, measurement errors, or design flaws—it is hoped that the combined results of many heterogeneous studies will reveal whether a program effect is present and under what conditions it can be maximized.

The major problem introduced by the shift to multiple small-scale evaluations is that of finding appropriate decision rules for combining results from different studies and for interpreting variations in outcomes across studies. Considerable progress has been made in the development of *meta-analysis* techniques (for example, see Glass, 1977; Hunter, Schmidt, & Jackson, 1982) for deriving statistical summaries of the effects obtained from studies using different measures of outcomes. The application of these techniques, however, reveals clearly the role of subjective judgment in determining how best to reduce and aggregate a set of complex results.

The multiple replication approach is being increasingly tried in evaluation research. To date there have been four independent Negative Income Tax Experiments, seven different evaluations of *Sesame Street,* and numerous studies of school desegregation and prison rehabilitation programs (see Cook, 1981). In addition, *secondary analyses* of major evaluation studies have proliferated (for example, see Boruch, Wortman, Cordray, et al., 1981) in which large data sets are reanalyzed by different investigators using different statistical techniques involving different design assumptions. As a result, today's policy-maker is faced not with a single evaluation outcome to guide decision making, but with myriad competing interpretations and alternative conclusions about available research results. While this state of affairs may not satisfy a need for cognitive simplicity, it probably represents the most appropriate interface between evaluation research and the political decision-making process.

In-House Versus External Evaluation

Along with large-scale nationally coordinated studies, the policies of most federal agencies with respect to evaluation research in the 1960s and 1970s promoted the organizational separation of program administration from program evaluation. Such a policy is based on a checks-and-balances theory of management and has the advantage of removing evaluation activities from the budgetary control and constraints of program implementation. In many, if not most, cases, the evaluation is separately funded, and the evaluators are not employed by social service agencies but represent outside research firms or academic departments. This particular model maximizes the independence of evaluation research functions from program staff.

In their summary evaluation of federally funded evaluation research projects, Bernstein and Freeman (1975) concluded that "academic-type" evaluations generally produced higher quality research than "entrepreneurial-type" evaluations. But they also found that research quality was positively correlated with the degree of interdependence between program and evaluation staff, and that, overall, projects in which evaluation and service delivery staffs were part of the same organization produced a higher proportion of high-quality research studies than did projects in which evaluation and program staffs came from different organizations. Since that study, a number of other researchers have criticized the separation of evaluation and program implementation as potentially detrimental to research quality and interpretability of evaluation data. As Campbell (1979, p. 71) points out, "External evaluators tend to lack the essential qualitative knowledge of what happened. The chronic conflict between evaluators and implementors, which will be bad enough under a unified local direction, tends to be exacerbated . . . the relevance of the measures to local program goals and dangers is weakened." Campbell also notes that the separation of administration and evaluation is not parallel to the prevailing model in the experimental sciences, where the researcher who develops the theory and designs the research program also directs the data collection.

A number of alternative models for the relationship between project and evaluation staff have been developed. In one model, the service agency itself maintains an in-house staff to plan and conduct evaluation studies. In this model, the evaluation function is kept separate from program delivery, but both evaluation and program staff answer to the same administration. Another model, which was implemented on an experimental basis by the National Institute of Education in the late 1970s, is called "stakeholder-based evaluation" (Bryk, 1983). The ideal behind this model is that evaluation research design and priorities should be responsive not only to the goals of program staff, but to all groups involved in the program—policymakers, funding agencies, and community organizations. Stakeholder groups are given the opportunity to participate in planning all aspects of evaluation design, data collection, and analysis, in the hopes of assuring that the evaluation results will be relevant to the goals and concerns of interested parties. In many ways, the implementation of the stakeholder model maximizes the politicization of evaluation research, in sharp contrast to a "disinterested scientist" model.

RESEARCH DESIGN ISSUES
IN EVALUATION

Apart from issues surrounding the role of evaluation research in political decision making, many of the more technical aspects of the design and conduct of evaluation studies are also the subject of continuing debate. Conflicts regarding appropriate design and analysis strategies reflect both the different disciplinary background of evaluation researchers and disagreements about the goals and purposes of evaluation research. Some of the major differences in research approaches are discussed below.

Quantitative Versus Qualitative Research

Although the original rationale for program evaluation research emphasized the introduction of quantitative-experimental methodology to the decision-making process, criticisms of the legitimacy of such a model for program evaluation quickly arose (for example, see Weiss & Rein, 1969; Guttentag, 1971). In some sense, this criticism reflects the prevailing controversy between qualitative, "humanistic" and quantitative, "scientific" approaches that is characteristic of most of the social sciences in general. In evaluation research, this controversy is represented in two extreme forms along the quantitative-qualitative dimension. On the one extreme are pure outcome evaluations in which quantitative measures of program effects are derived from test scores or institutional records, and no other forms of information on the program or the target population are incorporated in the evaluation design. At the other extreme are "case-study" evaluations, represented by the Model Cities evaluations and NIE's "Experimental Schools" program, in which anthropologists are used as observers to document the program and its effects on the local population. These latter studies involve no quantitative assessment or comparative baseline information.

In between these two extremes are research programs that attempt to combine "process" evaluation with outcome assessment. Process measures usually involve the use of observers and/or interviews with program personnel to document relevant aspects of program implementation, staff morale, and the social and political context in which the program operates. Such qualitative evidence is considered supplementary to quantitative data and is used to qualify and extend the results of the outcome assessment. The major difficulty associated with process-outcome evaluations is the unavailability of consensually agreed-upon methods for integrating the two sources of information about program impact in the interpretation of evaluation outcomes.

Other research approaches have also been proposed that attempt to avoid the sharp distinction between quantitative and qualitative methodologies. Among these are various adaptations of methods employed in other applied fields, including systems analysis from organizational research (Wooldridge, 1981), and techniques derived from epidemiology, geography, philosophy, operations research, and art (see Smith, 1981).

Internal Versus External Validity

In their classic treatment of experimental research design, Campbell and Stanley (1966) drew a distinction between internal and external validity of causal hypothesis-testing research. Internal validity refers to the legitimacy of making a causal inference about the results of a particular study—did the experimental treatment produce a difference in the dependent measure in this particular instance. External validity, on the other hand, refers to the generalizability of such results to other settings and populations. In a further elaboration of this distinction, Cook and Campbell (1979, chap. 2) discuss the trade-offs inherent in attempting to maximize both types of validity, recognizing that the precision and control needed to assure internal validity may at times sacrifice external validity. Nevertheless, they conclude that internal validity should take priority in both basic and applied research, as the *sine qua non* of causal inference.

The primacy of internal validity for evaluation research has been challenged in a number of quarters (for example, see Cronbach et al., 1980). For those whose major concern is policy relevance of findings, issues of external validity often take precedence. An overemphasis on internal validity can lead to the neglect of historical and social processes that are integral to program effects (Berk & Rossi, 1976). Clearly, achieving internal validity at the cost of isolating a program from all of the social and political context in which it would ordinarily be delivered would be carrying the sacrifice of external validity too far for evaluation needs. However, such contextual isolation of effects is not necessarily inherent to internal validity, and results that are highly generalizable but uninterpretable with respect to estimating program effects would certainly be equally useless for purposes of evaluation.

Experimental Versus Statistical Control

Closely related to the issues associated with maximizing internal validity of evaluation research results is the question of whether statistical adjustments can be used to substitute for experimental control in estimating program effects. True experimental design requires that all relevant conditions—including characteristics of the subject population—other than the experimental treatment (program) of interest be either held constant or randomly distributed between treatment conditions. Since these design criteria are often difficult to meet in program evaluation settings, there are considerable practical pressures toward utilization of variations on "quasi-experimental" designs (Cook & Campbell, 1979) or nonexperimental designs that rely on statistical modeling of the relevant social processes.

In the past decade, increasingly sophisticated structural equation models, largely derived from econometric techniques, have been developed to estimate causal effects from both cross-sectional and longitudinal correlational data. All of these analytic techniques rely heavily on certain assumptions regarding measurement reliability, inclusion of all relevant variables, and correct specification of the functional relationships among variables in the system. Knowing whether such assumptions are correct or appropriate for a particular data set requires not only understanding of the mathematical models underlying the statistical analyses, but also knowledge of relevant social theory and intimate familiarity with the nature of the data and the conditions of data collection. Changing the assumptions on which analyses are based can alter dramatically the estimates of effects that are obtained. Using somewhat different assumptions about measurement error in analyses of the Head Start evaluation data, for instance, resulted in estimates of program effect that varied from slightly negative to somewhat positive (Magidson, 1977). Thus, in many ways, reliance on statistical alternatives to experimental designs requires considerably more understanding of the evaluation setting and more interpretive judgment on the part of the evaluation researcher, along with a greater tolerance for uncertainty.

OVERVIEW OF THE VOLUME

Most of the fundamental issues regarding the nature and purposes of evaluation had been identified in the early 1970s and were reflected in the contributions prepared for the initial *Handbook of Evaluation Research.* In this abridged version of the *Handbook,* we have attempted to represent selectively those contributions that have best stood the test of time in the sense of providing perspective on those methodological and political issues that have since emerged as major preoccupations in the field of program evaluation research.

The criteria for inclusion of chapters in this volume represent the collective judgment of a diverse set of evaluation researchers. In 1981, members of the Evaluation Research Society were polled as to their use of articles in the 1975 *Handbook* both for personal reference and classroom assignments. Of the chapters that received multiple nominations, those that, in the editors' judgment best represented the range of issues discussed in the section above were selected for inclusion. In addition, each selection has been supplemented by a set of references to relevant materials that have appeared since the publication of the original article. These bibliographic materials are intended to provide the reader with a state-of-the-art summary of developments in evaluation research methodology during the past decade.

The first section of the volume includes chapters concerned with the political and social context within which program evaluation is undertaken. Together, the three contributions in this section deal with issues regarding the sensitive relationship between research and policy decision making, the fine line between evaluation of programs and of people, and the role of evaluation research in social experimentation and social change. The chapters by Weiss and Gurel give particular attention to the potential for conflict between goals and values of evaluators and administrators and identify some of the subtle but powerful effects that organizational realities may have on the design and conduct of evaluation studies. The Sjoberg chapter takes a somewhat broader view from the perspective of the sociology of knowledge and points out some of the political and ethical assumptions that are implicit in evaluation research methods. The references appended to these articles reflect the continuing debate that these issues engender in the field and the increased sophistication among evaluation researchers about the political realities in which their work is embedded.

The selections in the second section of the volume complement those in the first section in that they present alternative models for the conduct of evaluation studies that reflect different conceptualizations of the nature of evaluation and its role in policy decisions. The chapters by Deming and Campbell focus on the logic and applicability of traditional scientific methods to the purposes of program evaluation. The Campbell article—which is a classic on the issues of experimental design—is concerned with the validity of the conclusions to be drawn from evaluation studies as a function of the quality of the research design employed.

Further variations on experimental design for evaluation settings are suggested in the updated bibliography appended to these articles. A very different technique for the conduct of evaluations is represented in the article by Edwards, Guttentag, and Snapper, which is derived from the work in the area of decision analysis. More recent applications of "multiattribute utility analysis" to a broad range of evaluation situations are presented in the updated reference list for this chapter.

Somewhat different perspectives on the nature of program evaluation are suggested by a focus on ecological issues and a concern with the influence of attributes of the environment on the health and mental health of individuals and populations. The selections in the third section of this volume represent approaches to evaluation research derived from work in social ecology. Susser reviews the logic and method of epidemiological investigation, with particular emphasis on the intimate relationship between human welfare and the quality of the environment. The chapter by Struening illustrates the method of social area analysis as applied to evaluation problems, including experimental studies of innovation or change in service delivery systems. Further applications of these methods are illustrated in the supplemental bibliographies appended to the chapters.

The following section moves into more technical aspects of evaluation research methodology, beginning with consideration of measurement issues associated with assessment of outcomes. The selection in this section is an adapted version of those portions of Nunnally's book on psychometric theory dealing with technical issues most relevant to the measurement of change. Because no single excerpt can adequately represent all of the measurement issues that are of concern to evaluation researchers, this chapter is followed by an extensive bibliography, organized by subtopics, to provide an overview of this critical area.

Other technical issues associated with the use of multivariate statistical procedures in analyses of the results of evaluation studies are covered in the next section of this volume. Eber describes the logic of multivariate analysis techniques and their application to evaluation research, including data reduction procedures, detection of group differences, and use of multiple regression. The following chapter, by Cohen, describes the flexibility of multiple regression as a general data-analytic system and demonstrates its equivalence to selected analysis of variance designs. On the other side of the picture, the chapter by Campbell and Erlebacher criticizes the use of analysis of covariance as a substitute for adequate experimental design and illustrates how such analyses can misrepresent treatment effects in the evaluation of compensatory education programs. Controversies over the appropriate use of statistical adjustments in evaluation research have led to an extensive literature in applied statistics, which is selectively reviewed in the supplemental bibliographies in this section of the volume.

The final section of this volume is concerned with the use and communication of evaluation research results to relevant decision makers. The Levin chapter provides a model of cost-effectiveness analysis and the utilization of evaluation research results in the measurement of program effectiveness. The last chapter, by Davis and Salasin, proposes guidelines for enhancing the effective application and dissemination of evaluation results to new settings. Improving the utilization of evaluation research findings in decision making and program planning has been a continuing concern of evaluation researchers, and a comprehensive bibliography on this topic completes the present volume.

REFERENCES

Anderson, S., S. Ball, R. Murphy, et al. *Encyclopedia of educational evaluation.* San Francisco: Jossey-Bass, 1975.

Bennett, C. A. and A. A. Lumsdaine. (eds.). *Evaluation and experiment: Some critical issues in assessing social programs.* New York: Academic, 1975.

Berk, R. A. and P. H. Rossi. Doing good or worse: Evaluation research politically re-examined. *Social Problems,* 1976, 23, 337-349.

Bernstein, I. N. and H. E. Freeman. *Academic and entrepreneurial research: The consequences of diversity in federal evaluation studies.* New York: Russell Sage, 1975.

Boruch, R., P. Wortman, D. Cordray, et al. *Reanalyzing program evaluations.* San Francisco: Jossey-Bass, 1981.

Bryk, A. S. (ed.). *Stakeholder-based evaluation.* San Francisco: Jossey-Bass, 1983.

Campbell, D. T. Reforms as experiments. *American Psychologist,* 1969, 24, 409-429.

Campbell, D. T. Assessing the impact of planned social change. *Evaluation and Program Planning,* 1979, 2, 67-90.

Campbell, D. T. and J. C. Stanley. *Experimental and quasi-experimental designs for research.* Chicago: Rand McNally, 1966.

Cicirelli, V. G. et al. *The impact of Head Start.* Athens: Westinghouse Learning Corporation and Ohio University, 1969.

Cline, M. G. et al. *Education as experimentation: Evaluation of the Follow Through planned variation model.* Cambridge, MA: Abt Associates, 1975.

Coleman, J. S. et al. *Equality of educational opportunity.* Washington, DC: Government Printing Office, 1966.

Cook, T. D. Dilemmas in evaluation of social programs. In M. Brewer and B. Collins (eds.), *Scientific inquiry and the social sciences.* San Francisco: Jossey-Bass, 1981.

Cook, T. D. and D. T. Campbell. *Quasi-experimentation: Design and analysis issues for field settings.* Chicago: Rand McNally, 1979.

Cronbach, L. J. Course improvement through evaluation. *Teachers College Record,* 1963, 64, 672-683.

Cronbach, L. J. et al. *Toward reform of program evaluation: Aims, methods, and institutional arrangements.* San Francisco: Jossey-Bass, 1980.

Fairweather, G. W. *Methods for experimental social innovation.* New York: John Wiley, 1967.

Fairweather, G. W. et al. *Creating change in mental health organizations.* New York: Pergamon, 1974.

Garfinkle, I. and E. M. Gramlich. A statistical analysis of the OEO experiment on performance contracting. *Journal of Human Resources,* 1973, 8, 275-305.

Glass, G. V (ed.). *Evaluation studies review annual* (Vol. 1). Beverly Hills, CA: Sage, 1976.

Glass, G. V Integrating findings: The meta-analysis of research. *Review of Research in Education,* 1977, 5, 351-379.

Guttentag, M. Models and methods in evaluation research. *Journal for the Theory of Social Behavior,* 1971, 1, 75-95.

Hunter, J., F. Schmidt, and G. Jackson. *Meta-analysis: Cumulating research findings across studies.* Beverly Hills, CA: Sage, 1982.

Kershaw, D. and J. Fair. *The New Jersey income-maintenance experiment.* New York: Academic, 1976.

Levine, R. A., M. A. Solomon, G. M. Hellstern, and H. Wollman (eds.).*Evaluation research and practice: Comparative and international perspectives.* Beverly Hills, CA: Sage, 1981.

Magidson, J. Toward a causal model approach for adjusting for preexisting differences in the nonequivalent control group situation: A general alternative to ANCOVA. *Evaluation Quarterly,* 1977, 1, 399-420.

Main, E. D. A nationwide evaluation of the MDTA institutional job training. *Journal of Human Resources,* 1968, 3, 159-170.

McLaughlin, M. W. *Evaluation and reform: The Elementary and Secondary Education Act of 1965/Title I.* Cambridge, MA: Ballinger, 1975.

Riecken, H. W. and R. F. Boruch (eds.). *Social experimentation: A method for planning and evaluating social intervention.* New York: Academic, 1974.

Rivlin, A. and P. M. Timpane (eds.). *Planned variation in education: Should we give up or try harder?* Washington, DC: Brookings Institution, 1975.

Rossi, P. H. and K. C. Lyall. *Reforming public welfare.* New York: Russell Sage, 1976.

Rossi, P. H. and W. Williams. (Eds.). *Evaluating social programs: Theory, practice, and politics.* New York: Seminar, 1972.

Scriven, M. The methodology of evaluation. In R. Tyler, R. Gagne, and M. Scriven (eds.) *Perspectives on curriculum evaluation.* Chicago: Rand McNally, 1967.

Smith, N. L. (ed.). *Federal efforts to develop new evaluation methods.* San Francisco: Jossey-Bass, 1981.

Suchman, E. *Evaluation research.* New York: Russell Sage, 1967.

Weiss, C. H. (ed.) *Evaluating action programs: Readings in social action and education.* Boston: Allyn & Bacon, 1972.

Weiss, C. H. Doing science or doing policy. *Evaluation and Program Planning,* 1981, 4, 397-402.

Weiss, R. S. and M. Rein. The evaluation of broad-aim programs: A cautionary case and a moral. *Annals of the American Academy of Political and Social Science,* 1969, 385, 133-142.

Wholey, J. S. *Evaluation: Promise and performance.* Washington, DC: Urban Institute, 1979.

Wooldrige, R. J. (ed.). *Evaluation of complex systems.* San Francisco: Jossey-Bass, 1981.

II

POLITICS, ETHICS, AND VALUES
IN EVALUATION RESEARCH

2

EVALUATION RESEARCH IN THE POLITICAL CONTEXT

CAROL H. WEISS

Bureau of Applied Social Research
Columbia University

Evaluation research is a rational enterprise. It examines the effects of policies and programs on their targets (individuals, groups, institutions, communities) in terms of the goals they are meant to achieve. By objective and systematic methods, evaluation research assesses the extent to which goals are realized and looks at the factors associated with successful or unsuccessful outcomes. The assumption is that by providing "the facts," evaluation assists decision-makers to make wise choices among future courses of action. Careful and unbiased data on the consequences of programs should improve decision-making.

But evaluation is a rational enterprise that takes place in a political context. Political considerations intrude in three major ways, and the evaluator who fails to recognize their presence is in for a series of shocks and frustrations. First, the policies and programs with which evaluation deals are the creatures of political decisions. They were proposed, defined, debated, enacted, and funded through political processes; and in implementation they remain subject to pressures, both supportive and hostile, which arise out of the play of politics. Second, because evaluation is undertaken *in order to* feed into decision-making, its reports enter the political arena. There evaluative evidence of program outcomes has to compete for attention with other factors that carry weight in the political process. Third, and perhaps least recognized, evaluation itself has a political stance. By its very nature, it makes implicit political statements about such issues as the problematic nature of

AUTHOR'S NOTE: Paper presented at the annual meeting of the American Psychologic Association, Montreal, August 30, 1973.

some programs and the unassailableness of others, the legitimacy of program goals, the legitimacy of program strategies, the utility of strategies of incremental reform, and even the appropriate role of the social scientist in policy and program formation.

Knowing that there are political constraints and resistances is not a reason for abandoning evaluation research; rather it is a precondition for usable evaluation research. Only when the evaluator has insight into the interests and motivations of the other actors in the system, understands the roles that he himself is consciously or inadvertently playing, realizes the obstacles and opportunities that impinge upon the evaluative effort, and the limitations and possibilities for putting the results of evaluation to work—only with sensitivity to the politics of evaluation research can the evaluator be as creative and strategically useful as he should be.

PROGRAMS ARE POLITICAL CREATURES

Evaluation research assesses the effects of social programs, which in recent years have increasingly been governmental programs and larger in scale and scope than the programs studied in earlier decades. There have been important evaluations of job training programs, compensatory education, mental health centers, community health services, Head Start and Follow Through, community action, law enforcement, corrections, and other government interventions. Most evaluation efforts have been addressed to new programs; while there have been occasional studies of long-established traditional services, it is the program into which new money is being poured that tends to raise the most immediate questions about viability and continuation.

The programs with which the evaluator deals are not neutral, antiseptic, laboratory-type entities. They emerged from the rough-and-tumble of political support, opposition, and bargaining; and attached to them are the reputations of legislative sponsors, the careers of administrators, the jobs of program staff, and the expectations of clients (who may be more concerned with hanging on to the attention, services, and resources available than with long-run consequences). The support of these groups coalesces around the program. But the counterpressures that were activated during its development remain active, and it remains vulnerable to interference from legislatures, bureaucracies, interest groups, professional guilds, the media. It is affected by interagency and intra-agency jockeying for advantage and influence.

The politics of program survival is an ancient and important art. Much of the literature on bureaucracy stresses the investment that organizations have in maintaining their existence, their influence, and their empires. As Halperin (1971) succinctly notes:

> Organizational interests, then, are for many participants a dominant factor in determining the face of the issue which they see and the stand which they take. . . . Organizations with missions strive to maintain or to improve their (1) autonomy, (2) organizational morale, (3) organizational "essence," and (4) roles and missions. Organizations with high-cost capabilities are also concerned with maintaining or increasing (5) budgets.

It is not only around evaluation that social scientists bemoan the political factors that distort what they see as rational behavior. An economist recently noted:

> ... you may go through a scientific analysis to answer the question of where the airport should be located, but an altogether different decision may finally emerge from the bureaucracy. [Margolis, 1971]

Bureaucrats, or in our terms program administrators and operators, are not irrational; they have a different model of rationality in mind. They are concerned not just with today's progress in achieving program goals, but with building long-term support for the program. This may require attention to factors and to people who can be helpful in later events and future contests. Administrators also must build and maintain the organization—recruit staff with needed qualifications, train them to the appropriate functions, arrange effective interstaff relations and communications, keep people happy and working enthusiastically, expand the influence and mission of the agency. There are budgetary interests, too, the need to maintain, increase, or maximize appropriations for agency functioning. Clients have to be attracted, a favorable public image developed, and a complex system managed and operated. Accomplishing the goals for which the program was set up is not unimportant, but it is not the only, the largest, or usually the most immediate of the concerns on the administrator's docket.

Particularly when an organization is newly formed to run new programs, its viability may be uncertain. If the organization is dealing with marginal clienteles, it can fall heir to the marginal repute of its clients, and it is likely to have relatively low public acceptance. Organizational vulnerability can become the dominant factor in determining what actions to take, and the need to build and maintain support can overwhelm the imperatives to achieve program goals.

In sum, social programs are the creatures of legislative and bureaucratic politics. The model of the system that is most salient to program managers—and the components of the system with which they are concerned—are bound to be different from the model of the social scientist/evaluator. Their view is probably no less rational. In fact, evidence suggests that programs can and do survive evaluations showing dismal failure to achieve goals. They are less likely to survive a hostile congressional committee, newspaper exposes, or withdrawal of the support of professional groups.

There have been occasional references in the evaluation literature to the need to pay attention to the achievement of organizational "system" objectives as well as to the achievement of program goals (e.g., Schulberg and Baker, 1968; Weiss, 1970), but the notion has never caught on. So evaluators continue to regard these concerns of program staff as diversions from their true mission, and give them no points on the scorecard for effectiveness in the politics of organizational survival.

The disparity in viewpoint between evaluation researchers and program managers has consequences for the kind of study that is done, how well it is done, and the reception it gets when completed. Obviously the political sensitivities of program managers can dim their receptivity to any evaluation at all, and when a study *is* undertaken, can limit their cooperation on decisive issues of research design and data collection (Weiss, 1973). Again at the completion of the study, their political perspectives will lessen the likelihood that they view the evaluative findings as conclusive or the need to act on them as imperative. Even rigorously documented evidence of outcomes may not outweigh all their other interests and concerns.

More subtly, some of the political fallout shapes the very definition of the evaluation study. As an example let us look at the specification of program goals which become the evaluator's criteria for effectiveness. Because of the political processes of persuasion and negotiation required to get a program enacted, inflated promises are made in the guise of program goals. Public housing will not only provide decent living space; it will also improve health, enhance marital stability, reduce crime, and lead to improved school performance. Because statements of goals are designed to secure support for programs, they set extravagant levels of expectation. Furthermore, the goals often lack the clarity and intellectual coherence that evaluation criteria should have. Rather than being clear, specific, and measurable, they are diffuse and sometimes inherently incompatible. Again, it is the need to develop coalition support that leaves its mark. Holders of diverse values and different interests have to be won over, and in the process a host of realistic and unrealistic goal commitments are made.

Given the consequent grandiosity and diffuseness of program goals, there tends to be little agreement, even within the program, on which goals are real, real in the sense that effort is actually going into attaining them, and which are window dressing. With this ambiguity, actors at different levels in the system perceive and interpret goals in different ways. What the Congress writes into legislation as program objectives are not necessarily what the secretary's office or the director of the program see as their mission, nor what the state or local project managers or the operating staff actually try to accomplish. The evaluator is faced with the task of sifting the real from the unreal, the important from the unimportant, perhaps even uncovering the covert goals that genuinely set the direction of the program but are unlikely to surface in open discussion, and discovering priorities among goals. Unless he is astute enough to direct his research toward authentic goals, he winds up evaluating the program against meaningless criteria. Unless he is skillful enough to devise measures that provide valid indicators of success in this complex web of expectations, he runs the risk of having his report disowned and disregarded. It is not uncommon for evaluation reports to meet the disclaimer: "But that's not what we were trying to do."

While the evaluation study is in progress, political pressures can alter or undermine it. Let us look at one final example of how organizational politics can affect the shape of evaluation research. Programs do not always keep to their original course; over time, often a short span of time, they can shift in activities and in overall strategy and even in the objectives they seek to attain. They are responding to a host of factors: budget cutting or budget expansion, changes in administration or in top officials, veering of the ideological winds, changes in congressional support, public appraisal, initiation of rival agencies and rival programs, pervasive client dissatisfaction, critical media coverage. Whereas the evaluator wants to study the effects of a stable and specifiable stimulus, program managers have much less interest in the integrity of the study than in assuring that the program makes the best possible adaptation to conditions. Which leaves the evaluator in a predicament. He is measuring outcomes of a "program" that has little coherence: What are the inputs? To what are the outcomes attributable? If the program succeeds, what activities should be replicated? If the program fails, what features were at fault? Unless programs under study are sheltered from the extremes of political turbulence, evaluation research produces outcome data that are almost impossible to interpret. On the other hand, to expect programs to remain unchanging laboratory treatments is to ignore the political imperatives. In this regard, as in others, programs have a logic and a rationality of their own.

THE POLITICS OF HIGHER ECHELON DECISION-MAKING

Much evaluation research is sponsored not by individual projects or by managers of federal programs but by superordinate levels, such as the director of the agency or the secretary or assistant secretary of the federal department, and the reports often go to cognizant officials in the Office of Management and Budget (OMB) and the White House and to members of Congressional committees. If the organizations that run programs have a vested interest in their protection, these higher-level decision-makers can view the conclusions of evaluation research with a more open mind. They are likely to be less concerned with issues of organizational survival or expansion and more with ensuring that public policies are worth their money and produce the desired effects. Of course, some legislators and Cabinet or sub-Cabinet officials are members of the alliance that supports particular programs; but it is generally true that the further removed the decision-maker is from direct responsibility for running the program, the more dispassionately he considers the evidence.

This of course does not mean that policy-makers venerate outcome data or regard it as the decisive input for decision. They are members of a policy-making system that has its own values and its own rules. Their model of the system, its boundaries and pivotal components, goes far beyond concern with program effectiveness. Their decisions are rooted in all the complexities of the democratic decision-making process, the allocation of power and authority, the development of coalitions, the trade-offs with interest groups, professional guilds, and salient publics. How well a program is doing may be less important than the position of the congressional committee chairman, the political clout of its supporters, or the other demands on the budget. A considerable amount of ineffectiveness may be tolerated if a program fits well with the prevailing values, satisfies voters, or pays off political debts.

What evaluation research can do is clarify what the political trade-offs involve. It should show how much is being given up to satisfy political demands and what kinds of program effects decision-makers are settling for or foregoing when they adopt a position. It will not be the sole basis for a decision, and legitimately so: other information and other values inevitably enter a democratic policy process. But evidence of effectiveness should be introduced to indicate the consequences that various decisions entail.

As a matter of record, relatively few evaluation studies have had a noticeable effect on the making and remaking of public policy. There are some striking exceptions, and in any case, our time frame may be too short. Perhaps it takes five or ten years or more before decision makers respond to the accumulation of consistent evidence. There may need to be a sharp change in administration or a decisive shift in expectations. But to date, devastating evidence of program failure has left some policies and programs unscathed, and positive evidence has not shielded others from dissolution (Rossi, 1969). Clearly other factors weigh heavily in the politics of the decision process.

Perhaps one of the reasons that evaluations are so readily disregarded is that they address only official goals. If they also assessed programs on their effectiveness on political goals—such as showing that the Administration was "doing something," placating interest groups, enhancing the influence of a particular department—they might learn more about the measures of success valued by decision makers. They might show why some programs survive despite abysmal outcomes, why some that look fine on indicators of goal achievement go down the drain, and which factors have the most influence on the making and persistence of policy. Just as economic cost-benefit analysis added the vital dimension of cost to analysis of outcomes, *political-benefit* analysis might help to resolve questions about political benefits and foregone opportunities.

It is true that many public officials in the Congress and the Executive Branch sincerely believe that policy choices should consistently be based on what works and what does not. It is also true that, like all the other actors in the drama, policy-makers respond to the imperatives of their own institutions. One seemingly peripheral but consequential factor is the time horizon of the policy process. Presidents, governors, legislators have a relatively short time perspective. They want to make a record before the next election. Appointed officials in the top positions of government agencies tend to serve for even shorter periods. Their average tenure in federal departments is a little over two years (Stanley, Mann, and Doig, 1967). The emphasis therefore tends to be on takeoffs not on landings. It is often more important to a politically astute official to launch a program with great fanfare to show how much he is doing than to worry about how effectively the program serves people's needs. The annual cycle of the budget process also has the effect of foreshortening the time perspective. When decisions on funding level have to be made within twelve months, there is little time to gather evidence (at least competent evidence) on program outcomes or to consider it.

What does it take to get the results of evaluation research a hearing? In a discussion of policy analysis (of which evaluation research is one phase), Lindblom (1968) states that differences in values and value priorities constitute an inevitable limitation on the use of objective rational analysis. As we have already noted, maximizing program effectiveness is only one of many values that enter decisions. Therefore, Lindblom (1968: 34, 117) explains, the way that analysis is used is not as a substitute for politics but as a

> tactic in the play of power. . . . It does not avoid fighting over policy; it is a
> method of fighting. . . . And it does not run afoul of disagreement on goals or

values . . . because it accepts as generally valid the values of the policy-maker to whom it is addressed.

It does appear that evaluation research is most likely to affect decisions when it accepts the values, assumptions, and objectives of the decision-maker. Research evidence is pressed into service to support the preexisting values and programmatic objectives of decision-makers. This means obviously that decision-makers heed and use results that come out the way they want them to. But it suggests more than the rationalization of predetermined positions. There is a further important implication that those who value the *criteria* that evaluation research uses, those who are concerned with the achievement of official program goals, will pay attention as well. The key factor is that they accept the assumptions built into the study. Whether or not the outcome results agree with their own wishes, they are likely to give the evidence a hearing. But evaluation results are not likely to be persuasive to those for whom other values have higher priority. If a decision maker thinks it is important for job trainees to get and hold on to skilled jobs, he will take negative evaluation findings seriously; but if he is satisfied that job training programs seem to keep the ghettos quiet, then job outcome data mean much less.

THE POLITICS IMPLICIT IN EVALUATION RESEARCH

The third element of politics in the evaluation context is the stance of evaluation itself. Social scientists tend to see evaluation research, like all research, as objective, unbiased, nonpolitical, a corrective for the special pleading and selfish interests of program operators and policy-makers alike. Evaluation produces hard evidence of actual outcomes, but it incorporates as well a series of assumptions; and many researchers are unaware of the political nature of the assumptions they make and the role they play.

First, evaluation research asks the question: How effective is the program in meeting its goals? Thus, it accepts the desirability of achieving those goals. By testing the effectiveness of the program against the goal criteria, it not only accepts the rightness of the goals, it also tends to accept the premises underlying the program. There is an implicit assumption that this type of program strategy is a reasonable way to deal with the problem, that there is justification for the social diagnosis and prescription that the program represents. Further, it assumes that the program has a realistic chance of reaching the goals, or else the study would be a frittering away of time, energy, and talent. These are political statements with a status quo cast.

For many programs, social science knowledge and theory would suggest that the goals are not well reasoned, that the problem diagnosis and the selection of the point and type of intervention are inappropriate, and that chances of success are slight. But when the social scientist agrees to evaluate a program, he gives it an aura of legitimacy.

Furthermore, as Warren (1973) has noted, by limiting his study to the effects of the experimental variables—those few factors that the program manipulates—the evaluator conveys the message that other elements in the situation are either unimportant or are fixed and unchangeable. The intervention strategy is viewed as the key element, and all other conditions that may give rise to, sustain, or alter the problem are brushed aside. In particular, most evaluations—by accepting a program emphasis on services—tend to ignore the social and institutional structures within which the problems of the target groups are generated and sustained. The evaluation study generally focuses on identifying changes in those who receive program services compared to those who do not, and holds constant (by randomization or other techniques) critical structural variables in the lives of the people.

Warren suggests that there is an unhappy convergence between the preferred methodology of evaluation research—the controlled experiment—and the preferred method of operation of most single-focus agencies. Agencies tend to deal in piecemeal programs, addressing a single problem with a limited intervention, and

> . . . for various reasons of practice and practicality they confine themselves to a very limited, relatively identifiable type of intervention, while other things in the life situation of the target population are . . . left unaltered. . . . The more piecemeal, the fewer the experimental variables involved, the more applicable is the [experimental] research design. [Warren, 1973: 4, 9]

Methodologically, of course, experimental designs can be applied to highly complex programs (which is what factorial designs are about), but in practice there does seem to be an affinity between the experiment and the limited focus program. And if there is anything that we should have learned from the history of social reform, it is that fragmented program approaches make very little headway in solving serious social problems. An hour of counseling a week, or the introduction of paraprofessional aides, or citizen representation on the board of directors—efforts like these cannot possibly have significant consequences in alleviating major ills.

Another political statement is implicit in the selection of some programs to undergo evaluation, while others go unexamined. The unanalyzed program is safe and undisturbed, while the evaluated program is subjected to scrutiny. What criteria are used in selecting programs to evaluate? Obviously, newness is one criterion. The old established program is rarely a candidate for evaluation research. It is the new and (perhaps) innovative program that is put on trial while the hardy perennials go on, whether or not they are accomplishing their goals, through the sheer weight of tradition.

Other criteria for selecting programs for evaluations are even more overtly political. Thus in a discussion of program analysis, Schultze (1968) makes two recommendations: (1) program analysts should give more consideration to programs that do not directly affect the structure of institutional and political power than to programs that fundamentally affect income distribution or impinge on the power structure, and (2) analysts can be more useful by studying new and expanding programs than long-existing programs with well-organized constituencies (cf. Hatry, Winnie, and Fisk, 1973: 110-111). There are persuasive reasons for such prescriptions. Evaluators, like all other analysts, who ignore the political constraints of special interests, institutional power, and protective layers of alliances, may confront the decision maker with troublesome information. If time after time they bring in news that calls for difficult political choices, if they too often put him in a position that is politically unviable, they may discredit evaluation research as a useful tool. Nevertheless, there are serious political implications in restricting evaluation to the unprotected program and the program marginal to the distribution of economic and political power.

The structure of the evaluation research enterprise also has political overtones. Evaluation is generally commissioned by the agency responsible for the program, not by the recipients of its efforts. This is so obvious and taken for granted that its implications are easily overlooked. Some of the consequences are that the officials' goal statements form the basis for study and if recipients have different needs or different ends in mind, these do not surface. Another probability is that the evaluator interprets his data in light of the contingencies open to the agency: the agency is the client, and he tries to gear his recommendations to accord with realistic practicalities. Furthermore, study findings are reported to decision-makers and managers, and usually not to program participants; if the findings are negative, officials may not completely bury the report (although sometimes they try), but they can at least release it with their own interpretations: "We need more money," "We need more time," "The evaluation was too crude to measure the important changes that took place." (For further common defenses, see Ward and Kassebaum in Weiss, 1972: 302.) To the extent that administrators' interpretations shape the understanding of the study's import, they constrain the decisions likely to be made about the program in the future and even to influence the demands of the target groups. An evaluation report showing that Program A is doing little good, if interpreted from the perspective of the participants in the program, might well lead to very different recommendations from those developed by an agency-oriented evaluator or a program official.

Most of these political implications of evaluation research have an "establishment" orientation. They accept the world as it is, as it is defined in agency structure, in official diagnoses of social problems, and in the types of ameliorative activities that are run. But the basic proclivity of evaluation research is reformist. Its whole thrust is to improve the way that society copes with social problems. While accepting program assumptions, evaluation research subjects them to scrutiny; its aim is to locate discrepancies between intent and actual outcome.

In fact, social science evaluators tend to be more liberal in orientation than many of the agencies they study (Orlans, 1973). Their perspectives inevitably affect their research. No study collects neutral "facts." All research entails value decisions and to some degree reflects the researcher's selections, assumptions, and interpretations. This liberal bias of much evaluation research can threaten its credibility to officialdom. Thus, a federal assistant secretary writes:

> The choices of conceptual frameworks, assumptions, output measures, variables, hypotheses, and data provide wide latitude for judgment, and values of the researcher often guide the decisions to at least some degree. Evaluation is much more of an art than a science, and the artist's soul may be as influential as his mind. To the extent that this is true, the evaluator becomes another special interest or advocate rather than a purveyor of objectively developed

evidence and insights, and *the credibility of his work can be challenged.*
[Lynn, 1973: 57; italics added]

In this statement, there seems to be an assumption that such a thing as "objectively developed evidence" exists and that assumptions and values are foreign intrusions. But the message that comes through is that "objectively developed evidence" is that which develops only out of government-sanctioned assumptions and values. Certainly evaluators should be able to look at other variables and other outcomes, wanted and unwanted, in addition to those set by official policy.

The intrinsically reformist orientation of evaluation research is apparent in its product. Evaluation conclusions are the identification of some greater or lesser shortfall between goals and outcomes, and the usual recommendations will call for modifications in program operation. The assumptions here are (1) that reforms in current policies and programs will serve to improve government performance without drastic restructuring and (2) that decision-makers will heed the evidence and respond by improving programming. It is worthwhile examining both these assumptions, particularly when we take note of one major piece of intelligence: evaluation research discloses that most programs dealing with social problems fail to accomplish their goals. The finding of little impact is pervasive over a wide band of program fields and program strategies. True, much of the evaluation research has been methodologically deficient and needs upgrading (Mushkin, 1973; Campbell and Erlebacher, 1970), but there is little evidence that methodologically sounder studies find more positive outcomes. Numbers of excellent studies have been carried out, and they generally report findings at least as negative as do the poor ones. Moreover, the pattern of null results is dolefully consistent. So despite the conceptual and methodological shortcomings of many of the studies, the cumulative evidence has to be taken seriously.

What does the evaluation researcher recommend when he finds that the program is ineffective? For a time, it may be a reasonable response to call attention to possible variations that may increase success: higher levels of funding, more skilled management, better trained staff, better coordination with other services, more intensive treatment, and so on. If these recommendations are ignored, if the political response is to persist with the same low-cost low-trouble program, there is not much more that the social scientist can learn by evaluating participant outcomes. If program changes are made, then further evaluation research is in order. But there comes a time when scores or even hundreds of variants of a program have been run, for example, in compensatory education or rehabilitation of criminal offenders, and none of them has shown much success. If it was not evident before, it should be clear by then that tinkering with the same approaches in different combination is unlikely to pay off. There needs to be serious reexamination of the basic problem, how it is defined, what social phenomena nurture and sustain it, how it is related to other social conditions and social processes, and the total configuration of forces that have overwhelmed past program efforts. Fragmented, one-service-at-a-time programs, dissociated from people's total patterns of living, may have to be abandoned; and as Moynihan (1970) has suggested, integrated policies that reach deeper into the social fabric will have to be developed. What this suggests is that in fields where the whole array of past program approaches has proved bankrupt, the assumption is no longer tenable that evaluation research of one program at a time can draw useful implications for action or that piecemeal modifications will improve effectiveness (Weiss, 1970).

As for the other major premise on which the utility of evaluation research is based, that policy-makers will heed research results and respond by improving programming, there is not much positive evidence either. We have noted how the politics of program survival and the politics of higher policy-making accord evaluative evidence relatively minor weight in the decisional calculus. It is when evaluation results confirm what decision-makers already believe or disclose what they are predisposed to accept that evaluation is most apt to get serious attention. Thus, for example, the Nixon Administration was willing to listen to the negative findings about the Johnson Great Society programs. As Schick (1971) has pointed out, evaluation research is comfortably compatible with a government perspective of disillusionment with major program initiatives, stock-taking, and retrenchment. The fiscal year 1973 budget submitted to Congress proposed to cut out or cut back programs that were not working. The evaluation researcher—now that somebody was paying attention to findings—was cast in the role of political hatchet man. Because evaluation researchers tend to be liberal, reformist, humanitarian, and advocates of the underdog, it is exceedingly uncomfortable to have evaluation findings used to justify an end to spending on domestic social programs. On the other hand, it is extremely difficult for evaluators to advocate continuation of programs they have found had no apparent results. The political dilemma is real and painful. It has led some social scientists to justify continued spending on avowedly ineffective programs to preserve the illusion that something is being done. Others have called for continued spending, whatever the outcome, so as not to lose the momentum of social progress. Others justify the programs in ways that they used to belittle in self-serving program staff: the programs serve other purposes, the evaluations are not very good, the programs need more money, they need more time. My own bent is to find some truth in each of these justifications, but they tend to be declarations based on social ideology and faith, rather than on evidence that these factors are responsible for the poor showing or that the programs are achieving other valued ends.

What would be a responsible position for evaluation research? It seems to me that there are a few steps that can be taken. One reform in evaluation research would be to put program goals in sensible perspective. Among the many reasons for the negative pall of evaluation results is that studies have accepted bloated promises and political rhetoric as authentic program goals. Whatever eager sponsors may say, day care centers will not end welfare dependency, and neighborhood government will not create widespread feelings of citizen efficacy. Programs should have more modest expectations (helping people to cope is not an unimportant contribution), and they should be evaluated against more reasonable goals.

Another course would be to evaluate a particularly strong version of the program before, or along with, the evaluation of the ordinary levels at which it functions.

This would tend to show whether the program at its best can achieve the desired results, whether accomplishments diminish as resource level or skills decline, and how intensive an effort it takes for a program to work. If the full-strength "model" program has little effect, then it is fruitless to tinker with modest, low-budget versions of it.

More fundamentally, however, it seems to me that now in some fields there is a limit to how much more evaluation research can accomplish. In areas where numbers of good studies have been done and have found negative results, there seems little point in devoting significant effort to evaluations of minor program variants. Evaluation research is not likely to tell much more. There is apparently something wrong with many of our social policies and much social programming. We do not know *how* to solve some of the major problems facing the society. We do not apply the knowledge that we have. We mount limited-focus programs to cope with broad-gauge problems. We devote limited resources to long-standing and stubborn problems. Above all, we concentrate attention on changing the attitudes and behavior of target groups without concomitant attention to the institutional structures and social arrangements that tend to keep them "target groups."

For the social scientist who wants to contribute to the improvement of social programming, there may be more effective routes at this point than through evaluation research. There may be greater potential in doing research on the processes that give rise to social problems, the institutional structures that contribute to their origin and persistence, the social arrangements that overwhelm efforts to eradicate them, and the points at which they are vulnerable to societal intervention. Pivotal contributions are needed in understanding the dynamics of such processes and in applying the knowledge, theory, and experience that exist to the formulation of policy. I suspect that in many areas, this effort will lead us to think in new categories and suggest different orders of intervention. As we gain deeper awareness of the complexities and interrelationships that maintain problem behavior, perhaps we can develop coherent, integrated, mutually supportive sets of activities, incentives, regulations, and rewards that represent a concerted attack and begin to deserve the title of "policy."

How receptive will established institutions be to new ways of looking at problems and to the new courses of action that derive from them? We suggested earlier that decision-makers tend to use research only when its results match their preconceptions and its assumptions accord with their values. There will certainly be resistance to analysis that suggests changes in power relations and in institutional policy and practice; but legislatures and agencies are not monoliths, and there may well be some supporters, too. As time goes on, if confirming evidence piles up year after year on the failures of old approaches, if mounting data suggest new modes of intervention, this will percolate through the concerned publics. When the political climate veers toward the search for new initiative, or if sudden crises arise and there is a scramble for effective policy mechanisms, some empirically grounded guidelines will be available.

Of course, there remains a vital role for evaluation research. It is important to focus attention on the consequences of programs, old and new, to keep uncovering their shortcomings so that the message gets through, and to locate those programs that do have positive effects and can be extended and expanded. It is important to improve the craft of evaluation so that we have greater confidence in its results. To have immediate and direct influence on decisions, there is a vital place for "inside evaluation" that is consonant with decision-makers' goals and values—and perhaps stretches their sights a bit. There is also a place for independent evaluation based on different assumptions with wider perspectives, and for the structures to sustain it. One of the more interesting roles for evaluation is as "social experimentation" on proposed new program ventures, to test controlled small-scale prototypes before major programs are launched and gain good measures of their consequences.

Nevertheless, given the record of largely ineffective social programming, I think the time has come to put more of our research talents into even earlier phases of the policy process, into work that contributes to the development of schemes and prototypes. I believe that we need more research on the social processes and institutional structures that sustain the problems of the society. I have hope that this can contribute to understanding which factors have to be altered if change is to occur and, in time, to more effective program and policy formation.

REFERENCES

Campbell, Donald T. and Albert Erlebacher, "How Regression Artifacts in Quasi-Experimental Evaluations Can Mistakenly Make Compensatory Education Look Harmful," in J. Hellmuth (ed.) *Compensatory Education: A National Debate,* vol. 3. New York: Brunner/Mazel, 1970.

Caplan, Nathan and Stephen D. Nelson, "On Being Useful: The Nature and Consequences of Psychological Research on Social Problems." *American Psychologist,* 28, 3: (1973) 199-211.

Halperin, Morton H., "Why Bureaucrats Play Games." Reprint 199. Washington, D.C.: Brookings Institution, 1971.

Hatry, Harry P., Richard E. Winnie and Donald M. Fisk, *Practical Program Evaluation for State and Local Government Officials.* Washington: The Urban Institute, 1973.

Lindblom, Charles E., *The Policy-Making Process.* Englewood Cliffs, N.J.: Prentice-Hall, 1968.

Lynn, Laurence E., Jr., "A Federal Evaluation Office?" *Evaluation,* 1, 2: (1973) 56-59, 92, 96.

Margolis, Julius, "Evaluative Criteria in Social Policy," pp. 25-31 in T. R. Dye (ed.) *The Measurement of Policy Impact.* Florida State University, 1971.

Moynihan, Daniel P., "Policy vs. Program in the '70's." *The Public Interest,* no. 20: (1970) 90-100.

Mushkin, Selma J., "Evaluations: Use with Caution." *Evaluation* 1, 2: (1973) 30-35.

Orlans, Harold, *Contracting for Knowledge.* San Francisco: Jossey-Bass, 1973.

Rossi, Peter, "Practice, Method, and Theory in Evaluating Social-Action Programs," pp. 217-234 in J. L. Sundquist (ed.) *On Fighting Poverty: Perspectives from Experience.* New York: Basic Books, 1969.

Schick, Allen, "From Analysis to Evaluation." *Annals of the American Academy of Political and Social Science* 394: (1971) 57-71.

Schulberg, Herbert C. and Frank Baker, "Program Evaluation Models and the Implementation of Research Findings." *American Journal of Public Health* 58, 7: (1968) 1248-1255.

Schultze, Charles L., *The Politics and Economics of Public Spending.* Washington, D.C.: Brookings Institution, 1968.

Stanley, David T., Dean E. Mann and Jameson W. Doig, *Men Who Govern: A Biographical Profile of Federal Political Executives.* Washington, D.C.: Brookings Institution, 1967.

Ward, David A. and Gene G. Kassebaum, "On Biting the Hand that Feeds: Some Implications of Sociological Evaluations of Correctional Effectiveness," pp. 300-310 in Carol H. Weiss (ed.) *Evaluating Action Programs: Readings in Social Action and Education.* Boston: Allyn and Bacon, 1972.

Warren, Roland, "The Social Context of Program Evaluation Research." Paper presented at Ohio State University Symposium on Evaluation in Human Service Programs, June 1973.

Weiss, Carol H., "The Politics of Impact Measurement." *Policy Studies Journal* 1, 3: (1973) 179-183.

———, *Evaluation Research: Methods of Assessing Program Effectiveness.* Englewood Cliffs, N.J.: Prentice-Hall, 1972.

———, "The Politicization of Evaluation Research." *Journal of Social Issues* 26, 4: (1970) 57-68.

REFERENCE UPDATE

Selected by Carol H. Weiss

Berk, R. A. and P. H. Rossi. Doing good or worse: Evaluation research politically re-examined. *Social Problems,* 1976, 3: 337-349.

Caplan, N. The two-communities theory and knowledge utilization. *American Behavioral Scientist,* 1979, 22 (3): 459-470.

Cherns, A. *Using the social sciences.* London: Routledge & Kegan Paul, 1979.

Ciarlo, J. A. (ed.). *Utilizing evaluation: Concepts and measurement techniques.* Beverly Hills, CA: Sage, 1981.

Cochran, N. Society as emergent and more than rational: An essay on the inappropriateness of program evaluation. *Policy Sciences,* 1980, 12 (2): 113-129.

Cronbach, L. J. et al. *Toward reform of program evaluation.* San Francisco: Jossey-Bass, 1980.

Frankel, C. (ed.). *Controversies and decisions: The social sciences and public policy.* New York; Russell Sage, 1976.

Hayes, C. D. (ed.). *Making policies for children: A study of the federal process.* Washington, DC: National Academy Press, 1982.

Lindblom, C. E. *The policy-making process.* (2nd ed.). Englewood Cliffs, NJ: Prentice-Hall, 1980.

Orlans, H. *Contracting for knowledge.* San Francisco: Jossey-Bass, 1973.

Rein, M. and S. H. White (1978) Can policy research help policy? In H. E. Freeman (ed.) *Policy studies review annual* (Vol. 2). Beverly Hills, CA: Sage, 1978.

Rule, J. B. *Insight and social betterment.* New York: Oxford University Press, 1978.

Saxe, L. and D. Koretz (eds.). Making evaluation research useful to Congress. *New Directions for Program Evaluation,* 1982, 14 (special issue).

Schulberg, H. C. and J. M. Jerrell (eds.) *The evaluator and management.* Beverly Hills, CA: Sage, 1979.

Schwarz, P. A. Program devaluation: Can the experiment reform? In E. Loveland (ed.) Measuring the hard-to-measure. *New Directions for Program Evaluation,* 980, 12 (special issue).

Weiss, C. H. (ed.) *Using social research in public policy making.* Lexington, MA: D. C. Heath, 1977. (a)

Weiss, C. H. Research for policy's sake: the enlightenment function of social science research. *Policy Analysis,* 1977, 3 (4): 531-545.

Weiss, C. H. Improving the linkage between social research and public policy. In L. E. Lynn, Jr. (ed.) *Knowledge and policy: The uncertain connection.* Washington, DC: National Academy of Sciences, 1978.

Weiss, C. H. Knowledge creep and decision accretion. *Knowledge: Creation, Diffusion, Utilization,* 1980, 1 (3).

Weiss, C. H. Use of social science research in organizations; The constrained repertoire theory. In H. D. Stein (ed.) *Organization and the human services.* Philadelphia: Temple University Press, 1981.

Weiss, C. H. Policy research in the context of diffuse decision-making. *Journal of Higher Education*, 1982, 53 (6).
Weiss, C. H. Ideology, interests, and information: The basis of policy positions. In D. Callahan and B. Jennings (eds.) *Ethics, the social sciences, and policy analysis*, New York: Plenum, 1983.
Weiss, C. H. with M. J. Bucuvalas. *Social science research and decision-making*. New York: Columbia University Press, 1980.
Wildavsky, A. *Speaking truth to power*. Boston: Little, Brown, 1979.
Zweig, F. M. (ed.). *Evaluation in legislation*. Beverly Hills, CA: Sage, 1979.

3

THE HUMAN SIDE OF EVALUATING HUMAN
SERVICES PROGRAMS: PROBLEMS AND PROSPECTS

LEE GUREL

American Psychiatric Association

PROLOGUE

Increasingly in recent years, evaluation has been viewed as an integral and essential, even if often neglected, part of a wide range of service programs funded by public monies. Program evaluation was obviously not invented in the middle of the twentieth century, but one need only look at the mushrooming evaluation literature to see how the field has expanded in the last 10 to 15 years. This rapid growth coincides historically with the emphases on rationalized decision-making associated with the early years of Robert McNamara's tenure in the Department of Defense. These emphases were subsequently formalized throughout the federal government by the (then) Budget Bureau's October 1965 Bulletin # 66-3 requiring agencies to implement the Planning, Programming and Budget system, an essential element of which was the requirement that program effectiveness and efficiency be evaluated in cost-benefit terms. While the specifics of the Bureau of the Budget directive became obscured under the Nixon administration, the pressures for institutionalizing program evaluation have, if anything, increased. Given ever-present shortages of funds available for human services, continuing pressures for intensified evaluation of public service programs are almost a certainty.

Paralleling the growth of evaluation activity, there has been a not unexpected proliferation of the evaluation literature. However, it was not long ago that students of evaluation ventured forth with little more than Suchman's now almost classic

AUTHOR'S NOTE: Separate parts of this chapter have been presented on three previous occasions: Invited Address to the Third Annual Research Seminar, South Florida Chapter of the National Association of Social Workers, Miami, April 1971; Presidential Address, Division of Psychologists in Public Service, Division 18 of the American Psychological Association, at its annual meeting, Honolulu, September 1972; and Invited Address to the 25th Annual Institute on Hospital and Community Psychiatry, Miami Beach, September 1973.

and somewhat elementary monograph (Suchman, 1967) and a general admonition from their mentors that evaluators need clear statements of program objectives and support from top management. Evaluation has proven to be much more complicated than that, and what are examined in this chapter are some of those complications still inadequately covered in the existing literature. These aspects of the evaluation process have to do, not with technical and methodological issues, but with the organizational context, the structural constraints and requirements, and, most of all, the interpersonal interactions which influence program evaluation efforts. The thesis presented here is that these issues have the most profound consequences for the success or failure of evaluative activity. My hope is that readers who are or who become involved in evaluation studies will be forewarned as to the problems and be better prepared to resolve those that can be resolved or to at least defuse those for which there is simply no good solution.

Most of the material in this chapter derives from a 15-year experience in evaluation of several parts of the Veterans Administration's program of medical care, especially its program of psychiatric care. However, I would not lead the reader on a retrospective odyssey had my reading and contacts with evaluators in other fields not convinced me that the principles and examples to be cited are by no means unique and, in fact, have considerable generalizability. Nor do I intend to bore the reader with either an apologia for mistakes I as an evaluator have made or with hostile criticism of program managers with whom I once worked. Rather, what I hope to demonstrate is that the problems of evaluation discussed here are not to be interpreted as evidence that program managers are "the bad guys" who embody evil, while program evaluators are "the good guys" who embody virtue. Those of us who are evaluators often act as though we had a moral imperative to search out truth, and we not infrequently regard those who hinder our quest as malevolent—or worse. What I hope to illustrate is that program managers and evaluators alike are simply human beings made of flesh and blood, that they are, therefore, imperfect humans, and that their seemingly imperfect behavior can be better understood through examining their social roles, their personal characteristics, and the situational demands and constraints acting on them.

PARTICIPANTS IN EVALUATION

We can distinguish at least four parties to any attempt at evaluation of human services programs. First, there is the sponsoring authority which legitimates or authorizes or orders the provision of services. This can be a board of directors, the Congress, a state legislature, the (now) Office of Management and Budget, or whatever. Let me point out in connection with material in the next section that it would be a mistake to neglect the fact that these kinds of sanctioning bodies possess the real life-or-death power over both service programs and their evaluation and that, because program managers are exquisitely responsive to them, sponsoring authorities can and often do figure centrally in evaluation efforts.

Next, there is the program administrator or executive, or, as I shall refer to him here, the program manager. And, of course, just as there are levels of programs nested within programs and corresponding levels of evaluation, so, too, there can be several levels of program managers. A third group which can strongly affect the outcome of evaluative activity are the program staff who operate or execute the program and who are often the source of the evaluator's data. Finally, the fourth party to any evaluation effort is the evaluating agency, be it a person or a group of people assembled into an evaluation staff.

There can be other concerned parties, of course, depending on the particular situation: program clients, outside commercial interests, the news media, consultants, and the like. The four I have identified seem to me to be universally present in any evaluation effort. All four figure in the discussion that follows, but we will be primarily concerned with the program manager and the program evaluator, since it is my thesis that it is their divergent characteristics, plus the nature of their interaction and the context in which it occurs, which most centrally affect the outcome of program evaluation.

THE CONTEXT FOR EVALUATION

Looking first at the context within which manager and evaluator interact, I will call attention to four considerations: (1) the conflicting superordinate organizational goals to which the program manager and the program evaluator subscribe, (2) the stereotype of scientific omnipotence, (3) the extension of rigorous evaluation to areas of public service only recently considered exempt from external scrutiny, and (4) the recourse to evaluation as a panacea for programs in failing health. Even just listing these four issues should serve to establish the point that evaluation efforts are necessarily launched into troubled waters.

Commitment to Conflicting Organizational Goals

Any number of students of organization have noted that, whatever its stated and unstated goals, every organization has two superordinate sets of goals. One has to do with stability and survival; the other has to do with growth and change. And the two always operate to a significant degree to pull the organization in different directions. The important point here is that program managers tend to identify themselves primarily with the organization's stability, while the evaluator is necessarily identified with the forces of innovation which pose a threat to stability.

This seemingly obvious point assumes special significance in the evaluation of public service programs, since most of them are conducted or sponsored by hierarchical, bureaucratic, governmental agencies. Almost by definition, the supervisory echelons to which evaluators report, whether the evaluators are from within or from without an agency, are comprised of people committed to organizational stability. An important concern of management is with not making waves, with not rocking the boat. In contrast, evaluation is necessarily a force which leads to disequilibrium, no matter how minimal or transitory. Seen in this light, a medical analogy seems quite appropriate. The organizational body which serves as unwilling host to the evaluation is in much the same position as the human body when its homeostatic equilibrium is disrupted by an unwelcome pathogen against which it must mobilize its various defenses. So, too, will the forces committed to organizational equilibrium seek to resist the intrusion of agents identified with change.

As an aside, it might be noted that, if John Gardner is correct in arguing that the survival of organizations and social institutions depends on self-renewal through growth and change (Gardner, 1963), then the process described is indeed ironic. However, the irony of it does not alter the problem of organizational resistance to evaluation, nor does it eliminate the need for evaluators to understand its relevance for introducing an evaluation program.

Stereotype of Scientific Omnipotence

A second consideration has to do with the extent to which our society over-estimates the ability of science and technology to solve any and all problems. A September 1973 editorial in *Science* reported a Harris poll indicating the great confidence which the public has in scientists—greater confidence, in fact, than in the Supreme Court, the Congress, and the executive branch! After all, we live in an age when men walk on the moon, when people are kept alive by mechanical kidneys and hearts, when laser beams are used to guide bombs and to do eye surgery—all this in the less than 50 years since Lindbergh's crossing of the Atlantic seemed incredible. Surely, if given the resources, social scientists would be able to help eliminate poverty, to teach Johnny to read, to improve our mental health, to design more responsive political institutions, and so on. Obviously, any such expectations are doomed.

The dramatic accomplishments of the physical sciences notwithstanding, the social and behavioral sciences do not have even the beginnings of a technology to improve substantially the quality of our lives, even if the resources for such efforts were suddenly to become available. Nevertheless, the optimistic aura persists, and program managers, like others in the society, tend to share such views. It has been my experience that, as a result, many managers entertain a more or less unrealistic set of expectations for what evaluators can help them accomplish, the extent of their erroneous perception varying with the extent to which the evaluator is credentialed as a scientist.

Evaluating the Previously Unevaluated

A third portent of future difficulty lies in the fact that, historically speaking, the whole notion of formal evaluation has been totally foreign to most human services programs. We need only consider the degree to which organized medicine has fought bitterly to forestall attempts at evaluating the quality of medical care. And what is true for medicine has been equally true for many other service programs and institutions: prisons, educational programs, churches, training programs for the disabled or disadvantaged, and the like. There was never any question but what such institutions and their programs did "good" things and provided useful services; the idea was simply not entertained until fairly recently that one could and should determine whether the programs and the services were accomplishing what they were supposed to accomplish.

Nor is it sufficient to say that evaluation is novel and therefore abstractly threatening to those involved in these kinds of activities. The threat is much more real and immediate. Two facets of this threat merit explication.

The first of these, no matter how dimly perceived, is that evaluation may address itself to the most basic assumptions on which programs and the professional lives of their operators are based. Suppose, for example, that rigorous evaluation of mental health practices consistently failed to confirm benefits commensurate with the resources expended. Where would such a finding leave practitioners? Or, in the field of education, it is one thing for an evaluator to contrast the effectiveness of teaching techniques A and B. But suppose that, over a number of evaluations, it is ultimately established that, not only are techniques A, B, and C through Z essentially equivalent, but that none of them achieves stated educational goals—or achieves them to any greater degree than is accomplished by letting children loose on the streets. Picture, if you will, the terror which would strike into the hearts of thousands of schoolteachers. Better yet, let your mind play with the possibilities of evaluating church programs!

My examples are admittedly more than a little strained, but the issue is one of enormous significance. Mental health practitioners do not just offer mental health services, and teachers do not just teach. They believe in mental health and in education, often in a particular set of theories or methods, for example, psychotherapy a la Jung or free expression a la Summerhill. Many of the services only recently confronted with the prospect of evaluation are built on sets of assumptions and personal philosophies deriving from the accumulated biases and preconceptions which pass for conventional wisdom. In certain areas, such as mental health services, this assumptive framework can command emotional commitments as compelling as a set of religious beliefs. Only the most intrepid of program managers and service providers could be expected to be other than hostile to an inquiry which could conceivably render totally meaningless their personal and professional investments in these assumptive frameworks.

A second kind of threat inherent in evaluation may be more immediate but is no less profound in its impact. Simply stated, evaluation poses a serious threat to whatever degree of power the program manager may exercise. Whether through guile or through naivete, the evaluator may seek to pass off his work as a neutral activity intended only to develop knowledge for knowledge's sake. However, program managers, especially if they have clawed their way up the administrative ladder, are not likely to be taken in by the evaluator's assurances, no matter how innocently offered. They recognize that information and knowledge are not neutral quantities once they enter into the public domain. Knowledge is power. Depending on whether the information is withheld and, if disseminated, how and where it is disseminated, information can be made to serve political ends. The inherently political nature of evaluation has been dealt with at length in another chapter. The point here is that most program managers are probably well aware that they can use evaluation results to suit their own political ends and their own attempts to hold power—and that these results could just as easily be made to serve the opposing political ends and power needs of subordinates and supervisors, to say nothing of a host of potential critics and competitors.

Evaluation as Panacea

The three considerations just noted serve, it seems to me, as a backdrop for practically any evaluation. A fourth issue, somewhat related to the second, appears to be widely prevalent, but it is by no means as universal.

It was noted above that the social and behavioral sciences do not possess sufficiently precise technology for grappling with the urgent societal problems which daily diminish and complicate the quality of our lives. It is commonly argued that this observation was one of the sobering lessons to come out of the attempt to implement President Lyndon Johnson's plans for the Great Society. However, the lack of experience, skills, and tools did not stop attempts to resolve social problems. People operated programs as best they knew how, the limitations of the available tools notwithstanding. In retrospect, it is now easy to understand why some programs soon found themselves in trouble; but, for present purposes, we are not concerned with performing a postmortem on specific Great Society programs. These situations serve only as a paradigm for the more general instance of programs operating without adequate know-how and therefore running into various difficulties. Programs for delivering mental health services have for decades now illustrated this phenomenon. The point is that, lacking technologically sound expertise, human services programs are doomed to being beset at times by massive problems of one kind or another.

All too frequently, it is precisely when the program is in trouble, particularly when the trouble is a threat to program funding, that the evaluator is called in. Whether or not the problem is specifically financial, the pressures for evaluation in such instances usually come from outside the program management and operators, not uncommonly from a critical and dissatisfied sponsoring authority. It takes little imagination to visualize the chilly reception evaluation and the evaluator will receive from program managers under these circumstances.

The history of the VA's Psychiatric Evaluation Project and its several reorganization-bred successors is instructive as an illustration of how program evaluation is called on when programs are in trouble. Out of nine major evaluation studies, one was generated by the evaluation group itself, and one came from elsewhere in the agency. The others all had their origins in pressures and queries which were conveyed with varying amounts of criticism and/or congressional or Budget Bureau threats of financial reprisal. One study, for example, was largely in response to a Bureau of the Budget attack on what was then the very costly cornerstone of the agency's plans for delivery of institutional psychiatric services. On another occasion, the agency received a rather innocuous query about one of its programs from a prestigious—but probably powerless—group at the level of a presidential commission. My own later contact with the originator of the inquiry convinced me it was just that, an inquiry, and that it carried no covert message of criticism. In the meantime, however, the agency had undertaken several defensive actions, one of which was to mount a large-scale evaluation of the program. On still another occasion, a powerful congressional critic unleashed a withering attack on a program activity in which several levels of management took considerable—and, as it turned out, unjustified—pride; the agency response was again a hastily mounted evaluation study.

Because they are instructive in several respects, these illustrations will be referred to again in connection with a discussion of the need for evaluators to understand what groups are pushing for the evaluation and what their motivations are for doing so. For the present, the major point of these examples is that evaluation is often management's begrudging response to threat. What is not so apparent and what may perhaps be even more important here, is that, no matter how the evaluation may itself be feared and unwelcome, a self-deluding feeling can be generated that the program will now somehow be made well. It is as though the medical specialist has now been called in and will be bringing with him a cureall or another "magic bullet."

Such a false hope is all the more likely if the evaluator had to oversell the evaluation proposal and its potential benefits to managers of the jeopardized program. He may even have believed sincerely that he was going to be of great help in getting the program off the hook! The program operators and management are in turn only too willing, under the circumstances, to accept the evaluator's promises as a ray of hope that the program, no matter how moribund, is going to weather its crisis and be made whole again. This is not to say that such feelings displace the program staff's feelings of threat and suspicion at being, as they may perceive it, "investigated." The point is that all of these feelings will coexist in one big, churning knot of ambivalence toward the evaluation and evaluator.

Having identified these four considerations, it should be apparent that the stage upon which the program manager and the program evaluator will interact is structured in ways that predispose that interaction to serious conflict, as each plays out his respective hopes, anxieties, suspicions, ambivalences, and unrealistic expectations. Some additional considerations more specific to the context of mental health program evaluation are dealt with below.

SOME CHARACTERISTICS OF MANAGERS AND EVALUATORS . . .

Having considered the milieu within which they interact, it is instructive to look at some of the background, personal, and role characteristics of managers and evaluators. Given limitation of space, I shall present a composite picture, hoping to capture and reflect salient group features without doing too much violence to the individual. Of necessity, some managers and evaluators better fit the generalized image than do others, and it is recognized that there are exceptions to the overall characterization. Let me first make clear, however, that I do not consider here as evaluators persons who do not derive from some kind of scientific or technical background and who have not had specific, even if minimal, training in evaluation methodology; it is true that persons with administrative or managerial backgrounds sometimes function on an ad hoc basis as program evaluators, but they are excluded from consideration here.

. . . and How They Differ

An attempt to assemble some of the characteristics of managers and evaluators produces an interesting result. It soon becomes apparent that one can practically go down the two sides of a sheet headed with their names, and, whatever characteristic is listed on one side, one can almost invariably list on the other side an essentially polar opposite of that characteristic. As I shall specify in more detail, the point to be noted in the discussion to follow is the extent to which program managers and program evaluators are simply cut out of different kinds of cloth.

Several ways in which managers and evaluators differ have already been alluded to. Most important of these was that managers are necessarily identified with program survival and preserving the status quo, while evaluators are more closely identified with innovation and changing the status quo. As a corollary, the one approaches analysis and evaluation in terms of their potential for program defense, while the other views them in terms of program assessment and appraisal. Both may say sincerely that they want the facts that evaluation can yield, but it should be recognized that they may want them for very different reasons.

Also, the program manager (unless he is some kind of out-and-out fraud) believes deeply in the validity and worth of his program, its possible flaws notwithstanding, and he is vitally involved in seeing that the program succeeds. The evaluator usually has no such commitment to the values and ultimate success of the program; if anything, he approaches the program with a thoroughly ingrained skepticism, and, not infrequently, with an attitude of cynicism toward human service programs in general.

There is, however, one interesting exception to the evaluator's skepticism. He is probably as deeply committed to an ethic of evaluation and to his role as manager of an evaluation program as the manager is to the operating program. So we have a situation of quid pro quo. On the one hand, the manager's commitment is met with skepticism toward the operating program; on the hand, the evaluator's commitment is met with ambivalence toward the evaluation program.

Bureaucrat vs. Scientist

The differences just noted flow naturally from differences in role. There is another major set of differences between manager and evaluator. These, it seems to me, flow equally naturally from the fact that the one—and it is unfortunate that pejorative terminology is necessary, but it best communicates my conceptual framework of the differences—is a bureaucrat, and the other is a scientist.

The program manager is a "company man" or, to use Whyte's now popular phrase, an "organization man." He is unswervingly loyal to the organization, denies even to himself its faults, and is so strongly identified with it that his own personality becomes submerged in it. He derives security from his identification with the organization and looks to it as his primary source of personal advancement and recognition. When need be, he can be counted on to subordinate his own interests, and even his personally held principles, to what he perceives as the interests of the organization generally and "the management team" specifically.

The evaluator, on the other hand, most often identifies himself as a scientist and an individualist. Not infrequently, he delights in a few iconoclastic swipes at the petty stupidities which seem to abound in any organization. He looks for recognition, less from his associates in the organization, and more from his associates in the professional groups with which he identifies. To obtain such recognition, he seeks to contribute to the expansion of knowledge in his professional field, usually by publishing in the professional literature. My own experience has been that the evaluator's taking time for publication can be particularly annoying to a program manager concerned with the immediate utility of evaluation results for program and organizational defense; the latter very much resents the evaluator's use of time and other resources for activities not clearly and immediately related to organizational goals as he perceives them.

On the other hand, the evaluator can be as frustrated as the manager is resentful over his inability to communicate with his peers. However, the problem goes beyond just journal publication. The more central issue is what constitutes an adequate completion and wrap-up of a study. For the manager, since the evaluation effort is only one of many activities to which he attends, completion can be a series of progress reports which establishes the probable trend of the final results. I have even known managers to be content with just a memorandum or with a brief verbal report. How formal a wrap-up the manager requires is in large part a reflection of his involvement with the evaluation effort, an issue considered in more detail below. His investment, however, can never match that of the evaluator for whom doing the evaluation was a major commitment. Thus, the evaluator will ordinarily want to surround his report of findings with all the fanfare and elaborate packaging possible as evidence of both his personal accomplishment and the importance of the completed work. In a word, he wants reinforcement.

Aside from the intrinsic rewards of the work itself, evaluators tend to derive satisfaction from either the impact of their work on programming or from the recognition of their professional peers, depending on the balance between their identifications with the organization and with their profession. A manager who is content with a verbal report which he stores as information somewhere in the back of his head cuts the evaluator off from both these sources of satisfaction.

Pursuing the matter a step further, let us suppose the evaluator is administratively responsible to the manager. (Although what is to be described could as easily occur if manager and evaluator were both responsible to a supervisor who shared the manager's views.) The manager can operationalize his satisfaction with minimal reporting by assigning the next evaluation effort long before the preceding one is completed to the evaluator's satisfaction. Over a period of time, evaluators thus amass yellowing books of computer output and file drawers full of obsolescent data for addressing no-longer-relevant questions. The mountains of paper are matched by the mammoth frustration well known to psychologists as the Zeigarnik Effect, the annoyance and frustration of not being able to complete something one is very much involved in.

Also in connection with publication, what will be terribly distressing to most managers I have known or heard about is the possibility that the evaluator, committed as he is to an ethic of full and complete disclosure of data, may publicly say something to put the program in an unfavorable light. It makes no difference that the evaluator may be accurate in his analysis and have mountains of data to support his conclusions. To go public with what could be construed as criticism— and what organization cannot be legitimately criticized?—is perceived by the faithful "company man" as whistle-blowing, a "crime" of awesome proportions

(Branch, 1971). No matter the evaluator has published or wishes to publish in some obscure journal. Whatever might possibly rebound to make the organization look bad is seen as an attack. Which, of course, it is, in the sense that the highlighting of imperfections erodes a structure which the manager is committed to defend and to which he has pledged his loyalty. That is, the manager perceives attack because what is being undermined by even the mildest constructive criticism is not just a program or organization, but a set of values, a source of security, and whatever else the program means to the manager as a person.

The latter point was illustrated for me by the reception accorded a paper presented at an annual, predominantly intra-VA conference of mental health researchers and practitioners. On prior occasions, I had reported a study, or some manageable piece of it, much as I would deliver a research paper to an audience of other psychologists: rationale, hypotheses, subjects, procedure, and so on. On the occasion in question, I presented an overview of several years of group effort and several lines of evidence which strongly suggested that the programs evaluated had a number of shortcomings and were generally not achieving the levels of effectiveness publicized by program managers.

Responses to my "disclosures" fell pretty much into two discrete categories, and these were associated with two different role-types. Some very positive, even enthusiastic, reactions came from people who were not centrally involved in the program and who did not figure importantly, or even at all, in the power hierarchy which managed the programs. On the other hand, the nature of the response from the management in-group is best conveyed by its leader's comment that, "I hear you offended some of the boys down in [meeting site]; I'm sorry I couldn't be there because some of them were pretty upset." The manager's immediate subordinates were less direct. One suggested that, "The paper was OK, but it would have been nice if you had had some brightly colored charts to go with the talk." The paper was equally OK with another subordinate, except that he "sort of wished [I] had gone more into presenting the data"—which, of course, was exactly what had had little impact on several previous occasions. Still another simply wondered, "How many friends did you lose out there today?"

Without going into other evidence on which I based my interpretation of these comments, I believe that what was being expressed by these several program managers was distress that a program with which they were closely identified had been, as they perceived it, not just evaluated, but attacked. Worse yet, the so-called attack had been made publicly (having been picked up and distributed by one of the wire services). While most evaluators are likely to be generally aware of the kinds of sensitivities described here, I have not known them to appreciate fully the depth of feeling involved and the extent to which mere criticism may be interpreted as an attack on activities the manager holds dear. What to the evaluator is nothing more than reporting the facts can be seen by the manager as anything from malicious sabotage to vicious assault.

Sciencing Around

Another facet of the bureaucrat-scientist conflict of values can be seen in the manager's growing impatience with what he describes as the evaluator's "sciencing around," a set of behaviors which the evaluator sees as a necessary search for precision. The program manager is willing to settle for whatever is good enough for a given job; he is, to use the title of a perfectly delightful book, a "satisficer" (Levin, 1970). Not only is the program manager not committed to the evaluator's goal of scientific accuracy, he sees the never-ending search for precision as so much lost time and wasted effort.

The preceding is not meant to imply that there is something wrong with the program manager's views of what evaluation should be. If blame were to be assigned, an objective assessment might more often determine that it is the evaluator who is at fault. Whereas both serve themselves, the program and the organization, the evaluator, to the extent that he identifies himself as a scientist, also sees himself as serving the so-called broader scientific community. Consequently, the evaluator often tends to perceive what he was hired to do and what he is doing as being research. Whether deliberately or inadvertently, he loses sight of the critical distinctions between research and evaluation and thinks of himself as doing something he describes as evaluative research. Whatever it is called, it may or may not possess the policy and decision-making implications which are the sine qua non of evaluation on which the program manager rightfully insists. Whether the activity meets criteria of scientific respectability, a matter of great concern to the evaluator, will ordinarily matter very little to the manager. What does matter to the manager is that the evaluation be done quickly and that it have implications for planning and administrative action. Such implications are, of course, the hallmarks that distinguish evaluation from research, but the distinction is frequently overlooked by the researcher-turned-evaluator or the evaluator-would-be-researcher.

A list of motivational and personal differences between the manager and evaluator is easily extended. The manager is politically sensitive; the evaluator's orientation toward rules and internal political machinations borders on cavalier dismissal— again, an attitude not likely to endear him to the program manager. The one clearly values conformity, the other nonconformity. The one is a doer, a man of action; the other is far more contemplative and deliberate.

I would add only one final point here, and that concerns the person trained in some scientific field, who does some evaluation, and who later becomes an administrator. Depending on the amount of time spent in administrative roles, my experience has been that such a person more nearly resembles the program manager than he does the evaluator. While this may seem like a minor, or even irrelevant, point, it will be seen to be of significance in the concluding discussion on prospects for the future.

THE MANAGER-EVALUATOR INTERACTION

And so the stage is set, the actors in place, and the interaction of manager and evaluator begins. In order for there to be any chance of their mounting a successful evaluation, I believe that this interaction necessarily starts off as impossibly frustrating and demanding to the point of being exhausting—or so the initial contacts are likely to be experienced. For purposes of discussion, we can identify four separate areas of potential friction.

Identifying Program Objectives, Rationale, and Procedures

To begin with, the evaluator must pin the manager down to specific and detailed answers to a list of questions not unlike those that newspaper reporters are taught to ask: who, what, when, where, how, and how much. What are the program objectives, both immediate and ultimate; for what target population; what changes are anticipated as indication that the objectives have been met; when and how will changes be manifested; what kinds of activities are supposed to produce those changes; how much change; how are program activities intended to produce change to be conducted; where and for what length of time; with how much and what kinds of resource inputs?

It is not just that such questions are embarrassing in the sense that they highlight deficiencies in the program planning process—and there almost have to be such deficiencies, since most human service programs are hastily mounted or have grown Topsy-fashion over time. The problem is that they are extremely difficult questions, the first question—the issue of program objectives—being the most difficult of all. Yet the evaluator cannot proceed with the design of a meaningful evaluation unless he has the answers; one cannot operationalize objectives into criterion measures, for example, until one knows those objectives.

Short of a separate paper, it is difficult to convey adequately the extent of mutual frustration and antagonism that can be generated by trying to elicit from program managers an organized statement of the program's ultimate objectives, the major operating goals, the subgoals, the relation of program activities to achieving subgoals, and how some goals, once achieved, will become activities to achieve higher goals. Program managers seem to get fixated at either listing off detailed activities of the program, or, at the other extreme, they offer some vague super-objective, such as helping people to lead more useful lives.

Some of my evaluator associates have speculated that the difficulty of obtaining statements of objectives reflects the influence of covert goals as primary but unstated objectives. The notion is that managers wittingly or otherwise have hidden agendas which are not made explicit in planning the evaluation—as, for example, the real objectives of methadone treatment having to do with cutting down on street crime rather than with rehabilitating heroin addicts. Such explanations may possess some limited validity, especially to the extent that enhancing the prestige and influence of special interest groups constitutes a hidden agenda. However, my own experience suggests that nothing quite so sinister is operating. In fact, rather than anything remotely Machiavellian, I have been impressed with the extent to which program officials simply do not think in the kinds of terms that recognize the pervasive influence of program objectives on program operation and evaluation. Admittedly, I have not dealt extensively at the very apex of agency management, but, at several levels of management below that, I have found an enormous preoccupation with getting started and moving off, with very little awareness that going somewhere necessarily implies having a series of intermediate destinations leading to an ultimate destination and some plans about the mechanics of the trip. (It should be a great boon to evaluators if the present-day emphasis on management by objectives takes root and replaces management by expediency, otherwise known as flying by the seat of the pants!)

Motivations for Evaluation

Let us assume that the evaluator has managed to obtain answers to the questions posed above, and goes to his office to design the evaluation. That would be most unfortunate if it implied that the evaluator neglected to explore thoroughly the motivations which led to plans for an evaluation. More than any other step in the whole process of planning and executing an evaluation, it is this failure to explore the background of and the motivations for the evaluation that explains for me why so many evaluation projects eventually falter along the way, why so many conflicts develop between manager and evaluator, and, ultimately, why the results of evaluation studies, rare though they may be, have so little impact on programming.

The evaluator too often pays only the most cursory attention to finding out who wants what, why they want it, how much they are willing to invest to get it, and what they plan to do with it when they have it. The possible effects of this neglect can be staggering. Probably the most far-reaching of these is a gross mismatch between the scope of the evaluation and the issues it is intended to address. In particular, it is possible to mount an extensive and costly evaluation for the flimsiest and the most irrelevant of reasons. Again, the history of the VA Psychiatric Evaluation Project (PEP) referred to earlier is instructive on this point.

Although not a party to the initial planning of the venture, my review of memoranda after I joined the group suggested to me a euphonious phrasing for describing PEP's origins: that the initial PEP study of mental hospital effectiveness developed out of a unique confluence of budgetary and professional interest in the outcomes achieved by modern psychiatric treatment methods. I liked the phrase and used it often in various presentations describing the study. At the time, I was only vaguely aware that "unique confluence of budgetary and professional interests . . ." might be a euphemism for (1) the Bureau of the Budget pressuring the VA to justify in terms of documented improvement in patient outcomes the higher operating costs of its newer mental hospitals, (2) program managers already convinced that higher costs were justified doing little more than just going along with an evaluation whose only conceivable outcome was confirming that more money bought better treatment results, and (3) researchers, one of whom would probably head the proposed evaluation, arguing for opposite strategies of evaluation which not accidently coincided with their respective preexisting research interests.

Thus was mounted a multi-year, multi-million dollar project employing 25 to 30 full-time mental health professionals and 15 to 20 clerks and technicians, and requiring the occasional data collection efforts of hundreds of treatment staff. It was not until some years later, while talking with several of those since-relocated managers—in some instances even their replacements had been replaced—that I fully realized how little investment these managers had had in the evaluation. Not only did each have his/her own idea of the project's original purposes, but none of them was really very clear on what those purposes were. The senior program official ultimately responsible for the new program emphasis was perhaps an exception; he was quite clear as to what the evaluation was all about. His question to me was, "What ever happened to that study they started about the time I left that was supposed to prove I had made the right decision [in initiating the program]?"

The lessons to be learned from even this one bit of history are enough to fill another chapter of this volume. For present purposes, I will simply repeat that mounting an evaluation requires the most thoroughgoing kind of planning and, specifically, an intensive scrutiny of the motivations of the parties involved. This by no means implies that there is anything sinister about the participants' reasons for initiating the evaluation and that they should be made to undergo "third-degree" questioning. Viewed negatively, all that is being advanced is the admonition that one avoid through better planning the kind of evaluation that nobody wants: the evaluation that ends up addressing the wrong questions, in the sense of questions in which managers are not really interested; the evaluation that is actually a research project in disguise and does not have a built-in assurance that policy implications will be forthcoming; the evaluation whose financial and other resource costs are out of all proportion to the importance of the issues being addressed; the "quick-and-dirty" look-see which tries to answer questions that can only be answered satisfactorily by a much more intensive effort.

General rules of thumb are risky, but I have found it useful to think of the time requirements for an overall evaluation effort as being roughly divisible into thirds: as much time for planning and tooling up as for data collection and an equal amount of time for analysis and reporting. And it is in the very first planning stages that the kinds of questions listed earlier must be explored—all the way from who wants what kinds of information from the study to how that information will be of value and what differences it will make to somebody to have it. Typically, the pressures to get underway with the evaluation are almost irresistable, and they not infrequently reinforce one another. The evaluator, the manager, and the sponsoring authorities may have different reasons for haste, but they all want to see something get started. Too often, the something that gets started is different from the kind of effort that would be wanted by all the concerned parties if the evaluation were adequately planned. The point can be illustrated by another bit of PEP history mentioned earlier.

What was described as an innocuous request for information from a prestigious group came to the VA during the period when data were still being collected for the first PEP study. Nevertheless, there was little choice but to proceed with new data collection. Top VA management had determined that its best course in responding to the inquiry was the familiar stalling technique of we-can't-reply-yet-because-we're-studying-the-problem. The study that was subsequently—albeit quickly—initiated came down the chain of command in the usual fashion. Only four or five steps on the administrative level were involved. However, by the time the evaluation staff started work on the evaluation plan, the lack of any real managerial commitment to the study had been lost sight of. To make matters worse, the evaluation staff, motivated by their own research interests and reinforced by research-minded consultants, expanded the study plan into something they felt would be more scientifically challenging. In this case, the evaluators ended up answering questions that nobody but they themselves had asked.

Are the instances recounted above only atypical, idiosyncratic anecdotes? Obviously, I am convinced that they are not or I would not be citing them. Each of us has to answer in terms of our own experience and our exposure to the experience of others. As stated, I have been impressed often enough and strongly enough by the problem of unclarified and dissimilar motivations that I accord it unquestioned first place among the possible reasons so much evaluation effort comes to naught.

Two final points by way of postscript. I have had enough exposure to other situations that I can state categorically that the examples cited are by no means unique to the Veterans Administration or to the federal bureaucracy. Except that I am familiar with them only in a consultant role, comparable situations from state government settings could just as well have been described; it is only through the exercise of great restraint that I have refrained from recounting in detail one such chilling sequence which almost ended in an evaluation whose scope required resources several times greater than that of the operating program.

The second postscript echoes a point made at the outset. Although the reader is free to conclude otherwise, I would still maintain that there are no real villains in the incidents cited. However, if responsibility for these and similar misadventures were to be fixed, I would more likely fault the evaluator than the manager. Managers know that evaluation is "good." They come to the evaluator for whatever it is that evaluation can offer to the solution of management problems and without really knowing what it is they are getting into. And, where this is true, instead of being responsive to the manager's need for instant information and a limited inquiry yielding a narrowly restricted set of answers, the evaluator derides the manager's limited purposes and imposes his own preconception that more central issues should be more extensively investigated. Deliberately or otherwise, the evaluator also manages to frame the broader inquiry he would prefer to pursue in ways more likely to yield information of general professional interest. The manager's naivete and haste offer an alluring snare in which evaluators are seemingly only too willing to become entrapped.

Demands on Operating Staff

One of the inevitable results of expanding an inquiry is an increase in the evaluator's demands on the operating staff, and this constitutes a third area in which manager and evaluator can interact in mutually stressful ways. The position of staff has to be understood as one where they probably know little about the relation of the evaluation to future conduct of the program. Any little knowledge or interest they may have could hardly be interpreted as commitment by even the most sanguine observer. What the staff perceive most clearly is that extra work is being required of them in the form of interviews, or rating scales, or special arrangements of some kind. The point to be noted is that the program manager is sooner or later going to be caught in the middle between operating staff and evaluator. Either staff will complain that too much is being required on top of their—as they see it—vastly more important regular duties, or the evaluator is going to complain that he is not getting the staff cooperation he needs and would the program manager please do something about it.

It might be argued that staff participation need not become a source of difficulty in the manager-evaluator interaction if (1) the staff are adequately involved in planning the evaluation, (2) their participation is recognized and rewarded, and (3) they receive feedback about the course of the evaluation. Such may well be true, and, on general principles, I strongly endorse any moves in these directions. But I am unaware of any positive examples where these efforts have actually eliminated problems of staff cooperation (excluding from consideration research-like studies originated by the staff or worked out with them as a mutual endeavor, a quite different situation). Earlier, problems that could be resolved were distinguished from those that could only be ameliorated; adequately rewarding service staff for collecting evaluation data is one of those problems for which I know of no truly effective solutions.

Implied in what has gone before, but meriting separate attention, is a fourth area in which the manager-evaluator interaction may result in conflict. Evaluation can quite legitimately encompass the gamut from a set of observations and a narrative description of the program to full-blown pre-post comparison of randomly assigned experimentals and controls. As a general rule, the more rigorous the design, the more the evaluator will need to pressure the manager to operate the program in ways required by the design and, more critically, to refrain from program changes that might tend to invalidate the evaluation. It should be obvious that what the evaluator really requires and what he is implicitly asking for when he wants to do a highly rigorous evaluation is that he be given control of the conduct of the program. Whether or not he should have control and whether or not the manager could agree to such an arrangement is immaterial for our purposes. The important point is that the mere presentation of the situation is enough to open a Pandora's box full of impossible, conflict-laden problems: the withholding of services from otherwise eligible clients, management accountability for program success, redistribution of power, the necessity of midstream changes to correct program deficiencies, and so on. Some writers have even gone so far as to suggest that dilemmas such as these render inappropriate the use of rigorous methodologies in evaluating large-scale public service programs. Personally, I tend to disagree with such views, but the fact remains that, given the usual preference of the evaluator, plus the somewhat naive desire of the manager that the evaluation be very scientific, the use of more rigorous methodologies and the attendant problems of program control constitute another major source of potential conflict in the manager-evaluator interaction.

Up to this point, then, the discussion has dealt with (1) how the context within which evaluation of public service programs is conducted militates against the success of the evaluation venture, (2) how the potential for failure is reinforced by the disparate personal and role characteristics of evaluators and managers, and (3) how the interaction of evaluator and manager in mounting and conducting the evaluation is fraught with potential conflict.

There is no guarantee, even under the best of circumstances, that evaluation results will have some payoff in terms of being utilized to improve a program. But, as a general rule, the more difficulties of the kinds discussed here, the less the likelihood of the evaluation findings having any impact.

SOME THOUGHTS ON THE FUTURE

This chapter was introduced with the view that, as long as a service program is funded by public monies, there will always be pressures for evaluating it. As Klerman (1974) recently pointed out, that assumption is all the more valid in 1974 in view of the country's deepening economic retrenchment and political conservatism. With the prospect of increased public pressures for evaluation as a backdrop, the discussion has focused on some relatively unrecognized issues whose explication should help further the institutionalizing of program evaluation as a routine, ongoing part of program operations. While the content was in many ways ample grounds for pessimism about the future of evaluation, the intent was not to argue that the enormous difficulties attending evaluation cannot be overcome.

In fact, one basis for optimism resides in the very fact of increasing public pressures. As the notion of accountability at all levels of service delivery takes hold, there is no direction in which to move except for evaluation to gain acceptance as an integral part of program operation. At many points in the chapter, we spoke of an evaluation project or an evaluation effort or an evaluation study. The fact of the matter is that evaluation is at this point in time still very much an on-again, off-again kind of activity. As pressures increase, there will be no choice but for evaluation to be instituted as a continuing part of service delivery systems.

One facet of this inevitability is particularly relevant to the content of this chapter. The discussion has stressed problems and pitfalls in the expectation that clarification will lead to correction. If left to their own devices, I am confident that managers and evaluators would slowly learn to be more accommodating to one another and would eventually learn to work more productively together. One of the bases for that faith derives from what was noted about evaluators-turned-managers. What this observation seemed to indicate was that situational determinants play a critical role in producing the kinds of characteristics displayed by both managers and evaluators. Such an interpretation is, of course, consistent with a much larger body of social psychological research now coming into prominence, such as the mock prisoner research and the pseudo-patient studies. To the extent that their behaviors are situationally determined, and to the extent that the situation changes in the directions indicated, it is probably not overly optimistic to hope for a more effective collaboration between manager and evaluator than has characterized their interaction to date.

SUMMARY

In summary, then, what has been presented here is a series of considerations in support of the view that the major barriers to successful evaluation are not technical and methodological, though these are certainly important and worthy of further effort, but are rather the structural constraints and requirements and the interpersonal relationships which characterize the evaluation endeavor. It is paradoxical that influences which are in many respects somewhat irrational should assume so important a role in a venture which, in origin and intent, represents the height of rationality. However, this has been the nature of my experiences with the evaluation enterprise, and I have presented them with the hope that being forewarned will help in mounting more successful evaluation projects in the future.

REFERENCES

Branch, T. Courage without esteem: Profiles in whistle-blowing. *Washington Monthly,* 1971, 3 (3): 23-40.

Gardner, J. W. *Self-Renewal: The Individual and the Innovative Society.* New York: Harper & Row, 1963.

Klerman, G. Current evaluation research on mental health services. *American Journal of Psychiatry,* 1974, 131: 783-787.

Levin, A. *The Satisficers.* New York: McCall, 1970.

Suchman, E. A. *Evaluative Research: Principles and Practice in Public Service and Social Action Programs.* New York: Russell Sage Foundation, 1967.

REFERENCE UPDATE

Selected by Lee Gurel

Coursey, R. D., R. Mitchell, and J. Friedman. Staff participation in program evaluation. In R. D. Coursey, G. A. Spector, S. A. Murrell, and B. Hunt (eds.) *Program evaluation for mental health: Methods, strategies and participants.* New York: Grune & Stratton, 1977.

DeYoung, D. J. and R. F. Conner. Evaluation preconceptions about organizational decision making: Rational versus incremental perspective. *Evaluation Review,* 1982, 6: 431-440.

Glaser, E. M. and S. H. Taylor. Factors influencing the success of applied research. *American Psychologist,* 1973, 28: 140-146.

Kelman, H. C. *A time to speak: On human values and social research.* San Francisco: Jossey-Bass, 1968.

Meld, M. B. The politics of evaluation of social programs. *Social Work,* 1974, 19: 448-455.

Page, S. and E. Yates. Fear of evaluation and reluctance to participate in research. *Professional Psychology,* 1974, 5: 400-408.

Sharpe, L. J. The social scientist and policymaking: Some cautionary thoughts and transatlantic reflections. In C. Weiss (ed.) *Using social research in public policy making.* Lexington, MA: D. C. Heath, 1977.

Sichel, J. L. *Program evaluation guidelines: A research handbook for agency personnel.* New York: Human Sciences Press, 1982.

Vallance, T. R. Social science and social policy: Amoral methodology in a matrix of values. *American Psychologist,* 1972, 27: 107-113.

Weiss, C. H. Evaluation in relation to policy and administration. In J. Zusman and C. R. Wurster (eds.) *Program evaluation: Alcohol, drug abuse, and mental health services.* Lexington, MA: D. C. Heath, 1975.

Wortman, P. M. Evaluation research: A psychological perspective. *American Psychologist,* 1975, 30: 562-575.

4

POLITICS, ETHICS AND EVALUATION RESEARCH

GIDEON SJOBERG

University of Texas

The more one delves into the massive literature on evaluation research, the more cognizant one becomes of the deep-seated ethical and political implications of the social scientist's efforts, whether direct or indirect, to evaluate the performance of individuals or the programs of on-going organizations. The political and ethical dilemmas are especially troublesome in the evaluation of experimental programs.

An examination of the relevant literature has persuaded me of the need for a far more disciplined and critical analysis of evaluation research than is currently available. Suchman, in his summary work, *Evaluative Research* (1967), analyzes the problems in a well-reasoned and balanced manner, yet "brackets" many of the key political issues and overlooks the central ethical dilemmas involved in this kind of research. So too, Hyman and his associates (1962, 1967), who rank among the leading methodologists concerned with evaluation in sociology, skirt the fundamental ethical and political problems associated with their own work. Although a number of social scientists have in recent years become sensitive to various ethical and political aspects of the research process, they have not incorporated the issues involved into their methodology or, more narrowly, into their methodology for evaluation research (e.g., Caro, 1971).

Much of the failure to grasp the implications of political and ethical issues stems from the social scientist's limited, even distorted, conception of the research process. Typically methodologists have no means of incorporating relevant ethical and political issues into a research design. Because of this situation, I shall briefly outline a counterorientation toward the dominant methodological perspectives in social science. Such will then lay the basis for an analysis of the impact of political and ethical factors upon evaluation research and for my presentation of an alternative approach to the evaluation of the performance of individuals and of projected social programs.

A REORIENTATION TOWARD METHODOLOGY

Although there are basic similarities in the nature of the scientific method in the natural and the social sciences, there are essential differences in the nature of reality in the natural and social realms. The two involve different relationships between the researcher and his subject matter, and this calls for different kinds of research procedures. Thus, although we subscribe to the principle of the unity of science on the abstract level, we reject the notion that the actual research procedures employed in the natural and in the social sciences are or can be the same.

The unrealistic view of the research process adhered to by most social scientists and philosophers of science has hindered the advance of research methodology and the social scientist's ability to cope with the problems that confront him in actual practice. The conceptualization of the scientific process as expressed in most treatises on social research makes it impossible to grapple with the political and ethical issues that arise (Sjoberg and Nett, 1968), especially in the area of evaluation research.

Social Research as a Social Enterprise

If we are to deal with the inadequacies of the traditional formulations, it is essential to recognize that social research is a social enterprise. And although the social scientist's actions differ in some fundamental respects from those in everyday life, the scientific method nevertheless consists of a system of rules or norms created by and sustained by scientists. Such norms relate to those procedures for the collection and analysis of data, all refined for the purpose of acquiring "objective knowledge" about the social order.

If we conceptualize social research as a social enterprise, we can more readily recognize that the scientist is a variable in the research design. Indeed it is empirically demonstrable that the scientist's political commitments or ideology and his ethical orientations enter to some degree into the formulation and execution of the research design.

We must remember that the scientist, while he is a member of a broader community of scholars, also belongs to the social order, particularly a nation-state and various subsystems therein. The scientist carries over, unwittingly or not, many of his general social commitments into the research situation. Although a social researcher may, through reflective consciousness, be able to objectify his (her) political and ethical commitments, and even reduce their impact upon the research process, no scholar can fully eliminate their impact upon her (his) work.

Too frequently the political and ethical commitments of the researcher are taken for granted. Most contemporary social scientists are unaware of their ethical orientation, one that emphasizes the "public interest" and accepts the nation-state as the source of the "ultimate good." Even when scholars adhere to other ethical principles, the impact of the latter upon the research design is typically not explicated or acknowledged.

The role of political factors is more readily discerned. The political constraints upon research in particular have come dramatically to light in recent years. Certainly social scientists must expect to encounter opposition to their activities in any democratic order, and the constraints upon their actions when they carry out research in other societies is far more pronounced. Still, most methodologists have not incorporated the political variable into their research design.

A number of psychologists, Orne (1962) and Rosenthal (1966) among them, have documented the impact of the experimenter's beliefs and values upon the outcome of "controlled" experiments. Rosenthal, for one, seems to assume the impact of the experimenter can be controlled through more carefully designed experiments. While the impact of the researcher may be reduced through ingenious experiments, the control of ethical and political contingencies through carefully designed experiments is unfeasible in most research situations, if for no other reason than such experiments, calling as they do for purposive manipulation of subjects or organizations, are incompatible with many democratic ideals and with the interests of particular power groups. More generally, there are many kinds of social issues that can not be studied via careful experimental designs.

After examining the activities of social researchers, I am forced to conclude that most treatises on research methods propound ideal norms which often have no, and at best only a vague, relationship to what occurs in practice. The actual norms adhered to by the researcher may even be at odds with the ideal ones. Or there are areas of social research where the norms have not yet been explicated. Many of these gaps result from a failure to recognize the relationship of the researcher to the research design.

We need to be particularly concerned with explicating the practical, taken-for-granted, norms of research, For example, Lazarsfeld and Rosenberg (1955: 15), when discussing the selection and construction of indicators, speak of the speculative phase of this task. They fail to recognize that, even in this so-called speculative phase, they and others adhere to certain general rules in the selection of indicators. Researchers typically select indicators that are compatible with or acceptable to the dominant power orientation within the society or subgroup being investigated. Thus Lazarsfeld and Thielens, in their study *The Academic Mind* (1958), developed indicators for ranking colleges and universities in American society that reflect criteria associated with the high-status universities, not low-status ones. Recognition of such a norm, or guiding principle, is essential if we are to analyze the indicators that are employed in research projects.

We can clarify our methodological orientation by contrasting it with that set forth, for instance, by Denzin (1970). In the last chapter of his book, Denzin acknowledges the impact of political and ethical factors upon the research process. Yet he follows the format of detailing the idealized pattern of how research should be conducted and then viewing the ethical and political factors that distort this ideal design. With this perspective, Denzin, like so many other methodologists, is unable to demonstrate how the differing political and ethical commitments of researchers can lead to different research designs, the use of varying procedures for collecting data and divergent modes of analysis. Our conceptualization makes it possible to view the political and ethical commitments of scholars as an integral element of the formulation of particular research strategies.

The research process is far more complex than has been depicted by scholars (cf.

Smith, 1969). Typically there is a kind of "circular causation" that results in the emergence of the final design. The format—statement of the problem, collection of the data, and analysis of the results—is typically imposed upon the research process in an ex-post-facto manner. In practice, the researcher's political and ethical orientation and the broader social constraints placed upon him are such that the procedures for collecting data feed back upon the first stages of the design; so too the type of analysis affects the choice of research procedures; and so on. Changes in strategy during the course of the research project typically lead to a revision of the overall design. The picture of the research process, as idealized in print, is generally a crude approximation to actuality.[1]

Theory Construction

Research is necessarily carried out within some particular theoretical framework. But the question of theory and its meaning has been the subject of widespread debate, despite the efforts in recent years to oversimplify and mechanize the mode of theory construction (e.g., Stinchcombe, 1968).

Two broad traditions with respect to theory building exist in social science (Sjoberg and Nett, 1968). One school of thought focuses upon the assumptions scholars make about human nature and social reality and how these lead to different interpretations of the social order. These assumptions, which Gouldner (1970) calls "domain assumptions," deal with such matters as whether the individual or the collectivity should be the basic unit of analysis, whether a social order is basically oriented toward tension and conflict or whether it is oriented toward consensus, whether the actors in a social system are "rational" or whether they are "irrational," whether they are oriented toward self-interest or toward altruism. Wallace (1969) has offered one classification of these assumptions and has shown, through illustrative readings, how they are central for an understanding of why sociologists interpret social life in very different ways.

The second tradition in theory building emphasizes the logical form of inquiry. Most social scientists today have been heavily influenced by the natural sciences. As such, most research is oriented toward the testing of hypotheses, notably the statement of relationships between variables. Ideally these hypotheses or propositions should be derived from a complex set of axioms or postulates. Thus those scholars oriented toward this perspective tend to uphold the logico-deductive model as the one toward which the scientist should strive, although most social scientists work with less than ideal norms, even with propositions that form a loose system.

But the logico-deductive model is only one of the logical systems employed by social scientists. The logic of analogy and that of the dialectic are two other significant forms. Moreover, there is a relationship between some of the researchers' domain assumptions and the logical forms they employ. Thus scholars who utilize the logic of analogy fit existing or emerging social patterns into preexisting categories. This is the basis of legal reasoning with its emphasis upon precedent (Berman, 1968); so too, sociologists such as Goffman (1959) use the categories of the theater for interpreting everyday life. This logical orientation has a "conservative" bent to it. Those who examine the relationship among variables, either in relative isolation or in the context of some logico-deductive system, rely upon the categories of the system, but these categories are modified in light of empirical tests. Popper (1962: 5-7, 34-37) seems to have been correct when he equated the logico-deductive method with a commitment to political liberalism. The logic of the dialectic, especially as we employ it, is oriented toward building new categories and thus is associated with a more critical, though optimistic, view of human nature and social reality. Certain implications of the relationships of the domain assumptions and the logic of inquiry should become clearer in our analysis of evaluation research.

Toward a Critical Perspective

We have argued that the research process is a social enterprise and that political and ethical factors affect the structure of the research design, and we have sought to delineate the nature of theory construction. Our conception of the researcher as a variable in the research design and our view of theory construction are inter-related in several respects. For one thing, the scientist's ethical and political orientations are a part of his domain assumptions, which in turn are related to the logical structure the scientist employs.

Our methodology makes it possible to explicate some of the taken-for-granted assumptions in evaluation research. That various assumptions about human nature and reality—notably political and ethical ones—markedly affect the methods of evaluation and how these in turn are associated with the researcher's logic require explication. Much of the debate over evaluation research, as with most research efforts, is muddled by the failure to clarify the different assumptions held by scholars as they formulate the research design and carry out their projects.

Herein I adopt a modified sociology-of-knowledge orientation. I am employing this perspective as a means of "exposing" some of the assumptions that underlie evaluation research. Some ethnomethodologists have also sought to uncover "tacit assumptions" about the social order, including the world of scientists, but for them this unmasking process seems to have become an end in itself. Methodologists must probe still further: they must seek out alternative solutions to research problems, including those faced in evaluation research, and thus strive to attain relative transcendence over the ethical and political issues that permeate the research enterprise.

THE NATURE OF EVALUATION RESEARCH

Evaluation is implicit in all social orders. A society's status or stratification system rests upon some form of evaluation. Men and women are evaluated in one way or another throughout their entire lifetime. And this evaluation process is fraught with tensions and dilemmas. Nowadays university students in the United States are claiming the right to evaluate or grade their professors while simultaneously arguing that formal grading of themselves as students should be abolished. Thus, "Who should evaluate whom?" and "What indicators should be employed in the process?" are questions that cannot be disassociated from the structure within organizations, as well as that within the society at large.

Evaluation research, in contrast to social evaluation more generally, has taken on far more restricted meaning. Hyman and his associates (1962) limit their attention to those forms of evaluation that involve fact-finding regarding the results of planned social action. Suchman (1967) defines evaluation as the determination of the results attained by some activity designed to accomplish a particular value or objective. He then argues that the scientific method is the most promising means for determining the relationship of the stimulus to the objective.

This narrowing of the scope of evaluation research has been fostered by events of the 1960s, when social scientists were asked to judge the effectiveness of various programs or policies designed to change segments of the social order, for example, the poverty program. But to limit our attention to evaluation of the negative or positive impact of planned social intervention is too restricted a focus for our purposes.

Social scientists evaluate activities or programs that have been under way for years in order to assess the impact of certain variables (such as size and morale of personnel) upon different organizations' abilities to attain a stated goal or goals. In addition we must take account of the manifold efforts of scholars to develop and refine testing and measurement devices for use in evaluating clients or organizational personnel as well. These instruments can be administered and interpreted by others than the social scientists who devised them.

Our rather broad conception of evaluation is, we believe, in keeping with the activities of social scientists. And this perspective makes it easier to understand the manifold relationships of politics and ethics to evaluation research.

THE SOCIAL CONTEXT OF EVALUATION RESEARCH

Not only has evaluation research been furthered by recent social forces within modern society but changes in the social structure and the value system that stem from the shift from an industrial to a postindustrial order will have widespread repercussions upon it in the years ahead.

If we look back over the past several decades, we find that the increased bureaucratization of modern society has been associated with a rising interest in evaluation research. Even today, after substantial criticism on both theoretical and empirical grounds, Weber's conception of bureaucracy, with its emphasis upon rationality, remains a dominant image of how industrial-urban life is and should be organized.

The bureaucratic model rests upon the principle of dominance or hierarchy. Although various positions in the structure are interrelated in complex ways, the overall pattern is one of superordination and subordination. It is within this context of dominance that the notion of universalism is applied in, say, the selection and promotion of personnel. It is within this context that the principle of rationality is applied. In practice, however, persons in positions of power determine what is "rational": they select what to them seems to be the most efficient means for attaining the goal in question (e.g., Sjoberg, Brymer, and Farris, 1966).

If we can judge by the results, notably the greatly increased affluence of modern industrial society, the organizational revolution has proved to be highly effective in the economic sphere. Fewer and fewer workers are needed to produce a given amount of goods. At no period in history has humankind experienced such a high standard of living where so many are freed from the contraints of production in order to survive. Although a sizable sector of the population remains near the subsistence level, the relatively great expansion of affluence in the past several decades has been the most striking feature of highly industrialized nations such as the United States and a number in Western Europe.

Some credit for this affluence must be given to the increased knowledge that economists have acquired concerning the functioning of the economic system. Although they quarrel among themselves, they have formulated conceptual tools that have perceptibly furthered economic and industrial growth. Moreover, the application of their ideas rests in part upon the accumulation of more and more factual knowledge about the economic order. Policy makers rely upon numerous economic indicators to make decisions, and these indicators in turn require that vast amounts of data be collected.

Associated with this movement toward the rationalization of an economy dominated by big business, big labor, and big government, we have witnessed a marked shift in the nature of the labor force. Automation, in particular, has led to a decreased need for blue-collar workers in the manufacturing sector, and the increased affluence has facilitated a sharp increase in the size of a service-oriented labor force. Fuchs (1968) speaks of the United States as the first service economy. More and more segments of the economy have become oriented toward providing services in the areas of health, education, and welfare. In turn, large-scale educational, health, and welfare organizations, through which the expanded services are dispensed, have become part of the American scene in the past few decades.

Many of the issues surrounding evaluation research have arisen out of studies of the service sector. Researchers in the vanguard of the "social indicator movement" have been developing indicators for health, education, and welfare activities to enable them to measure the impact of various policy decisions upon the kind of social services provided (e.g., Bauer, 1966; Gross, 1969). So too, we have witnessed the rise of the PPB (planning, programming, and budgeting system) within the federal government (e.g., Shultze, 1968). Instituted by Hitch and his associates in the Department of Defense, this orientation has been adopted as a means of rationalizing the expenditures of funds in health, education, and welfare. The movement toward the PPB system has been fostered by economists who have sought to apply some of the broader principles used to measure efficiency in the production sector to the service sector.

Although the widely heralded PPB system has been promoted as a means for attaining greater efficiency in the allocation of resources, this system and the use of social indicators are efforts to make the persons who dispense funds accountable for their actions to both politicians and the public at large. Politicians, in particular, want "hard data" by which to evaluate the effectiveness of programs that are becoming increasingly costly. Thus evaluation research has two functions: judging the effectiveness or efficiency of programs and providing some basis for holding those who spend public funds on particular programs accountable for their decisions.

However, scholars who advocate the increased use of social indicators, as well as evaluation research more generally, have typically overlooked various fundamental issues. At the very time when efforts are being made to ensure that bureaucracies in the areas of health, education, and welfare function efficiently, these bureaucracies have come under severe attack for over-concern with efficiency and system maintenance at the expense of their clients' interests or welfare. During the 1960s the welfare state developed to the point where its basic contradictions became apparent. Now key segments of the population have come to challenge openly the manner in which these organizations have been attaining their goals. Thus the relevance of the phrase "the crisis of institutions" (White and Sjoberg, in press).

The proponents of evaluation research simply have not grappled with the dilemmas inherent in modern bureaucratic systems, for example, the fact that bureaucracy, with its emphasis upon hierarchy and efficiency, runs counter to the demands for equality and justice (Sjoberg, Brymer, and Farris, 1966). How is it possible to provide equality of opportunity in a system that is hierarchically oriented? Indeed, many of the measurement devices used in the evaluation of clients have been oriented toward the maintenance of hierarchy. The proponents of particular evaluation efforts have failed to recognize the contradictions in the programs they are evaluating.

One reason for this lack of recognition is that most social scientists, in line with Weber's bureaucratic model, have carried out their research in accordance with the principle that scarcity, not plentitude, is the central problem in modern society. Although I am well aware that the problem of scarcity remains an urgent one for many Americans, the United States is nevertheless moving toward the stage where economic affluence is theoretically possible for a vast sector of the populace.

Evaluation researchers have become captives of Weber's bureaucratic model in still other ways. To achieve efficiency one needs to have well-defined goals. Evaluation researchers frequently complain about the ambiguity, vagueness, or multiplicity of goals in the programs they evaluate. But they fail to recognize the objective possibility that vagueness, ambiguity, and multiplicity of goals are essential if *client-centered* bureaucracies, in contrast to organizations that are oriented to the production of goods, are to satisfy the legitimate demands and interests of their clients.

A considerable body of research and social analysis suggests that client-centered organizations tend to require goals that are multiple and ambiguous. Contemporary client-centered bureaucracies, patterned as they are upon production-oriented systems, are too rigid and inflexible to attain the goals for which they were created. Many of the political and ethical issues in evaluation research grow out of the fact that the organizational structures which researchers take for granted have been under severe attack and must be reordered if a viable postindustrial order is to emerge. This fundamental change cannot be accomplished through application of traditional evaluation procedures.

THE POLITICAL IMPLICATIONS OF EVALUATION RESEARCH

A number of scholars have argued that evaluation research is fundamentally a political enterprise. In justifying this position, Cohen contends that "Evaluation is a technique for measuring the satisfaction of public priorities; to evaluate a social action program is to establish an information system in which the main questions involve the allocation of power, status, and other public goods" (Cohen, 1970: 232). It follows that if we are to objectify the political dimension of evaluation research, we must understand the ideological orientation of the researcher, as well as the political constraints imposed upon him.

As suggested above, evaluation researchers typically take the structural constraints of the system they are evaluating for granted. This holds even when evaluation is used as a basis for reform or manipulation. Moreover, researchers generally align themselves with the dominant groups in the system. Although we are not committed to the notion of a homogeneous elite in America, there are marked differences between the advantaged and the disadvantaged, and the vast majority of social scientists side with the former rather than the latter. Such a "system orientation" influences the evaluation of all programs, notably experimental ones. To clarify these issues we can examine some of the functions of current evaluation research.

Evaluation as a Means of Reform and Manipulation

One of the best-developed intellectual rationales for evaluation research as a means for reform is set forth by Janowitz (1966: viii) in his foreword to Street et al., *Organization for Treatment: A Comparative Study of Institutions for Delinquents:*

> ... this research follows the "enlightenment" model ... it focuses on developing a fundamental understanding of the institution jointly by both the social scientists and professional practitioners. In the enlightenment model, there is a continuity of interest and interaction between the researcher and the practitioner.

Janowitz (1966: ix) goes on to state:

> As the authors shared their findings with the executives, the most pervasive impact was to develop in the executive an understanding of the extent to which they were operating with a deficit of information and of how they could ... develop more information about their own inmates and organizations.

In this instance, a stimulas had been introduced, that is, information about the system which was shared with executives, and then a follow-up study was initiated.

The principle underlying this approach was to assist the executives of these organizations to move from a custodial to a treatment model for delinquents. The authors of this study were concerned with delineating the conditions necessary to create and maintain a precarious social structure, the treatment-oriented correctional institution. In this reform model of evaluation research, the emphasis was upon working through the power structure for modification of institutions for delinquents.

Evaluation research can also be used for manipulation of organizational personnel or clients (although what may be reform and manipulation may depend upon the actor's definition of the situation). Unfortunately there is a paucity of data concerning instances where evaluation procedures have been used by leaders of organizations for manipulating personnel (cf. March, 1965). Because the goals of health, education, and welfare organizations are often ambiguous and even contradictory, administrators are in a position to advance certain goals at the expense of others while at the same time sustaining an image of fairness and universality. "Objective measurement instruments" provide the means for attaining universalism. But even "hard data" are not immune to diverse interpretations.

The use of evaluation instruments in academia, notably for judging teaching effectiveness, provides opportunities for manipulation. My own observations, conversations with persons in different academic settings, and incidental comments in the literature, all suggest that these instruments can and do serve the political ends of administrators.

Administrators of educational institutions, even under ideal conditions, must weigh a number of different criteria in making judgments about who is or is not a good teacher. Almost all teacher evaluation instruments utilize a variety of criteria as "indicators" of good teaching (e.g., McKeachie, 1969). Etzioni and Lehman (1969), in analyzing the problems inherent in the use of indicators, rightly speak of "fractured measurement." By this they mean that no one indicator can capture the "meaning" of a concept such as good teaching. Thus we must rely upon multiple indicators. What Etizioni and Lehman fail to grasp is that the indicators employed are not always consistent with one another. Indeed some concepts, such as good teaching, may embody implicit contradictions.

Who is a good teacher? One who appeals to a few especially talented students and who can stimulate them where others cannot? Or the teacher who tries to reach the widest spectrum of students possible? And how should we evaluate the teacher whose primary aim is the "recovery" of possible "failures"? In addition, what about the teacher who is thought to perform poorly in the classroom but who is effective in communicating with students on a personal level and, indeed, dedicates long hours to them outside the formal classroom situation? Because evaluation forms stress classroom performance, this person falls outside the generally accepted teaching model as defined by the key indicators on most measurement instruments. We must recognize that there have been a variety of teaching models from Socrates to the present day and that the measurement of what is good teaching takes place within a relatively circumscribed framework (cf. McKeachie, 1963).

Given the fact that what is good teaching can be defined in various ways, measurement instruments can be used as rationalizations for administrative decisions. If a teacher is considered to have an abrasive personality or if he is a controversial political figure, it becomes rather easy for an administrator to select particular items on a measurement test—say, the finding that a teacher did not spend sufficient time in his office—and, by an arbitrary weighting procedure, to devalue the teacher overall.

More generally, as indicated above, administrators are in a position to push forward certain models of teaching, such as the consensus model wherein the professor appeals to a large number of students rather than to a selected few. In a variety of subtle ways the administrator can interpret and manipulate findings about teacher evaluation to suit his purposes, especially in situations where it is difficult to hold the administrator accountable for his actions.

Evaluation as a Means for Sustaining Power or Structural Arrangements

Although this category overlaps with the above, our emphasis here is different. Measurement instruments, developed for evaluating either the organization's personnel or its clients, are also utilized by the leadership within bureaucracies to sustain themselves as well as the broader class and power alignments.

With respect to the formulation of social indicators, used as the basis for evaluations, Biderman (1966: 131) writes:

> The greater the organization, self-awareness, and political power of interest groups, the more likely we are to find statistical and other systematic indicators relating to the social and economic conditions and trends that these groups believe affect their welfare.

> Furthermore, it is more than likely that the indicators will reflect the dominant ideological orientations of the most powerful and articulate groups affected by the phenomena measured.

Add to this the fact that evaluation is often carried out by persons in positions of some power, and that they help in deciding upon the indicators to be employed, and we can more readily understand why, for example, the accreditation of Parsons College became a cause célèbre. Koerner, after reviewing the evaluation of Parsons College by the North Central Association of Colleges and Secondary Schools, observes that, although there were many reasons for disaccrediting Parsons College, "most of the errors and weaknesses of which Parsons was guilty from 1955 to 1967 can be found today in more institutions in good standing than Parsons' critics would care to admit" (Koerner, 1970: 214). A double standard was evoked because Parsons College and its president had become too controversial. President Roberts' avowed goal of having a college reap financial rewards by teaching the rejects of other colleges and universities was a threat to the established order within higher education.

The relationship of evaluation to political considerations is by no means a simple one. Biderman (1966), in his highly useful essay on social indicators, analyzes at some length the Uniform Crime Reports, which have perhaps been the most significant noneconomic indicator in American society. These reports have been the basis for formulating policy and for evaluating the results of policy decisions in the area of "law and order."

Nevertheless, these statistics are the product of a complex and decentralized bureaucratic system. Any revision in the indicators would entail some changes in the administrative system of the agencies that "generate" these data. Moreover, Biderman contends that the Uniform Crime Reports have a built-in basis for inflating the crime rate over time. For example, a theft involving $50.00 or more is still recorded as a larceny, a major crime, even though economic inflation has greatly decreased the purchasing value of this amount.

Actually the problem of the Uniform Crime Reports relates back to Biderman's observation concerning the relationship of indicators to the power structure. Such acts as murder, forcible rape, robbery, aggravated assault, burglary, larceny, and auto theft (the so-called major crimes) are associated with the lower rather than the middle and upper classes. A typical white-collar crime such as embezzlement simply does not appear in the index of major crimes.

Biderman suggests that the validity of the Uniform Crime Reports is so questionable that we might be better off with no crime indicators at all. Certainly the implications that these indicators have for reinforcing the class and power arrangements must constantly be kept in mind.

But it is in the economic and educational arena that indicators or measurement instruments have the most transparent implications for class and power relationships. Economic indicators, such as that reflecting the cost of living, have been subject to considerable debate. Special interest groups have sought to gain an economic advantage by having indicators defined so as to favor them.

Moreover, if we judge by patterns in the educational sphere in recent years, we can look forward to an increased hostility by many groups in America to the indicators and measurements that have been employed as screening devices from elementary through graduate school. These instruments play a major role in sustaining existing class and power arrangements.

Psychologists have shown considerable sensitivity to the attacks against their instruments (e.g., Anastasi, 1967). The critics range from some intellectuals to members of minority groups who reason that the tests discriminate against them. Unfortunately, many of the justifications for psychological tests have not dealt with the manner in which these have supported the privileged groups in society. Anastasi, while cognizant of some of the issues involved, fails to grasp the central relationship between testing and social structure. Tests and measurements are intimately related to the needs of bureaucracies. The latter's more privileged members have a stake in sustaining the use of certain kinds of tests and measurements. Thus Anastasi, for instance, does not consider the possibility that if the "culturally deprived" are to advance, we must do more than resocialize individuals; we must change the structure. It is not possible to overcome the problem faced by minorities simply by working with individuals. Many blacks, Chicanos, and other minorities are quite rational when they call for structural change and for abolition of the measuring instruments that support present arrangements.

In line with this reasoning, the recent questioning of SAT scores, which have for some time been utilized as a crucial screening device for entrance into many colleges and universities, is highly informative. The Report of the Commission on Testing (1970) has indicated that there are a variety of skills and knowledge that are related to education and are meaningful to the broader society—for instance, leadership and aesthetic talent—and which fall outside the scope of the SAT instrument. This Commission's views support our own perspective. With the rise of an affluent society, alternative modes of academic success can be tolerated, and moreover it becomes essential to take into account a wide variety of social and intellectual skills. The SAT requires fundamental revisions because it is associated with a power structure and mobility system that has come under attack.

We can expect similar criticisms of the Graduate Record Examination to arise. It is ironic that many social science departments continue to accept GRE scores so uncritically even when the available evidence raises serious questions about their validity as a predictor of academic success. I would suggest that the GRE has served to restrict the recruitment of persons with diverse talents into graduate schools. This instrument, like the SAT, has been oriented toward a narrow conception of education that is not in keeping with the emerging postindustrial order.

Experimental Programs and Evaluation Research

Nowhere is the tendency to sustain the status quo more clearly dramatized than in the evaluation of experimental social programs. We hypothesize that the overriding pattern is for the dominant bureaucratic structures, or the existing power arrangements, to impose their indicators upon experimental programs. This in turn undermines the very efforts to formulate viable alternatives.

Ward and his associates (1967) suggest that innovation prison reform systems typically are not judged to be successful. However, they do not seem to explore the full range of reasons for their findings. One that they overlooked is that new programs were judged by traditional categories or indicators. Therefore, through a kind of self-fulfilling prophecy, innovative efforts do not suceed. Innovation calls not only for new programs but for new modes of evaluation.

The efforts to evaluate the poverty programs of the 1960s bear mute testimony to the difficulties researchers encounter when evaluating fledgling social experiments. The efforts to provide means for compensatory education for the socially disadvantaged serve as a case in point. More specifically we can consider the Head Start program which was the pearl of the Office of Economic Opportunity's program.

The Head Start program was an effort to provide compensatory education for disadvantaged children. And it was subjected to extensive evaluation. For within the OEO there existed the Office of Research, Plans, Programs, and Evaluation, a product of the social pressures for evaluation discussed above. Thus there was a built-in structural support for evaluation of the Head Start program, and this ultimately led to a study by the Westinghouse Learning Corporation (Ohio University), which carried out an ex-post-facto examination of this experiment (e.g., Williams and Evans, 1969).

There are several significant aspects to the Westinghouse study, which concluded that the Head Start program had little, if any, impact upon the educational progress of the children involved. For one thing, the Westinghouse researchers, while recognizing that the Head Start program had numerous objectives, focused upon the cognitive and affective dimensions of the children's success. The supporters of the evaluation effort argued that this particular set of indicators did not deny the multiplicity of goals; they maintained that cognitive improvement was the primary goal of Head Start and moreover was an activity which reflected the success of other activities (Williams and Evans, 1969: 124). This argument is in keeping with our earlier contention that evaluators tend to impose a unidimensional framework upon a multidimensional world. But this orientation reflects only one way of evaluating educational success. After all, one conclusion of the Westinghouse study was that the parents of Head Start enrollees reported substantial participation in the activities of educational centers. The increased involvement of parents in the educational process could have had considerable long-run impact upon their children's educational attainment, although their participation might have had no real consequence for the Head Start program.

Actually, scholars generally agree that the methodology employed in this research effort deviated markedly from the ideal norms for social research. The nature of the research design—with the lack of an effective control group, the nature of the sample, and the admitted lack of reliability and validity of the indicators (they were used because they were the "best available")—makes it difficult to interpret the meaning of the results. Yet, after the proper apologia, the researchers drew some rather definitive conclusions as to the program's lack of success.

But it would be surprising, on theoretical grounds alone, to have found major cognitive improvement in children who had spent a year or less in the Head Start program. The utilization of traditional categories for measuring educational achievement, plus the diversity of the social order and the factors that impinge upon a child's socialization and learning patterns, would lead one to hypothesize that such a program as Head Start would have little, if any, significant impact upon educational improvement. To break the cycle for the educationally disadvantaged would take more than a modest effort. The assumptions about learning and about the child's relationship to the school and the broader society by the Head Start officials and by the Westinghouse researchers are open to serious question.

The arguments concerning compensatory programs in education, including that of Head Start, took a somewhat different twist in the debate resulting from Jensen's study of IQ tests (1969). Jensen contended that there is a basic difference between the IQ of blacks and that of whites. He reasoned that compensatory education, and he cited various experimental programs, has not been (and will not be) able to overcome the differences resulting from an inherently genetic basis. By resting his case upon differences in the nature of human nature, Jensen provided an ideological justification for the maintenance of existing structural arrangements.

Numerous social scientists have severely criticized Jensen's work. In the main their criticisms reflect the way in which assumptions about the nature of human nature affect the interpretation of data. The measurement of intelligence, even as Jensen defines it, is still a sociocultural process, although he seeks to explain the sociocultural differences in terms of genetic variables.

Stinchcombe (1969), whose criticism of Jensen rests heavily upon domain assumptions that are congruent with my own, contends that the social environment is highly complex, not as undifferentiated as Jensen suggests. Stinchcombe singles out one of Jensen's findings—that IQ scores for blacks are somewhat higher than for whites in early childhood and that these shift afterwards—and argues that it is the more complex environment of the white children that leads them, as they grow older, to acquire cognitive skills greater than those of children in the black community.

Overall the debate about the Head Start program and Jensen's judgment about compensatory education underscore the difficulties of evaluating any efforts that deviate from traditional patterns. These difficulties have in turn led practitioners to make political adjustments with respect to the formulation of social experiments. One pattern consists of "creaming." In order to demonstrate that a new program is worthy of support, administrators select those clients who are most likely to succeed. Thus, in an experiment on the social impact of housing subsidies in Boston (Tilly, Feagin, and Williams, 1968: 118), we find that the persons to be subsidized were screened in such a manner as to help ensure the success of the experiment. Still other means will continue to be employed by supporters of new experiments if they are to circumvent evaluations that are "biased against" innovation.

ETHICS AND EVALUATION RESEARCH

When examining the relationship of ethics to social research, social scientists have typically dealt with this problem without explicit recognition of the ethical commitments that inform their actions, a pattern related to our thesis that methodologists have not incorporated the fact that the researcher is a variable in the research design.

Elsewhere Vaughan and I (1971) have argued that, taking a world view, the dominant ethical orientation of social scientists has been associated with the categories or value orientations of their particular nation-states. When social scientists reason that ethical commitments are private concerns or that professional associations should, in the name of value neutrality, refuse to take public stands on issues affecting humankind, they tacitly accept the nation-state as a given and come to work within its guidelines. More narrowly, social scientists frequently identify with the large-scale bureaucratic organizations that either support or are supported by the nation's legal framework. Up to a point a scientist can justify his loyalty to an organization or the nation-state. But system loyalty, if it becomes an end in itself, poses serious difficulties for any scholar.

We must recognize that the products of scientific endeavor have been used both for good and for ill. The results of the natural scientists' efforts were employed in Nazi Germany to commit the crime of genocide against the Jews and in the United States to bomb Hiroshima and Nagasaki. In Nazi Germany loyalty to the system became the dominant ideology for justifying the acceptance of the acts of inhumanity against the Jews.

One major step in overcoming some of the ethical dilemmas facing social scientists is to recognize the implications of the fact that science is a human enterprise. Science, if it is to survive, must be predicated upon respect for human dignity. The legal-rational principle, which Weber saw as the basis of legitimacy for the central activities of modern society, is too nation-state specific. We cannot define the idea of human dignity within the context of any one nation-state but only in terms of some transnational category. The emphasis upon human dignity is consistent with, in fact built into, a major premise of the scientific method, namely, that scientists are concerned with the general rather than the particular.

At this point, we are confronted with the problem of defining "human dignity." We must proceed beyond those philosophers or social scientists who stress survival and biological needs; we must emphasize the unique feature of men and women, their sociocultural environment. We define human dignity in terms of people's ability to pursue alternative courses of action, to have available to them significant structural choices. The idea of alternatives, when defined in terms of significant structural choices, stresses the actors' ability to control their own destinies, at least to some degree. Freedom is not to be equated, as is done by a number of sociologists, with mere adherence to norms. Such an assumption would permit one to argue that Hitler's Germany and Stalin's Russia were lands of the free. Nor is freedom to be equated with psychological freedom for self-actualization without regard to the needs of other persons. Human dignity is especially enhanced when humans are free to participate in the construction of structurally meaningful choices. Such can only be attained where there is a built-in tension between the individual and the group or subgroups and the broader society. Only then can scholars look beyond their commitment to the system in which they live.

In light of the aforementioned ethical orientation, it is possible to reanalyze the orientation of most evaluation research. It has been social-system, or more generally nation-state, oriented, and within this context social scientists have too frequently accepted the power structure's definition of what is right and what is wrong. This has made it difficult for social scientists to deal adequately with the notion of human dignity not only for persons in other sociocultural settings but also for the powerless within the researcher's own nation-state.

Our perspective leads us to challenge at least two commonplace commitments of social scientists. One is that enunciated by Moynihan: "The role of social science lies not in the formulation of social policy, but in the measurement of its results" (1970: xxix). Moynihan's argument, even when qualified somewhat, still leaves the researcher committed to system categories, to the acceptance of the power groups, and, more narrowly, the administrative apparatus, definition of right and wrong. It is ironic that Moynihan, who has been committed to developing policy at the highest levels in Washington, has in effect relegated other social scientists to a position where they should not challenge his enunciations.

Still another viewpoint of social scientists needs to be reexamined if one accepts our orientation toward ethics. Some writers, such as Becker (1963, 1967), state that researchers can stand on only one side at a time, and moreover, that they should typically be committed to defending the underdog. Gouldner (1968) has charged that mere identification with the underdog does not lead one to challenge the structure that keeps the disadvantaged in their place. Moreover, Becker's thesis (1963: 172-173) that a social scientist can align himself only with one group at a time makes it impossible for the evaluation researcher to seek some means for transcending the structural hiatus between the privileged and the underprivileged.

Researchers must do more than accept the categories of the system when they carry out their evaluations. They cannot unquestionably accept the categories of the underprivileged if they are to carry out their role effectively. In order to think in terms of significant alternatives, researchers must first adopt a critical perspective. The function of criticism is underscored in the field of mental health. In the late fifties and early sixties, we witnessed a number of evaluations of mental health programs; but these were often carried out with an uncritical acceptance of the society's (and power groups') definition of what is normal. The psychiatrists Szasz (1961) and Laing (1960) and the sociologist Scheff (1966) have, each in his own way, raised questions as to who really is mentally ill. These scholars, as critics, have questioned the very goals of those organizations that treat the "mentally ill." To the degree that such a scholar as Szasz is correct in his stance, the label of mental illness does much to degrade humankind. It confines human beings within social cages from which they find it difficult, if not impossible, to escape. In many instances researchers involved in the evaluation of mental health programs have helped to place locks upon these cages. It is in this sense that the "liberal model" espoused by Janowitz (1966), with its emphasis upon the use of evaluation as a basis for modifying correctional institutions for juvenile delinquents, can be called into question. It is conceivable that many of the so-called delinquents in the institutions he studied should not have been labeled as delinquents at all.

But criticism alone will not advance the cause of human dignity. We must formulate research orientations that emphasize the development of alternative structural arrangements that transcend some of the difficulties inherent in the present-day social order.

TOWARD A NEW EVALUATION METHODOLOGY

We have sought to explicate some of the taken for granted assumptions in present-day evaluation research. We have reasoned that the political and ethical orientations of social scientists have led them to work within system categories, often those defined by the power groups.

The ethical and political dilemmas in most evaluation research are magnified during periods of rapid change. Researchers, reasoning via the logic of analogy, implicitly assume that the categories of the emerging postindustrial, post-welfare order are analogous to the categories of the traditional industrial-urban one, which is dominated by bureaucracies oriented toward the efficient use of scarce resources.

We have suggested that social criticism becomes an essential ingredient of evaluation research. Consider the field of family planning. Here evaluation studies have been mainly concerned with analyzing the effectiveness of various family planning programs in reducing population growth (e.g., Berelson and others, 1966). But as Kingsley Davis (1967, 1970) has suggested, this orientation is woefully inadequate. Davis contends that if we are to resolve the major population problems facing the modern world, we must restructure the family system so that people will be motivated to have fewer children. Although Davis does not indicate just how we might restructure the family, the existing programs for controlling population growth, and by implication those that have been subjected to evaluation studies, are doomed to failure.

But we must proceed beyond criticism to a more constructive form of analysis. Our approach to evaluation research is based upon what we term "countersystem analysis," a form of dialectical reasoning (Sjoberg and Cain, 1971). A countersystem is a negation of and logical alternative to the existing social order (or social structure) in question and is therefore a kind of "utopian model."

Social scientists are able to construct a number of countersystems with respect to any given social arrangement. They vary according to the assumptions about the social order that are taken as givens. Thus, Fanon (1965) negated the modern industrial-urban order and constructed a countersystem that excluded industrialization and urbanization. Still other countersystem (or utopian) models have been constructed upon the premise that industrialization and urbanization should be sustained, though with the proviso that major elements of the social structure be remade.

Countersystem analysis provides social scientists with some distinct methodological advantages. One of these is that they can employ the countersystem as a standard for evaluating the on going order. The latter does not have to be evaluated on its own terms. And new programs need not be seen simply as deviations from the on-going order; they are also deviations from the ideal order.

To be sure, we must be wary of reifying, as many radical thinkers are prone to do, the countersystem model. Many intellectuals have constructed utopian dreams and then have assumed that these should automatically become a reality. Moreover, there is the danger that a utopian model itself may embody serious limitations. Our own orientation is that both the categories or standards of the system and those of the countersystem are essential in evaluating programs of social action.

At this point, it is possible to suggest an application of our framework to the realm of education, to evaluation of the success of graduate school programs and of college teachers. The evaluations of graduate programs, be these on the university or the departmental level, and to a somewhat lesser degree the evaluations of teachers, have emphasized uniformity (unidimensionality) and the dominant success indicators of the broader society. Too frequently scholars and administrators judge graduate school programs in terms of the publication record of the faculty and their students.

In contrast to the emphasis upon uniformity and success, a countersystem approach would emphasize those programs that help students avoid failure and would place a premium upon faculty and students developing a variety of intellectual and social commitments, not solely those measured by publications. As a utopian dream this countersystem would be difficult, if not impossible, to implement. But it does present a standard by which to evaluate traditional or experimental programs. Moreover, in an affluent, postindustrial order, many elements of the countersystem model may not only be realizable but also essential for meeting the demands and potentialities of the emerging order.

Consider the many activities in which graduate schools could engage. Students could not only be educated to become successful scholars, but they could utilize graduate education as a basis for an avocation. Intellectual pursuits might provide many persons with more meaning in life than presently stems from most leisure-time activities. Graduate schools could also stress the education of persons for policy posts or for upgrading schools and colleges that teach the disadvantaged. And so on.

We could also set forth a variety of criteria for defining good teaching as well, criteria that are typically unmeasured by present-day instruments. How many instruments, for example, include criteria by which administrators or colleagues could positively value a teacher who helps students avoid failure? There are still other criteria mentioned earlier in this essay that do not currently form part of evaluation efforts.

One objection to our proposal is: How would it be possible to eliminate poor graduate programs or ineffective teachers? One could not do so by employing the standards of the countersystem per se. But it certainly seems reasonable to expect that we should begin evaluating graduate programs and teachers not only in terms of their successes but also in terms of the casualties of their efforts. Is it not feasible, indeed necessary, to balance off the successes against the failures and rule out those programs or teachers where the ratio of failure to success is too great?

A number of graduate schools and graduate departments have taken a degree of satisfaction in the failures they produce. A good deal of folklore in sociology concerns programs where in times past few students could overcome the hurdles. Some programs during the 1960s kept many students around but permitted few of them to graduate. The striking negative features of this kind of educational activity have not received the serious attention they deserve. When evaluating programs in terms of the number of failures versus the number of successes we, of course, should take into account the efforts toward prescreening of candidates. A program that accepts persons who are defined by society as "high risks" should not be evaluated on the same basis as one that carefully prescreens its students. To reiterate: a just evaluation of a program should balance off its negative features against its positive ones.

A somewhat similar evaluation effort could be carried out with respect to teaching. It should be possible to establish a rather broad range of socially meaningful indicators. Then we could weigh the negative against the positive features of teachers' activities, and it should be possible to establish outer limits where the contributions of particular teachers are outweighed by the casualties that result from their actions. In practice it is easier to cope with a system's teachers than with its programs. Students can more readily move from one teacher to another than from one school to another.

However one may view my countersystem orientation,[2] and only a brief sketch of its implications is provided here, I am convinced that, because of the deepseated impact of political and ethical factors upon evaluation research, more attention must be given to formulating alternative methodologies (cf. Scriven, 1967; Weiss and Rein, 1969). The emphasis upon experimental designs (cf. Suchman, 1967; Rossi, 1969), although these are useful under certain conditions, often seems

misplaced. The deviations from the ideal norms of the experimental design, resulting from the impact of the researcher upon the research process, are usually so
marked as to cast doubt upon the results. In addition, experimental designs lead
researchers to analyze innovative programs in terms of the control group. This in
effect means that researchers employ system variables without benefit of a countersystem perspective. My concern is not with de-emphasizing research but with
placing it within a broader perspective and avoiding undue reliance upon technical
virtuosity.

CONCLUSIONS

Some recapitulation and integration of our argument is in order. Our discussion
began with an analysis of the researcher's role in the research design. Thus far
methodologists have been unwilling to make the major leap of reconceptualizing
the research design so as effectively to take account of social factors that structure
the research from its inception on through the analysis of the findings. Once this is
done, the research process becomes more complex and problematic than books on
research methods would have us believe.

We also briefly discussed theory building, which has at least two significant
dimensions: the logical structure (or form) and the assumptions about human
nature and social reality. The relationship between the researcher as a variable in
the research design and our conception of theory building is most clearly seen when
we recognize the impact of the researcher's assumptions about human nature and
social reality upon the research process. In discussing evaluation research we have
attempted to illustrate how researchers typically accept the power structure as
given and thus come to align themselves, unwittingly or otherwise, with the
dominant groups in the system. They have typically accepted the indicators
determining success defined by the dominant groups in the society, as well as the
latter's definitions of the "public good" or the "national interest" as standards for
evaluating social programs.

Although researchers necessarily must work within a societal or nation-state
context, they also have a responsibility to science and to the principle of human
dignity to recognize the broader political and ethical implications of their efforts.
The tendency of the "social indicator school" to over-identify with the dominant
groups within the nation-state raises serious questions that must be honestly faced.

I have suggested one means of avoiding the dilemmas of research evaluation: the
use of countersystem analysis. This logical orientation, if properly employed, offers
researchers one means of transcending the inherent tension between the advantaged
and the disadvantaged in a society and, just as important, between the advantaged
and the disadvantaged on a global scale. It is unfortunate that evaluation researchers
become so locked into their own framework that they do not attempt to understand the implications of their efforts, not just for the programs they seek to
evaluate but for all humankind.

The orientation toward research that I have espoused commits me to views
about human nature and social reality that are quite different from those held by
most evaluation researchers. The ambiguity and paradoxes in social life, and the

tensions between individuals and groups and between groups and the broader society, have positive as well as negative features. I would not impose upon social life an evaluation process that demands uniformity or unidimensionality, although I have recognized that some form of evaluation must and will occur. Ultimately I am more concerned with the consequences of evaluation than with the narrow technical proficiency that has all too frequently dominated efforts in this significant social realm.

NOTES

1. My intent, as suggested above, is not to rid social research of a standardized set of rules or ideal norms for collecting and analyzing data. My concern is with formulating these so that they can be more useful than those currently espoused. Researchers, especially in conducting evaluation studies, cannot adhere to many of the research procedures that writers of research textbooks or monographs say ought to be followed. The ideal norms should be cast in a more realistic manner. Moreover, many actual norms that are implicitly accepted by researchers should be raised to the level of consciousness and elevated to the realm of ideal norms. I accept the need for a tension between those rules that researchers ought to follow and those that they can or do follow, but the discrepancy between the two should not become so great as to encourage hypocrisy.

2. Countersystem analysis should also prove useful for coping with the "unanticipated consequences" of research programs. Although I cannot pursue the problem herein, I believe that, by thinking in terms of the negation of and logical alternatives to the intended consequences of a program, one might be able to anticipate some of the unanticipated consequences of purposive social action. Unfortunately the unanticipated consequences of purposive action are seldom treated by evaluation researchers, at least in an explicit manner.

Clearly the unanticipated consequences of planned social intervention can be of great significance. For instance, a few years ago I served as a consultant to the Wesley Community Agency's research and social action program (San Antonio, Texas). Buford Farris and Richard Brymer, among others, were seeking to develop an alternative type of organization, one that would serve high-risk families or juveniles. In looking back upon the efforts of this Agency, we see many unanticipated consequences to their program. One of these was the training of persons who later came to head agencies elsewhere and who sought to transfer features of the Wesley model to other settings. A narrow and short-range view of social experiments can lead researchers to overlook the significant implications, both positive and negative, of a social program.

REFERENCES

Anastasi, A. Psychology, psychologists, and psychological testing. *American Psychologist,* 1967, 22: 297-306.

Bauer, R. A. (ed.) *Social indicators.* Cambridge, Mass.: M.I.T. Press, 1966.

Becker, H. *Outsiders.* New York: Free Press, 1963.

———. Whose side are we on? *Social Problems,* 1967, 14: 239-247.

Berelson, B., and others. *Family planning and population programs.* Chicago: University of Chicago Press, 1966.

Berman, H. J. Legal reasoning. Pp. 197-204 in *International encyclopedia of the social sciences, IX.* New York: Macmillan, 1968.

Biderman, A. D. Social indicators and goals. In R. A. Bauer (ed.), *Social indicators.* Cambridge, Mass: M.I.T. Press, 1966.

Caro, F. G. (ed.) *Readings in evaluation research.* New York: Russell Sage Foundation, 1971.

Cohen, D. K. Politics and research: evaluation of social action programs in education. *Review of Educational Research,* 1970, 40: 213-238.

Davis, K. Population policy: will current programs succeed? *Science,* November 10, 1967, 158: 734-736.

–––. The climax of population growth. *California Medicine,* 1970, 113: 33-39.

Denzin, N. *The research act.* Chicago: Aldine, 1970.

Etzioni, A. and E. W. Lehman. Some dangers in 'valid' social measurement. In B. M. Gross (ed.), *Social intelligence for America's future.* Boston: Allyn Bacon, 1969.

Fanon, F. *The wretched of the earth.* New York: Grove Press, 1965.

Fuchs, V. R. *The service economy.* New York: National Bureau of Economic Research, 1968.

Goffman, E. *The presentation of self in everyday life.* Garden City: Doubleday, Anchor Books, 1959.

Gouldner, A. The sociologist as partisan: sociology and the welfare state. *American Sociologist,* 1968, 3: 103-116.

–––. *The coming crisis of Western sociology.* New York: Basic Books, 1970.

Gross, B. M. (ed.) *Social intelligence for America's future.* Boston: Allyn and Bacon, 1969.

Hyman, H. H. and C. R. Wright. Evaluating social action programs. In P. F. Lazarsfeld, H. Sewell, and H. L. Wilensky (eds.), *The uses of sociology.* New York: Basic Books, 1967.

Hyman, H. H., C. R. Wright and T. K. Hopkins. *Applications of methods of evaluation.* Berkeley and Los Angeles: University of California Press, 1962.

Janowitz, M. Foreword. In D. Street, R. D. Vinter, and C. Perrow, *Organization for treatment.* New York: Free Press, 1966.

Jensen, A. R. How much can we boost IQ and scholastic achievement? *Harvard Education Review,* 1969, 39: 1-123.

Koerner, J. D. *The Parsons College bubble.* New York: Basic Books, 1970.

Laing, R. D. *The divided self.* Chicago: Quadrangle Books, 1960.

Lazarsfeld, P. F. and M. Rosenberg (eds.). *The language of social research.* New York: Free Press, 1955.

Lazarsfeld, P. F. and W. Thielens, Jr. *The academic mind.* New York: Free Press, 1958.

McKeachie, W. J. Research on teaching at the college and university level. In N. L. Gage (ed.), *Handbook of research on teaching.* Chicago: Rand McNally, 1963.

–––. Student ratings of faculty. *AAUP Bulletin,* 1969, 55: 439-444.

March, J. G. (ed.) *Handbook of organizations.* Chicago: Rand McNally, 1965.

Moynihan, D. P. *Maximum feasible misunderstanding.* New York: Free Press, 1970.

Orne, M. T. On the social psychology of the psychological experiment. *American Psychologist,* 1962, 17: 776-783.

Popper, K. *Conjectures and refutations.* New York: Basic Books, 1962.

Report of the Commission on Testing. *Righting the Balance, I.* New York: College Entrance Examination Board, 1970.

Rossie, P. Practice, method, and theory in evaluating social-action programs. In J. L. Sandquist (ed.), *On fighting poverty.* New York: Basic Books, 1969.

Rosenthal, R. *Experimenter effects in behavioral science.* New York: Appleton-Century-Crofts, 1966.

Scheff, T. J. *Being mentally ill.* Chicago: Aldine, 1966.

Schultze, C. L. The politics and economics of public spending. Washington, D.C.: Brookings Institution, 1968.

Scriven, M. The methodology of evaluation. In S. Tyler, R. M. Gagne, and M. Scriven (eds.), *Perspectives on curriculum education.* Chicago: Rand McNally, 1967.

Sjoberg, G., R. Brymer and B. Farris. Bureaucracy and the lower class. *Sociology and Social Research,* 1966, 50: 325-327.

Sjoberg, G. and L. D. Cain, Jr. Negative values, countersystem models, and the analysis of social systems. In H. Turk and R. L. Simpson (eds.), *Institutions and Social Exchange: The Sociologies of Talcott Parsons and George C. Homans.* Indianapolis: Bobbs-Merrill, 1971.

Sjoberg, G. and R. Nett. *A methodology for social research.* New York: Harper and Row, 1968.

Sjoberg, G. and T. R. Vaughan. The sociology of ethics and the ethics of sociology. In E. Tiryakian (ed.), *The phenomenon of sociology.* New York: Appleton-Century-Crofts, 1971.

Smith, J. O. Social research in a psychiatric setting: the natural history of a research project. Dissertation. Ohio State University, 1969.

Smith, M. S. and J. S. Bissell. Report analysis: the impact of Head Start. *Harvard Educational Review,* 1970, 40: 51-104.

Stinchcombe, A. L. *Constructing social theories.* New York: Harcourt, Brace, and World, 1968.

———. Environment: the cumulation of events. *Harvard Educational Review,* 1969, 39: 511-522.

Suchman, E. *Evaluative research.* New York: Russell Sage Foundation, 1967.

Szasz, T. S. *The myth of mental illness.* New York: Hoeber-Harper, 1961.

Tilly, C., J. R. Feagin and C. Williams. *Rent supplements in Boston.* Cambridge, Mass.: Joint Center for Urban Studies of the Massachusetts Institute of Technology and Harvard University, 1968. Mimeo.

Ward, D. A. Evaluations of correctional treatment: some implications of negative findings. In S. A. Yefsky (ed.), *Law enforcement science and technology.* London: Academic Press, 1967.

Wallace, W. (ed.) *Sociological theory.* Chicago: Aldine, 1969.

Weiss, R. S. and M. Rein. The evaluation of broad-aim programs: a cautionary case and a moral. *The Annals,* 1969, 385: 133-142.

White, O. Jr. and G. Sjoberg. The emerging 'new politics' in America. In M. D. Hancock and G. Sjoberg (eds.), *Politics in the post-welfare state.* New York: Columbia University Press, in press.

Williams, W. and J. W. Evans. The politics of evaluation: the case of Head Start. *The Annals,* 1969, 385: 118-132.

REFERENCE UPDATE

Selected by Elmer L. Struening

Abbott, A. Professional ethics. *American Journal of Sociology,* 1983, 88 (5).

Barnes, J. A. *Who should know what? Social science, privacy and ethics.* Cambridge: Cambridge University, 1979.

Berk, R. S. and P. H. Rossi. Doing good or worse: Evaluation research politically re-examined. *Social Problems,* 1976, 23: 337-349.

Berman, G., H. C. Kelman, and D. P. Warwick (eds.). *The ethics of social intervention.* Washington, DC: Hemisphere, 1978.

Boruch, R. F. and J. S. Cecil (eds.). *Solutions to ethical and legal problems in social research.* New York: Academic, 1983.

Caro, F. G. Leverage and evaluation effectiveness. *Evaluation and Program Planning,* 1980, 3 (2): 83-89.

Gorry, G. A. and T. J. Goodrich. On the role of values in program evaluation. *Evaluation Quarterly,* 1978, 2 (4).

Graycar, A. Political issues in research and evaluation. *Evaluation Quarterly,* 1979, 3 (3): 460-471.

Hackler, J. C. The dangers of political naivete and excessive complexity in evaluating delinquency prevention programs. *Evaluation and Program Planning,* 1978, 1 (4): 273-283.

Hendrickson, L. and L. Barber. Evaluation and politics: A critical study of a community school program. *Evaluation Review,* 1980, 4 (6): 769-787.

Keeley, M. A social justice approach to organizational evaluation. *Administrative Science Quarterly,* 1978, 23: 272-292.

Korr, W. S. How evaluators can deal with role conflict. *Evaluation and Program Planning,* 1982, 5 (1): 53-58.

Levine, A. and M. Levine. The social context of evaluation research; A case study. *Evaluation Quarterly,* 1977, 1 (4).

Neigher, W. and C. Windle. Ethical problems in program evaluation: Advice for trapped evaluators. *Evaluation and Program Planning,* 1978, 1 (2): 97-108.

Perloff, R. and E. Perloff (eds.) Values, ethics, and standards in evaluation. *New Directions for Program Evaluation*, 1980, 7 (special issue).

Rezmovic, E. L., T. J. Cook, and L. D. Dobson. Beyond random assignment: Factors affecting evaluation integrity. *Evaluation Review*, 1981, 5 (1) 51-67.

Sheinfeld, S. N. and G. L. Lord. The ethics of evaluation researchers: An exploration of value choices. *Evaluation Review*, 1981, 5 (3): 377-391.

Sieber, J. E. (ed.). *The ethics of social research* (2 vols.). New York: Springer-Verlag, 1982.

Sjoberg, G. and T. R. Vaughan. A moral context for social research: A review essay on the ethics of social research. *Hastings Center Report*, 1983, 13.

Stein, R. E. K. and D. J. Jessop. An ethics committee to aid in implementing a randomized clinical trial. *Controlled Clinical Trials*, 1983, 4: 37-42.

III

CONCEPTUALIZATION AND DESIGN
OF EVALUATION STUDIES

5

THE LOGIC OF EVALUATION

W. EDWARDS DEMING

WHAT IS EVALUATION?

The point of view here will be that evaluation is a pronouncement concerning the effectiveness of some treatment or plan that has been tried or put into effect. The purpose of this chapter will be to explain some of the problems in the design and interpretation of a study whose aim is to evaluate the effectiveness of some treatment or plan; also to point out some of the difficulties of studying by retrospect the cause of success or failure, or the cause of a disease or of a specific alleged cure therefor. Emphasis will be placed on ways to improve the reliability of evaluation by understanding and avoiding possible misuses of statistical techniques in evaluation.

It is fascinating to look around us and to observe how often people apply some treatment in the hope of producing a desired effect, then claim success if events turn in their favor, but suppress the whole affair if they do not.

A governor put 200 additional policemen on the highways to decrease the rate of accidents (he hoped). Serious accidents dropped from 74 to 63 the month following his action. Was this decrease attributable to the policemen, as he claimed? The answer seems at first to be so obvious: yes, of course. But wait. If every accident be independent of every other accident, then the student of statistical theory would recognize the number of accidents in a given period of time as a Poisson variate. He would then accept the square root of the number of accidents as a random variable distributed normally with variance ¼. The difference between the square roots of the number of accidents in two months would be distributed normally about O with variance ¼ + ¼. On this basis, one would calculate

$$t = \frac{\sqrt{74} - \sqrt{63}}{\sqrt{¼ + ¼}} = .94$$

for the t-value of the observed difference.

Without any calculation at all, one could only say that (1) any two months will be different; and (2) the decrease in accidents was consistent with the hypothesis that the governor's efforts had some effect. What does the above calculation add to our knowledge? It tells us that it would be rash to conclude that the data establish the hypothesis, for the small value of t admits a competing hypothesis, namely, that the observed difference was simply a random fluctuation, the kind of difference that would turn up in scoop after scoop of black and white beans drawn from a bushel of black and white beans mixed and remixed between scoops. Lack of independence between accidents, such as icy roads that persist over several days, would only decrease t, and would weaken further any argument that the governor's efforts were successful. We therefore see no statistical evidence from the figures given that the governor's efforts had any effect. Maybe they did. We shall never know.

Examples that show results that went in the wrong direction are hard to find: they get buried, not published. No one is around to take the negative credit for a failure.

A mother tries to persuade a child, by precept, example, or punishment, to cease and desist from some practice or habit. How effective is she? A young man saves money and gives up his job for a year in order that he may go to school. He applies education to himself, in the hope of improving in the future his economic and social status in life. He may eventually evaluate his decision: he may be satisfied that he did the right thing, or he may decide otherwise. By what criteria should he evaluate his decision?

Do fluorides in the drinking water retard greatly the decay of teeth? Does smoking cause cancer? Is marijuana really harmful? How effective is Head Start? In what way? Do seat belts save lives? How effective are loss leaders in a grocery store? What can go wrong in a test market?

Did the Federal Reserve Board make some right moves in the depression of 1969-1972? Will Variety A of wheat, sown in some specified area next year, show a yield at least 5 more bushels per acre than Variety B? Is EXTHRX effective as an antidepressant? For what kind of patients? What are some of the side effects, and how long before they appear? Does a certain plan of parole and education achieve the goals claimed in advance?

How effective are incentives for reenlistment in the Navy? What is the loss to a grocer who runs out of stock Saturday noon of a popular item? What is the cost of a defective item that goes out from a manufacturer to a consumer?

A prototype of some assembly or machine (e.g., an airplane) is put together for test. Will tests of the prototype predict the performance of machines that will later come out of regular production? Why not?

May one estimate from the results of an accelerated test establish the length of life of a lamp, or of a vacuum tube, or of a vacuum cleaner, or the mean time to failure of a complex apparatus? Why not? Or if so, how?

A flash of lightning brightens the landscape. A clap of thunder hits our ears a few seconds later. We never raise a question about the cause of the thunder; we agree that the lightning caused it, and we do not try to convince anyone that the thunder caused the lightning. Innoculation for smallpox is effective. Cholera in London came from drinking water that came from wells. Certain treatments and drugs for tuberculosis are effective. Most of these statements, well accepted now, were learned without benefit of statistical design.

Social programs and wide-scale tests of treatments are unfortunately laid out almost always so that statistical evaluation of their effectiveness cannot be evaluated. Government regulations on safety of mechanical and electrical devices are meaningless. And what about the side effects from noxious by-products of catalytic converters?

No one can calculate by statistical theory in advance, or even afterward, the effect of changes in interest rates, the impact of a merger, or of a step taken by the Federal Reserve Board. A statistically designed test is impossible, though accidental comparisons may of course turn up.

A firm advertises in magazines and newspapers and other media, or by direct mail, to increase sales. Adequate design of the experiment is usually difficult, and not even attempted. As a result, the effectiveness of the campaign is still in doubt after the experiment, just as it was before. An increase in sales could be the result of the campaign, but there are usually half a dozen competing hypotheses such as the effects of nonresponse or of other failures in cooperation of respondents, errors in response, changes in economic conditions, impact of competition, new products, new models, any one of which could explain what was observed.

The advantages of evaluation with the help of a statistical designed experiment, when such a thing is possible, are better grounds for understanding the results, speed, and economy. But we have to learn to use statistical inferences that are conditional, relating only to special conditions.

When men arrive at a consensus on cause and effect, they have solved, temporarily at least, a problem in evaluation. Textbooks in statistics and in the social sciences are replete with methods and examples of evaluation (not necessarily called by this name), without warning of pitfalls. The most important lesson we can learn about statistical methods in evaluation is that circumstances where one may depend wholly on statistical inference are rare.

NEED FOR CARE IN DEFINITIONS OF TERMS

There has never in man's history been an era of greater effort toward safe drugs, safe automobiles, safe apparatus, safety on the job, decrease in pollution, war on poverty, aids to underprivileged children, and all sorts of well-meant social programs. The problems of evaluation of these efforts are compounded by failure to define terms operationally, as well as by failure to lay down criteria by which to weigh gains and advantages against losses and disadvantages. A drug that helps thousands may be harmful to a few people. Is it safe?

Any adjective that is to be used in evaluation requires an operational definition, which can be stated only in statistical terms. Unemployed, improved, good, acceptable, safe, round, reliable, accurate, dangerous, polluted, flammable, on-time performance (as of an airline or train) have no meaning except in terms of a stated statistical degree of uniformity and reproducibility of a test method or criterion.

There is no such thing as the true value of anything.

The label on a blanket reads "50% wool." What does this mean? Half wool, on the average, over a month's production? Or does it relate somehow to this blanket that we purchased? By weight? If so, at what humidity? The bottom half of the blanket is wool and the top half is something else? Is the blanket 50% wool? Does 50% wool mean that there must be some wool in any random cross-section the size of a half dollar? If so, how many cuts shall be tested? How must they be selected? What criterion must the average satisfy? And how much variation between cuts is permissible? Obviously, the meaning of 50% wool requires statistical criteria. Words will not suffice.

FOUR REQUIREMENTS FOR AN EFFECTIVE SYSTEM OF EVALUATION

The four requirements for an effective system of evaluation are:

1. A meaningful operational measure of success or of failure, satisfactory to experts in the subject matter, of some proposed treatment applied to specified material,[1] under specified conditions. (Examples: a medical criterion of recovery or improvement in some affliction: a criterion for recognition of a definite and notable increase in production of wheat or of rice; a criterion for recognition of a definite and notable improvement of quality of a textile or of a carburetor; a criterion for improvement in quality of transmission of signals; a criterion for recognition of a definite and notable increase in the speed of learning a language.)

2. Some satisfactory design of experiments, tests, surveys, or examination of data already recorded. The design of a new study will include selection of samples of the specified material; a record, for the duration of each phase of the study, of certain specified environmental conditions that appear to be important; procedures for carrying out the investigation; and statistical controls to aid supervision of the investigation.

3. Methods for presentation and interpretation of the results of the experiments, tests, survey, or other investigation, that will not lead to action different from the action that would be taken on the basis of the original data.[2] The data must include a record of the environmental conditions, including test method, questionnaire, perhaps the names of the observers. They must include a description of the frame.

4. Some official or some group of people authorized to take action (with or without evidence).

LIMITATIONS OF STATISTICAL INFERENCE

A statistical study, prospective or retrospective, proceeds by investigation of some or all of the material in a frame.[3] A complete investigation is called a census. The frame is an aggregate of tangible units of material of some kind, any or all of which may be selected and investigated. The frame may be lists of people, dwelling units, schoolchildren, areas, blocks and plots in agricultural trials, business establishments, materials, manufactured parts, or other units that would supposedly yield useful results if the whole frame were investigated.

A point often forgotten is that the results of statistical inference refer only to the material in the frame that was studied, the instrument of test, and the method of using it, and to the ranges of economic and physical conditions and stresses within which there was randomization. Statistical inference ends with the frame and the environmental conditions under which the frame was studied. The theory of probability cannot help us outside these limits.

All probabilities are conditional and all statistical inference likewise, being conditional on the frame and the environmental conditions of the experiment. Any probability calculated from an experiment, if it has any use at all, is a prediction that future experiments on samples of material drawn by random numbers from the same frame, tested in the same way, and under the same environmental conditions, would show about the same results within calculable limits. Unfortunately, in an analytic study (next section), where the aim is to provide a basis for action on a process (if we get any good at all out of the experiment), the environmental conditions will be different from those that governed the experiment. It follows that any estimate or other evaluation based on an experiment can be used in an analytic study only on the authority of an expert in the subject matter who is willing to offer a judgment on whether the results are applicable to other conditions.

A good question to ask in the early stages of preparation of a study is this: What will the results refer to? How do you propose to use them?

ENUMERATIVE STUDIES CONTRASTED WITH ANALYTIC STUDIES

Effective use of statistical methods requires careful distinction between enumerative studies and analytic studies, with continual recognition of the limitations of statistical inference. The aim of any statistical study is to provide a basis for action. There are two broad types of action:

Enumerative—Action on the frame.
Analytic—Action on the cause-system (process) that produced the frame and will produce more frames in the future.

The methods of statistical design and of statistical inference are different for the two types of action. Failure to make the distinction between them has led to uninspired teaching of statistical methods and to misguided inferences.[4]

In an enumerative study, action will be taken on the frame and will depend purely on the estimate of the number or proportion of the people or materials in the frame that have certain characteristics (sometimes on the maximum or minimum). The action does not depend on how or why man or nature produced the frame. Examples:

1. We may need to know how many children by age there are in a certain region whose diet is below a minimum tolerable level (perhaps in calories, perhaps in vitamin or protein content). The reason to make the count is to know how much food to supply and what kind.
2. A quick count of the number of people left without homes and without food by a flood or earthquake. A vital question is how many people, adults, infants, and infirm are in need of the necessities of life.

3. The census of the U.S. for congressional apportionment, district by district.
4. A census of a city taken as a basis for an increase in financial support from the state.
5. We may need to know the total debits and credits in dollars on the books of some railway for services that they performed jointly with other railways during the past year. The frame could be, for example, 3 million interline abstracts in the files of this railway.
6. An inventory of certain materials is to be taken to assess the total value of an inventory. This inventory may determine the selling price of the material, or it may find its way into the auditor's annual report, or it may be used for tax purposes.
7. Cores bored from bales of wool selected by random numbers from a shipload of wool as it is unloaded, and analyzed by a chemist for clean content, determine the price and the duty to be paid on the whole shipload.
8. A telephone company may make a field inspection of the equipment it owns to determine the present worth of this equipment as a basis for rates for service.

In an analytic study, the aim is to try to learn something about the cause-system (process) to be in a position to change it or to leave it alone, whichever appears to be better for the future benefit of man or of his pocketbook. The frame studied (material or people) in an analytic problem is not of interest in itself. A complete census or study of the entire frame (all the people in an area, or all of last week's product) is still only a sample of what the cause system can produce, and did.

There is no finite multiplier of the form $1/n - 1/N$ in an estimate of variance in an analytic study. This same multiplier is of course very important in an enumerative study, as it reduces the sampling variation to zero for a complete census, that is, when $n = N$.

Some studies serve both enumerative and analytic uses. The census of any country, aside from enumerative uses (number of representatives or number of councilmen for an area, allocation of water, electricity, teachers) furnishes information by which economists, sociologists, and agricultural experts construct and test theories of migration, fertility, growth of the population, aging of the population, consumption of food, the aim being to understand better the changes in fertility and longevity that take place in the distribution of the population by sex, age, education, income, employment, occupation, industry, and urbanization. One aim among other aims might be to alter the causes of poverty and malnutrition.

A study of accounts receivable, primarily for an enumerative purpose, namely, this year's financial statement, may also yield information that is helpful in reducing errors of certain types in the future.

TWO POSSIBLE MISTAKES IN AN ENUMERATIVE STUDY

One may make either one of two types of error in taking action on the basis of an enumerative study. To take a concrete example, we are about to purchase a load of ore. The price to pay will depend on the results of assay of samples of the ore. We may, as a result of the sampling and assay:

1. Pay more by an amount D than the ore is worth;

or

2. Sell it for less by an amount D′ than it is worth.

We must pause at these words. We talk as if it were possible to find out what the load of ore is worth. We can proceed only if we are willing to accept some method as a master standard. Thus, we might agree that the master standard shall be the result of assays that follow a specified procedure on a large number of samples of the ore, more than we think are necessary for our purchase to be made presently. In practice, we take enough samples to provide a useful estimate of the master standard.

Statistical theory enables us to minimize the net economic loss in such problems from too much testing and from not enough testing.[5]

Techniques that are useful in enumerative studies are theory of sampling, including, of course, theory for optimum allocation of effort, losses in precision in estimates for the whole of a frame when differential sampling fractions are specified in order to get separate estimates for a particular stratum. Confidence intervals and fiducial intervals are useful in inference. Controls by appropriate statistical techniques of the instruments and of the methods of using them, and control of field-work, are essential for reliability and economy, and to understand the results. Calculation of the risk of being wrong in an inference from a statistically designed study in an enumerative problem is in the nature of a mathematical consequence.[6]

Unfortunately, as we shall see, no such beauty of theory exists in an analytic study.

TWO POSSIBLE MISTAKES IN AN ANALYTIC STUDY

There are also two types of mistake in taking action in an analytic study. These mistakes are totally different in nature from the mistakes of using an enumerative study. In an analytic problem:

1. We may adopt Treatment B in preference to A based partly or wholly on a statistical study, only to regret later our action to adopt it;

or

2. We may fail to adopt B, retain A, only to regret later our failure to adopt B.

One may make either mistake, with or without the help of an experiment, and it requires no high degree of education to make them. It is easy to bet on the wrong horse, to use an ineffective method of advertising, to purchase and install a machine that turns out later on to be a mistake, to plant the variety of wheat with the lesser outturn, misjudge a drug, approve social legislation that turns out to backfire, and so on.

The aim in the use of statistical theory should be to develop rules that will minimize in the long run the net loss from both mistakes. How to use statistical inference in analytic problems has received, so far, scant treatment in the statistical literature.

We shall not pause here for an example, as one will appear later. Suffice it to say here that, in contrast with the possible errors of using an enumerative study, we cannot, in an analytic study, calculate or govern by statistical methods the risks of making either error. The reason is that our action will be tested on future material, not yet produced, and we know not in advance what these future conditions may be. Even if we knew, we do not know except by substantive knowledge how they would affect the cause-system (treatment) of the future.

The watchmaker works on your watch and claims after a few weeks that it keeps perfect time. You wear it under other conditions—other temperatures, movements, irregular winding—and it loses time or becomes erratic. The watchmaker evaluates himself on the performance of your watch on the job, not by the record in his shop. This is why he tells you to bring the watch back after a few weeks so that he may adjust it if necessary.

The season, date, climate, rainfall, levels, dosage, length of treatment, age, ranges of concentration, pressure, temperature, speed, or voltage, or other stresses that may affect the performance of the process will be different in the future. Two varieties of wheat tested at Rothamsted may show that Variety B delivers under certain conditions much greater yield than Variety A. But does this result tell you which variety would do better on your farm in Illinois? Can you evaluate from the experiment at Rothamsted the probability of going wrong in adopting Variety B in Illinois? No. Tests of varieties of wheat lead to valid statistical inference only for the climate, rainfall, and soil that the study was conducted on. We shall never meet these conditions again. Yet the results, carefully presented, may be useful in the hands of the expert in the subject matter.

We must face the fact that it is impossible to calculate from the data of an experiment the risk of making the wrong choice. The difficulty is that there is no statistical theory that will predict from data of the past what will happen under economic or physical conditions outside the range of the study. We can only be sure that conditions outside this range will be encountered. There is thus no such thing as the power of a statistical test. (These assertions conflict sharply with books and teaching on tests of hypotheses, to which I will return later with a comment.)

Generalization to people from results of medical tests on rats is a perennial problem. Statistical theory can only tell us about rats. Generalization to people is the responsibility of the expert in the subject matter (chemistry, or various specialisms in medical science).

The aim of evaluation is to provide a basis for action in the future, with the aim to improve the product, or to help people to live better, whatever be the definition of better. Evaluation is a study of causes. Evaluation is thus analytic, not enumerative.

USE OF JUDGMENT-SAMPLES

It is hazardous to try to estimate or generalize from a judgment-sample to a portion or all of the frame whence the sample was selected. Use of a judgment-sample instead of a percentage or total of the frame for this purpose is worth no more than the reputation of the man that signs it. The reason is that there is no way except by judgment to set limits on the margin of uncertainty of the estimate.

Nevertheless, judgment-samples serve at times a very useful purpose by throwing light on a comparison of treatments. In spite of the fact that we are permitted to carry out a comparison of treatments only on patients who are highly abnormal (usually patients who do not need either treatment, or which neither treatment can help), or at a selected location such as Rothamsted, it is comforting to note that if the two treatments appropriately randomized and tested under these special conditions turn out to show results different by as much as D, then we have learned something: we may assert that the two treatments are materially different in some way—chemically, socially, psychologically, genetically, or otherwise. This we may assert even though we may never again use the treatments with patients like the ones tested, nor raise wheat under the same environmental conditions. The establishment of a difference of economic or scientific importance under any conditions may constitute important new knowledge.

Such a result, however, does not permit generalization: we cannot assert by statistical inference that other patients, nor other pupils, nor two varieties of wheat raised in some other location would show similar differences. Further experimentation would be required.

Randomization within a judgment-sample of plots within blocks (for trials of wheat), or of patients (for comparison of treatments) removes an important area of doubt and justifies the use of probability for conditional inferences. To understand the power of randomization within a judgment-sample of plots, one need only reflect on the contributions to our knowledge and economy that have emanated from the Rothamsted Experimental Station.

One could even go so far as to say that all analytic studies are carried out on judgment-samples of materials and environmental conditions, because application of the results will be to conditions beyond the boundaries of the experiment. This is why substantive judgment is so important in an analytic study.

We may often minimize the doubts about a series of experiments by choosing conditions for the study that will approximate (in the judgment of substantive experts) the conditions to be met in the future. Or, there may be a chance to run tests over a wide range of conditions. Thus, for tests of a variety of wheat, we might be able to run comparative experiments under different conditions of rainfall, irrigation, soil, climate, and length of growing season. One might, by substantive judgment, not by statistical theory, feel safe in planting or in not planting one of the varieties under test. In other words, one might, by substantive judgment, in fortunate circumstances, claim that the risk of the error of type 1 in a given analytic study is very small.

Thus, the law in physics that F = ma requires no qualification. A student in physics learns it once for all time. Originated by Sir Isaac Newton in London, it appears to hold in Liverpool, Tokyo, Chicago.

The advantage brought into a state of statistical control—stable in the Shewhart sense[7]—is that we may use statistical theory to predict the characteristics of tomorrow's product.

EFFECTIVE STATISTICAL INFERENCE

The aim of statistical inference in an analytic problem should be to give the expert in the subject matter the best possible chance to take the right action, that is, to reduce to a minimum the losses from the two types of mistake. A careful description of the conditions of the experiment are, as Shewhart emphasized,[8] an important part of the data of the experiment: the expert in the subject matter requires this kind of information (unfortunately too often omitted by statisticians).

There is no knowledge without temporal spread, which implies prediction.[9] In most analytic problems, the substantive expert must contribute heavily to the conclusions, the knowledge, that can be drawn out of a study.

Statistical inference in an analytic problem is most effective when it is presented as conclusions valid for the frame studied and for the range of environmental conditions specified for the tests. It is important to make clear that conclusions drawn by statistical theory may not hold under other conditions, and that other conditions may well be encountered.

Tests of a medical treatment, to be useful to future patients, would specify ranges of dosage, length of treatment, severities and other characteristics of the illness treated, and observation of side effects; otherwise, there would be serious difficulties in evaluating of the test results. "The comparison was carried out over a period of three weeks. No side effects were observed." Consumer research on some products can be nigh meaningless without reference to the season, climate, and economic conditions, for example, studies on consumption of soft drinks, or of analgesics, or of intentions to travel.

The theory of sampling and design of experiment are important in analytic studies. Optimum allocation of effort in analytic studies often differs from optimum allocation of effort in enumerative studies, though there is no literature to cite. Analysis of variance is useful as a rough tool of inference, to be followed up with more careful analysis. The trouble with analysis of variance is that it obscures trends and differences between small segments. The same caution holds for factor analysis and for cluster analysis. Any technique can be useful if its limitations are understood and observed.

Techniques of analysis that are most efficient in analytic problems include run charts to detect trends and differences between small classes. A run chart is simply a plot of results in order of age, time, duration of test, stress, or geographic location. A scatter diagram is often helpful. A distribution, simple though it be, is a powerful tool. Extreme skewness and wiggles detect sources of variation and lead to improved understanding of the process. The Mosteller-Tukey double square-root paper is useful, even when results are moderately correlated and do not follow strictly the binomial distribution.[10]

STATISTICAL TESTS OF HYPOTHESES

Unfortunately, as already stated, no statistical technique will evaluate the risks in an analytic problem. A brief note in the negative about testing hypotheses belongs here. The sad truth is that so-called tests of hypotheses, tutored well but not wisely in books and in teaching, are not helpful in practical problems, and as a system of logic, are misleading.[11] Two different treatments or two different varieties are never equal under any set of conditions: this we know without spending a nickel on an experiment. A difference between two treatments, though far too small to be of any economic or scientific consequence, will show up as "significantly different" if the experiment be conducted through a sufficient number of trials. A difference may be highly significant, yet be of no economic nor scientific importance. Obviously, such a test conveys no knowledge.

Likewise, tests of whether the data of a survey or an experiment fit some particular curve is of no scientific or economic importance. $P(x^2)$ for any curve, for any system, approaches zero as the number of observations increases. With enough data, no curve will fit.

The question that one faces in using some curve or relationship is whether it leads to a useful conclusion for experience in the future, or whether some other curve would do better? How robust are the conclusions?

Examples in the books on tests of hypotheses and in teaching are usually analytic in nature, but are treated as if they were enumerative, with inferences applicable to neither type.

Likewise, the teaching of regression estimates usually makes no distinction between (a) estimates of a total count in a frame, or the average per unit (enumerative uses), and (b) estimates of parameters (analytic). The techniques are different, the theory of optimum allocation of effort is different, and the uses even more so.

To state usefully the analytic problem in symbols, we first require from the substantive expert the number D, the difference that he requires between the two treatments (processes) to warrant action, which might of course be to continue the experiment. He needs an answer to the question

$$\text{Is } B \geq A + D ?$$

What we really need to know is whether the difference D will persist under conditions other than those that govern the experiment. As the manager of a large firm put it to his statistician, in consideration of two possible sizes of product, how much would it cost to carry out experiments that would tell him with fair certainty whether size B of the product would bring in 15% more dollars in sales than size A would bring. Here, $D = .15$. If the difference is less than 15%, it would not be worthwhile (in the judgment of the manager) to change the size: above 15%, it would be.

The appropriate statistical design will depend on the value of D.

For an example, one need only open any book on mathematical statistics, or any journal in psychology or biometrics. To avoid innuendo, in Table 5.1 I give an example close to hand.[12] The characteristic is somnambulism in children.

There is no mention of what difference D might be important. Moreover, the results must surely be obscured by difficulties in observation: "The behavioral findings presented in this report were obtained from a parent or guardian, usually the child's mother" (p. 2). The questionnaire was left at the home, picked up later. There is no mention of any test on the reliability of such observations.

TABLE 5.1 UNPLEASANT DREAMS

Sex	Frequently	Not often	Never	Unknown
Both	1.8	41.8	52.1	4.3
Boys	2.0	41.2	52.0	4.8
Girls	1.6	42.4	52.1	3.9

While 10% of children in the national study were reported to have done some sleepwalking, only about 1% did so frequently. The data in the table, however, are sufficient to clearly establish the statistical significance of the relationship (χ^2_4 = 35.3 for boys and 24.4 for girls, $P < .001$ for both boys and girls).

In my own experience, correlation between two informers or observers on such characteristics can only be described as disappointing, even at the extreme ends of the scale, where theory tells us that agreement should be good if both observers are independent and equal.[13] One could conclude that the differences between boys and girls in this study are measures of differences between observers, mostly mothers, instead of differences between boys and girls.

AN EXAMPLE OF AN ANALYTIC STUDY

Suppose that the problem is to decide whether the cause-system has the value p or p', or how much it has changed over a period of time, and why. As an example, p might be the birthrate per schizophrenic female in the state of New York in one 3-year period (e.g., 1934-1936) and p' the rate 20 years later (1954-1956), after drugs for schizophrenia had come into general use by most psychiatrists. The substantive problem is to find why the rate changed, if it changed. The plan is to study the records of patients that entered the hospitals in the state of New York over the two periods. The first step would be to screen the case notes of a sample of patients admitted in the specified periods, to decide which female patients within the prescribed range of age (i.e., 20 to 39) were schizophrenic. The results of the study are highly dependent on just who is classified in this screening as schizophrenic; hence the screening must be carried out by psychiatrists who are willing to abide by an accepted glossary. There must be controls in the form of independent judgments of a subsample of cases to measure the variance between psychiatrists and to develop an identifiable system of diagnosis. The statistical problem is more than to estimate p - p'.

The next step would be further examination of the case notes of the females classified as schizophrenic to discover whether they were on drugs in or out of the hospital, how many children had been born to them before admission, and to trace these females over a period of years to discover how many more children they had over a span of years, and how much time they spent in the hospital. It would be a simple matter, when the results are in, to calculate the overall change p - p'. But how would one use the standard error so calculated? Clearly, it would have little meaning and less use. The problem of interpreting the results would be difficult, even with the most skillful statistical design and interviewing of patients and informants. The problem is not one in statistical significance. It is for this reason that extreme accuracy in an analytic study is wasted effort.

A change in rate from p to p′ by an amount D would be established or refuted only by examination in detail by age, size of community, orientation of the hospital. Useful statistical tools would be scatter diagrams aided by the sign test, and comparison of cumulative distributions.

We could go wrong in our conclusion, but unfortunately there is no statistical test we can apply to the data of the study that can tell us the risk of ascribing the change in birthrate to the use of drugs which decrease the time spent in the hospital, increase the time spent at home, when the experts decide in later years that drugs were not the cause of the change in birthrate. Neither is there a statistical test to tell us the contrary risk of eliminating drugs as a cause, when the experts decide in later years that drugs were definitely a contributing factor.

ANOTHER EXAMPLE

There are two methods of packing coffee into tins. Method A is the machinery already on the floor and the customary way of using it. Method B is new machinery that its manufacturer claims will turn out the work more rapidly and hit closer to any prescribed weight, so that with his machinery it is not necessary to put as many additional grains of coffee into a can to meet requirements of minimum weight as it is with the machinery in use. One machine of the new type is to be set up along a production line next week, and it is proposed to test it against the standard method of the past. It is hoped to reach a decision within a few weeks on whether the new machinery would be sufficiently advantageous to warrant the cost of replacement.

Would it be good management to try to be guided entirely on the results? One could run the two methods side by side and get figures, but what could he infer from these figures? Would the figures predict unforeseeable events such as time out for repairs, ability of the manufacturer of B to supply parts and service? The new machinery may not require repairs for six months, at the end of which time it may start to deteriorate.

Another possible difficulty is that the test to be run during the next few weeks could be unfair to the new machinery because the men that will operate it will be either operators of the regular machinery; or if sent in from the outside, they will hardly have a chance to accustom themselves to the new environment before the test will be running. As a further point, in spite of the manufacturer's efforts, Machine B may not be installed properly: it may require adjustments over a period of weeks.

Certain decisive results are of course possible. The new machinery may break down continually, or it may distinctly outclass the standard machinery and methods, with little danger (on engineering judgment, not statistical) of running into heavy costs of maintenance.

If forced, anybody could, at the end of a test, or with no test, make one decision or the other: (1) adopt the new machinery; (2) stay with the old machinery. Management would perhaps decide later that they had made a wise decision, or an unwise one. More likely, they would never raise a question about their decision, nor be able to provide any information about it.

THE RETROSPECTIVE METHOD

This is a method of evaluation that is much used, even though the hazards of wrong conclusions are great unless the observations are interpreted with care. It may therefore be useful to explain the method in simple terms and to offer a few words of caution. In the retrospective method, one divides into groups (diseased, not diseased) a population as it exists today, and inquires into the past histories of the individuals in these groups. The aim is of course to discover whether the past histories are different in any meaningful way and thus to discover the causes of the differences observed today between the two groups. The method is tempting, by reasons of economy, speed, and simplicity: we do not need to follow over a long period of time the people or animals or plants that we wish to study, with all the problems of tracing people as they move about. Still more tempting, the retrospective method does not require us to try to divide a sample of people into two groups, A and B, and say to Group A, you people are not to smoke during the next 20 years, and to Group B, you people are to smoke 2 packs a day for the next 20 years (all of which is of course fantastic).

The following example explains the retrospective method (oversimplified, as every term requires a lengthy operational definition):

Cause 1 (C1): he was a smoker 20 years ago.
Cause 2 (C2): he was not a smoker 20 years ago.
Effect 1 (E1): alive now, diseased.
Effect 2 (E2): alive now, not diseased.

By examination of a proper sample of people living today, we may divide those **that have attained a certain age, say 50, into four groups, shown in Table 5.2,** into which we have entered the observed frequencies, x_{ij}. Now suppose that the frequencies off the diagonal were zero ($x_{12} = x_{21} = 0$). Every person diseased today was a smoker 20 years ago. Every person not diseased today was not a smoker 20 years ago. Could we conclude that smoking 20 years ago caused disease

TABLE 5.2

Cause (from history)	Result (observed today)		
	E 1 (diseased)	E 2 (not diseased)	Total
C 1 (smoked)	x_{11}	x_{12}	$x_{1.}$
C 2 (did not smoke)	x_{21}	x_{22}	$x_{2.}$
Total	$x_{.1}$	$x_{.2}$	$x_{..}$

today? No, but the retrospective method can raise question marks for further study.

The trouble with the retrospective method is that it studies only the survivors. We can study today only the survivors of 20 years ago. One must admit the possibility, and investigate it, that all the deaths that occurred over the interval of 20 years were nonsmokers; that smoking toughens one's resistance to diseases other than the specified disease, and that a smoker thus has a better chance to live 20 years, even though, at the end of that period, he will already have contracted the specified disease.

It is easy to make a wrong inference by a computation of chi-square for the 2 x 2 table under discussion. The survivors we study today are not a sample of the people who were alive 20 years ago. The survivors alive today do not tell us all that we need to know about the effects of the suspected causes that operated 20 years ago. We need to know what happened to the nonsurvivors. Where are the rest of the people, not alive today, who were alive 20 years ago? What happened to them? We cannot calculate limits of uncertainty on conclusions concerning suspected causes of disease drawn purely from observations on today's survivors. This is the great failing of the retrospective method, and it is serious.

Must we throw away the information acquired in a retrospective study? No, do not throw it away; supplement it. The retrospective method raises questions, hypotheses to study. The next step is to fill in the gaps, perhaps by making use of small prospective studies, pointed directly at the target. Unfortunately, one must wait for results.

NOTES

1. Following Frank Yates, I use the word *material* to denote people, patients, business establishments, accounts, cases, animals, agricultural products, industrial products, or anything else.

2. Shewhart's Rule 2, from Walter A. Shewhart, *Statistical Method from the Viewpoint of Quality Control* (Graduate School, Department of Agriculture, Washington, 1938), p. 92.

3. The concept of the frame was first defined but without use of any specific term by F. F. Stephan, American Sociological Review 1 (1936): 569-580.

4. The contrast between enumerative and analytic studies is set forth in chapter 7 of Deming, *Some Theory of Sampling* (Wiley, 1950; Dover, 1966). See also chapter 31 in *New Developments in Survey Sampling* by Norman L. Johnson and Harry Smith (Wiley-Interscience, 1969).

5. Richard H. Blythe, "The Economics of Sample-Size Applied to the Scaling of Sawlogs," The Biometrics Bulletin [Washington] 1 (1945): 67-70. Leo Törnqvist, "An Attempt to Analyze the Problem of an Economical Production of Statistical Data." Nordisk Tidsskrift for Teknisk Økonomi 37 (1948): 263-274.

6. Some pitfalls in estimation are described in chapter 31 in *New Developments in Survey Sampling* by Norman L. Johnson and Harry Smith cited earlier.

7. Walter A. Shewhart, *Statistical Method from the Viewpoint of Quality Control* (Graduate School, Department of Agriculture, 1939), chap. 3.

8. Ibid.

9. C. I. Lewis, *Mind and the World-Order* (Scribners, 1929), chaps. 6 and 7.

10. Frederick Mosteller and John W. Tukey, "The Uses and Usefulness of Probability Paper," Journal of the American Statistical Association 44 (1949): 174-212. The double square-root paper is manufactured by the Codex Book Company of Norwood, Mass.

11. Joseph Berkson, "Tests of Significance Considered as Evidence," Journal of the American Statistical Association 37 (1942): 325-335; Carl Earhardt, "Statistics, a Trap for the Unwary," Obstetrics and Gynecology 14 (Oct. 1959): 549-554; J. Wolfowitz, "Remarks on the Theory of Testing Hypotheses," The New York Statistician 18 (March 1967); W. Edwards Deming, "Boundaries of Statistical Inference," being chapter 31 in New Developments in Survey Sampling by Norman L. Johnson and Harry Smith (Wiley, 1969); Denton E. Morrison and Ramon E. Henkel, The Significance Test Controversy (Aldine, 1970).

12. Relationships among (sic) parent ratings of behavioral characteristics of children, National Center for Health Statistics, series 11, no. 121, Oct. 1972.

13. John Mandel, "Flammability of Children's Sleep-Wear," Standardization News [Philadelphia], May 1973, p. 11.

6

REFORMS AS EXPERIMENTS

DONALD T. CAMPBELL

Northwestern University

The United States and other modern nations should be ready for an experimental approach to social reform, an approach in which we try out new programs designed to cure specific social problems, in which we learn whether or not these programs are effective, and in which we retain, imitate, modify, or discard them on the basis of apparent effectiveness on the multiple imperfect criteria available. Our readiness for this stage is indicated by the inclusion of specific provisions for program evaluation in the first wave of the "Great Society" legislation, and by the current congressional proposals for establishing "social indicators" and socially relevant "data banks." So long have we had good intentions in this regard that many may feel we are already at this stage, that we already are continuing or discontinuing programs on the basis of assessed effectiveness. It is a theme of this article that this is not at all so, that most ameliorative programs end up with *no* interpretable evaluation (Etzioni, 1968; Hyman and Wright, 1967; Schwartz, 1961). We must look hard at the sources of this condition, and design ways of overcoming the difficulties. This article is a preliminary effort in this regard.

AUTHOR'S NOTE: The preparation of this paper has been supported by National Science Foundation Grant GS1309X. Versions of this paper have been presented as the Northwestern University Alumni Fund Lecture, January 24, 1968; to the Social Psychology Section of the British Psychological Society at Oxford, September 20, 1968; to the International Conference on Social Psychology at Prague, October 7, 1968 (under a different title); and to several other groups. Requests for reprints should be sent to Donald T. Campbell, Department of Psychology, Northwestern University, Evanston, Illinois 60201.

Many of the difficulties lie in the intransigencies of the research setting and in the presence of recurrent seductive pitfalls of interpretation. The bulk of this article will be devoted to these problems. But the few available solutions turn out to depend upon correct administrative decisions in the initiation and execution of the program. These decisions are made in a political arena, and involve political jeopardies that are often sufficient to explain the lack of hard-headed evaluation of effects. Removing reform administrators from the political spotlight seems both highly unlikely, and undesirable even if it were possible. What is instead essential is that the social scientist research advisor understand the political realities of the situation, and that he aid by helping create a public demand for hard-headed evaluation, by contributing to those political inventions that reduce the liability of honest evaluation, and by educating future administrators to the problems and possibilities.

For this reason, there is also an attempt in this article to consider the political setting of program evaluation, and to offer suggestions as to political postures that might further a truly experimental approach to social reform. Although such considerations will be distributed as a minor theme throughout this article, it seems convenient to begin with some general points of this political nature.

POLITICAL VULNERABILITY FROM KNOWING OUTCOMES

It is one of the most characteristic aspects of the present situation that *specific reforms are advocated as though they were certain to be successful.* For this reason, knowing outcomes has immediate political implications. Given the inherent difficulty of making significant improvements by the means usually provided and given the discrepancy between promise and possibility, most administrators wisely prefer to limit the evaluations to those the outcomes of which they can control, particularly insofar as published outcomes or press releases are concerned. Ambiguity, lack of truly comparable comparison bases, and lack of concrete evidence all work to increase the administrator's control over what gets said, or at least to reduce the bite of criticism in the case of actual failure. There is safety under the cloak of ignorance. Over and above this tie-in of advocacy and administration, there is another source of vulnerability in that the facts relevant to experimental program evaluation are also available to argue the general efficiency and honesty of administrators. The public availability of such facts reduces the privacy and security of at least some administrators.

Even where there are ideological commitments to a hard-headed evaluation of organizational efficiency, or to a scientific organization of society, these two jeopardies lead to the failure to evaluate organizational experiments realistically. If the political and administrative system has committed itself in advance to the correctness and efficacy of its reforms, it cannot tolerate learning of failure. To be truly scientific we must be able to experiment. We must be able to advocate without that excess of commitment that blinds us to reality testing.

This predicament, abetted by public apathy and by deliberate corruption, may prove in the long run to permanently preclude a truly experimental approach to social amelioration. But our needs and our hopes for a better society demand we make the effort. There are a few signs of hope. In the United States we have been able to achieve cost-of-living and unemployment indices that, however imperfect, have embarrassed the administrations that published them. We are able to conduct censuses that reduce the number of representatives a state has in Congress. These are grounds for optimism, although the corrupt tardiness of state governments in following their own constitutions in revising legislative districts illustrates the problem.

One simple shift in political posture which would reduce the problem is the shift from the advocacy of a specific reform to the advocacy of the seriousness of the problem, and hence to the advocacy of persistence in alternative reform efforts should the first one fail. The political stance would become: "This is a serious problem. We propose to initiate Policy A on an experimental basis. If after five years there has been no significant improvement, we will shift to Policy B." By making explicit that a given problem solution was only one of several that the administrator or party could in good conscience advocate, and by having ready a plausible alternative, the administrator could afford honest evaluation of outcomes. Negative results, a failure of the first program, would not jeopardize his job, for his job would be to keep after the problem until something was found that worked.

Coupled with this should be a general moratorium on ad hominem evaluative research, that is, on research designed to evaluate specific administrators rather than alternative policies. If we worry about the invasion-of-privacy problem in the data banks and social indicators of the future (e.g., Sawyer and Schechter, 1968), the touchiest point is the privacy of administrators. If we threaten this, the measurement system will surely be sabotaged in the innumerable ways possible. While this may sound unduly pessimistic, the recurrent anecdotes of administrators attempting to squelch unwanted research findings convince me of its accuracy. But we should be able to evaluate those alternative policies that a given administrator has the option of implementing.

FIELD EXPERIMENTS AND QUASI-EXPERIMENTAL DESIGNS

In efforts to extend the logic of laboratory experimentation into the "field," and into settings not fully experimental, an inventory of threats to experimental validity has been assembled, in terms of which some 15 or 20 experimental and quasi-experimental designs have been evaluated (Campbell, 1957, 1963; Campbell and Stanley, 1963). In the present article only three or four designs will be examined, and therefore not all of the validity threats will be relevant, but it will provide useful background to look briefly at them all. Following are nine threats to internal validity.[1]

1. *History:* events, other than the experimental treatment, occurring between pretest and posttest and thus providing alternate explanations of effects.
2. *Maturation:* processes within the respondents or observed social units producing changes as a function of the passage of time per se, such as growth, fatigue, secular trends, etc.
3. *Instability:* unreliability of measures, fluctuations in sampling persons or

components, autonomous instability of repeated or "equivalent" measures. (This is the only threat to which statistical tests of significance are relevant.)

4. *Testing:* the effect of taking a test upon the scores of a second testing. The effect of publication of a social indicator upon subsequent readings of that indicator.

5. *Instrumentation:* in which changes in the calibration of a measuring instrument or changes in the observers or scores used may produce changes in the obtained measurements.

6. *Regression artifacts:* pseudo-shifts occurring when persons or treatment units have been selected upon the basis of their extreme scores.

7. *Selection:* biases resulting from differential recruitment of comparison groups, producing different mean levels on the measure of effects.

8. *Experimental mortality:* the differential loss of respondents from comparison groups.

9. *Selection-maturation interaction:* selection biases resulting in differential rates of "maturation" or autonomous change.

If a change or difference occurs, these are rival explanations that could be used to explain away an effect and thus to deny that in this specific experiment any genuine effect of the experimental treatment had been demonstrated. These are faults that true experiments avoid, primarily through the use of randomization and control groups. In the approach here advocated, this checklist is used to evaluate specific quasi-experimental designs. This is evaluation, not rejection, for it often turns out that for a specific design in a specific setting the threat is implausible, or that there are supplementary data that can help rule it out even where randomization is impossible. The general ethic, here advocated for public administrators as well as social scientists, is to use the very best method possible, aiming at "true experiments" with random control groups. But where randomized treatments are not possible, a self-critical use of quasi-experimental designs is advocated. We must do the best we can with what is available to us.

Our posture vis-à-vis perfectionist critics from laboratory experimentation is more militant than this: the only threats to validity that we will allow to invalidate an experiment are those that admit of the status of empirical laws more dependable and more plausible than the law involving the treatment. The mere possibility of some alternative explanation is not enough—it is only the *plausible* rival hypotheses that are invalidating. Vis-à-vis correlational studies and common-sense descriptive studies, on the other hand, our stance is one of greater conservatism. For example, because of the specific methodological trap of regression artifacts, the sociological tradition of "ex post facto" designs (Chapin, 1947; Greenwood, 1945) is totally rejected (Campbell and Stanley, 1963: 240-241; 1966: 70-71).

Threats to external validity, which follow, cover the validity problems involved in interpreting experimental results, the threats to valid generalization of the results to other settings, to other versions of the treatment, or to other measures of the effect:[2]

1. *Interaction effects of testing:* the effect of a pretest in increasing or decreasing the respondent's sensitivity or responsiveness to the experimental

variable, thus making the results obtained for a pretested population unrepresentative of the effects of the experimental variable for the unpretested universe from which the experimental respondents were selected.

2. *Interaction of selection and experimental treatment:* unrepresentative responsiveness of the treated population.

3. *Reactive effects of experimental arrangements:* "artificiality"; conditions making the experimental setting atypical of conditions of regular application of the treatment: "Hawthorne effects."

4. *Multiple-treatment interference:* where multiple treatments are jointly applied, effects atypical of the separate application of the treatments.

5. *Irrelevant responsiveness of measures:* all measures are complex, and all include irrelevant components that may produce apparent effects.

6. *Irrelevant replicability of treatments:* treatments are complex, and replications of them may fail to include those components actually responsible for the effects.

These threats apply equally to true experiments and quasi-experiments. They are particularly relevant to applied experimentation. In the cumulative history of our methodology, this class of threats was first noted as a critique of true experiments involving pretests (Schanck and Goodman, 1939; Solomon, 1949). Such experiments provided a sound basis for generalizing to other *pretested* populations, but the reactions of unpretested populations to the treatment might well be quite different. As a result, there has been an advocacy of true experimental designs obviating the pretest (Campbell, 1957; Schanck and Goodman, 1939; Solomon, 1949) and a search for nonreactive measures (Webb, Campbell, Schwartz, and Sechrest, 1966).

These threats to validity will serve as a background against which we will discuss several research designs particularly appropriate for evaluating specific programs of social amelioration. These are the "interrupted time-series design," the "control series design," "regression discontinuity design," and various "true experiments." The order is from a weak but generally available design to stronger ones that require more administrative foresight and determination.

INTERRUPTED TIME-SERIES DESIGN

By and large, when a political unit initiates a reform it is put into effect across the board, with the total unit being affected. In this setting the only comparison base is the record of previous years. The usual mode of utilization is a casual version of a very weak quasi-experimental design, the one-group pretest-posttest design.

A convenient illustration comes from the 1955 Connecticut crackdown on speeding, which Sociologist H. Laurence Ross and I have been analyzing as a methodological illustration (Campbell and Ross, 1968; Glass, 1968; Ross and Campbell, 1968). After a record high of traffic fatalities in 1955, Governor Abraham Ribicoff instituted an unprecedentedly severe crackdown on speeding. At the end of a year of such enforcement there had been but 284 traffic deaths as compared with 324 the year before. In announcing this the Governor stated, "With the saving of 40 lives in 1956, a reduction of *12.3%* from the 1955 motor vehicle death toll, we can say that the program is definitely worthwhile." These results are graphed in Figure 6.1, with a deliberate effort to make them look impressive.

In what follows, while we in the end decide that the crackdown had some beneficial effects, we criticize Ribicoff's interpretation of his results, from the point of view of the social scientist's proper standards of evidence. Were the now Senator Ribicoff not the man of stature that he is, this would be most unpolitic, because we could be alienating one of the strongest proponents of social experimentation in our nation. Given his character, however, we may feel sure that he shares our interests both in a progressive program of experimental social amelioration, and in making the most hard-headed evaluation possible of these experiments. Indeed, it was his integrity in using every available means at his disposal as Governor to make sure that the unpopular speeding crackdown was indeed enforced that make these data worth examining at all. But the potentials of this one illustration and our political temptation to substitute for it a less touchy one, point to the political problems that must be faced in experimenting with social reform.

Keeping Figure 6.1 and Ribicoff's statement in mind, let us look at the same data presented as a part of an extended time series in Figure 5.2 and go over the relevant threats to internal validity. First, *History*. Both presentations fail to control for the effects of other potential change agents. For instance, 1956 might have been a particularly dry year, with fewer accidents due to rain or snow. Or

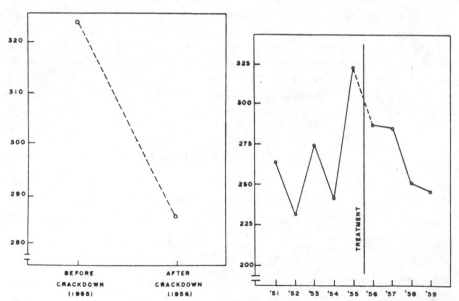

Figure 6.1 Connecticut traffic fatalities

Figure 6.2 Connecticut traffic fatalities. (Same data as in Figure 1 presented as part of an extended time series.)

there might have been a dramatic increase in use of seat belts, or other safety features. The advocated strategy in quasi-experimentation is not to throw up one's hands and refuse to use the evidence because of this lack of control, but rather to generate by informed criticism appropriate to this specific setting as many *plausible* rival hypotheses as possible, and then to do the supplementary research, as into weather records and safety-belt sales, for example, which would reflect on these rival hypotheses.

Maturation. This is a term coming from criticisms of training studies of children. Applied here to the simple pretest-posttest data of Figure 6.1, it could be the plausible rival hypothesis that death rates were steadily going down year after year (as indeed they are, relative to miles driven or population of automobiles). Here the extended time series has a strong methodological advantage, and rules out this threat to validity. The general trend is inconsistently up prior to the crackdown, and steadily down thereafter.

Instability. Seemingly implicit in the public pronouncement was the assumption that all of the change from 1955 to 1956 was due to the crackdown. There was no recognition of the fact that all time series are unstable even when no treatments are being applied. The degree of this normal instability is the crucial issue, and one of the main advantages of the extended time series is that it samples this instability. The great pretreatment instability now makes the treatment effect look relatively trivial. The 1955-56 shift is less than the gains of both 1954-55 and 1952-53. It is the largest drop in the series, but it exceeds the drops of 1951-52, 1953-54, and 1957-58 by trivial amounts. Thus the unexplained instabilities of the series are such as to make the 1955-56 drop understandable as more of the same. On the other hand, it is noteworthy that after the crackdown there are no year-to-year gains, and in this respect the character of the time series seems definitely to have changed.

The threat of instability is the only threat to which tests of significance are relevant. Box and Tiao (1965) have an elegant Bayesian model for the interrupted time series. Applied by Glass (1968) to our monthly data, with seasonal trends removed, it shows a statistically significant downward shift in the series after the crackdown. But as we shall see, an alternative explanation of at least part of this significant effect exists.

Regression. In true experiments the treatment is applied independently of the prior state of the units. In natural experiments exposure to treatment is often a cosymptom of the treated group's condition. The treatment is apt to be an *effect* rather than, or in addition to being, a cause. Psychotherapy is such a cosymptom treatment, as is any other in which the treated group is self-selected or assigned on the basis of need. These all present special problems of interpretation, of which the present illustration provides one type.

The selection-regression plausible rival hypothesis works this way: Given that the fatality rate has some degree of unreliability, then a subsample selected for its extremity in 1955 would on the average, merely as a reflection of that unreliability, be less extreme in 1956. Has there been selection for extremity in applying this treatment? Probably yes. Of all Connecticut fatality years, the most likely time for a crackdown would be after an exceptionally high year. If the time series showed instability, the subsequent year would on the average be less, *purely as a function of that instability.* Regression artifacts are probably the most recurrent form of self-deception in the experimental social reform literature. It is hard to make them intuitively obvious. Let us try again. Take any time series with variability, including one generated of pure error. Move along it as in a time dimension. Pick a point that is the "highest so far." Look then at the next point. On the average this next point will be lower, or nearer the general trend.

In our present setting the most striking shift in the whole series is the upward shift just prior to the crackdown. It is highly probable that this caused the crackdown, rather than, or in addition to, the crackdown causing the 1956 drop. At least part of the 1956 drop is an artifact of the 1955 extremity. While in principle the degree of expected regression can be computed from the autocorrelation of the series, we lack here an extended-enough body of data to do this with any confidence.

Advice to administrators who want to do genuine reality-testing must include attention to this problem, and it will be a very hard problem to surmount. The most general advice would be to work on chronic problems of a persistent urgency or extremity, rather than reacting to momentary extremes. The administrator should look at the pretreatment time series to judge whether or not instability plus momentary extremity will explain away his program gains. If it will, he should schedule the treatment for a year or two later, so that his decision is more independent of the one year's extremity. (The selection biases remaining under such a procedure need further examination.)

In giving advice to the *experimental* administrator, one is also inevitably giving advice to those *trapped* administrators whose political predicament requires a favorable outcome whether valid or not. To such trapped administrators the advice is pick the very worst year, and the very worst social unit. If there is inherent instability, there is no where to go but up, for the average case at least.

Two other threats to internal validity need discussion in regard to this design. By *testing* we typically have in mind the condition under which a test of attitude, ability, or personality is itself a change agent, persuading, informing, practicing, or otherwise setting processes of change in action. No artificially introduced testing procedures are involved here. However, for the simple before-and-after design of Figure 1, if the pretest were the first data collection of its kind ever publicized, this publicity in itself might produce a reduction in traffic deaths which would have taken place even without a speeding crackdown. Many traffic safety programs assume this. The longer time-series evidence reassures us on this only to the extent that we can assume that the figures had been published each year with equivalent emphasis.[3]

Instrumentation changes are not a likely flaw in this instance, but would be if recording practices and institutional responsibility had shifted simultaneously with the crackdown. Probably in a case like this it is better to use raw frequencies rather than indices whose correction parameters are subject to periodic revision. Thus per capita rates are subject to periodic jumps as new census figures become available correcting old extrapolations. Analogously, a change in the miles per gallon assumed in estimating traffic mileage for mileage-based mortality rates might explain a shift. Such biases can of course work to disguise a true effect. Almost certainly, Ribicoff's crackdown reduced traffic speed (Campbell and Ross, 1968). Such a decrease in speed increases the miles per gallon actually obtained, producing a concomitant drop in the estimate of miles driven, which would appear as an inflation of the estimate of mileage-based traffic fatalities if the same fixed approximation to actual miles per gallon were used, as it undoubtedly would be.

The "new broom" that introduces abrupt changes of policy is apt to reform the record keeping too, and thus confound reform treatments with instrumentation change. The ideal experimental administrator will, if possible, avoid doing this. He will prefer to keep comparable a partially imperfect measuring system rather than lose comparability altogether. The politics of the situation do not always make this possible, however. Consider, as an experimental reform, Orlando Wilson's reorganization of the police system in Chicago. **Figure 6.3** shows his impact on petty larceny in Chicago—a striking *increase!* Wilson, of course, called this shot in advance, one aspect of his reform being a reform in the bookkeeping. (Note in the pre-Wilson records the suspicious absence of the expected upward secular trend.) In this situation Wilson had no choice. Had he left the record keeping as it was, for the purposes of better experimental design, his resentful patrolmen would have clobbered him with a crime wave by deliberately starting to record the many complaints that had not been getting into the books.[4]

Those who advocate the use of archival measures as social indicators (Bauer, 1966; Gross, 1966, 1967; Kaysen, 1967; Webb et al., 1966) must face up not only to their high degree of chaotic error and systematic bias, but also to the politically motivated changes in record keeping that will follow upon their public use as social indicators (Etzioni and Lehman, 1967). Not all measures are equally susceptible. In **Figure 6.4, Orlando Wilson's** effect on homicides seems negligible one way or the other.

Of the threats to external validity, the one most relevant to social experimentation is *Irrelevant Responsiveness of Measures.* This seems best discussed in terms of

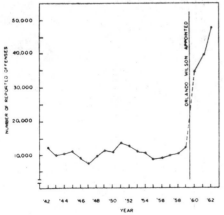

Figure 6.3 Number of reported larcenies under $50 in Chicago, Illinois, from 1942 to 1962 (data from *Uniform Crime Reports for the United States,* 1942-62).

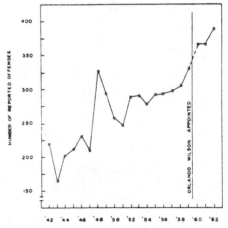

Figure 6.4 Number of reported murders and nonnegligent manslaughters in Chicago, Illinois, from 1942 to 1962 (data from *Uniform Crime Reports for the United States,* 1942-62).

the problem of generalizing from indicator to indicator or in terms of the imperfect validity of all measures that is only to be overcome by the use of multiple measures of independent imperfection (Campbell and Fiske, 1959; Webb et al., 1966).

For treatments on any given problem within any given governmental or business subunit, there will usually be something of a governmental monopoly on reform. Even though different divisions may optimally be trying different reforms, within each division there will usually be only one reform on a given problem going on at a time. But for measures of effect this need not and should not be the case. The administrative machinery should itself make multiple measures of potential benefits and of unwanted side effects. In addition, the loyal opposition should be allowed to add still other indicators, with the political process and adversary argument challenging both validity and relative importance, with social science methodologists testifying for both parties, and with the basic records kept public and under bipartisan audit (as are voting records under optimal conditions). This competitive scrutiny is indeed the main source of objectivity in sciences (Polanyi, 1966, 1967; Popper, 1963) and epitomizes an ideal of democratic practice in both judicial and legislative procedures.

The next few figures return again to the Connecticut crackdown on speeding and look to some other measures of effect. They are relevant to the confirming that there was indeed a crackdown, and to the issue of side effects. They also provide the methodological comfort of assuring us that in some cases the interrupted time-series design can provide clear-cut evidence of effect. Figure 6.5 shows the

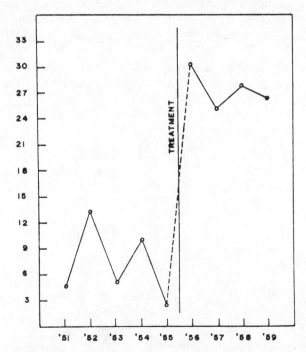

Figure 6.5   Suspensions of licenses for speeding, as a percentage of all suspensions.

jump in suspensions of licenses for speeding—evidence that severe punishment was abruptly instituted. Again a note to experimental administrators: with this weak design, *it is only abrupt and decisive changes that we have any chance of evaluating.* A gradually introduced reform will be indistinguishable from the background of secular change, from the net effect of the innumerable change agents continually impinging.

We would want intermediate evidence that traffic speed was modified. A sampling each year of a few hundred five-minute highway movies (random as to location and time) could have provided this at a moderate cost, but they were not collected. Of the public records available, perhaps the data of Figure 6.6, showing a reduction in speeding violations, indicate a reduction in traffic speed. But the effects on the legal system were complex, and in part undesirable. Driving with a suspended license markedly increased (Figure 6.7), at least in the biased sample of those arrested. Presumably because of the harshness of the punishment if guilty, judges may have become more lenient (Figure 6.8) although this effect is of marginal significance.

The relevance of indicators for the social problems we wish to cure must be kept continually in focus. The social indicators approach will tend to make the indicators themselves the goal of social action, rather than the social problems they but imperfectly indicate. There are apt to be tendencies to legislate changes in the indicators per se rather than changes in the social problems.

To illustrate the problem of the irrelevant responsiveness of measures, Figure 6.9 shows a result of the 1900 change in divorce law in Germany. In a recent reanalysis of the data with the Box and Tiao (1965) statistic, Glass (Glass, Tiao, and Maguire, 1971) has found the change highly significant, in contrast to earlier statistical analyses (Rheinstein, 1959; Wolf, Luke, and Hax, 1959). But Rheinstein's emphasis would still be relevant: This indicator change indicates no likely improvement in marital harmony, or even in marital stability. Rather than reducing them, the legal change has made the divorce rate a less valid indicator of marital discord and separation than it had been earlier (see also Etzioni and Lehman, 1967).

CONTROL SERIES DESIGN

The interrupted time-series design as discussed so far is available for those settings in which no control group is possible, in which the total governmental unit has received the experimental treatment, the social reform measure. In the general program of quasi-experimental design, we argue the great advantage of untreated comparison groups even where these cannot be assigned at random. The most common of such designs is the nonequivalent control-group pretest-posttest design, in which for each of two natural groups, one of which receives the treatment, a pretest and posttest measure is taken. If the traditional mistaken practice is avoided of matching on pretest scores (with resultant regression artifacts), this design provides a useful control over those aspects of history, maturation, and test-retest effects shared by both groups. But it does not control for the plausible rival hypothesis of *selection-maturation interaction*—that is, the hypothesis that the selection differences in the natural aggregations involve not only differences in mean level, but differences in maturation rate.

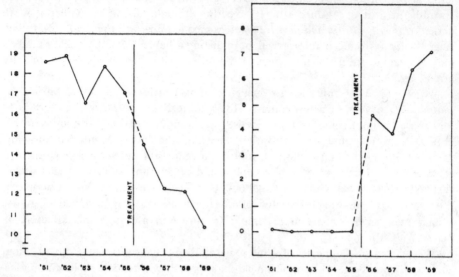

Figure 6.6 Speeding violations, as a percentage of all traffic violations.

Figure 6.7 Arrested while driving with a suspended license, as a percentage of suspensions.

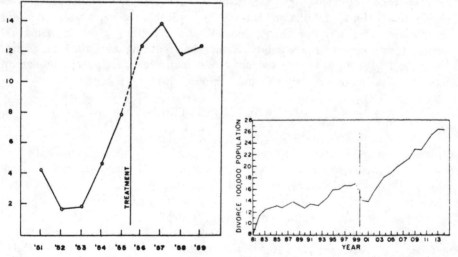

Figure 6.8 Percentage of speeding violations judged not guilty.

Figure 6.9 Divorce rate for German Empire, 1881-1914

This point can be illustrated in terms of the traditional quasi-experimental design problem of the effects of Latin on English vocabulary (Campbell, 1963). In the hypothetical **data of Figure 6.10B, two alternative interpretations remain open** Latin may have had effect, for those taking Latin gained more than those not. But, on the other hand, those students taking Latin may have a greater annual rate of vocabulary growth that would manifest itself whether or not they took Latin. Extending this common design into two time series provides relevant evidence, as **comparison of the two alternative outcomes of Figure 6.10C and 6.10D** shows. Thus approaching quasi-experimental design from either improving the nonequivalent control-group design or from improving the interrupted time-series design, we **arrive at the control series design. Figure 6.11 shows this for the** Connecticut speeding crackdown, adding evidence from the fatality rates of neighboring states. Here the data are presented as population-based fatality rates so as to make the two series of comparable magnitude.

The control series design of Figure 6.11 shows that downward trends were available in the other states for 1955-56 as due to history and maturation, that is, due to shared secular trends, weather, automotive safety features, etc. But the data also show a general trend for Connecticut to rise relatively closer to the other states

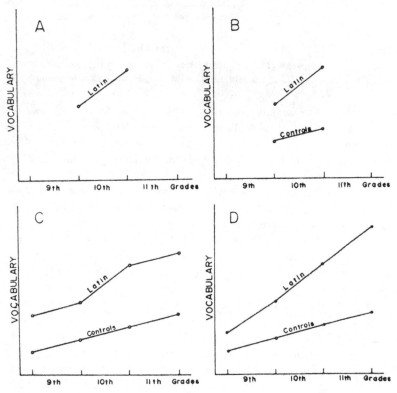

Figure 6.10   Forms of quasi-experimental analysis for the effect of specific course work, including control series design.

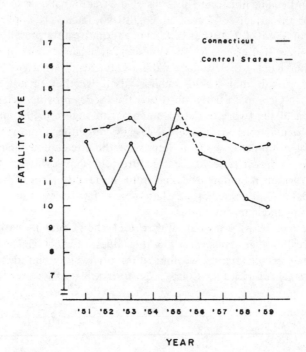

Figure 6.11   Control series design comparing Connecticut
fatalities with those of four comparable
states.

prior to 1955, and to steadily drop more rapidly than other states from 1956 on.
Glass (1968) has used our monthly data for Connecticut and the control states to
generate a monthly difference score, and this too shows a significant shift in trend
in the Box and Tiao (1965) statistic. Impressed particularly by the 1957, 1958, and
1959 trend, we are willing to conclude that the crackdown had some effect, over
and above the undeniable pseudo-effects of regression (Campbell and Ross, 1968).

The advantages of the control series design point to the advantages for social
experimentation of a social system allowing subunit diversity. Our ability to
estimate the effects of the speeding crackdown, Rose's (1952) and Stieber (1949)
ability to estimate the effects on strikes of compulsory arbitration laws, and
Simon's (1966) ability to estimate the price elasticity of liquor were made possible
because the changes were not being put into effect in all states simultaneously,
because they were matters of state legislation rather than national. I do not want to
appear to justify on these grounds the wasteful and unjust diversity of laws and
enforcement practices from state to state. But I would strongly advocate that social
engineers make use of this diversity while it remains available, and plan cooperatively their changes in administrative policy and in record keeping so as to provide
optimal experimental inference. More important is the recommendation that, for
those aspects of social reform handled by the central government, a purposeful
diversity of implementation be envisaged so that experimental and control groups

be available for analysis. Properly planned, these can approach true experiments, better than the casual and ad hoc comparison groups now available. But without such fundamental planning, uniform central control can reduce the present possibilities of reality testing, that is, of true social experimentation. In the same spirit, decentralization of decision making, both within large government and within private monopolies, can provide a useful competition for both efficiency and innovation, reflected in a multiplicity of indicators.

THE BRITISH BREATHALYSER CRACKDOWN

One further illustration of the Interrupted Time Series and the Control Series will be provided. The variety of illustrations so far have each illustrated some methodological point, and have thus ended up as "bad examples." To provide a "good example," an instance which survives methodological critique as a valid illustration of a successful reform, data from the British Road Safety Act of 1967 are provided in Figure 6.12 (Ross, Campbell, and Glass, 1970).

The data on a weekly-hours basis are only available for a composite category of fatalities plus serious injuries, and Figure 6.12 therefore uses this composite for all three bodies of data. "Weekend nights" comprises Friday and Saturday nights from 10:00 p.m. to 4:00 a.m. Here, as expected, the crackdown is most dramatically effective, producing initially more than a 40% drop, leveling off at perhaps 30%, although this involves dubious extrapolations in the absence of some control comparison to indicate what the trend over the years might have been without the crackdown. In this British case, no comparison state with comparable traffic conditions or drinking laws was available. But controls need not always be separate groups of persons, they may also be separate samples of times or stimulus materials (Campbell and Stanley, 1966: 43-47). A cigarette company may use the sales of its main competitor as a control comparison to evaluate a new advertising campaign. One should search around for the most nearly appropriate control comparison. For the Breathalyser crackdown, commuting hours when pubs had been long closed seemed ideal. (The "commuting hours" figures come from 7:00 a.m. to 10:00 a.m. and 4:00 p.m. to 5:00 p.m. Pubs are open for lunch from 12:00 to 2:00 or 2:30, and open again at 5:00 p.m.)

These commuting hours data convincingly show no effect, but are too unstable to help much with estimating the long term effects. They show a different annual cycle than do the weekend nights or the overall figures, and do not go back far enough to provide an adequate base for estimating this annual cycle with precision.

The use of a highly judgmental category such as "serious injuries" provides an opportunity for pseudo effects due to a shift in the classifiers' standards. The overall figures are available separately for fatalities, and these show a highly significant effect as strong as that found for the serious injury category or the composite shown in Figure 6.12.

More details and the methodological problems are considered in our fuller presentation (Ross, Campbell, and Glass, 1970). One rule for the use of this design needs emphasizing. The interrupted Time Series can only provide clear evidence of effect where the reform is introduced with a vigorous abruptness. A

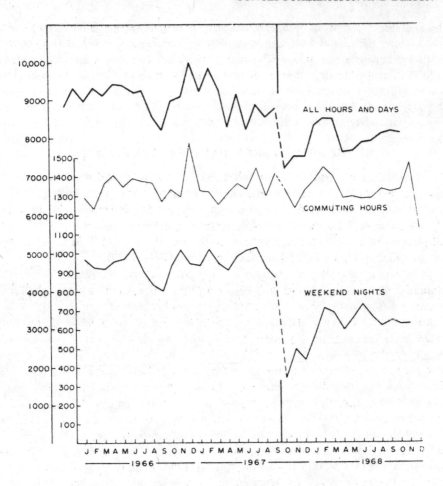

Figure 6.12   British traffic fatalities plus serious injuries,
before and after the Breathalyser crackdown
of October 1967 (seasonally adjusted.)

gradually introduced reform has little chance of being distinguished from shifts in secular trends or from the cumulative effect of the many other influences imping- ing during a prolonged period of introduction. In the Breathalyser crackdown, an intense publicity campaign naming the specific starting date preceded the actual crackdown. Although the impact seems primarily due to publicity and fear rather than an actual increase of arrests, an abrupt initiation date was achieved. Had the enforcement effort changed at the moment the act had passed, with public awareness being built up by subsequent publicity, the resulting data series would have been essentially uninterpretable.

REGRESSION DISCONTINUITY DESIGN

We shift now to social ameliorations that are in short supply, and that therefore cannot be given to all individuals. Such scarcity is inevitable under many circumstances, and can make possible an evaluation of effects that would otherwise be impossible. Consider the heroic Salk poliomyelitis vaccine trials in which some children were given the vaccine while others were given an inert saline placebo injection—and in which many more of these placebo controls would die than would have if they had been given the vaccine. Creation of these placebo controls would have been morally, psychologically, and socially impossible had there been enough vaccine for all. As it was, due to the scarcity, most children that year had to go without the vaccine anyway. The creation of experimental and control groups was the highly moral allocation of that scarcity so as to enable us to learn the true efficacy of the supposed good. The usual medical practice of introducing new cures on a so-called trial basis in general medical practice makes evaluation impossible by confounding prior status with treatment, that is, giving the drug to the most needy or most hopeless. It has the further social bias of giving the supposed benefit to those most assiduous in keeping their medical needs in the attention of the medical profession, that is, the upper and upper-middle classes. The political stance further-ing social experimentation here is the recognition of randomization as the most democratic and moral means of allocating scarce resources (and scarce hazardous duties), plus the moral imperative to further utilize the randomization so that society may indeed learn true value of the supposed boon. This is the ideology that makes possible "true experiments" in a large class of social reforms.

But if randomization is not politically feasible or morally justifiable in a given setting, there is a powerful quasi-experimental design available that allows the scarce good to be given to the most needy or the most deserving. This is the regression discontinuity design. All it requires is strict and orderly attention to the priority dimension. The design originated through an advocacy of a tie-breaking experiment to measure the effects of receiving a fellowship (Thistlethwaite and Campbell, 1960), and it seems easiest to explain it in that light. Consider as in **Figure 6.13, pre-award ability-and-merit dimension, which would have** some rela-tion to later success in life (finishing college, earnings 10 years later, etc.). Those higher on the premeasure are most deserving and receive the award. They do better in later life, but does the award have an effect? It is normally impossible to say

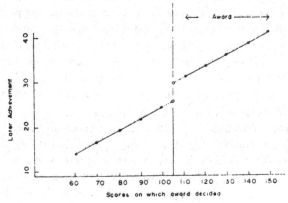

Figure 6.13   Tie-breaking experiment and regression dis-continuity analysis.

because they would have done better in later life anyway. Full randomization of the award was impossible given the stated intention to reward merit and ability. But it might be possible to take a narrow band of ability at the cutting point, to regard all of these persons as tied, and to assign half of them to awards, half to no awards, by means of a tie-breaking randomization.

The tie-breaking rationale is still worth doing. but in considering that design it became obvious that, if the regression of premeasure on later effects were reasonably orderly, one should be able to extrapolate to the results of the tie-breaking experiment by plotting the regression of posttest on pretest separately for those in the award and nonaward regions. If there is no significant difference for these at the decision-point intercept, then the tie-breaking experiment should show no difference. In cases where the tie breakers would show an effect, there should be an abrupt discontinuity in the regression line. Such a discontinuity cannot be explained away by the normal regression of the posttest on pretest, for this normal regression, as extensively sampled within the nonaward area and within the award area, provides no such expectation.

Figure 6.13 presents, in terms of column means, an instance in which higher pretest scores would have led to higher posttest scores even without the treatment, and in which there is in addition a substantial treatment effect. Figure 6.14 shows a series of paired outcomes, those on the left to be interpreted as no effect, those in the center and on the right as effect. Note some particular cases. In instances of granting opportunity on the basis of merit, like 6.14a and 6.14b (and Figure 6.13), neglect of the background regression of pretest on posttest leads to optimistic pseudo-effects: in Figure 6.14a, those receiving the award do do better in later life, though not really because of the award. But in social ameliorative efforts, the setting is more apt to be like Figure 6.14d and e, where neglect of the background regression is apt to make the program look deleterious if no effect, or ineffective if there is a real effect.

The design will of course work just as well or better if the award dimension and the decision base, the pretest measure, are unrelated to the posttest dimension, if it is irrelevant or unfair, as instanced in Figure 6.14a, h, and i. In such cases the decision base is the functional equivalent of randomization. Negative background relationships are obviously possible, as in Figure 6.14j, k, and l. In Figure 6.14m, n, and o are included to emphasize that it is a jump in intercept at the cutting point that shows effect, and that differences in slope without differences at the cutting point are not acceptable as evidences of effect. This becomes more obvious if we remember that in cases like m, a tie-breaking randomization experiment would have shown no difference. Curvilinear background relationships, as in Figure 6.14p, q, and r, will provide added obstacles to clear inference in many instances, where sampling error could make Figure 6.14p look like 6.14b.

As further illustration, Figure 6.15 provides computer-simulated data, showing individual observations and fitted regression lines, in a fuller version of the no-effect outcome of Figure 6.14a. Figure 6.16 shows an outcome with effect. These have been generated[5] by assigning to each individual a weighted normal random number as a "true score," to which is added a weighted independent "error" to generate the

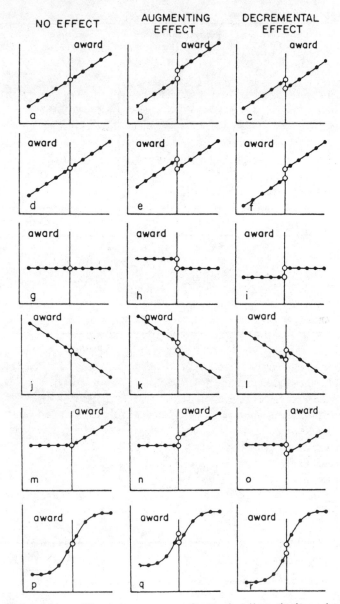

NO EFFECT   AUGMENTING   DECREMENTAL
                     EFFECT   EFFECT

Figure 6.14   Illustrative outcomes of regression discontinuity analyses.

"pretest." The "true score" plus another independent "error" produces the "post-test" in no-effect cases such as Figure 6.15. In treatment-effect simulations, as in Figure 6.16, there are added into the posttest "effects points" for all "treated" cases, that is, those above the cutting point on the pretest score.

This design could be used in a number of settings. Consider Job Training Corps applicants, in larger number than the program can accommodate, with eligibility

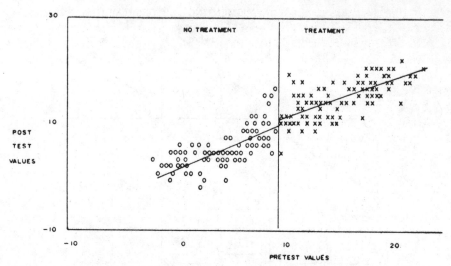

Figure 6.15   Regression discontinuity design: No effect.

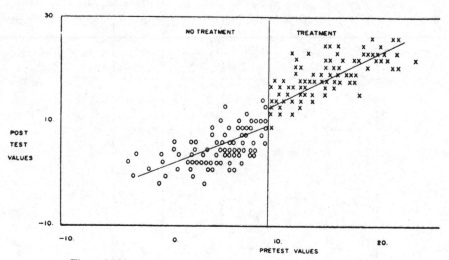

Figure 6.16   Regression discontinuity design: Genuine effect.

determined by need. The setting would be as in Figure 6.15d and e. The base-line decision dimension could be per capita family income, with those at below the cutoff getting training. The outcome dimension could be the amount of withholding tax withheld two years later, or the percentage drawing unemployment insurance, these follow-up figures being provided from the National Data Bank in response to categorized social security numbers fed in, without individual anonymity being breached, without any real invasion of privacy—by the technique of Mutually Insulated Data Banks. While the plotted points could be named, there is no need that they be named. In a classic field experiment on tax compliance, Richard Schwartz and the Bureau of Internal Revenue have managed to put together sets of personally identified interviews and tax-return data so that statistical analyses such as these could be done, without the separate custodians of either interview or tax returns learning the corresponding data for specific persons (Schwartz and Orleans, 1967; see also Schwartz and Skolnick, 1963).

Applied to the Job Corps illustration, it would work as follows: Separate lists of Job Corps applicants (with social security numbers) would be prepared for every class interval on per capita family income. To each of these lists an alphabetical designation would be assigned at random. (Thus the $10.00 per week list might be labeled M; $11.00, C; $12.00, Z; $13.00, Q; $14.00, N, etc.) These lists would be sent to Internal Revenue, without the Internal Revenue personnel being able to learn anything interpretable about their traineeship status or family income. The Internal Revenue statisticians would locate the withholding tax collected for each person on each list, but would not return the data in that form. Instead, for each list, only the withholding tax amounts would be listed, and these in a newly randomized order. These would be returned to Job Corps research, who could use them to plot a graph like Figures 6.10 and 6.11, and do the appropriate statistical analyses by retranslating the alphabetical symbols into meaningful, base-line values. But within any list, they would be unable to learn which value belonged to which person. (To ensure this effective anonymity, it could be specified that no lists shorter than 100 persons be used, the base-line intervals being expanded if necessary to achieve this.) Manniche and Hayes (1957) have spelled out how a broker can be used in a two-staged matching of doubly coded data. Kaysen (1967) and Sawyer and Schechter (1968) have wise discussions of the more general problem.

What is required of the administrator of a scarce ameliorative commodity to use this design? Most essential is a sharp cutoff point on a decision-criterion dimension, on which several other qualitatively similar analytic cutoffs can be made both above and below the award cut. Let me explain this better by explaining why National Merit scholarships were unable to use the design for their actual fellowship decision (although it has been used for their Certificate of Merit). In their operation, diverse committees make small numbers of award decisions by considering a group of candidates and then picking from them the N best to which to award the N fellowships allocated them. This provides one cutting point on an unspecified pooled decision base, but fails to provide analogous potential cutting points above and below. What could be done is for each committee to collectively rank its group of 20 or so candidates. The top N would then receive the award. Pooling cases across committees, cases could be classified according to number of ranks above and below the cutting point, these other ranks being analogous to the award-nonaward cutting point as far as regression onto posttreatment measures was concerned. Such group ranking would be costly of committee time. An equally good procedure, if committees agreed, would be to have each member, after full discussion and freedom to revise, give each candidate a grade, A+, A, A-, B+, B, etc., and to award the fellowships to the N candidates averaging best on these ratings, with no revisions allowed after the averaging process. These ranking or rating units, even if not comparable from committee to committee in range of talent, in number of persons ranked, or in cutting point, could be pooled without bias as far as a regression discontinuity is concerned, for that range of units above and below the cutting point in which all committees were represented.

It is the dimensionality and sharpness of the decision criterion that is at issue, not its components or validity. The ratings could be based upon nepotism, whimsey, and superstition and still serve. As has been stated, if the decision criterion is utterly invalid we approach the pure randomness of a true experiment. Thus the weakness of subjective committee decisions is not their subjectivity, but the fact that they provide only the one cutting point on their net subjective dimension. Even in the form of average ratings the recommended procedures probably represent some slight increase in committee work load. But this could be justified to the decision committees by the fact that through refusals, etc., it cannot be known at the time of the committee meeting the exact number to whom the fellowship can be offered. Other costs at the planning time are likewise minimal. The primary additional burden is in keeping as good records on the nonawardees as on the awardees. Thus at a low cost, an experimental administrator can lay the groundwork for later scientific follow-ups, the budgets for which need not yet be in sight.

Our present situation is more apt to be one where our pretreatment measures, aptitude measures, reference ratings, etc., can be combined via multiple correlation into an index that correlates highly but not perfectly with the award decision. For this dimension there is a fuzzy cutoff point. Can the design be used in this case? Probably not. **Figure 6.17 shows the pseudo-effect possible if the award decision** contributes any valid variance to the quantified pretest evidence, as it usually will. The award regression rides above the nonaward regression just because of that valid variance in this simulated case, there being no true award effect at all. (In simulating this case, the award decision has been based upon a composite of true score plus **an independent award error.) Figure 6.18 shows a fuzzy cutting point** plus a genuine award effect.[6] The recommendation to the administrator is clear:

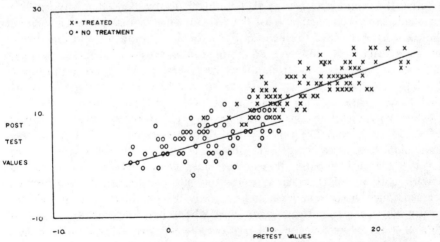

Figure 6.17   Regression discontinuity design: Fuzzy cutting point, pseudo treatment effect only.

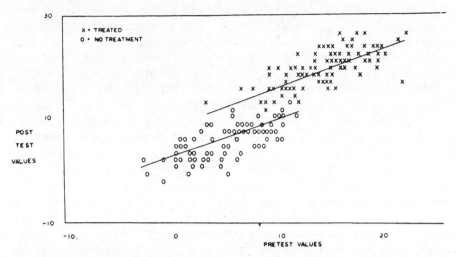

Figure 6.18   Regression discontinuity design: Fuzzy cutting point, with real treatment plus pseudo treatment effects.

aim for a sharp cutting point on a quantified decision criterion. If there are complex rules for eligibility, only one of which is quantified, seek out for follow-up that subset of persons for whom the quantitative dimension was determinate. If political patronage necessitates some decisions inconsistent with a sharp cutoff, record these cases under the heading "qualitative decision rule" and keep them out of your experimental analysis.

Almost all of our ameliorative programs designed for the disadvantaged could be studied via this design, and so too some major governmental actions affecting the lives of citizens in ways we do not think of as experimental. For example, for a considerable period, quantitative test scores have been used to call up for military service or reject as unfit at the lower ability range. If these cutting points, test scores, names, and social security numbers have been recorded for a number of steps both above and below the cutting point, we could make elegant studies of the effect of military service on later withholding taxes, mortality, number of dependents, etc.

This illustration points to one of the threats to external validity of this design, or of the tie-breaking experiment. The effect of the treatment has only been studied for that narrow range of talent near the cutting point, and generalization of the effects of military service, for example, from this low ability level to the careers of the most able would be hazardous in the extreme. But in the draft laws and the requirements of the military services there may be other sharp cutting points on a quantitative criterion that could also be used. For example, those over 6 feet 6 inches are excluded from service. Imagine a five-year-later follow-up of draftees grouped by inch in the 6 feet 1 inch to 6 feet 5 inches range, and a group of their counterparts who would have been drafted except for their heights, 6 feet 6 inches to 6 feet 10 inches. (The fact that the other grounds of deferment might not have been examined by the draft board would be a problem here, but probably not insurmountable.) That we should not expect height in this range to have any relation to later-life variables is not at all a weakness of this design, and if we have indeed a subpopulation for which there is a sharp numerical cutting point, an internally valid measure of effects would result. Deferment under the present system is an unquantified committee decision. But just as the sense of justice of United States soldiers was quantified through paired comparisons of cases into an acceptable Demobilization Points system at the end of World War II (Guttman, 1946; Stouffer, 1949), so a quantified composite index of deferment priority could be achieved and applied as uniform justice across the nation, providing another numerical cutting point.

In addition to the National Data Bank type of indicators, there will be occasions in which new data collections as by interview or questionnaire are needed. For these there is the special problem of uneven cooperation that would be classified as instrumentation error. In our traditional mode of thinking, completeness of description is valued more highly than comparability. Thus if, in a fellowship study, a follow-up mailed out from the fellowship office would bring a higher return from past winners, this might seem desirable even if the nonawardees' rate of response was much lower. From the point of view of quasi-experimentation, however, it would be better to use an independent survey agency and a disguised purpose, achieving equally low response rates from both awardees and nonawardees, and avoiding a regression discontinuity in cooperation rate that might be misinterpreted as a discontinuity in more important effects.

RANDOMIZED CONTROL GROUP EXPERIMENTS

Experiments with randomization tend to be limited to the laboratory and agricultural experiment station. But this certainly need not be so. The randomization unit may be persons, families, precincts, or larger administrative units. For statistical purposes the randomization units should be numerous, and hence ideally small. But for reasons of external validity, including reactive arrangements, the randomization units should be selected on the basis of the units of administrative access. Where policies are administered through individual client contacts, randomization at the person level may be often inconspicuously achieved, with the clients unaware that different ones of them are getting different treatments. But for most social reforms, larger administrative units will be involved, such as classrooms, schools, cities, counties, or states. We need to develop the political postures and ideologies that make randomization at these levels possible.

"Pilot project" is a useful term already in our political vocabulary. It designates a trial program that, if it works, will be spread to other areas. By modifying actual practice in this regard, without going outside of the popular understanding of the term, a valuable experimental ideology could be developed. How are areas selected for pilot projects? If the public worries about this, it probably assumes a lobbying process in which the greater needs of some areas are only one consideration, political power and expediency being others. Without violating the public tolerance or intent, one could probably devise a system in which the usual lobbying decided upon the areas eligible for a formal public lottery that would make final choices between matched pairs. Such decision procedures as the drawing of lots have had a justly esteemed position since time immemorial (e.g., Aubert, 1959). At the present time, record keeping for pilot projects tends to be limited to the experimental group only. In the experimental ideology, comparable data would be collected on designated controls. (There are of course exceptions, as in the heroic Public Health Service fluoridation experiments, in which the teeth of Oak Park children were examined year after year as controls for the Evanston experimentals [Blayney and Hill, 1967].)

Another general political stance making possible experimental social ameliora-tion is that of *staged innovation.* Even though by intent a new reform is to be put into effect in all units, the logistics of the situation usually dictate that simul-taneous introduction is not possible. What results is a haphazard sequence of convenience. Under the program of staged innovation, the introduction of the program would be deliberately spread out, and those units selected to be first and last would be randomly assigned (perhaps randomization from matched pairs), so that during the transition period the first recipients could be analyzed as experi-mental units, the last recipients as controls. A third ideology making possible true experiments has already been discussed: randomization as the democratic means of allocating scarce resources.

This article will not give true experimentation equal space with quasi-experimentation only because excellent discussions of, and statistical consultation on, true experimentation are readily available. True experiments should almost always be preferred to quasi-experiments where both are available. Only occa-sionally are the threats to external validity so much greater for the true experiment that one would prefer a quasi-experiment. The uneven allocation of space here should not be read as indicating otherwise.

MORE ADVICE FOR TRAPPED ADMINISTRATORS

But the competition is not really between the fairly interpretable quasi-experiments here reviewed and "true" experiments. Both stand together as rare excellencies in contrast with a morass of obfuscation and self-deception. Both to emphasize this contrast, and again as guidelines for the benefit of those trapped administrators whose political predicament will not allow the risk of failure, some of these alternatives should be mentioned.

Grateful Testimonials

Human courtesy and gratitude being what it is, the most dependable means of assuring a favorable evaluation is to use voluntary testimonials from those who have had the treatment. If the spontaneously produced testimonials are in short supply, these should be solicited from the recipients with whom the program is still in contact. The rosy glow resulting is analogous to the professor's impression of his teaching success when it is based solely upon the comments of those students who come up and talk with him after class. In many programs, as in psychotherapy, the recipient, as well as the agency, has devoted much time and effort to the program and it is dissonance reducing for himself, as well as common courtesy to his therapist, to report improvement. These grateful testimonials can come in the language of letters and conversation, or be framed as answers to multiple-item "tests" in which a recurrent theme of "I am sick," "I am well," "I am happy," "I am sad" recurs. Probably the testimonials will be more favorable as: (a) the more the evaluative meaning of the response measure is clear to the recipient—it is completely clear in most personality, adjustment, morale, and attitude tests; (b) the more directly the recipient is identified by name with his answer; (c) the more the recipient gives the answer directly to the therapist or agent of reform; (d) the more the agent will continue to be influential in the recipient's life in the future; (e) the more the answers deal with feelings and evaluations rather than with verifiable facts; and (f) the more the recipients participating in the evaluation are a small and self-selected or agent-selected subset of all recipients. Properly designed, the grateful testimonial method can involve pretests as well as posttests, and randomized control groups as well as experimentals, for there are usually no placebo treatments, and the recipients know when they have had the boon.

Confounding Selection and Treatment

Another dependable tactic bound to give favorable outcomes is to confound selection and treatment, so that in the published comparison those receiving the treatment are also the more able and well placed. The often-cited evidence of the dollar value of a college education is of this nature—all careful studies show that most of the effect, and of the superior effect of superior colleges, is explainable in terms of superior talents and family connections, rather than in terms of what is learned or even the prestige of the degree. Matching techniques and statistical partialings generally undermatch and do not fully control for the selection differences—they introduce regression artifacts confusable as treatment effects.

There are two types of situations that must be distinguished. First, there are those treatments that are given to the most promising, treatments like a college education which are regularly given to those who need it least. For these, the later concomitants of the grounds of selection operate in the same direction as the treatment: those most likely to achieve anyway get into the college most likely to produce later achievement. For these settings, the trapped administrator should use the pooled mean of all those treated, comparing it with the mean of all untreated, although in this setting almost any comparison an administrator might hit upon would be biased in his favor.

At the other end of the talent continuum are those remedial treatments given to those who need it most. Here the later concomitants of the grounds of selection are poorer success. In the Job Training Corps example, casual comparisons of the later unemployment rate of those who received the training with those who did not are in general biased against showing an advantage to the training. This seems to have been the case in the major Head Start evaluation (Campbell and Erlebacher, 1970). Here the trapped administrator must be careful to seek out those few special comparisons biasing selection in his favor. For training programs such as Operation Head Start and tutoring programs, a useful solution is to compare the later success of those who completed the training program with those who were invited but never showed plus those who came a few times and dropped out. By regarding only those who complete the program as "trained" and using the others as controls, one is selecting for conscientiousness, stable and supporting family backgrounds, enjoyment of the training activity, ability, determination to get ahead in the world—all factors promising well for future achievement even if the remedial program is valueless. To apply this tactic effectively in the Job Training Corps, one might have to eliminate from the so-called control group all those who quit the training program because they had found a job—but this would seem a reasonable practice and would not blemish the reception of a glowing progress report.

These are but two more samples of well-tried modes of analysis for the trapped administrator who cannot afford an honest evaluation of the social reform he directs. They remind us again that we must help create a political climate that demands more rigorous and less self-deceptive reality testing. We must provide political stances that permit true experiments, or good quasi-experiments. Of the several suggestions toward this end that are contained in this article, the most important is probably the initial theme: Administrators and parties must advocate the importance of the problem rather than the importance of the answer. They must advocate experimental sequences of reforms, rather than one certain cure-all, advocating Reform A with Alternative B available to try next should an honest evaluation of A prove it worthless or harmful.

MULTIPLE REPLICATION IN ENACTMENT

Too many social scientists expect single experiments to settle issues once and for all. This may be a mistaken generalization from the history of great crucial experiments in physics and chemistry. In actuality the significant experiments in the physical sciences are replicated thousands of times, not only in deliberate replication efforts, but also as inevitable incidentals in successive experimentation and in utilizations of those many measurement devices (such as the galvanometer) that in their own operation embody the principles of classic experiments. Because we social scientists have less ability to achieve "experimental isolation," because we have good reason to expect our treatment effects to interact significantly with a wide variety of social factors many of which we have not yet mapped, we have much greater needs for replication experiments than do the physical sciences.

The implications are clear. We should not only do hard-headed reality testing in the initial pilot testing and choosing of which reform to make general law; but once it has been decided that the reform is to be adopted as standard practice in all administrative units, we should experimentally evaluate it in each of its implementations (Campbell, 1967).

CONCLUSIONS

Trapped administrators have so committed themselves in advance to the efficacy of the reform that they cannot afford honest evaluation. For them, favorably biased analyses are recommended, including capitalizing on regression, grateful testimonials, and confounding selection and treatment. *Experimental administra-*

tors have justified the reform on the basis of the importance of the problem, not the certainty of their answer, and are committed to going on to other potential solutions if the one first tried fails. They are therefore not threatened by a hard-headed analysis of the reform. For such, proper administrative decisions can lay the base for useful experimental or quasi-experimental analyses. Through the ideology of allocating scarce resources by lottery, through the use of staged innovation, and through the pilot project, true experiments with randomly assigned control groups can be achieved. If the reform must be introduced across the board, the interrupted time-series design is available. If there are similar units under independent administration, a control series design adds strength. If a scarce boon must. be given to the most needy or to the most deserving, quantifying this need or merit makes possible the regression discontinuity analysis.

NOTES

1. This list has been expanded from the major previous presentations by the addition of *Instability* (but see Campbell, 1968; Campbell and Ross, 1968). This has been done in reaction to the sociological discussion of the use of tests of significance in nonexperimental or quasi-experimental research (e.g., Selvin, 1957; and as reviewed by Galtung, 1967, pp. 358-389). On the one hand, I join with the critics in criticizing the exaggerated status of "statistically significant differences" in establishing convictions of validity. Statistical tests are relevant to at best 1 out of 15 or so threats to validity. On the other hand, I join with those who defend their use in situations where randomization has not been employed. Even in those situations, it is relevant to say or to deny, "This is a trivial difference. It is of the order that would have occurred frequently *had* these measures been assigned to these classes solely by chance." Tests of significance, making use of random reassignments of the actual scores, are particularly useful in communicating this point.

2. This list has been lengthened from previous presentations to make more salient Threats 5 and 6 which are particularly relevant to social experimentation. Discussion in previous presentations (Campbell, 1957: 309-310; Campbell and Stanley, 1963: 203-204) had covered these points, but they had not been included in the checklist.

3. No doubt the public and press shared the Governor's special alarm over the 1955 death toll. This differential reaction could be seen as a negative feedback servosystem in which the dampening effect was proportional to the degree of upward deviation from the prior trend. Insofar as such alarm reduces traffic fatalities, it adds a negative component to the autocorrelation, increasing the regression effect. This component should probably be regarded as a rival cause or treatment rather than as artifact. (The regression effect is less as the positive autocorrelation is higher, and will be present to some degree insofar as this correlation is less than positive unity. Negative correlation in a time series would represent regression beyond the mean, in a way not quite analogous to negative correlation across persons. For an autocorrelation of Lag 1, high negative correlation would be represented by a series that oscillated maximally from one extreme to the other.)

4. Wilson's inconsistency in utilization of records and the political problem of relevant records are ably documented in Kamisar (1964). Etzioni (1968) reports that in New York City in 1965 a crime wave was proclaimed that turned out to be due to an unpublicized improvement in record keeping.

5. J. Sween and D. T. Campbell, "Computer programs for simulating and analyzing sharp and fuzzy regression-discontinuity experiments." In preparation.

6. There are some subtle statistical clues that might distinguish these two instances if one had enough cases. There should be increased pooled column variance in the mixed columns for a true effects case. If the data are arbitrarily treated as though there had been a sharp cutting point located in the middle of the overlap area, then there should be no discontinuity in the

no-effect case, and some discontinuity in the case of a real effect, albeit an underestimated discontinuity, since there are untreated cases above the cutting point and treated ones below, dampening the apparent effect. The degree of such dampening should be estimable, and correctable, perhaps by iterative procedures. But these are hopes for the future.

REFERENCES

Aubert, V. Chance in social affairs. *Inquiry*, 1959, 2: 1-24.

Bauer, R. M. *Social indicators*. Cambridge, Mass.: M.I.T. Press, 1966.

Blayney, M. R., and I. N. Hill. Fluorine and dental cares. *The Journal of the American Dental Association* (Special Issue), 1967, 74: 233-302.

Box, G. E. P., and G. C. Tiao. A change in level of nonstationary time series. *Biometrika*, 1965, 52: 181-192.

Campbell, D. T. Factors relevant to the validity of experiments in social settings. *Psychological Bulletin*, 1957, 54: 297-312.

———. From description to experimentation: Interpreting trends as quasi-experiments. In C. W. Harris (ed.) *Problems in measuring change*. Madison: University of Wisconsin Press, 1963.

———. Administrative experimentation, institutional records, and nonreactive measures. In J. C. Stanley (ed.) *Improving experimental design and statistical analysis*. Chicago: Rand McNally, 1967.

———. Quasi-experimental design. In D. L. Sills (ed.) *International Encyclopedia of the Social Sciences*. New York: MacMillan and Free Press, 1968. Vol. 5, pp. 259-263.

Campbell, D. T., and A. Erlebacher. How regression artifacts in quasi-experimental evaluations can mistakenly make compensatory education look harmful. Pp. 455-463 in J. Hellmuth (ed.) *Compensatory education: A national debate*. Vol. III of *The disadvantaged child*. New York: Brunner/Mazel, 1970.

———, and D. W. Fiske. Convergent and discriminant validation by the multitrait-multimethod matrix. *Psychological Bulletin*, 1959, 56: 81-105.

———, and H. L. Ross. The Connecticut crackdown on speeding; Time-series data in quasi-experimental analysis. *Law and Society Review*, 1968, 3 (1): 33-53.

———, and J. C. Stanley. Experimental and quasi-experimental designs for research on teaching. In N. L. Gage (ed.) *Handbook of research on teaching*. Chicago: Rand McNally, 1963. Reprinted as *Experimental and quasi-experimental design for research*. Chicago: Rand McNally, 1966.

Chapin, F. S. *Experimental design in sociological research*. New York: Harper, 1947.

Etzioni, A. "Shortcuts" to social change? *The Public Interest*, 1968, 12: 40-51.

———, and E. W. Lehman. Some dangers in "valid" social measurement. *Annals of the American Academy of Political and Social Science*, 1967, 373: 1-15.

Galtung, J. *Theory and methods of social research*. Oslo: Universitetsforloget; London: Allen & Unwin; New York: Columbia University Press, 1967.

Glass, G. V. Analysis of data on the Connecticut speeding crackdown as a time-series quasi-experiment. *Law and Society Review*, 1968, 3 (1): 55-76.

———, G. C. Tiao, and T. O. Maguire. Analysis of data on the 1900 revision of the German divorce laws as a quasi-experiment. *Law and Society Review*, 1971.

Greenwood, E. *Experimental sociology: A study in method*. New York: King's Crown Press, 1945.

Gross, B. M. *The state of the nation: Social system accounting*. London: Tavistock Publications, 1966. Also in R. M. Bauer, *Social indicators*. Cambridge, Mass.: M.I.T. Press, 1966.

——— (ed.) Social goals and indicators. *Annals of the American Academy of Political and Social Science*, 1967, 371: Part 1, May, pp. i-iii and 1-177; Part 2, September, pp. i-iii and 1-218.

Guttman, L. An approach for quantifying paired comparisons and rank order. *Annals of Mathematical Statistics*, 1946, 17: 144-163.

Hyman, H. H., and C. R. Wright. Evaluating social action programs. In P. F. Lazarfeld, W. H. Sewell, and H. L. Wilensky (eds.) *The uses of sociology*. New York: Basic Books, 1967.

Kamisar, Y. The tactics of police-persecution oriented critics of the courts. *Cornell Law Quarterly,* 1964, 49: 458-471.

Kaysen, C. Data banks and dossiers. *The Public Interest,* 1967, 7: 52-60.

Manniche, E., and D. P. Hayes. Respondent anonymity and data matching. *Public Opinion Quarterly,* 1957, 21 (3): 384-388.

Polanyi, M. A society of explorers. In *The tacit dimension* (chap. 3). New York: Doubleday, 1966.

–––. The growth of science in society. *Minerva,* 1967, 5: 533-545.

Popper, K. R. *Conjectures and refutations.* London: Routledge and Kegan Paul; New York: Basic Books, 1963.

Rheinstein, M. Divorce and the law in Germany: A review. *American Journal of Sociology,* 1959, 65: 489-498.

Rose, A. M. Needed research on the mediation of labor disputes. *Personnel Psychology,* 1952, 5: 187-200.

Ross, H. L., and D. T. Campbell. The Connecticut speed crackdown: A study of the effects of legal change. In H. L. Ross (ed.) *Perspectives on the social order: Readings in sociology.* New York: McGraw-Hill, 1968.

Ross, H. L., D. T. Campbell, and G. V. Glass. Determining the social effect of a legal reform: The British "Breathalyser" crackdown of 1967. *American Behavioral Scientist,* 1970, 13 (4): 493-509.

Sawyer, J., and H. Schechter. Computers, privacy, and the National Data Center: The responsibility of social scientists. *American Psychologist,* 1968, 23: 810-818.

Schanck, R. L., and C. Goodman. Reactions to propaganda on both sides of a controversial issue. *Public Opinion Quarterly,* 1939, 3: 107-112.

Schwartz, R. D. Field experimentation in sociological research. *Journal of Legal Education,* 1961, 13: 401-410.

–––, and S. Orleans. On Legal sanctions. *University of Chicago Law Review,* 1967, 34: 274-300.

Schwartz, R. D., and J. H. Skolnick. Televised communication and income tax compliance. In L. Arons and M. May (eds.) *Television and human behavior.* New York: Appleton-Century-Crofts, 1963.

Selvin, H. A critique of tests of significance in survey research. *American Sociological Review,* 1957, 22: 519-527.

Simon, J. L. The price elasticity of liquor in the U.S. and a simple method of determination. *Econometrica,* 1966, 34: 193-205.

Solomon, R. W. An extension of control group design. *Psychological Bulletin,* 1949, 46: 137-150.

Stieber, J. W. *Ten years of the Minnesota Labor Relations Act.* Minneapolis: Industrial Relations Center, University of Minnesota, 1949.

Stouffer, S. A. The point system for redeployment and discharge. In S. A. Stouffer et al., *The American soldier. Vol. 2, Combat and its aftermath.* Princeton: Princeton University Press, 1949.

Suchman, E. A. *Evaluative research: Principles and practice in public service and social action programs.* New York: Russell Sage, 1967.

Sween, J., and D. T. Campbell. A study of the effect of proximally auto-correlated error on tests of significance for the interrupted time-series quasi-experimental design. Available from the author, 1965. (Multilith)

Thistlethwaite, D. L., and D. T. Campbell. Regression-discontinuity analysis: An alternative to the ex post facto experiment. *Journal of Educational Psychology,* 1960, 51: 309-317.

Walker, H. M., and J. Lev. *Statistical inference.* New York: Holt, 1953.

Webb, E. J., D. T. Campbell, R. D. Schwartz, and L. B. Sechrest. *Unobtrusive measures: Nonreactive research in the social sciences.* Chicago: Rand McNally, 1966.

Wolf, E., G. Lüke, and H. Hax. *Scheidung und Scheidungsrecht: Grundfrägen der Ehescheidung in Deutschland.* Tübigen: J. C. B. Mohr, 1959.

REFERENCE UPDATE

Selected by Donald T. Campbell

Campbell, D. T. Focal local indicators for social program evaluation. *Social Indicators Research*, 1976, 3: 237-256.

Campbell, D. T. Assessing the impact of planned social change. *Evaluation and Program Planning*, 1979, 2: 67-90.

Campbell, D. T., R. F. Boruch, R. D. Schwartz, and J. Steinberg. Confidentiality-preserving modes of access to file and to interfile exchange for useful statistical analysis. *Evaluation Quarterly*, 1977, (2): 269-299.

Cook, T. D. and D. T. Campbell. *Quasi-experimentation: Design and analysis for field settings.* Boston: Houghton Mifflin, 1979.

Judd, C. M. and D. A. Kenny. *Estimating the effects of social interventions.* Cambridge: Cambridge Univesity Press, 1981.

McCleary, R. and R. A. Hay, Jr. *Applied time series analysis for the social sciences.* Beverly Hills, CA: Sage, 1980.

Riecken, H. W. and R. F. Boruch (eds.). *Social experimentation: A method for planning and evaluating social intervention.* New York: Academic, 1974.

Trochim, W. M. K. Methodologically based discrepancies in compensatory education evaluations. *Evaluation Review*, 1982, 6 (4): 443-480.

7

A DECISION-THEORETIC APPROACH
TO EVALUATION RESEARCH

WARD EDWARDS

University of Southern California

MARCIA GUTTENTAG

and

KURT SNAPPER

George Washington University

Two themes dominate the current literature on evaluation. One major theme is "Clean it up," meaning that programs should be as similar as possible to experiments, so that classical experimental designs and statistics can be used to evaluate them (Suchman, 1967; Campbell, 1974; Riecken et al., 1975). Researchers who adopt this view, a position not commonly held by program people, are fond of citing the few score examples of programs that have been designed, at least initially, as experiments, for example, the negative income tax (Boruch, 1973; Watts, 1969). Their efforts are primarily devoted to illustrating the usefulness and power of experimental designs when used for evaluation (Campbell, 1974; Gilbert, Light, and

AUTHORS' NOTE: We are grateful to John Busa and Saul Rosoff of the Office of Child Development for their help in the development of the decision-theoretic process within that agency.

Mosteller, 1974), in the belief that the central task of evaluation is to reach stronger casual inferences.

A more muted refrain, in a minor key, is chanted by a diverse group of skeptics. Their theme is, "Evaluation will not make a difference." Given the muddiness and complexity of organizational and bureaucratic practices, the separation between researchers and political decision makers, and the potent political context of many programs, they emphasize how rarely evaluation data are used in final program decisions. These critics locate the core problem of evaluation in the large, perhaps unbridgeable, gap between evaluation data and the decisions of policy makers (Weiss, 1972; Weiss and Rein, 1970; Williams and Evans, 1969). They are pessimistic about the likelihood of ever linking the two.

Both themes are valid. Much that is useful to doing and understanding evaluation has been produced by each group.

Yet the viewpoint of this article is that neither one addresses the central issue of evaluation research, which is the requirement for a usable conceptual framework and methodology that links *inferences about states of the world, the values of decision makers, and decisions.*

To understand why such a linkage is crucial to evaluation research methodologies, we will first discuss the distinctive characteristics of of evaluation research questions and contexts, and the ways in which evaluation research problems can be distinguished from other research problems. Then we will present a conceptual and methodological framework for evaluation research, essentially the ideas of decision analysis specialized to evaluation research interests. Within this framework the three elements—inferences, values, and decision—though distinct, combine in what we consider a logically compelling way. The role of casual inferences and experimentation will be discussed, including the dangers of the pseudo-experiment. The topic of handling political and bureaucratic complexities within the approach will be examined. The concrete steps of proposed methodology will then be presented, with an example of its use.

EVALUATION FOR DECISION

Evaluations, we believe, exist (or perhaps only should exist) to facilitate intelligent decision-making. The scientist who conducts evaluation research, and even his sponsor, may be interested in various hypotheses about the program (or whatever it is) being evaluated out of sheer intellectual curiosity. And an evaluation research program will often satisfy curiosities. But if it does no more, if it does not improve the basis for decisions about the program and its competitors, then it loses its distinctive character as *evaluation* research and becomes simply research. Most significant programs, we believe, are evaluated because some decision maker wants help in figuring out what to do. Sometimes there are clear-cut alternatives; occasionally they can even be meaningfully compared with one another. More often, programs of rather different characters with rather different purposes are competing for money. Perhaps the most common decision question of all is "Should we go on doing this or should we try something else, including doing nothing?"

STAKES, AS WELL AS ODDS, CONTROL DECISIONS

Decision makers, not researchers, make decisions. While the decision maker always should be, and sometimes is, willing to consider the evidence bearing on his options and his choice among them, virtually never is he willing to delegate to that evidence, or its finder, the task of being decisive. Nor, we believe, should he. Every human decision does, and should, depend on the answers to two questions: what are the odds, and what's at stake. Most research evidence bears directly on the first of these two questions, and at best indirectly on the second. But the second is the most important. Moreover, for every real-world decision the stakes are complicated, multidimensional, and high. For example, an educational program which, on the evidence, in fact educates no one may nevertheless be desirable. Perhaps it is addressed to a disadvantaged group and contributes to the feeling of members or leaders that the group's needs are being felt and responded to. Or perhaps some officeholder needs to be able to point to the program's existence to prove that he kept his campaign promises. Or both. As citizens, we may question whether these are proper reasons for continuing an educationally useless program. As evaluation researchers, however, we clearly fail in understanding the decision problem unless we recognize that these value dimensions are relevant to it. If we want to help the decision maker, our task is to provide him with techniques appropriate to assess the strength and relevance of each of these reasons for continuing or not continuing the program, to aggregate these values appropriately, and then to reach a decision that takes them all into account, each to the extent that its importance justifies.

INCONSISTENT VALUES HELD BY DISAGREEING GROUPS CONTROL MOST DECISIONS

So far we have written as though decisions were made by a single decision maker, with a single, though multidimensional, set of values. For any significant decision, that is absurd. Most organizations have identifiable decision makers. Their role in significant decisions was well summarized by Harry Truman's famous desk sign "The buck stops here." Our point about that sign, different from Truman's, is that the buck seldom started on Truman's desk. It started elsewhere—typically, in dozens of places. Options were formulated, values and costs were assessed. Most commonly, "the buck," by which we mean the decision, never reached Truman's desk; a choice was made by some decision-making group subordinate to him and presented to him, if at all, only for ratification. If it did reach him as a genuine decision problem, it was accompanied by extensive staff studies spelling out the relevant stakes and odds, and typically recommending one option over the others.

Whose values, then, are to be maximized? Occasionally, those of the decision maker, as understood by those who serve and advise him. More often, some amalgam of the values of many different groups all with stakes in the decision. A technology for explicating, comparing, and when possible, reconciling, and ultimately aggregating such inconsistent values of groups in conflict is clearly needed for social decision making. The germs of it exist, though much remains to be done.

Evaluation researchers can ignore this problem of group values in conflict only if they choose, as they often do, to ignore the problem of values altogether, typically by assuming some simple value as the only relevant one. Sometimes, this works well. Doctors, for example, can avoid many value problems by assuming that life is preferable to death and health to sickness. On those assumptions, value questions can be bypassed in favor of more researchable questions such as whether a given procedure does in fact contribute to preservation of life or restoration of health. But we need only to mention recent public discussions of euthanasia, abortion, and preservation of the lives of fetuses with severe genetic defects to illustrate that the values that should bear on medical decisions are often more complicated than that, and to suggest the danger of simplistic, ill-thought-through, unexplicated value systems. (For a careful study of the costs of such casual values, combined with other ingredients of seat-of-the-pants decision-making, in a medical context, see Fryback, 1974. That study also illustrates how decision-theoretical procedures, in this case Bayesian probabilistic inference, can reduce these costs—in Fryback's example, by almost 50%.)

FIVE COMPLAINTS ABOUT FOLKWAYS OF EVALUATION RESEARCHERS

Folkway 1: Reification of Programs

We have frequently encountered the idea that a program is a fixed, unchanging object, observable at various times and places. A common administrative fiction, especially in Washington, is that because some money associated with an administrative label (e.g., Head Start) has been spent at several places and over a period of time, that the entities spending the money are comparable from time to time and from place to place. Such assumptions can easily lead to evaluation-research disasters. Programs differ from place to place because places differ.

This topic is tricky. All entities subject to multiple observation vary, as every experimenting psychologist plagued by within-group individual differences and test-retest unreliability sorrowfully knows. Even batches of vaccine, or even individual doses within a batch, may vary in potency. The question is whether the variations from one observation to another associated with planned action (e.g., different levels of an independent variable) are large or small relative to those associated with spontaneous intra- or interentity variability. That, of course, is typically the question that an experiment sets out to answer, and often an experiment is needed to answer it. But, especially in the domain of social programs, it may be obvious by casual observation that program variability from time to time or from place to place is so large that no reasonable independent variable can be expected to have comparable variance-producing potency. In such cases, experimentation will be at best irrelevant; at worst, severely misleading.

That is no excuse for the evaluation researcher to throw up his hands in despair! The decision maker or decision-making organization *must* do something; the evaluation researcher should help as best he can. And, even in such situations, he can help a great deal.

Folkway 2: Insistence on Casual Inferences

We have often heard research-trained individuals in funding agencies say "If you cannot answer 'why,' don't bother to ask 'what.'" This sort of statement is philosophically dubious, and can lead both to bad science and bad decision-making. The definition of casual inference lies outside the scope of this paper (see, for example, Harre and Secord, 1972). Radical behaviorists typically assert that questions beginning "Why . . ." are really questions beginning "What . . ." ill phrased. Model-builders might disagree, asserting that "What . . ." refers to data while "Why . . ." refers to models. We think this is what those who insist on "Why . . ." questions in evaluation contexts really have in mind. But, as we have already suggested, evaluation-research contexts seldom permit enough precision for the construction of useful models. And a bad model often is worse than none, because its plausibility may turn off fruitful lines of study or action.

Whether or not a model is useful to a decision maker depends on the decision. Imagine, for example, that it were found that Head Start programs work, and that the reason they work is not because of anything that happens to children within the programs but rather because participants are selected, or select themselves, from among those more likely to succeed in school later. From a scientist's point of view this might be considered as a "What . . ." and its accompanying "Why. . . ." From a decision maker's point of view, it is simply two "Whats": his decision about whether or not to continue Head Start programs would presumably depend on the relative importance to him of selecting early those who later will succeed in school and of modifying the chances of success of Head Start participants. It is easy to imagine goal structures in which either value, or both, might be important.

Folkway 3: Pseudo-experiments

Our graduate school teachers of research design, statistical methods, and the like clearly are doing an extraordinarily effective job of selling experimental research as the high road to knowledge. (We have already commented on the frequently inappropriate assumption that knowledge of the kind obtainable from experiments is the crucial antecedent to appropriate decision.) Researchers who have been trained to believe that they must make inferences, that inferences are statistical, and that good statistical inferences grow from experiments therefore find themselves in dilemmas resulting from the intractable, insistently flexible diversity of the real world and programs embedded in it. Experimental and quasi-experimental designs are treated as Procrustean beds, into which programs must fit in order to be evaluated. The result is what we call pseudo-experiments.

One familiar phenomenon in pseudo-experiments is the insistence that the program being studied remain invariant while the data about it are being collected. Programs normally do not remain invariant (though sometimes they do), and a program in need of change is unlikely to remain unchanged to suit the needs of the evaluator. A much more likely outcome is disguised, unadvertised change.

Almost equally familiar is the control group that does not control. Often it is unclear what it is a control for. Defining a suitable control group in a real setting that depends on voluntary participation is difficult. Medical researchers, for example, must resort to double-blind procedures in which neither patient nor doctor knows whether the drug being administered is one under test or a placebo. How can a social experiment be comparably controlled? Usually, it cannot. Sometimes there are obvious absurdities like matching an experimental city to a "comparable" control city. Less dramatic examples of the same difficulty include control schools, control teachers, control classes, control neighborhoods, and so on. Campbell (1974) argues that only random assignment of subject to treatments can provide really appropriate control groups. He chooses his examples from a field (remedial education) in which suitable control groups may be possible, though even in that field a set of control classes to be compared with a set of experimental classes may be easier to ask for than to obtain. But how can a set of control observations be made to help in evaluating a city-wide program? The necessary condition is a large enough set of entities that can in some sense be considered comparable, and that can be randomly assigned to experimental and control treatments. How often is that condition fulfilled?

The most common solution to this sort of problem is the pre-post design, in which each entity being observed serves as its own control. While this approach is considerably better than no control group at all, it leaves much to be desired, especially when the number of entities that can be observed is small (e.g., one). It confounds spontaneous variation and time-related variation with variation due to treatment, even when ideally done. More important, it is often difficult to do. Certain Alcohol Safety Action Programs, for example, attempted to use this kind of control by setting up roadside surveys in which drivers were stopped by a policeman and asked to take a voluntary breath test. These roadside surveys were conducted before and after community action programs designed to reduce the number of drunk drivers. Among the numerous difficulties of this procedure, one obvious one is that, since the test was voluntary, the drunks could and often did refuse to take it. If that refusal rate among drunks were constant, it would make little difference to the effectiveness of the control. But there is every reason to suppose that the word about being able to refuse with impunity got around, so that more drunks refused before than after the community program, thus providing spurious evidence of program effectiveness.

Don't get us wrong. We are against sin, and believe in both motherhood and control groups. It is almost always nice to have one set of numbers to compare with another set. However, in many evaluation research contexts, such comparisons, even (or perhaps especially) when made with highly sophisticated statistical tools, are more often than not misleading.

The convergent validity approach, where possible, is one way to avoid being misled.

A roadside survey finding of fewer drunk drivers after community action than before, by itself, merits little more than a "Hmm. Interesting." If accompanied by a decrease in drunk-driving arrests (along with some reason to believe that police effort was constant before and after), the interest increases. And a finding of fewer personal-injury accidents than before would raise the interest to fever pitch, especially if other cities not participating in the program should not show such decrease. Each of these comparisons, by itself, is dubious; in none of them is the control an adequate protection against various kinds of error. Indeed, the conjunction of all of these comparisons would by no means be conclusive, given the degree to which motives other than devotion to pure science can influence the collection of social statistics at the source, and their subsequent processing. Yet the more different lines of evidence point in the same direction, the more persuaded we are likely to become.

To summarize: pseudo-experiments should be avoided if possible, but often it will not be possible. In some cases they may well be worth doing. But in such cases, convergent validity is essential to establish confidence in a conclusion, and the more different lines of evidence converge, the better.

How can a sufficient number of measures be assured so that convergent validity is possible? The use of a conceptual framework which forces the evaluation researcher into multiple measurement is needed. The approach that will be described creates just such a multiple measurement requirement of the evaluation researcher.

Because the conditions for internal validity are not met and error variance abounds in the usual pseudo-experiment in evaluation, the program is considered a failure, since significant effects are not found. But the failure to find such effects is the result of faults in the study, rather than faults in the program. In recent years, the federal government has bet with the null hypothesis, rather than against it, in the social experiments it has sponsored (e.g., negative income tax) in what may be an unconscious awareness of the problems in those evaluations which try to find positive effects of programs using classical procedures.

Folkway 4: Planning vs. Formative Evaluation vs. Summative Evaluation

Social programs often need continuous feedback to permit wise program management and adaptation, either to correct errors or to adapt to changing circumstances. The phrase *formative evaluation* was invented to describe this kind of feedback. It is often distinguished from *summative evaluation,* which is supposed to be the final verdict on the program. And both are distinguished from the planning that occurred before the program ever started.

Why? Obviously the decision problems faced at all three stages are essentially the same. Is this program a good idea? If so, what can we do to make it work as well as possible? If not, how can we devise something better, given our constraints?

As a program progresses, at least four kinds of changes occur. First, the values of both those served by the program and the program people change, both in response to experience with the program and in response to other, external causes. Second, the program evolves, changes shape and character. Third, the external societal circumstances to which the program is a response change. And fourth, knowledge of program events and consequences accumulates. All four of these kinds of changes affect the answer to the decision problem, and all four are continuous.

In our view, the ideal evaluation technique would be equally continuous. It would assess program merit continuously, taking into account all four kinds of changes, and would permit exploration of the merits of alternative programs that could be had by changing this one, whether the changes were great or small. We believe that decision technology can do this.

Especially important, we think, is the possibility of direct comparison between the extent to which the values the program was intended to serve were expected to be served, and the extent to which they were actually served. Obviously this cannot be done unless those values, almost always multidimensional, can be quantified and aggregated.

In short, we cannot see any hard-and-fast lines to distinguish program evaluation at different stages in its life span. We therefore squirm about language or methods that imply such distinctions, or suggest that different techniques are appropriate for different states of program evaluation.

Folkway 5: The Baseball Statistician's Approach

Our phrase "the baseball statistician's approach" characterizes a very common, and in many ways very sensible approach to evaluation research, one rather unlike the experimentalist's approach we have discussed. The experimentalist wants to test a hypothesis; the baseball statistician wants to describe a phenomenon as thoroughly as possible. So he gathers information, usually as detailed as possible, about the program he is evaluating. He then reports it—again, usually in as detailed a way as possible. We call this the baseball statistician's approach because it is in fact used for evaluative purpose in baseball. Box scores and similar essentially narrative descriptions of what happened are the raw materials; relatively simple statistics like batting averages, earned run averages, and the like are about as sophisticated as the data processing typically gets.

When this approach is applied to anything as complicated as a large social program, it is likely to be costly and voluminous. It is also quite likely to be useful, as it is in baseball. It provides a program manager with detailed feedback, which can be very timely, about what is going on in his program. It provides decision makers with a set of numbers at least some of which must be relevant to their interests and the program's purposes. And it provides sponsors with evaluation reports that are thick and heavy enough to be thorough, and detailed enough to be thoroughly unread. As owners of the Kinsey reports will agree, a massive and unreadable book with an indexing system that permits retrieval of an occasional stimulating statistic can be a useful and appealing product of a research project.

Consider a program that sets out to reduce the incidence of drunk driving by providing severe punishments for drunks and remitting them if the culprit "volunteers" to participate in a supervised Antabuse program. (Antabuse is a drug which, if present in the body, makes you violently ill if you take even one drink.) The program may require that the participant seek therapy from community agencies, but supply no funds for that therapy. In these circumstances, the baseball statistician will certainly be able to document the number of participants, the length of their participation, the number of dropouts, and the number of drunk-driving arrests and accidents. He may also be able to document the increase of social agency work load. If roadside surveys have been used, he may be able to provide whatever pre-post information they offer about the incidence of drunk driving. He will almost certainly be unable to examine what happens to participants and to others using community therapy services because of the increased load without increased funds. He will almost certainly be unable to examine the emotional consequences of depriving drinkers of their drug. He may or may not be able to provide statistics bearing on increased case loads for police and courts which are likely to accompany such a program; it is unlikely that he can assess the effect of these case loads on the quality of justice in that community. He can calculate the direct dollar costs of the program itself, to the extent that they are paid from program funds, but he almost certainly cannot calculate the total direct dollar costs to the community, since many of those costs are paid by community agencies and are not easily separable from non-program-related costs.

The decision maker wants to know "Was this program a good idea? Should it be continued? If so, at what level of funding and with what funding expectations from other agencies? Should it be taken as a model for programs in other communities? If so, how can leaders in those other communities be persuaded to accept its costs?" The baseball statistician cannot tell him the answers to any of these questions, though he can offer literally thousands or hundreds of thousands of numbers that bear on them in one way or another. Because the decision maker cannot understand or assimilate thousands of numbers, all only indirectly related to the question at hand, he has no choice but to select out a few, combine them with a large dose of intuition and political savvy, and make a seat-of-the-pants decision.

If forced to choose between the experimentalist's and the baseball statistician's approaches to program evaluation, we will choose the latter almost every time. Fact-gathering, however dull it may be, is indispensable to everything that comes after. And a reasonably exhaustive compendium of relevant facts about a program can, in principle and sometimes in practice, be interrogated by a decision maker about whatever he really wants to know.

But we feel that fact-gathering in itself has two severe deficiences as an evaluation method. The first, already indicated, is that too many facts are almost as difficult to use for decision making as too few. Indexing, summarizing, and information retrieval techniques tend to be the weakness of every baseball statistician's evaluation. And the more remote the decision maker is from the scientists who designed the program and/or ran the evaluation study, the more severe the difficulty becomes. This, we feel, explains one of the paradoxes of our time: in a government in which practically everything is studied, restudied, and evaluated to death, most decision makers feel simultaneously inundated with information they cannot effectively use and unable to obtain the rather small set of simple answers they need in order to make wise decisions. The complaint comes from Presidents, members of Congress, heads of government departments, and their counterparts in business; and we think the complaint is thoroughly justified. Too much information is almost as useless as too little. No one (not even the librarians or the computer-memory designers) feels other than queasy about the information explosion.

The other difficulty of the baseball statistician's approach to evaluation is that it has virtually nothing to say about values. Almost inevitably these will escape the baseball statistician's number dredge, because they reside in the decision maker's head (or, more often, in the collective and disagreeing heads of the various organizations with a say in the decision), not in the detailed facts of the program itself.

AN OVERVIEW OF DECISION ANALYSIS AS IT APPLIES TO EVALUATION

Figure 7.1 is a block diagram of flow chart indicating the processes that lead up to a decision. In this and following block diagrams, rectangles enclose operations, and circles enclose the informational inputs to or outputs from operations. Arrows of course indicate direction of information flow. Only one instance exists within Figure 7.1 (and none in the other flow charts) in which informational outputs combine without intervening operations to produce other informational outputs. The list of available acts combines with the list of states relevant to outcomes of acts to generate the table of outcomes without any intervening processing because an outcome is, by definition, the intersection of an act and a state; for, in less mathematical language, an outcome is what happens if a given act is chosen and a particular state of the world turns out to obtain.

The main conclusion to which an initial look at Figure 7.1 must inevitably lead is that decision making fully analyzed is complicated. It divides into four phases. The first consists of recognition of a decision problem and definition of its nature and dimensions, the raw materials of a decision process. The second is called probability evaluation in Figure 7.1; other names used for the same process in other contexts are diagnosis, intelligence evaluation, data gathering and interpretation, and the like. It is itself a complicated process. Figure 7.1 indicates, in typical Bayesian fashion, that the output is a set of posterior probabilities of states, but less formal judgments of probability, like those contained in such intuitive processes as conventional medical diagnosis, and such formal ones as the acceptance or rejection of statistical hypotheses also fit here and might be substituted for the Bayesian version of the process by those less convinced of the Bayesian point of view.

A more detailed Bayesian version of what goes on in probability evaluation is given in Figure 7.2, which translates into flow diagram form some of the basic ideas of an information processing system called PIP (see Edwards, 1971), but applies just about equally well to any formal application of Bayesian ideas that distinguished between priors and likelihoods.

We believe that Bayesian techniques have much to offer evaluation research— unfortunately, too much to go into here. For expositions of the Bayesian position in statistics itself, see Edwards, Lindman, and Savage (1963) or Phillips (1973). For illustrations of how to use Bayesian inference in decision-making, see Raiffa (1968), Schlaifer (1969), or any of a dozen recent texts on the subject, mostly addressed to business school audiences. For an exciting example of application of Bayesian tools for evaluation alternative options in medical diagnosis, see Fryback (1974).

The essence of what these procedures have to offer evaluation researchers, we think, is flexibility. They do not make use of artificial devices such as null

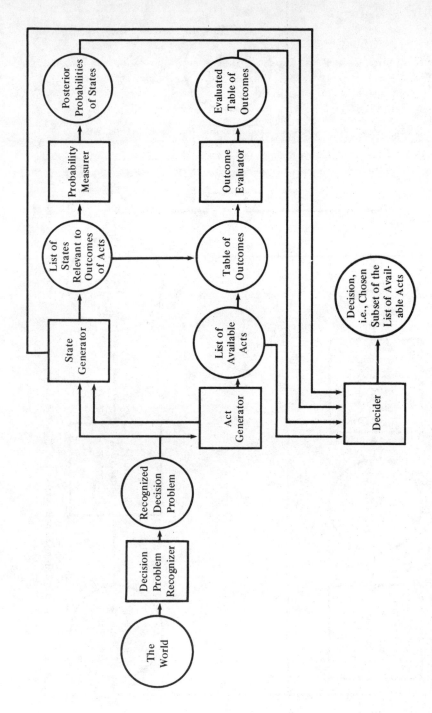

FIGURE 7.1   A block diagram or flow chart of the processes that lead up to a decision.

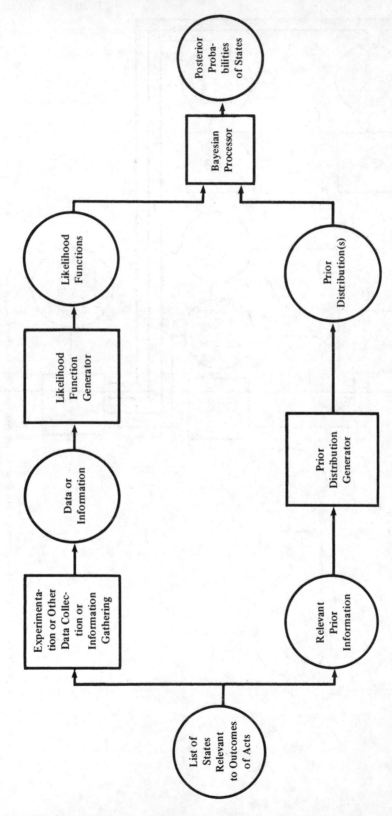

FIGURE 7.2 A flow chart of processes involved in probability evaluation. This is an elaboration of the "Probability Evaluation" block of Figure 1.

hypotheses. They permit, in fact, encourage, quantitative combination of evidence from different sources, different lines of inquiry, and different techniques of investigation. In particular, they make it easy to combine, in a formally appropriate numerical way, judgments with experimental or other empirical data. And they combine very naturally with the value judgments that are the main topic of this paper to produce wise decisions.

The third phase of decision making, as outlined in Figure 7.1, is outcome evaluation. "Evaluation" here means literally that: the attachment of values, preferably in numerical form, to outcomes. And those values are not probabilities; in our preferred version of the evaluation process, values are explicit, numerical answers to the question, "Is that particular outcome good or bad, and how good or how bad?" Another way of putting the question to be answered in outcome evaluation is: "Suppose I could know for certain that this particular act would lead to this particular outcome, and suppose I then chose this act. How attractive would its outcome be to me, or to someone, or to some collection of people?"

Note that outcomes, not acts, are evaluated. We often think of values as being attached to acts. That is in a sense appropriate, since the whole purpose of obtaining values of outcomes and probabilities of states is to permit the simple computation that associates an expected value with an act. In the special case of no uncertainty (i.e., some state has probability 1, or, more often, you treat it as though it had probability 1 even though you know that unlikely alternative states exist), each act has only one outcome, and so the value of the outcome is also the value of the act.

The fourth phase of decision making, as outlined in Figure 7.1, is actual choice among acts. It is based on the values of outcomes and the probabilities of states (or the intuitive substitutes for these numbers). In general, it is a rather trivial process. In a pick-one-act situation, one simply picks the act with the highest value, or expected value. In a pick-several-acts situation, more complex decision rules may be used, but they are still logically simple, and have essentially the character either that the acts that have the highest values, or the acts that return most value per unit of cost, are selected. Special situations, such as competitive games, gambler's-ruin problems, and sequential decision problems lead to still other, computationally more complex decision rules, but the input numbers are still the same.

Of these various processes, probability evaluation and outcome evaluation come closest to the heart of what evaluation research is typically supposed to be about. One contention of this chapter is that these two distinct operations have been lumped together under the label "evaluation research"; that they are different; that they require quite different kinds of procedures to provide answers; and that answers to both are typically necessary for wise decision making.

OUTCOME EVALUATION USING MULTI-ATTRIBUTE UTILITY ANALYSIS

Outcomes could be evaluated in many direct ways. Perhaps the most commonly used direct way is to equate outcome with price. The phrase "that's so cheap it can't be any good" is true enough, often enough, to illustrate the phenomenon, and its frequent falsity illustrates how unsatisfactory the procedure is. Price depends more on the relation between supply and demand than on value. Air is free, but if some predatory corporation or country had a monopoly on it, would you not be willing to pay any amount within your means for a year's supply?

A more reasonable procedure, often used, is simply to consider the outcome and make a direct intuitive value judgment. We all do this every day; experts, such as diamond appraisers, make good livings by doing it exceptionally well with a limited field of expertise. While such judgments are most often phrased in language that is vague, categorical, or both, they can be expressed directly in numbers. Miller, Kaplan, and Edwards (1969) showed that a resource allocation system designed around such numbers far outperformed a system based on intuitive judgments. Yet this, too, is an extremely primitive way of making value judgments.

Most outcomes have value for a number of different reasons, that is, on a number of different dimensions. A remedial education program may contribute to the education of those receiving it. If so, the number of those people and the extent of the contribution made to each may be relevant to the value of the program. The cost of the program, in money, in teaching talent, in student time, and perhaps in educational materials and facilities, is also relevant. The durability of the educational gain is relevant. The program's target population may be relevant. The generalizability of the remedial education techniques used over students, over teachers, over settings, over cultures, and so on may be considered relevant. All of these considerations will, and should, enter into a decision about whether to continue, expand, or terminate the program. Other considerations may enter as well. The city in which the program is located may be on politically harmonious terms with the funding organization, or may not. The program may have no educative value whatever, and may nevertheless provide employment for otherwise unemployed teachers and administrators.

The program may offer opportunities for private profit, ranging from sale of textbooks to graft. It may keep off the street youths who otherwise would be smoking pot, shoplifting, committing assaults, and the like. At the other extreme, a superlatively successful program may disrupt the schools to which its graduates go by presenting its teachers with demands they cannot meet. And so on.

All these considerations—along with many others—may enter into a decision about whether to continue, expand, or terminate a program. Clearly this multiplicity of value dimensions presents a multiplicity of problems. Who determines what dimensions are relevant, and how relevant each is? How is that set of judgments made and used? How is the location of each possible outcome of each act being considered on each relevant dimension of value measured, judged, or otherwise discovered? Finally, what combination of judgmental transformation and arithmetical aggregation is used to translate all this input information into outcome evaluations?

An explicit technology, or, more precisely, several competing versions of an explicit technology, exists to answer some of these questions. Its name is multi-attribute utility measurement, and expositions of various versions of it have been presented by Raiffa (1968), Keeney (1972a), Edwards (1971), and others.

The version we present here, adapted from Edwards (1971), is oriented toward easy communication and use in environments in which time is short and decision makers are numerous and busy. Further, it is a method that is psychologically meaningful to decision makers, who are required to give judgments that are intuitively reasonable. Still, unpublished studies strongly argue that the simple rating-scale procedures described below produce results essentially the same as much more complicated procedures involving imaginary lotteries.

The essence of multi-attribute utility measurements, in any of its versions, is that each outcome to be evaluated is located on each dimension of value by a procedure that may consist of experimentation, naturalistic observation, judgment, or some combination of these. These location measures are combined by means of an aggregation rule, most often simply a weighted linear combination. The weights are numbers describing the importance of each dimension of value relative to the others. In every application of multi-attribute utilities we know of, such numbers are judgmentally obtained. A flow diagram of this process is contained in Figure 7.3, which is an expansion of the block called "Outcome evaluation" in Figure 7.1.

Our implementation of Figure 7.3 consists of ten steps:

Step 1: Identify the person or organization whose utilities are to be maximized. If, as is often the case, several organizations have stakes and voices in the decision, they must all be identified. People who can speak for them must be identified and induced to cooperate.

Step 2: Identify the issue or issues (i.e., decisions) to which the utilities needed are relevant. The same objects or acts may have many different values, depending on context and purpose. In general, utility is a function of the evaluator, the entity being evaluated, and the purpose for which the evaluation is being made. The third argument of that function is sometimes neglected.

Step 3: Identify the entities to be evaluated. Previously, we have indicated that they are outcomes of possible actions. For example, the value of a dollar is the value of whatever you choose to buy with it; the value of an education is the value of the things that can be done with—but not without—it. Since it is always necessary to·cut the decision tree somewhere—to stop considering outcomes as opportunities for further decisions and instead simply to treat them as outcomes with intrinsic values—the choice of what to call an outcome becomes largely one of convenience. Often, in practice, it is sufficient to treat an action itself as an outcome. This amounts to treating the action as having an inevitable outcome, that is, of assuming that uncertainty about outcomes is not involved in the evaluation of that action.

Step 4: Identify the relevant dimensions of value. The first three steps were more or less philosophical. The first answered the question: Whose utility? The second answered the question: Utility for what purpose? The third answered the question: Utility of what entities? With step 4 we come to the first technical task: Discover what dimensions of value are important to the evaluation of the entities we are interested in.

As Raiffa (1969) has noted, goals ordinarily come in hierarchies. But it is often practical and useful to ignore their hierarchical structure, and instead to specify a simple list of goals that seem important for the purpose at hand. Goals, for this

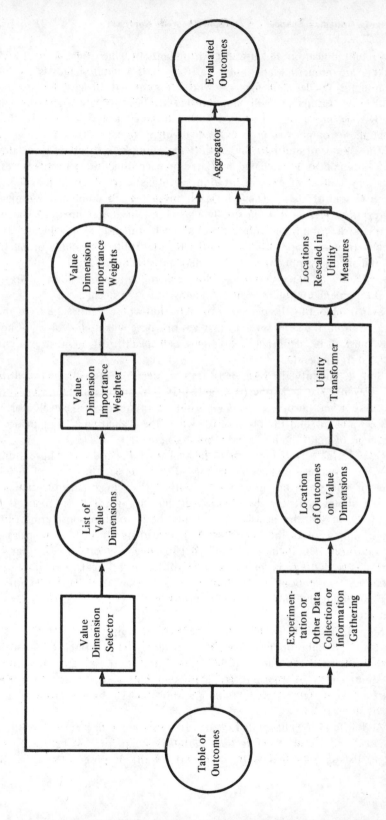

FIGURE 7.3   Illustration of the average scale values of all recommendations on four representative values (E, F, G, H).

154

purpose, should not be stated as target numbers (e.g., reduction of drinking-driver accidents by 50%), but rather as dimensions (reduction of drinking-driver accidents).

It is important not to be too expansive at this stage. The number of relevant dimensions of value should be kept down, for reasons that will be apparent shortly. This can often be done by restating and combining goals, or by moving upward in a goal hierarchy, thereby using fewer, more general values. Even more important, it can be done by simply omitting the less important goals. There is no requirement that the list evolved in this step be complete, and much reason to hope that it will not be.

Step 5: Rank the dimensions in order of importance. This ranking job, like Step 4, can be performed either by an individual, or by representatives of conflicting values acting separately, or by those representatives acting as a group. Our preferred technique is to try group processes first, mostly to get the arguments on the table and to make it more likely that the participants start from a common information base, and then to get separate judgments from each individual. The separate judgments will differ, of course, both here and in the following step.

Step 6: Rate dimensions in importance, preserving ratios. To do this, start by assigning the least important dimension an importance of 10. (We use 10 rather than 1 to permit subsequent judgments to be finely graded and nevertheless made in integers.) Now consider the next-least-important dimension. How many times more important (if any) is it than the least important? Assign it a number that reflects that ratio. Continue on up the list, checking each set of implied ratios as each new judgment is made. Thus, if a dimension is assigned a weight of 20, while another is assigned a weight of 80, it means that the 20 dimension is ¼ as important as the 80 dimension. And so on. By the time you get to the most important dimensions, there will be many checks to perform; typically, respondents will want to revise previous judgments to make them consistent with present ones. That's fine; they can do so. Once again, individual differences are likely to arise.

Step 7: Sum the importance weights, divide each by the sum, and multiply by 100. This is a purely computational step which converts importance weights into numbers that, mathematically, are rather like probabilities. The choice of a 0-to-100 scale is, of course, purely arbitrary.

At this step, the folly of including too many dimensions at Step 4 becomes glaringly apparent. If 100 points are to be distributed over a set of dimensions, and some dimensions are very much more important than others, then the less important dimensions will have non-trivial weights only if there are not too many of them. As a rule of thumb, 8 dimensions is plenty, and 15 is too many. Knowing this, you will want at Step 4 to discourage respondents from being too finely analytical: rather gross dimensions will be just right. Moreover, it may occur that the list of dimensions will be revised later, and that revision, if it occurs, will typically consist of including more rather than fewer.

Step 8: Measure the location of each entity being evaluated on each dimension. The word "measure" is used rather loosely here. There are three classes of dimensions: purely subjective, partly subjective, and purely objective. The purely subjective dimensions are perhaps the easiest; you simply get an appropriate expert to estimate the position of that entity on that dimension on a 0-to-100 scale, where 0 is defined as the minimum plausible value on that dimension and 100 is defined as the maximum plausible value.

A partly subjective dimension is one in which the units of measurement are objective, but the locations of the entities must be subjectively estimated.

A wholly objective dimension is one that can be measured rather objectively, in objective units, before the decision. For partly or wholly objective dimensions, it is necessary to have the estimators provide not only values for each entity to be evaluated, but also minimum and maximum plausible values, in the natural units of each dimension.

The final task in Step 8 is to convert measures to the partly subjective and wholly objective dimensions into the 0-to-100 scale in which 0 is minimum plausible and 100 is maximum plausible.

A linear transformation is almost always adequate for this purpose; errors produced by linear approximations to monotonic nonlinear functions are likely to be unimportant relative to test-retest unreliability, interrespondent differences, and the like.

Now all entities have been located on the relevant value dimensions, and the location measures have been rescaled. In what sense, if any, are the scales comparable? The question cannot be considered separately from the question of what "importance," as it was judged at Step 6, means. Formally, judgments at Step 6 should be designed so that when the output of Step 7 (or of Step 6, which differs only by a linear transformation) is multiplied by the output of Step 8, equal numerical distances between these products on different dimensions correspond to equal changes in desirability. For example, suppose entity A has a location of 50 and entity B a location of 10 on value dimension X, while A has a location of 70 and B a location of 90 on value dimension Y (only X and Y are relevant). Suppose further that dimension Y is twice as important as dimension X. Then A and B should be equivalent in value. (The relevant arithmetic is: for A, $50 + 2(70) = 190$; for B, $10 + 2(90) = 190$. Another way of writing the same arithmetic, which makes clearer what is meant by saying that equal numerical differences between these products on different dimensions correspond to equal changes in desirability, is $(50 - 10) + 2(70 - 90) = 0$.) It is important that judges understand this concept as they perform both Steps 6 and 8.[1]

Step 9: Calculate utilities for entities. The equation is $U_i = \sum_i w_j u_{ij}$, remembering that $\sum_j w_j = 100$. U_i is the aggregate utility for the ith entity. w_j is the normalized importance weight of the jth dimension of value, and u_{ij} is the rescaled position of the ith entity on the jth dimension. Thus w_j is the output of Step 7 and u_{ij} is the output of Step 8. The equation, of course, is nothing more than the formula for a weighted average.

Step 10: Decide. If a single act is to be chosen, the rule is simple: maximize U_i. If a subset of i is to be chosen, then the subset for which $_i U_i$ is maximum is best.

A special case arises when one of the dimensions, such as cost, is subject to an upper bound, that is, there is a budget constraint. In that case, Steps 4 through 10 should be done ignoring the constrained dimension. Then the ratios U_i/C_i should be calculated; these are the famous benefit-to-cost ratios. Actions should be chosen in decreasing order of that ratio until the budget constraint is used up. (More complicated arithmetic is needed if programs are interdependent or if this rule does not come very close to exactly exhausting the budget constraint.) This is the only case in which the benefit-to-cost ratio is the appropriate figure on which to base a decision. In the absence of budget constraints, cost is just another dimension of value, to be treated on the same footing as all other dimensions of value, entering into U_i with a minus sign, like other unattractive dimensions. In effect, in the general case it is the benefit-minus-cost difference, not the benefit-over-cost ratio, that should usually control action.

An important caveat needs to be added concerning benefit-to-cost ratios. Such ratios assume that both benefits and costs are measured on a ratio scale, that is, a scale with a true zero point and ratio properties. The concepts both of zero benefit and zero cost are somewhat slippery on close analysis. A not-too-bad solution to the problem is to assume that you know what zero cost means, and then attempt to find the zero point on the aggregate benefit scale. If that scale is reasonably densely populated with candidate programs, an approach to locating that zero point is to ask the decision maker "Would you undertake this program if it had the same benefits it has now, but had zero cost?" If the answer is yes, the program is above the zero point on the benefit scale; if the answer is no, it is below the zero point. In the Office of Child Development example discussed below, this procedure was tried, and seemed to work quite well. It permitted quite precise location of a zero point on the benefit scale. Ratio judgments of benefits to see if they were consistent with this zero point could have been tried, but were not.

The multi-attribute utility approach can easily be adapted to cases in which there are minimum or maximum acceptable values on a given dimension of value by simply excluding alternatives that lead to outcomes that transgress these limits.

Flexibilities of the Method

Practically every technical step in the preceding list has alternatives. For example Keeney (1972b) has proposed use of a multiplicative rather than an additive aggregation rule. Certain applications have combined multiplication and addition. The methods suggested above for obtaining location measures and importance weights have alternatives; the most common is the direct assignment of importance weights on a 0-to-100 scale. (We consider this procedure inferior to the one described above, but doubt that it makes much practical difference in most cases.)

Independence Properties

Either the additive or the multiplicative version of the aggregation rule assumes value independence. Roughly, that means that the extent of your preference for location a_2 over location a_1 of dimension A is unaffected by the position of the entity being evaluated on dimensions B, C, D. . . . Value independence is a strong assumption, not easily satisfied. Fortunately, in the presence of even modest amounts of measurement error, quite substantial amounts of deviation from value independence will make little difference to the ultimate number U_i, and even less to the rank ordering of the U_i values. (For recent discussions of the robustness of linear models, on which this assertion depends, see Dawes and Corrigan [1974].) A frequently satisfied condition that makes the assumption of value independence very unlikely to cause trouble is monotonicity; that is, the additive approximation will almost always work well if, for each dimension, either more is preferable to less or less is preferable to more throughout the range of the dimension that is involved in the evaluation, for all available values of the other dimensions. When the assumption of value independence is unacceptable even as an approximation, much more complicated models and elicitation procedures that take value dependence into account are available.[2]

A trickier issue than value independence is what might be called environmental independence. The number of administrators, secretaries, and others involved in a program is extremely likely to be positively correlated with the number of people served by the program. Yet these two dimensions may be value-independent; the correlation simply means that programs involving few workers and many people served are unlikely to present themselves for evaluation.

Interpersonal and Intergroup Disagreements[3]

Nothing in the preceding discussion ensures that different respondents will come up with similar numbers, and such agreements are indeed rare.

We might expect that the magnitude of interpersonal disagreement produced by this procedure would be less than that produced by simply arguing about what to do. Gardiner (1974), in an application of the method described above, found just that. His stimuli were hypothetical applications for building permits in the California town of Venice. His subjects were members of the California Southern Coastal Commission, and others interested in the development of the California coastline, from both developer and conservationist points of view. (California law requires that all permits for building within 1,000 yards of the high-tide line be approved by the relevant regional Coastal Commission before building can commence.) His subjects both rated these permit requests on a wholistic numerical scale and applied an 8-dimensional multi-attribute utility technique. When one of the more extreme conservationists was compared with one of the more development-oriented subjects, the wholistic ratings correlated -.50. But the U_i's for the same permit requests and subjects correlated +.59. In addition, two groups of subjects were formed reflecting differing viewpoints with respect to the permits, and group evaluations were collected for each of the 14 permits using group wholistic ratings and group U_i's. These group ratings were then compared using an ANOVA (permit by group for mean permit worth). The results showed that the two groups differed significantly when wholistic ratings were compared (reflected by a significant interaction effect accounting for 12% of the variance) but that when compared using group U_i's this interaction virtually disappeared (no significant interaction effect and only 2% of the variance accounted for). In other words, use of the multi-attribute utility technique had turned substantial disagreement into modest agreement.

Why? A plausible answer is suggested by Gardiner's data. When making wholistic evaluations, those with strong points of view tend to concentrate on those aspects of the entities being evaluated that most strongly engage their biases. But the multi-attribute procedure does not permit this; it separates judgment of the importance of a dimension from judgment of where a particular entity falls on that dimension. These applications, though they varied on various dimensions that are relevant to the environmentalist-versus-builder arguments, also varied on other dimensions not involved in that sort of issue. Agreement about those other dimensions tends to water down disagreement on controversial dimensions in a multi-attribute utility procedure.

Although multi-attribute utility measurement procedures can be expected to reduce the magnitude of disagreements, they cannot and should not eliminate them. What then?

We distinguish between two kinds of disagreements. Disagreements at Step 8 seem to us to be essentially like disagreements among different thermometers measuring the same temperature. If they are not too large, we have little compunction about taking an average. If they are, then we are likely to suspect that some of the thermometers are not working properly and to discard their readings. In general, we think that judgmentally determined location measures should reflect expertise, and typically we would expect different value dimensions to require different kinds of expertise and therefore different experts. In some practical contexts, we can avoid the problem of disagreement at Step 8 entirely by the simple expedient of asking only the best available expert for each dimension to make judgments about that dimension.

Disagreement at Steps 5 and 6 are another matter. These seem to us to be the essence of conflicting values, and we wish to respect them as much as possible. For that reason, we feel that the judges who perform Steps 5 and 6 should be either the decision maker(s) or well-chosen representatives. Considerable discussion, persuasion, and information exchange should be used in an attempt to reduce the disagreements as much as possible.

This will seldom reduce them to zero. For some organizations, we can at this point invoke once more Truman's desk sign "The buck stops here," this time with Truman's intended meaning. One function of an executive, boss, or decision maker is to resolve disagreements among subordinates. He can do this in various ways: by substituting his judgment for theirs, by picking one of them as "right" and rejecting the others, or, in the weighted-averaging spirit of multi-attribute utility measurement, by assigning a weight to each of the disagreeing subordinates and then calculating weighted-average importance weights.

If there is no decision maker to resolve disagreement, we can only carry through the evaluation separately for each of the disagreeing individuals or groups, hoping that the disagreements are small enough to have little or no action implications. And if that hope is not fulfilled, we have no suggestions to offer beyond the familiar political processes by means of which society functions in spite of conflicting interests. We offer technology, not miracles.

AN EXAMPLE FROM THE OFFICE OF CHILD DEVELOPMENT (OCD)

The multi-attribute utilities method was used in the planning process of OCD. Following the steps of the multi-attribute utilities method, the organization whose utilities were to be maximized (Step 1) was OCD. The issues to which the utilities needed were relevant (Step 2) were plans for fiscal years 1974 and 1975-1979. The entities to be evaluated (Step 3) were of two kinds: recommendations for broad strategies that could be pursued by OCD and recommendations for specific program initiatives that fell within each broad strategy. Step 3 was conducted concurrently with Step 4, the identification of relevant dimensions of value. Both of these processes are described below.

We set out initially to measure three kinds of values separately: benefits to children and families (which might be considered "external" utilities), benefits to OCD as an agency in HEW (or "internal" benefits), and cost.

A small work group was assembled at OCD to develop the value dimensions. This group consisted of the Acting Director, Saul Rosoff, other members of the OCD staff, some of the Associate Regional Directors, and some child development consultants. In two days of discussion, the value dimensions work group decided on the following dimensions of benefits to children and families:

- Promote service continuity/eliminate fragmentation (includes idea of coordination).
- Invest in prototype/high-leverage programs.
- Enhance families' sense of efficacy and ability to obtain and use resources necessary for the healthy development of children.
- Promote child health.
- Maximize the number of children affected.
- Increase developmentally appropriate opportunities for choice and self-direction among older children.
- Increase probability that children will acquire skills necessary for successful performance of adult roles.
- Develop leadership capacity in communities served.
- Make the public and institutions more sensitive to the developmental needs of children.
- Contribute to knowledge expansion and/or use of knowledge for program planning.
- Individualize services and programs.
- Stimulate pluralistic child care delivery systems that provide for parental choice.
- Promote self-respect and mutual regard among children of diverse racial, cultural, class, and ethnic backgrounds.
- Enhance parental involvement in program planning and management.

This list of 14, presented here unordered, was refined from a much longer list that had been freely generated by group members. Overlapping values, duplications, and subsets of values already listed were refined and combined during the course of group discussion.

The group also developed a separate list of value dimensions that were oriented toward OCD and its internal role in HEW. These were:

- Use money for leverage, not services.
- Interagency coordination at federal, state, and local levels.

- Administrative feasibility.
- Make political leadership more sensitive to the needs of children.
- Promote understanding by and support from groups OCD works with and/or relates to.
- Influence national child care policy.
- Course of action capable of rational explication.
- Produce tangible short-term results.
- Maximize support by OCD staff.
- Make best use of OCD resources and personnel.
- Improve OCD's information base.
- Improve stewardship and accountability.

The above list resulted from a similar process of refinement accomplished during group discussion.

Next, each member of the value dimensions work group was asked to rank order the dimensions and to assign importance weights individually (Step 5).

At the same time that the value dimensions work was in progress, recommendations for broad strategies and for individual programs were being assembled. These came from a large number of sources. Major reports to OCD and to HEW, which contained a number of recommendations, were summarized. Recommendations were solicited from members of the OCD staff and from the Office of the Assistant Secretary for Planning and Evaluation in HEW. In addition, the Secretary's National Advisory Committee on Children, the National Academy of Science's Child Development Group, the Associate Regional Directors of OCD, and representatives of minority organizations, as well as child development experts throughout the country, were asked to submit recommendations for broad strategies and specific programs. The current strategies and programs also formed a part of this group of recommendations. Several hundred recommendations were assembled as the result of this process. At present, these recommendations are being refined and combined where redundant (Guttentag, 1973).

The following are a random sample of some of the concrete recommendations which were the result of the first phase:[4]

OCD should undertake a *feasibility study* to explore the whole area of providing training to child care givers, using modern technology—video, through both PBS and/or closed circuit (cable) outlets, films, cassettes, etc.

Cost: $50,000   Time: 1 year

*   *   *   *   *   *   *   *   *   *

Presently there are no official national standards for the administration of foster care licensing ... in terms of personnel requirements, workload, or what is expected of a licensing service. CB should design a strategy for upgrading the quality of child foster care licensing in State welfare and health departments, including specification of the education and experience needed to qualify licensing personnel at operating, supervisory, and administrative levels; in-service training guidelines for licensing authorities; and its own plan for providing consultation and monitoring through self-study guides and other forms of evaluation. This should be developed cooperatively with CSA.

Cost: $1,500,000   Time: 3 years

*   *   *   *   *   *   *   *   *   *

OCD should support research on the effects of social climate, physical settings, crowding, and other environmental, non-program variables on the social and cognitive development of children in school settings. Initially, OCD should fund 4 or 5 independent *feasibility* studies, at $20,000–$25,000 each, to determine a research strategy.

Cost: $100,000   Time: 1 year

*   *   *   *   *   *   *   *   *   *

OCD should determine the feasibility of training and utilizing community residents as homemakers, or high school students as parent apprentices, in order to visit and assist families in which parents are overburdened with caring for old or sick relatives, meeting the needs of large families, house-keeping under difficult circumstances, etc. Many disadvantaged parents are unable to spend time in activities with their young children because of other demands in the home. Homemakers or parent apprentices could take over some of these responsibilities so that parents could be free to engage in activities with their younger children.

Cost: $100,000   Time: 1 year

*   *   *   *   *   *   *   *   *   *

OCD should develop and periodically disseminate a "State of the Child Report" describing the status of children and youth in the Nation within a given time frame.

As part of this effort, OCD should cooperate with the National Child Center for Social Statistics and others in developing the Report's statistical and narrative requirements.

Cost: $150,000   Time: 1 year

*   *   *   *   *   *   *   *   *   *

OCD should conduct longitudinal studies of the effects on children of transracial adoptions.

Cost: $500,000   Time: 3 years
(longitudinal research)

As a result of the importance weighting, only 13 value dimensions survived from the original list, that is, received any significant importance weights. These dimensions came from both the list of values to children and families and values to OCD. To facilitate translation from decision-theoretical jargon into government jargon, the words "value dimension" were replaced by the word "criterion."

The 13 surviving criteria were:

Criterion A (Importance weight = .007)
The extent to which a recommended activity is likely to foster service continuity/coordination and elimination of fragmentation, or is likely to contribute to this goal.

Criterion B (Importance weight = .145)
The extent to which a recommended activity represents an investment in a

prototypical and/or high-leverage activity, or is likely to contribute to the development of prototypical/high-leverage programs.

Criterion C (Importance weight = .061)

The extent to which a recommended activity increases or is likely to contribute to an increase in families' sense of efficacy and their ability to obtain and use resources necessary for the healthy development of children.

Criterion D (Importance weight = .052)

The extent to which a recommended activity is likely to increase the probability that children will acquire the skills necessary for successful performance of adult roles, or is likely to contribute to that goal.

Criterion E (Importance weight = .036)

The extent to which a recommended activity is likely to contribute to making the public and institutions more sensitive to the developmental needs of children.

Criterion F (Importance weight = .048)

The extent to which a recommended activity is likely to promote the individualization of services or programs, or is likely to contribute to this goal.

Criterion G (Importance weight = .043)

The extent to which a recommended activity is likely to stimulate the development of pluralistic child care delivery systems that provide for parental choice, or is likely to contribute to the expansion of such systems.

Criterion H (Importance weight = .014)

The extent to which a recommended activity is likely to promote self-respect and mutual regard among children from diverse racial, cultural, class, and ethnic backgrounds, or is likely to contribute to this goal.

Criterion I (Importance weight = .009)

The extent to which a recommended activity is likely to result in effective interagency coordination at federal, state, and local levels, or is likely to contribute to this goal.

Criterion J (Importance weight = .160)

The extent to which a recommended activity is consonant with administration and departmental policies and philosophy, or reflects prevailing public and social thinking.

Criterion K (Importance weight = .120)

The extent to which a recommended activity is likely to make public leadership more sensitive to the needs of children.

Criterion L (Importance weight = .145)

The extent to which a recommended activity is likely to influence national child care policy in a positive way.

Criterion M (Importance weight = .032)

The extent to which a recommended activity is capable of rational explication, that is, the extent to which it represents a logical extention of past results and conclusions, is indicated on theoretical grounds, or fulfills prior commitments.

Criterion N (Importance weight = .129)

The extent to which a recommended activity is likely to produce tangible, short-term results, that is, the extent to which it is likely to produce or contribute to the production of solid conclusions, benefits, or results within a relatively short period of time.

There was some interpersonal disagreement about what the precise weights should be, although analysis showed that the disagreement was not systematically related to the race, sex, or organizational locus of the respondent. However, there was excellent agreement about what the most important dimensions were, in terms of rank order across individuals. The method proved to be useful for identifying the most important dimensions, although it did not produce, nor was it intended to produce, uniformity of weights across individuals. Figure 7.4 illustrates that there may be differences between the importance weights of individual participants, but that medians, or some other measure of central tendency, can more or less reflect the group consensus. Scatter plots of the type shown in Figure 7.4 were used as inputs about the group's values to the Acting Director of the Office of Child Development when later in the process he decided on the final importance weights.

Following the next step of the process, each of the research recommendations had to be scaled for each value dimension. Individuals who did the scaling were told to think of an imaginary scale of 0 to 1,000. Their task was to estimate the extent to which a research recommendation contributed to a particular value or criterion. Since this task required some knowledge of the past work in each area of research, staff members of the Office of Child Development, with considerable familiarity with the research programs, were asked to make these judgments. Typically, three individuals judged each value dimension and each individual was assigned three value dimensions. In this way, three different scores were generated for each recommendation on each value. Figure 7.5 shows, for values E, F, G, and H, the location of each specific research recommendation. Note that all the recommendations fall below 500 on Criterion G, but some recommendations are above 750 on Criterion H, making a substantial contribution. Such differences also hold for individual judge data, and are not artifacts either of averaging or of assignments of different judges to different criteria.

Following Step 9 in the process, utilities were then calculated for each research recommendation for all of the values taken together (A through N).

Figure 7.6 shows rescaled utilities for the recommendations thus far. These rescaled utilities run from precisely 0 to precisely 1,000, because that is how they were calculated. The actual range of outputs of Step 9 was something like 200 to 550; a linear transformation was used to produce the rescaled numbers in Figure 7.6.

Figure 7.7 gives the benefit-to-cost ratios for the recommendations developed in this phase of the process. The numbers indicate specific recommendations; the "/" simply indicated that two recommendations were approximately tied.

This approach to planning and evaluation is an iterative one. At every step it is possible, indeed desirable, that the usefulness of the outcome be reconsidered.

(text continues on p. 168)

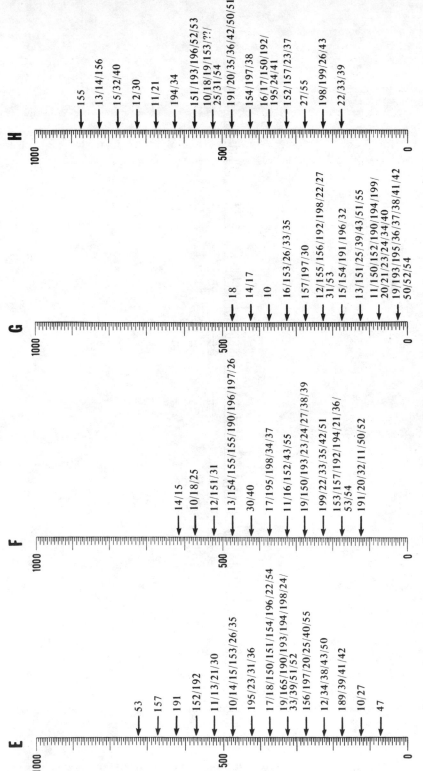

FIGURE 7.4 Illustration of the average scale values of all recommendations on four representative values (E, F, G, H).

165

FIGURE 7.5   Standardized utilities for recommendations (First phase).

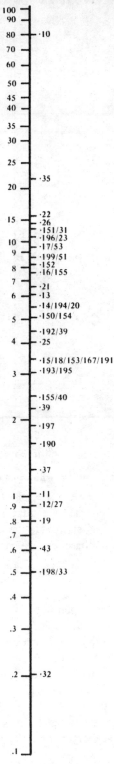

FIGURE 7.6 Benefit-to-cost ratios for the recommendations (First phase).

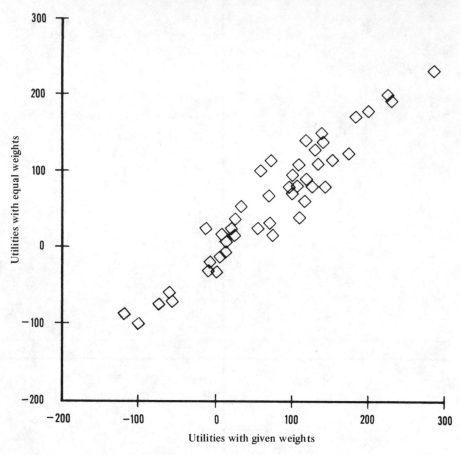

FIGURE 7.7   Recalculation of utilities with equal weights.

It became clear after the first phase, in which 13 value criteria had been applied to several hundred research recommendations, that both the values and recommendations could be clarified and made more general. In the following section, we will deal with the second phase and the changes made in value criteria in the research recommendations.

Phase Two—Values

The discussion of value dimensions in the first phase reflects a first cut at determining the structure of the agency's values. While refining the value dimensions, it became apparent that the agency's values were *hierarchically* structured (Raiffa, 1969), so that most of the values were subordinate to a relatively small number of superordinate values. Instead of depicting the agency's values as two sets of values, it was appropriate to identify the superordinate value dimensions. The process was facilitated by the fact that, in analyzing the weights attached by participants, there was excellent agreement about which values should be ranked highest, although there was disagreement about their precise weights.

After a discussion of the analysis with the Director and key participants, the Director decided that five value dimensions adequately reflected the agency's value structure. The decision was made, therefore, to utilize only these five superordinate values in the evaluation of substantive areas.

These five values, roughly equal in importance, were all considerably more important than any of the others. (See the earlier list of 13, which include these 5.) These value dimensions, which were then used in the second phase, were B, J, K, L, and N from the initial list. Their renormalized importance weights were:

Value Dimensions		Weight
(J)	Consistent with departmental policy	.23
(L)	Influences national child care policy positively	.21
(B)	Prototype/high-leverage activity	.21
(N)	Produces tangible short-term results	.18
(K)	Makes public leadership more sensitive to children's needs	.17

The total of the non-renormalized weights is .699 or .70. The other eight value criteria, which are really subordinate hierarchical values, have a combined importance weight of only .30. While it is important to agree precisely upon what set of values will be used, Figure 7.8 shows that it is less important to agree upon what their weights are. Figure 7.8 indicates that a recalculation of utilities with equal weights assigned to the five values produces scores that correlate highly with the utilities calculated using the individual weights generated by the Office of Child Development Acting Director. This illustrates that, although people may believe that they are in disagreement, sharing common values should help to lead them to make the same decision, the same phenomenon Gardiner (1974) found.

Phase Two—Recommendations

As was described earlier, in the initial phase research recommendations were solicited from a wide variety of outside groups, for example, child development specialists, Office of Child Development staff, and current as well as previously considered research and programs of the Office of Child Development. Several hundred recommendations were solicited and refined. During the first phase, the values were applied to each of the several hundred recommendations and utilities were derived.

It became apparent, however, that there were some problems with recommendations (entities) defined as specifically as these were. First, because the recommendations had been solicited in an inductive manner, some important substantive areas were not covered. Second, a particular recommendation might well be one way, perhaps not the best way, of attacking its topic. Relatively minor improvements might lead to substantially higher utilities.

This became clear early in the process. In the second phase, therefore, a deductive approach to the research recommendations was used. This was done by mapping out a comprehensive taxonomy of all the possible competing major research options. The substantive areas in which OCD had previously done research

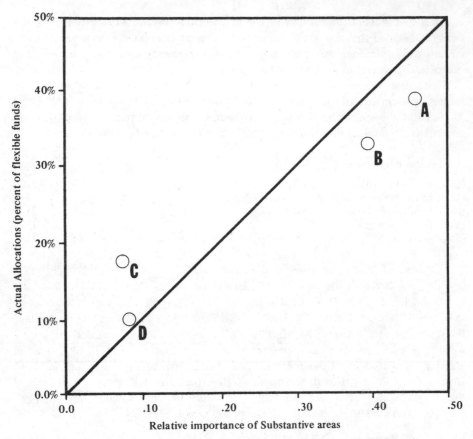

(Substantive areas: A—Children at risk and the child welfare system; B—Child development and the family; C—Child advocacy; D—Television and children.)

FIGURE 7.8   Final decisions: the relative importance of the substantive areas.

or had programs were reviewed. Extensive panel meetings with outside experts also identified other salient issues which were considered in the overall plan. Position papers were solicited on a number of these issues. What emerged during the second phase was an identification of broad research topics and themes. These general research foci subsumed most of the previously generated concrete, specific recommendations.

The broad substantive research and program areas included the following: (a) children at risk and the child welfare system; (b) child development and the family; (c) child advocacy; (d) television and children.

Finally, using the five final value dimensions, each of the broad research and program areas was evaluated (Step 8). In Step 9, utilities were established for each of the general recommendations. The utility analysis indicated how the OCD research and development budget could be allocated across different categories of projects. The analysis also indicated how much money each substantive area could receive given the results of the utility analysis.[5]

The rule used was that the amount of money each area would receive was directly proportional to the utility of that area. Under certain assumptions, this allocation rule maximizes the overall utility of the specific projects that would be funded. However, because the analysis did not involve the specific assessment of discrete research and development projects, this rule was used only as a rough rule-of-thumb, and was provided to the OCD Director as overall guidance.

At Step 10, the step of decision, the Director of the Office of Child Development, with the value dimensions in hand, but at first without the utilities which were the result of the judgments of the staff and a number of outside groups, intuitively allocated the flexible funds across the broad substantive areas. The Director's intuitive allocation and the guidance from the utility analysis were then compared. Although the agreement was good, it was by no means perfect.

As a result of the discrepancies between his own judgments and the utility analysis, the Director decided that, if possible, funds previously allocated for child advocacy would be reduced. He also decided that, since additional funds were expected from the termination of cutbacks in ongoing projects, that these monies would be distributed between the two areas that appeared to be funded at too low a level, given the utility analysis. In this case, the conformity between the Director's intuitive decisions and the utility analysis guidance was quite close, so that the analysis did not induce major changes in emphasis. However, it did affect the Director's decisions about how additional flexible funds would be allocated. When comparisons were made between fiscal year 1973 and fiscal year 1974, the differences and changes in budget emphases follow the 1974 utility analysis.

How does one go back from the broad substantive areas to specific research projects? Once the allocations across the broad substantive areas had been made, highly detailed and specific project specifications were worked out by the OCD staff. It is possible to use either the same or a separately generated set of specific research values to apply to the research recommendations within each substantive area.

The Office of Child Development research plan was then sent to the Office of Human Development and to the Assistant Secretary for Planning and Development in HEW. Each of these agencies makes decisions about the final research plan. Under ideal circumstances, each of these agencies should have made its values explicit and used the same utilities analysis system as had the Office of Child Development. If this had been done, it would have been possible for each of these agencies to know precisely where the differences and similarities in values between them lay. But the simultaneous conversion of several government agencies to a new methodology is too much to ask!

Social Psychology of the Process

Until this point, only the content of the decision-theoretic planning and evaluation process has been described. A large part of the actual process, however, is social in nature. This section deals with the ways in which group processes were used in the development of the OCD plan.

At Step 2, the identification of the issue or issues to which the utilities needed are relevant, a group may or may not be involved. The definition of the issue or issues can, in the case of an agency or program where goals are multiple, be a target for debate.

Generally, however, groups become involved only at Step 4, the identification of the relevant dimensions of value. The multi-attribute utility technique does not specify whether or not face-to-face groups should be used. The agency can decide how it wants these relevant dimensions of value to be generated.

In past work, we have found that having the dimensions of value generated in a face-to-face group is quite useful for the agency. Individuals frequently agree more about values than they would predict. Since no values are excluded and no arguments occur, the value dimension generation process is often useful in providing information to members of a group about their own values.

When there are groups that clearly have different values inside and outside the program to be evaluated, it is often useful to have each group generate its own values independently. Then information about these values can be provided to every other group. Again, it is important to emphasize that, because at this stage there is no judgment of relative importances, the information generated is useful and unthreatening to each group.

Steps 5 and 6 can also be done either by face-to-face groups or by individuals whose rankings are later combined. Generally, the face-to-face group process is better if it is possible. It is better because the process tends to build a group consensus on the ordering of the values. When, however, there are clearly diverse groups, both within and outside a program or agency, it is most useful to permit each of these groups (or representatives of them) to perform their own rank ordering and importance weighting as a face-to-face group.

This is useful for three reasons. First, each group builds a consensus about its own values vis-a-vis the programs. This makes it possible to exchange information about the relative ordering of values between groups, so that discussions between groups about value differences can be quite explicit and quantified. This pleasantly cuts down the noise of rhetoric. Second, the same evaluation data can be fed back to each group. The same data, in a matrix in which values, rank order, and/or importance weights differ considerably, will yield very different final conclusions and decisions. Thus, a number of groups can, using the same data, come to very different conclusions about whether a program or programs are meeting their goals. This then provides them with a substantive basis for discussions with one another. Third, consensus is not a sine qua non of the evaluation process. If a number of different groups generate very different values, then data must be gathered which indicate how contemplated actions bear on every one of the values. This forces the evaluation researcher into multiple measurement. In addition, it means that decision makers receive research data on issues that may be foreign to their own values, but quite germane to the values of other groups, for example, persons affected by a program. The result of this value diversity is a much greater richness of evaluation information. All concerned groups benefit.

At Step 8, the measurement of the entity being evaluated on each dimension, the best choice is to use experts. At the planning stage, one presumes that whatever research or other evaluation data are available must be combined in some way to generate a location measure. Therefore, it is best to use individuals who are able to make such judgments expertly.

The Integration of Planning and Evaluation

Only the OCD research plan has so far been described. Earlier, we asserted that the planning and evaluation process could and should be integrated. How, then, does one proceed from a research plan of this kind to the evaluation process?

As has been earlier noted, a matrix has been generated as part of the multi-attribute utility planning process. All of the values that have been rank ordered and importance weighted are in the matrix. The rows of the matrix consist of the programs, subprograms, and so on, that is, the entities being evaluated. The columns are the value dimensions. In each cell of the matrix, there is a location judgment of the extent to which program 1 is likely to contribute to value A, and the like. In the planning stage, this judgment has been made using all the available data on the program. Where programs do not exist, and are potential new options, these judgments are no more than educated guesses.

As the program proceeds, data are gathered. In cases in which the educated guess used in planning was specific enough to be modified by an observed number (e.g., number of participants in a voluntary program), the standard techniques of Bayesian statistics can be used to update initial guesses as data accumulate. In the OCD case, most of the value dimensions used were so abstract that numbers observable during a program are unlikely to represent them, though they obviously bear on them. In such cases, the entries in the matrix should still be updated, either by the direct use of expert judgment or by some more formal process, such as further decomposition of each value via the value hierarchy concept.

Thus the original evaluation structure used in planning the program can also be used to evaluate it as it proceeds, and to assess its merits when it is over.

However, values (here interpreted as importance weights) change as programs proceed, as circumstances change, as time passes. The weights appropriate this year may not be appropriate next year. This suggests that two different evaluative questions, both based on the same updated location measures, can and should be asked. One is "How does the present program measure up to the expectations we had for it when we planned it?" The other is "Given this year's values, how does the present program look? Should it be changed? If so, how?"

It is fairly often reasonable to define a value dimension as a goal. A very abstract dimension can often be operationalized by specifying some measure or set of measures such that attainment of them constitutes success, and failure to attain them constitutes failure. Then the probability of success can be treated as the location measure, and can be updated as data accumulate by standard Bayesian procedures. We will illustrate this technique in two examples, one hypothetical and one real.

A SIMPLE EXAMPLE INTEGRATING PLANNING AND EVALUATION

Suppose that a large city has a program for identifying and treating health problems, and that different "models" are being evaluated. Accordingly, 400 children are randomly assigned as "clients." Staffing patterns vary among the first three models. Model 1 is staffed by one full-time medical doctor and one full-time paraprofessional; Model 2 is staffed by one half-time medical doctor and five full-time paraprofessionals; and Model 3 is staffed by one one-fourth-time medical doctor and seven full-time paraprofessionals. Model 4 is a control, or no-treatment group, and indicates how well children do outside the program models. Staff members are randomly assigned to the different models (except Model 4), and the models are comparable in terms of total funding level, total salaries, equipment, medicine, access to ancillary services, and the like. All 400 children are tested on the first day of the program and retested after one year. Steps in a decision-theoretic approach to evaluation would proceed as follows. (The numbering does not correspond to that in the list of ten steps to evaluation via multi-attribute utility given earlier.)

Step 1: Identify Program Goals

Typically, program goals are consistent with the decision maker's values, and it is possible to make explicit the program's goals and their relative importance to the decision maker. Suppose that the program has three separate goals: to improve physical health, to improve mental health, and to improve social competency. In many instances, such broad goals must be subdivided and partitioned into subgoals that can be assessed separately. But this example is simplified by the assumption that these goals can be used without further elaboration. (This corresponds to Step 5 of our original list.)

Step 2: Determine the Relative Importance of Goals

Since the hypothetical program is targeted on health problems. It is plausible to assume that improving physical health is the most important and that improving social competency is the least important goal. Following our procedure, we assign an arbitrary importance weight of 10 to the least important goal (social competency), and the remaining two goals are weighed relative to the least important goal. Assume that the relative importance of these goals is expressed by weights of 10 (social competency), 20 (mental health), and 80 (physical health). (This corresponds to Step 6 of our original list.)

Step 3: Identify Probabilistic Measures of Goal Attainment

In this step operational definitions of the program's goals are specified. The appropriate measures may be very complex and difficult to measure, or they may be simply defined and amenable to measurement. For this example we will use simple, dichotomous goals, and the criterion for success will be whether a client exceeds predefined standards. For each goal, the location measure will be the probability that a (randomly chosen) client will exceed the standard.

Step 4: Estimate Prior Probabilities of Goal Attainment

Prior to implementation of programs there are typically few or no data about program maximization of goals. Nevertheless, decision makers have subjective prior probabilities which should guide the planning process and govern the selection of activities. Recall that Guttentag (1973) refers to a planning process built upon wholly subjective, prior information. For the present example, suppose that the subjective prior probabilities for each goal are given in Table 7.1. These prior probabilities suggest that we initially expect Model 1 to be the best according to all goals, except that it is equal in value to Model 2 in terms of achieving the physical health goal. (This corresponds to Step 8 of our original list.)

Step 5: Calculate Prior Utilities

In this example, the worth of a model will be determined by the expected number of clients who achieve each goal, and the importance of each goal. Since the expected number is proportional to the prior probability, the prior utility for each model is

$$U_i = \sum_j (W_j \cdot P_{ij})$$

where W_j is the weight for the jth goal, and P_{ij} is the prior probability that a client in the ith model will achieve the jth goal. In words, the prior utility for a given model is proportional to the sum of the prior probabilities, each multiplied by the appropriate importance weight.

Step 6: Measure Goal Attainment

In this example there is an operational definition of goals, and pertinent data are frequency counts of goal achievement on retest. For the hypothetical example, we might assume that the proportions are given in Table 7.2. Clearly, these data run counter to prior expectations—on goals 2 and 3, Models 2 and 3 do better than Model 1. The computation, in Step 8, of posterior utilities will indicate how these data should change prior opinion about the value of these models.

Step 7: Calculate Posterior Probabilities

Before posterior utilities can be calculated, it is appropriate to revise the probabilities associated with goal attainment. Bayes's theorem (e.g., see Edwards, Lindman, and Savage, 1963) is the algorithm used to revise probabilities; the beta

TABLE 7.1

Model	Prior Probability of Client's Achieving Goal			Prior Utility
	Goal 1	Goal 2	Goal 3	
1	.40	.80	.60	54.00
2	.40	.75	.50	52.00
3	.30	.60	.45	40.50
4	.10	.30	.35	17.50

TABLE 7.2

Model	Proportion of Clients Achieving Goal		
	Goal 1	Goal 2	Goal 3
1	62/100	40/100	40/100
2	55/100	85/100	50/100
3	35/100	90/100	65/100
4	10/100	35/100	40/100

distribution is used as a prior in this example. Because the assessment of prior distributions can be controversial, we arbitrarily assume that the parameters of the prior beta distribution sum to 1.0. (This amounts to assuming that all prior opinions were very weakly held.) Using the prior distribution and the probabilities of the data for each model (described by the binomial distribution), the posterior probabilities (means of the posterior distributions) shown in Table 7.3 are derived.

(Note that the posterior probabilities in Table 7.4 are very nearly equal to the sample proportions in Table 7.3. This is an example of "stable estimation," since data exert a much larger effect on the posteriors that the priors do. If, however, there is little or no sample information, the posterior probabilities will be close to the prior probabilities. Thus, this method reflects the diagnosticity of data from program evaluation and provides a mathematically appropriate rule for modifying opinion about programs.)

TABLE 7.3

Model	Posterior Probabilities of Client's Achieving Goal			Posterior Utility
	Goal 1	Goal 2	Goal 3	
1	.62	.47	.41	61.90
2	.55	.86	.51	66.30
3	.35	.91	.66	52.80
4	.10	.35	.40	19.00

TABLE 7.4

Comparison Group	Prior Probability of Cient's Achieving Goal					Prior Utility
	Goal 1	Goal 2	Goal 3	Goal 4	Goal 5	
Graduates	.23	.30	.10	.07	.30	45.75
Nongraduates	.15	.22	.06	.12	.45	34.80

Step 8: Calculate Posterior Utilities

The computational formula for posterior utilities is (except for minor notational changes) identical to the equation in Step 5: to calculate posterior utilities, simply replace the prior probabilities in Step 5 with the posterior probabilities from Step 7. The posterior utilities are shown in Table 7.3.

This hypothetical example illustrates how evaluation data can be directly related to the decision maker's values, and how these data can be used to revise prior assessments of the worth of programs. By assessing the worth of each model across all dimensions at once, the utility score incorporates tradeoffs between goals or values. Note, for example, that Model 2 has a higher overall posterior utility than Model 1, although Model 1 has a somewhat higher posterior probability on Goal 1 than Model 2 does. These data indicate that the data from evaluation should induce the decision maker to rate Model 2 as a better investment than Model 1, and reverse his prior rank ordering.

An Example from the Career Education Project

Currently, a decision-theoretic approach is being used by the Career Education Project (CEP), Educational Development Center, Inc. A goal of this project is to reach potential members of the labor force, especially "homebased" women, and counsel them about career education or training opportunities. One way of evaluating this project is to specify goals in terms of status in education or training activities. The general approach can be illustrated using data from a formative stage of the project; these are follow-up for clients who terminated the service with the stated intention of enrolling in an education or training activity. (The tentative plans are for the latest evaluation to include a control group and a more complete set of goals.) For the follow-up study, the goals and importance weights (in parentheses) are: Goal 1, Client Enrolled and Completed ETR (90); Goal 2, Client Enrolled and Participating in ETR (60); Goal 3, Client Enrolled and Waiting for ETR to Begin (30); Goal 4, Client Tried to Enroll but Failed to Resolve Constraints (15); and Goal 5, Client Enrolled but Dropped ETR (10).

To evaluate the differential impact of the counseling service on different subgroups of clients, many comparative analyses were made. Utility is calculated for each separate subgroup. For example, high school graduates were compared to nongraduates. After appropriate instructions, subjective prior probability estimates were made by a project member; these, along with the prior utilities (calculated from Step 5) are shown in Table 7.4.

These prior probabilities were subjective estimates about what goal attainment would be six months after clients left the service. Data for these clients were obtained by talking with them after the six-month delay. Actual results are indicated in Table 7.5, which shows the posterior probabilities and utilities.

Murphy (1974) has suggested that comparing prior and posterior probabilities may highlight ways in which the program is not performing as expected. Disparity between the wholly subjective priors and the data-based posteriors could indicate that the program should be modified, or that additional research efforts might be

TABLE 7.5

Comparison Group	Posterior Probability of Client's Achieving Goal					Posterior Utility
	Goal 1	Goal 2	Goal 3	Goal 4	Goal 5	
Graduates	.21	.45	.05	.11	.18	50.85
Nongraduates	.29	.30	.01	.19	.21	49.35

required. In particular, such analyses may show that a program should be modified to better meet the needs of specific subgroups of clients.

In these analyses of the follow-up studies, no control group or randomization was used. Thus, self-selection among clients is a distinct possibility. Nevertheless, utility measures such as these indicate how classes of clients are interacting with the program and—regardless of their personal or demographic characteristics—indicate differences in outcomes for client groups. Thus, the utility scores are useful, even under nonexperimental conditions.

These illustrations show how the method discussed in this paper can be used in both nonexperimental conditions (e.g., the CEP follow-up study) and experimental conditions (the hypothetical example and the CEP evaluation plan). This flexibility is a major advantage over more conventional approaches, which are generally unrelated to planning or resource allocation decisions.

NOTES

1. This section on independence is more technical than the remainder of the paper. It can be skipped by those who are comfortable with simply making independence assumptions as a way of getting on with the job of evaluation, but should be read and pondered by those interested in the technical properties of multi-attribute utility measurement.

2. We are grateful to David Seaver, who first called the issue discussed in the following paragraphs to our attention.

3. Much of this material was originally presented in Guttentag (1973).

4. Much of this material will appear in a forthcoming issue of *Evaluation* (see Guttentag and Snapper, in press).

5. Snapper (1973) has described the hierarchical version of the multi-attribute utility model that was actually used in calculations. His notation is different from that used in this paper, so his argument is here paraphrased and the equations are given a form consistent with the notation used throughout.

When OCD attempted to use the nonhierarchical version of multi-attribute utility measurement, it became clear that the values to be served were at a very different level of abstraction from the specific projects; the logical and conceptual linkages between projects and values were therefore unclear. For that reason, a four-level hierarchical model was adopted. At the top level were the five value dimensions already chosen; the index j runs over them. Next below them came substantive areas (e.g., child advocacy, children at risk and the child welfare system); it was assumed that each substantive area had value within each of the value dimensions. The index k runs over them. Next below substantive areas came issues. Since different issues may arise within each substantive area, the index h_k runs over the issues within the kth substantive area. Finally, the index i runs over specific projects. If u_{ijkh_k} is the location measure of the ith research project with respect to value dimension J, substantive area k, and issue within that substantive area h_k, the w's are the importances, and U_j is the aggregate value of the ith research project, then in this notation

$$U_i = \sum_j \left[w_j \left\{ \sum_k w_k \left(\sum_{h_k} w_{h_k} u_{ijkh_k} \right) \right\} \right]$$

subject to the following sum constraints:

$$\Sigma_j w_j = 1$$
$$\Sigma_k w_k = 1$$

For each value of k, $\Sigma_k w_{h_k} = 1$.

This hierarchical formulation of the multi-attribute utility model established logical and conceptual linkages between the value dimensions and specific projects, thereby meeting the first criticism. But how can a budget be allocated without the need for dubious cost estimates? As Snapper noted: "In many forward-planning contexts, the actual set of projects (or options) is unknown at the time budget allocation is required. This occurs, for example, when "directive" research involves project recommendations solicited from the field. When the set of projects is not complete . . . it is impossible . . . to apply the benefit-to-cost algorithm. . . . However, there are several bureaucratic techniques for allocating funds prior to the receipt of specific projects. The most plausible is to allocate funds to substantive areas in proportion to the importance weights."

Snapper went on to point out that benefit-to-cost rules will select projects with modest benefits only if their costs are correspondingly modest, and will select projects with large costs only if they also produce large benefits; that is, the rule produces a high positive correlation between benefit and costs for selected projects. Thus allocation of funds in proportion to importance weight approximates the result of a full benefit-to-cost analysis, since those weights are crucial to calculation of benefits.

The goal, then, is to allocate funds proportionally to w_k. Rather than directly estimating w_k, this was done by using the equation

$$w = w_j w_{k_j}$$

The term w_{k_j} is a judgment of the extent to which substantive area k satisfies, or fulfills, value dimension j. Of course

$$\sum_{k_j} w_{k_j} = 1.$$

Using this equation and the Director's estimates, the calculated importance weights w_k for the four substantive areas were:

Substantive Area	Importance Weight
Children at risk and the child welfare system	.46
Child development and the family	.39
Child advocacy	.08
Television and children	.07

6. Unlike the hypothetical example, the CEP application involves a multinomial distribution, and the prior distribution is Dirichlet rather than beta; however, the computation of posterior probabilities and utilities is analogous to that used in the binomial example.

REFERENCES

Boruch, Robert F. "Problems in research utilization: Use of social experiments, experimental results and auxiliary data in experiments." *Annals of the New York Academy of Sciences: Critical Human Behavioral Research Issues in Social Intervention Programs,* June 22, 1973, 218: 56-77.

Campbell, Donald T. "Assessing the impact of planned social change." Lecture given at Conference on Social Psychology, Budapest, Hungary, May 1974.

–––. "Making the case for randomized assignment to treatments by considering the alternatives: six ways in which quasi-experimental evaluations in compensatory education tend to underestimate effects." Reconstruction and extension of lecture presented to the conference on Central Issues in Social Program Evaluation. In C. A. Bennet and A. Lumsdaine, *Central Issues in Social Program Evaluation,* in press.

Dawes, R. M. and B. Corrigan. "Linear Models in decision making." *Psychological Bulletin,* 1974, 81: 97-106.

Edwards, Ward. "Social utilities." *The Engineering Economist,* Summer Symposium Series, VI, 1971.

Edwards, W., H. Lindman and L. J. Savage. "Bayesian statistical inference for psychological research." *Psychological Review,* 1963, 70: 193-242.

Edwards, W., L. D. Phillips, W. L. Hays, and B. C. Goodman. "Probabilistic information processing systems: Design and evaluation." *IEEE Transaction on Systems Science and Cybernetics,* 1968, SSC-4: 248-265.

Fryback, Dennis Gene. "Subjective Probability Estimates in a medical decision making problem." Ph.D. thesis, University of Michigan, 1974.

Gardiner, Peter C., "The Application of decision technology and Monte Carlo simulation to multiple objective public policy decision making: A case study in California coastal zone management." Ph.D. dissertation, University of Southern California, 1974.

Gilbert, John P., Richard J. Light and Frederick Mosteller. "Assessing social innovations: An empirical base for policy." In C. A. Bennett and A. Lumsdaine (eds.) *Central Issues in Social Program Evaluation,* in press.

Guttentag, M. "Subjectivity and its use in evaluation research." *Evaluation,* 1973, 1 (2).

Guttentag, M. and K. J. Snapper. "Plans, evaluations, and decisions." *Evaluation,* in press.

Harre, Ron and Paul Secord. *The Explanation of Social Behavior.* Oxford: Blackwell and Mott, 1972.

Keeney, R. L. "Utility functions for multi-attributed consequences." *Management Science,* 1972a, 18, 276-287.

–––. "Multiplicative utility functions." Technical Report #70, Operations Research Center. Boston: M.I.T., 1972b.

Miller, L. W., R. J. Kaplan, and W. Edwards. "JUDGE: A laboratory evaluation." *Organizational Behavior and Human Performance,* 1969, 4: 97-111.

Murphy, J. F. "Multi-attribute utility analysis: an application in social utilities." Career Education Project Technical Report (74-1, July 1974).

Phillips, L. D. *Bayesian Statistics for Social Scientists.* New York: Crowell, 1973.

Raiffa, H. *Decision Analysis: Introductory Lectures on Choices Under Certainty.* Reading, Mass.: Addison-Wesley, 1968.

–––. Preferences for multi-attribute alternatives. The RAND Corp., Memorandum RM-5968-DOT/RC, April 1969.

Riecken, H. W., R. F. Boruch, D. T. Campbell, N. Caplan, T. K. Glennan, J. Pratt, A. Rees, and W. Williams. *Experimentation as a Method for Planning and Evaluating Social Innovations.* New York: Seminar Press, 1975.

Schlaifer, R. *Analysis of Decisions Under Uncertainty.* New York: McGraw-Hill, 1969.

Snapper, K. J. and C. Peterson. "Information seeking and data diagnosticity." *Journal of Cognitive Psychology,* 1971, 87: 429-433.

Suchman, E. *Evaluation Research.* New York: Russell Sage, 1967.

Watts, H. W. "Graduated work incentives: An experiment in negative taxation." *American Economic Review,* 1969, 59: 463-472.

Weiss, C. H. *Evaluation Research.* Englewood Cliffs, N.J.: Prentice-Hall, 1972.

Weiss, R. S. and M. Rein. "The evaluation of broad-aim programs: Experimental design, its difficulties, and an alternative." *Administrative Science Quarterly,* 1970, 15: 97-109.

Williams, W., and J. W. Evans. "The politics of evaluation: The case of Head Start." *The Annals,* 1969, 385: 118-132.

REFERENCE UPDATE

Selected by Ward Edwards and Kurt Snapper

In 1975, we noted that multiattribute utility measurement was a general-purpose tool for evaluation. An explosion of successful applications to real problems has occurred since then. Edwards (1980) reviewed 27 instances of application and cited 18 publications. Some of the most important applications have not been reported in open scientific literature at all. Some such reports are classified; some are company confidential; many are never written down because the users are executives interested in making decisions rather than researchers interested in publishing papers.

Probably the largest collection of successful real applications in open literature arises in medicine. The journal *Medical Decision Making* has been publishing four issues a year since 1981. About half the papers in each issue use one version or another of multiattribute utility measurement in connection with some real medical decision. One regular feature of the journal is a report of clinical rounds at the New England Medical Center, edited by Dr. Stephen G. Pauker. Each such report presents a case in which a bedside decision analysis was made to select a course of treatment; most of these cases use the tools of multiattribute utility measurement. Utilities are usually expressed as quality-adjusted life years (QALY). Since that journal contains so many reports of real applications, we will not cite them separately here; interested users should browse through the journal.

Organization of evaluation literature along topical rather than methodological lines explains the widespread lack of recognition of the explosive growth of multiattribute utility evaluation since the early 1970s. The diversity of journals and technical reports to search, and of topics to which the technique has been applied, ensures that no one— certainly not either of us—is aware of the frequency of application or able to cite all of the relevant literature.

Aschenbrenner, M. K. and W. Kasubek. *Challenging the Cushing Syndrome: Multiattribute evaluation of cortisone drugs.* University of Mannheim, n.d.

Bajgier, S. M. and H. Moskowitz. *Public risk assessment evaluation of drinking water quality.* Report 596. Krannert Graduate School of Management, Purdue University, 1977.

Barclay, S. and C. R. Peterson. *Multiattribute utility models for negotiations.* Technical Report 76-1. Arlington, VA: Defense Advanced Research Projects Agency.

Bauer, V. and M. Wegener. Simulation, evaluation and conflict analysis in urban planning. *Proceedings of the Institute of Electrical and Electronics Engineers,* 1975, 63: 405-413.

Beach, L. R., B. P. Townes, F. L. Campbell, and G. W. Keating. Developing and testing a decision aid for birth planning decisions. *Organizational Behavior and Human Performance,* 1976, 15: 99-116.

Bell, D. E. *A decision analysis of objectives for a forest pest problem.* Research Report 75-43. Laxenburg, Austria: International Institute for Applied Systems Analysis, 1975.

Brown, R. V., C. W. Kelly, R. R. Stewart, and J. W. Ulvila. *The timeliness of a NATO response to an impending Warsaw Pact attack.* Technical Report DT/TR 75-7. Arlington, VA: Advanced Research Projects Agency, 1975.

Brown, R. V., C. R. Peterson, and J. W. Ulvila. *An analysis of alternative Mideastern oil agreements.* Technical Report DT/TR 75-6. Arlington, VA: Rome Air Development Center, Office of Naval Research and Defense Advanced Research Projects Agency, 1975.

Brown, R. V., D. A. Seaver, and R. C. Bromage. *An analysis of the community anti-crime funding decision.* Technical Report 80-2. Falls Church, VA: Decision Science Consortium, 1980.

Buehring, W. A., W. K. Foell, and R. L. Keeney. *Energy/environment management: Application of decision analysis.* Research Report 75-14. Laxenburg, Austria: International Institute for Applied Systems Analysis, 1975.

Chen, M. M., J. W. Bush, and D. L. Patrick. Social indicators for health planning and policy analysis. *Policy Sciences,* 1975, 6: 71-89.

Chinnis, J. O., C. W. Kelly, R. D. Minckler, and M. F. O'Connor. Single channel ground and airborne radio system (SINCGARS) evaluation model. Technical report, Decisions & Designs, 1975.

Dyer, J. S. and R. F. Miles, Jr. An actual application of collective choice theory to the selection of trajectories for the Mariner Jupiter/Saturn 1977 project. *Operations Research,* 1976, 24 (2): 220-224.

Edwards, W. How to use multiattribute utility measurement for social decision making. *IEEE Transactions on Systems, Man and Cybernetics,* 1977, 7: 326-340.

Edwards, W. Technology for director dubious. In K. R. Hammond (ed.) *Judgment and decision in public policy formation.* Boulder, CO: Westview, 1978.

Edwards, W. Multiattribute utility measurement: Evaluating desegregation plans in a highly political context. In R. Perloff (ed.) *Evaluator interventions: Pros and cons.* Beverly Hills, CA: Sage, 1979.

Edwards, W. Multiattribute utility for evaluation: Structures, uses, and problems. In M. Klein and K. Teilmannn (eds.) *Handbook of criminal justice evaluation.* Beverly Hills, CA: Sage, 1980. (a)

Edwards, W. Reflections on and criticisms of a highly political multiattribute utility analysis. In L. Cobb and R. M. Thrall (eds.) *Mathematical frontiers of behavioral and policy sciences.* Boulder, CO: Westview, 1980. (b)

Edwards, W., G. W. Fischer, and C. W. Kelly. *Decision theoretic aids for inference, evaluation, and decision making: A review of research and experience.* Technical Report TR 78-1-30. Arlington, VA: Advanced Decision Technology Program, Defense Advanced Research Projects Agency, 1978.

Edwards, W. and M. Guttentag. Experiments and evaluations: A re-examination. In C. A. Bennett and A. Lumsdaine (eds.) *Evaluation and experiment: Some critical issues in assessing social programs.* New York: Academic, 1975.

Edwards, W., M. Guttentag, and K. Snapper. Effective evaluation: A decision theoretic approach. In C. A. Bennett and A. Lumsdaine (eds.) *Evaluation and experiment: Some critical issues in assessing social programs.* New York: Academic, 1975.

Edwards, W., M. Guttentag, and K. Snapper. Un enfoque de toma de decisiones en la investigacion evaluativa. In G. E. Finley and G. Marin (eds.) *Avances en psicologia contemporanea.* Mexico City: Editorial Trillas, 1979.

Edwards, W. and J. R. Newman. *Multiattribute evaluation.* Beverly Hills, CA; Sage, 1982.

Edwards, W., W. Stillwell, and F. H. Barron. *Credit applications: A validation of multiattribute utility techniques against a real world criterion.* Technical Report 80-1. Los Angeles: Social Science Research Institute, University of Southern California, 1980.

Edwards, W., W. Stillwell, and D. von Winterfeldt. *Value tree analysis of energy supply alternatives.* Technical Report 81-2. Los Angeles: Social Science Research Institute, University of Southern California, 1981.

Edwards, W. and D. von Winterfeldt. Public disputes about risky technologies: Stakeholders and arenas. In J. Menkes, V. Covello, and J. Mumpower (eds.) *Contemporary issues in risk analysis.* New York: Plenum, 1983.

Edwards, W., D. von Winterfeldt, and D. Moody. Simplicity in decision analysis: An example and a discussion. In D. Bell (ed.) *Decision making: Descriptive, normative, and prescriptive interactions.* Cambridge, MA: Harvard Business School, 1983.

Gardiner, P. and W. Edwards. Public values: Multiattribute utility measurement in social decision making. In M. Schwartz and A. Kaplan (eds.) *Human judgment and decision processes: Formal and mathematical approaches.* New York: Academic, 1975.

Golabi, K., C. W. Kirkwood, and A. Sicherman. Selecting a portfolio of solar energy projects using multiattribute preference theory. *Management Science,* 1981, 27: 174-189.

Gustafson, D. H. and D. C. Holloway. A decision theory measuring severity in illness. *Health Services Research,* 1975, Spring: 97-106.

Herner, S. and K. Snapper. The application of multi-criteria utility theory to the evaluation of information systems. *Journal of the American Society for Information Science,* 1978, 29: 289-296.

Jauch, L. R. and W. F. Glueck. Evaluation of university professors' research performance. *Management Science,* 1975, 22 (1): 66-75.

Kaplan, R. M., J. W. Bush, and C. C. Berry. Health status: Types of validity and the index of well-being. *Health Services Research,* 1976, 11 (3): 478-507.

Keefer, D. L. *A decision analysis approach to resource allocation planning problems with multiple objectives.* Unpublished doctoral dissertation, University of Michigan, 1976.

Keeney, R. L. *Energy policy and value tradeoffs.* Research Memorandum 75-76. Laxenburg, Austria: International Institute for Applied Systems Analysis, 1975.

Keeney, R. L. *A utility function for examining policy affecting salmon in the Skeena River.* Research Report 76-5. Laxenburg, Austria: International Institute for Applied Systems Analysis, 1976.

Keeney, R. L. *Evaluation of proposed pumped storage sites.* San Francisco: Woodward-Clyde Consultants, Inc., 1977.

Keeney, R. L. *Siting energy facilities.* New York: Academic, 1980.

Keeney, R. L. and K. Nair. *Evaluating potential nuclear power plant sites in the Pacific Northwest using decision analysis.* Professional Paper 76-1. Laxenburg, Austria: International Institute for Applied Systems Analysis, 1976.

Keeney, R. L. and H. Raiffa. *Decisions with multiple objectives: Preferences and value tradeoffs.* New York: John Wiley, 1976.

Moskowitz, H., J. Evans, and I. Jimenez-Lerma. *Development of a multiattribute value function for long range electrical generation expansion.* Report 670. Krannert Graduate School of Management, Purdue University, 1978.

O'Connor, M. F. *The application of multiattribute scaling procedures to the development of indices of water quality.* Report 7339. Center for Mathematical Studies in Business and Economics, University of Chicago, 1973.

O'Connor, M. F., T. R. Rhees, and J. J. Allen. *A multiattribute utility approach for evaluating alternative naval aviation plans.* Technical Report 76-16. Arlington, VA: Defense Advanced Research Projects Agency, 1976.

Otway, H. J. and W. Edwards. *Application of a simple multiattribute rating technique to evaluation of nuclear waste disposal sites: A demonstration.* Research memorandum 77-31. Laxenburg, Austria: International Institute for Applied Systems Analysis, 1977.

Rozelle, M. A. *The incorporation of public values into public policy.* Unpublished doctoral dissertation, Arizona State University, 1982.

Snapper, K. J. with MetroStudy Foundation, Inc. *The District of Columbia's CETA summer youth employment program: An empirical assessment.* Washington, DC: MetroStudy Foundation, Inc., 1979.

Snapper, K. J. and D. A. Seaver. *Application of decision analysis to program planning and evaluations.* Technical Report 78-1. Washington, DC: Decision Science Consortium, Inc., 1978.

Snapper, K. J. and D. A. Seaver. *The irrelevance of evaluation research for decision making.* Technical Report 80-7. Falls Church, VA: Decision Science Consortium, Inc., 1980. (a)

Snapper, K. J. and D. A. Seaver. *The irrelevance of evaluation research for decision making: Case studies from the Community Anti-Crime Program.* Technical Report 80-12. Falls Church, VA: Decision Science Consortium, Inc., 1980. (b)

Snapper, K. J. and D. A. Seaver. The use of evaluation models for decision making: Application to the Community Anti-Crime Program. *Evaluation and Program Planning,* 1980, 3: 197-209. (c)

Snapper, K. J. and D. A. Seaver. Program decisions: Evaluating a bird in the hand versus two in the bush. *Evaluation and Program Planning,* 1981, 4: 325-334.

Snapper, K. J., T. Sutherland, and M. Peterson. *Decision-analytic methods for evaluating energy contingency plans.* Technical Report 81-2. Fox Mill, VA: Planning Systems Associates, Inc., 1981.

IV

EVALUATION THROUGH SOCIAL ECOLOGY

8

EPIDEMIOLOGICAL MODELS

M. SUSSER
Columbia University

In current definition, epidemiology is the study of the distribution and determinants of states of health in human populations. The modern epidemiologist studies the occurrence, the evolution, and the causes of health disorders, maintains surveillance over trends, and seeks methods to prevent or control their occurrence. For these purposes, the enumeration of health disorders is a first step; and the next step is the study of their relationship to society and habitat, that is, the way they vary in the population and the attributes and circumstances with which they are associated.

Populations are central to epidemiological study. Whereas case studies deal only with numerators, population studies give the numerators meaning by relating the cases to the population from which they are drawn, thus, creating a standard of comparison, without which no conclusion can be reached on the abnormality or distinctiveness of any phenomenon.

Epidemiology shares this procedure, in a general way, with other sciences that study populations, for instance the social sciences, human biology, and population genetics. The study of populations also involves the study of society, for states of health do not exist in a vacuum apart from people. People form societies, and any study of the attributes of people is also a study of the manifestations of the form, the structure, and the processes of social forces.

The disciplines studying society differ one from another in the selection of the particular substance of study. At the same time, by differentiating itself through its choice of states of health, epidemiology shares common ground with other medical sciences. It differs from other medical sciences in that the unit of observation is

EDITORS' NOTE: Abstracted from *Causal Thinking in the Health Sciences: Concepts and Strategies of Epidemiology,* Copyright © 1973, Oxford University Press, and reprinted by permission of the publishers.

populations and not individuals. Epidemiology brings into medicine, with this unit of observation, another level of organization.

The level of organization of populations and societies introduces a set of variables[1] over and above those germane to individuals. These variables are complex and numerous, and their use in medicine creates a body of knowledge about states of health different from that obtained in clinical and laboratory medicine and complementary to it. The study of disease in individuals can suggest the nature of the disordered state of functioning and its progress through time. Studies of individuals cannot determine, even in a series of cases, the limits of the disorder in relation to normality or securely predict its onset, progress, and outcome. To garner this knowledge the epidemiological method, which provides data both sufficient in number and chosen in a manner that permits meaningful comparisions, must be used. Only by such comparisons is it possible to comprehend all the aspects of a disease process at different points in time. The spectrum to be comprehended starts with the antecedent factors that cause disease, moves to the precursors that may enable the prediction and prevention of disease, and passes through the full span of clinical manifestations, course, and eventual outcome.

SURVEY METHOD

The survey is the general method that establishes the real relation between two or more variables in a population in numerical terms (Hyman, 1955). Surveys rely on the information that can be elicited and collated from existing sources (not only records, but people who can say how they feel or what happened). The survey sets up suitable mechanisms to collect the information. In its broad sense, the term survey can be made to include the *secondary analysis* of existing data collected for purposes other than the study in hand, for instance, from registers of vital statistics, from hospital records, and from censuses. For example, in the London of 1662, parishes reported deaths by cause in weekly "bills of mortality." Originally intended as a plague warning to allow the wealthier classes time to leave the city, the aggregated figures were used by John Graunt (1662) to study the population in relation to the environment. He found differences in mortality between the sexes and between urban and rural areas, noted changes in causes of death over time, and offered statistical interpretations of his findings. His approach to the study was that of secondary analysis of existing data accumulated in registers. More commonly, the term describes the planned collection of data for a specific study by means of the *field survey*.

One use of surveys is *descriptive,* to set our norms and limits of the distribution of variables in numerical terms. Surveys quantify the attributes of populations, of environments, and of periods of time. They provide an understanding of a selected problem, its size, its nature, among whom and where it is to be found, and, indeed, whether the problem exists.

A second use of surveys is *explanatory* or *analytical:* to compare different populations in relation to environments and trends in time and to account for the variations between them. To explain relationships and establish causes, specific variables or combinations of variables must first be conceived and then isolated, and the effects of their presence or absence predicted. In the explanatory survey, the prediction or hypothesis is tested by seeking out circumstances in which the effects of the presence and absence of the supposed cause can be observed and compared. The comparisons can be made as valid as possible through the proper use of techniques of sampling (the numerators in the rates compared relate to denominators that represent known populations), techniques of data collection (as much information as needed is obtained and is unbiased, replicable, and means what we say it does), and of research design (an efficient means of answering the question one aims to answer is used).

The essence of the analytical survey is the comparison of similarities and dissimilarities in the past, the present, or the awaited experience of populations. The field survey is most often retrospective. The retrospective survey is commonly a *case-control* study and starts with the case of established disorder (MacMahon and Pugh, 1970). Thus, a population of cases that manifests given effects is chosen for observation, and the history of supposedly causal past events and experiences in the population is compared with a control population that does not manifest the effects. The prospective survey is normally a *cohort* study and starts with the experience thought to give rise to disorder. Thus, a population exposed to a given experience is chosen for observation, and the development of cases in that population is compared with a control population not so exposed.[2] In either case, the survey is influenced by events. A survey can exercise no direct control over the variables that are the object of study; it must exploit and observe the unfolding of the natural and the social environment through history.

The survey and the epidemiological or social experiment share the basic design of the survey method by which the effects of different group experiences are compared. Thus, a survey, even if done from records after the event, to some degree approximates the epidemiological experiment by the way in which it reconstructs the past experience of the population. The essential comparisons made in case-control, cohort, and experimental studies can all be represented in the fourfold table such as Table 8.1.

The cells of the table represent the frequency in a population with which both a manifestation or effect (the dependent variable) and an experience or hypothetical cause (the independent variable) occur both separately and together. In other words, the table represents the degree to which the two variables are associated with each other. The letters a, b, c, and d stand for the numbers of individuals in each cell. Whatever the study design, the cells of the table show all four possible combinations of any two characteristics in a survey population.

TABLE 8.1

Independent Variable	Dependent Variable		
	Present	Absent	Total
Exposed	a	b	a + b
Unexposed	c	d	c + d
Total	a + c	b + d	a + b + c + d

In a case-control study, individuals are first identified, and classified into case and control groups by the presence or absence of the manifestation under study. In the table, the group of cases is represented by a + c, the group of controls by b + d. The frequencies of the independent variable in the two groups are then compared. That is,

$$\frac{a}{a + c} \text{ is compared with } \frac{b}{b + d}$$

A higher frequency or exposure in the group of cases points to the association of the two study variables.

In cohort and experimental studies, individuals are first identified and classified according to whether they were exposed or not to the experience under study. In the table the group exposed is represented by a + b, the unexposed control group by c + d. The frequencies of the dependent variable among both groups is then compared. That is,

$$\frac{a}{a + b} \text{ is compared with } \frac{c}{c + d}$$

Here a higher frequency of cases in the exposed group points to the association of the two variables.

CONCEPTS OF ENVIRONMENT

The results a survey can yield follow strictly from the nature and specificity with which steady variables are conceived and isolated. Different concepts of reality lead to the selection of different types of variables. In science generally, as in other areas of study, concepts play a major role in determining modes of thought. Concepts are the organizing principles by which facts are brought together and woven into a coherent whole. Concepts thus determine the particular explanations sought for the phenomena observed and even the phenomena chosen for observation. Early in the nineteenth century, medicine and the public health movement were dominated by the miasma theory of Sydenham and others that foul emanations from impure soil and water cause disease. At that time, investigation sought to prove the ill effect of miasma; prevention tried to eliminate the sources of miasma in slums and poor sanitation. Thus Edwin Chadwick published the Report on the Sanitary Condition of the Labouring Population of Great Britain in 1842 (MacMahon and Pugh, 1970). This work, inspired by the "miasma" theory, relates area mortality to drainage. After Jacob Henle had formulated the conditions that needed to be met to prove the germ theory (Rosen, 1937) and, some twenty years later, Louis Pasteur had demonstrated the existence of microorganisms, a quite different course of investigation was followed. Microorganisms became the object of the search for causes, and containment of their spread the object of prevention.

Yet the concepts of miasma and of germs both proved effective when applied to disease prevention. Evidently different theories can often work equally well as guides to action. Assumptions lie behind all scientific theories; the governing assumptions of a faulty theory may be sufficiently general to permit a broad range of effective action within its terms. In brief, concepts and theory enable predictions to be tested and choices to be made among paths of action. But different theories can lead to equally successful action in the same situation. One theory is better than another only when it is faced with more specific tests which require narrower assumptions, which the less effective theory cannot meet. Although justified by both the miasma theory and the germ theory, sanitation prevents only one broad class of infectious diseases. Immunization chemotherapy, and antibiotics are needed to prevent others. The concept of the *environment* as a source of disease goes back to the Hippocratic writings. In the book, *Ave, Nube, Places,* the authors speculated on the relationship between disease and the physical environment of climate, water, soil, and prevailing winds. In doing so, they distinguished the environment from the *host,* as represented by the individual constitution. Only in the seventeenth century, however, did it become apparent with the world of John Graunt that understanding of the environment required the numerical approach to populations, as surveys. Quantitative studies of disease mortality became the foundation of the Public Health movement. Thus Edwin Chadwick's famous Report May 1842 is a compilation of many local surveys. The quote below, from Chadwick (1842: 151), is set out on the model of a "before and after" experiment and describes the condition of the population of Wisbech by mortality rates before its exposure to the experience of living in an area that had been drained, and again after. The independent variable postulated as cause is drainage; the dependent variable is deaths.

On reference to a very perfect account of the baptisms, marriages, and burials, in Wisbech, from 1558 to 1826, I find that in the decennial periods, of which 1801, 1811, and 1821, were the middle years, the baptisms and burials were as under:

	Baptisms	Burials	Population in 1801
1796 to 1805	1627	1535	4710
1806 to 1815	1654	1313	5209
1816 to 1825	2165	1390	6515

In the first of the three periods the mortality was 1 in 31; in the second, 1 in 40; in the third, 1 in 47; the latter being less than the mean mortality of the Kingdom for the last two years. (See *Registrar General's Second Report*, p. 4, folio edition.) These figures clearly show that the mortality has wonderfully diminished in the last half century, and who can doubt but that the increased salubrity of the fens produced by drainage is a chief cause of the improvement.

A more sophisticated research design than control by the "before and after" comparison of an environment was the comparison by Chadwick (1842: 103) of a drained area with an undrained area at three parallel points in time. This comparison provided a control for the historical factors, presumably shared by both areas, that might have brought about a decline in mortality and protected against wrongly attributing such a decline in the drained area to drainage. Writes Chadwick,

The following has been the proportion of deaths to the population in the two towns:

	Beccles	Bungay
Between the years 1811 and 1821	1 in 67	1 in 69
Between the years 1821 and 1831	1 in 72	1 in 67
Between the years 1831 and 1841	1 in 71	1 in 59

You will therefore see that the rate of mortality has gradually diminished in Beccles since it has been drained, whilst in Bungay, notwithstanding its larger proportion of rural population, it has considerably increased.

The Ditchingham Factory may have given a greater increase of population to Bungay than I have allowed for, but on the other hand, the Roman Catholics and the Independents bury many of their dead in their own ground, which I have not calculated upon. Since writing the above, I have been over to Bungay, to examine more particularly the state of its drainage, which is much worse than I had any idea of. If their population should much increase, their mortality will increase much faster.

The numerical approach to the understanding of public health problems related to the environment taken by Chadwick was followed by epidemiologists throughout the nineteenth century, and by the end of the century was well established in epidemiological thinking.

The discovery of microorganisms and their effects thus gave impetus to the search for specific agents that caused specific conditions. This search still continues. At the same time, from the standpoint of the development of causal models, this great spurt in medical research diminished awareness of the rarity of one-to-one relationships and of the complex relationships between causes and effects that exist in the real world. The concept of specific agents as causes of disease enlarged knowledge, but the concept was adequate only up to a point. Like the miasma theory, the germ theory failed to explain many medical observations and had to be rethought before further advance became possible.

Pasteur's work and thought opened up another major area of research, that of immunity and host resistance. In 1880, Pasteur developed immunizing procedures in chicken cholera and produced immunity by inoculating hens with attenuated organisms—a method he extended soon after to anthrax, swine erysipelas, and rabies.

The many developments around the idea that resistance to specific infections depended on specific immune mechanisms again emphasize the importance of the initial concept. By 1798 Edward Jenner had managed to publish his paper (refused by the Royal Society) on smallpox vaccination, in which he put an observation of folk medicine to scientific test. But until the concept of immunity was clearly formulated, the practice of vaccination was confined to the one condition in which Jenner had discovered it to be effective. Between the development of smallpox and diphtheria immunization there was the lapse of a century. New concepts were a prerequisite for generalization from the particular practice of smallpox vaccination to the practice of immunization against a wide range of diseases.

From the point of view of the epidemiologist, the focus on the host is an important element of the concept of immunity. The host had always been the prime object of medical study by the nature of medicine as a social institution concerned with the care of sick individuals. But the concern had been with the manifestations of disorder rather than the host's own capacity to shape the manifestations of disorder.

AGENT, HOST, AND ENVIRONMENT

For many investigators of the early era of microbiology, the physical environment became all important in the search for the specific agents that caused specific diseases. The environment tended to be seen as a source, or a vehicle, of specific agents rather than as a shaping force with many interacting elements.

Epidemiologists of the time emphasized infectious diseases, often to the exclusion of all other diseases from their interests. Their professional responsibilities for the prevention and control of disease, however, obliged epidemiologists also to investigate the environmental sources of infectious agents and modes of transmission of infection. Their work demanded a broad concept of disease that syntehsized the triad of agent, host, and environment.

Schistosomiasis, or bilharzia, will serve to illustrate[3] the use and limitations of these three elements in a causal analysis. The life cycles of the agent, the flatworms *Schistosoma mansoni* and *Schistosoma haematobium* alternate between man and certain species of snails (see Figure 8.1).

Man is the primary host in which *S. mansoni* and *S. haematobium* undergo their adult and sexual life; they embed themselves in no other mammal. Each subspecies of schistosome also has an intermediary host and seeks out various snail species as hosts of predilection. The free-living forms that alternately infect humans and snails can exist only in water. Thus, the life cycle of the schistosome could not have evolved if man had not habitually dwelt, bathed, and excreted in the vicinity of pools or slow-running streams infested by snails. Human beings are part of the ecology of the schistosome, and human ways of life made their infection by the schistosome possible. This epidemiological model can be represented as a simple causal sequence of events between agent, host and environment (Figure 8.2).

The necessary environment of the intermediate forms of the schistosome is quiet waters. The snails that are host to these intermediate forms also need or prefer special environments. The human host of the schistosome can survive in most environments, but man perfers some environments to others, and he changes the environment to suit himself. Man developed tools, family life, and the social organization of group society; he came to live in increasingly dense aggregates of people. These developments in turn modified the relationship between the schistosome and its human hosts.

Bilharzia is mentioned in a papyrus of ancient Egypt, and signs of it have been found in mummies. In modern Egypt, social and economic development, by altering the physical environment, have given a new advantage to this disease of antiquity. When water use and excretion remain promiscuous in the absence of sanitation, then the closer the settlement to water and the denser it is, the heavier

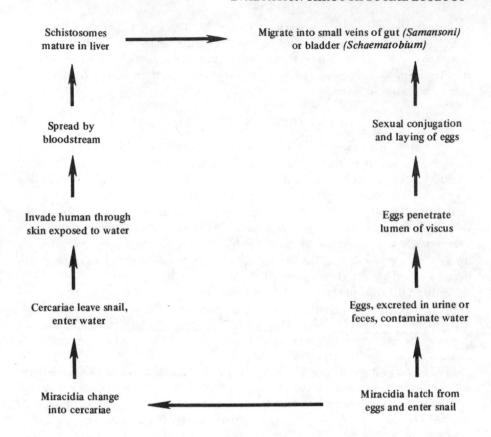

FIGURE 8.1 Exhibit 3: Life cycle of schistosoma.

the rate of infection in a population. The traditional form of irrigation in Egypt was to collect the flood waters of the Nile in basins, to water fields from the basins once a year, and to allow the land to dry out in the off season. Nowadays, the waters of the Nile are collected in huge reservoirs, and water is released gradually over the whole year through a network of canals. This perennial system of irrigation makes better use of the land, produces more food, and creates a favorable environment for the people, so that more of them survive to live there. At the same time, the irrigation system creates an environment permanently damp and full of vegetable matter that is favorable to snails and cercariae. In this new environment created by economic development, habits of water use and excretion remained the same as the population grew, and the prevalence of bilharzia rose. In the areas where the traditional form of irrigation is practiced, the rate of infection is about 6% among the population. In areas watered from the reservoirs, it is often 60%.

Even in this example, chosen for its simplicity, there are complex relations between agent, host, and environment. The environment and, in this instance, the prevalence of the agent itself can alter the response of the host to the agent. Many

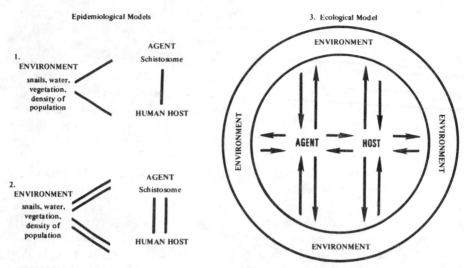

FIGURE 8.2   Exhibit 4: Schistosomiasis: epidemiological and ecological models.

Egyptian adults show little reaction to bilharzia infection, and it seems that they acquire a degree of resistance from frequent exposure in their youth. Persons newly exposed to the parasite do not show such resistance and have more severe reactions. When Napoleon's troops were billeted in the Nile delta during his Egyptian campaign, they apparently suffered marked reactions to bilharzia, as did British troops in Egypt in World Wars I and II. Thus immunity to an infecting agent varies in populations with opportunities for exposure, with previous experience of infection, and with age at first exposure. Resistance to infection probably varies also with other factors unrelated to the agent, such as nutrition.

The epidemiology of bilharzia is further complicated by the fact that, while the reactions of the human host to infection are modified by the pervasiveness of the agent in the environment, the host population in turn influences the pervasiveness of the agent by its role in distributing it. The host population exposes snails to infection through promiscuous excretion, eliminates snails or the vegetation on which they depend, or alters its own habits of excretion and bathing.

The simple sequential causal model (Figure 8.2.1) has developed into a model in which the triad of agent, host, and environment are engaged in processes of reciprocal interaction (Figure 8.2.2). A complex ecological model (Figure 8.2.3)[4] is a still better representation of reality: agent and host are engaged in continuing interactions with an enveloping environment.

ABSTRACTING VARIABLES FROM ECOLOGICAL MODELS

In the ecological model, the interrelationships are appropriately described by terms like "web," "network," or "configuration." Nearly all the interactions among factors in the particular system already examined are reciprocal and multiple, and the terms "agent," "host," and "environment" and the associated concepts, can be used to describe ecological relationships though they are not precise enough to describe causal relationships.

The triad of agent, host, and environment helped epidemiologists to focus on different classes of factors, especially with communicable disease, and so to tease out their relations. But when the elements of all three components interact, analysis in terms of cause becomes clumsy. The activity and survival of both host and agent depend on environment, are altered by it, and in turn alter the environment. Before a disease becomes manifest with a characteristic distribution in a population, many elements of the triad interact with each other in manifold fashion.

Current genetic models (Edwards, 1969) have developed in a way remarkably similar to epidemiological models. Few characteristics are now attributed to single genes, as they were in the simple and elegant Mendelian model. For instance, the heritable components of a characteristic that has a continuous distribution, say IQ or blood pressure, are assumed to be polygenic and to result from a number of genes at several loci on the chromosome. Each gene may be polymorphic, in that each gene may express itself in different forms and each form in different degrees. These many forms of expression allow for a subtle and complex interaction of heredity with the environment. The interaction produces change and diversity in the characteristics and health disorders of populations.

Thus current genetics, in common with epidemiology, uses models of multiple causality. Even where the heritable component of a particular characteristic appears to be large, the models are compatible with dramatic changes in the frequency of the characteristic produced by change in the environment. The current rates of occurrence of tuberculosis and rheumatic fever, diseases for which a genetic element seems established, have dwindled to a small fraction of the rates that existed a half-century ago. The scale and rate of these changes indicate that they are environmental in origin. Current genetic models allow for such interaction of genetic forms with environmental forces.

To handle these complexities, variables must be conceived in a way that makes them accessible to being counted, qualified, and manipulated. Ecological systems or, at any rate, segments of systems, can be simplified to models comprised of related variables. The function of such models is either to predict or to represent, and thus help develop and clarify statements about causal relationships.

The *predictive* function is perhaps the most widespread use of explicit model building. Such models begin with the relationships between variables known to exist in present and past trends. From these relationships future trends can be extrapolated and predicted within estimated margins of error. The assumption (not always valid) is made that known relationships will remain constant and hold in the future and that past trends will continue.

Predictive models are an essential aid to planning, a process that aims to devise rational responses to estimated future needs. A rational response implies that one makes particular choices among courses of action in the expectation that what follows from the choice can to some degree be predicted. Planning proceeds, therefore, by predicting the effects of various interventions using assumptions about causal relationships. In terms of variables, the planner assigns alternative values to the various independent variables included in the system, and he then assesses the effects of these alternatives on the dependent variables (Navarro and Parker, 1970).

The *representational* function of models is to represent existing or postulated relationships in simplified form. The representations serve at least three sub-functions: organizing, mediating, and analyzing.

The *organizing* function of models is illustrated in the previous discussion of epidemiological and ecological models. Such models organize and synthesize a complex of related factors into coherent forms (see Figure 8.2).

The *mediating* function of models is less familiar. The model reveals the common ground between formulations that appear distinct or even disparate at first sight. The ecological model for schistosomiasis developed in the preceding discussion has such a mediating function. The model mediates between the traditional epidemiological formulation of agent, host, and environment and the multivariate formulations that quantify the relationships among the many variables of the ecological system.

The *analyzing* (explanatory) function involves models that pose alternatives among the possible relations between variables. The scientific procedure is then to test the consistency of the alternative explanations, hypotheses, and theories in particular situations. An ideal test will eliminate one or more of the competing hypotheses.

The work of MacDonald (1957) will serve to illustrate how complex ecological relations, set out in Figure 8.2 for schistosomiasis, can be reduced to a system of variables that can be handled and analyzed by epidemiologists. Writes MacDonald (1965):

> A following set of programmes . . . completes these observations by testing over a long period, 20 years, the effects of equal reduction in contamination, snails, exposure, and worm longevity by treatment, supported by reduction of exposure, to a degree at which some of them at least would be expected to produce ultimate eradication. The effect of reduced contamination to one 15,000th of excreta reaching water, which represents a very high standard of sanitation, is virtually negligible over the entire period. The effects of snail control and control of exposure in the form of entry to water are virtually identical during most of the period of fall, though during the later stages control of exposure is somewhat more effective, resulting in a slightly earlier disappearance of the infection. Ultimate disappearance following either of these methods is delayed for over 20 years, throughout all of which effective measures would have to be carried out, and even improvement to a level approaching perfection would only slightly reduce the time involved, to 14 or 15 years, owing to the long mean length of life postulated for the worms, 3 years. By contrast, the combination of systematic treatment with either reduction of exposure or snail control produces a rapid result, the final effects of which are visible between 4 and 5 years after the start.

In his schistosomiasis model (Figure 8.3), MacDonald introduced four main sets of variables:

1. A fertility factor measured the over-all output of eggs by the schistosome infecting the human host. The chance of the worms sexually pairing and producing eggs depends on the worm load in the body systems of the human host and on the longevity of the worms.
2. A contamination factor measured the number of schistosome eggs introduced into the local water. This factor depends on the number of excreted eggs carried into the water (determined by the excretory habits and methods of sanitation of the human hosts).
3. A snail factor measured the output of cercariac by infected snails. This factor depends mainly on the density of the susceptible snail population in the water contaminated by schistosome eggs. Snail density determines the chances of a snail's being infected by the miracidia generated by the eggs, as well as the number of cercariac excreted by the snails into the water.
4. An exposure factor measured the chance of cercariae excreted by the snail's infecting the human host. This factor depends on the number and extent of the contacts with infected water made by potential hosts.

MacDonald used his model to predict the effectiveness of several approaches to eradication of the disease in a community. He found that there was a critical number of worms in a given environment, a "break point," above which numbers would increase until they reached a stable infection level and below which numbers would decrease and disappear. Figure 8.3 illustrates the effects of four different control programs on the prevalence of the human host population. The model predicted that sanitation alone would prove ineffectual, that the most effective approach would prove to be a combination of measures intensively applied at a local level, and that the most rapid benefits at the least cost would be the improvement of mass therapeutic methods. Although the predictions of this model have not been tested and validated, as have those of other models, predictions seem to be in rough accord with past experience of preventive programs.[5]

Whereas the success of some disease eradication programs has encouraged model builders, the failures have instructed them. These failures are of two main types:

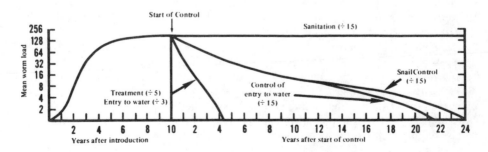

FIGURE 8.3   Exhibit 5

biological and mathematical. On the biological side, the models cannot be universal. The processes of transmission are not everywhere the same, and as a result, programs that work in Ceylon do not work in Ethiopia. On the mathematical side, the models are too simple to encompass all the relevant variables, that is, immunity, vector resistance, and human migration. Social and political contexts are often not quantifiable. In addition, for models that try to represent causal sequences, the time dimension is especially significant. Processes evolve through time, and adequate models that must simulate the continuing unfolding of interacting events often need the assistance of electronic computers, a tool only recently available.

While the merits of various models may be argued, it is agreed that the concept of abstract variables with general properties is a heuristic one for epidemiologists.

SYSTEMS AND ORGANIZATIONAL LEVELS

Any multivariate model is an abstraction from a system, as a segment of a system. The concept of a "system" implies a set of factors connected with each other in terms of a coherent structure or coherent function. The circulatory system comprises heart and blood vessels; the nervous system comprises the brain, spinal cord, and the peripheral and autonomic nerves. The human body is a system in itself at a higher and more complex level of organization than each of the physiological systems of the body. Society comprises a system of persisting and ordered relationships at a still more complex level of organization. The universe is a system of vast and cosmic scale; the DNA molecule, or any atom, a system of minuscule scale.

Systems define the limits of a particular level of organization and the structure and function within those limits. Because the factors contained in the system are related and connected, change or activity in one sector of the system is likely to have an effect on another sector.

Systems also relate to one another; they contain each other like the boxes of a Chinese conjuring trick. The universe has a simultaneous existence, and each level of organization is encompassed by a more complex level or organization. Atoms are encompassed by molecules, molecules by chromosomes, chromosomes by cells, and cells by tissues. Organs and physiological systems are encompassed by individuals and individuals by social groups.

All these systems are linked. The conceptualization and isolation of 26 systems and subsystems is solely for purposes of study and understanding. Thus the limits of the systems and subsystems studied are defined by those dimensions of time, place, and structure that contain the independent and dependent variables selected. The subsystem, thus, begins with the independent variables and ends with dependent variables. The focus of study may be, so to speak, horizontal and confined to a single level of organization. If the study cuts vertically across levels, the focus will include more than one level.

DIRECT AND INDIRECT CAUSE

One of the problems of inference posed by a study that cuts across levels of organization, or indeed by any complex system of variables, is the question of direct and indirect cause. Associations between cause and effect are direct or indirect according to those decisions of research design or analysis that define the variables to be included in the system or in the segment of the system under study.

The cause is direct if a change in the causal factor (or independent variable) is capable of producing a change in an effect (or dependent variable) with two critical provisos: First, that there are no known intervening variables; and second, that cause and effect relate to the same level of organization within a system.

The cause is indirect when either of the two provisions is not satisfied: Either a sequence of linked factors exists or another level of organization is interposed between the cause under study and its outcome. If the first proviso is not satisfied, there is a known sequence of linked factors that intervenes between the independent and dependent variables included in the defined causal system chosen for study, and the system can be represented as follows:

$$X_1 \longrightarrow X_2 \longrightarrow X_3 \cdots \cdots Y$$

For example, breathing air polluted by cigarette or other smoke (independent variable X_1) causes damage to the respiratory epithelium (intervening variable X_2); this damage increases the susceptibility of the epithelium to infection (intervening variable X_3) and results in chronic bronchitis (dependent variable Y).

The second proviso implies that a cause is indirect if the causal factor on one level of organization in a system is related to an effect located at a different level of organization indicated by the unit of observation used. The unit may be, for example, country, state, residential area, household, or individual. Thus the circumstances of social class could be said to be a direct cause of the variation of mortality rates. This conclusion could be reached by showing that area mortality rates vary consistently with the social class composition of areas, even when such other known factors as age and sex, which influence mortality rates, are controlled. However, individuals represent a different level of organization from social groups. To try to attribute the death of an individual to his social class position is at once to become aware that additional factors must intervene between social position and causes of death. The analyst is nudged, as it were, into stating hypotheses to explain the links between social class and the causes of individual deaths.

Chadwick's report (1842) related area mortality to drainage. Drainage was the causal factor, mortality, the outcome in local communities defined by administrative area. In these tables, Chadwick examined independent and dependent variables relating to phenomena located at the same level of organizational complexity, that is, as defined by administrative area.

In terms of the system Chadwick had chosen to isolate for analysis, he had discovered a direct relationship, a relationship that both the time-order of the variables and the replication of the results across the country suggested was causal. With these findings, therefore, he had grounds enough to go ahead and institute area sanitation nationwide without doing violence to causal logic. The method of sanitation Chadwick introduced probably saved more human lives than any other single health measure up to the post-World War II era. The success of his policy, propounded on the basis of a mistaken etiological theory, was more than a lucky accident. The policy was based on an entirely reasonable inference of causality.

William Farr was involved with these problems during the same historical period and made his great contribution as chief statistical medical officer of the General Registry Office in London starting in 1832. The outstanding historical value of these British statistics, even though they were started later than some others in Europe, rests on the fact that from the beginning Farr collected and analyzed the data for specific causes of death. Thus, by specifying the cause of death, he advanced the process of refinement of variables and opened up a new field of investigation and analysis vital statistics.

In his analyses of the vital statistics of England and Wales, Farr examined specific causes of death in relation to many independent variables. Table 8.2 is Farr's tabulation of the correlation between altitude and deaths from cholera (Farr, 1852: lxiv), the most feared scourge of the times.

Commented Farr, "The difference between the number of persons to an acre in the mean of 38 districts, and in all London, as separately calculated, arises in consequence of several districts of large area being thrown into the divisor in the latter case, while the effect of taking the mean of 38 districts is to render the population of each district of equal amount."

In this analysis, Farr set out a direct ecological relationship of the type used by Chadwick. He took the hypothesized environment cause, altitude, as the independent study variable and related it to cholera death rates as the dependent variable. Both the independent and dependent variables were characteristics of administrative areas and are thereby units at the same level of organization.

From this analysis, however, Farr concluded wrongly that "elevation of habitations reduces the effects of cholera to insignificance." The relationship Farr

TABLE 8.2   CHOLERA MORTALITY AND ALTITUDE. A. LONDON DISTRICTS ARRANGED ACCORDING TO THE ELEVATION OF THEIR SOIL. B. MORTALITY FROM CHOLERA IN LONDON TO 10,000 OF THE POPULATION, AT SIXTEEN DIFFERENT ELEVATIONS FROM 0 TO 350 FEET.

Number of districts	Elevation in feet above Trinity high-water mark	Observed Average						
		Annual mortality to 10,000 persons living		Number of persons to		Average annual value of		Poor rate in the of house rent 1842-43
		Cholera (1849)	All causes (1838-44)	An acre	A house	Houses	House and shop room to each person	
							£	
16	Under 20	102	251	74	6.8	31	4.645	.072
7	20 - 40	65	237	105	7.6	56	7.358	.071
8	40 - 60	34	235	184	8.5	64	7.342	.056
3	60 - 80	27	236	152	8.8	52	6.374	.049
2	80 - 100	22	211	44	7.7	38	5.183	.036
1	100	17	227	102	9.8	71	7.586	.043
1	350	8	202	5	7.2	40	5.804	- - -
Mean of 38 districts		66	240	107	7.6	46	5.985	.064
All London		62	252	29	.7	40	5.419	.063

observed was local and not general. The lower reaches of the Thames, as it flowed through London, became increasingly contaminated by sewage. The contaminated water supply that caused most of the cholera in London was thereby brought into association with low altitude. Thus, Farr had developed a testable hypothesis, but he had not searched far enough for instances to contradict it. Although Chadwick was right and Farr wrong in inferring the causes of high mortality in certain areas, both had developed legitimate hypotheses from their observations of *ecological units*. From there, however, neither could go further in establishing direct causes of death in *individuals* because the unit of observation was not individuals but the population of defined administrative areas, a different organizational level.

Like Farr, John Snow began his studies of cholera with data relating cholera deaths to administrative areas; at that level of organization, he postulated water supplies contaminated by sewage as the causal factor. But Snow took his hypothesis much further. About thirty years before Koch and Pasteur described the "Vibrio" as the agent in cholera, he postulated an invisible, self-reproducing living agent as the cause of the manifestations of cholera in individuals. So precise a hypothesis about individuals implied a linked sequence of events between data for areas and data for individuals which could not be tested at the level of organization of admininstative areas.

Snow demonstrated the precision of his hypothesis by extending his investigations to other levels of organization where the units of observation were smaller than administrative areas. Early in his studies, Snow tabulated cholera mortality rates of the 1849 outbreak for the districts of London in rank order, and set against these rates the company responsible for the water supply. Snow showed an obvious association of the water supplied by the Southward and Vauxhall and the Lambeth Waterworks with the high rates of death from cholera (Table 8.3, from Snow, 1855: 62-63). This was a direct relationship at the ecological level.

Snow pointed out that five years later, in the 1853 outbreak, a change had come about: the Southwark and Vauxhall Company water supply was still associated with high cholera mortality, but the Lambeth supply seemed not to be (Table 8.4, from Snow, 1855: 69). Snow found that the Lambeth Company had moved its waterworks to a point higher up the Thames, thus obtaining a supply of water free from the sewage of London. William Farr had provided this lead for Snow in his weekly return of births and deaths from the General Registry Office.

Now by narrowing his focus down to a different level of organization, namely, households, Snow produced his most convincing evidence of the relationship of water supply to individual cholera deaths. These studies illustrate the principle that, as soon as the dependent variable is observed and specified at a level of organization different from the independent variable, the postulated causal relationship is made indirect. Thus, in trying to relate the water supply to areas of deaths in households, Snow was dealing with an indirect relationship. Between area water supply and household deaths, there had to be intervening factors at the household level. The next logical step in investigation was to reveal these factors.

As is often true in epidemiological studies, obtaining the data relating to this smaller and more refined unit of observation required Snow to conduct a special

TABLE 8.3 MORTALITY FROM CHOLERA, AND THE WATER SUPPLY, IN THE DISTRICTS OF LONDON IN 1849
(DISTRICTS ARE ARRANGED IN THE ORDER OF THEIR MORTALITY FROM CHOLERA)

District	Population mid-1849	Deaths from cholera	Deaths by cholera to 10,000 inhabitants	Annual value of house & shop room to each person in £	Water supply
Rotherhithe	17,208	352	205	4.238	Southwark and Vauxhall Water Works, Kent Water Works, and Tidal Ditches
St. Olave, Southwark	19,278	349	181	4.559	Southwark and Vauxhall
St. George, Southwark	50,900	836	164	3.518	Southwark and Vauxhall, Lambeth
Bermondsey	45,500	734	161	3.077	Southwark and Vauxhall
St. Saviour, Southwark	35,227	539	153	5.291	Southwark and Vauxhall
Newington	63,074	907	144	3.788	Southwark and Vauxhall, Lambeth
Lambeth	134,768	1,618	120	4.389	Southwark and Vauxhall, Lambeth
Wandsworth	48,446	484	100	4.839	Pump wells, Southwark and Vauxhall, river Wandle
Camberwell	51,714	504	97	4.508	Southwark and Vauxhall, Lambeth
West London	28,829	429	96	7.454	New River
Bethnal Green	87,263	789	90	1.480	East London
Shoreditch	104,122	789	76	3.103	New River, East London
Greenwich	95,954	718	75	3.379	Kent
Poplar	44,103	313	71	7.360	East London
Westminster	64,109	437	68	4.189	Chelsea
Whitechapel	78,590	506	64	3.388	East London
St. Giles	54,062	285	53	5.635	New River
Stepney	106,988	501	47	3.319	East London
Chelsea	53,379	247	46	4.210	Chelsea
East London	43,495	182	45	4.823	New River
St. George's, East	47,334	199	42	4.753	East London
London City	55,816	207	38	17.676	New River
St. Martin	24,557	91	37	11.844	New River
Strand	44,254	156	35	7.374	New River
Holborn	46,134	161	35	5.883	New River
St. Luke	53,234	183	34	3.731	New River
Kensington (except Paddington)	110,491	260	33	5.070	West Middlesex, Chelsea, Grand Junction
Lewisham	32,299	96	30	4.824	Kent
Belgrave	37,918	105	28	8.875	Chelsea
Hackney	55,152	139	25	4.397	New River, East London
Islington	87,761	187	22	5.494	New River
St. Pancras	160,122	360	22	4.871	New River, Hampstead, West Middlesex
Clerkenwell	63,499	121	19	4.138	New River
Marylebone	153,960	261	17	7.586	West Middlesex
St. James, Westminster	36,426	57	16	12.669	Grand Junction, New River
Paddington	41,267	35	8	9.349	Grand Junction
Hampstead	11,572	9	8	5.804	Hampstead, West Middlesex
Hanover Square & May Fair	33,196	26	8	16.754	Grand Junction
London	2,280,282	14,137	62	---	

TABLE 8.4   CHOLERA DEATH RATES BY CHIEF WATER COMPANIES SUPPLYING
DISTRICTS, GROUPED BY SOURCES OF COMPANY WATER

| Water companies | Sources of supply | Aggregate of districts supplied chiefly by the respective companies | | |
		Population	Deaths by cholera in 13 weeks ending Nov. 19	Deaths in 100,000 inhabitants
(1) Lambeth and (2) Southwark and Vauxhall	Thames, at Thames Ditton and at Battersea	346,363	211	61
Southwark and Vauxhall	Thames at Battersea	118,267	111	94
(1) Southwark and Vauxhall (2) Kent	Thames, at Battersea the Ravens-bourne in Kent; ditches and walls	17,605	19	107

field survey. It so happened that the overlap of the water supply provided by the two companies was so intimate that an ideal opportunity for observation was created. Snow described the situation:

> ... As there is no difference whatever, either in the houses or the people receiving the supply of the two Water Companies, or in any of the physical conditions with which they are surrounded, it is obvious that no experiment could have been devised, which would have been devised, which would more thoroughly test the effect of water supply on the progress of cholera than this, which circumstances placed ready made before the observer.
>
> The experiment, too, was on the grandest scale. No fewer than three hundred thousand people of both sexes, of every age and occupation, and of every rank and station, from gentlefolks down to the very poor, were divided into two groups without their choice, and, in most cases, without their knowledge; one group being supplied with water containing the sewage of London, and, amongst it, whatever might have come from the cholera patients, the other group having water quite free from such impurity.
>
> To turn this grand experiment to account, all that was required was to learn the supply of water to each individual house where a fatal attack of cholera might occur.

The data from the investigation carried out by Snow are shown in Table 8.5 (Snow, 1855: 86).

Here the Southwark and Vauxhall Company consumers were at a relative risk of cholera deaths of more than 8 to 1 compared with Lambeth Company consumers. The conviction arising from this study is greatly strengthened by the direct relation shown between independent and dependent variables with a smaller unit of observation. Despite the epidemiologist's insistence on studying populations, his ultimate

TABLE 8.5 CHOLERA DEATH RATES BY COMPANY SUPPLYING
HOUSEHOLD WATER

Company	Number of houses	Deaths from cholera	Deaths in each 10,000 houses
Southwark and Vauxhall Company	40,046	1,263	315
Lambeth Company	26,107	98	37
Rest of London	256,423	1,422	59

concern is with health, disease, and death as it occurs in individuals. In the analyses by district, there was no way of knowing if all individuals were exposed to the same water supply. In Snow's analysis persons grouped in households and exposed to particular water supplies are specified with great precision. The distribution is almost in imitation of random assignment.

Snow's work stands as a classic in epidemiology. By his procedures of method and inference, he solved a major problem and established a model for all who followed him. He was careful to seek out the intervening links of indirect causal chains, including the indirect relationships created by moving from one level of organization to another and by intervening variables. Thus Snow was able to reinterpret the variable contaminated water (which had confounded Farr's work and led him into the error of attributing cholera mortality to residence at low altitude) as the intervening variable between cholera mortality and place or residence.

In epidemiology and the social sciences, turbulence, willfulness, and low levels of predictability are manifest characteristics of the subjects of study. By the same token, the process of causal analysis, central to all science, is here most crucial.

NOTES

1. A variable is an abstract term representing a particular property (e.g., age, sex, or income) of the units under observation (e.g., persons or groups of persons). Thus, a variable is a measure comprising all the differing values or qualities of the property among the units under the study (e.g., "males" and "females" are the values of the property "sex" in the unit "persons"). An effect is a dependent variable and a cause is an independent variable.

2. Cohort studies need not be prospective in relation to the position of the investigator in time. The criteria by which the study populations, or cohorts, are selected for entry to observation must be attributes or experiences that precede the events to be studied among them, but it is feasible and often economical to reconstruct study populations and the events that befell them from historical records.

3. There are many cases in New York City, all imported from elsewhere. That schistosomiasis should appear in New York, the epitome of the megalopolis, is a commentary in itself on the intimate relations between social forces and the distribution of disease.

4. The main distinction between epidemiology and ecology is that, while epidemiology is centered on the state of health of man, ecology is not anthropocentric but embraces the interrelations of all living things. Epidemiology could be described as human ecology, or that large part of human ecology relating to states of health.

5. In China the story seems to be a different one. The disease caused by Schistosoma japonicum is reported to be serious and even devastating. Eradication is known to be complicated, and various approaches are being used. Mass treatment is being undertaken; night soil

is collected and stored until the heat generated kills the excreted ova; and snails are destroyed by filling in old canals or burying the snails on the banks. The attack is carried out by the technique of the "human sea," by which many thousands of people are mobilized in communal effort. Several country districts are reported to have been cleared by these means, with dramatic improvement in the people's health (Horn, 1969; Cheng, 1971).

Chairman Mao wrote about this problem: "After reading in the *People's Daily* of how schistosomiasis was wiped out in Yukiang County, so many fancies crossed my mind that I could not sleep. In the warm morning breeze, as sunlight fell on my window, I looked toward the distant sourthern sky and in my happiness wrote the following lines." His poem, "Farewell to the God of Plague," refers to a famous physician, Hua To, and to two mythical emperors, Yao and Shun.

> Green streams, blue hills—but all to what avail?
> This tiny germ left even Hau To powerless;
> Weeds choked hundreds of villages, men wasted away;
> Thousands of households dwindled, phantoms sang with glee.
> On earth I travel eighty thousand li a day,
> Ranging the sky I see myriad rivers,
> Should the cowherd ask tidings of the God of Plague,
> Say; Past joys and woe have vanished with the waves.
> The spring wind blows amid ten thousand willow branches,
> Six hundred million in this sacred land all equal Yao and Shun.
> Flowers falling like crimson rain swirl in waves at will;
> Green mountains turn to bridges at our wish;
> Gleaming mattocks fall on heaven-high peaks;
> Mighty arms moved rivers, rock and earth.
> We ask the God of Plague; Where are you bound?
> Paper barges aflame and candlelight illuminate the sky.

REFERENCES

Chadwick, E. (1842) *Report on the Sanitary Condition of The Labouring Population of Great Britain.* Reprinted 1965; Edinburgh: Edinburgh University Press.

Cheng, Tien-Hsi (1971) Schistosomiasis in Mainland China: A Review of research and control programs since 1949. *Amer. J. Trop. Med. & Hyg.* 20: 26-53.

Edwards, J. H. (1969) Familial Predisposition in Man. Pp. 58-64 in C. E. Ford and H. Harris (eds.) *New Aspects of Human Genetics.* London: British Medical Bulletin, vol. 25.

Farr, W. (1885) *Vital Statistics: A Memorial Volume of Selections From the Reports and Writings of William Farr.* Edited by N. Humphries. London: Sanitary Institute.

——— (1852) *Report on the Mortality of Cholera in England in 1848-49.* London: H. M. Stationery Office.

Graunt, J. (1662) *Natural and Political Observations.* Made upon the Bills of Mortality (London: T. Roycraft). Reprinted 1939 (Baltimore: John Hopkins Press).

Horn, J. S. (1969) *Away With All Pests.* New York: Monthly Review Publications. Pp. 94-106.

Hyman, H. (1955) *Survey Design and Analysis.* New York: Free Press.

MacDonald, G. (1965) The Dynamics of Helminth Infections, with special Reference to Schistosomes. *Trans. Roy. Soc. Trop. Med. Hyg.* 59(5): 489-506.

——— (1957) *The Epidemiology and Control of Malaria.* London: Oxford University Press.

MacMahon, B., and T. F. Pugh. *Epidemiology: Principles and Methods.* Boston: Little, Brown.

Navarro, V. and R. D. Parker. (1970) Models in health services planning. Pp. 181-198 in W. W. Holland (ed.) *Data Handling in Epidemiology.* London: Oxford University Press.

Rosen, G. (1937) Social aspects of Jacob Henle's medical thought. *Bull. Inst. Hist. Med.* 5:509-37.

Simon, J. (1890) *English Sanitary Institutions.* London: Cassell.
Snow, J. (1855) *On the Mode of Communication of Cholera.* 2nd ed., much enlarged; London: J. Churchill. Reprinted 1936 as *Snow on Cholera* (New York: Commonwealth Fund).
Wilcocks, C. (1962) *Aspects of Medical Investigation in Africa.* London: Oxford University Press.

REFERENCE UPDATE
Selected by M. Susser and Elmer L. Struening

Alwin, D. F. and R. M. Hauser. The decomposition of effects in path analysis. *American Sociological Review*, 1975, 40: 37-47.
Alwin, D. F. and R. C. Tessler. Causal models, unobserved variables, and experimental data. *American Journal of Sociology*, 1974, 80: 58-86.
Anderson, J. G. Constructing causal models: Critical issues. In L. Sechrest, S. G. West, M. A. Phillips, R. Redner, and W. Yeaton (eds.) *Evaluation studies review annual* (Vol. 4). Beverly Hills, CA: Sage, 1979. (a)
Anderson, J. G. Constructing causal models: Problems of units of analysis, aggregation, and specification. In L. Sechrest, S. G. West, M. A. Phillips, R. Redner, and W. Yeaton (eds.) *Evaluation studies review annual* (Vol. 4). Beverly Hills, CA: Sage, 1979.
Anderson, M. Directly transmitted infectious diseases: Control by vaccination. *Science*, 1982, 215: 1053-1060.
Asher, H. B. *Causal modeling.* Beverly Hills, CA: Sage, 1977.
Bentler, P. M. Multivariate analysis with latent variables: Causal modeling. *Annual Review of Psychology*, 1980, 31: 419-456.
Bentler, P. M. and J. A. Woodward. Nonexperimental evaluation research: Contributions of causal modeling. In L. Datta and R. Perloff (eds.) *Improving evaluations.* Beverly Hills, CA: Sage, 1979.
Blalock, H. M., Jr. *Causal inferences in nonexperimental research.* Chapel Hill: University of North Carolina Press, 1964.
Bogue, D. J. and E. L. Bogue. *Essays in human ecology.* Chicago: Community and Faculty Study Center, University of Chicago, 1976.
Breslow, N. and N. Day. Statistical analysis of case control studies in cancer research. In World Health Organization, *The analysis of case control studies.* IARC Scientific Publication 32, 1980.
Brooks, C. H. Infant mortality in SMSAs before Medicaid: Test of a causal model. In L. Sechrest, S. G. West, M. A. Phillips, R. Redner, and W. Yeaton (eds.) *Evaluation studies review annual* (Vol. 4). Beverly Hills, CA: Sage, 1979.
Deegan, J. Specification error in causal models. *Social Science Research*, 1974, 3: 235-259.
Duncan, O. D. Partials, partitions, and paths. In E. F. Borgatta and G. W. Bohrnstedt (eds.) *Sociological Methodology 1970.* San Francisco: Jossey-Bass, 1970.
Duncan, O. D. *Introduction to structural equation models.* New York: Academic, 1975.
Hauser, R. and A. Goldberger. The treatment of unobservable variables in path analysis. In H. L. Costner (ed.) *Sociological methodology 1971.* San Francisco: Jossey-Bass, 1971.
Heise, D. R. Causal inference from panel data. In E. F. Borgatta and G. W. Bohrnstedt (eds.) *Sociological methodology 1970.* San Francisco: Jossey-Bass, 1970.
Humphreys, L. G. and C. K. Parsons. A simplex process model for describing differences between cross-lagged correlation. *Psychological Bulletin*, 1979, 86 (2): 325-334.
Kim, J. O. and C. W. Mueller. Standardized and unstandardized coefficients in causal analysis. *Sociological Methods and Research*, 1976, 4: 423-438.

Knox, E. G. Strategy for rubella vaccination. *International Journal of Epidemiology*, 1980, 9: 13-23.

Li, C. C. *Path analysis: A primer*. Pacific Grove, CA: Boxwood, 1975.

Lilienfeld, A. M. and D. E. Lilienfeld. *Foundations of epidemiology* (2nd ed.). New York; Oxford University Press, 1980.

Long, J. S. Estimation and hypothesis testing in linear models containing measurement error. *Sociological Methods and Research*, 1976, 5: 157-206.

MacMahon, B. and T. F. Pugh. *Epidemiology: Principles and methods*. Boston: Little, Brown, 1970.

McPherson, J. M. and C. J. Huang. Hypothesis testing in path models. *Social Science Research*, 1974, 3: 127-139.

Rogosa, D. A critique of cross-lagged correlation. *Psychological Bulletin*, 1980, 88 (2): 245-258.

Schlesselman, J. J. *Case control studies; Design, conduct, analysis*. New York: Oxford University Press, 1982.

Specht, D. A. and R. D. Warren. Comparing causal models. In D. R. Heise (ed.) *Sociological methodology 1976*. San Francisco: Jossey-Bass, 1976.

Susser, M. *Causal thinking in the health sciences: Concepts and strategies in epidemiology*. New York: Oxford University Press, 1973.

Tanaka, J. S. The evaluation and selection of adequate causal models: A compensatory education example. *Evaluation and Program Planning*, 1982, 5 (1): 11-20.

9

SOCIAL AREA ANALYSIS AS A METHOD OF EVALUATION

ELMER L. STRUENING

As interest in the specialities of community medicine and community mental health has evolved, emphasis has been placed on the delivery of comprehensive health and mental health services to populations residing in defined geographic or catchment areas. Service delivery systems are assumed to be responsible for the health and mental health status of the residents of their catchment areas. Although the effectiveness of service delivery systems is partially dependent upon the quality of their relationships with catchment area populations or communities, the under-standing of this interaction has yet to receive serious attention in the literature of program evaluation. As a result, our knowledge of the determinants of the selective use of health and mental health facilities by catchment area populations and of the effectiveness of these facilities in maintaining the health status of their commu-nities according to accepted epidemiological criteria is still in the early stages of development (McKinlay, 1972; Williams and Ozarin, 1968).

Ideally, representatives of service delivery systems and elected members of their catchment areas would formulate a hierarchy of priorities as a guide to the use of available resources. Within the limits of a stated budget, the specific objectives of the service system would be derived from ordered priorities and stated, in opera-tional terms, as meaningful questions to be answered by evaluation research studies. The results of such studies would then be used for deciding whether or not the service system meets its stated objectives. If it does not, theoretically sound changes in the service delivery system would be in a constant state of systematic change, guided by feedback from evaluation studies, with the general goal of evolving to a system of optimal effectiveness.

This ideal state of affairs seldom, if ever, exists in our health and mental health delivery systems. As a consequence the field of evaluation research has not pro-duced a well-developed applied science complete with a comprehensive set of

AUTHOR'S NOTE: A portion of this chapter appeared originally in Struening, E.L., "Approaches to Evaluation: Social Area Analysis," *International Journal of Health Services*, 1974, Vol. 4, No. 3, pp. 503-514. Copyright 1974 Baywood Publishing Company, Inc. Reprinted by permission.

constructs and their reliable and valid measures. Nor has it developed a system-atically acquired body of knowledge acceptable to the scientific community and sufficiently general to apply in a variety of settings without question. What appears to be available are methods, measures, and concepts primarily borrowed from other disciplines and applied in an unsystematic manner to a variety of problems in a variety of settings. The time is ripe for the development of general evaluation methodologies which have application in a number of settings so that an accumula-tive set of substantive findings can be generated.

The general purpose of this chapter is to describe and demonstrate a method-ology designed to promote the understanding of relationships between health and mental health delivery systems and residents of the catchment areas they serve. Emphasis is placed on explaining the selective use of services and evaluating the effects of change as it is introduced into the service system. Principles of epidem-iology, the methodology of modern social area analysis, and selected multivariate statistical methods are discussed and integrated into a set of procedures for evaluating health and mental health delivery systems with catchment area responsi-bilities. The role of evaluation research is briefly discussed; three levels of evalua-tion are defined. A brief history of social area analysis is given, with illustrations of area analysis in descriptive, correlational, and controlled evaluation studies.

THE ROLE OF EVALUATION RESEARCH

Evaluation research is generally thought of as a speciality within the applied sciences, with general emphasis placed on assessing the effectiveness of human service systems and with particular focus on the relative effectiveness of their treatment, service, or educational programs. Evaluation studies are generally preoc-cupied with providing answers to carefully formulated questions and not with testing hypotheses or with making predictions derived from theories. While the formulation of hypotheses regarding the outcomes of evaluation should help to conceptualize the study in greater depth, leading to the important issue of why, for example, differential reactions to treatment occur, this is seldom done. This approach to evaluation may partly explain the superficial nature of many evalua-tion studies. As the knowledge of this field grows, producing well-defined con-structs, organized into meaningful theories capable of predicting (health and mental health) relevant behavior, it seems likely that evaluators will make more direct use of theory in conceptualizing studies, or at least be more aware of the theoretical assumptions implicit in their work.

The role of evaluation research differs from that of conventional research in its explicit attempt to make value judgments. Evaluation research goes beyond hypoth-esis testing, if it is concerned with that at all. It is generally directed toward determining what is most effective, valuable, desirable, or useful, rather than simply whether or not a hypothesis was supported. It is concerned with the determination of relative value.

This concern of evaluation research with the relative value of human endeavor places it squarely in the middle of social and political controversy. Evaluation takes place in a social and organizational context and is therefore influenced by the particular value orientations, vested interests, and political forces which surround each study. On one hand, properties of this social and organizational context may greatly facilitate the conduct and use of the implications of the evaluation study; on the other hand, the social and political forces may impede the conduct of the study and, in the extreme, distort or suppress the results. Thus the political and social climates of evaluation studies are potentially stormy and, to be successfully completed, require a thorough understanding of the context in which they are to be conducted.

The above conditions suggest that the project directors of evaluation studies must possess attributes somewhat different from the laboratory oriented scientist. For a detailed discussion of how politics and values are involved in evaluation research, please see chapters by Weiss, and those by Sjoberg and by Gurel in Volume II in this *Handbook*. These chapters document in some detail the sources of cooperation and conflict in the evaluation process. Whatever conditions obtain, it seems important to move toward objective, quantifiable methods of evaluation which are sufficiently relevant to answer important questions about the effectiveness of human service delivery systems and convincingly accurate to all parties involved in the evaluation process.

A DEFINITION OF EVALUATION RESEARCH

In the limited perspective of this chapter, the subject matter of evaluation research is restricted to the evaluation of human service systems. Even within this limited sphere, evaluation research is complex in nature and does not lend itself to simple and precise definition. It is insufficient to reduce it to the classical experimental method because, as a developing discipline, much work needs to be done in the conceptual, descriptive, and measurement aspects of development. A definition should include the range of activities currently involved and necessary to promote growth of the discipline.

Evaluation research is defined as the application of scientific principles, methods, and theories to identify, describe, conceptualize, measure, predict, change, and control those factors or variables important to the development of effective human service delivery systems.

The definition of *effective* at both the construct and operational levels involves both the theoretical and value orientations of those engaged in the evaluation process. These orientations influence the *selection* or *development* of outcome or criterion variables, the interpretation of results, and the implications of the results for changing the service delivery system. Controversy arising from evaluation studies probably derives more from differences in the value orientations of those with vested interests, such as administrators and evaluators, than from the specific problems of actually doing the study.

Evaluation research is conceived at four levels: (1) descriptive, (2) correlational or comparative, (3) experimental, and (4) theory construction. Theory is implicated, either implicitly or explicitly, at all four levels.

Descriptive evaluation research is preoccupied with *what is* and *how much,* or the descriptive statistics of the measure of an important construct or characteristic. It is concerned with the comprehensive description of human service systems, their component parts and programs, the populations they serve, and the environments in which the populations live. This requires the creation of conceptual frames of reference and the development of constructs and their operational definitions of measures. Evaluation research, like the social sciences from which it borrows, suffers from an abundance of overlapping and poorly defined constructs which are either inadequately defined or defined by a number of measures with questionable psychometric properties. As a result the evaluator often finds it necessary to develop appropriate measures or to use those of marginal utility that are available in the literature. Thus evaluation research, as a field in the early, developmental stages, will find it necessary to expend considerable energy at the descriptive level before moving to correlational and experimental studies.

The correlational or comparative level of evaluation is concerned with relationships among measures developed at the descriptive level. Critical examination of relationships among measures describing a health or mental health delivery system may raise meaningful questions which can be answered by subsequent experimental studies or may result in immediately useful causal inferences regarding, for example, the implications of social status in the use of service facilities. While inferences from correlations or the comparison of groups from a population of interest may provide valuable insights into the what goes on, for example, in a service delivery system, experimental studies are needed to understand the value of new and innovative programs relative to established programs.

The experimental approach to evaluation is generally viewed as the most important type of evaluation research. The general logic of the experimental design requires the comparison of experimental and control groups, to which subjects were randomly assigned, on a measure of change on some outcome variable of interest, such as symptom reduction. Experimental usually implies something new or innovative. Therefore, experimental designs are usually concerned with discovering the relative effectiveness of new approaches to a problem compared with older, more traditional approaches. Thus, while descriptive and correlational studies yield valuable information about a service delivery system or a treatment modality, results of the more rigorous experimental studies are needed to demonstrate the effectiveness of innovation as a basis for introducing change into the delivery system.

The fourth level of evaluation, that of theory construction, is generally not accepted as the province of evaluation research. As an applied science, the role of evaluation research is restricted to the application of that which is already known or accepted to a particular problem. However, as previously indicated, that which is already known or developed is frequently inadequate. Populations investigated in university settings, frequently representing only a narrow segment of society, are too restricted to produce results on which comprehensive theories of behavior can be constructed. Therefore, it seems that theories of behavioral change could fruitfully grow out of evaluation studies focused on those influences or treatments designed to produce change. Most health and mental health systems hope to promote physical, intellectual, and emotional growth, or change, in all populations involved in their delivery systems. In both client and community populations there is a desire to educate toward the prevention of disease and mental illness and toward the appropriate use of health and mental health facilities. In the staff population there is an ever-present need to acquire and apply new knowledge so that health and mental health delivery systems reflect the latest advancements in the many relevant disciplines. This difficult enterprise requires the integration of disparate theories of behavior and behavioral change from clinical, social psychological, sociological, and anthropological frames of reference and the cooperation of theoretical and applied scientists if the final results are to be useful to the evaluator. At the rate that universities and human service delivery systems are joining forces to develop a comprehensive theory of behavior relevant and useful to understanding the behavior of the general population, it seems important for evaluation researchers to become more interested in the theoretical sources of their applied work, and in theory construction, if evaluation research is to evolve into a mature discipline.

ISSUES IN SERVICE DELIVERY: A BASIS FOR ASKING QUESTIONS

With the above definitions in mind, we turn now to selected issues in service delivery to catchment area (CA) populations which provoke meaningful questions that can be answered by different levels of evaluation research, using the methodology of social area analysis.

The Issue of Equity

Equity is defined as serving all citizens of a CA according to their medical and mental health needs. This implies the design and deployment of competent service delivery systems that are effectively used by all populations, especially those at high risk, in both preventive and secondary roles. To achieve the goal of equity in service delivery, information about the health and mental health status of the CA population is needed. Planners, administrators, and evaluators must have reasonably accurate information about the distribution of health and mental health problems in subpopulations (usually defined by age and sex) as they vary over geographical subareas comprising the CA if they are to design effective programs related to the pattern of risk in the CA. Generation of this type of information involves the disciplines of epidemiology and demography. By revealing the relevant characteristics of the CA as they vary over subareas, both in frequency and rate format, the descriptive level of evaluation is illustrated.

The Issue of Context

Community medicine and mental health professionals involved in service delivery are becoming more aware that the social, physical, and normative context in which people live affects their health and behavior in important and subtle ways. To understand the health and behavior of a population, it now seems necessary to understand the particular environments in which the people live. Over large cities there is enormous variability in housing, transportation, medical services, income, refuse collection, family stability, spatial mobility, sociocultural values, life-styles, belief systems about the causes of mental and physical illness, and so forth, all of which bear some relationship with the health and mental health status of the citizen population. Relationships among selected characteristics of environments and the health and mental health status of their residents provide a basis for causal inference with implications for designing strategies of intervention that will reduce incidence and prevalence rates. Inferences made from patterns of relationships illustrate the correlational level of evaluation.

The Issue of Change

Human service systems often become committed to, and subsequently defensive about, their particular style of service delivery. To improve service effectiveness, there is a need to experiment with new or alternative forms of service delivery by comparing their relative effectiveness with currently used methods under controlled experimental conditions. Thus the introduction of change in service systems requires evaluation research studies at the third level if change is to be systematic and rational rather than haphazard and unplanned.

The Issue of Theory

With the rebirth of interest in ecology, the role of environment as it effects man is receiving increased attention. A particular aspect of this interest is the relationship of environments with the health and mental health of their inhabitants. A still more specialized facet are the conceptions and attitudes of people about the prevention and treatment of physical and mental disorders and their selective use of facilities responsible for treating these disorders. As yet our knowledge in these areas is fragmented, inconsistent, and controversial. There is a need for dynamic theories linking the well-being and behavior of people to characteristics of their environments, especially behavior relevant to self care and the use of services. Well-designed experimental evaluation studies carried out in a variety of settings may provide a worthwhile basis for constructing such theories.

Community medicine and community mental health, then, are experiencing the growing pains of early development, particularly with respect to relationship between the service delivery system and the community to be served. A number of important questions on such issues as the equity, effectiveness, and accountability of service systems occur as one conceptualizes the interaction and interdependence between service systems and their CA populations. While a considerable literature has partial answers for some of the questions, the need for a body of organized knowledge, based on the systematic observation of service-community relationships, is unmet.

The following section provides a sample of three types of questions which might occur as one attempted to understand the environment of CA residents, the facilities providing them with medical and mental health services, and the nature of their interactions.

A SAMPLE OF MEANINGFUL QUESTIONS

Questions of Description

Demography. What are the major demographic characteristics of the CA which, according to the literature, are likely to be related to the health and mental health status of CA residents? To what extent do these characteristics vary over subareas, such as census blocks or tracts of the CA?

Epidemiology. What are the major health and mental health problems observed in the CA and how do their rates vary over subareas and among various subpopulations of the CA? To what extent do age-specific death rates vary over the subareas of the CA?

Physical Environment. What is the quality of the environment surrounding the citizens of the CA, including factors, such as housing, transportation, and refuse collection, which are hypothetically linked to, for example, general morale and the use of service facilities.

Social Context. What are the dominant belief systems and levels of knowledge about physical and mental illness, their nature, cause and cure?

Community Resources. What support systems, in the form of family structures, extended families, ethnic cohesion, religious groups, social welfare agencies, social and political clubs, and so forth, exist in the CA and provide avenues of education, communication, and help during crisis situations.

Questions of Relationship or Comparison

Poverty and Health. To what extent do measures of poverty account for variability in rates of disease in various subpopulations of the CA?

Sociocultural Factors and Facility Use. To what extent does variation in sociocultural values over subareas of the CA account for variation in the use of health services?

Social Class and Mental Health. Is variability in the inpatient/outpatient ratio of mental health service use over the subareas of the CA primarily a function of variability in social class variables?

Environment and Mortality. Which characteristics of subareas of the CA play the most important role in predicting age-specific mortality rates?

Family Structure and Mental Disorders. With age controlled, is marital status a significant factor in the mental health of the CA population? Is marital status an important variable in predicting the use of mental health facilities?

Ethnicity and Use of Mental Health Facilities. Is variation in ethnic composition over the subareas of the CA an important variable in predicting the use of mental health facilities?

Transportation and Facility Use. Are the location, quality, and efficiency of transportation facilities important determinants of the use of health and mental health facilities?

Family Structure, Poverty, and Infant Health. What is the relative contribution of variables measuring family structure and poverty in accounting for variability in rates of premature birth and neonatal and postneonatal mortality?

Questions of Change or Experimentation

Facility Location. Is proximity a factor in the use of health and mental health facilities? Does the installation of new clinics in areas of high risk result in serving more citizens at a reduced cost per service rendered?

Education. Are recent mothers more likely to seek a postpartum examination following exposure to a health education program?

Training. Do inservice training programs for paraprofessionals, which carry the immediate reward of high school or college credit, increase the morale and effectiveness of this category of personnel?

Service Delivery Style. Do components of service organized as teams function more effectively than components in which staff members are organized along occupational categories?

Monitoring of Drugs. Do education programs for staff members, focused on drug characteristics and their appropriate prescription and evaluation, result in more effective treatment? Do drug education programs for patients, including the purpose of the drugs, its potential benefit, and possible side effects, result in fewer complaints, greater compliance with instructions, and more rapid recovery rates among patients?

Patient Role. In controlled experiments does the education of patients to be inquiring and knowledgeable about their medical and mental problems and clear about their roles in the treatment and recovery program make a difference in terms of time and rate of recovery?

Answers to the above questions can be provided by different levels of evaluation research studies using a variety of strategies and methods. We turn now to the methods of modern social area analysis, an objective and systematic methodology for understanding characteristics of small geographic areas and their resident populations. In the following sections, social area analysis will be defined and illustrated at the descriptive, correlational, and experimental levels.

THE METHODOLOGY OF SOCIAL AREA ANALYSIS

Review articles on the historical development of this methodology will be found in Cartwright (1969) and Bell (1967). Objective procedures for developing indexes from census tract data were published by Shevky and Williams (1949). Modifications of these procedures appeared in Shevky and Bell (1955). In the same year Tryon (1955) published a monograph in which multivariate statistical procedures were applied to identify salient dimensions in a correlation matrix of census variables and to relate these dimensions, describing characteristics of citizens living in defined areas (census tracts), to their voting behavior, rates of mental illness, and other forms of behavior. These methods, generally referred to as social area analysis, are most comprehensively presented in Tryon and Bailey (1970).

Within the limits described here, social area analysis is defined as a set of integrated procedures designed to study characteristics of groups or subpopulations of people who live in defined geographical areas, such as census tracts, census blocks, enumeration districts (Houser and Duncan, 1959) or "natural" neighborhoods or communities. More specifically, the interest is in characteristics or attributes which meaningfully differentiate areas or their resident populations, and have important relationships with the health status of residents. The relationships of variables describing groups and their environments with variables describing their health status provide a basis for inferring causal priorities and for planning intervention programs.

It is, of course, meaningful to conceptualize and measure properties of groups or subpopulations living in defined geographical areas just as one conceptualizes and measures properties of individuals or objects. For example, a group could be described in terms of the percent of its members completing college; similarly, an individual in the same age range could be described on the same dichotomous variable: completed college versus did not complete college. In a similar manner the group being described is one of a sample of groups representing some population of groups, while the individuals represent some known population of individuals. Our purpose is to make valid conclusions about either population from studying a sample drawn from it. It is incorrect to make conclusions about populations of individuals from the study of a sample of groups. To do so constitutes a kind of error that is known as the "ecological fallacy."

Measures of properties of groups can be appropriately manipulated to answer specific questions or to test hypotheses. For example, measures of two characteristics of a sample of groups could be correlated to estimate the magnitude of the relationship of the two characteristics in the population of groups. In an urban setting, the correlation of age-corrected death rates with rates of overcrowded housing or poverty income, with a sample of census tracts as the units of observation, would provide some insight into the relationship between environment and health. The relationship of premature births with the percent of mothers using medical facilities during pregnancy, observed over the health areas of New York City, provides preliminary information on the importance of appropriate health care and identifies those areas of the city where intervention in the form of more effective facilities or health education programs is needed. Following intervention, changes in the use of medical facilities and the subsequent changes in prematurity rates, if they occur, can be observed. The effectiveness of types of intervention can also be compared if the target areas and populations are similar.

A HYPOTHETICAL APPLICATION OF SOCIAL AREA ANALYSIS

To apply the above procedures to a CA served by a health service, let us imagine the area occupied by approximately 400,000 people, subdivided into 100 census tracts with a mean population of about 4,000 residents per block. N, or the number of areas, is equal to 100 or the 100 groups of people which compose both the sample and population of interest. Subgroups from each of the 100 areas, such as all women giving birth during a certain time period, could be selected for study, in which case the number of observed groups would again be 100.

To limit our perspective, let us assume that our primary concerns are with the health of pregnant women, newborn babies, and people over 65 years of age, and with the selective use of health services by these groups.

Describing the Catchment Area

Our first step might be the location of target populations, their distribution over the CA, their predicted increase or decrease in size over time, and salient health characteristics and living conditions. Birthrates vary widely over the areas of large cities, and it is important to locate areas of the CA where rates are especially high and where pregnant women and newborns are at high risk (Struening et al., 1973). While high birthrates are generally associated with such factors as high premature birthrates and high infant mortality rates, this may not be true for a limited area of a large city.

In conceptualizing the effective delivery of services, consideration of both birth concentration and the possible increase or decrease in the number of births may be important. Trends in the latter may be derived from birth figures of the past ten years, usually available through vital statistics. Such factors as mobility, the building of new housing, and the relaxation of abortion laws may have important and unanticipated influences on birthrate changes. Living conditions, such as over-crowded housing and poverty income, and family disorganization, as indicated by divorce and separation rates, are, as characteristics of area populations, generally strongly associated with high rates of low birth weight and infant mortality (Struening et al., 1973). Since extremely low birth weight is associated with developmental problems and subsequently with learning problems, the medical planner can anticipate that a range of services will be required to meet the needs of this high-risk group. The issue of the possibility of prevention, as compared with the extensive, long-term treatment often required by children with developmental problems, is important in the planner's deliberations (Stein, Susser, and Guterman, 1973).

A health problem of increasing dimensions is effective service delivery to older citizens, many of whom live well beyond 75 years and are not able to make the difficult trip to outpatient services. Thus, transportation or easy access to medical services is a major factor of effective service to the elderly. The breakdown of the extended family and the low social value placed on the elderly are additional influences affecting treatment of the elderly. The specific family situation is apparently extremely important; widows generally die at higher rates than married subjects at the same age levels (Kraus and Lilienfeld, 1959). In New York City approximately 19% of the men over 65 are widowed, while approximately 54% of the women over 65 are widowed. Over 65% of the men over 65 are married while 31% of the women over 65 are married. Approximately 10% of either group did not marry and another 5% reported divorce or separation status.

Rates of widowhood for both men and women over 65 vary greatly over the census tracts of New York City: 10 to 43% for men and 41 to 68% for women. Thus, the living situations of the elderly, easily available in census data, have important implications for service delivery administrators. Although the relative importance of these implications must be derived from empirical studies relating, for example, widowhood status to appropriate use of medical facilities, data describing the living conditions and social context of the elderly are available though such sources as social welfare statistics, census records, and vital statistics.

The records kept by a health service can provide a useful description of the client or patient population. By noting the age, sex, and census tract of residence of each client over a given time period, frequency of use of each age-sex combination can easily be determined. Rates of use can be computed by dividing the number of clients from each corresponding census tract, yielding a comparable set of rates and a basis for identifying high- or low-use populations in the CA. The rates of use by more specific categories of clients can easily be obtained by dividing, for example, the number of women clients over 65 by the number of women of that age category in each census tract. Study of this distribution of rates will readily identify those areas with high, low, and average use patterns. Results of such work might provoke the testing of a hypothesis that married women over 65 are more likely to use the health services than are widowed women of the same age range. If marital status is recorded in client files, rates of use by the two groups could be compared in each census tract. It may be that the hypothesis will hold only in certain census tracts where, for example, many of the widows are living alone and thus do not have someone to help them get to the doctor.

In summary, descriptive statistics tell a limited but useful and sometimes hypothesis-provoking story. Frequencies, the result of simply counting, tell the administrator how many in each meaningful category are in the community as potential users and in the client's files as actual users. Variations in rates of use, linked to subareas of the CA, identify high-user and low-user areas and suggest the hypothesis of differential risk levels or perhaps inappropriate use of services. Rates of certain categories, such as premature birth or neonatal death, take on meaning by comparison with national or city standards. Assuming relatively high rates, the politically astute administrator may use these data to increase his budget or secure federal funding.

Although descriptive statistics as a primitive form of evaluation are useful and provocative of further inquiry, they also have definite limitations. They provide answers to questions of "what is" or "how many," but offer little basis for the important questions of "why" and "of what relative importance are causal factors?" That is, descriptive statistics provide only a weak basis for causal inference and the identification of causal priorities.

We turn now to more powerful forms of statistical analysis to provide a firmer basis for causal inference and the development of intervention strategies.

Studies Involving Comparison and Correlation

Let us first consider the issue of the selective use of health services by catchment area residents. Clinicians and administrators involved in service delivery and planning may have specific ideas or hypotheses regarding the selective use of services. The evaluator or epidemiologist may derive hypotheses from environmental stress theory or the role of family structure in appropriate health care.

Dependent variables would be selected from service system records. As previously indicated age, sex, and the census tract of residence are essential in describing the client population using the services over a given time period. Additional classification data, such as marital status, occupation, services rendered, diagnosis, and so forth, may provide further understanding of the relative importance of factors related to service use in selected categories of clients. The client population should be sufficiently large so that census tracts are represented by reliable and valid samples which, ideally, differentiate census tracts on continua of frequency and rate.

Dividing service users by two categories of sex and five categories of age would result in 10 dependent variables. If both frequency and rate formats are used, we would have 20 variables describing each of the 100 census tracts in terms of the use of medical services. Totals for each sex, and a grand total expressed as frequencies and rates, would yield a total of 26 variables.

Our next job is to develop a rationale for selecting variables which have the best chance of predicting variability in rate of service use for the ten categories of users. This is the time for conjecture and the raising of questions. Do elderly people living in areas with high rates of single-room occupants fail to use medical services? Do pregnant unmarried teenagers shy away from medical examinations? Is distance a factor in seeking treatment, or is the convenience of mass transportation? Is the median education level of women aged 14-44 in census tracts related to their use of medical facilities during pregnancy? Is the rate of movement of people into census tracts from outside the state a factor in their use of the medical services? Is the rate of marital stability a factor in the use of medical services by women aged 20-44? Are high death rates directly or inversely related to high rates of service use? Is ethnicity related to rates of service use, especially when English is not the preferred language?

The above questions are examples of those that might occur to clinicians, administrators, evaluators, epidemiologists, and perhaps a sample of clients as they think about characteristics of census tract populations which might affect the use of medical services. In seeking answers to these questions, or in testing this set of hypotheses, measures of the designated variables would be derived from census data, vital statistics, social welfare data, and other sources to form a set of independent variables. That is, we are interested in those characteristics of census tract populations and subpopulations which account for variability in rates of medical service use for ten categories of clients composed of age-sex combinations.

For illustrative purposes, let us consider variables in rate format only. All independent variables would be expressed in percentages, such as the percentage of women between 20 and 44 who have not completed high school, the percentage of people who have migrated from another state, rates of death for men between 45 and 64, and so forth.

Next, a 33 by 33 correlation matrix with 13 dependent and 20 independent variables in rate format would be computed, resulting in 528 correlation coefficients. A systematic examination of results could start with relationships among the dependent variables to assess the extent to which census tracts are ranked in approximately the same order by the 13 use-rate variables. Is medical service use a unidimensional phenomenon, or are, for example, rates for men uncorrelated with rates for women over the 100 census tracts? Are use rates for the elderly related to use rates for the very young? If, for example, use rates for elderly men are correlated with use rates for elderly women at a magnitude of 0.85 or above, the two variables could possibly be combined in future work. Use rates for small children would almost certainly be highly correlated and could be combined without loss of information. Thus, correlations among the 13 dependent variables would clarify the organization and structure of medical use rates over census tracts as influenced by the age and sex classification system (Struening et al., 1970).

The relationships among the 20 independent variables could be studied for the same structural properties. Study of the patterns of relationship among the 20 variables will almost certainly indicate several groups of variables with moderate to high correlations within each group and relatively low correlations among variables with different group membership. Each variable group will probably define a meaningful construct such as social alienation or socioeconomic status. The procedures of cluster analysis (Tryon and Bailey, 1970) and factor analysis (Comrey, 1973; Harmon, 1967) effectively identify the important dimensions measured by the 20 variables. By using either this formal and objective method of scaling or more subjective, judgmental methods of variable clustering, the groups of variables can be combined into variable composites or factor/cluster scores with high reliability. In previous studies of the dimensionality of census data, theoretically meaningful constructs were inferred from the groups of highly correlated variables. For example, Bloom (1968) identified and combined census variables into four cluster scores which described the census tracts of Pueblo, Colorado, and defined the following constructs or terms: socioeconomic affluence, young marrieds, social isolation, and social disequilibrium. The above procedure can be reversed by selecting census tract variables to define constructs which are theoretically or empirically related to health status and the use of medical facilities.

Regardless of the particular approach, it is possible to reduce a sample of census variables to somewhere between four and nine highly reliable, theoretically meaningful, and relatively independent composite scores which comprehensively describe the environments of census tract residents.

By reducing, through factor or cluster analysis, the 20 independent variables to five composite scores and by eliminating one of the 13 dependent variables by combining rates of use by very young (age 0-5) males and females, we have a manageable set of 17 variables which describe census tracts and their respective client populations. These variables may be statistically manipulated to answer questions or test hypotheses.

We might first tackle the general question: to what extent do characteristics of census tracts predict the selective use of medical services? Patterns of relationship of the five independent composite variable scores with each service delivery variable should provide at least partial answers to the question: Why do residents of certain tracts make extensive use of medical services while residents of other tracts make minimal use of the services? The five independent variables may play strikingly different roles in predicting service use rates by the very old and the very young. Social isolation may be dominant in the very young. Studies of this type are sparse, and there is little or no organized knowledge based on replicated results which might guide the evaluator. However, common sense, a sensitive ear to the ideas of service clinicians, and interpretations of even fragmentary results of other studies will help to make the results meaningful, raise additional questions, and provide one type of information for changes in service delivery.

More rigorous and comprehensive data analysis procedures may of course be applied to this data set of 17 variables observed on the 100 census tracts. Using multiple regression procedures, one could estimate the extent to which differences among residents of census tracts on variables of service use could be accounted for by a weighted, linear combination of the five independent composite scores which describe the environments of the census tract residents. Such analyses would establish the degree of predictive power which characteristics of the environment have in accounting for differences in the rate of service use over tracts. Again, it would be of interest to observe the relative weight which each independent variable receives in accounting for rate differences.

Partial correlation coefficients, where four of the five independent variables are held constant, would help determine the importance of one characteristic of the environment in accounting for rate differences when the other four characteristics are partialled out or held constant. Application of this procedure would result in five partial correlation coefficients as one more basis for inferring causal priorities.

Study and interpretation of the above results should provide a reasonably firm basis for designing changes in service delivery. It may at times be wise to test inferences regarding the cause of service use rates by surveying populations of census tracts with low, medium, and high rates of use. Such medical-sociologic surveys would be excellent training for students in health occupations. All results, considered within the political-economic context in which service delivery takes place, should lead to change. The next section presents a strategy for evaluating the effects of change.

THE EXPERIMENTAL EVALUATION OF INNOVATION

Kurt Lewin is among those credited with the statement that the best way to understand a social system is through attempting to change it (Marrow, 1969). The foregoing sections have provided methods for describing communities divided into geographic areas and for inferring causal priorities in the use of health services. Assuming that change is desirable in a particular area of health care, how do we procede, using social area analysis methodology? The logic of experimentation dictates that we influence, or attempt to change, similar populations with different stimuli or programs and observe the relative change in the populations being compared. Within a social area analysis framework, similar populations are defined as residents of areas with similar profiles on a number of characteristics which comprehensively describe the area residents.

To follow through with our hypothetical study of the residents of 100 census tracts, let us assume that the rates of seeking a physical examination following the delivery of a child are below a desirable level and that the health service is committed to doing something about it. However, the health service would also like to know the most effective method of convincing this population of recent mothers to obtain a thorough postpartum examination. Recent figures indicate that approximately 50% now complete the examination. Two methods of influence are developed. One, method A, is a personal letter from the subject's doctor urging her to return for the examination, stressing its importance and also assuring her that in all probability there will be no problem. The second method, labeled B, involves a visit to the subject's home by a congenial, mature woman, trained as an obstetric assistant, who talks with the subject, conveying to her essentially the content of the letter sent in method A. A third method, method C, is the one currently used in the hospital, where a nurse discusses the importance of the postpartum examination with the subject during her hospital stay.

Areas of the CA with similar profiles on both the independent and dependent variables previously described would be identified by profile analytic methods, referenced in Fleiss and Zubin (1969) and applied by Tryon and Bailey (1970). Census tracts with very similar profiles would be assigned to methods A, B, and C, resulting in three experimental areas with highly similar characteristics. In addition, rates of postpartum examination would be computed for each experimental area to assure us of essentially similar populations on this variable.

Following a pilot study to test the methodology, the study would be implemented and changes would be observed in the two experimental groups relative to each other and to the control group. After the collection of sufficient data to make valid conclusions, additional changes in the health delivery system could be made to encourage proper health care following the birth of a child. Such changes might include the installation of a satellite clinic in an area of high birthrates or the training of a home visiting team to provide home examinations to mothers unable to make clinic visits. The message of the visiting woman could be varied to determine whether its influence varies with different types of women. An interesting study of this type was completed by Lehmann (1970).

A similar type of evaluation strategy could, of course, be applied to estimate the effects of change in the delivery of mental health services. The effectiveness of satellite clinics, sensitive to the sociocultural values and life-styles of their clients and area residents, could be evaluated by comparing their service use patterns with those of more traditional clinics providing services to residents living in similar areas. The influence of different types of mental health education programs, placing emphasis on the early detection or prevention of mental disorders, could be evaluated by comparing the types of services requested by clients from similar areas, but participating in different mental health education programs.

A key issue in providing mental health services is for example, the source of referral of clients. The referral network is one important connection between the service system and the community it serves. The nature of the referral network is a function of both the type of community served and the service delivery style.

If, for example, a large proportion of clients are brought in by the police and require hospitalization, while out-patient services receive minimal use, the service system would be dominated by in-patient services where clients request service only when their mental disorders are severe or they are forcibly brought in by the police. If, on the other hand, a large proportion of clients came to out-patient services accompanied by a relative or friend and referred by a family member or social organization in the community, then a different style of service delivery is manifest.

If one makes the assumption that referral sources are related to levels and types of mental disorders received, and subsequently, to the pattern of services rendered, then service administrators could ask a number of pertinent questions: With what pattern of services should I spend allocated funds in order to best serve the mental health needs of CA residents? Is it possible to alter referral sources so that service dollars play a more preventive role? Is it possible to attract clients through new referral sources before their level of disorder is severe enough to require hospitalization? Can rates of hospitalization for discharged patients be lowered by developing referral sources and making more effective use of out-patient and rehabilitation services? What role can consultation and educational services play in developing more effective referral networks?

Once referral sources and patterns of service have been conceptualized as important issues, plans for changing selected aspects of service delivery procedures or for creating new referral sources can be developed. The effects of introducing these changes into program components serving a given area could be compared over time, in a time series design, to see if desirable results, in terms of referral source and services rendered, are achieved.

In a more rigorous experimental framework, planned changes to improve referral sources and to increase preventive services could be introduced to a defined area while an area with a very similar resident and client population continued the usual style of service delivery. Changes in referral source and services rendered could be compared at various time intervals to estimate the efforts of planned change.

It would take little effort to think of additional factors that could conceivably play important roles in service delivery. The social area method, in the experimental framework, involves the introduction of new methods of service delivery to similar areas in order to observe their relative effectiveness in achieving some service delivery goal or standard of performance.

Application of social area analysis need not be limited to relationships between service delivery systems and their CA populations and organizations. A study of Brandon in the second volume of this Handbook illustrates area analysis applied to New York City. This study identifies the relative role of social area characteristics, type and cost of services, and proximity of services in predicting the rate of use of inpatient and out-patient services by selected age-sex populations residing in 338 health areas of New York City. In Chapter 11, Brandon clearly indicates the complexity of factors which influence the selective use of services by applying multiple regression procedures to area or aggregate data. Chein (1963) in New York City and Cartwright and Howard (1966) in Chicago have applied social area analysis to the study of deviant behavior, while as previously mentioned, Tryon (1955) has used the same approach in relating area characteristics to voting behavior. Studies by the author and colleagues (1970) have analyzed the relationships of area attributes to the health, mental health and behavior of area residents. Work by Bloom (1968) and Levy and Rowitz (1973) illustrate the use of area analysis with psychiatric hospitalization as the dependent variable.

SUMMARY

Systematic study is needed to provide understanding of the complex relationships between human service delivery systems and the populations they serve. More generally planners and administrators need to know more about situational or environmental factors which influence the health, mental health, and behavior of people experiencing those situations or environments.

Because our level of knowledge regarding the successful fit of characteristics of groups to be served with the style of human services rendered is fragmentary and inconclusive, it seems that all levels of evaluation—descriptive, comparative or correlational, and experimental—are urgently needed. It is hypothesized that theory construction will take on a more important, integrative role as empirical development progresses. Appropriate applications of social area analysis, particularly focused on the experimental evaluation of the effects of innovation, promise to add to our understanding of area populations, their selective use of human service delivery systems, and the types of changes needed to make services optimally effective.

REFERENCES

Bell, W. Urban neighborhoods and individual behavior. In *Problems of Youth: Transition to Adulthood in a Changing World,* edited by M. Sherif and C. W. Sherif. Chicago: Aldine, 1967.

Bloom, B. L. An ecological analysis of psychiatric hospitalizations. *Multivariate Behavioral Research,* 1968, 3(4): 423-464.

Cartwright, D. S. Ecological variables. Pp. 155-218 *in Sociological Methodology,* edited by E. F. Borgatta. San Francisco: Jossey-Bass, 1969.

Cartwright, Desmond S. and Kenneth Howard. Multivariate analysis of gang delinquency: I Ecologic influences. *Multivariate Behavioral Research,* July 1966, 1: 321-371.

Chein, I. *Some Epidemiological Vectors of Delinquency and Its Control: Outline of a Project.* Research Center for Human Relations, New York University, 1963. Mimeo.

Comrey, A. L. *A First Course in Factor Analysis.* New York and London: Academic Press, 1973.

Fleiss, J. L. and J. Zubin. On the methods and theory of clustering. *Multivariate Behavioral Research,* 1969, 4(2): 235-250.

Harman, H. H. *Modern Factor Analysis.* Chicago: University of Chicago Press, 1967.

Hauser, P. M. and O. D. Duncan. (eds.) *The Study of Population.* Chicago: University of Chicago Press, 1959.

Kraus, A. S. and Lilienfeld. Some epidemiologic aspects of the high mortality rate in the young widowed group. *J. Chron. Dis.,* 1959, 10 (3): 207-218.

Lehmann, S. Personality and compliance: A study of anxiety and self-esteem in opinion and behavior change. *J. Pers. Soc. Psychol.,* 1970, 15 (1): 76-80.

Levy, L. and L. Rowitz, *The Ecology of Mental Disorder.* Behavioral Publications, New York, 1973.

McKinlay, J. B. Some approaches and problems in the study of the use of services—An overview. *J. Health Soc. Behav., 1972, 13(2): 115-152.*

Marrow, A. J. *The Practical Theorist: The Life and Work of Kurt Lewin.* New York: Basic Books, 1969.

Shevky, E. and W. Bell. *Social Area Analysis.* Stanford: Stanford University Press, 1955.

Shevky, E. and M. Williams. *The Social Areas of Los Angeles: Analysis and Typology.* Berkeley and Los Angeles: University of California Press, 1949.

Stein, Z., M. Susser, and A. Guterman. Screen programme for prevention of Down's syndrome. *Lancet*, 1973, 1(7798): 305-310.

Struening, E. L., S. Lehmann, and J. G. Rabkin. Context and behavior: A social area study of New York City. In *Behavior in New Environments*, edited by E. B. Brody. Beverly Hills, Calif.: Sage Publications, 1970.

Struening, E. L., J. G. Rabkin, and H. Peck. Migration and ethnic membership in relation to social problems. In *Behavior in New Environments*, edited by E. B. Brody. Beverly Hills, Calif.: Sage Publications, 1970.

Struening, E. L., J. G. Rabkin, P. Cohen, G. Raabe, G. Muhlin and J. Cohen. Family, ethnic and economic indicators of low birth weight and infant mortality: A social area analysis. *Ann. N. Y. Acad. Sci.*, 1973, 218: 87-107.

Tryon, R. C. *Identification of Social Areas by Cluster Analysis.* Berkeley and Los Angeles: University of California Press, 1955.

–––. Predicting group differences in cluster analysis: The social area problem. *Multivariate Behavioral Research*, 1967, 2: 453-475.

–––. Comparative cluster analysis of social areas. *Multivariate Behavioral Research*, 1968, 3(2): 213-232.

––– and D. E. Bailey. *Cluster Analysis.* New York: McGraw-Hill, 1970.

Williams, R. H. and L. D. Ozarin (eds.) *Community Mental Health.* San Francisco: Jossey-Bass, 1968.

REFERENCE UPDATE
Selected by Elmer L. Struening

Andersen, R. Health status indices and access to medical care. *American Journal of Public Health,* 1978, 68 (5): 458-462.

Anderson, T. R. and J. A. Egeland. Spatial aspects of social area analysis. *American Sociological Review*, 1961, 26 (3): 392-398.

Bagley, C. and S. Jacobson. Ecological variation of three types of suicide. *Psychological Medicine*, 1976, 6: 423-427.

Bell, R. A., H. F. Goldsmith, E. Lin, R. K. Hirzel, and S. Sobel. *Social indicators for human service systems.* Louisville: Department of Psychiatry and Behavioral Sciences, School of Medicine, University of Louisville, 1982.

Blau, P. Structural effects. *American Sociological Review*, 1960, 25, 178-193.

Bloom, B. L. A census tract analysis of socially deviant behaviors. *Multivariate Behavioral Research*, 1966 (July): 307-320.

Bloom, B. L. *Changing patterns of psychiatric care.* New York: Human Sciences Press, 1975.

Brandon, R. N. Differential use of mental health services: Social pathology or class victimization? In M. Guttentag and E. L. Struening (eds.) *Handbook of evaluation research* (Vol. 2). Beverly Hills, CA: Sage, 1975.

Braucht, G. N. Interactional analysis of suicidal behavior. *Journal of Consulting and Clinical Psychology*, 1979, 47 (4): 653-669.

Braucht, G. N., F. Loya, and K. J. Jamieson. Victims of violent death: A critical review. *Psychological Bulletin*, 1980, 87 (2): 309-333.

Campbell, D. E., B. N. Steenbarger, T. W. Smith, and R. J. Stucky. An ecological systems approach to evaluation: Cruising in Topeka. *Evaluation Review*, 1982, 6 (5): 625-648.

Catalano, R. and C. D. Dooley. Economic predictors of depressed mood and stressful life events in a metropolitan community. *Journal of Health and Social Behavior*, 1977, 18: 292-307.

Converse, P. E. Survey research and the decoding of patterns in ecological data. In M. Dogan and S. Rokkan (eds.) *Quantitative ecological analysis in the social sciences.* Cambridge: MIT Press, 1969.

Dangermond, J. Planning applications for social area analysis. In A. Livingood (ed.) *Social indicators*. Louisville: Urban Studies Center, University of Louisville, 1975.

Feather, J. Using macro variables in program evaluation. *Evaluation and Program Planning*, 1982, 5 (3): 209-215.

Firebaugh, G. A rule for inferring individual-level relationships from aggregate data. *American Sociological Review*, 1978, 43: 557-572.

Goodman, A. B. and A. Hoffer. Ethnic and class factors affecting mental health clinic service. *Evaluation and Program Planning, 1979, 2 (2): 159-171.*

Goodman, L. *Some alternatives to ecological correlations. American Journal of Sociology*, 1959, 64: 610-625.

Goodstein, J., A. Zautra, and D. Goodhart. A test of the utility of social indicators for behavioral health service planning. *Social Indicators Research*, 1978, 10: 273-295.

Gordon, R. A. Issues in the ecological study of delinquency. *American Sociological Review*, 1967, 32: 927-944.

Hammond, J. L. Two sources of error in ecological correlations. *American Sociological Review*, 1973, 38: 764-777.

Harburg, E., J. Erfurst, J. Havenstein, C. Chape, W. Schull, and M. Schork. Socioecological stress, suppressed hostility, skin color, and black-white male blood pressure: Detroit. *Psychosomatic Medicine*, 1973, 35: 276-296.

Hargreaves, W. A. and E. A. DeLay. Program evaluation in a rural community mental health center. *Community Mental Health Journal*, 1979, 15 (2): 104-118.

Hauser, R. M. Contextual analysis revisited. *Sociological Methods and Research, 1974*, 2: 365-375.

Herbert, D. T. (ed.) *Social areas in cities, vol. 1: Spatial processes and form.* New York: John Wiley, 1976.

Herbert, D. T. *Social areas in cities: Processes, patterns and problems.* New York: John Wiley, 1978.

Holzer, C., D. J. Jackson, and D. Tweed. Horizontal synthetic estimation: A strategy for estimating small area health-related characteristics. *Evaluation and Program Planning*, 1981, 4 (1): 29-34.

Janson, C. G. Factorial social ecology: An attempt at summary and evaluation. *Annual Review of Sociology*, 1980, 6: 433-456.

Kay, F. D. Applications of social area analysis to program planning and evaluation. *Evaluation and Program Planning*, 1978, 1 (1): 65-78.

Kleinman, J. C. Age-adjusted mortality indexes for small areas; Applications to health planning. *American Journal of Public Health*, 1977, 67 (9): 834-840.

Langbein, L. I. and A. J. Lichtman. *Ecological inference.* Beverly Hills, CA: Sage, 1978.

Lee, A. S. and H. F. Goldsmith. Small area indicators and social change. *Evaluation and Program Planning*, 1981, 4 (1): 83-94.

Milcarek, B. I. and B. G. Link. Handling problems of ecological fallacy in program planning and evaluation. *Evaluation and Program Planning*, 1981, 4 (1): 23-28.

Muhlin, G. L., P. Cohen, E. L. Struening, L. E. Genevie, S. R. Kaplan, and H. Peck. Behavioral epidemiology and social area analysis: The study of blackout looting. *Evaluation and Program Planning*, 1981, 4 (1): 35-42.

National Institute of Mental Health. *A typological approach to doing social area analysis.* DHEW Publication (ADM) 76-262. Washington, DC: Government Printing Office, 1975.

Neser, W. B., H. A. Tyroller, and J. C. Cassel. Social disorganization and stroke mortality in the black population of North Carolina. *American Journal of Epidemiology*, 1971, 93 (3).

Piasecki, J. R. and E. K. Gould. Social area analysis in program evaluation and planning. *Evaluation and Program Planning*, 1981, 4 (1): 3-14.

Rabkin, J. and E. L. Struening. *Ethnicity, social class and mental illness.* Working Paper 17. New York: Institute on Pluralism and Group Identity, American Jewish Committee, 1976.

Schuessler, K. Analysis of ratio variables: Opportunities and pitfalls. *Ameriacan Journal of Sociology*, 1974, 80: 379-396.

Schweitzer, L. and H. Kierszenbaum. Community characteristics that affect hospitalization and rehospitalization rates in a municipal psychiatric hospital. *Community Mental Health Journal*, 1978, 14 (1): 63-73.

Schweitzer, L. and S. Wen-Huey. Population density and the rate of mental illness. *American Journal of Public Health*, 1977, 67 (2): 1165-1172.

Scott-Samuel, A. Social area analysis in community medicine. *British Journal of Preventive and Social Medicine*, 1977: 199-204.

Siegel, C. and A. Goodman. Differences in white-nonwhite community mental health center service utilization patterns. *Evaluation and Program Planning*, 1978, 1 (1): 51-63.

Smith, N. L. Techniques for the analysis of geographic data in evaluation. *Evaluation and Program Planning*, 1979, 2 (2): 119-126.

Strobino, D. M. Evaluation of perinatal services: An application of social area analysis. *Evaluation Review*, 1982, 6 (1): 127-139.

Struening, E. L., B. I. Milcarek, J. Pittman, and F. Winsor. Community and institutional determinants of psychiatric hospitalization: The ecological match. In E. Gottheil, A. T. McLellan, and K. A. Druley (eds.) *Matching patient needs and treatment methods in alcoholism and drug abuse*. Springfield, IL: Charles C Thomas, 1981.

Valkonen, T. Individual and structural effects in ecological research. In M. Dogan and S. Rokkan (eds.) *Quantitative ecological analysis in the social sciences*. Cambridge: MIT Press, 1979.

Warheit, C. J., C. E. Holzer, and L. Robbins. Social indicators and mental health planning: An empirical case study. *Community Mental Health Journal*, 1979, 15: 21.

Wechsler, H. and T. F. Pugh. Fit of individual and community characteristics and rates of psychiatric hospitalization. *American Journal of Sociology*, 1967, 73: 331-338.

Wennberg, J. and A. Gittelsohn. Small area variations in health care delivery. *Science*, 1973, 182: 1102-1108.

Zwick, R., V. Neuhoff, L. A. Marascuilo, and J. R. Levin. Statistical tests for correlated proportions: Some extensions. *Psychological Bulletin*, 1982, 92 (1): 258-271.

V

MEASUREMENT ISSUES
IN EVALUATION RESEARCH

10

THE STUDY OF CHANGE IN EVALUATION RESEARCH: PRINCIPLES CONCERNING MEASUREMENT, EXPERIMENTAL DESIGN, AND ANALYSIS

JUM C. NUNNALLY

If one inspects examples of evaluation research discussed in these volumes and in other places, it is apparent that the term evaluation research is generally concerned with the effectiveness of programs of social improvement. Thus, social improvement is involved in the introduction of the Peace Corps into a new country, the institution of community mental health programs, development of family planning programs, and the introduction of "new math" in a school system. In all cases the effort of the program is to improve some existing state of affairs among people; in all cases the effort of evaluation research is to document the amounts and kinds of improvements that actually occur, if any.

Of course, if a new program of social improvement actually is effective, people who participate in the program should improve during the course of their participation. This is another way of saying that they change over the time of participation. Thus it may be said that evaluation research is intimately related to the study of change.

As will be discussed more fully later, the introduction of a new program of social improvement is analogous to a "treatment" like that in the typical controlled experiment. Not only are experiments relating to programs of social improvement concerned with change, but all experiments of any kind with people are concerned with change. Thus, in the course of investigating the effectiveness of different drugs

AUTHOR'S NOTE: Appreciation is expressed to McGraw-Hill Book Co. for permission to borrow extensively from the following book for material adapted for this chapter: J. C. Nunnally, *Psychometric Theory* (New York: McGraw-Hill, 1967). Appreciation is also expressed to Robert L. Durham and William H. Wilson for their assistance.

on moods of depressed patients, the essence of the experiment is to document any changes that occur as a function of the drug administrations. Similarly, in comparing the effectiveness of three methods of instruction in foreign languages, in essence the experiment is concerned with changes in proficiency as a function of the different treatments.

Although it can be said that all experimentation is in essence concerned with change, there are some special problems of logic and technique in the study of change in evaluation research that either do not occur at all or occur to a lesser degree in the typical experiment with people. Consequently, this chapter is devoted to a discussion of problems that frequently arise in the study of change in evaluation research. The issues will be discussed in the logical order that they should occur to the scientist: measurement, then research design, and finally statistical analysis.

ILLUSTRATIVE PROBLEMS OF MEASUREMENT IN THE STUDY OF CHANGE

The theory and methodology of psychological measurement are discussed in Chapters 9 and 10 of the *Handbook of Evaluation Research,* Volume 1 (Struening and Guttentag, 1975). However, some special issues arise in evaluation research concerning the degree or type of measurement employed. Such issues will be discussed in this section.

Constructing Measures Ex Post Facto

It should go without saying that measures employed to evaluate a program concerning social improvement should be constructed before rather than after the program is under way. However, there still are many examples of programs that are completed before any effort is made to develop adequate measuring instruments. Surely no professional researcher would commit such a faux pas; but where adequate professional researchers have not been involved, examples are legion of this blunder occurring. An example was mentioned previously where the author was once asked for advice on evaluating a program of "new math" in a public school system after the program had been in effect for a year. It is surprising to find that even some administrative officials involved in various programs of social improvement apparently think that professional researchers can, by some form of legerdemain, pull adequate measuring instruments out of a hat at any time for any circumstance.

An exception to the principle that measures should be selected or constructed before new programs are undertaken is that in which the measuring instruments naturally grow out of the program while it is under way. An example would be in performing content analyses of changes during group psychotherapy. Whereas experimenters probably could formulate many of the content coding categories before the inception of the program, some of the important categories would make themselves known only after the therapy sessions had been going on for some time. It might, for example, become apparent after a number of sessions had occurred that special issues arose in those groups that were conducted by female rather than male therapists. Consequently, in midstream of performing content analyses of therapy sessions, experimenters would need to add some additional coding categories relating to this unforeseen issue. The new coding categories not only could be used henceforth in analyzing the program, but also could be applied retrospectively to the transcripts of earlier sessions.

Reactivity of Measurements

A problem that is encountered frequently in evaluation research is that pretest measures interact with treatment conditions in a program being evaluated. An example would be in the evaluation of neighborhood discussion groups as a way of reducing race prejudice. Before the group sessions are started, a pretest is given which consists of questions relating to race prejudice such as the following:

	Yes	*No*
1. When Negroes move into a neighborhood that was formerly all white, property values usually decrease.	_____	_____
2. Negroes are rapidly moving into professional positions in medicine, law, etc.	_____	_____
3. It is doubtful that the average intelligence of Negroes is as high as that of whites.	_____	_____

Rather obviously such a pretest measure would alert group members regarding issues and differentially sensitize them to various topics that arose in the discussion. After a series of group sessions extending over several months, the same inventory is given to all subjects. Large differences are found between pretest and posttest scores, but the differences may be due entirely to reactivity from participating in the pretest. The results would generalize only to those situations in which pretests were administered before group sessions were started, but this might not be the plan of the individuals who are developing the program. To prevent such reactivity, a better research design is one in which tests are given only at the end of a training program and in which the group that receives the training program is compared with a control group.

The only major exception to the foregoing principle is in a situation where the number of subjects necessarily is quite small, and thus every ounce of statistical muscle is needed. The major advantage of using a repeated measures design in which the same subjects are administered a pretest and a posttest is that the statistical power of comparisons frequently are substantially higher than in employing a between-groups design in which a treatment group is compared with a control group. For example, this circumstance might arise in an extensive program to train high-level personnel, such as airline pilots. Pilots who participate in the usual training program are compared with pilots who are given a radically new type of training in instrument flying. Unless there is strong suspicion that pretest measures would interact with treatment conditions, statistical power probably could be increased by employing both a pretest and a posttest. Campbell and Stanley (1968) have discussed numerous issues concerning appropriate designs when reactivity of measurement is a potential problem.

There are a number of steps one can take to ensure that pretest measures are not interacting with treatment conditions in evaluation research. First, as was mentioned above, there are research designs in which this is not a problem. Second, in some instances one can employ measures that logically are nonreactive. Numerous such measures are discussed by Webb, Campbell, Schwartz, and Sechrest (1966). Two examples (not from Webb et al.) are as follows. A series of TV films is used in schools to increase interest in a wide variety of reading topics. Over the months following the films, the success of the program can be measured in part by the numbers and kinds of books checked out of the school library as compared to the situation before the films were shown. Another example is that of evaluating the success of a series of spot announcements on radio regarding the availability of free advice on birth planning. The success of the announcement can be measured in part by the relative increase in numbers of phone calls seeking appointments at the end of each broadcast and the overall increases from before until after the series is presented. However, the problem in so much evaluation research is that the purposes and content of measures are rather obvious, and consequently the measures potentially will interact with treatments.

Another approach to handling problems of reactivity is to learn at an early stage of the game whether pretest measures actually are interacting with treatments. The logic of employing research designs for this purpose is discussed by Campbell and Stanley (1968). If the reactivity is found to be very slight in the special research, one can employ simpler research designs for subsequent research on evaluating a program of action without worrying about reactivity of measurement.

A fourth potential approach to handling reactivity of measurement is to disguise the items in traditional tests of abilities and sentiments. For reasons which will be discussed later in this chapter, this approach usually fails.

Faking of Responses

A problem related to reactivity of measurement is that of faking. In many programs of evaluation research (even good ones), the people who operate the program are highly committed to their evaluations even before the research evidence is in. Sometimes they are convinced that a program is working poorly and want to prove that such is the case. This might occur when an agency of a local government investigates the effectiveness of a youth correction program. The people who conduct the research, or who engage others to do so, may strongly feel that the program is generally bad. If the people who hold this point of view actually conduct or otherwise influence the research activity, there are many ways in which data could be faked to support that point of view. (Here the word "faked" is being used in a very general sense concerning any methods that unfairly sample, analyze, or interpret research results. The faking may be of a patent, dishonest form in which the individual purposely distorts information; or the individual may be so committed to the outcome that, by one defense mechanism or another, he fools himself.)

The more frequently occurring situation is that in which the people who conduct evaluation research are highly committed to the positiveness of the program being evaluated. Most new social programs (e.g., a new type of school instruction or the Peace Corps) originate because of the messianic zeal of the progenitors. Obviously it is very difficult for such persons to face up to the possibility that evaluation research will prove the program to be ineffective.

Faking can enter into evaluation research in many different ways. Psychotherapy patients usually want to please their therapist by indicating they have improved even if they have not. In rating the improvement of youth in a program of training for delinquent boys, the manager of the program might pick raters who sympathize with his points of view rather than other equally competent people in the institution who have different points of view. In comparisons of two groups that were subjected to different types of training programs, the test constructor might deliberately favor one group by selecting items specifically because they were considered more extensively in one method of training than the other.

Of course, one of the primary ways to prevent faking from markedly influencing results is to have the research conducted mainly by individuals who have very little personal stake in the outcome. In addition, there are other ways to lower the influence of faking. Another way, where it is feasible, is to employ the types of unobtrusive measures discussed and illustrated previously (Webb et al., 1966). Relatedly, a second principle is to ensure that as much as possible of the data generating and gathering process is out of the hands of individuals who are invested in the outcomes of evaluation research. For example, rather than have ratings made by people who function in a program of social action, it would be advisable to have such ratings made by trained persons who are not involved in the program being evaluated.

If the measuring instruments are easily faked (as most measures of sentiments, as opposed to abilities, are), a fourth principle is to try to reduce faking by specifically warning subjects of the need for strict objectivity, even if the real truth is unkind. Of course, such admonitions do not constitute a cure-all against faking, but it is surprising how frequently subjects are not carefully instructed in that way. Depending on the situation, various assurances can be given to subjects which promote objectivity. In many cases subjects can be told by research workers that the personnel of a program of social action (e.g., a job training program) will not see individual responses on questionnaires. In some cases, one can even go to the extent of specifically telling subjects not to place their names on questionnaires.

A fifth method is one that almost always fails, but it has absorbed so much energy from research workers, that it should be mentioned. When working with sentiments, behavioral scientists have spent a great deal of time and money in the effort to develop highly deceptive but valid measures of attitudes, values, and personality characteristics. One approach is with "sneaky" items. An example is a multiple-choice test with items like "If you were reincarnated, what type of person would you like to be?" Many other Machiavellian attempts have been made with projective tests, pupillary response, and numerous supposed physiological correlates of emotions. Valid indicators of sentiments have *not* yet come from work with such variables. (See discussions of these issues in Guilford, 1959, and in Nunnally, 1967.)

It is necessary to make a careful distinction between measures that are deceptive in the sneaky sense illustrated above and the previously mentioned and illustrated types of unobtrusive measures. The latter also are deceptive in the sense of trying to get the individual to give away his own private feelings based on test items or other types of stimuli whose relationship to the traits in question are quite elliptical and remote. Thus, if in an unobtrusive measure one estimates the amount of alcoholic consumption in a household by counting the number of bottles found in the garbage each week, the measure is hidden from the view of the subject but rather obviously related to the trait in question. In contrast if one knocks on a man's door and asks him which one of ten magazines he thought would be more appropriate for an orphanage, the measure certainly is deceptive but not likely to be very predictive of alcoholic consumption in the household. Many years of trying to develop such measures have resulted mainly in disappointment.

Extent of Measurement Problem

The difficulty of constructing adequate measures for evaluation research varies considerably with the questions that those measures are intended to answer. If the program being evaluated largely concerns training in human capabilities, the measurement problems usually are rather straightforward. Examples are (1) the measurement of changes in knowledge about forestry brought about by a government financed training program, (2) the measurement of progress in swimming classes by objective indicators of performance and instructor's ratings, and (3) the use of commercially distributed achievement tests to measure the effects of special schooling on the culturally disadvantaged. However, sometimes the capability being investigated is much more illusive, such as capability with respect to public speaking, creativity, or effectiveness in job situations. Such characteristics present real challenges to measurement. They may be approached through ratings, various types of documentary evidence, and specially constructed achievement tests.

Rather than being concerned with improvement in capabilities (in the usual sense of the term), many programs that are evaluated concern habits and dispositions in daily life. Examples are (1) consumption of alcoholic beverages, (2) reckless driving, and (3) acts of courtesy. Problems of measuring such dispositions range from the absolutely trivial to the nearly insurmountable. At one extreme, there is no problem at all to "weigh the evidence" in a program to reduce obesity. In contrast, it would be much more difficult to obtain objective measures of improvements in highway safety of individuals (unless one monitored each person in his daily driving). However, even with some of the more illusive dispositions, it is possible to obtain measurements of changes in group performance even if one cannot finely measure such performance in individuals.

The most controversy concerning measurement in evaluation research has not been concerned with capabilities, as discussed above, but with what has been referred to as sentiments—attitudes, values, and preferences. In this realm the opaque instruments tend to be invalid, and the transparent instruments leave lingering doubts about faking. If the cautions that were mentioned previously with respect to faking are followed, then there is no major reason straightforward inventories and rating scales cannot be used as valid measuring instruments in nearly all evaluation research. Long ago the author came to the conclusion that generally the most valid, economical, sometimes the only, way to learn about a person's sentiments is simply to ask him.

Subjective Assessments

Some of the most important human traits involved in evaluation research presently can be measured only in terms of subjective assessments rather than in terms of more objective means. For example, an individual's satisfaction with a series of training sessions in first aid necessarily would require a measurement of the participant's feelings about the course of instruction. Thus, in one sense or another, they would be required to rate their feelings about the program. In other instances, it would be necessary to obtain subjective assessments from persons in supervisory roles in a training program. This would be true, for example, in evaluating the progress of students in flight training programs of the Armed Forces. Because much anguish has been expressed concerning the need to employ such subjective assessments in evaluation research (and indeed, quite widely in research throughout the behavioral sciences), it would be worthwhile to consider the matter in some detail here.

The word "subjective" frequently is tossed about uncritically in a way that refers to at least four major issues concerning psychological measurement. First, objective measures have been distinguished from subjective measures in terms of the presence or absence of ostensive indicators of the trait in question. If a student correctly solves 26 of 32 problems on a test, then evidence regarding capability in that topic is present for everyone to see. If a program of evaluation research concerns training programs in underdeveloped countries regarding the production of rice, then the piles of rice coming from the fields can be witnessed and weighed in such a way that all present can witness the product. The effectiveness of spot announcements on TV regarding the availability of free birth planning assistance programs could be indexed partly in terms of the number of individuals applying. These examples concern the ostensiveness of data used to obtain dependent measures in evaluation research.

In many of the measures employed in the behavioral sciences, the data underlying measurements methods are not evidenced directly in palpable, sensory experience; but rather they are evidenced in the personal reactions of individuals. Thus, when an individual says that he prefers chocolate ice cream over vanilla ice cream, there are no ostensive data to back up the assertion. Of course, one could always investigate whether the individual purchased chocolate rather than vanilla ice cream when given the option, but that is not the same matter as measuring stated preferences. More germane to the issue of evaluation research, if supervisors rate trainees in a job-training program on a 7-point scale concerning motivation for employment, then the data underlying the measurement are literally in the head of the person making the ratings. In this sense, such ratings have been referred to as subjective. It is not necessarily bad that measures are subjective regarding the ostensiveness or lack of it in the measurement process; rather, the bad features that sometimes are present come because of some correlated problems, which will be discussed next.

Human impressions used to develop measures of psychological traits are referred to as subjective for another reason, namely because it is difficult to explicitly instruct subjects as to how to perform their rating tasks. An example was mentioned previously of that concerning supervisors' ratings of the motivation of students for employment. The 7-step scale used for that purpose might be indexed by "average, slightly above average, much above average," and so on. As any investigator knows, it becomes somewhat embarrassing if the respondent wants to know exactly what is meant by the terms and how he should distinguish between, for example, slightly above average and much above average. Although some general suggestions can be given in the printed instructions, admittedly the respondent is left largely to use the rating scale in a way that seems appropriate. Thus, the data themselves not only are subjective, but the method for making appraisals is subjective, in the sense that it relies on the intuitions of the respondent.

A third way in which many measures are said to be subjective concerns the sheer variability in results from rater to rater and from occasion to occasion. Because such sources of variability act as measurement error in most circumstances, it can be said that ratings tend to have only a modest reliability at best. For example, whereas one would expect two forms of an intelligence test to correlate at least .90, one would be very happy indeed to find that two supervisors made ratings of 40 trainees that correlated at least .60. The term subjective frequently is used where people differ markedly among themselves about events, and for this reason the word subjective frequently is used with respect to rating methods.

The word subjective is employed in a fourth important way with respect to rating methods used in evaluation research, namely that the results are influenced by numerous artifacts concerning the way people make ratings and in the rating tasks themselves. As one example, the rating given any person on any trait is markedly influenced by the group with which the individual is compared. An example would be in a training program for lifeguards. At the end of the program, supervisors make ratings on a number of traits concerning future job performance. One of the trainees, Fred Wilkerson, finds himself in an unusually capable, highly motivated, class of trainees. Fred would have looked good in a typical group of trainees; but in comparison to this premium group, he is given rather poor ratings by supervisors. Another artifact that occurs in ratings is that of the "halo effect." This is the tendency to rate people as all good or all bad on different traits rather than be more selective in making individual ratings. These and other artifacts in ratings are discussed in detail by Guilford (1954).

That rating methods are subjective in the first way mentioned above (lack of ostensiveness in the data) should pose no major problem for evaluation research. Many things are inherently subjective in that regard, and indeed a search for so-called objective indicators might be illogical. An example would be in having ladies rate their men friends in terms of overall desirability. The myriad underlying traits would be illusive and perhaps intractable to measurement. If one really is interested in the lady's evaluations rather than why she makes the choices that she does, the simplest approach is to have the individual rate the men by one psychometric device or another. The second way in which ratings are said to be subjective causes some problems in the construction of measurement methods, but these are by no means insurmountable. There are better ways to construct rating scales and better ways to instruct subjects in their use (e.g., see discussion in Nunnally, 1967, chap. 14).

The third and fourth ways in which ratings are said to be subjective do constitute workaday problems in evaluation research. Ratings typically are not highly reliable; and although methods are available for increasing the reliability, a good dose of measurement error usually remains. A cardinal way to increase reliability is to employ multiple raters and average their responses, for example, three supervisors rating the participants in a training program. Artifacts of measurement also can be reduced markedly by the way in which rating scales are constructed and administered. Although there is not enough space here to go into the many special issues concerning the construction and use of rating scales, the reader who is not already familiar with these matters should avail himself of summaries of the available literature. These are presented in Guilford (1954) and Nunnally (1967). Up to the present time, much evaluation research has relied in large part on self-ratings and ratings by others; and although such measurement methods have their problems, they probably will be relied on heavily in the future.

THE SELECTION AND DEVELOPMENT OF MEASURES
FOR THE STUDY OF CHANGE

Of course, before it is possible to investigate changes that occur in people with respect to programs of sound improvement, it is necessary to have measures that document such changes. General principles for the selection and development of measurement methods are discussed in Struening and Guttentag (1975, chaps. 4 and 5). Some special issues that arise with respect to the study of change are discussed as follows.

Construction of Measures on the Basis of Change

Because evaluation research is concerned with the study of change, it is easy to fall into the semantic trap of assuming that measurement methods should be constructed on the basis of empirical evidence concerning the amount of change found in research. An approach that has been attempted in that regard is as follows. The program of social improvement concerns a new type of group psychotherapy. For constructing a test of the effectiveness of changes in psychotherapy, a large item pool is assembled, populated with items concerning a wide variety of values, opinions, and personality characteristics. Each item is rated as either "Agree" or "Disagree." The pool of items is administered to a sample of subjects before they undertake the group therapy and after the sessions of group therapy are completed. Then, so the reasoning goes, the items that show the most change from before to after are the ones most sensitive to the changes that occurred during the therapy sessions. A comparison is made of the percentages of agreements (in decimal form, p values). Items are rank-ordered in terms of the absolute magnitude of such differences, and the items that differ most in this regard are selected to form a test for the measurement of change over the period of psychotherapy. This approach has something to say for itself, in that it is grounded in the raw empiricism of what actually changes over the period of psychotherapy; however, the liabilities of this approach far outweigh the apparent advantages.

The major problem with the above approach is that, at best, it would lead to a test which simultaneously measured a hodgepodge of possibly unrelated attributes. Thus, the collection of items used to form a test might concern introversion-extroversion, aggressiveness, tendency to accept opposing opinions, freedom from anxiety, and a host of other separable traits. Also, since the number of items relating to each trait would depend fortuitously upon the number of items originally tossed into the pool, the factorial composition of the conglomerate measure would be rather arbitrary. Consequently, even if in a statistical sense the measure served to index the amount of change that occurred during the therapy sessions, it would be all but impossible to understand the changes that occurred in underlying personality traits.

Even if it were logically defensible to select items for the measurement of change in terms of differences in p values from before to after, the approach might take great advantage of chance. Even if all subjects flipped coins to decide their answers on the before measure and the after measure, there would be differences in p values which could be used for the selection of items.

A third problem with this approach is that not all items which change markedly in p value from before to after any program necessarily are valid indicators of what occurred in the program. An example would be a multiple-choice item in which subjects were asked the name of the course instructor. Before the course was undertaken, many persons would not know; after the course was completed, almost everyone would know the instructor's name. The sheer logic of this approach would indicate this to be a highly valid item, which is nonsense, of course. Changes in p values from before to after a program provide only raw circumstantial evidence rather than direct evidence of validity.

Another approach that has been advocated for constructing measures based on actual changes during a program of social improvement concerns the percentages of individuals who change their scores from before to afterward. It should be obvious that this index is not necessarily related to that of changes in p values discussed above. Thus, before the program is undertaken, 50% of the people could agree with the item, and afterward 50% of the people could agree with the item; but the 50% of the people who agreed before could be the 50% of the people who disagreed afterward.

An example of constructing tests on the basis of before-after changes would be with respect to the item, "I look forward to getting up each morning and facing a new day." From before to after the sessions of group therapy, it might be found that 40% of the participants changed their answers—from agree to disagree or vice versa. So the argument goes, this means that the particular item is relatively sensitive to changes that occur in the particular type of group therapy.

The selection of items in terms of percentages of changes over a program of social improvement has the major faults of selecting items in terms of changes in p values plus an even more insidious fault of its own. At best, the method would lead to a conglomerate of items for which a total score would be largely uninterpretable.

This method also would tend to take advantage of chance and in many cases would not produce replicable results. This method also provides only rough circumstantial rather than direct evidence regarding validity of individual items. An important additional problem with this method is that it would lead to the selection of highly unreliable items for the eventual test. Obviously, according to the standard for selecting items, a good item would be one in which subjects actually flip coins to determine their answers before and afterward. In this case, the expectation is that 50% of the people would change their responses from before to afterward—either from agreement to disagreement or vice versa. Although in some cases one might find larger percentage reversals (e.g., from 70% agreeing to 80% disagreeing), in the analysis of such shifts it would be unusual to find items that changed as much as 50%.

Neither of the two approaches discussed above has proven successful in evaluation research, and both are condemned as general approaches for the measurement of change. The approaches discussed in the following section are far more appropriate.

Selection of Measures for the Study of Change

Far better than to construct measures ad hoc for particular investigations of change is to select existing measures that have proven themselves with respect to criteria discussed in chapter 3 of Psychometric Theory (Nunnally, 1967, 1978). Such measures should have the charactersitics of being (1) constructed in such a way as to be homogeneous in content, (2) highly reliable with respect to various sources of measurement error, and (3) of known factorial composition as determined by factor analysis of various types of capabilities and sentiments. Even in very large-scale programs of research, it takes years to develop standard measures of psychological characteristics that meet these standards. In particular, gathering evidence for construct validity is a matter that takes numerous years, at best. Consequently, it is usually foolhardy for those who are entering a program of evaluation research (which usually is limited both in terms of time and funds) to undertake the development and standardization of most of the measures that will be employed. The far better part of valor and the far better part of common sense is to seek suitable measures from those that have been ripening over the years.

Although the particular program of evaluation research may require tests of attributes not previously investigated in detail, this more frequently is the exception rather than the rule. More frequently, when investigators dive into a heavy program of developing their own measurement methods for evaluation research, they are either unaware of the psychometric standards that must be applied or unaware of much research that has been done to develop the measurement methods needed. In some cases the individual who is responsible for performing evaluation research is pardonably unacquainted with existing measures of human traits which can be found in the literature concerning the behavioral sciences. In that case, he probably would be helped considerably by inspecting (1) *The Seventh Mental*

Measurements Yearbook (Buros, 1972), (2) *Tests in Print* (Buros, 1961), (3) catalogues from commercial testing firms, (4) textbooks on educational and psychological measurement (e.g., Nunnally, 1970, 1972), and (5) some of the professional journals in the behavioral sciences. Through these sources and consultation with individuals who specialize in behavioral measurement, the investigator who is new to the field probably will find that measures of most psychological traits have been investigated by numerous people in the past; even if in many cases those investigations have not been highly successful in producing the necessary yardsticks.

CHANGE SCORES

Because evaluation research is in essence concerned with change from before to after people have undergone a program of social improvement, it is tempting to assume that the basic psychometric datum with which one works is the change score. Thus, if one is making comparisons of intelligence test scores at two points in time (symbolized by X_1 and X_2), it is assumed that the interest is in $X_2 - X_1$ and that such scores should be computed as one of the first steps in performing analyses. Actually, both the history of the problem and the logic of investigation indicate that the last thing one wants to do is to think in terms of or to compute such change scores unless the problem makes it absolutely necessary. As is generally known, the major problem in working directly with change scores is that they are ridden with a *regression effect*. The problem is illustrated in Figure 6.1. The variables X_1 and X_2 can be thought of as the raw scores obtained on the same test at two points in time, or the raw scores obtained on alternative forms of a test administered at two points in time. As necessarily must be the case, there is a regression line; and if the correlation is less than unity, the phenomena of regression toward the mean is present. If one computes change scores, he finds that the people who scored above the mean on the first occasion tend to have negative change scores, and that the people who scored below the mean on the first occasion tend to have positive change scores—all of this being purely an artifact of the way such scores are computed and the phenomena of regression toward the mean.

A horrible example is often cited (surely apocryphal) where a whole experiment was misinterpreted because of regression toward the mean. In this case a school teacher wanted to try out three different methods of instruction in reading speed in her class corresponding respectively to three groups in terms of scores at the beginning of the semester on a test of reading speed. The top third of the class was given one method of training; the middle third was given another method; and the bottom third was given still a third method. At the end of the semester, the test was readministered, and the statistical analyses were made of the change scores. The teacher found that the training given to the top third of the students actually hurt their reading speed, because the mean score was somewhat lower than it was at the beginning of the semester. The method of instruction provided for the bottom third of the students apparently worked very well, because their mean went up substantially. Apparently the instruction given to the middle third of the students had very little effect, because their mean was essentially the same as it was at the beginning

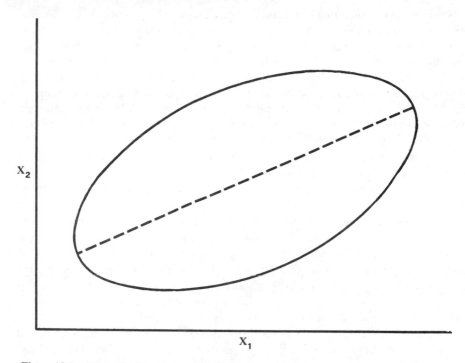

Figure 10.1 Regression line and correlation contour for scores on a test administered at two points in time.

of the semester. Of course, in these days to accuse anyone of performing such an experiment or being unaware of the serious limitations of change scores would be to attack a straw man; but the example does serve to illustrate the need either not to work with change scores at all or to work with some modification of them.

The modification of change scores that has been advocated most frequently is that of *residual change scores.* Quite simply, residual change scores consist of deviations of scores on a second occasion from those predicted by regression analysis from a knowledge of scores on a first occasion. Thus, in Figure 10.1 all scores above the regression line would have positive residual change scores, and all those below the regression line would have negative residual change scores. The advantage of working with residual change scores is that they circumvent the regression effect inherent in absolute change scores $(X_2 - X_1)$. However, this is not the end of a happy story, because a great deal of ink has been spilled over exactly how to compute such residual change scores. (An extensive review of the arguments is given in Cronbach and Furby, 1970.) Such residual change scores encounter both conceptual and psychometric problems.

The major psychometric problem with residual change scores is that they fail to take account of the measurement error inherent in both measurements. Thus, if X_2 were administered on the day following X_1 rather than an appreciable time later, scores would not be exactly the same, the correlation would probably be appreciably less than unity, and residual change scores could be computed and inspected.

Of course, such residual change scores would be due almost entirely to measurement error (unless the trait actually changed overnight) rather than to any systematic change in people. To take account of the measurement error inherent in residual change scores, it has been advocated that the correlation between X_1 and X_2 be corrected for attenuation before residual change scores are computed. However, there are questions as to exactly how that should be done. For example, should one correct the correlation only for measurement error in the first measurement, or should one make a double correction for measurement error to take account of the reliability inherent in the second measurement as well?

Numerous complex mathematical models have been developed for obtaining so-called pure measures of change (e.g., as discussed by Lord, 1963). However, the mathematical models involved are based on arguable assumptions about the logic of measuring change and presume that, in practice, one has much better evidence regarding reliabilities of scores and other psychometric characteristics of the before and after measures than usually is true in evaluation research. Also, individual experts concerned with the statistical issues involved express their own lack of certainty regarding proper procedures to be used in general, and various experts disagree with one another about proper procedures.

As a general rule it is wise to avoid working with change scores if at all possible. To summarize some of the major faults, they are (1) based on somewhat shaky assumptions, (2) derived by mathematical models which are controversial and frequently unfeasible in practice, (3) difficult for some people to understand, and are open to misinterpretation, and (4) as can be seen above, computationally rather complex. As Cronbach and Furby (1970) show, most problems regarding the measurement of change can be handled without thinking in terms of, or actually working with, residual change scores.

The major exception to the above statements regarding the avoidance of change scores is in the circumstance where evaluation research specifically concerns individual differences in the tendency to change in some way. An example would be that of individual differences in changes in reading comprehension test scores as a function of a particular type of training. A major concern for the investigator might be that of who changes more and who changes less. It might be desired to measure the amount of change, compute change scores, and then correlate such change scores with various measures of personality, ability, and characteristics of home environment. If it is feasible to employ it, a research design is available that allows one to estimate change scores in a sensible manner. The design circumvents most of the major problems that have plagued models for determining change scores. The design will be illustrated in the simple situation where a control group is compared with a treatment group on a single dependent measure. The logic can be extended to complex designs and multiple dependent measures. The design is as follows. An available group of subjects is randomly sorted into a treatment group and a control group. Both groups are tested at the same time before the treatment is applied. After the treatment is applied, subjects in both groups are retested with the same measure. (To take account of practice effects, alternate forms of the test could be employed, with counterbalancing within each group as to which form is used as pretest and which form is used as posttest.) The data obtained in this way would permit a separate correlational analysis for the control group and for the treatment group. The regression lines and scatter plots could be depicted in the same figure. Hypothetical results in that regard are shown in Figure 10.2.

The bivariate statistical properties of the results for the control group are precisely what one would expect to find from the treatment group *if the treatment had no effect.* Because the two groups are randomly sorted originally, it is to be expected that the means, standard deviations, and other parameters of the pretest distributions will be the same. The posttest results for the treatment group could differ in these ways from the control group. In Figure 10.2, the two groups are shown as having the same pretest mean but different posttest means, which is what the experimenter hoped for when he designed the experiment. Although they are depicted in Figure 10.2 as being essentially the same, the standard deviation on the pretest for the treatment group could be different from that on the control group, and also the slopes of the two regression lines could be different. Of course, differences between means, variances, and regression slopes all provide interesting evidence regarding the treatment effect. What is important to realize in this circumstance is that change scores in the treatment group can be computed directly from the regression line in the control group. If a person in the treatment group is above the regression line for the control group, then he has a positive change score

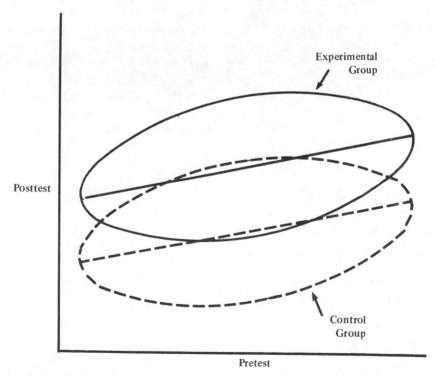

Figure 10.2   Regression lines and correlation contours for an experimental group and a control group on a pretest and a posttest measure.

equal to the indicated amount. Similarly, if a person in the treatment group is below the regression line for the control group, then he has actually lost ground by the amount indicated. One would compute residual change scores in the usual way for the treatment group, except that he would use the regression line obtained from the control group. This is a very sensible approach to the measurement of change scores.

The assumption that evaluation research requires the computation of some type of change scores is forced on the investigator by the same type of semantic innuendo that leads to the assumption that tests should be constructed in such a way as to capitalize on such change scores (as discussed in the previous section of this chapter). Actually, one could specialize in evaluation research for numerous years and never find an instance in which it was necessary actually to compute, inspect, analyze, or otherwise take direct action with respect to the change scores of *individuals*. As will be seen in subsequent sections of this chapter, nearly all of the problems concerning the changes that occur in evaluation research can be handled more simply and defensibly with respect to *group trends* without having to think in terms of or actually compute any type of change score for each individual in the investigation.

RESEARCH DESIGNS IN THE STUDY OF CHANGE

An ideal experiment has three essential features. First, experimental manipulations should concern only the treatment variable(s) and not some other, unsuspected (confounding) variable(s). Second, the dependent variables should be indexed by good measures—good in the sense of being reliable, otherwise well-standardized, valid, and practicable (Nunnally, 1967, 1978). Third, there should be an explicit plan for applying the treatments (independent variables) to subjects and measuring their effects on dependent variables. This section is concerned with the plan, or experimental design, as it is called. Of course, whole books have been written on general issues concerning experimental design and analysis; consequently, the discussion in this section will necessarily be limited to some issues that are particularly important for evaluation research. The opinions expressed in this section were influenced heavily by the writings of Campbell and his associates (e.g., Campbell and Stanley, 1968; and Campbell, 1969).

Types of Design

Following will be a discussion of some basic distinctions among types of experimental designs. Subsequently, designs that represent particular issues relating to these distinctions will be discussed in more detail.

Experimental versus quasi-experimental designs. Campbell and his associates make a distinction between true experimental designs and so-called quasi-experimental designs (e.g., Campbell and Stanley, 1968). True experimental designs are those in which it is possible to rule out all or most of the obvious, possible confounding variables in the experiment. A simplified example is that of evaluating the effect of a drug on the moods of hospitalized, depressed patients. All of the depressed patients in a hospital are randomly divided into two groups, with equal numbers of subjects in each group. The patients in the other group are given a sugar pill which closely resembles in appearance the actual drug. The patients do not know which pill they are receiving, and the persons administering the pill do not know which pill they are administering. Dependent measures concern psycho-physiological processes, self-ratings of moods, and ratings by attendants concerning adjustment status of patients. One can see that in this simple example all of the major, possible confounding variables are controlled. For example, since the subjects are randomly assigned to groups, there is no reason to believe that they would differ on the average with respect to the dependent measures any more than could be expected by chance alone.

If it were necessary to sacrifice any of the three types of controls mentioned above in the study of a drug, then one would no longer be working with a true experimental design but rather with a quasi-experimental design. For example, for one reason or another, it might have been necessary to give the drug to all patients in one ward and compare them with patients in another ward who received the placebo, rather than randomly divide the total pool of subjects into an experimental and a control group. Measures are taken on all subjects at only one point in time—after the course of treatment has been completed for subjects in the experimental group. The reader can easily think of numerous, potential confounding variables in this experiment. As one example, the two groups of patients might have differed on the average initially in terms of the dependent measures. This would be so if there had been a tendency of the hospital staff to place more severely disturbed patients in one part of the hospital rather than another, which is quite likely the case. Another confounding variable would be differences in the general atmosphere of the two wards, related to differences of personnel, physical surroundings, social structure among patients, and myriad other things. When it is unethical or unfeasable to employ a true experimental design, either the phenomena must go uninvestigated or a quasi-experimental design must be employed instead. In essence, a good quasi-experimental design is one in which additional information is obtained which provides considerable circumstantial evidence regarding what the outcome would be if a true experimental design actually could be employed.

Temporal components. In evaluation research it is important to consider the amount of time over which measures of dependent variables will be applied. In most evaluation research, the time span itself is not so long as to be an important consideration. Typically, such evaluation research concerns a program of human improvement that lasts no more than six months or a year. This would be true of programs concerning (1) "new math" introduced into the fourth grade, (2) structured personal interviews intended to bring high school dropouts back to school, and (3) treatment for alcoholics. In these and other examples of evaluation research, typically most of the data on dependent measures would be obtained by the end of one year. Follow-up studies might be conducted over the next several years, but rarely does a program of evaluation research cover more than three years. When projects do cover more than three years, serious problems occur in terms of research design, measurement, and analysis. For example, if the research program concerned periodic application of dependent measures at yearly intervals from age five to age ten, it probably would not be possible to apply the same measure to all those age groups. If a test contained written material at all, it obviously could not be employed with preschoolers. Regardless of the type of test, a test that would be of the right difficulty level for five-year-olds would be trivially easy for ten-year-olds. Many other severe problems occur in studies that span more than about three years. Such studies are developmental, in that they concern significant portions of the lives of the subjects. Extensive discussions concerning many aspects of the methodology of developmental research are presented in Nesselroade and Reese (1972).

Numbers of observations. A related issue to that of the amount of time over which observations are made is that of the number of observations in an experiment. One could have an experiment that lasted for 10 years but in which only two periods of observation occurred, in a pretest and in a posttest. In contrast, one could have an experiment that lasted only 30 days but in which testing occurred on each day. The reason that it is important to consider the number of observations is that it relates to problems of measurement and research design. Regarding the former, if the same measure is used over and over, there are quite likely to be "practice effects" of various kinds. Regarding experimental design, some of the quasi-experimental designs to be discussed later require numerous observations (applications of dependent measures) to help rule out potentially confounding variables. Also, as will be discussed later, in some types of research there are advantages to having only one observation period, after experimental treatments have been applied.

Experimental Designs

As mentioned above, true experimental designs form the backbone of science. Some important issues concerning experimental designs in evaluation research are discussed as follows.

Assignment of subjects. In the behavioral sciences, the bedrock essential for any true experimental design is the random assignment of subjects to treatment conditions. The design may entail only one independent variable, such as (1) presence or absence of a particular type of instruction in mathematics, (2) different levels of a particular drug administered to depressive patients, or (3) four levels of practice on a learning task. In practice, the number of levels on an independent variable range from two (usually a comparison of a treatment condition with a control condition) up to eight or more. The design may entail a number of independent variables rather than only one, such as a factorial design with (1) three levels of amount of practice, (2) four levels of amount of problem difficulty, and (3) five amounts of delay before testing for retention.

However simple or complex the design, the essence of the true experimental design is that the available pool of subjects is randomly sorted into the various cells. The only restriction usually employed in this regard is that an equal number of people be placed into each cell. By the process of randomly assigning people to cells of the design (as with a table of random numbers), some of the cells will be filled before others, which necessitates ignoring these cells and allocating the remaining subjects in a random manner to cells not yet filled. This process of randomization requires first, a statement of the experimental design, and second, a designation of the total group of subjects available. The designation of the group available is not so much a matter of sampling, in the statistical sense, as it is of defining the population over which the results can be generalized. A typical group defined in this way is that of the first 100 students in Introductory Psychology who sign up for an experiment as part of a course requirement to participate in research. If the experiment concerned a simple 2 x 2 factorial design, then 25 students would be randomly placed in each of the four cells of the design. Then, the implicit intention is to obtain results that are generalizable to college students of the same *kind,* although one might not be able to say specifically what that meant.

A possibility that has been mentioned by various authors is that of improving on sheer randomization by matching the subjects in various cells of an experimental design in terms of some variable that is likely to be important for the outcome, for example, matching subjects on level of intelligence before comparing them on two methods of learning arithmetic. Such matching might reduce the amount of experimental error; however, it would be feasible only in very simple experimental designs, for example, comparing an experimental group with a control group. Even in that case, it would hardly be worth the trouble unless the number of subjects available was quite limited, for example, less than 20 subjects for each cell of the design. The possibility of matching subjects in this way is mentioned only in passing with respect to true experimental designs because it is mentioned both seriously and actually used in practice with some of the quasi-experimental designs discussed later.

Of course, the beauty of randomly assigning subjects to cells of an experimental design is that the procedure *absolutely guarantees* that subjects will not differ on the average with respect to any characteristic more than could be expected by chance alone prior to participation in experimental treatments. By "chance alone" is meant the probability distributions associated with the random sorting of subjects into treatment cells. Thus, the subjects in an investigation of methods of training in arithmetic would vary in terms of height, intelligence, social class, personality characteristics, and many other human traits before being introduced to experimental treatments. After being randomly allocated to cells of the design, subjects would still vary within cells with respect to all such human traits; and the sheer act of randomly allocating subjects would lead to a predictable amount of variation in average values of these traits over the cells of experimental designs. However, the randomization process would ensure that there were no systematic influences tending to make the average value of any extraneous variable higher in one cell than in another. Also, the random fluctuations that occur because of the process of sorting people into cells are taken account of in methods of statistics used to analyze results of the experiment.

Comparison groups. The most important consideration with respect to experimental designs is the groups that are compared. The simplest of all possible true experimental designs is that in which the available pool of subjects is randomly sorted into two groups; one group is given the treatment and the other is not, and dependent measures are applied after the treatment to both groups. Following the lead of Campbell (e.g., Campbell and Stanley, 1968), a capital O will be used to stand for an observation or period of testing, and an X will be used to represent some type of treatment. This design can be symbolized as follows:

$$X \; O_a$$
$$O_b$$

The two randomly selected groups are referred to as a and b, respectively. With this type of symbolism, each row represents a different group (or cell) in the experimental design. Although this is a very simple design, it has many virtues. It is probably used more widely than any other for evaluation research. An example would be that of taking a group of 100 mentally retarded preschool children and randomly dividing them into a treatment group and a control group. The treatment group would be given a variety of forms of stimulus enrichment, for example, numerous toys that lead to the discovery of simple principles concerning physical reality. These special experiences would be withheld from the control group. The observation (posttest) would consist of achievement test scores, quantitative skills, and other topics at the end of the first grade. The goal of the treatment would be to enhance learning rates during the first grade.

The posttest-only design can easily be extended to any number (k) of treatments:

$$X_a \quad O_a$$
$$X_b \quad O_b$$
$$X_c \quad O_c$$
$$\cdot \qquad \cdot$$
$$\cdot \qquad \cdot$$
$$\cdot \qquad \cdot$$
$$X_k \quad O_k$$
$$O_1$$

An example of a posttest-only design having multiple treatments would be that in which different types of stimulus enrichment were given to different, randomly determined groups of mental retardates (e.g., passive stimulus enrichment versus active opportunity to manipulate objects), and these in turn were compared with a control group. In some cases the term "control group" is a misnomer because it implies that no experiences relative to the dependent variable (observation) occur at all during the time that the experimental groups are receiving their respective treatments. The logic of the posttest-only design is the same regardless of the number of treatment conditions or independent variables.

The posttest-only design can easily be extended to accommodate more than one independent variable. For example, a factorial design could manipulate the effects of different kinds of practice and amounts of practice on the development of motor coordination in young children.

Rather than a posttest only, a method that has been advocated and frequently used in evaluation research is that with a pretest as well as a posttest. An example would be evaluating the effectiveness of a series of films on health care with a questionnaire. Typical questions would be: "How frequently do you brush your teeth each day?" and "Approximately how many carbonated drinks do you consume each week?" All of the types of designs that can be employed with the posttest-only design also can be employed in a situation where both a pretest and a posttest are obtained. In a true experimental design, the available group of subjects would be randomly allocated to the various treatment conditions.

Potentially, the major advantage of the pretest-posttest design is that it allows one to obtain more information (statistical power) than would be true for a posttest-only design. The potential advantages could be important when (1) the number of subjects in each cell necessarily is small, (2) subjects vary widely with respect to the dependent measure in comparison to anticipated effects of the independent variables, and (3) the correlation within cells of before and after measures of dependent variables are expected to be high. All of these conditions would hold in the following circumstances. Methods are investigated for increasing the IQs of children in highly impoverished city areas. Three methods of training are to be compared with one another and with a control group. Because of the amount of time and funds required to undertake each of the three special training programs (treatments), it is feasible to have no more than about 50 children for each group. A total group of 200 children then is randomly divided into three treatment groups and a control group. It is important to determine not only the statistical significance of differences among the groups but also to precisely document the exact amounts of such differences. Consequently, it is necessary for experimental error to be reduced to the very minimum possible. The pretest shows that the average measured IQ is 85; more important, it is found that the standard deviation of the scores is large (about that of the normative population as a whole). Although it is hypothesized that the treatments will produce improvements over the control group and perhaps have different average effects from one another, it is anticipated that there will be a rather high correlation between pretest and posttest measures *within* each of the groups (e.g., on the order of .70 or higher). Because the research problem has all of the characteristics mentioned above, indicating the need for a pretest-posttest design, such a design definitely should be employed in this case.

In contrast to the above example, it usually is *unwise* to employ a pretest-posttest design rather than employ a posttest-design only. In most evaluation research, all three of the above circumstances that encourage one to use a pretest-posttest design are not present. Frequently the standard deviation of pretest measures is not large in comparison to the expected effects of treatments and/or the correlation between pretest and posttest measures is not high. These conditions probably would hold in comparing the effects of different drugs on the moods of depressed patients in mental hospitals. Most patients would rate themselves as rather glum, and there would not be a large standard deviation in that regard. Pretest and posttest measures probably would not correlate highly, both because of the small standard deviation on each occasion, and because moods tend to fluctuate in all people from day to day.

Most important, in the above and most other types of evaluation research, the available group of subjects is not so limited in number as to require the time and expense of applying a pretest and of encountering a very real hazard. The hazard mentioned above is that of employing an experimental arrangement in which the pretest *sensitizes* subjects to some aspects of the forthcoming treatment condition. An example would be that previously mentioned of studying the effectiveness of a series of films on health care. If the pretests were administered soon before subjects viewed the films, the questionnaire itself would alert subjects to look for and retain information relative to the questions. An example would be the case in which part of a film stressed the importance of brushing teeth at least three times a day, including after lunch. One can imagine the impact this would have on an individual who indicated in the pretest that he only brushed his teeth twice a day, or less. On receiving the advice that it was very important to brush teeth after lunch, the respondent is likely to have taken special note of this in the light of his previous responses to the questionnaire.

An even more blatant example of the sensitization (interaction) of the pretest with the treatment condition would be where the films concerned racial prejudice. In the context of a love story, the film might entail a subtle presentation of the difficulties of Mexican-Americans in this country. Members of the audience might not fully grasp all of the subtle effects of ethnic prejudice shown in the film. However, if only the day before they were required to respond to questionnaires concerning their own feelings and beliefs about Mexican-Americans, they probably would be much more alert to issues regarding prejudice in the films. Whereas such effects are referred to as sensitization, more generally they should be spoken of as interaction of pretest and treatment. Although in some types of research this interaction has predictable effects, in others the effect might be quite surprising. In any case where the treatment concerns an increase in knowledge, the interaction should result in more improvement from the treatment then would occur if a posttest only were administered. In other cases, however, the effect might be very difficult to predict. An example would be that of a series of films intended to improve attitudes toward life in the armed forces. A pretest might not only sensitize people to the content of the films, but also have a boomerang effect. The pretest might have alerted subjects to the effort to manipulate their attitudes by use of the films, thus causing them to resist any changes in that regard, or even move toward more negative positions.

Potentially another problem with the pretest-posttest design is that the two testings will interact, which is usually referred to as a "practice effect." However, in most instances this is not a serious problem. In many cases the degree of such practice effects is known from previous studies, and known to be slight. This is true in the illustrative experiment concerning the measurement of intelligence before and after treatments. If a no-treatment control group is employed, interactions of measures (and also natural changes over time) can be separated out from the treatment effects. Also, in some types of research it is possible to employ alternate forms of a measuring instrument which at least partly rule out practice effects. This would be true in the study concerning intelligence if there were two forms available for the test. In the pretest, half of the subjects in each treatment group could receive one test and the other half would receive the other test. In the posttest, subjects would receive the alternate form. This would supply all of the information necessary to separate the major component of practice effects from the treatment effects.

Research designs have been developed which further provide information about interaction of pretests with treatments and interactions of pretests with posttests. One such design is as follows:

$$0_{a1} \quad X_a \quad 0_{a2}$$
$$X_b \quad 0_{b2}$$
$$0_{c1} \quad \quad 0_{c2}$$
$$0_{d2}$$

In the first row of the design, we have a complete pretest-posttest treatment in which measures are administered before and after. In the second row the same treatment is applied, but there is a posttest only. The third row represents a control group in which both pretests and posttests are given, but there is no intervening treatment. The fourth row symbolizes a condition in which only a posttest is given. The subscripts on observations indicate the time at which the observations (dependent measures) are taken. A comparison of the group in row 1 with that in row 2 would indicate the size of the interaction of pretest with treatment. A comparison of results from groups depicted in rows 3 and 4 would indicate the degree of interaction between pretests and posttests. If the mean posttest scores are not very different for the two groups, it indicates that the interaction was slight. If the mean difference on posttest measures for the two treatment conditions was slight, the data could be pooled. If mean differences on the posttest measure were small for the two control groups, the data could be combined. A simple comparison then could be made of the pooled treatment data with the pooled control data. This would lead to a very simple test of the difference between the treatment condition and the control condition. However, if differences within treatment groups and/or within control groups are relatively large, then the situation becomes rather messy. In particular, if the differences within the two types of groups are not very similar, the results become largely uninterpretable.

Rather than waste more time on the topic, it is better to say that such elaborate designs as those depicted above for testing artifacts in pretest-posttest designs are definitely not worth the trouble. If the experimenter has enough subjects available and resources that are required by elaborate designs like the four-group design above, then it would be utterly foolish to use the pretest-posttest design rather than the posttest-only design. In that case there would be no interaction of pretests with treatments or interactions of pretests with posttests. Not to employ the posttest-only design would be as foolish as the individual with a chronic ailment who bought only half of the medicine prescribed for his illness so that he could pay for many visits to the doctor's office in order to learn in precise detail about his deteriorating condition.

In summary, the posttest-only design is the workhorse of evaluation research, and with certain exceptions, should remain so. Pretest-posttest designs should be used only when the three conditions discussed above prevail and there is reason to believe that pretest treatment interactions and pretest-posttest interactions are slight. Pretest-posttest interactions can be reduced considerably in some instances by employing alternative forms of measuring instruments, but it is very difficult to reduce appreciably pretest-treatment interactions.

Methods of analysis. There are no major problems in analyzing the results of true experiments in evaluation research. Whether the pretest-posttest design or the posttest-only design is employed, an abundance of statistical methods are available (e.g., those discussed by Kirk, 1968, and by Winer, 1971). Indeed, it is easy to get the feeling that the statistical machinery is overly elegant for the data we frequently feed into it. Generally speaking, heavy reliance is placed on the linear model in statistics, which considers variance manifested in an independent variable as being decomposable into uncorrelated additive components respectively concerning (1) treatment effects, (2) their interactions, (3) interaction of subjects and observations in a repeated measurements design, and (4) a residual component attributable to experimental error.

The first step in analyzing data from true experimental designs usually is to perform an overall analysis of variance to test for significance of main effects and interactions. This is no problem at all in the posttest-only design. In the pretest-posttest design, a problem (usually slight) occurs because of possible correlated errors from pretest to posttest. For example, people might tend to repeat some test-taking strategies from the first to the second testing, such as the tendency to guess when in doubt rather than be conservative in that regard. Such correlated errors would tend to increase the correlation between pretests and posttests, and thus reduce the error term below what it would be if such practice effects were not present. This is not a major problem because (1) there is little reason to believe that such correlated errors occur on most measures and (2) the research results should be taken seriously only if they are significant at a level which leaves little room to worry about such small artifacts.

As so many people have said over the last decade, tests of statistical significance alone provide only the most meager form of evidence regarding the results of experiments. To issue this warning again here should be on the order of attacking a straw man, but unfortunately there are still many research workers who overly glorify the importance of "hypothesis testing" with inferential statistics. Tests of statistical significance alone are best regarded as "wastebasket tests"; that is, if the data do not measure up in this regard, it probably would be better to toss the data sheets into the wastebasket than to try to make sense of them in any other way. Beyond providing comfort that *something* happened as a function of the treatments, such significant tests provide very little information indeed.

If data survive the wastebasket test, then three additional types of information should be obtained. First, if the independent variable(s) are on an ordered metric, then tests for various trends should be made. By an ordered metric is meant an independent variable measurable on a rank-order scale, an interval scale, or a ratio scale. Examples on an interval scale would be intelligence test scores and ratings of attitudes toward the United Nations. Of course, analysis of variance designs frequently entail dependent variables that are not in terms of an ordered metric, such as comparisons of people from different occupations and comparisons of the effects of different types of drugs. If the independent and dependent variables are expressed in terms of an ordered metric, it is important to learn to what extent the trend is linear, quadratic, or otherwise. Also, the percentages of variance explained by the different trends provide very important information. Thus, if the linear trend explains 90% of the variation of the means of treatment groups and higher order components explain only the remaining 10%, this means that the trend can be spoken of as essentially linear.

The second type of analysis which should be performed in many cases is that of asserting statistical confidence bands about mean effects. This procedure might indicate, for example, that the odds are 99 out of 100 that the learning rate produced by one method of instruction is at least 50% better than that produced by another method of instruction. The logic and technique of developing such confidence bands are discussed in most advanced books on statistics (e.g., Kirk, 1968, and Winer, 1971).

The third thing one should do in addition to running tests of statistical significance is to compute various indices showing the strength of relationship between independent and dependent variables. A simple example would be that of comparing a treatment group with a control group, in which a t test shows that the two are significantly different. Although the test of significance would provide some assurance regarding the genuineness of the apparent difference, it would not necessarily provide any information at all about the amount of difference between the treatment group and the control group. The amount of difference could be obtained by the point-biserial correlation. It would mean a great deal of difference whether this correlation were, say, .60 rather than .20. The major measures employed to document the degree of relationship between independent and dependent variables are all variants of the product-moment correlation coefficient. These methods can be applied not only to the simple situation of comparing a control group with a treatment group, but also to any number of levels of a treatment group and to any number of combinations of such independent variables in a factorial design. These methods are discussed by Kirk (1968) and by Winer (1971).

Quasi-experimental Designs

As mentioned previously, essentially a quasi-experimental design is one in which some potentially important confounding variables are not controlled. It was said that essentially what one does in this situation is to obtain extra information (over that which would be obtained from a true experimental design) in order to weave a net of circumstantial evidence regarding the "reality" of observed findings. Evaluation research usually takes place in the crucible of ongoing important life activities of individuals, and consequently it frequently is either unethical or unfeasible to randomly divide subjects up for treatments or to do other things that would be needed to obtain precise experimental control. Here an effort will be made to summarize some of the most important considerations from the writings of Campbell and his associates; also, the author will state some opinions of his own regarding the nature of quasi-experimental designs and their place in evaluation research.

Pre-experimental designs. To place in focus principles underlying quasi-experimental designs, Campbell and Stanley (1968) present three pre-experimental designs. The lack of experimental control in these designs is so obvious that it points up the need to provide additional information before any conclusions can be reached from research. A very crude form of pre-experimental design is as follows:

$$X \quad O$$

In the design, some type of treatment is applied and subsequently observations are made. An example would be that of introducing a new food supplement program in elementary schools for children in impoverished areas. At the end of the school year, children are given brief medical examinations to index general health and freedom from various symptoms of disorder. On the basis of such statistics and ratings, it is concluded that the children are in reasonably good health (a conclusion, of course, which cries out for a normative comparison with children in general of the same age group). On the basis of this impressionistic information, the researchers conclude (incorrectly, of course) that the food supplement program has actually benefited the children's health. The possible rival hypotheses relating to confounding variables are quite obvious. First, as mentioned, measurements taken at the observation period would have no meaningful basis of comparison in this case. However, in some uses of this pre-experimental design, comparison bases are available either in terms of norms or at least in terms of the impressions of the experimenters. Regarding the former possibility, norms for general health might have been available from a national survey or at least a sample throughout a geographic region. Similarly, in other uses of this pre-experimental design, there may be considerable normative data available, for example, in the form of standardized tests of achievement in various topics. When such standardized bases of comparison are not available, the "experimenters" frequently have some impressionistic standards in their heads. This probably would have been the case with the study of changes in general health as a function of nutritional supplements. The physicians performing the physical examinations probably were comparing the children in the study with children from the same socioeconomic environments who had not participated in the experimental program of food supplements. However, such comparisons are shaky at best, for reasons too obvious to merit detailed discussion.

A second fault of the above pre-experimental design is that it provides no evidence regarding the crucial issue of whether or not the treatment had any effect on the dependent variable(s). To reach any safe conclusions at all in that regard, the necessary starting point would be at least to add a pretest. This leads to the second pre-experimental design:

$$O_1 \quad X \quad O_2$$

The major uncontrolled variable in the second pre-experimental design is that of natural changes as a function of time and events, rather than by the experimental treatment per se. There are numerous ways in which this can occur. For example, in a study of the effectiveness of communication programs concerning birth planning, any evaluation research that ranged over several years might be confounded by changes in attitudes of young people that had nothing at all to do with the communication programs. Psychological dispositions in that regard have been so cyclic over the last 40 years that natural changes over periods of several years would constitute potentially important confounding influences. Even over shorter periods of time, rapid changes frequently occur in the social milieu, which could induce large changes from pretest to posttest measures regardless of intervening experimental treatments. An example would be that of studying the effectiveness of group discussions on attitudes toward various aspects of an ongoing war. The pretest is given while the war is still on, treatments concerning group discussions go on over a period of two months, but a cease-fire is signed the day before posttest measures are to be given. The possible confound would be painfully obvious to the experimenter.

A second rival hypothesis concerning the one group, pretest-posttest design, concerns possible regression toward the mean. This condition would exist if the group of subjects being investigated had been preselected either on the pretest independent variable or on some variable that correlated substantially with the pretest variable. The former would be the case if children for a training program in remedial reading were selected initially in terms of their low scores on a reading achievement test and the same test was used for the posttest measure. The second possibility is illustrated in the situation where the children are selected not on the basis of the reading achievement test but on the basis of low scores on an IQ test. Because the two types of tests would correlate substantially, the experimental group would be well below average on reading comprehension as well as IQ. In either case, it is expected that there will be a regression toward the mean when subjects are selected because they are above or below average with respect to the pretest and posttest measures. This matter was discussed in detail earlier in this chapter and in *Psychometric Theory*. In addition to the two faults discussed above of this type of design, it also suffers from all of the problems concerning pretest-posttest designs mentioned with respect to true experiments. To reiterate, the major confounding variables are interaction of pretest with treatment and interaction of the two testings with each other.

A third type of experimental design employs a control group at the posttest period only, but the two groups involved are not formed randomly from some larger group. Instead, the groups were intact before the experiment was undertaken. This design can be symbolized as follows, with a dashed line between the rows representing the two groups signifying intact groups rather than randomly sampled groups.

$$\underline{X} \; - \; - \; \underline{O_a} \atop O_b$$

Examples of this type of pre-experimental design are legion in evaluation research. An example is that of trying out a new program of dormitory counseling for students at a college. There are two large men's dormitories available for the study. The counseling program is undertaken throughout one semester in one dormitory, and no changes are made in the other dormitory. Afterward dependent measures are administered concerning progress in school, self-ratings, and peer-ratings of various kinds.

An obvious rival hypothesis with this type of design is that men in the two dormitories differed initially with respect to the traits involved in the dependent measures. There are many ways in which this could happen. For example, it might be that the entire football team was housed in one of the dormitories. Campbell and Stanley (1968) mentioned a number of other confounding variables in this type of design, for example, possible differences between the two groups because of more willingness of the members of one group to participate in the research.

It is necessary to carefully distinguish between experiments comparing *intact* groups and ones that will be discussed later concerning *contrasted* groups. In studying intact groups, at least the intention is to compare groups that are approximately comparable with respect to traits involved in the dependent measures. Thus, in the previous example, by applying the treatment to one section of a course rather than another, it is hoped that the students in the two groups do not differ markedly on the average in terms of traits relating to the dependent variable. In many instances, this is a reasonable assumption; consequently, one should not rule out altogether evidence coming from this pre-experimental design. As will be discussed more fully later, contrasted groups are selected *because* it is thought that they differ markedly with respect to some important psychological traits.

From pre-experimental to quasi-experimental designs. Of course, if there were no practical or ethical problems involved, the wise experimenter always would change or extend the previously mentioned and other pre-experimental designs into true experimental designs. Illustrative of the fact that this is not always practicable is the situation in which it would be necessary to isolate schoolchildren from one another in their training in different methods of teaching foreign languages. To make comparisons among intact groups in the usual classroom situation might result in "group effects" where the feelings of children were communicated to one another, and this in turn influenced dependent measures. However, the alternative of giving separate instruction to each student in isolation from the others probably would be completely out of the question in terms of manpower and other resources.

That the employment of a true experimental design is not always ethical is evidenced in a study of two types of memorization tasks in deaf and normal children. It goes without saying that the experimenter would not take a large group of normal children and randomly deafen half of them in order to ensure that the niceties of true experimental designs were obtained. In these instances, and other instances that are far less obvious, it is necessary to employ quasi-experimental designs. Campbell and his associates have discussed numerous principles regarding a wide variety of such designs (e.g., Campbell and Stanley, 1968). Here only several major issues will be discussed.

One of the major problems incurred in research is the inability to achieve a true experimental design by the random assignment of subjects to groups. Previously, it was mentioned that some pre-experimental designs require the use of intact groups. As mentioned there, these problems frequently are not serious unless subjects are preselected on the dependent variable or on measures that correlate substantially with the dependent variable. Real problems arise, however, when the groups being compared are known to differ markedly in at least some traits. Examples of that would be comparing deaf with normals, males with females, mental hospital patients with persons outside, and groups from different countries. If a posttest-only design is used with such contrasted groups, differences on the posttest quite likely are because of initial differences among the groups rather than anything having to do with experimental treatments. A statistician could argue that it is absolutely hopeless to perform impeccable research by making comparisons among such groups. However, the problems will not go away simply because they pose problems for research. If the person actually is interested in differences among such contrasted groups, he must make comparisons among them and apply as many safeguards as possible against the intrusion of confounding variables.

The simplest type of design for contrasted groups is that in which the only "treatment" consists of group membership, and the members of each group are tested with respect to some attribute of interest. An example would be that of comparing political attitudes of people in different occupations, which would be symbolized as follows:

$$O_a$$
$$O_b$$
$$O_c$$
.

.

.

$$O_k$$

Differences in scores obtained for the above k groups could be submitted to analysis of variance and other types of statistical comparisons. If one is interested in differences in psychological traits of occupational groups or any other groups, then such comparisons are straightforward. However, because the groups differ from one another in so many ways, it might be very difficult to determine *why* the groups differ on the trait-being investigated. Also, the groups may differ from one another because of artifacts in the measurement procedures rather than because of any real differences among them. For example, if white interviewers interview both black and white adults regarding political attitudes, the presence of the white interviewer might make the black respondents give answers that are not representative of their true feelings. As another example, mental patients may show differences from normal persons in terms of various types of perceptual tasks, not because they really are deficient in their perceptual abilities, but because they are anxious and are distracted by their own personal problems. There are many other artifacts of measurement that could produce illusory differences among contrasted groups.

If the evaluation research concerns differences among contrasted groups when no treatment condition is applied, the major safeguard is to weave a network of circumstantial evidence over time regarding hypothesized differences. One should be quite chary of differences obtained in one setting with only one type of measure of an attribute. Thus, one should place very little faith in the comparison of one group of schizophrenic patients with one group of normal subjects on only one measure relating to perceptual accuracy. If essentially the same finding is obtained in other locales, and comparisons are made on a wide variety of measures concerning perceptual accuracy; then the circumstantial evidence accumulates to the point where considerable confidence can be placed in the tenability of the hypothesis at issue. In essence, when contrasted groups differ so markedly as deaf from normal and schizophrenic from normal, it is necessary to establish a type of construct validity, not unlike that discussed in the previous chapter with respect to the development of measures of psychological traits.

A research method that has been employed frequently in comparing the effects of treatments on contrasted groups is to match subjects from the two groups on one or more variables. An example would be that of a new method of teaching reading skills in the first grade in which a comparison is made of the amount of progress shown by children from a highly impoverished city area with children from a much more affluent area of the same city. A pretest shows that the average level of reading skill is very different for the two groups before the special method of instruction is applied. The experimenter puts children from the two groups in pairs such that their scores on the test of reading comprehension are very similar. In this way, the experimenter obtains two groups that have very similar average scores on the pretest and very similar standard deviations. This could be a disastrous approach to studying the issue. By matching subjects in this way, the experimenter would be selecting children with comparatively high reading scores in the lower socioeconomic group and children with comparatively low reading scores in the higher socioeconomic group. Then, purely because of measurement error in the test, there would be a regression toward the mean on the posttest. This would make it appear that the children from the lower socioeconomic group actually lost ground in terms of reading skills, and that the children from the higher socioeconomic group gained considerably. These would be the expected results regardless of any intervening treatment, and such regression effects could either produce artifactually significant findings from the experiment or at least muddy the waters considerably. There are many other problems that arise from attempts to match subjects in different treatment groups, or in treatment and control groups, for example, the unanswerable question as to whether subjects have been matched on *all* of the major possible confounding variables. When the experiment does not concern contrasted groups, matching usually is not worth the effort. When the experiment concerns contrasted groups, matching is a very hazardous practice that is definitely not recommended. Far better is to try to take account of initial differences between contrasted groups by research designs and methods of analysis discussed subsequently.

In some situations where either intact or contrasted groups are compared, observations are available on a number of occasions before the treatment and after the treatment. Essentially, the advantage of having multiple observations before and/or after the treatment is that it provides an indication of the amount of normal variation in the phenomenon from time to time, irrespective of a treatment condition. An example would be that of comparing the achievement test scores in mathematics in the third through seventh grade for children in two schools in the same community. The study is performed retroactively for students who currently are in the seventh grade and have remained in schools from the third grade up to that time. In one of the schools (A), a new approach to teaching mathematics was introduced throughout the fifth grade, but this was not done in the other school (B). Because the achievement test is given routinely each year, there is no problem in having comparable measurements available for each of the five years. Some possible types of results are shown in Figures 10.3 through 10.5. Evidence for a treatment effect when there are multiple observations before and after the treatment over time consists of a sharp interaction from before to after the treatment for the two or more groups being compared, as seen in Figure 10.3. In Figure 10.4, the apparent change in school A is illusory because it is matched by a proportional change in school B. Rather than the treatment having any particular effect, the steepening curve probably is because of other (unknown) changes in instruction and general social milieu of the two schools. Another possibility is that the national norms for the test in question were obtained somewhat differently than in previous years, in such a way as to increase the apparent competence of students in these two schools in comparison to the national norms.

The results in Figure 10.4 suggest that the treatment had no effect at all on the students in school A beyond what would be expected from the usual instruction, as evidenced in school B. In Figure 10.5 such a sharp interaction is witnessed at the end of the fifth grade, but the increase in average performance shown for school A at the end of the fifth grade dwindles back to approximately the same level as before the treatment by the time testing is performed at the end of the seventh grade. This strongly suggests that the special training had only a temporary effect, and in the long-run the students in school A would have been as well off to have received the same training as students in school B. Of course, in a situation where there are multiple observations before and after testing, there are many other such results that would not have been nearly as clear as those depicted in Figures 10.3 through 10.5. Unless striking results are obtained like those depicted in the figures, usually it is quite hazardous to make any firm interpretations at all of studies concerning intact or contrasted groups.

In some evaluation research, no control condition at all is available for comparing effects of the treatment. This would be the case in the previous example if data were available only for school A. Studies where pre- and post-measures are available on a number of occasions before and after the experiment are referred to as *time-series experiments.* Usually when the name is employed, one has available at least three or more sets of observations before and after the experimental treatment. A typical design would be as follows:

$$O_1 \quad O_2 \quad O_3 \quad O_4 \quad X \quad O_5 \quad O_6 \quad O_7 \quad O_8$$

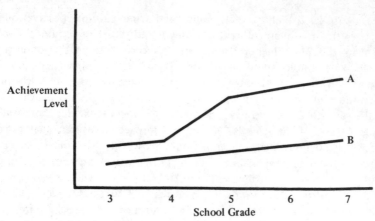

Figure 10.3   Comparison of an experimental group (A) with a control group (B) which indicates that the treatment had a definite effect.

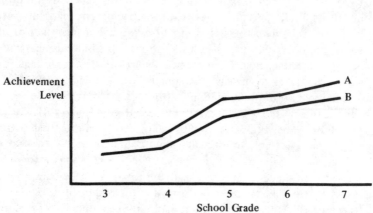

Figure 10.4   Comparison of an experimental group (A) with a control group (B) in which the apparent effect of the treatment is illusory.

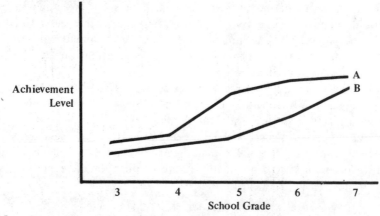

Figure 10.5   Comparison of an experimental group (A) with a control group (B) in which the treatment effect was only temporary.

Some of the many possible results from examining this time-series are depicted in Figure 10.6. In condition a, the curve goes up from before to after the treatment; but it was going up at the same rate before the treatment and continues up at the same rate after the treatment. Consequently, there is no reason to believe that the treatment had any effect. Curve b also goes up from before to after the treatment, but the variations both before and after treatment provide no confidence that the apparent treatment effect is real. In condition c, there is circumstantial evidence that the apparent increase from before to after the treatment is "real." However, since the curve goes back down to the same level as before the treatment, any effects of the treatment apparently were quite temporary. Strong circumstantial evidence for the occurrence of a treatment effect is presented in condition d.

For reasons which were discussed previously, the time-series experiments, without any form of comparison group (intact group or contrasted group), provide at best only very rough circumstantial evidence for a treatment effect. With any one-group experiment, many rival hypotheses are available to explain results. If there is only a pretest or a pretest and posttest, so many rival hypotheses are available that such designs are referred to as pre-experimental. When only a treatment group is available and no comparisons can be made either with an intact group or even a contrasted group, then no amount of observation before and after will permit the experimenter to reach strong conclusions about the results.

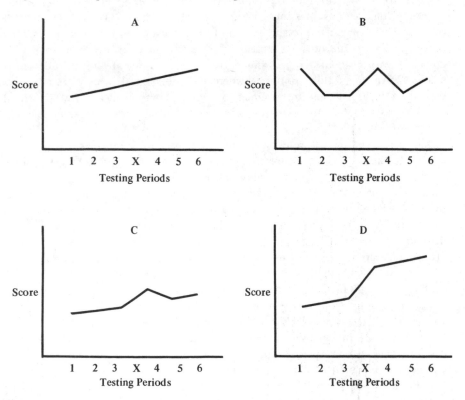

Figure 10.6   Four different types of results that could be obtained from a time-series study.

Methods of analysis. Whereas statistical methods for the analysis of true experiments generally are straightforward, methods of analysis for quasi-experimental designs are controversial in many cases. Methods for analyzing quasi-experimental designs are discussed in detail by Campbell and Stanley (1968); only some of the major principles will be discussed here. The better quasi-experimental designs have two features, which we will assume to be the case in discussing methods of analysis. First, there is a control group, which, however, usually consists of an intact similar group or a purposefully drawn contrasted group rather than a random sample of available subjects. Second, observations are made before and after the treatment on both the treatment group(s) and the control group. In some cases there may be more than one observation before and after the treatment is applied.

When either an intact group or a contrasted group is employed as a control group (or as one of two or more treatment groups), there is always the possibility that groups differ from one another on the pretest measure before treatments are applied. Examples were given previously of how this could be so. It has been recommended that covariance analysis (COVARAN) be used as a general tool for partialing out the effects of pretest differences on posttest differences. Covariance analysis actually has been employed for that purpose in many quasi-experimental designs.

At the present state of knowledge about the use of COVARAN, it is a *distinct mistake* to employ this method of analysis with quasi-experimental designs. First, there are some serious questions regarding the meaning of COVARAN in any type of statistical analysis. For example, even if the pretest measure can be partialed out of the results of the posttest measure, how does one control for variables which correlate with both the pretest and posttest variable but are not included in the analysis? An illustration would be where the pretest and posttest measure concerned an experiment on improvement of reading comprehension. Two classrooms are used as intact groups for the experiment, one classroom receiving a special treatment, the other acting as a control group. COVARAN is used to adjust for initial differences in the pretest measure for analysis of differences on the posttest measures. However, if the groups differ substantially with regard to reading comprehension initially, they also probably differ with respect to general intelligence. Then, if the pretest measure of reading comprehension is statistically held constant by COVARAN from the posttest measure, the two groups still could differ substantially in terms of average IQ. The sheer difference in IQ could affect differences between groups on the posttest measure even if the effect due to the pretest measure were held constant. Several questions of this kind arise about the logic of COVARAN and its use in all types of experimentation.

The second problem with the use of COVARAN with quasi-experimental designs is that the assumptions are frequently violated. A cardinal assumption is that the within-groups regression slope is the same for all groups. This assumption is quite likely to be false in comparing intact groups and even more so in contrasted groups, for example, in comparing pretest and posttest scores for normal persons and schizophrenic mental patients after both have participated in a treatment concerning training of motor skills. There are many reasons the regression slope might be different in the two groups, for example, there could be an "end effect" in normals because the task is so easy that many subjects make the highest score possible, which in turn would tend to produce a nonlinear scatter plot and thus a reduced linear regression slope.

A third reason COVARAN should not be used in quasi-experimental designs is that there is quite a hassle about how to take account of measurement error (test reliability) in employing this class of statistical methods. This matter is discussed and illustrated by Werts and Linn (1971). The problem is that, if some correction due to measurement error is not made, then COVARAN undercorrects the posttest measure for differences in the pretest measure. If the reliabilities are far from unity (e.g., less than .90), either some type of correction for measurement error must be made or the statistical results obviously will be fallacious. Also, as Werts and Linn demonstrate (1971), the distortion may either result in an overly liberal or overly conservative statistical test of the differences between comparison groups.

Unfortunately, the experts are still arguing about how to adjust statistical parameters of COVARAN to take account of measurement error. Even if a logically acceptable solution were found, it apparently would entail the gathering of considerable data regarding the measurement error inherent in the pretest and posttest. Data of this kind usually are not available in most evaluation research, which means that the research time and effort would be increased considerably to gather this new information. Even if data concerning measurement of reliability were available from previous investigations, it would be hazardous to use such data because reliability coefficients might be different in previous research from those in the study at hand. Also, unless the data obtained from a previous study or from the study being conducted were based on a large number of subjects (e.g., at least 300), the reliability coefficients would be ridden with sampling error, and consequently any corrections based upon the reliability coefficients would provide rather poor estimates.

There is a much better general approach to analyzing quasi-experimental designs than COVARAN. The approach consists of considering differences between pretest and posttest measures as constituting a within-subjects factor in repeated measurements analysis of variance designs. Comparisons of treatments with one another and/or with a control group could also be a within-subjects factor, but usually this is a between-groups factor instead. Thus, the usual quasi-experimental design entails a within-subjects, repeated measurements factor, and a between-groups factor or factors. The major result of interest is the *interaction of treatment conditions with comparison groups*. A very simple example is presented in Figure 10.7. Here we have an imperfect control group, in the sense that an intact group happens to differ substantially on the pretest from the treatment group, or a contrasted group purposefully is chosen. In this case, imagine that standard deviations within groups on the pretest measure are small relative to the mean difference, hence the difference is statistically significant and large in terms of amount of variance explained. Rather than try to covary these differences, it is better to examine the interaction of the two groups with pretest and posttest measures. Although the two groups differed substantially on the pretest, they differ much more on the posttest.

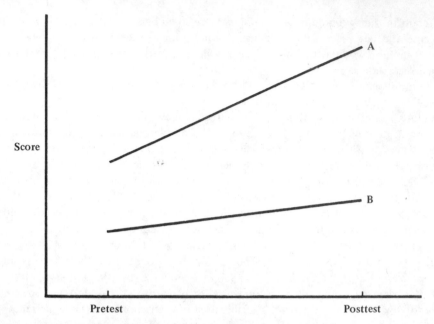

Figure 10.7   Comparison of an experimental group (A) with a control group (B) before and after the experimental treatment.

The interaction variance can be examined straighforwardly for statistical significance (e.g., as discussed in Kirk, 1968; Winer, 1971).

Analyses of more complex experimental designs also usually involve interactions of observations with treatment conditions. A complex example would be that of multiple pretests and posttests in comparing a number of different treatments with a control group. In this case all groups are nonrandomly sampled; rather they are either intact groups or contrasted groups. Differences in average scores over time on the multiple pretests would be evidence of differences in general standings of the groups before the treatment is applied. Interactions of groups and pretest measures would be evidence of different growth functions (differences in maturation or effects of social events on the groups). Similar analysis could be performed on posttest scores. Of most interest, however, would be various interaction terms concerning pretest and posttest scores for the different treatments. Of interest would be interactions of groups with immediate pretest and posttest scores, mean scores over all pretest and posttest occasions, and selective other interaction terms. Tests of significance can be performed on these. However, since a number of such tests might be performed in a post hoc manner depending on the obtained results, it would be wise to be conservative in interpretation of statistical tests, that is, to place faith in only a high level of statistical significance, such as the .01 level or lower probability. Measures of strength of association can be obtained for all main effects and interactions in analysis of variance designs (cf. Winer, 1971: 428-430). Such measures of association will provide suggestions regarding the size of differences among treatment conditions and their implications for the workaday world in which evaluation research is conducted.

REFERENCES

Buros, O. K. *Tests in print.* Highland Park, N.J.: Gryphon Press, 1961.
———. *Seventh Mental Measurements Yearbook.* Highland Park, N.J.: Gryphon Press, 1972.
Campbell, D.T. Reforms as experiments. *American Psychologist,* 1969, 24: 409-429.
Campbell, D. T. and J. C. Stanley. *Experimental and quasi-experimental designs for research.* Chicago: Rand-McNally, fourth printing, 1968.
Cronbach, L. J. and L. Furby. How we should measure "change"—or should we? *Psychological Bulletin,* 1970, 74: 68-80.
Guilford, J. P. *Psychometric methods.* 2nd ed.; New York: McGraw-Hill, 1954.
———. *Personality.* New York: McGraw-Hill, 1959.
Kirk, R. E. *Experimental design: Procedures for the behavioral sciences.* Belmont, Cal.: Wadsworth, 1968.
Lord, F. M. Elementary models for measuring change. In C. W. Harris (ed.) *Problems in measuring change.* Madison: University of Wisconsin Press, 1963.
Nesselroade, J. R. and H. W. Reese (eds.) *Life-span developmental psychology.* New York: Academic Press, 1972.
Nunnally, J. C. *Psychometric theory.* New York: McGraw-Hill, 1967.
———. *Psychometric theory.* 2nd ed. New York: McGraw-Hill, 1978.
———. *Introduction to psychological measurement.* New York: McGraw-Hill, 1970.
———. *Educational measurement and evaluation,* 2nd ed.; New York: McGraw-Hill, 1972.
——— and R. L. Durham. Validity, reliability, and special problems of measurement in evaluation research. In E. L. Struening and M. Guttentag (eds.) *Handbook of evaluation research* (Vol. 1). Beverly Hills, CA: Sage, 1975.
Nunnally, J. C. and W. H. Wilson. Method and theory for developing measures in evaluation research. In E. L. Struening and M. Guttentag (eds.) *Handbook of evaluation research* (Vol.1). Beverly Hills, CA: Sage, 1975.
Webb, E. J., D. T. Campbell, R. D. Schwartz, and L. Sechrest. *Unobtrusive measures: Nonreactive research in the social sciences.* Chicago: Rand-McNally, 1966.
Werts, C. E. and R. L. Linn. Analyzing shool effects ANOVA with a fallible covariate. *Educational and Psychological Measurement,* 1971, 31: 95-104.
Winer, B. J. *Statistical principles in experimental design.* 2nd ed.; New York; McGraw-Hill, 1971.

REFERENCE UPDATE

Selected by Elmer L. Struening

GENERAL ISSUES IN MEASUREMENT

Bass, B. M. The substance and the shadow. *American Psychologist,* 1974, 29 (12): 870-886.
Bejar, I. I. Biased assessment of program impact due to psychometric artifacts. *Psychological Bulletin,* 1980, 87 (3): 513-524.
Blair, J. and R. Czaja. Locating a special population using random digit dialing. *Public Opinion Quarterly,* 1982, 46 (4): 585-590.
Blalock, H. M., Jr. The measurement problem: A gap between the language of theory and research. In H. M. Blalock, Jr., and A. B. Blalock (eds.) *Methodology in social research.* New York: McGraw-Hill, 1978.
Blalock, H. M., Jr. *Conceptualization and measurement in the social sciences.* Beverly Hills, CA: Sage, 1982.
Bohrnstedt, G. W. and E. F. Borgatta (eds.) *Social measurement: Current issues.* Beverly Hills, CA: Sage, 1981.
Bradburn, N. M., S. Sudman, and Associates. *Improving interview method and questionnaire design.* San Francisco: Jossey-Bass, 1980.
Cannell, C., P. Miller, and M. Oskenberg. Research on interviewing techniques. In S. Leimhardt (ed.) *Sociological methodology 1981.* San Francisco: Jossey-Bass, 1981.

Gaito, J. Measurement scales and statistics: Resurgence of an old misconception. *Psychological Bulletin*, 1980, 87 (3): 564-567.

Ghiselli, E. E., J. P. Campbell, and S. Zedeck. *Measurement theory for the behavioral sciences*. San Francisco: W. H. Freeman, 1981.

Heilman, J. Uses of direct and indirect measures: A case study of program impact in the energy conservation field. *Evaluation Review*, 1982, 6 (1): 61-78.

Heise, D. R. Some issues in sociological measurement. In H. L. Costner (ed.) *Sociological methodology 1973-1974*. San Francisco: Jossey-Bass, 1974.

Kish, L. *Survey sampling*. New York: John Wiley, 1965.

Labouvie, E. W. Measurement of individual differences in intraindividual changes. *Psychological Bulletin*, 1980, 88 (1): 54-59.

Lazerwitz. B. Sampling theory and procedures. In H. M. Blalock Jr., and A. B. Blalock (eds.) *Methodology in social research*. New York: McGraw-Hill, 1978.

Messick, S. Constructs and their vicissitudes in educational and psychological measurement. *Psychological Bulletin*, 1981, 89 (3): 575-588.

Milcarek, B. I. and E. L. Struening. Evaluation methodology: A selective bibliography. In E. L. Struening and M. Guttentag (eds.) *Handbook of evaluation research* (Vol. 1) Beverly Hills, CA: Sage, 1975.

Nunnally, J. C. and W. H. Wilson. Method and theory for developing measures in evaluation research. In E. L. Struening and M. Guttentag (eds.) *Handbook of evaluation research* (Vol. 1). Beverly Hills, CA: Sage, 1975.

Orwin, R. G. and R. F. Boruch. RRT meets RDD: Statistical strategies for assuring response privacy in telephone surveys. *Public Opinion Quarterly*, 1982, 46 (4): 560-571.

Schuman, H. and O. D. Duncan. Questions about attitude survey questions. In H. L. Costner (ed.) *Sociological methodology 1973-1974*. San Francisco: Jossey-Bass, 1974.

Sudman, S. *Applied sampling*. New York: Academic, 1976.

Sudman, S. Estimating response to follow-ups in mail surveys. *Public Opinion Quarterly*, 1982, 46 (4): 582-584.

Webb, E., D. T. Campbell, R. Schwartz, L. Sechrest, and J. Grove. *Nonreactive measures in the social sciences*. Boston: Houghton Mifflin, 1981.

Zeller, R. A. and E. G. Carmines. *Measurement in the social sciences*. New York: Cambridge University Press, 1980.

FACTOR ANALYSIS, SCALE CONSTRUCTION, AND QUESTIONNAIRE DEVELOPMENT

Bollen, K. A. A confirmatory factor analysis of subjective air quality. *Evaluation Review*, 1982, 6 (4): 521-536.

Cattell, R. B. *Factor analysis*. New York; Harper & Row, 1952.

Cattell, R. B. Factor analysis: An introduction to essentials. (I) The purpose and underlying models. (II) The role of factor analysis in research. *Biometrics*, 1965, 21: 190-215, 405-435.

Comrey, A. L. *A first course in factor analysis*, New York: Academic, 1973.

Filstead, W. J. et al. Developing a multidimensional clinical rating scale: Evaluating mental health services. *Evaluation review*, 1982, 6 (4): 559-576.

Gorsuch, R. L. *Factor analysis* (2nd ed.). Hillsdale, NJ: Erlbaum, 1983.

Guilford, J. P. *Psychometiric methods* (2nd ed.). New york: McGraw-Hill, 1954.

Guilford, J. P. The invariance problem in factor analysis. *Educational and Psychological Measurement*, 1977, 37: 11-19.

Harman, H. H. *Modern factor analysis* (3rd ed.). Chicago: University of Chicago Press, 1976.

Horn, J. L. An empirical comparison of various methods for estimating common factor scores. *Educational and Psychological Measurement*, 1965, 25: 313-322.

Kaiser, H. F. The varimax criterion for analytic rotation in factor analysis. *Psychometirka*, 1958, 23: 187-200.

Kim, J. -O. and C. Mueller. *Introduction to factor analysis*. Beverly Hills, CA: Sage, 1978. (a)

Kim, J. -O. and C. Mueller, *Factor analysis*. Beverly Hills, CA: Sage, 1978. (b)

Kruskal, J. B. and M. Wish. *Multidimensional scaling.* Beverly Hills, CA: Sage, 1981.

Labaw, P. *Advanced questionnaire design.* Cambridge, MA: Abt, 1980.

Lord, F. M. and W. R. Novick. *Statistical theories of mental test scores.* Reading, MA: Addison-Wesley, 1968.

Oppenheim, A. N., *Questionnaire design and attitude measurement.* New York; Basic Books, 1966.

Rummel, R. J. *Applied factor analysis.* Evanston, IL: Northwestern University Press, 1970.

Sorbom, D. and K. G. Joreskog. *Coramm: Confirmatory factor analysis with model modification, user's guide.* Chicago: National Educational Resources, Inc., 1976.

Stinchcombe, A. l. A heuristic procedure for interpreting factor analysis. *American Sociological Review,* 36: 1080-1084.

Weiss, C. H. Interviewing in evaluation research. In E. L. Struening and M. Guttentag (eds.) *Handbook of evaluation research* (Vol. 1). Beverly Hills, CA: Sage, 1975.

THE STUDY OF CHANGE

Algina, J. and S. F. Olejnik. Multiple group time-series design: An analysis of data. *Evaluation Review,* 6 (2): 203-232.

Baltes, P. B., H. W. Reese, and J. R. Nesselroade. *Life-span developmental psychology: Introduction to research methods.* Monterey, CA: Brooks/Cole, 1977.

Bronfman, B. H. A time-series analysis of urban renewal allocations: The application of a method. *Evaluation Review.* 1980, 4 (5): 657-664.

Campbell, D. T. Assessing the impact of planned social change. *Evaluation and Program Planning,* 1979, 2 (1); 67-90.

Dooley, D. and R. Catalano. Economic change as a cause of behavioral disorder. *Psychological Bulletin,* 87 (3): 450-468.

Forehand, G. A. (ed.). Applications of time series analysis to evaluation. *New Directions for Program Evaluation,* 1982, 16 (special issue).

Glenn, N. D. *Cohort analysis.* Beverly Hills, CA: Sage, 1977.

Group for the Advancement of Psychiatry. *Psychiatric research and the assessment of change* (Vol. 6). New York: Author, 1966.

Guthrie, D. Analysis of dichotomous variables in repeated measures experiments. *Psychological Bulletin,* 1981, 90 (1): 189-195.

Horne, G. P., M. C. K. Yang, and W. B. Ware. Time series analysis for single-subject designs. *Psychological Bulletin,* 1982, 91 (1): 178-189.

Howard, G. S. and S. E. Maxwell. Linked raters' judgments: A more sensitive index of change. *Evaluation Review,* 1982, 6 (1): 140-146.

Kessler, R. C. and D. Greenberrg. *Linear panel analysis: Models of quantitative change.* New York: Academic, 1981.

Labouvie, E. W. The concept of change and regression toward the mean. *Psychological Bulletin,* 1982, 92 (1): 251-257.

McCleary, R. and R. A. Hay. *Applied time series analysis.* Beverly Hills, CA: Sage, 1980.

Maltz, M. D. and R. McCleary. The mathematics of behavioral change: Recidivism and construct validity. *Evaluation Quarterly,* 1977, 1 (3): 421-438.

Myers, J. L., J. V. DiCecco, J. B. White, and V. M. Borden. Repeated measurements on dichotomous variables: Q and F tests. *Psychological Bulletin,* 1982, 92 (2): 517-525.

Nesselroade, J. R., S. M. Stigler, and P. B. Baltes. Regression toward the mean and the study of change. *Psychological Bulletin,* 1980, 88 (3): 622-637.

Rogosa, D., D. Brandt, and M. Zimowski. A growth curve approach to the measurement of change. *Psychological Bulletin,* 92 (3); 726-748.

Stollmack, S. Comments on "The mathematics of behavioral change." *Evaluation Quarterly,* 1979, 3 (1): 118-123.

Whittaker, G. F. The evaluation of a merged hospital system; Application of the interrupted time series design. *Evaluation Review,* 1981, 5 (1): 68-89.

THE RELIABILITY OF RATINGS, SCALES, AND OTHER MEASURES

Alwin, D. and D. Jackson. Measurement models for response errors in surveys; Issues and applications. In K. Schuessler (ed.) *Sociological methodology 1980*. San Francisco: Jossey-Bass, 1980.

Armor, D. J. Theta reliability and factor scaling. In H. L. Costner (ed.) *Sociological methodology 1973-1974*. San Francisco: Jossey-Bass, 1974.

Bartke, J. J. The intraclass correlation coefficient as a measure of reliability. *Psychological Reprints*, 1966, 19: 3-11.

Bohrnstedt, G. W. A quick method for determining the reliability and validity of multiple-item scales. *American Sociological Review*, 1969, 34: 542-548.

Carmines, E. G. and R. A. Zeller. *Reliability and validity assessment*. Beverly Hills, CA: Sage, 1979.

Cohen, J. A coefficient of agreement for nominal scales. *Educational and Psychological Measurement*, 1960, 20: 37-46.

Cohen, J. Weighted kappa: Nominal scale agreement with provision for scaled disagreement or partial credit. *Psychological Bulletin*, 1968, 70: 213-220.

Conger, A. J. Integration and generalization of kappas for multiple raters. *Psychological Bulletin*, 1980, 88 (2): 322-328.

Crittenden, K. S. and R. J. Hill. Coding reliability and validity of interview data. *American Sociological Review*, 1972, 37: 1073-1080.

Finney, H. C. Improving the reliability of retrospective survey measures: Results of a longitudinal field survey. *Evaluation Review*, 1981, 5 (1): 207-229.

Fleiss, J. L., J. C. M. Nee, and J. R. Landis. Large sample variance of kappa in the case of different sets of raters. *Psychological Bulletin*, 1978, 86 (5).

Fleiss, J. L., R. L. Spitzer, J. Endicott, and J. Cohen. Quantification of agreement in multiple psychiatric diagnosis. *Archives of General Psychiatry*, 1972, 26: 168-171.

Lahey, M. A., R. G. Downey, and F. E. Saal. Intraclass correlations: There's more there than meets the eye. *Psychological Bulletin*, 1983, 93 (3).

Link, S. W. Correcting response measures for guessing and partial information. *Psychological Bulletin*, 1982, 92 (2): 469-486.

Linn, R. L. and C. E. Werts. Errors of inference due to errors of measurement. *Educational and Psychological Measurement*, 1973, 33: 531-543.

Mitchell, S. K. Interobserver agreement, reliability, and generalizability of data collected in observational studies. *Psychological Bulletin*, 1979, 86 (2); 376-390.

Nicewander, W. A. and J. M. Price. Dependent variable reliability and the power of significance tests. *Psychological Bulletin*, 1978, 85 (2): 405-409.

Shrout, P. E. and J. L. Fleiss. Intraclass correlations; Uses in assessing rater reliability. *Psychological Bulletin*, 1979, 86 (2): 420-428.

Sutcliffe, J. P. On the relationship of reliability to statistical power. *Psychological Bulletin*, 1980, 88 (2): 509-515.

Wheaton, B., B. Muthen, D. Alwin, and G. Summers. Assessing reliability and stability in panel models. In D. Heise (ed.) *Sociological methodology 1977*. San Francisco: Jossey-Bass, 1977.

Wiley, D. R. and J. A. Wiley. The estimation of measurement error in panel data. *American Sociological Review*, 1970, 35: 112-117.

THE VALIDITY OF MEASURES AND EXPERIMENTS

Althauser, R. P. and T. A. Heberlein. Validity and the multitrait—multimethod matirix. In E. F. Borgatta et al. (eds.) *Sociological methodology 1970*. San Francisco; Jossey-Bass, 1970.

Berkowitz, L. and M. Donnerstein. External validity is more than skin deep: Some answers to criticisms of laboratory experiments. *American Psychologist*, 1982, 37 (3): 245-257.

Bernstein, I. N. Validity issues in evaluative research: An overview. In I. N. Bernstein (ed.) *Validity issues in evaluative research*. Beverly Hills, CA: Sage, 1976.

Bernstein, I. N., G. W. Bohrnstedt, and E. F. Borgatta. External validity and evaluation research: A codification of problems. In I. N. Bernstein (ed.) *Validity issues in evaluative research*. Beverly Hills, CA: Sage, 1976.

Bracht, G. H. and G. V Glass. The external validity of experiments. *American Educational Research Journal*, 1968, 5: 437-474.

Campbell, D. T. and D. W. Fiske. Convergent and discriminant validation by the multitrait-multimethod matrix. *Psychological Bulletin*, 1959, 56: 81-105.

Cronbach, L. J. Coefficient alpha and the internal structure of tests. *Psychometrika*, 1951, 16: 297-334.

Cronbach, L. J. Validity. In C. W. Harris (ed.) *Encyclopedia of educational research* (3rd ed.). New York: Macmillan, 1960.

Cronbach, L. J. and P. E. Meehl. Construct validity in psychological tests. *Psychological Bulletin*, 1955, 52; 281-302.

Drasgow, F. Biased test items and differential validity. *Psychological Bulletin*, 1982, 92 (2): 526-531.

Embretson, S. W. Construct validity: Construct representation versus nomothetic span. *Psychological Bulletin*, 1983, 93 (1): 179-197.

Ford, M. E. The construct validity of egocentrism. *Psychological Bulletin*, 1979, 86 (6): 1169-1188.

Heath, L. Differential validity: Another threat to compensatory education evaluations. *Evaluation and Program Planning*, 1979, 2 (1): 25-32.

Heise, D. R. and G. W. Bohrnstedt. Validity, invalidity, and reliability. In E. F. Borgatta and G. W. Bohrnstedt (eds.) *Sociological methodology 1970*. San Francisco: Jossey-Bass, 1970.

House, E. R. *Evaluating with validity*. Beverly Hills, CA: Sage, 1980.

Howard, G. S. On validity. *Evaluation Review*, 5 (4); 567-576.

Krause, M. S. and J. C. Jackson. The validity of some routine evaluative data: A study. *Evaluation Review* 1983, 7 (2): 271-275.

Lana, R. E. Pretest sensitization. In R. Rosenthal and R. L. Rosnow (eds.) *Artifact in behavioral research*. New York: Academic, 1969.

Loevinger, J. Objective tests as instruments of psychological theory. *Psychological Reports*, 1957, 3 (monograph supplement): 635-694.

Messick, S. Test validity and the ethics of assessment. *American Psychologist*, 1980, 35 (11): 1012-1027.

Nunnally, J. C. and R. L. Durham. Validity, reliability, and special problems of measurement in evaluation research. In E. L. Struening and M. Guttentag (eds.) *Handbook of evaluation research* (Vol. 1). Beverly Hills, CA: Sage, 1975.

Smith, N. L. and D. N. Caulley. Post-evaluation determination of a program's generalizability. *Evaluation and Program Planning*, 2 (4): 297-302.

Willson, V. L. Time and the external validity of experiments. *Evaluation and Program Planning*, 1981, 4 (3): 229-238.

SOURCEBOOKS FOR MEASURES

Bonjean, C. M., R. J. Hill, and S. D. McLemore. *Sociological measurement: An inventory of scales and indices*. San Francisco; Chandler, 1967.

Brodsky, S. L. and O. Smitherman. *Handbook of scales for research in crime and delinquency*. New York: Plenum, 1983.

Chun, K.-T., S. Cobb, and J. R. P. French, Jr. *A guide to 3,000 references on instrument construction and selected applications*. Ann Arbor: Institute for Social Research, University of Michigan, 1975.

Comrey, A. L., E. E. Backer, and E. M. Glaser (eds.). *A sourcebook of mental health measures*. Human Interaction Research Institute, 1973.

Johnson, O. G. and J. W. Bommarito. *Tests and measurements in child development: A handbook*. San Francisco: Jossey-Bass, 1971.

Lake, D. G., M. B. Miles, and R. B. Earle, Jr. *Measuring human behavior: Tools for the assessment of social functioning*. New York: Teachers College Press, 1973.

McReynolds, P. (ed.). *Advances in psychological assessment* (Vol. 1). Palo Alto, CA: Science and Behavior, 1968.

McReynolds, P. (ed.). *Advances in psychological assessment* (Vol. 2). Palo Alto, CA: Science and Behavior, 1971.

McReynolds, P. (ed.). *Advances in psychological assessment*, (Vol. 3). San Francisco: Jossey-Bass, 1975.

Miller, D. C. *Handbook of research design and social measurement* (3rd ed.). New York: David McKay, 1977.

National Institute on Drug Abuse. *Drug abuse instrument handbook*. Washington, DC: Government Printing Office, 1977.

Price, J. L. *Handbook of organizational measurement*. Lexington, MA: D. C. Heath, 1972.

Robinson, J. P., A. Athansiou, and K. B. Head. *Measures of occupational attitudes and occupational characteristics*. Ann Arbor: Institute for Social Research, University of Michigan, 1968.

Robinson, J. P., J. G. Rusk, and K. B. Head. *Measures of political attitudes* (rev. ed.). Ann Arbor: Institute for Social Research, University of Michigan, 1968.

Robinson, J. P. and P. R. Shaver. *Measures of social psychological attitudes*. Ann Arbor. Institute for Social Research, University of Michigan, 1973.

Shaw, M. E. and J. M. Wright. *Scales for the measurement of attitudes*. New York: McGraw-Hill, 1967.

Straus, M. A. *Family measurement techniques: Abstracts of published instruments, 1935-1965*. Minneapolis: University of Minnesota Press, 1969.

Walder, D. K. *Socioemotional measures for preschool and kindergarten children*. San Francisco: Jossey-Bass, 1973.

Waskow, I. E. and M. B. parloff (eds.). *Psychotherapy change measures*. Washington, DC; National Institute of Mental Health, 1975.

Wiley, D. R. and J. A. Wiley. The estimatin of measurement error in panel data. *American Sociological Review*, 1970, 35: 112-117.

VI

DATA-ANALYTIC METHODS

11

MULTIVARIATE METHODOLOGIES FOR EVALUATION RESEARCH

HERBERT W. EBER

HISTORY AND DEVELOPMENT

When the social sciences emerged from the armchair of the natural philosopher and began the application of scientific method to psychology, sociology, economics, and similar areas, the model of the scientific method was that provided by the older, "established," physical sciences. The model emphasized laboratories, equipment, rigorous experiments under controlled conditions, and most important, the study of one variable at a time, all other variables being held constant.

The young sciences accepted the model but found compliance with its requirements difficult to impossible. "All other variables" refused to become or remain constant. Actually, they had never been really constant in physics. All billiard balls are not really alike, billiard tables do not have perfect surfaces or cushions, and even astronomers had found the exasperation of the "personal equation."

However, the magnitude of error introduced by the inconstancy of "other variables" in the physical sciences was trivial during the early years; measurements themselves were of limited accuracy, and the main effects under study were so gross that their obvious parameters overshadowed the minor errors.

Not so in the social sciences. Experiments using organic subjects, animal or human, usually obtained variance of the same magnitude between subjects as between conditions. For example, comparison among the effects of several methods of memorizing showed (unwanted) differences among subjects. While Ebbinghaus solved that problem by studying primarily his own memory processes, a better solution seemed required.

Univariate statistical models provided the required technique. In general, these models were of two types, though later these were shown to be simply two ways of looking at the same thing.

The basic concept was that variance is additive and that total variance can thus be partitioned into two major components, a *lawful* part and an *error* part. Lawful was defined as resulting from the variable under study; error was that variance due to those "other variables" that refused to remain constant.

It was shown that *error* provided a basis for judging the significance of *lawful variance*. Clearly, intuitively, if *error* is so large that *lawful* is hardly perceptible by comparison, then all may be error. Conversely, if *lawful* looms large by contrast with *error*, then theory is supported (or destroyed) and the experiment has been successful. In time, the theoretical basis of such judgments was defined and codified. Statistical inference had become a handmaiden to the social (and later the physical) scientist.

The two types of models mentioned above resulted from two types of *lawfulness* that had been hypothesized. Where theory was oriented toward differences in outcome resulting from differences in the variable under examination, *lawfulness* was defined as between-groups (of subjects) variance while *error* was variance within groups. Techniques such as the t-test, and later more extensive types of "analysis of variance" resulted.

Where theory looked at relationships of two variables (perhaps an "independent" and a "dependent," perhaps not), *lawfulness* was defined as covariance of the relationship, while error was all else. Correlational techniques of many kinds were the product of this approach.

It is intuitively obvious to many students, and it can be shown both mathematically and empirically, that complete translation from one type of model to the other is simple and complete. Nevertheless, historical factors produced two "schools" of statistical thought, emphasizing different approaches to different problems, and at times each vigorously defending the "rightness" of its technology. An association of analysis-of-variance with experimental rigor versus correlational methods with naturalistic observation became historically meaningful, despite being substantively unnecessary and irrelevant.

In time, both schools grasped the larger utility of the concept that variance can be partitioned. The t-test became the F-test; analysis-of-variance became analysis-of-covariance. Simple correlation led to multiple correlation and regression theory, and in turn to factor analysis.

With the advent of the electronic computer, what had been the demanding (and even exhausting) technique used by a few became the technology available to all social (and other) scientists. The ability actually to carry out the calculations that had seemed desirable served as a spur to development. Multivariate statistical methods had arrived, and the last two decades have seen not only the development of theory, but the coming of age of a group of scientists whose familiarity with that theory permits the ready use of multivariate technology.

The mathematics of the multivariate approaches to statistical inference need not concern us in this discussion. They are not inordinately difficult, but are of interest primarily to the specialist, and the notation and precise conceptualization can become complex. Excellent treatments in as much detail as may be desired are readily available, for example, in Cooley and Lohnes (1971), Cattell (1966), or Overall and Klett (1972).

At the level of understanding required for the user of these techniques, however, the issues are not beyond the present concern. All multivariate techniques are based upon the familiar concept that variance can be subdivided, allocated, analyzed, related to other variance, compared, and so forth. Moreover, all multivariate techniques are extensions into more general terms of concepts whose univariate antecedents were a special case. In exactly the same way that plane geometry can be conceptualized as a special case (two dimensions, Cartesian metric) of a much larger, more general family of geometries, so a t-test may be considered as a very simple, special case of discriminant functions.

Without minimizing the very real and extensive competence required of the multivariate statistician, and the large number of procedures whose judicious use can be of major help to the evaluation researcher, it is nevertheless fair to say that there are essentially only three types of problems, and two of these are alternate versions of the same thing. Understanding these three (or two) types is not difficult.

DATA REDUCTION MODELS

There is a class of problems in which the researcher has a larger number of observations than he can easily interpret. Perhaps there are multiple measurements upon a number of subjects, perhaps on a number of occasions, perhaps obtained through a number of methods. The task is to reduce this complexity to a more easily conceptualized pattern; it is not primarily a matter of statistical inference or proof.

A number of specific techniques have been developed to achieve desired types of data reduction. Factor analysis is probably the best-known name of a procedure in this area, but cluster analysis, image analysis, and component analysis all describe techniques of this type.

Important methodological issues are represented by the names of the techniques and by other issues discussed by multivariate analysts, not only in the area of technique but also in areas of philosophy of science and definition of goals. However, these are not our major concern in this chapter. Rather, we shall examine the basic (simplified) strategy of all such methods.

The basic method is the partitioning of variance and the grouping together of those variables, subjects, occasions which show relatively small variance among themselves, while showing large variation from other groupings. These things that "go together" are then conceived as a type, a factor, an influence.

At the simplest level, a reduction in complexity occurs, and this is helpful in dealing with the data. One test score on each of a dozen factors represents an easier way of describing persons than 100 test scores from as many measurements. If the analysis has been properly performed, then little useful accuracy is lost in the reduction of the number of scores, and a great deal of convenience has been gained.

On the other hand, some factor-cluster analysts are far from content with gains in convenience. They wish to use the methods to search for underlying causes, basic types, and similar explanatory concepts. While such efforts have sometimes generated more in the way of controversy than utility, the reverse has also been true. Years of programmatic research in an area have developed conceptual structures eminently suitable for scientific theorizing (e.g., Cattell, 1965; Guilford, 1967; French et al., 1963).

In the more immediate world of evaluation research, data reduction by such techniques has classified patients or clients, analyzed demographic variables, subdivided states into regions and countries into voting blocs, suggested (multiple) production criteria, and reduced the complexity of many other problems. Whenever an evaluation specialist finds a problem with multiple variables, he is likely to perform some of these data reduction analyses to help bring the ultimate issues of the research into more manageable focus.

A (SIMPLIFIED) EXAMPLE OF DATA REDUCTION IN EVALUATION RESEARCH

In a massive study of the Alabama Vocational Rehabilitation System, the writer (Eber, 1966, 1967) analyzed file record data from three groups of rehabilitation clients. Included among these data were various aspects of rehabilitation outcome. Substantial controversy existed at that time (and still does) regarding what may be called the "true" criterion of rehabilitation success. The results of the study may be an instructive example of the use of factor analysis, or data reduction technique, in aiding conceptual clarity.

The raw data describing each of several hundred clients included:

1. Degree of disability as judged by OASI pension decisions
2. Age
3. Work status at case closure
4. Mobility (can client get around) at acceptance
5. Mobility at closure
6. Prestige status of closure job (if any)
7. Earnings during week of closure
8. Was the counselor the job placement agent?
9. Amount of money spent for diagnosis
10. Amount of money spent for prostheses
11. Amount of money spent—TOTAL
12. Was case closed "successful"?
13. Was client alive at closure?
14. Were any services (beyond diagnosis) ever given?
15. Had client worked after the onset of disability, but before rehab acceptance?
16. Amount of wages claimed ever earned
17. Employed at follow-up?
18. Work status at follow-up
19. Earnings at follow-up
20. Public assistance at follow-up

21. Was client "happy" at follow-up?
22. Has client been reactivated?
23. Has client received "services to a closed case"?
24. Was client drawing OASI disability benefits at follow-up?

An interesting, and misleading question might be "Which of these 24 variables represents the *real* outcome criterion?" or "Which one of the 24 variables tells me, the decision maker, how well the client did?"

Some more meaningful questions could be:

A. How many "outcomes" are there? One? Two? Twenty-four?
B. If there are fewer than 24 "outcomes," how best do we define them?
C. What relationship exists, if any, between various types of outcome?

Factor analysis was performed as a way of answering the latter questions. The results are shown in Table 11.1, where an "X" represents how much a variable "belongs" in the factor and a blank, that it does not.

The first dramatic result of the analysis is a clear answer to question A. There are *two* outcome factors, not one, not twenty-four. In fact, analysis of the variables that "belong" versus those that do not suggests a clear meaning for the two factors, *short-range success* and *long-range success*.

TABLE 11.1   LOADINGS OF 24 VARIABLES ON TWO OUTCOME FACTORS

Variable	Factor I	Factor II
1. OASI benefit at intake	-XX	-X
2. Age		-XX
3. Status at closure	XXX	
4. Mobility at acceptance	XXX	
5. Mobility at closure	XXX	
6. Prestige, closure job	XXX	
7. Earnings, week of closure	XXX	
8. Counselor placement	X	
9. Money spent, diagnosis	X	-X
10. Money spent, prosthesis		-X
11. Money spent, total		-X
12. Closed "success"	XXX	
13. Alive at closure	X	
14. Ever served	X	
15. Work history after disability	X	
16. Highest claimed wage		-X
17. Employed at follow-up		XXXX
18. Status at follow-up		XXXX
19. Earnings at follow-up		XX
20. Public assistance at follow-up		-X
21. "Happy" at follow-up		XXXX
22. Reactivated?	-X	
23. "Service to closed case"	-XX	
24. OASI benefit at follow-up		-XX

Second, definition of the two factors is easily accomplished. *Short-range success* could be defined by a weighted composite of variables 3, 5, 6, 7, and 12; *long-range success* by a similar composite of variables 17, 18, 19, 21, and (−) 24.

Third, the analysis shows a correlation of .57 between the two factors. Interpretation? Short-range and long-range success are positively correlated but are not, apparently, the same thing.

Moreover, the relationship of individual variables to outcome can now be defined well enough for further study. For example, it would appear that counselor placement effort is helpful in the short run but *not* in the long-range result. If verified in a second study, such evidence could affect the way the decision maker allocates counselor effort.

It should be emphasized that the data here have been simplified, and are in fact part of a much larger, more complex study. Nevertheless, what has been cited is part of the results, and demonstrates the utility of data reduction technique to the evaluation researcher.

GROUP DIFFERENCE MODELS

This is a class of problems in which impact of independent variables upon one or more dependent variables is to be evaluated by comparisons among groups of subjects. Typically, the researcher may classify subjects into experimental and control groups, and search for evidence of impact by between-group comparison.

The basic technique is that lawful, predicted (or theoretically predictable) variance between groups is compared with random, unpredicted (perhaps unpredictable) variance within groups. The impact of treatments, programs, classifications, and so on should make the between-group variance large by comparison with the error term, and impact is judged by *how* large.

Standard statistical tests exist, based upon both theoretical and empirical evidence, that answer the question "how large is large enough?" Typically, they approach the problem in terms of the probability that differences as large as those observed could have occurred purely by chance. In this, the multivariate techniques are no different from the simpler, univariate ones. By treating the total, or at least large subsets of the data simultaneously, the multivariate methods tend to allow for the full complexity of the data to emerge in the findings. On the other hand, these techniques tend to "capitalize on chance" less than repeated univariate analysis of the same data. For example the graduate student who evaluates two groups of rats by twenty different measures, performs twenty t-tests, finds one "significant at the .05 level," reports on that one, and forgets the rest may be more apocryphal than real. Nevertheless, comparable if less obvious distortions of statistics are reported in the literature, and not always by students.

Multivariate methods are based, by and large, upon the so-called linear model. That is, multiple linear equations in multiple unknowns are solved. Often, a "best fit" of that solution is evaluated against how good the "fit" is likely to be by chance. The power of that linear model to provide "good fit" for *any* data has often been underestimated, most often by those who use the model unknowingly.

The multivariate methods for evaluating group differences have grown out of the "analysis-of-variance" model. From two groups to many; from random selection to designed, multifactorial experiments; from a single dependent variable to many; the expansion of models to include complex cases has made the techniques constantly more valuable in the sense that the simplification of the laboratory has become less and less a prerequisite.

The power and flexibility of multivariate group comparisons is well illustrated by the frequently used *multiple discriminant function.* A number of measures are obtained on each of a (it is hoped, large) number of subjects; the latter are classified into groups on the basis of the researcher's hypotheses. Each group represents some treatment or condition. The question asked is: "Within the complex multispace provided by the variables, what is the best possible separation of groups that can be achieved by giving each variable a single weight. The function gives literally an equation for the *best* such separation that can be achieved. How good is this "best" separation is then evaluated by significance tests, and the separation achieved is mathematically *removed* from the data.

The same question is asked again, but the removal of the first function rephrases it as ". . . what is the best possible *further* separation. . . ?" The process of defining a function, removing it, defining another, and so on continues until the number of functions is n-1 or k-1, whichever is smaller (n = number of variables, k = number of groups).

As might be expected from any mathematical technique that maximizes ("best"), each succeeding separation of the groups is less clear (or at least no clearer) than the one before. Each function is tested for significance, and spurious ones are dropped. The significant functions may then correspond to hypotheses about the groups.

As is true of data reduction methods, the calculations would be horrendous without electronic computers. Also, the mathematics of the model are quite demanding, and programming a computer to perform such a process is a significant job. Fortunately, none of this presents a barrier to the use of these techniques. Standard computer programs are available for most machines, and statisticians can readily arrange the use of whatever is, in their judgment, most appropriate.

AN EXAMPLE OF THE GROUP DIFFERENCE APPROACH

Miss A and Mrs. B are teachers of special classes for retarded children. A budget cut requires that only one of them be retained for the following year. They are of equal seniority and equal formal qualifications, and both desire to continue on the job. The administrator wants to find some fair basis for a choice between them; he proposes that their students' data be examined for possible evidence of the teachers' competence.

For each student, the data consist of:

Achievement test scores at entrance
Achievement test scores after the class year

Number of involvements in disciplinary problems

IQ as reported by the school psychologist, obtained before the student was exposed to Miss A or Mrs. B.

The data are shown in Table 11.2. It is suggested that the reader examine this table and evaluate the evidence before reviewing the analysis below.

Obviously, "eyeball" methods are of little help with such data. With an adding machine, one might get means, but then which ones are significant? Moreover, even if a substantial mean difference appeared in "post test" data, how much compensation would be necessary for any differences in "pre test" data? Finally, the scores are somewhat correlated, and that makes the analysis even more complex.

The relevant parts of the discriminant analysis are shown in Table 11.3; all numbers have been rounded off for ease of reading. The function tells us:

1. The best separation of Miss A's and Mrs. B's students that can be achieved is not very significant. Virtually *any real* evidence of qualifications would be

TABLE 11.2   STUDENT DATA FROM TWO SPECIAL CLASSES

		Pre			Post			Discipline	
		Reading	Spelling	Arithmetic	Reading	Spelling	Arithmetic	Problems	IQ
Miss A:	John	2	3	2	2	3	3	1	68
	Bill	0	1	1	1	2	3	5	77
	Mary	3	2	0	4	2	1	0	70
	Ann	4	4	3	4	4	4	0	74
	Alice	1	1	5	2	1	5	3	61
	Harry	2	2	4	5	2	4	1	71
Mrs. B:	Jane	2	2	4	4	1	4	0	66
	Martha	0	2	0	0	2	1	2	59
	Bob	2	6	3	2	5	4	4	78
	Allen	4	0	2	4	0	2	4	74
	Martin	0	3	2	4	2	2	1	75
	Helen	2	5	2	5	5	4	0	73

TABLE 11.3   DISCRIMINANT FUNCTION: MISS A VERSUS MRS. B

	Variable	Weight	Description
Pre	Reading	0	On this function, Mrs. B's
	Spelling	4	students are higher than
	Arithmetic	-3	Miss A's
Post	Reading	1	
	Spelling	-4	
	Arithmetic	2	Significance
Discipline		1	X^2 (df = 8) = 10
IQ (pre)		-1	sig = .30

better than these data provide. The significance level of .30 means that the findings would have occurred by accident 30% of the time, hardly overwhelming odds. Scientists want odds of 20:1 ($p < .05$) for *suggestive* findings; these odds are not even 3:1.

2. Even what *is* shown is a mixture of preexisting conditions and possible influence of the teachers. The largest weights in the function (pre and post spelling) suggest either that Mrs. B's students have deteriorated in this ability, or that Miss A's have improved. Inspection of the data suggests the former. It would seem that Mrs. B began with students whose arithmetic was poor, emphasized that aspect, and perhaps obtained some small improvement. While doing this, she neglected spelling, where her students pre-tested fair, and these scores deteriorated. (A better explanation is still that nothing consistent is shown by these data.)

3. The administrator is advised to look elsewhere for justification as to which teacher to retain.

RELATIONSHIP MODELS

At first glance, models that examine "co-variation," that is, co-occurring variance in two or more measures, seem quite different from group difference models. Historically, that apparent difference has been the cause of two major "schools" of statistics. In fact, however, there is little difference.

Suppose that a measure of some type has been made upon each of several hundred subjects, and that these subjects can be logically classified into three groups (perhaps "drug," "placebo," and "control"). The task is to evaluate the impact of the drug upon the measured (dependent) variable. Obviously, this is true for the group difference model.

Alternatively, suppose we define two variables in addition to the measured (dependent) one. The first such variable is "has been given *the drug*," and on this variable, members of the "drug" group are assigned a score of 1, while both "placebo" and "control" group members get a score of 0. Then, the second constructed variable is "has been given something," with a score of 1 for members of the "drug" *and* the "placebo" group, 0 for the controls.

It should be evident that all our knowledge about the subjects is now represented by three variables, one measured and two *constructed* to show group membership. What may be less evident, but is equally true, is that all statistical measures that can be derived from the original data by the *group difference* model can be as easily derived from these constructed data and the *relationship model*. Not only will the results of the analysis be the same, but the exact same numbers will be obtained, and this is true regardless of what "scores" are used to signify group membership on the constructed variables.

Conversely, we could restructure the data in another way. Let us define six groups instead of three by using the measured variable as a grouping method. Let us say that all subjects who score above the mean will be in the "high" group, all below the mean in the "low" group. Obviously, we now have six groups, in the format shown in Figure 11.4, and a simple chi-square test of statistical significance can be used.

TABLE 11.4

	Drug	Placebo	Control
High	G_{hd}	G_{hp}	G_{hc}
Low	G_{ld}	G_{lp}	G_{lc}

Note however that "high" and "low" does *not* contain all the knowledge we have of the subjects. This approach will yield *essentially similar* results, but the method of analysis is less sensitive and makes use of only part of the data.

Actually, any data of the group difference type can always be equally well represented as relationships, but not necessarily vice versa. In this sense, what appear to be distinct approaches are, in fact, quite closely related. Moreover, it is never necessary to force data into categories when, in fact, continuous measures were initially available. Such a procedure may reduce computing complexity but must, inevitably, use the information contained in the data less efficiently. With the availability of computers, complexity of calculation is, or should be, a trivial consideration in most cases.

An example of a problem falling "naturally" into the relationship model is provided by the development of a *regression equation* to predict some *criterion*. Given a (large) group of subjects whose status upon some criterion variable, presumably one of a substantive importance, is known; given further, for each subject, a number of other scores representing status on other, *predictor* variables; the questions asked are: (1) "How well can the variance in the criterion be predicted (explained?) by a composite of predictor scores?" and (2) "What is the formula for the best such composite?"

The *linear regression* model provides answers to these questions. It solves, essentially, for a "best fit" among a system of linear equations in multiple unknowns. Each equation represents one subject, with (unknown) weights given to each predictor score. If the number of equations (subjects) were exactly equal to the number of unknowns (predictor weights), an exact solution could be obtained by the methods familiar to high school algebra. With fewer equations than unknowns, the solution is impossible; with (the usual) more equations than unknowns, we obtain a "best fit," and again, the power of the linear model to obtain such a best fit is substantial.

The results of the calculations will include a multiple correlation coefficient which answers the question "How well . . ." and a set of "beta" weights which constitute the formula. Because the model must, by definition, yield a "best fit," there will be some concern about how well the formula will work with a different set of subjects. In other words, an issue of *cross validation* must be resolved, analogous to the question of chance differences among groups. Both theoretical and practical answers to this question of "shrinkage" of a multiple correlation are well known; both use the obvious fact that data based upon a large number of observations are more stable than those based upon fewer. Good estimates of "How good . . ." can be made.

However, as with all best fit models, the ultimate proof is most convincing when a new set of data *cross validate* at an appropriate level of significance. The concept that the initial analysis yields an *hypothesis* to be tested by further study is not so often honored by social scientists as might be ideal; still, that must remain the ultimate test, in relationship models as in other (multivariate *and* univariate) approaches.

STRATEGY OF ANALYSIS

The foregoing discussion makes a strong case for the use of multivariate techniques whenever the data required for such analysis exist. They usually do exist, and simplified, univariate analysis usually requires that available data be ignored.

It is desirable, however, that the picture not be overdrawn. While it is true that simpler models usually lose information, and that the more comprehensive techniques can never yield less information than the simpler ones, this does not rule out the possibility that a simple model may yield the most effective and desirable insight for a particular problem in a specific context.

Particularly in evaluation research, the scientist's role is not exclusively one of discovering relationships that conform to the canons of rigorous inquiry. To be sure, that is part of the task, and the emphasis upon objectivity, replication (or at least replicability), conceptual rigor, and dissemination of methods *and* results are the hallmark of the scientific method. However, most research is undertaken for a purpose, and that purpose is rarely more clearly defined than in evaluation research. Someone needs or wants to use the information developed, usually as a guide to decision making.

Given that there is a consumer of research, a user of the information developed by a scientific enterprise, then the researcher's job must include the communication of his findings to their user *in such form that they are correctly understood*. The "pure" scientist, whose consumers are primarily others of his own background and interest, may legitimately communicate in as complex and rigorous a manner as may to him seem appropriate to the issue. He may, and usually will, demand of his reader such expertise as may be necessary to understand all appropriate ramifications of the findings.

The "pure" scientist assumes that the reader of his report has no limitations, either of capacity or of expertise. If the subject is best presented as a set of 47 equations, whose understanding requires intimate knowledge of a dozen esoteric mathematical concepts, then that is the way the information will be presented. The "consumer" who is not sufficiently expert to understand must either obtain the required expertise or abandon the information.

In evaluation research, and in fact in *any* applied research, findings must be communicated to a different consumer. Were that user of the information oriented toward technical and esoteric competence, he would likely have little need for the evaluation researcher. More important, the specialization of roles in a complex society makes it unlikely that orientation toward complex scientific issues and toward sociopolitical decision making will coexist in the same person. Therefore, the evalation researcher must accept the responsibility for communication to what may best be described as the highly intelligent layman. He must present his findings without demanding that the reader share his scientific expertise. In this task, the judicious reexamination of findings by models whose results are easy to communicate may become part of the total picture.

Thus, the evaluation researcher must analyze the data from two standpoints, his own attempt to achieve the most complete and rigorous possible understanding of the results, and his need to communicate the relevant parts of those results to the consumer. The two parts of the task may well require complementary, but different, statistical models.

In his attempt to clarify the relationships underlying a set of data, the evaluation researcher most often should take advantage of the comprehensive models offered by multivariate methods. He can never, in this way, lose information. Any *legitimate* result that can emerge from univariate analysis *must* emerge at least equally clearly from the more comprehensive multivariate technology. The inclusion of additional relevant variables in an analysis will reduce the error variance. Since that error component forms the denominator in the F-ratio (or acts in an analogous manner in other statistics), valid significance levels from a univariate analysis must be at least equally significant (usually more significant) in the more comprehensive model.

The exception occurs when irrelevant variables are included, increasing the "degrees of freedom" without increasing lawful variance. In that case, what would otherwise be significant appears less so, but one must distinguish here between what was known to be irrelevant *before* the analysis and what was discovered to be irrelevant *in* the analysis. We are back to the student and his 20 t-tests, one significant at the .05 level. The decision that the other 19 are "irrelevant," *after* the analysis, is simply cheating. The multivariate result of *no significance* is correct; the apparent univariate result of significance is obviously wrong.

Thus the investigator should begin his analysis of a set of data by including the maximum permissible number of relevant variables. "Permissible" must be defined in terms of degrees of freedom. Without discussing this sometimes technical concept, it is intuitively obvious that a mathematical equation with a sufficient number of possible adjustments (degrees of freedom) can be made to fit an elephant. "Goodness of fit," upon which concept all statistical tests of significance are based, is meaningless if the data are such that a *bad* fit cannot occur.

The initial question asked of his data by the evaluation researcher should be: "Is *anything* other than random variation in the data system evident?" If the answer to that question is in the negative, further analysis is not only useless but virtually guaranteed to produce misleading results. The ability to find "meaningful and significant" results in an isolated area of the data by throwing away what is (now) defined as irrelevant is an asset to the fortune-teller. Unfortunately, that ability is not found only among such practitioners.

In his role as statistical consultant to projects where massive data sets are the rule, the author has repeatedly been impressed with the rationalization capacities of investigators (including himself). An analysis yields nonsignificant results, but the few trends that are suggested as *possible* areas for further study are "so obviously sensible and in line with theory/knowledge/intuition/clinical judgment (chose one)" that they *must* be real truths emerging from statistical obfuscation. When, by error or design, the author has reversed the signs, and thus the direction of apparent relationships of half the variables in question, the trends are still equally "obviously . . .".

Just as the power of the linear model to fit *any* data set should not be underestimated, so the capacity of the scientist to rationalize *any* results must be taken into account. The evaluation researcher must first demand of the data some solid evidence that "something other then nothing is indicated." Failure to adhere to this standard cannot help but vitiate any further evidence obtained.

Now it is a fact that real data obtained by competent observers using reasonably good measures usually show very clearly that lawful variance exists. The more comprehensive the analysis, the less chance that lawful relationships which exist will have been missed by failure of representation in the data set. This is the basis for the suggestion that comprehensive analysis by multivariate techniques is the best strategy at the beginning.

Assuming then that the comprehensive analysis has been completed and that lawful variance has been identified, the researcher next faces the task of communicating results to the user of the information. The findings must be expressed in ways that will permit the decision maker to anticipate probable consequences of various courses of action. If the decisions to be made are sufficiently important to warrant the gathering and analysis of a second data set, this final state of evaluation research can use the most powerful method of predicting results of decisions with increased accuracy.

That method is cross-validation of major hypotheses derived from the first (comprehensive) analysis. The researcher selects or produces a data set representing those major factors that emerged from the first study as candidates for action to be taken. Here now is the place for "designed experiments," for systematic variation of combinations of (few) factors. Also, here is the place for simpler statistics, for more specific but less comprehensive models.

Since the first experiment yielded proof of lawful variance, this cross-validation can focus upon the specific impact of a small number of manageable factors. The results can now be expressed in less esoteric concepts than before. Assuming that cross-validation is successful, the probable impact of action taken can be predicted fairly accurately. On the other hand, failure of cross-validation can yield dual benefits, preventing useless (or possibly even harmful) action, and permitting the researcher to clarify and correct erroneous concepts.

Thus, while a single evaluation research project usually obtains best results from a comprehensive, multivariate analysis of data, a cycle of research, incorporating more than one project, may best proceed from complex to simpler models, from comprehensive to narrower goals, from general conceptualization to precise definition. In the latter stages of the cycle, univariate or simple multivariate models achieve optimum utility.

SOME SUGGESTIONS FOR CONDUCTING, MANAGING, AND UTILIZING MULTIVARIATE RESEARCH

The complexity of the models used in multivariate procedures, and the facility with which these models can be applied through the use of electronic computers, give rise to a new type of problem which has been inaccurately but graphically described as "GIGO," namely "garbage in, garbage out." The description is inaccurate because it is not inevitably true; multivariate (and other) statistical analysis is a matter of separating the wheat from the chaff, of separating lawful variance from random variance. The suspicion that the information used may include a substantial proportion of error should not necessarily prevent the researcher from proceeding.

Social scientists are accustomed to hearing criticisms regarding the fallible nature of their data, even while some researchers who make these criticisms utilize extremely fallible data as if those data were perfect. A psychiatrist of the writer's acquaintance recently obtained, on a large sample of patients, both their age and their date of birth. Calculating age from the date of birth, and correlating that calculated age with the "age" reported by the patients, he obtained a correlation of only .91. Clearly such a simple datum as age is fallible. Similarly, it is suggested that a person's sex is by no means a clear-cut datum; otherwise, there would be no need for sophisticated chromosome tests of Olympic athletes who claim to be women but who strike observers of women's events at the Olympics as possibly being impostors.

The question is not whether there is error in the data, but whether the effects of error on the findings may be minimized, so that the meaningful variance can be given a chance to show itself. Multivariate techniques are the most sophisticated ones available for this process; however, the very sophistication and complexity of the multivariate models gives rise to some new problems against which definitive steps have to be taken by the researcher, the administrator, and the user of research findings. These problems reside in the area of the data definitions, and of the relationships between the multivariate operations performed and the application of the model to the specific case at hand.

At the simplest level, keypunchers make mistakes, and most computer programs do not successfully identify these mistakes. Many researchers are impatient with the painstaking editing of data that should be a prerequisite before an analysis is begun. Such editing is not easily done by the computer or by any other method. Often, a printed listing of the data cards and the trained eye of the researcher are the most appropriate combination in the search for ridiculous errors. There is evidence that this step is all too rarely executed.

Then there is the problem of missing data. A number of conventions are used for the representation of missing data, and there are too many cases where the user of an available computer program did not assure himself that missing data would be appropriately handled. Many programs are written in Fortran, with Fortran input and output conventions. When that is done, a blank entry among numeric data is read as a zero, and no error message results. The researcher may well proceed, blindly unaware of the fact that missing data have occurred and have been interpreted by the computer program as scores which lie 341 standard deviations below the mean.

Conventions for representing missing data which do not utilize blanks in the data set can be equally dangerous. The ubiquitous practice of representing a missing data item by a 9, a 99, and 999, or some such "ridiculous" value can be quite effective unless the researcher neglects to tell the computer what has been done. In this case, missing data are likely to be interpreted as 300-odd standard deviations *above* the mean, and again there is no error message to tell the user that he has made a ridiculous error.

Among the conventional methods of handling missing data, once assuming that they have been properly identified as "missing," one suggestion (Cohen and Cohen, 1973) deserves special mention. Let the missing data value be replaced by the mean for that item, thus effectively neutralizing it. Then, construct another variable in which the "missingness" of the data is represented. Analyze both, and it may turn out that "missingness" is a more powerful predictor than the data value itself.

A fictional example provided by Cohen and Cohen concerns IQ data "missing" from files of students who had been classified as mentally retarded. Analysis gave strong evidence that data had not been lost on a random basis. A "retarded" student whose IQ data were missing showed strong probability of having been classified for administrative convenience rather than on the basis of the data now (years later) missing.

At a more sophisticated level than missing data is the problem of distributions which depart radically from those assumed by the statistic being used. The writer is not a purist, and has relatively little patience with compulsive discussions of the fine points regarding assumptions about the shape of data distributions which may or may not be satisfied by a particular set of scores. At the same time, gross deviations from the assumed shape of a distribution may lead to insignificant results where more careful attention to such shape would have permitted a clearer definition of the data and resulting greater ease in finding lawful variance. Here again, the very facility of the electronic computing machinery serves to obscure relationships which would be evident, perhaps painfully so, to the researcher utilizing a hand calculator.

Most multivariate (and univariate) models are built upon assumptions about the shape of the distributions and of the relationships among variables which may frequently not be true for a real set of data. However, there is a good deal of evidence in the literature that replicable and significant results maybe obtained by ignoring the shape of the data distribution. When the purpose of the study is analytic—designed to provide understanding of the relationships among variables— rather than predictive, assumption failure is most likely to lead to erroneous inference.

There are some cases in which a knowledge of the nature of the data permits rational transformations which can make the resulting numbers more readily analyzed, and which will permit lawful variance to emerge more clearly than would otherwise be the case. One example is the logarithmic transformation, in which log X is substituted for the original observed data value X. The transformation is readily made in a computer program; it can literally be had for the asking.

There are variables used in evaluation research which have been studied and reported in the literature, and whose distribution shape is known to become more amenable to statistical and other interpretation when such a transformation is made. Examples of the log transform abound in psychophysical measurement. Within the ordinary ranges of stimulation, the relationship between perception and physical stimulation levels is virtually always best represented by the logarithmic equation. Many variables which involve human judgment of physical reality can be considered for such transforms, and similarly many growth curves which occur in nature fit this pattern quite well.

The question is not primarily one of correctness but rather of utility. Attention to the shape of the data, prior to entering them into multivariate analytic programs, can yield rich benefits in making lawful variance more visible and more easily interpreted than it would be if analytic programs were applied in a less sophisticated manner.

This leads finally to a more general point which concerns the collaboration between the administrator and user of research with the researcher himself. In general it requires repeated attempts to make clear, in the thinking of all concerned, the conceptual meaning in the substantive world of the operations that are performed upon and by the statistical model. The model, for example, permits certain kinds of transformations from the raw data variables to those derived data items which shall be analyzed. The question that must be asked, and answered, repeatedly is: "What does this operation *mean* when applied to these data?"

Our data permit correlations to be calculated, or covariance, or distance functions, or other coefficients of similarity or dissimilarity. What does each one of these represent in terms of the meaning of the data items? Which do we wish to analyze? Is there some rational basis for selecting one rather than the other?

It is at this point that general knowledge about the characteristics of various statistical coefficients and measures must be combined with intimate knowledge of the data, of how they were obtained, how they are given in the tables or cards used to represent them, and what the numbers really mean. It is suggested that the researcher should become so intimately knowledgeable in this regard that he can fully explain the impact of his statistical operations to an interested and intelligent layman. It is further suggested that those interested and intelligent laymen who function as administrators or users of research may well *insist* that this be done.

On the other hand, no serious examination of the data numbers by the researcher himself can substitute for that information regarding the data which is readily available to the substantive scientist, the administrator, the program director, and the research user. Collaborative effort stands to gain as much from these people as from the researcher's participation.

For example, in an evaluation of a rehabilitation program, the writer found that the results of a multivariate analysis failed to make the expected sense. He looked at the variables in question and found two variables which correlated .996. One variable represented the amount of welfare payment received out of funds that included federal money; the other represented the total amount received, regardless of source. Inspection of the data prior to the discovery of ridiculous results could have shown the offending correlation coefficient just as readily at that time as later. Inspection of the raw data, could have made the state of affairs obvious before even the correlation matrix was calculated, since the two data items were in adjoining columns and the equivalence of scores for almost every client upon these two data items would have been readily perceived. When the writer reported this finding to the administrator in charge of records, he responded, "Of course! During that year, there were *no significant* welfare funds in this state that did not include federal monies! The only reason we kept both data items is because federal regulations require both to be reported." The administrator knew the true facts of the case all the time, but no one asked him. He never had a chance to volunteer the information because he did not know what was being done with the data which his staff had helped to collect.

In this instance, the error was discovered because the findings were so obviously ridiculous that they alerted the researcher to the need for closer contact with the raw data and with those who understand the nature of those data. A much more serious example would be one in which a similar but not so blatant thing happened, for which the results of the study were not ridiculous but merely wrong. Leaving aside the man-hours wasted in the obtaining of the data and in their analysis, the real harm comes from the application of erroneous results. No amount of statistical sophistication can prevent such disasters; intimate communication among those who know various aspects of the problem is the only effective preventive measure.

Finally, let it be said that multivariate technology is by no means alone in being subject to the distortions inherent in insufficient understanding of the data and of the situation represented by the numbers. However, in the application of simpler models, errors are easier to find and the researcher remains closer to his data because he does not depend upon machine processes which he could not possibly duplicate. A single bivariate distribution plot can be inexpensively obtained and readily examined by the researcher, by simply looking at it. Under those conditions, ridiculous data items (such as apparent outliers which are, in fact, erroneous representations of missing data) can be readily seen, investigated, and corrected. In a multivariate analysis, however, there may be potentially several hundred or several thousand such bivariate distribution plots, making them expensive to obtain and impossible to examine carefully. Careful mapping of complex processes upon the substantive meaning represented by the data, repeated at every step of the analysis, becomes the only effective method of quality control.

SUMMARY

Multivariate methodologies for evaluation research have been presented as extensions of familiar statistical techniques. They fall generally into three types of models: data reduction, group differences, and relationships. The equivalence in most cases of the latter two has been stressed. Some strategies of analysis have been outlined, and suggestions for the utilization of multivariate techniques in evaluation research have been given.

The user of multivariate techniques is warned that the distance from the actual data sometimes created by the fact that a computer does the work may result in a larger number of errors in input and interpretation than when simple techniques are used. These errors may be avoided by careful examination of the raw data in combination with good communication between data analytic experts, substantive experts, and the research consumer.

REFERENCES

Cattell, R. B. *The Scientific Analysis of Personality*. Baltimore: Penguin, 1965.
Cattell, R. B. (ed.) *Handbook of Multivariate Experimental Psychology*. Chicago: Rand McNally, 1966.
Cohen, J. and P. Cohen. "A Method for Handling Missing Data in Multiple Regression/ Correlation." Paper presented at the Annual Meeting of the Society of Multivariate Experimental Psychology. November 1973.
Cooley, W. W. and P. R. Lohnes. *Multivariate Procedures in the Behavioral Sciences*. New York: Wiley, 1971.
Eber, H. W. Multivariate Analysis of a Vocational Rehabilitation System. *Multivariate Behavioral Research Monogram*. Number 66-1. For Worth, Tex.: TCU Press, 1966.
———. Multivariate Analysis of a Rehabilitation System: Cross Validation and Extension. *Multivariate Behavioral Research*, 1967, 2(4): 477-484.
French, J. W., R. B. Ekstrom and L. A. Price. *Manual of Kit for Reference Tests for Cognitive Factors*. Princeton: Educational Testing Service, 1963.
Guilford, J. P. *The Nature of Human Intelligence*. New York: McGraw-Hill, 1967.
Overall, J. E. and C. J. Klett. *Applied Multivariate Analysis*. New York: McGraw-Hill, 1972.

REFERENCE UPDATE
Selected by Elmer L. Struening

Baggaley, A. R. Multivariate analysis: An introduction for consumers of behavioral research. *Evaluation Review*, 5 (1): 123-131.
Bentler, P. M. multivariate analysis with latent variables: Causal modeling. *Annual Review of Psychology*, 1980, 31: 419-456.
Bentler, P. M. and D. G. Bonett. Significance tests and goodness of fit in the analysis of covariance structures. *Psychological Bulletin*, 1980, 88: 588-606.
Berk, R. A. and M. Brewer. Feet of clay in hobnail boots: An assessment of statistical inference in applied research. In T. D. Cook, M. L. D. Rosario, K. M. Hennigan, M. M. Mark, and W. M. K. Trochim (eds.) *Evaluation studies review annual* (Vol. 3). Beverly Hills, CA: Sage, 1978.
Bock, R. D. *Multivariate statistical methods in behavioral research*. New York: McGraw-Hill, 1975.
Cattell, R. B. (ed.). *Handbook of multivariate experimental psychology*. Chicago: Rand McNally, 1965.
DiCostanzo, J. L. and R. T. Eichelberger. Reporting ANCOVA results in evaluation settings. *Evaluation Review*, 1980, 4 (4): 419-450.
Fienberg, S. E. *The analysis of cross-classified categorical data*. Cambridge; MIT Press, 1977.
Finn, J. D. Multivariate analysis of repeated measures data. *Multivariate Behavioral Research*, 1969, 4: 391-413.
Finn, J. D. *A general model for multivariate analysis*. New York: Holt, Rinehart & Winston, 1974.

Hedges, L. V. Estimation of effect size from a series of independent experiments. *Psychological Bulletin*, 1982, 92 (2): 490-499.

Huitema, B. E. *The analysis of covariance and alternatives*. New York: John Wiley, 1980.

Judd, C. M. and D. A. Kenny. Process analysis: Estimating mediation in treatment evaluations. *Evaluation Review*, 1981, 5 (5): 602-619.

Kim, J. O. Multivariate analysis of ordinal variables. *American Journal of Sociology*, 1975, 81.

Koele, P. Calculating power in analysis of variance. *Psychological Bulletin*, 1982, 92 (2): 513-516.

Morrison, D. F. *Multivariate statistical methods* (2nd ed.). New York; McGraw-Hill, 1976.

Muthen, B. and G. Speckart. Categorizing skewed limited dependent variables: using multivariate probit regression to evaluate the California Civil Addict Program. *Evaluation Review*, 1983, 7 (2): 257-269.

Rosenthal, R. and D. B. Rubin. Comparing effect sizes of independent studies. *Psychological Bulletin*, 1982, 92 (2): 500-504.

Schuerman, J. R. Comments on statistical power in evaluative research design. In T. D. Cook, M. L. D. Rosario, K. M. Hennigan, M. M. Mark, and W. M. K. Trochim (eds.) *Evaluation studies review annual* (Vol. 3). Beverly Hills, CA: Sage, 1978.

Stevens, J. P. Power of the multivariate analysis of variance tests. *Psychological Bulletin*, 1980, 88 (3): 728-737.

Tukey, J. *Exploratory data analysis*. Reading, MA: Addison-Wesley, 1977.

12

MULTIPLE REGRESSION AS A GENERAL DATA-ANALYTIC SYSTEM

JACOB COHEN

New York University

Techniques for using multiple regression (MR) as a general variance-accounting procedure of great flexibility, power, and fidelity to research aims in both manipulative and observational psychological research are presented. As a prelude, the identity of MR and fixed-model analysis of variance/covariance (AV/ACV) is sketched. This requires an exposition of means of expressing nominal scale (qualitative) data as independent variables in MR. Attention is given to methods for handling interactions, curvilinearity, missing data, and covariates, for either uncorrelated or correlated independent variables in MR. Finally, the relative roles of AV/ACV and MR in data analysis are described, and the practical advantages of the latter are set forth.

If you should say to a mathematical statistician that you have discovered that linear multiple regression analysis and the analysis of variance (and covariance) are identical systems, he would mutter something like, "Of course—general linear model," and you might have trouble maintaining his attention. If you should say

AUTHOR'S NOTE: This work was supported by Grant No. MH 06137 from the National Institute of Mental Health of the United States Public Health Service. The author is grateful to the members of the Society of Multivariate Experimental Psychology for their constructive response when this material was presented at their annual meeting in Atlanta, Georgia, November 1966. This work profited greatly from detailed critiques supplied by Robert A. Bottenberg and Joe H. Ward, Jr., but since not all their suggestions were followed, they share no responsibility for any defects in the result. A detailed treatment of the procedures outlined here is available in Cohen and Cohen (1975).

Reprinted from *Psychological Bulletin,* 1968, Vol. 70, No. 6, pp. 426-433. Copyright 1968 by the American Psychological Association. Reprinted by permission of the publisher and author.

this to a typical psychologist, you would be met with incredulity, or worse. Yet it is true, and in its truth lie possibilities for more relevant and therefore more powerful exploitation of research data.

That psychologists would find strange the claimed equivalence of multiple regression (MR) and the fixed-model analysis of variance (AV) and covariance (ACV) is readily understandable. The textbooks in "psychological" statistics treat these matters quite separately, with wholly different algorithms, nomenclature, output, and examples.

MR is generally illustrated by examples drawn from the psychotechnology of educational or personnel selection, usually the prediction of some criterion (e.g., freshman grade point average) from predictors (e.g., verbal and quantitative score, high school rank). The yield is a multiple correlation (R) and a regression equation with weights which can be used for optimal prediction. The multiple R and the weights are subjected to significance testing, and conclusions are drawn about the effectiveness of the prediction, and which predictors do and do not contribute significantly to the prediction.

By way of contrast, AV and ACV are generally illustrated by pure research, manipulative experiments with groups subjected to different treatments or treatment combinations. Means and variances are found and main effect, interaction, and error mean squares computed and compared. Conclusions are drawn in terms of the significance of differences in sets or pairs of means or mean differences. More analytic yield of one or both of these systems is sometimes presented, but the above is a fair description of the respective thrusts of the two methods, and they are clearly different.

The differences are quite understandable, but the basis for this understanding comes primarily from the history and sociology of behavioral science research method and not from the essential mathematics. MR began to be exploited in the biological and behavioral sciences around the turn of the century in the course of the study of *natural* variation (Galton, Pearson, Yule). A couple of decades later, AV and ACV came out of the structure of (agronomic)experimentation, that is, of *artificial* or experimentally manipulated variation, where the treatments were carefully varied over the experimental material in efficient and logically esthetic experimental designs. The chief architect here was R. A. Fisher. These historical differences resulted in differences in tradition associated with substantively different areas and value systems in the psychological spectrum (cf. Cattell, 1966).

Yet the systems are, in the most meaningful sense, the same.

One of the purposes of this article is to sketch the equivalence of the two systems. In order to do so, it is necessary to show how nominal scales ("treatment," religion) can be used as "independent" variables in MR; the same is shown for "interactions." It is also necessary to demonstrate how multiple R^2 (and related statistics) can be computed from fixed-model AV and ACV output. Once the case is made for the *theoretical* equivalence of the two systems, the *practical* advantages of MR will be presented, which, given the foregoing, will be seen to constitute a very flexible general system for the analysis of data in the most frequently arising circumstance, namely, where an interval scaled or dichotomous (dependent) variable is to be "understood" in terms of other (independent) variables, however scaled.

A word about originality. Most of the material which follows was "discovered" by the author, only to find, after some painstaking library research, that much of it had been anticipated in published but not widely known works (chiefly Bottenberg & Ward, 1963; Li, 1964). Thus, no large claim for originality is being made, except for some of the heuristic concepts and their synthesis in a general data-analytic system realized by means of MR.

THE EQUIVALENCE OF THE SYSTEMS: NOMINAL SCALES AS INDEPENDENT VARIABLES IN MR

Some of the apparent differences in MR and AC/ACV lie in their respective terminologies. The variable being analyzed (from AV and ACV) and the criterion variable (from MR) are the same, and will be called the dependent variable and symbolized as Y. The variables bearing on Y, variously called main effect, interaction, or covariate in AV and ACV (depending on their definition and design function), and predictor variables in MR will be called independent variables, and symbolized as X_i (i = 1, 2, $\cdots$ k). Each X_i consumes *one* degree of freedom (df). In complex problems (e.g., factorial design, curvilinear analysis), it is convenient to define sets of the X_i, each such set representing a single research variable or factor.

In the conventional use of MR, the X_i are ordered quantitative variables, treated as equal interval scales. Thus, in a study of the prediction of freshman grade point average (Y), one might have X_1 = verbal aptitude score, X_2 = quantitative aptitude score, X_3 = percentile rank in high school graduating class, and X_4 = Hollingshead socio-economic status index. Thus, k = 4, and the question of sets need not arise (or, they may be thought of as four sets, each of a single variable). But what if one wanted to include *religion* among the X_i? Or alternatively, if the entering class were to be assigned randomly to four different experimental teaching systems, how would experimental group assignment be represented? More generally, how does one accommodate a purely nominal or qualitative variable as an independent variable in MR?

Imagine a simple situation in which a dependent variable Y is to be studied as a function of a nominal scale variable G, which has four "levels": groups G_1, G_2, G_3, and G_4. For concreteness, Y and G may be taken as having the following alternative meanings:

Research Area	Y		The G Set: G_1, G_2, G_3, G_4
Social Psychology	Attitude toward United Nations	Religion:	Protestant Catholic Jewish Other

Clinical Psychology	Suggestibility	Diagnosis:	Paranoid Schizophrenia
			Nonparanoid Schizophrenia
			Compulsive Neurosis
			Hysterical Neurosis
Physiological Psychology	Retention	Treatment:	Drug and Frontal Lesion
			Drug and Control Lesion
			No Drug and Frontal Lesion
			No Drug and Control Lesion

Formally, what is being posited is the assignment, not necessarily equally, of each of n cases into (four) mutually exclusive and exhaustive groups, no matter whether G is an organismic, naturally occurring variable or one created by the experimenter's manipulative efforts on randomly assigned subjects.

The expression of group membership as independent variables in MR can be accomplished in several ways, all equivalent in a sense to be later described. The intuitively simplest of these is "dummy" variable coding (Bottenberg & Ward, 1963; Suits, 1957).

Dummy Variable Coding

Table 12.1 presents various coding alternatives for the rendition of membership in one of four groups. Columns 1, 2, and 3 represent a dummy variable coding scheme. It involves merely successively dichotomizing so that each of $3(= g - 1)$ of the $4(= g)$ groups is distinguished from the remainder as one aspect of G. For example, on X_1 all subjects in G_1 are scored 1 and all others, without differentiation, are scored 0. Thus, this variable by itself carries only some of the information in the G variable as a whole, for example, Protestant versus all other, or Paranoid Schizophrenia versus all other. However, the three variables coded as in Columns 1, 2, and 3 together exhaust the information of the G variable. One might think that a fourth independent variable, one which distinguishes G_4 from all others, would be necessary, but such a variable would be redundant. In the usual MR system which uses a constant term in the regression equation, it requires no more than $g - 1$ independent variables (no matter how coded) to represent g groups of a G nominal scale. A fourth X_i here is not only unnecessary, but its inclusion would result in indeterminacy in the computation of the MR constants. This is an instance of a more general demand on the set of independent variables in any MR system: no independent variable in the set may yield a multiple R with the remaining inde-

TABLE 12.1 ILLUSTRATIVE CODING FOR A NOMINAL SCALE

Nominal scale variable	\multicolumn{15}{c	}{Columns}
	1	2	3	4	5	6	7	8	9	10	11	12	13	14	15
	X_1[a]	X_2	X_3	X_1	X_2	X_3	X_1	X_2	X_3	X_1	X_2	X_3	X_1	X_2	X_3
G_1	1	0	0	1	1	0	1	1	1	5	25	125	1	-7	0
G_2	0	1	0	1	-1	0	1	-1	-1	0	0	0	-1	-1	0
G_3	0	0	1	-1	0	1	-1	1	-1	-4	16	-64	-4	½	24
G_4	0	0	0	-1	0	-1	-1	-1	1	6	36	216	1	6	-1

a Independent variable.

pendent variables of 1.00. This constraint on the independent variables (in matrix algebraic terms, the demand that their data matrix be nonsingular or of full rank) would be violated if we introduced a fourth variable, since, in that case, any of the four X_i would yield $R = 1.00$ when treated as a dependent variable regressed on the other three. In terms that are intuitively compelling, one can see that members of G_4 are identified uniquely on the X_1, X_2, X_3 vector as 0, 0, 0, that is, as not G_1, not G_2, and not G_3, thus not requiring a fourth dichotomous X_i. G_4 is not being slighted; on the contrary, as will be shown below, it serves as a reference group. Any group may be designated for this role, but if one is functionally a control or reference group, so much the better.[1]

Before we turn to a consideration of X_1, X_2 and X_3 as a set of variables, let us consider them separately. Each can be correlated with the dependent variable Y. A set of artificial data was constructed to provide a concrete illustration. For n = 36 cases, a set of three-digit Y scores was written, the cases assigned to four groups and coded for X_i as described. The resulting product moment r's (point-biserial) were $r_{Y1} = -.5863$, $r_{Y2} = .0391$, and $r_{Y3} = .4965$. When squared, the resulting values indicate the proportion of the Y variance each distinction accounts for: $r^2_{Y1} = .3437$, $r^2_{Y2} = .0015$, and $r^2_{Y3} = .2465$. Thus, for example, the Protestant versus non-Protestant variable accounts for .3437 of the variance in Attitude toward the United Nations dependent variable, as represented in the sample.

Whether the .3437 value can be used as an estimator of the proportion of variance which G_1 versus remainder accounts for *in the population* of naturally occurring G depends on the way G was sampled. If the n cases of the sample were obtained by randomly sampling from the population as a whole so that the proportion of G_1 cases in the sample, n_1/n reflects their population predominance, .3437 estimates the proportion of variance in the natural population. However, if G was sampled to yield equal n_i in the g groups (or some other nonrepresentative numbers), the .3437 value is projectible to a similarly distributed artificial population. The statistical purist would abjure the use of r or r^2 (and R or R^2) in such instances, but if one understands that the parameters being estimated are for populations whose X_i characteristics are those of the sample, no inappropriate errors in inference need be made, and a useful analytic tool becomes available.

Although the separate r^2_{Yi} are analytically useful, our purpose is to understand the operation of X_1, X_2, X_3 as a set, since it is as a set that they represent G as the four-level nominal scale. The r^2_{Yi} cannot simply be added up to determine how much Y variance G accounts for, since dummy variables are inevitably correlated with each other. Mutually exclusive assignment means that membership in one group G_i necessarily means nonmembership in any other, G_j, hence a negative relationship. The product moment r (i.e., the phi coefficient) between such dichotomies, that is, between G_i and G_j or X_i and X_j when expressed in dummy variable form, is

$$r_{ij} = -\sqrt{\frac{n_i n_j}{(n - n_i)(n - n_j)}} \tag{1}$$

where n_i, n_j are the sample sizes of each group, and n is the total sample size over all g groups. When sample sizes are all equal, the formula simplifies to

$$r_{ij} = -\frac{1}{g-1} \qquad [2]$$

that is, the negative reciprocal of one less than the number of groups; thus, in our running artificial example, if we assume the four groups equal in size, the phi coefficients among the X_i dichotomies are all - $\frac{1}{3}$.

The fact that the independent variables representing group membership are correlated with each other poses no special problem for MR, which is designed to allow for this in whatever guise it appears. But it does alert us to the fact that the proportions of Y variance given by the r^2_{Yi} are overlapping. If we now compute the multiple R^2 using X_1, X_2, and X_3 as independent variables, the value we find in the artificial data is $R^2_{Y \cdot 123}$ = .4458. This is interpreted as meaning that G (religion, diagnosis, or treatment group membership) accounts for .4458 of the variance in the dependent variable Y, and in the exact sense ordinarily understood.

Identity with Analysis of Variance

Consider the more familiar AV analysis of these data. The Y scores can be assembled into the four G groups and a one-way AV performed. This yields the usual sums of squares for between groups (B SS), for within groups (W SS), and their total (T SS). If we determine the proportion of T SS which B SS constitutes, we have η^2 (eta square), the squared correlation ratio. This statistic has, as its most general interpretation, the proportion of variance of the dependent variable accounted for by G-group membership, or equivalently, accounted for by the group Y means. (Unfortunately, tradition in applied statistics textbooks and courses has focused on a narrow, special-case interpretation of η as an index of curvilinear correlation. For a broader view, see Cohen, 1965, pp. 104-105 and Peters & Van Voorhis, 1940, pp. 312-325 and, particularly, 353-357).

If we compute $\eta^2_{Y \cdot G}$ for the artificial data, we find

$$\eta^2_{Y \cdot G} = \frac{B\ SS}{T\ SS} = \frac{12127.0}{27205.6} = .4458 \qquad [3]$$

Thus, our MR coding procedure yields an $R^2_{Y \cdot 123}$ exactly equal to $\eta^2_{Y \cdot G}$, interpretable as the proportion of Y variance for which G accounts. The parallel goes further. It is demonstrable that the "shrunken" or df-corrected R^2 (McNemar, 1962, pp. 184-185) is identically the same as Kelley's "unbiased" squared correlation ratio, epsilon-square (Cohen, 1965, p. 105; Cureton, 1966; Peters & Van Voorhis, 1940, pp. 319-322).

Furthermore, if one tests either of these results for significance, one obtains identically the same F ratio, for identically the same df:

For the $R^2_{Y \cdot 123}$, using the standard formula (e.g., McNemar, 1962, p. 283)

$$F = \frac{R^2_{Y \cdot 123 \cdots k}/k}{(1 - R^2_{Y \cdot 123 \cdots k})/(n - k - 1)}$$

$$= \frac{R^2_{Y \cdot 123 \cdots k}/(g-1)}{(1 - R^2_{Y \cdot 123 \cdots k})/(n-g)}$$

$$= \frac{.4458/(4-1)}{(1-.4458)/(36-4)} = 8.580, \qquad [4]$$

for numerator (regression) df = k = g - 1 = 3 and denominator (residual or error) df = n - k - 1 = n - g = 32.

The significance of η^2 is, of course the signficance of the separation of the G groups' Y means, that is, the usual AV F test of the between-groups mean square (MS):

$$F = \frac{\text{between G groups MS}}{\text{within G groups MS}} = \frac{(B\ SS)/(g-1)}{(W\ SS)/(n-g)}$$

$$= \frac{(12127.0)/(4-1)}{(15078.6)/(36-4)} = \frac{4042.33}{471.21} = 8.580, \qquad [5]$$

for numerator (between G groups) df = g - 1 = 4 - 1 = 3, and denominator (within G groups, or error) df = n - g = 36 - 4 = 32.

These F ratios must be identical, since B SS = $(R^2_{Y \cdot 123 \cdots k})$ (total SS), and W SS - $(1 - R^2_{Y \cdot 123 \cdots k})$ (total SS). Formula 4 differs from Formula 5 only in that the total SS has been cancelled out from numerator and denominator.

The formulas help clarify the identity of the two procedures. We obtain another perspective on why 3(= g - 1) independent variables carry all the group membership information for 4(= g) groups, —there are only 3 df "associated with" G group membership. By either the MR or AV route the total SS (or variance) of Y has been partitioned into a portion accounted for by G group membership (or by G group Y means), and a portion not so accounted for (i.e., within group, residual, or "error"), the latter, by either route based on n - g df.

Conceptually, the F ratios can be understood to be the same because they are testing null hypotheses which are mathematically equivalent, even though they are traditionally differently stated:

$$\text{MR} : H_0 : \text{Population } R^2_{Y \cdot 123} = 0$$

$$\text{AV} : H_0 : \text{Population } m_1 = m_2 = m_3 = m_4 = m$$

If the AV H_0 is true, then knowledge of group membership and the use of group means leads to the same least squares prediction of the Y value of a given case as no knowledge, namely, the grand mean, thus one can account for none of the variance in Y by such knowledge, hence $R^2_{Y \cdot 123} = 0$, and conversely.

A full MR analysis also yields the regression coefficients and constant for the regression equation:

$$\dot{Y} = B_1 X_1 + B_2 X_2 + \cdots + B_k X_k + A \qquad [6]$$

where Y is the least-squares estimated ("predicted") value of $\dot{Y}$, the B_1 are raw score partial regression coefficients attached to each X_i, and A is the regression constant or Y-intercept, that is, the estimated value of Y when all X_i are set at zero. (Its computation is accomplished by including a "unit vector" with the X_i; see Draper & Smith, 1967.)

In any MR problem, a B_i coefficient gives the amount of the effect in Y expressed in Y units which is yielded by a unit increase in X_i. But since as dummy variables the X_i are coded 0 - 1, a unit increase means 1, membership in the group, rather than 0, nonmembership in the group. Solving for the values of the general regression Equation 6 for the artificial data, and using dummy variables, we obtain:

$$\hat{Y} = -30.34X_1 - .56X_2 + 21.22X_3 + 84.12$$

Since group membership is all-or-none, the B_i values give the *net* consequence of membership in G_i relative to G_4 for groups G_1, G_2, and G_3. Thus,

$$\hat{Y}_1 = \overline{Y}_1 = -30.34(1) - .56(0) + 21.22(0) + 84.12 = 53.78$$

$$\hat{Y}_2 = \overline{Y}_2 = -30.34(0) - .56(1) + 21.22(0) + 84.12 = 83.56$$

$$\hat{Y}_3 = \overline{Y}_3 = -30.34(0) - .56(0) + 21.22(1) + 84.12 = 105.34$$

And G_4 has not been slighted, since, substituting its scores on X_1, X_2, and X_3, we find:

$$Y_4 = \overline{Y}_4 = -30.34(0) - .56(0) + 21.22(0) + 84.12 = 84.12$$

Thus, one can understand that "B_4," the "missing" reference group's weight, is always zero, and that therefore $Y_4 = A$. The exact values of the B_i will vary, depending on which group is taken as the reference group (i.e., is coded $0, \cdots, 0$), but the differences among the B_i's will always be the same, since they are the same as the differences between the group Y means. That is, whichever the reference group, the separation of the B_i's in the example will be the same as that among the values -30.34, -.56, +21.22 and 0. (For example, if G_1 is taken as the reference group, the new B_i are 0, 29.78, 51.56, and 30.33, and the regression constant $A = \overline{Y}_1 = 53.78$.)

Not only are the B_i meaningful, but also the multiple-partial correlations with the criterion, that is, the correlation of Y with X_i, partialing out or holding constant all the other independent variables, which for the sake of notational simplicity, we designate p_i. With dummy variable coded X_i, p_i can be more specifically interpreted as the correlation between Y and the dichotomy made up of membership in G_i versus membership in G_0, the reference group. The p_i thus give, in correlational terms, the relevance to Y of the distinction between each G_i and the reference group.

Furthermore, the p_i, B_i, and β_i (the standardized partial regression coefficient) can be tested for significance by means of t (or equivalently, F with numerator df = 1). Indeed, the null hypothesis is the same for all three, —the respective population parameter equals zero. But for a given X_i, if any one of the three is zero, all are zero, and the value of t is identical for all three tests. For the artificial data, the results are

	X_1	X_2	X_3
B_i	-30.34	$-.56$	$+21.22$
β_i	$-.478$	$-.009$	$.334$
p_i	$-.464$	$-.010$	$.344$
t_i	-2.96	$-.05$	2.07

Thus, the G_1-G_4 distinction and also the G_3-G_4 distinction with regard to Y are significant (two tailed .01 and .05, with 32 df) while the G_2-G_4 is not. These are identically the results one would obtain for t tests between the respective Y means, using the within-group mean square (with 32 df) as the variance estimate.

The reader, having been shown the MR-AV identities, may nevertheless react, "O.K., that's interesting, but so what?" Other than the provision of correlational (or regression) values, no advantage of MR over AV is claimed for this problem. But if there were other independent variables of interest (main effects, either nominal, ordinal, or interval; interactions; covariates; nonlinear components; etc., whether or not correlated with G or each other), their addition to the G variable could proceed easily by means of MR, and not at all easily in an AV/ACV framework. This possibility is the single most important advantage of the MR procedure, and will receive further attention below.

To summarize, dummy variable coding of nominal scale data yields the multiple R^2 and F test (proportion of variance accounted for by group membership and an overall significance test) and the group Y means, but also information on the degree of relevance to Y of membership in any given group, G_i, relative to the remainder (r_{Yi}), and to a reference group in terms of either regression weights (B_i or β_i) or correlation (p_i), as well as specific significance tests on the relevant null hypotheses. The importance of dummy variable (or other nominal scale) coding lies not so much in its use when only a single nominal scale constitutes the independent variables, but rather in its ready inclusion with other independent variables in MR.

CONTRAST CODING

Another system for representing nominal data can be thought of as contrast or "issues" coding. Here, each independent variable carries a contrast (in the AV/ACV sense) among group means. Each subject is characterized for each contrast according to the role he plays in it, which depends upon his group membership. With all contrasts so represented, the MR analysis can proceed.

As an example, reconsider the representation of the G variable. We can contrast membership neither G_1 or G_2 versus membership in either G_3 or G_4. This could be substantively interpreted as, for example, majority versus minority religions, schizophrenic versus neurotic, or drug versus no-drug treatment condition. The coding or scoring of this issue may be rendered as in Column 4 in Table 12.1: the value of 1 is assigned the subjects in G_1 and G_2 and the value -1 to those in G_3 and G_4, as is done in the computation of orthogonal contrasts in AV (e.g., Edwards, 1960). Actually, any two different numbers can be used to render this issue by itself, but there are advantages for some purposes in using values which sum to zero. The simple correlation between the dependent variable and this X_1 is a point-biserial correlation (as were the dummy variable correlations) whose square gives directly the proportion of Y variance attributable to the G_1, G_2 versus G_3, G_4 distinction. For the artificial data, the $r^2_{Y1} = .2246$ ($r_{Y1} = -.4739$). This is a meaningful value which gives the size of the relationship in the sample. This r_{Y1} can be tested for significance, and confidence limits for it (or for r^2_{Y1}) can be computed by conventional procedures.

Other issues or contrasts can be rendered as independent variables. For example, a second issue which may be rendered is the effect on Y of the G_1 versus G_2 distinction, ignoring G_3 and G_4. A third issue may be the analogous G_3 versus G_4 distinction, ignoring G_1 and G_2. These are rendered, respectively, in Columns 5 and 6 in Table 12.1. Each yields an r and r^2 with the criterion which is interpretable, testable for significance, and confidence boundable.

Beyond the separate correlations of these three contrast variables, there is the further question of what their *combined* effect is on Y. We compute the $R^2_{Y \cdot 123}$ and F and obtain *exactly* the same values as when the arbitrary or dummy variable coding was used, .4458 and 8.580 (for the artificial data). This follows from the fact that the three independent variables satisfy the nonsingularity condition, that is, no one of them gives a multiple R with the other two of unity. This is a necessary *and sufficient* condition for *any* coding of g - 1 independent variables to represent G (see next section).

As before, the partial statistics, that is, the p_i, B_i and β_i and the common t test of their significance are also meaningful. If the independent variables all correlate zero with each other, the β_i will equal their respective r_{Yi}. That this must be the case can be seen from the fact that each r^2_{Yi} represents a *different* portion of the Y variance whose sum is the multiple $R^2_{Y \cdot 123}$ and thus the relationship $R^2_{Y \cdot 123} = \Sigma r_{Yi} \beta_i = \Sigma r^2_{Yi}$ must hold. The X_i as presented in Columns 4, 5, and 6 will be mutually uncorrelated if and only if the group samples sizes are equal. If they are not equal, the correlations among the X_i will be nonzero, which means that the contrasts or issues posed to the data are not independent. Such would be the case, in general, in the example if it were religion or diagnosis which formed the basis for group membership, and the actual natural population randomly sampled. Given unequal n_i for the four samples, although it is possible to make the three contrasts described above mutually uncorrelated, the coding of Columns 4, 5, and 6 does not do so. The scope of this article precludes discussion of the procedures whereby contrasts are coded so as to be uncorrelated. We note here merely that although it is always possible to do so, it is not necessarily desirable (see below).

Since, in AV terms, the between-groups SS can be (orthogonally) partitioned in various ways, there are sets of contrasts other than the set above which can be represented in the coding. A particularly popular set is that automatically provided by the AV factorial design. If the four groups of this example are looked upon as occupying the cells of a 2 x 2 design (an interpretation to which the physiological example of drug versus no drug, frontal lesion versus control lesion particularly lends itself), each of the usual AV effects can be represented as X_i by the proper coding. The first is the same as before, and contrasts G_1 and G_2 with G_3 and G_4, for example, the drug-no-drug main effect, reproduced as Column 7 of Table 12.1. The second main effect, for example, frontal-control lesion, contrasts G_1 and G_3 with G_2 and G_4 and is given by the coding in Column 8. This latter X_2 gives r_{Y2}, the (point-biserial) r for (e.g.) site of lesion with the dependent variable (e.g.) retention, and r^2_{Y2} is the proportion of Y variance accounted for by this variable.

The remaining df is, as the AV has taught us, the interaction of the two main effects, for example, Drug-No-Drug x Frontal-Control Lesion. It can always be rendered as a multiplicative function of the two single df aspects of the main effects. Here, it is simply coded as the product of each group's "scores" on X_1 and X_2 (given as Column 9 in Table 12.1): 1 x 1 = 1, 1 x –1 = –1, –1 x 1 = –1, and –1 x -1 = 1. Rendering the interaction as X_3, one can interpret it as carrying the information of that aspect of group membership which represents the *joint* (note, *not* additive) effect of the drug and frontal lesion conditions. Its (point-biserial) r_{Y3} is an expression in correlational terms of the degree of relationship between Y and the *joint* operation of drug and lesion site. r^2_{Y3} gives the proportion of Y variance accounted for by this joint effect.

In the example, these three issues are *conceptually* independent, thus it would be desirable that the X_i be uncorrelated, that is, $r_{12} = r_{13} = r_{23} = 0$. The coding values given in Columns 7, 8, and 9 of **Table 12.1** will satisfy this condition if (and only if) the sample sizes of the four cells are equal. (If not, other coding, not discussed here, would be necessary.)

The conceptual independence of the issues arises from the consideration that they are both manipulated variables. When this is the case, it is clearly desirable for them to be represented as mutually uncorrelated, since then the $\beta_{Yi} = r_{Yi}$ and the $R^2_{Y \cdot 123}$ is simply a sum of the separate r^2_{Yi}. Thus, the total variance of Y accounted for by group membership is unambiguously partitioned into the three separate sources. Further, the factorial AV F test values of each of the separate (one df) effects is *identical* with the t^2 of the analogous MR partial coefficients (β_i, B_i, or p_i).

However, whether one wishes to represent the issues as uncorrelated depends on whether they are conceptually independent and the differing n_i are a consequence of animals randomly dying or test tubes being randomly dropped on the one hand, or whether they carry valid sampling information about a natural population state of affairs. Assume Y is a measure of liberalism-conservatism and reconsider the problem with the groups reinterpreted as G_1: low education, low income ($n_1 = 160$), G_2: low education, high income ($n_2 = 20$), G_3: high education, low income ($n_3 = 80$), and G_4: high education, high income ($n_4 = 100$). These unequal and disproportional n_i carry valid sampling information about the univariate and bivariate distributions of education and income as defined here, the product moment r_{12} (phi) between them (coded as in Columns 7 and 8) equalling .4714. They may also be correlated with their interaction. One would ordinarily not wish to render these effects as uncorrelated, since the resulting X_i would be quite artificial, but rather by the coding given in Columns 7, 8, and 9, where, again, X_3 is simply the $X_1 X_2$ produuct.

Note that whether the X_i are correlated or uncorrelated, or whether the n_i are equal or unequal, *all* of these coding systems yield the same $R^2_{Y \cdot 123}$ and associated F.

Two systems of rendering nominal scale (group membership) information into independent variables have been described: dummy variable coding and contrast coding. They result in identically the same multiple R^2 (and associated F) but different per independent variable partial statistics which are differently interpreted. Either involves expressing the nominal scale of g levels (groups) into g - 1 independent variables, each carrying a distinct aspect of group membership whose degree of association and statistical significance can be determined.

Nonsense Coding

It turns out, quite contraintuitively, that if one's purpose is merely to represent G so that its R^2_Y and/or its associated F test value can be determined, it hardly matters how one codes $X_1, X_2, \cdots, X_{g-1}$. *Any* real numbers, positive or negative, whole or fractional, can be used in the coding subject only to the nonsingularity constraint, that is, no X_i may have a multiple R of 1.00 with the other independent variables.

Consider, for example, the values of Columns 10-12 of Table 12.1. The numbers for X_1 in Column 10 were obtained by random entry into a random number table and their signs by coin flipping. Column 11 for X_2 was constructed by squaring the entries in Column 10, and Column 12 for X_3 by cubing them. Powering the X_1 values assures the satisfaction of the nonsingularity constraint. Now, using these nonsense "scores" to code G and the same Y values of the artificial example, we find the *same* R^2_{Y123} of .4458 and F = 8.580.

Or, alternatively, the coding values of Columns 13, 14, and 15 were obtained by haphazard free association with a quick eyeball check to assure nonsingularity. They, too, yield $R^2_{Y \cdot 123}$ = .4458 and F = 8.580.

Why these, or any other values satisfying nonsingularity will "work" would require too much space to explain nontechnically. Ultimately, it is a generalization of the same principle which makes it possible to score a dichotomy with *any* two different values (not only the conventional 0 and 1) and obtain the same pointbiserial r^2 against another variable.

Of course, the statistics per X_i, that is, $r_{Yi}, p_i, B_i, \beta_i$, are as nonsensical as the X_i. But the regression equation will yield the correct group means on Y, and, as noted, R^2 and its F remain invariant. Thus, with the aid of an MR computer program and a table of random numbers (or a nonsingular imagination), one can duplicate the yield of an AV.

Apart from its status as a statistical curiosity, of what value is the demonstration that one can simulate an AV by means of an arbitrarily coded MR analysis? Not much, taken by itself. However, despite this disclaimer, it should be pointed out that for most investigators, the yield sought from the AV of such data is the significance status of the F test on the means, which the MR provides; the latter also "naturally" yields, in R^2, a statement of proportion of variance accounted for. True, this is identically available from the AV in η^2, but this is not generally understood and computed. The MR approach has the virtue of calling to the attention of the investigator the existence of a rho (relationship) value and its distinction from a tau (significance test) value (Cohen, 1965, pp. 101-106), an issue usually lost sight of in AV contexts (but, see Hays, 1963, pp. 325-333).

But if it hardly matters how we score G and still get the same $R^2_{Y\cdot123}$ and F ratio, we can score it in some meaningful way, one which provides analytically useful intermediate results, that is, by dummy variable or contrast coding. For other approaches to nominal scale coding, see Bottenberg and Ward (1963) and Jennings (1967).

ASPECTS OF QUANTITATIVE SCALES AS INDEPENDENT VARIABLES

As noted in the introduction, psychologists are familiar with the use of quantitative variables as independent variables in MR. This, indeed, is the only use of MR illustrated in the standard textbooks. Thus, given duration of first psychiatric hospitalization as the dependent variable Y, and as independent variables: age (X_1), Hollingshead SES Index (X_2), and MMPI Schizophrenia (Sc) score (X_3), the psychologist knows how to proceed. But MR provides opportunities for the analysis of quantitative independent variables which transcend this very limited approach.

Curvilinear Regression

From the enlarged conceptual framework of the present treatment of MR, we would say that this analysis is concerned with the *linear* aspects of age. SES, and Sc. There are other functions or aspects of these variables which can be represented as independent variables.

It has long been recognized that curvilinear relationships can be represented in linear MR by means of a polynomial form in powered terms. The standard Equation 6

$$\dot{Y} = B_1 X_1 + B_2 X_2 + \cdots B_k X_k + A$$

is linear in the X_i. If the X_i are $X_1 = Z, X_2 = Z^2, X_3 = Z^3, \cdots X_k = Z^k$, the equation is *still* linear in the X_i, even though not linear in the Z. The result of this strategem is that nonlinear regression of Y on Z can nevertheless be represented within the linear *multiple* regression framework, the "multiplicity" being used to represent various aspects of nonlinearity, the quadratic, cubic, etc. The provision of any given power u of Z, that is, Z^u allows for u - 1 bends in the regression curve of Y or Z. Thus Z^1 or Z provides for $1 - 1 = 0$ bends, hence a straight line, Z^2 provides for $2 - 1 = 1$ bend, Z^3 for 2 bends, etc. In most psychological research, provision for more than one or two bends will rarely be necessary.

It is the same strategem of polynomial representation further refined to make these aspects orthogonal to each other, which is utilized in the AV, also a linear model, in trend analysis designs.

A note of caution must be injected here. Such variables as Z, Z^2, and Z^3 are in general correlated, indeed, for score-like data, usually highly so. Table 12.2 presents some illustrative data. In this example, the correlations are .9479, .8840, and .9846. For reasons of ordinary scientific parsimony, unless one is working with a strong hypothesis, we normally think of them as a hierarchy: how much Y variance does Z account for? (.5834) If Z^2 is added to Z as a second variable, how much do both together account for? (.5949) The difference represents the increment in variance accounted for by making allowance for quadratic (parabolic) curvature. In the example, it is a very small amount, -.0115. If to Z and Z^2 we add Z^3, the multiple $R^2_{Y \cdot 123}$ becomes .5956, an increment over $R^2_{Y \cdot 12}$ of only .0007. Each of these separate increments, or the two combined can be tested for significance. In general, *any* increment to an $R^2_{Y \cdot A}$ due to the addition of B can be tested by the F ratio:

$$F = \frac{(R^2_{Y \cdot A,B} - R^2_{Y \cdot A})/b}{(1 - R^2_{Y \cdot AB})/(n - a - b - 1)} \qquad [7]$$

with df = b and (n - a - b - 1), where

$R^2_{Y \cdot A,B}$ is the incremented R^2 based on a + b independent variables, that is, predicted from the combined sets of A and B variables,

$R^2_{Y \cdot A}$ is the smaller R^2 based on only a independent variables, that is, predicted from only the A set,

a and b are the number of original (a) and added (b) independent variables, hence the number of df each "takes up."

This F test of an increment to R^2 is much more general in its applicability than the present narrow context, and its symbols have been accordingly given quite general interpretation. It is used several times later in the exposition, in other circumstances where, because of correlation among X_i, it provides a basis for judging how much a set of independent variables contributes *additionally* to Y variance accounting. Since what is added is independent of what is already provided for, this is a general device for partitioning R^2 into orthogonal portions. Since the size of such portions depends on the *order* in which sets are included, the hierarchy of sets is an important part of the investigator's hypothesis statement. The generality of Formula 7 is further seen in that Formula 4 is actually a special case of Formula 7, where $R^2_{Y \cdot A}$ is zero because no X_i are used (hence a = 0) and $R^2_{Y \cdot B}$ is the R^2 based on b (= k) df which is being tested, that is, an increment of R^2 from zero.

TABLE 12.2   ILLUSTRATIVE DATA ON POLYNOMIAL MULTIPLE REGRESSION

Variable	Correlations (r)			Cumulative R^2	Increment	pi
	Y	Z	Z^2			
Z (= X_1)	.7638			.5834	.5834	.1399
Z^2 (= X_2)	.7582	.9479		.5949	.0115	-.0116
Z^3 (= X_3)	.7268	.8840	.9846	.5956	.0007	.0419

Either set may have one or more independent variables. Thus, to test the increment of Z^2 to Z alone, assuming total n = 36,

$$F = \frac{(.5949 - .5834)/1}{(1 - .5949)/(36 - 1 - 1 - 1)} = \frac{.0115}{.4051/33} = .934$$

with df = 1 and 33 (a chance departure).
To test the pooled addition of both Z^2 and Z^3 to Z,

$$F = \frac{(.5956 - .5834)/2}{(1 - .5956)/(36 - 1 - 2 - 1)} = \frac{.0122/2}{.4044/32} = .483$$

with df = 2 and 32 (also a chance result).

The need for caution arises in that if one studies the results of the regression analysis which uses Z, Z^2 and Z^3, where the solution of the partial (regression or correlation) coefficients is simultaneous, not successive, the three variables are treated quite democratically. Each is partialed from the others without favor or hierarchy. Since such variables are highly correlated, when one partials Z^2 and Z^3 from Z, one is robbing Z of Y variance which we think of as rightfully belonging to it. Table 12.2 gives the p_i of the three predictors when one treats them as a set. The values are smaller (reflecting the mutual partialing), and may be negative (reflecting "suppression" effects). Because the p_i are so small, they may well be nonsignificant (as they are here), even though r_{YZ} is significant and any of the other variables may yield a significant increment. Thus, the significance interpretation of the regression of a set of polynomial terms simultaneously may be quite misleading when the usual hierarchical notions prevail.

On the other hand, if the analyst's purpose to portray a polynomial regression fit to an observed set of data, he can solve for the set simultaneously and use the resulting MR equation. For the data used for Table 12.2, the regression Equation 6 is:

$$\hat{Y} = 11.70X_1 - .50X_2 + .25X_3 + 55.90$$

the values being the B_i regression coefficients and constant, and the X_i successively Z, Z^2, and Z^3. One can substitute over the range of interest of Z and obtain fitted values of Y for purposes of prediction or of graphing of the function.

There are other means whereby curvilinear relationships can be handled in an MR framework. Briefly, one can organize an independent variable Z into g class intervals (ordinarily, but not necessarily equal in range) and treat the resulting classes as groups, coding them by the dummy variable technique described above. This results in g - 1 independent variables, each a segment of the Z range. The resulting $R^2_{Y \cdot G}$ is the amount of Y variance accounted for by Z (curvilinearly, if such is the case) and the Y means for the g intervals, computable from the resulting raw score regression equation, can be plotted graphically against the midpoints of the class intervals of Z to portray the function.

A more elegant method is the transformation (coding) of the Z values to *orthogonal* polynomials. This has the advantages in that the resulting X_i terms representing linear, quadratic, cubic, etc., components of the polynomial regression are uncorrelated with each other; thus each contributes a separate portion of the Y variance capable of being tested for significance. Unfortunately, this method becomes computationally quite cumbersome unless the Z values are equally spaced and with equal n_i per interval. The latter is the usual case when Z is an experimentally manipulated variable, where the standard trend analysis designs of the AV can be used (Edwards, 1960).

Finally, although the first few powers of a polynomial is a good *general* fitting function, in some circumstances, such transformations of Z as log Z, $1/Z$, or $Z^{1/2}$ may provide a better fit. Draper and Smith (1967) provide a useful general reference for handling curvilinearity (and other MR problems).

Joint Aspects or Interactions

Given two independent variables, $X_1 = Z$ and $X_2 = W$, one may be interested in not only their separate effects on Y, but also on their joint effect, over and above their separate effects. As noted above (Contrast Coding), where this was discussed in the narrow context of a 2 x 2 design, this joint effect is carried by a third independent variable, a score defined for each subject by the product of his Z and W scores, that is, $X_3 = ZW$. This variable contains this joint effect, which is identically the (first-order) interaction effect of AV, or the "moderator" effect of Saunders (1956). This identity is quite general, so that a triple interaction is carried by a triple product, say ZWV, etc. Furthermore, the above are all interactions or joint effects of *linear* aspects of the variables. The more complex interactions of nonlinear aspects, such as the linear by quadratic, or quadratic by cubic, made familiar by advanced treatments of AV trend analysis (Winer, 1962, pp. 273-278), would be represented by products of powered variables, for example ZW^2, Z^2W^3, each a single independent variable.

The presentation of joint effects as simple products in MR requires the same caution as in the polynomial representation of a single variable. (Indeed, a powered variable can be properly understood as a special case of an interaction, for example, Z^2 contains the Z by Z interaction.) If one uses simultaneously as independent variables $X_1 = Z$, $X_2 = W$, $X_3 = ZW$, the correlations of Z with ZW, and W with ZW will ordinarily not be zero, may indeed be large, and the partial coefficients for Z and W (β, B, p) will have lost to ZW some Y variance which properly is theirs (just as Z would be robbed of some of its Y variance by Z^2 and Z^3). The problem is solved as in the polynomial regression analysis: Find $R^2_{Y \cdot 123}$, the variance proportion accounted for by all three variables; then find $R^2_{Y \cdot 12}$, the amount accounted for *without* the interaction. The increment is tested for significance by the F ratio of Formula 7.

This, too, generalizes. In more complex systems, involving either more variables and higher order interactions or interactions among polynomial aspects (or both), one forms a hierarchy of sets of independent variables and tests for the significance of increments to R^2 by means of the same F ratio (Formula 7). For example, if one has three variables Z, W, and V, represented both linearly and quadratically with all their interactions, one possible way of organizing the variables is by means of the following sets:

A: Z, W, V

B: ZW, ZV, WV

C: ZWV

D: Z^2, W^2, V^2

E: $Z^2W, ZW^2, Z^2V, ZV^2, W^2V, WV^2$

F: Z^2W^2, Z^2V^2, W^2V^2

G: $Z^2W^2V^2$

One would then test $R^2_{Y \cdot AB} - R^2_{Y \cdot A}$, $R^2_{Y \cdot ABC} - R^2_{Y \cdot AB}$, etc., each by the F ratio for increments. When a set containing more than one variable is significant, one can "break out" each variable in it and test its increment for significance by the same procedure. Of course, one can elect to make all sets contain only one variable, but the number of resulting tests (in the example there would be 20) brings with it an increased risk of spuriously significant results over the complete analysis. This strategy parallels that of the AV, where the avoidance of this risk is implicit. In a 4 x 5 factorial design AV, for example, the interaction involves a single mean square based on 3 x 4 = 12 df which is tested by a single F test. One ordinarily does not test each of these 12 effects separately unless the set as a whole is significant. The principle, of course, obtains even for the main effects, involving sets of 3 and 4 df, where each set normally is tested "wholesale."

Other combinations and priorities of the X, Y, and Z variables are, of course, possible. This operation involves formulating hypotheses about what constitutes a relevant class of independent variables and the priorities of these classes. It depends not only on mechanical variance-stealing considerations, but also on substantive issues in the research and the judgment of the investigator.

Although the discussion in this section has been concerned with interactions among quantitative variables, the principles of forming interaction variables hold also for nominal variables, and for mixtures of variables. Let an "aspect" of a research variable such as religion or IQ be one of the X_i of the set which represent it. Then, for example, if the interaction of u aspects of one variable U and v aspects of another variable V are desired, one may form a total of uv interaction X_i, by multiplying each of the u aspects by each of the v aspects. Each of the resulting uv independent variables is a single (one df) variable which represents a specific aspect by aspect joint or interaction effect. Either U or V may be nominal or quantitative. Where nominal, their aspects may be dummy variables or contrasts; where quantitative, the aspects may be powered polynomial terms or missing data dichotomies (see below). One can thus generate such single interaction X_i as "majority-minority religious group by authoritarianism," "experimental group D versus control group by quadratic of stimulus intensity," etc. It is both convenient and enlightening to have each such joint aspect separately and unambiguously (but not necessarily orthogonally) represented in the set of independent variables. Their individual increment to R^2 and significance can then be determined.

Perhaps as important as being able to represent the interaction X_i in specific detail is the availability of the option *not* to represent some or all of them. The textbook paradigms for factorial design AV lead data analysts to dutifully harvest all possible interactions of all possible orders up to the highest, whether or not they are meaningful or interpretable or, if interpretable, communicable. There emanate from psychology departments many silent prayers to the spirit of R. A. Fisher that high-order interactions will not prove significant! Obviously, one need not (indeed cannot) analyze for all possible aspects including joint aspects of variables if for no other reason than the rapid loss of df for estimating error. The need to "specify the model," that is, the set of X_i to be studied in MR has the salutary effect of requiring an incisive prior conceptual analysis of the research problem. This goes hand in hand with the flexibility of the MR system, which makes readily possible the representation of the research issues posed by the investigator (i.e., multiple regression in the service of the ego!), rather than the canned issues mandated by AV computational routines.

Missing Data

In nonexperimental, particularly survey, research, it frequently occurs that some subjects are missing data on one or more (but not all) of the independent variables under study. Typically, the data are not missing randomly, but for reasons frequently related to values for other independent variables, and particularly to values for the dependent variable under study. For example, in a study of factors associated with the rehabilitation of drug addicts, reported weekly wages on last job is used as an independent variable, among others. Some respondents claim they do not recall or refuse to respond. As another example, consider a retrospective study of the school records of adult mental retardates where the recorded IQ is abstracted for use as an independent variable but found missing in some cases. In neither of these cases can one prudently assume that the mean of these cases on the X_i in question, other X_i, and, particularly, Y is the same as that for the cases with data present. The practice of excluding cases lacking some of the data has the undesirable properties of analyzing a residual sample which is unrepresentative to an unknown degree of the population originally sampled, as well as the loss of information (viz., the *fact* of data being missing) which may be criterion relevant.

MR provides a simple method for coping with this problem. Each such variable has *two* aspects, its value (where present) and whether or not the value *is* present. Accordingly, two independent variables are constructed: X_1 is the value itself, with the mean of X_1 for those cases where it is present entered for the cases where it is missing, and X_2 is the missing data aspect, a dummy variable dichotomy coded 0-1 for absent-present. These two aspects contain all the information available in the variable. Moreover, as scored, $r_{12} = 0$, hence X_1 and X_2 are each contributing an independent portion of the Y variance.

Actually, *any* value entered for the missing data in X_1 will "work" in the sense of accounting for Y variance, that is, the $R^2_{Y \cdot 12}$ will be the same. The use of the mean will uniquely result in $r_{12} = 0$, which may be advantageous interpretively. For some purposes, this advantage may be offset by using some (or any) other value, obviating the necessity of a prior computation of the mean.

The researcher, normally sensitive about tampering with data, may find the prospect of "plugging" empty spaces in his data sheet with means singularly unappealing. He may even correctly point out that this will have the effect of reducing r_{Y1} from what r_{YX} is for the subsample having X values present. In rebuttal, it must be pointed out that the subsample is not representative of the originally defined population, and the method proposed can be thought of as reflecting the fact that the population studied contains missing data, and fully incorporates this fact as positive information.

ANALYSIS OF COVARIANCE

Viewed from the perspective of the MR system, the fixed-model ACV turns out to be a rather minor wrinkle, and not the imposing parallel edifice it constitutes in the AV/ACV framework. A covariate is, after all, nothing but an independent variable, which, because of the logic dictated by the substantive issues of the research, assumes priority among the set of independent variables as a basis for accounting for Y variance. Consider a research in educational psychology in which the Y variable is some performance measure in children, X_1 is midparental education, X_2 is family income, and G, carried by the set X_3, X_4, X_5 represents some differential learning experience in four intact classes. This situation is a "natural" for ACV (assuming its assumptions are reasonably well met). One would think of it as studying the effect of learning experience or class membership on Y, using X_1 and X_2 as covariates. Thus considered, we are asking how much variance in Y (and its significance) the variables $X_3, X_4,$ and X_5 account for, *after* the variance due to X_1 and X_2 is allowed for, or held constant, or "partialed out" (the terms being equivalent). The form of the MR analysis to accomplish this purpose is directly suggested. Find $R^2_{Y \cdot 12345}$, the proportion of Y variance all independent variables account for. Then find $R^2_{Y \cdot 12}$, the proportion of Y variance attributable to the covariates education and income. Their difference is the increment due to group membership, which is tested for significance by the F test of Formula 7 used in a different design context above. Note that no problem arises if the four groups are defined by a 2 x 2 factorial. If X_3, X_4, X_5 are coded as in Columns 7, 8, 9 in Table 12.1 to represent the two main effects and their interaction, the respective ACV significance tests are performed by (Formula 7) F ratio tests of the increments $R^2_{Y \cdot 12345}$ - $R^2_{Y \cdot 1245}$ (for the main effect represented by X_3), $R^2_{Y \cdot 12345}$ - $R^2_{Y \cdot 1235}$ (for the main effect represented by X_4) and $r^2_{Y \cdot 12345}$ - $r^2_{Y \cdot 1234}$ (for the interaction or joint effect). Note that X_1 and X_2 are always included in the debited R^2, because of their priority in the issues as defined. This principle is readily generalized to designs of greater complexity.

That a covariate is nothing but another independent variable except for priority due to substantive considerations is evident when one considers a study formally almost identical to the above, now, however, done by sa social psychologist. Since there are four different classes and four different teachers, the classes ipso facto have had different learning experiences. But this research is concerned with the effects of parental education and income on the performance criterion, with group membership now the contaminant which must be removed, hence the covariate. Using the same set up and data, he would find $R^2_{Y \cdot 12345}$ - $R^2_{Y \cdot 345}$ as the combined effect of education and income, $R^2_{Y \cdot 12345}$ - $R^2_{Y \cdot 2345}$ as the net effect of education (i.e., over and above that of income as well as the covariates of class membership), and $R^2_{Y \cdot 12345} - R^2_{Y \cdot 1345}$ for the net effect of income, each F-testable as before. Thus, one man's main effect is another man's covariate.

The MR approach to ACV-like problems opens up possibilities for statistical control not dreamed of in ACV. We have just seen how purely nominal or qualitative variables (class membership) can serve as covariates. Beyond this, we can apply other principles which have been adduced above: (a) Any aspects of data can, by appropriate means, be represented as independent variables. (b) Any (sets of) independent variables can serve as covariates by priority assignment in variance accounting. Thus, for example, one can make provision for a covariate being nonlinearly related to Y (and/or to other independent variables) by writing a polynomial set of independent variables and giving the set priority; or, one can carry two variables *and* their interaction as a covariate set; or, one can even carry as a covariate a variable for which there are missing data by representing the two aspects of such a datum as two independent variables and giving them priority. Finally, one can combine the priority principle with those of contrast coding to achieve analytic modes of high fidelity to substantive research aims.

The ACV assumption that the regression lines (more generally, surfaces) of the covariates (U) on Y have the same slopes (more generally, regression parameters) between groups (V) is equivalent to the hypothesis of no significance for the set of uv interaction independent variables. This hypothesis can be F-tested as a Set B following the inclusion of U and V as Set A, using Formula 7.

DISCUSSION

In the introduction it was argued that MR and AV/ACV are essentially identical systems, and so they are, at least in their theory. In the actual practice of the data-analytic art, many differences emerge, differences which generally favor the MR system as outlined above.

Before turning to these differences, a closer look at their similarity in regard to statistical assumptions is warranted. This article has concerned itself only with the fixed-model AV/ACV, wherein it is assumed that inference to the population about the independent variables is for just those variables represented (and not those variables considered as samples) and that values on these variables are measured without error. This means that in a MR whose set of X_i include quantitative variates (e.g., scores), the population to which one generalizes, strictly speaking, is made up of cases having just those X_i values, only the Y values for any given combinations of values for the X_i varying; moreover, the Y distribution (and only this distribution) is assumed normal and of equal variance for all the observed combinations of X_i values. These seem, indeed, to be a constraining set of assumptions. However, the practical effect on the validity of the generalizations which one might wish to draw is likely to be vanishingly small. It seems likely that the substantive generalizations made strictly for the particular vectors of X_i values in the rows of the basic data matrix of the sample would hold for the slightly differing values which the population would contain if the sampling is random. As for the normality and variance homogeneity assumptions for Y, the robustness of the F test under conditions of such assumption failure is well attested to (for a summary, see Cohen, 1965, pp. 114-116). Particularly when reasonably large samples are used, itself desirable to assure adequate statistical power, no special inhibition need surround the drawing of inferences from the usual hypothesis testing, certainly no more so than in AV.

A discussion of the practical differences between MR and AV is best begun with a consideration of the nature of classical fixed-model AV. Its natural use is in the analysis of data generated by experimental manipulations along one or more dimensions (main effects), resulting in subgroups of observations in multifactor cells, treatment combinations. Each main effect is paradigmatically a set of qualitative distinctions along some dimension. These dimensions are conceptually independent of each other, and since they are under the control of the designer of the experiment, the data can, in principle, be gathered in such a way that the dimensions are actually mutually orthogonal in their representation in the data. (This condition is met by the proportionality of cell frequencies in all two dimensional subtables.) This also results in interactions being orthogonal to each other and to the main effects. Thus, the paradigm is of a set of batches (one batch per AV main effect or interaction) of qualitative independent variables, all batches mutually orthogonal.

Now, under such conditions, one *can*, as illustrated above, analyze the data by MR, but there is no advantage in so doing. The AV can be seen as a computational shortcut to an analysis by the linear model which analyzes by batches and capitalizes on the fact that batches are orthogonal. Thus, the classical fixed factorial AV is a special simplified case of MR analysis particularly suited to neat experimental layouts, where qualitative treatments are manipulated in appropriate orthogonal relationships. Later refinements allows for quantitative independent variables being exploited by trend analysis designs, but these, too, demand manipulative control in the form of equally spaced intervals in the dimension and equal sized samples per level if the computational simplicity is to be retained.

These designs are quite attractive, not only in their efficiency and relative computational simplicity, but also in the conceptual power they introduced to the data analyst, for example, interactions, trend components. They were presented in excellent applied statistics textbooks. Inevitably, they attracted investigators working in quite different modes, who proceeded to a Procrustean imposition of such designs on their research.

A simple example (not too much of a caricature) may help illustrate the point. Dr. Doe is investigating the effects of Authoritarianism (California F scale) and IQ on a cognitive style score (Y), using high school students as subjects. He is particularly interested in the F x IQ interaction, that is, in the possibility that r_{YF} differs as a function of IQ level. He gives the three tests, and proceeds to set up the data for analysis. He dichotomizes the F and IQ distributions as closely as possible to their medians into high-low groups and proceeds to assign the Y scores into the four cells of the resulting 2 x 2 fixed factorial design. He then discovers that the number of cases in the high-low and low-high cells distinctly exceed those in the other two, an expression of the fact that F and IQ are correlated. He must somehow cope with this disproportionality (nonorthogonality). He may (a) throw out cases randomly to achieve proportionality or equality; (b) use an "unweighted means" or other approximate solution (Snedecor, 1956, pp. 385-387); or (c) "fit constants by least squares" (Snedecor, 1956, pp. 388-391; Winer, 1962, pp. 224-227), which is, incidentally, an MR procedure.

Clearly, this is a far cry from experimentally manipulated qualitative variables. These are, in fact, naturally varying correlated quantitative variables. This analysis does violence to the problem in one or both of the following ways:

1. By reducing the F scale and the IQ to dichotomies, it has taken reliable variables which provide graduated distinctions between subjects over a wide range, and reduced them to two-point (high-low) scales, squandering much information in the process. For example, assuming bivariate normality, when a variable is so dichotomized, there is a reduction in r^2_{YX}, the criterion variance it accounts for, and hence in the value of F in the test of its significance, of 36%. This wilful degradation of available measurement information has a direct consequence in the loss of statistical power (Cohen, 1965, pp. 95-101, 118).

2. The throwing out of cases to achieve proportionality clearly reduces power, but, even worse, distorts the situation by analyzing as if IQ and F scale score were independent, when they are not. Other approximations suffer from these and/or other statistical deficiencies or distortions.

If Dr. Doe uses the MR-equivalent exact-fitting constants procedure, he has still given up computational simplicity, and, of course, the measurement information due to dichotomization. If he seeks to reduce the latter and also allow for the possibility of nonlinearity of Y on X_i regressions by breakdown of IQ and/or F scale into smaller segments, say quartiles, his needs for equality of intervals and cases will be frustrated, and he will not be able to find a computational paradigm, which, in any case, would be very complicated. It seems quite clear that, however considered, the conventional AV mode is the wrong way to analyze the data.

On the other hand, the data can be completely, powerfully, and relevantly analyzed by MR. A simple analysis would involve setting $X_1 = IQ$, $X_2 = F$ scale score, $X_3 = (IQ)(F)$. By finding $R^2_{Y \cdot 123} - R^2_{Y \cdot 12}$ and testing it for significance (or equivalently, by testing the significance of p_3), he learns how much the interaction contributes to Y variance accounting and its significance. Determinations of the values of r^2_{Y1}, r^2_{Y2}, $R^2_{Y \cdot 12}$, $R^2_{Y \cdot 12} - r^2_{Y \cdot 1}$, and $R^2_{Y \cdot 12} - r^2_{Y2}$ and testing each for significance fully exploits the information in the data at this level. If he believes it warranted, he can add polynomial terms for IQ and F score and their interaction in order to provide for nonlinearity of any of the relationships involved.

Another practical difference between MR and AC/ACV is with regard to computation. The MR procedure, in general, requires the computation and inversion of the matrix of correlations (or sums of squares and products) among the independent variables, a considerable amount of computation for even a modest number of independent variables. It is true that *classical* AV, whose main effects, interactions, polynomial trend components, etc., are mutually orthogonal, capitalizes on this orthogonality to substantially reduce the computation required. Whatever computational reduction there is in AV or MR depends directly on the orthogonality of the independent variables, which we have seen is restricted to manipulative experiments, and is by no means an invariant feature even of such experiments.

However, given the widespread availability of electronic computer facilities, the issue of the *amount* of computation required in the analysis of data from psychological research dwindles to the vanishing point, and is replaced by problems of programming. The typical statistical user of a typical computer facility requires that a computer program which will analyze his data be available in the program library. Such programs will have been either prepared or adapted for the particular computer configuration of that facility. Unfortunately, it is frequently the case that the available AV program or programs will not analyze the particular fixed AV design which the investigator brings. Some AV programs are wanting in capacity in number of factors or levels per factor, some will handle only orthogonal designs, some will handle only equal cases per cell, some will do AV but not ACV, some of those that do handle ACV can handle only one or two covariates. Many will not handle special forms of AV, for example, Latin squares.

On the other hand, even the most poorly programmed scientific computer facility will have at least one good MR program, if for no other reason than its wide use in various technologies, particularly engineering. All the standard statistical program packages contain at least one MR program. Although these vary in convenience, efficiency, and degree of informativeness of output, all of them can be used to accomplish the analyses discussed in this article. In contrast to the constraints of AV programs, the very general MR program can be particularized for any given design by representing (coding) those aspects of the independent variables of interest to the investigator according to the principles which have been described.

A note of caution: as we have seen, given even a few factors (main effects of nominal variables or linear aspects of quantitative variables), one can generate very large numbers of distinct independent variables (interactions of any order, polynomials, interactions of polynomials, etc.). The temptation to represent many such features of the data in an analysis must be resisted for sound research-philosophical and statistical reasons. Even in researches using a relatively large number of subjects (n), a small number of factors (nominal and quantitative scales) can generate a number of independent variables which exceed n. Each esoteric issue posed to the data costs a df which is lost from the error estimate, thus enfeebling the statistical power of the analysis.

This, ultimately, is the reason that it is desirable in research that is to lead to *conclusions* to state hypotheses which are relatively few in number. This formulation is not intended to indict exploratory studies, which may be invaluable, but by definition, such studies do not result in conclusions, but in hypotheses, which then need to be tested (or, depending on the research context, cross-validated). If one analyzes the data of a research involving 100 subjects by means of MR, and utilizes 40 independent variables, what does one conclude about 4 or 5 of them which prove to have partial regression weights "significant" at the .05 level? Certainly not that *all* of them are real effects, when one realizes that an overall null hypothesis leads to an expectation that 5% of 40, or 2 are expected by change. But which two?

A reasonable strategy depends upon organizing a hierarchy of sets of independent variables, ordered, by sets, according to a priori judgments. Set A represents the independent variables which the investigator most expects to be relevant to Y (perhaps all or some of the main effects and/or linear aspects of continuous variables). These may be thought of as *the* hypotheses of the research, and the fewer the better. Set B consists of next order possibilities (perhaps lower order interactions and/or some quadratic aspects). These are variables which are to be viewed less as hypotheses and more as exploratory issues. If there is a Set C (perhaps some higher order interactions and/or higher degree polynomials), it should be thought of as unqualifiedly exploratory. (If there are covariates in the design, they, of course, take precedence over all these sets, and would enter first.) The "perhaps" in the parenthetical phrases in this paragraph are included because it is *not* a mechanical ordering that is intended. In any given research, a central issue may be carried by an interaction or polynomial aspect while some main effect may be quite secondary. In most research, however, it is the simplest aspects of factors which are most likely to occupy the focus of the investigator's attention. However, the decision as to what constitutes an appropriate set depends on both research-strategic issues that go to the heart of the substantive nature of the research, and subtle statistical issues beyond the scope of this article. The latter are discussed by Miller (1966, pp. 30-35).

The independent variables so organized, one first does an MR analysis for Set A, then Sets A + B, then Sets A + B + C. Each additional set is tested for the increment to R^2 by means of the F test of Formula 7. A prudent procedure would then be to test for significance the contribution of any *single* independent variable in a set only if the set yields a significant increment to R^2. A riskier procedure would be to dispense with the latter condition, but then the results would clearly require cross-validation.

NOTE

1. It is of interest to note that information about the "omitted" group, here G_4 (more generally, G_0), is readily recovered. The value for the correlation of the dichotomy for that group with *any* variable Z (r_{Z0}) is a simple function of the r's of the other variables with Z (r_{Zi}) and the standard deviations of the X_i, namely

$$r_{Z0} = (- \Sigma_{i-1}^{g-1} r_{Z_i} \sigma_i)/\sigma_0$$

where

$$\sigma_i = [n_i(n - n_i)/n^2]^{1/2}, \text{ similarly for } \sigma_0.$$

When all groups are of the same size, this simplifies to

$$r_{Z0} = - \Sigma_{i-1}^{g-1} r_{Zi}$$

This relationship will hold whatever the nature of Z; it need not even be a real variable, —it will hold if Z is a factor in the factor-analytic sense, unrotated or rotated, with the r_{Zi} being factor loadings.

REFERENCES

Bottenberg, R. A. & J. H. Ward, Jr. *Applied multiple linear regression.* (PRL-TDR-63-6) Lackland AF Base, Texas, 1963.

Cattell, R. B. Psychological theory and scientific method. In R. B. Cattell (Ed.), *Handbook of multivariate experimental psychology.* Chicago: Rand McNally, 1966.

Cohen, J. Some statistical issues in psychological research. In B. B. Wolman (Ed.), *Handbook of clinical psychology.* New York: McGraw-Hill, 1965.

Cohen, J. & Cohen, P. *Applied multiple regression/correlation analysis for the behavioral sciences.* Hillsdale, New Jersey: Lawrence Erlbaum Associates, 1975.

Cureton, E. E. On correlation coefficients. *Psychometrika,* 1966, 31: 605-607.

Draper, N. & H. Smith. *Applied regression analysis.* New York: Wiley, 1967.

Edwards, A. E. *Experimental design in psychological research.* (Rev. ed.) New York: Rinehart, 1960.

Hays, W. L. *Statistics for psychologists.* New York: Holt, Rinehart & Winston, 1963.

Jennings. E. Fixed effects analysis of variance by regression analysis. *Multivariate Behavioral Research,* 1967, 2: 95-108.

Li, J. C. R. *Statistical inference.* Vol. 2. *The multiple regression and its ramifications.* Ann Arbor, Mich.: Edwards Bros., 1964.

McNemar, Q. *Psychological statistics.* (3rd ed.) New York: Wiley, 1962.

Miller, R. G., Jr. *Simultaneous statistical inference.* New York: McGraw-Hill, 1966.

Peters, C. C. & W. R. Van Voorhis. *Statistical procedures and their mathematical bases.* New York: McGraw-Hill, 1940.

Saunders, D. R. Moderator variables in prediction. *Educational and Psychological Measurement,* 1956, 16: 209-222.

Snedecor, G. W. *Statistical methods.* (5th ed.) Ames: Iowa State College Press, 1956.

Suits, D. B. Use of dummy variables in regression equations. *Journal of the American Statistical Association,* 1957, 52: 548-551.

Winer, B. J. *Statistical principles in experimental design.* New York: McGraw-Hill, 1962.

REFERENCE UPDATE
Selected by Jacob Cohen and Elmer L. Struening

Barton, R. R. and B. W. Turbull. Evaluation of recidivism data: Use of failure rate regression models. *Evaluation Quarterly,* 1979, 3 (4): 629-642.

Bohrnstedt, G. W. and L. Carter. Robustness in regression analysis. In H. L. Costner (ed.) *Sociological methodology 1971.* San Francisco: Jossey-Bass, 1971.

Cohen, J. *Statistical power analysis for the behavioral sciences* (rev. ed.). New York: Academic, 1977.

Cohen, J. Partialed products *are* interactions; partialed powers *are* curve components. *Psychological Bulletin,* 1978, 85: 858-866.

Cohen, J. Trend analysis the easy way. *Educational and Psychological Measurement,* 1980, 40: 565-568.

Cohen, J. "New look" multiple regression/correlation analysis and the analysis of variance/covariance. In G. Keren (ed.) *Statistical and methodological issues in behavioral sciences research.* Hillsdale, NJ: Erlbaum, 1982. (a)

Cohen, J. Set correlation as a general multivariate data-analytic method. *Multivariate Behavioral Research,* 1982, 17: 301-341. (b)

Cohen, J. and P. Cohen. General multiple regression analysis in drug research. In P. Bentler (ed.) *Drugs and research methodology*. Washington, DC: Government Printing Office, 1977.

Cohen, J. and P. Cohen. *Applied multiple regression/correlation analysis for the behavioral sciences* (2nd ed.). Hillsdale, NJ: Erlbaum, 1983.

Crane, J. A. The power of social intervention experiments to discriminate differences between experimental and control groups. In T. D. Cook, M. L. D. Rosario, K. M. Hennigan, M. M. Mark, and W. M. K. Trochim (eds.) *Evaluation studies review annual* (Vol. 3). Beverly Hills, CA: Sage, 1978.

Dretzke, B. J., J. R. Levin, and R. C. Serlin. Testing for regression homogeneity under variance heterogeneity. *Psychological Bulletin*, 1982, 91 (2): 376-383.

Duncan, O. D. Inheritance of poverty or inheritance of race? In D. P. Moynihan (ed.) *On understanding poverty: Perspectives from the social sciences*. New York: Basic Books, 1969.

Edwards, A. L. *An introduction to linear regression and correlation*. San Francisco: W. H. Freeman, 1976.

Fennessey, J. The general linear model. *American Journal of Sociology*, 1968, 74: 1-28.

Gordon, R. A. Issues in multiple regression. *American Journal of Sociology*, 1968, 73: 592-616.

Huynh, H. A comparison of four approaches to robust regression. *Psychological Bulletin*, 1982, 92 (2): 505-512.

Kenny, D. A. and J. S. Berman. Statistical approaches to the correction of correlational bias. *Psychological Bulletin*, 1980, 88 (2): 288-295.

Kerlinger, F. N. and E. J. Pedhazur. *Multiple regression in behavioral research*. New York: Holt, Rinehart & Winston, 1973.

Kleinbaum, D. G. and L. L. Kupper. *Applied regression analysis and other multivariable methods*. Boston: Duxbury, 1978.

Kriska, S. D. and G. W. Milligan. Multiple regression analysis for categorical data with an illustrative application in personnel selection. *Psychological Bulletin*, 1982, 92 (1): 193-201.

Laughlin, J. E. Comment on "Estimating coefficients in linear models: It don't make no nevermind." *Psychological Bulletin*, 1978, 85 (2); 247-253.

Lewis-Beck, M. S. *Applied regression: An introduction*. Beverly Hills, CA: Sage, 1980.

McIver, J. P. and E. G. Carmines. *Unidimensional scaling*. Beverly Hills, CA: Sage, 1981.

Mason, R. and W. G. Brown. Multicollinearity problems and ridge regression in sociological models. *Social Science Research*, 1975, 4: 135-149.

Ohls, J. C. The power of hypothesis tests in a regression context. *Evaluation Review*, 1980, 4 (5): 623-635.

Pedhazur, E. J. *Multiple regression in behavioral research; Explanation and prediction* (2nd ed.) New York: Holt, Rinehart & Winston, 1982.

Rockwell, R. C. Assessment of multicollinearity. *Sociological Methods and Research*, 1975, 3: 308-320.

Rogosa, D. Comparing nonparallel regression lines. *Psychological Bulletin*, 1980, 88 (2): 307-321.

Rozoboom, W. W. Ridge regression: Bonanza or beguilement? *Psychological Bulletin*, 1979, 86: 242-249.

Stolzenberg, R. M. Estimating an equation with multiplicative and additive terms, with an application to analysis of wage differentials between men and women in 1960. *Sociological Methods and Research*, 1974, 2: 313-331.

Wainer, H. Estimating coefficients in linear models: It don't make no nevermind. *Psychological Bulletin*, 1976, 83: 213-217.

Wainer, H. On the sensitivity of regression and regressors. *Psychological Bulletin*, 1978, 85 (2): 267-273.

Wilkinson, L. Tests of significance in stepwise regression. *Psychological Bulletin*, 1979, 86 (1): 168-174.

13

HOW REGRESSION ARTIFACTS IN QUASI-EXPERIMENTAL EVALUATIONS CAN MISTAKENLY MAKE COMPENSATORY EDUCATION LOOK HARMFUL

DONALD T. CAMPBELL
and
ALBERT ERLEBACHER

Northwestern University

Evaluations of compensatory educational efforts such as Head Start are commonly quasi-experimental or ex post facto. The compensatory program is made available to the most needy, and the "control" group then sought from among the untreated children of the same community. Often this untreated population is on the average more able than the "experimental" group. In such a situation the usual procedures of selection, adjustment, and analysis produce systematic biases in the direction of making the compensatory program look deleterious. Not only does matching produce regression artifacts in this direction, but so also do analysis of covariance and partial correlation. These biases of analysis occur both where pretest scores are available and in ex post facto studies.

It seems reasonably certain that this methodological error occurred in the Westinghouse-Ohio University study (Cicirelli, et al., 1969) and it probably has occurred in others purporting to show no effects or harmful effects from Head Start programs. The occurrence of such tragically misleading misanalyses must be attributed to the slow diffusion of the isolated warnings. These have been long

AUTHORS' NOTE: Supported in part by National Science Foundation Grant GS 1309X.

Reprinted from J. Helmuth (ed.) *Compensatory Education: A National Debate,* Vol. III of *The Disadvantaged Child.* New York: Brunner/Mazel, 1970, by permission of Brunner/Mazel.

available for the process of matching (e.g., McNemar, 1940, 1949; Thorndike, 1942; Hovland, Lumsdaine and Sheffield, 1949; Campbell and Clayton, 1961; Campbell and Stanley, 1963), and for ex post facto designs (Campbell and Stanley, 1963). But for analysis of covariance, the warning message is newer (Lord, 1960; Evans and Anastasio, 1968; Werts and Linn, 1969; see also Lord, 1967, 1969) and most references are wrong in their recommendations (e.g., Thorndike, 1942; Peters and Van Voorhis, 1940; Walker and Lev, 1953; Winer, 1962; Campbell and Stanley, 1963; McNemar, 1969).

The purpose of this essay is the didactic one of illustrating with a detailed example why these biases appear. The initial focus will be on the case of the superior control group. Subsequently, data assemblies which could misleadingly make compensatory education look effective will be discussed. Several of the sections that follow involve statistical technicalities which some readers will want to skip. It could be hoped that every reader will stick it out through the section on Matching. But however that may be, we would like to call attention of all readers to some general conclusions: (1) For the ex post facto situation to which the Westinghouse-Ohio University study was unavoidably limited, no satisfactory analysis is possible; (2) analysis of covariance in its usual forms is inadequate not only in such ex post facto settings, but also in those quasi-experimental settings where pretests are available; (3) for quasi-experiments with pretests similar in composition to the posttests, common-factor covariance adjustments developed by Lord (1960) and Porter (1967) may be appropriate. We would also like to call attention to the two nonstatistical sections at the end, especially the argument in favor of randomly assigned control groups.

For the purpose of illustration, we have generated computer-simulated data for two overlapping groups with no true treatment effect. Figure 13.1 shows the frequency distributions of these two groups. In the bottom portion are the two distributions representing the test scores obtained after the ameliorative treatment ("posttest"). It can be seen that the Experimental Group has a lower mean than the Control. However, as can be seen in the top portion of the figure, the difference between the two groups was already present prior to the treatment. The "pretest" shows precisely the same difference, except for the vagaries of random sampling.

With the data as displayed in Figure 19.1, few if any would be tempted to conclude that the treatment had any effect, helpful or harmful. However, our example is especially clear because we have kept the same means and standard deviations for the pretest and the posttest (as far as population parameters are concerned). Nevertheless we will be able to show that even in the present clear-cut instance of no treatment effects, the common quasi-experimental analysis techniques will result in serious biases.

Figures 13.2, 13.3, and 13.4 display the relationship between pretest (or covariate) and posttest scores within each group, separately and then combined. The relationships there displayed could have been reported more economically as correlation coefficients (the pretest-post correlations are .489 for the Experimental Group, .496 for the Control, where the theoretical population values are each

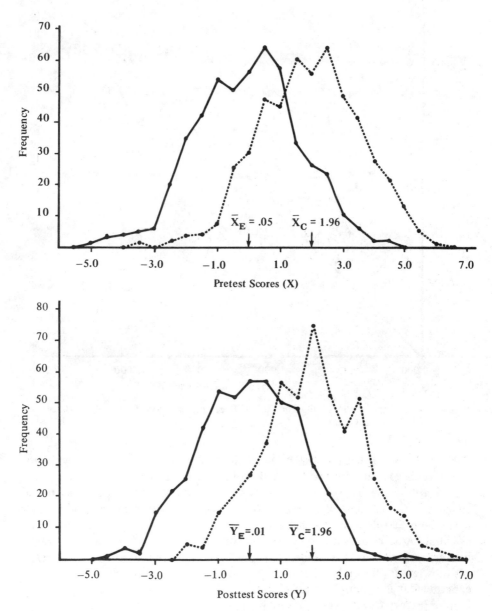

Figure 13.1 Pretest and posttest distributions (simulated data) for an instance of a superior Control Group (dashed lines) and no treatment effect in the Experimental Group (solid lines).

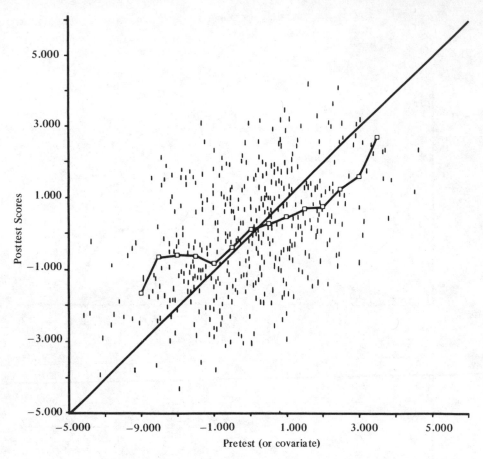

Figure 13.2   Scatter plot of the correlation of pretest and posttest scores for the Experimental Group.

.500); but we feel that the display of relationships as scatter diagrams provides the easiest route to an intuitive understanding of regression artifacts.

The truisms we are going to demonstrate with these simulated data are not at all specific to our mode of generating them. The similarity of pretest and posttest means and variances makes the didactic exposition easier to follow, but is not essential. Any simulation would do in which the mean difference and overlap between experimental and control group exists to the same degree in both pretest and posttest (as shown for example by the t ratio for the mean difference between experimental and control). Thus posttest means and variances could be larger than for the pretest. Or still less restrictively, any simulation will do which distinguishes between pretest values and the common factor (or true score component) shared by pretest and posttest, as by adding "error" or "unique variance" to the pretest as well as to the posttest. We believe that the reader may skip without loss the following paragraph on the details of our simulation.

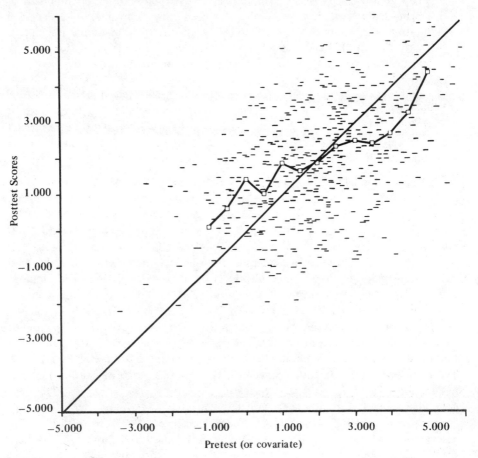

Figure 13.3   Scatter plot of the correlation of pretest and posttest scores for the Control Group.

The data were generated in the following way: A person's score was made up of three parts, added to each other. Thus for the pretest,

$$X_{ij} = G_{i.} + C_{ij} + E_{ij}, \text{ and}$$

for the posttest,

$$Y_{ij} = G_{i.} + C_{ij} + E'_{ij}, \text{ where}$$

X_{ij} is the pretest score of person j in Group i.
Y_{ij} is the postest score of subject j in Group i.
G_i is a group score common to all members of a group. It was taken as 0 for all members of the Experimental Group and 2 for all members of the Control Group. G is that portion of "true score" variance producing group differences.

C_{ij} is a common factor score for subject i j. It represents that component of "true score" variance accounting for persisting individual differences in ability within groups. C_{ij} was randomly chosen from a normal population with a mean of 0 and a standard deviation of 1. (In this simulation, neither pretest nor posttest contain "true score" components not shared with the other.)

E_{ij} and E'_{ij} are separate "error" scores for subject i j. They represent measurement errors. That is, if the same subject were tested again on the same test, because the test is not perfectly reliable, his E_{ij} would be different. E_{ij} and E'_{ij} were randomly chosen from a normal population with a mean of 0 and a standard deviation of 1.

In Figures 13.2, 13.3, and 13.4 there is a tally mark for each of 500 individuals in each of the highly overlapping distributions. Each "Experimental" individual is diagramed with a vertical mark, each of the generally superior "Control" individuals with a horizontal mark. For each class interval of pretest scores (width = .500 points), the mean posttest score has been plotted (the boxed or circled points) separately for each group. A meandering line connects these means. To understand the diagrams, look at the plots of individuals and means in a given area: Each mean is based upon the tallies of its type above and below it in a narrow vertical column, the boundaries of which are not shown but which can be inferred. Where the number of cases in a column was fewer than 6, no mean was plotted on the grounds that its small N would lead to misleading variability. Checking visually some of the plotted details will ensure comprehension. Begin at the left edge of Figure 13.2 The class interval -4.750 to -4.250 centered at 4.500, as read on the bottom line, has in the column it designates three cases, mean = 1.566, unplotted. The next column, centered around -4.000, with boundaries of -4.250 and -3.750, contains four cases, mean = -.2564, unplotted. The next interval, -3.750 to -3.250 has five cases, mean = -1.868, unplotted. In the next class interval, -3.250 to -2.750 there are six cases, mean = -1.643, providing our first plotted column mean, the boxed point above -3.000. From there rightward there is a plotted mean for the next 13 class intervals, plotted every .500 points, above points -2.500, -2.000, -1.500, -1.000, and so on. Small numbers still create instability, leading to the high value for the Experimental category centered at pretest +3.500, where one very high point produces a column (posttest) mean of +2.711, leading it to cross over the corresponding Control Group value, as seen in Figure 13.4.

The straight line running diagonally through Figures 13.2, 13.3, and 13.4 can be designated the identity diagonal and represents the set of values which all tallies would have taken had pretest and posttest scores been identical. Note that the line of column means for each of the groups lies below this identity diagonal in the higher range of its scores, and lies above the identity diagonal for lower half of its scores. The meandering line ideally should cross the identity diagonal at that point representing the intersection of the pretest and the posttest means. A straight line fitted by least squares to the column means would be the regression line of posttest on pretest. If the correlation were perfect, there would be no scatter, and this line would coincide with the identity diagonal. If there were zero correlation, that is if

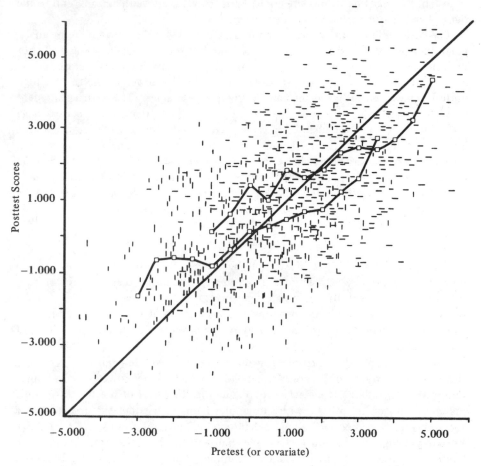

Figure 13.4   Scatter plot of the correlation of pretest and posttest scores for Experimental and Control Group. (Vertical tally marks represent Experimental Group children, horizontal tallys Controls)

pretest scores were totally useless in predicting posttest scores, then all column means would equal the posttest mean for the whole group (in universe values if not specific sample values) and the regression line would be perfectly horizontal. This case falls about halfway between. The correlation between pretest and posttest scores is .489 for the Experimental Group, and .496 for the Control Group, where the universe values determined by the formula for generating the scores are both .500.

In a usual presentation of regression phenomena, there would also be a presentation of the regression of pretest on posttest. However, to avoid needless visual complexity, we have omitted presentation in Figures 13.2, 13.3, and 13.4 of row means, that is of the mean pretest scores for each class interval of posttest scores. These values would be tipped away from the identity diagonal in the direction of the vertical, would be to the left of the identity value above the means, and to the right of the identity value below the means.

The often referred to but less often understood "regression toward the mean" is portrayed in the departure of the column means from the identity diagonal. For each class of pretest scores, the corresponding mean posttest score lies closer to the overall population mean, posttest values being thereby lower in the case of high pretest values, and higher in the case of low pretest values. (This verbal statement must be made more complex for situations in which pretest and posttest have different means and variances: For each pretest class interval, the corresponding mean score on the posttest is closer in standard-deviation units to the overall posttest mean than is the pretest class interval's distance from the pretest mean in pretest standard deviation units.) Note that *just as our Experimental and Control groups have different means on both pretest and posttest occasions, they thereby also have different regression lines.* This point will be expanded below.

MATCHING

With the details of the illustration before us, we can now look at several procedures commonly used in quasi-experimental situations to attempt to compensate for pretest inequality between experimental and control groups. Most widespread of these is *matching,* an ubiquitous error so supported by common sense that it is repeatedly reinvented as the way of "controlling for" initial inequalities of group means.

We have graphed, in Figures 13.1 through 13.4, an absolutely null case, in which the supposed "treatment" applied solely to the "Experimental Group" had absolutely no effect. Suppose we attempt to examine the effect of the treatment on a matched sample. Let us start with subsamples from each population matched on a specific pretest score, for example, 1.000 (class interval from .750 to 1.250). Looking at Figures 13.2 and 13.4, we see that, for the "Experimental" sample, the posttest mean is .478, for the "Control" sample (Figure 13.3 and 13.4), the mean is 1.850, a difference in the direction of the Experimental Group's becoming worse, the Control Group's becoming better. If we expand this matched sample by taking equal numbers of experimentals in each of the overlapping class intervals, we add further replication of this same bias, easily getting a highly significant effect. The proper interpretation of this effect is that scores in each group are regressing toward different means, which is inevitable if the groups do in fact have different means. It is to be hoped that the why of this error is by now intuitively obvious from the form of display used in Figures 13.2, 13.3, and 13.4.

One reason one is so often deceived by regression artifacts in the matching situation is that the matching score and the value of the dependent variable seem to be stated in the same, but actually are in different, metric languages. In the example above, the two pretest values of 1.000 are in the language of scores selected just because they had that value. The posttest values of .478 and 1.850 are actually means of scores that have been free to vary, and all of the effects of error and independence in the relationship between pretest and posttest have been thrown into these posttest means.

We could generate the opposite picture by starting with selected, matched posttest scores of 1.000 and looking for the mean pretest score corresponding to each. While row means have not been graphed in Figures 13.2, 13.3, and 13.4, you can probably confirm by visual inspection that the row (pretest) mean for the Experimental subjects whose posttest score is in the .750 to 1.250 interval is about .505, while that for the Control Group is 1.152. If one were a trapped director of a Head Start program who had to have experimental proof for the worth of a program which he knew on other grounds to be valuable, one could probably package this last result persuasively: "Of children scoring the same at time two, the Head Start children have gained .495 points while the Control children have lost .152." For a growth situation, the actual numerical values of our illustration are of course inappropriate in having pretest and posttest means the same. Normally both groups would have gained. Let us accommodate this by adding 1.000 to all posttest scores. This gets rid of the implausible loss on the part of the Control Group. Now our trapped director can say. "Of children scoring equally on the posttest, the Head Start children have gained 1.495 points, in comparison with a gain of only .848 on the part of the Control children." We recoil at such politically motivated sophistry, yet the analysis itself is no more fallacious than the complementary one we have fallen into inadvertently by matching on the pretest. The resulting implications for social policy might even be regarded as more benign, though neither bias is defensible.

Our simulated case has been based upon the psychometrician's traditional "true score" model. Along with this goes the derivation that a "fallible" ("obtained," "manifest") score is an unbiased estimate of the true score, given the normal definition of error as uncorrelated with true score. But this is correct only for *unselected* scores, that is, for total sets of scores that have been allowed to fall freely. Where scores have been selected *because* of their manifest values, they become biased estimates of true scores in the direction indicated by regression to the mean. Matching and any other classifying for analysis by obtained scores are just such biasing processes.

The magnitude of the pseudo-effect resulting from matching depends upon two parameters: First, the higher the pretest-posttest correlation, the less the regression. In a symmetrical situation such as this, or in a less symmetrical one when expressed in z scores, r directly shows the proportion of regression, or rather of nonregression. If the pretest-posttest correlation were .90, the scores would regress 1/10th of the distance toward the mean. In our simulation, the regression is 1/2 the way to the mean. Second, the larger the difference between group means, the more regression. Verbally stated, the farther the group means are apart, the farther the matched cases will be from their respective means, hence, the more regression. Visually, it is obvious that the larger the mean difference of the two overlapping clouds of tallies in Figure 13.4, the larger the separation between the two parallel plots of column means. In our example, the differences in the means of the two groups is about 2.00, and the regression pseudo-effect concomitant with a .50 correlation is half this, or about 1.00. If the mean difference were 4.00, the regression pseudo-effect would be half of that, or 2.00.

Matching on several variables simultaneously has the same logic and bias. The use of multiple matching variables may reduce the regression artifact, but will not remove it. It reduces it insofar as the multiple correlation of the several matching variables with the posttest is higher than the simple r of a single matching variable. Matching by means of qualitative dimensions or dichotomous variables has an equivalent bias. All such matching variables turn out to be imperfect indicators of the underlying variables we would like to match on. Parents' number of years of schooling have vastly different meanings from school to school, and within the same schools and classrooms. Living in the same neighborhood or block means widely different things as far as the educational quality of the home is concerned. Regression artifacts analogous to those of Figure 13.4 emerge. There is inevitably undermatching, in the sense that the population differences which one is trying to correct by matching are undercorrected by the matching process. The initial matching in the Westinghouse-Ohio University study was of this qualitative nature. This undermatching showed up on the socioeconomic status ratings subsequently made. Had they "corrected" their initial matching by further matching on the socioeconomic ratings, this composite would still have been an imperfect indicator of underlying achievement-ability; there would still have been undermatching, with resulting regression artifacts as in Figure 13.4, in the specific direction of making Head Start look damaging. Even had they had an achievement-ability pretest to match on, as some studies including Follow Through have, matching would produce this erroneous put down.

How can one tell which direction a matching bias will take? Only by having evidence on the nature of the population differences which matching attempted to overcome. Conceivably, in reporting a matching process, the researcher might neglect to say what kind of cases he found hard to get matches for, and what kind of cases existed in surplus in the control population. If so, we could not tell. In the Westinghouse-Ohio University study it *might* have been that matches were easily found for the most disadvantaged Head Start children, and hard to find for the

TABLE 13.1   MEANS OF SIMULATED DATA

| | Group | |
	Experimental	Control
Pretest	-0.047	1.956
Posttest	0.006	1.961
Population Values	0.000	2.000

TABLE 13.2   STANDARD DEVIATIONS OF SIMULATED DATA

| | Group | | Pooled Within Groups |
	Experimental	Control	
Pretest	1.644	1.602	1.625
Posttest	1.595	1.597	1.597
Population Values	1.414	1.414	1.414

TABLE 13.3   CORRELATION COEFFICIENT BETWEEN PRETEST AND POSTTEST

Group	r
Experimental	.489
Control	.496
Within Groups	.492
Population Value	.500

more advantaged ones: It *might* have been, but it was not. If it had been, then regression artifacts would have artifactually made Head Start look effective. Instead, it seems clear that, generally in the Westinghouse-Ohio University study, it was the most disadvantaged Head Starters who were hard to match and that the controls were selected from generally more able populations. The same direction of matching bias is probably prevalent in many of the small-scale studies of compensatory education also. Whereas it would probably be the case in most fields, as it is in pharmacology (Smith, Traganza and Harrison, 1969), that the less rigorously designed studies show the most favorable effects, it seems to be the reverse in compensatory education studies. For example, McDill, McDill and Sprehe (1969) review eleven studies of compensatory education. Of five using randomly assigned control groups, all show significant gains on some cognitive measures. Of five with quasi-experimental controls, only one shows a significant effect. While an examination of control group selection in each of these cases has not been done, pending that, the most plausible explanation seems to us to be the bias of the superior control group in the quasi-experimental studies.

In situations such as this where control samples are chosen to have pretest scores equaivalent to experimental samples, the question may be asked, "Since the Head Start children are an extreme group, why don't they regress toward the overall population mean just as much as do the matched controls?" Comparable questions emerge when psychotherapy applicants are matched with a control sample chosen to have equally maladjusted test scores (e.g., Campbell and Stanley, 1963; 1966: 11-12, 49-50). Why are these controls expected to regress to the population mean while the therapy applicants are not? An initial answer is that person-to-person matching on individual scores involves the misleading exploitation of score instability phenomena to a much greater degree than do the complex of processes which produced the Head Start sample or the psychotherapy applicants. These groups turn out to be extreme when measured, but were not selected on the basis of their extreme scores. It is selection on the basis of extreme individual scores that creates most strongly the conditions under which obtained scores become biased estimates of true scores.

This is not to deny some small degree of regression toward a mean of all children on the part of the Head Start children. But since the Head Start children were not selected on individual characteristics, but rather as members of neighborhoods or school districts, the degree of such regression would be trivial in magnitude in comparison with that of the control children selected because of individual attributes. The mean test level of the hundred or so children in a neighborhood is a very stable value compared with the score of a single child. The test-retest correlation for neighborhood average, computed over all of the neighborhoods of a city, will be very high, perhaps as high as .98 or .99, even with tests for which the test-retest correlation for children within a single neighborhood is only .50. These considerations become very confusing in the abstract. But in the applied situation one can tell the direction of the bias by the specific nature of the difficulties one has in finding matches, and by the differences prior to matching in the groups from which the matched cases are sought.

ANALYSIS OF COVARIANCE

The posttest means in our simulation were .006 and 1.961 for the Experimental and Control groups, respectively. The difference, 1.955, when tested by analysis of variance gives $F (1, 998) = 374.31$ which is, of course, statistically significant. Analysis of covariance, a technique commonly prescribed and used in the Westinghouse-Ohio University study to statistically "equate" groups, yields adjusted means of .491 and 1.476 for the two groups. Although the difference between these has been reduced to .985, we obviously have a serious undercorrection which is further demonstrated by the analysis of covariance $F (1, 997) = 90.80$, which is also very large and also statistically significant. The mean difference is of the same general magnitude as that produced by matching, and again, makes the experimental treatment look damaging. Our simulation is like a pretest, rather than a qualitatively different covariate, in that it is in the same metric as the posttest. The principle of undermatching due to error and unique factors in the covariate holds just as inexorably for the case of dissimilar covariates.

This underadjustment by the analysis of covariance has commonly been overlooked, and the resulting bias makes the statistical criticisms of the Westinghouse-Ohio University study by Smith and Bissell (1970) seem trivial in comparison. While we do not have enough information to estimate the magnitude of the bias, we can confidently state its direction on the basis of the reported group differences on the socioeconomic status rating used as a covariate. We can therefore confidently conclude that, had the Head Start programs actually produced no effects whatsoever, the mode of analysis used in the Westinghouse-Ohio University study would have made them look worse than useless, actually harmful.

Porter (1969) has pointed out that, in the Westinghouse-Ohio University tests of Summer Head Start programs, 44 of 56 have outcomes in the direction of Head Start's being worse than nothing, significantly different from a 50-50 split. For the summer programs, apparently, the true gains were not sufficient to overcome the inevitable regression artifacts coming from the fact that controls were selected from a superior population. For one-year programs, on some measures at least, the regression artifacts were overcome, but with the inevitable result that the true effects were underestimated to an unknown degree.

GAIN SCORES

In our particular analysis, with its stationary pretest-posttest structure chosen for a simplicity of presentation, analysis in terms of gain scores would have avoided

TABLE 13.4   MEANS ON POSTTEST ACCORDING TO PRETEST SCORE

Pretest Score	Experimental Group		Control Group	
	n	Posttest Mean	n	Posttest Mean
5.75 − 6.25	0	- - -	1	5.098
5.25 − 5.75	0	- - -	5	3.558
4.75 − 5.25	0	- - -	13	4.375
4.25 − 4.75	2	1.774	21	3.271
3.75 − 4.25	2	.954	27	2.699
3.25 − 3.75	6	2.711	41	2.413
2.75 − 3.25	10	1.625	48	2.485
2.25 − 2.75	23	1.252	64	2.320
1.75 − 2.25	26	.773	55	1.892
1.25 − 1.75	33	.716	60	1.631
.75 − 1.25	57	.478	45	1.850
.25 − .75	64	.293	47	1.029
- .25 − .25	56	.138	30	1.412
- .75 − - .25	50	- .349	25	.611
-1.25 − - .75	54	- .813	7	.114
-1.75 − -1.25	42	- .609	4	1.058
-2.25 − -1.75	35	- .583	4	- .340
-2.75 − -2.25	20	- .631	2	- .076
-3.25 − -2.75	6	-1.643	0	- - -
-3.75 − -3.25	5	-1.868	1	-2.205
-4.25 − -3.75	4	-2.564	0	- - -
-4.75 − -4.25	3	-1.566	0	- - -

the regression artifacts which both matching and analysis of covariance generated. Applied as a t test of the difference between the mean gain scores of the total Experimental Group versus the mean gain score of the total Control Group, such an analysis would have shown no effect. As can be seen from Firure 13.1, these means would be equal, both being essentially zero. (A comparison of gain scores for only the overlapping parts of the distributions would, of course, be biased, as described under Matching.) However, gain scores are in general such a treacherous quicksand, for example, are so noncomparable for high versus low scorers within any single sample, that one is reluctant to recommend them for any purpose. More important here is that, for the setting of compensatory education, the use of gain scores would involve an assumption that is certainly wrong. Again, the bias would be to make Head Start look damaging.

In a growth situation, unlike our simulation, the posttest mean would be higher than the pretest mean, for both Experimental and Control groups, and this would be so whether or not the treatment had an effect. In this situation, the crucial assumption of gain score analysis is that the absolute amount gained would have been the same for both Experimental and Control pupils under the condition of no treatment effect. This assumption is inconsistent with the fact that the groups differ at the time of the pretest. That difference no doubt is there because of a previously more rapid rate of growth on the part of the Control Group, which would be expected to continue during the period of the experimental treatment. Figure 13.5 illustrates the situation.

TABLE 13.5   MEANS ON PRETEST ACCORDING TO POSTTEST SCORE

| Posttest Score | Experimental Group | | Control Group | |
	n	Pretest Mean	n	Pretest Mean
6.25 − 6.75	0	- - -	1	2.877
5.75 − 6.25	0	- - -	3	4.459
5.25 − 5.75	0	- - -	4	4.406
4.75 − 5.25	1	3.266	14	3.153
4.25 − 4.75	0	- - -	16	3.746
3.75 − 4.25	2	2.036	25	2.762
3.25 − 3.75	3	1.719	51	2.719
2.75 − 3.25	14	1.420	41	2.407
2.25 − 2.75	21	1.790	52	2.256
1.75 − 2.25	29	.164	75	1.916
1.25 − 1.75	48	.340	52	1.862
.75 − 1.25	50	.505	57	1.152
.25 − .75	57	.623	37	1.338
- .25 − .25	57	- .048	27	1.143
- .75 − - .25	52	- .101	21	1.209
-1.25 − - .75	54	- .719	15	.841
-1.75 − -1.25	42	- .506	4	-1.102
-2.25 − -1.75	26	-1.281	5	- .771
-2.75 − -2.25	22	-1.623	0	- - -
-3.25 − -2.75	15	-1.259	0	- - -
-3.75 − -3.25	2	-1.971	0	- - -
-4.25 − -3.75	4	-3.325	0	- - -
-4.75 − -4.25	1	-1.966	0	- - -

In Figure 13.5 we have the growth curves for the two groups under the condition of no treatment effect. Between the ages of 4 and 5 when a treatment was given, the Control Group increased 8 units in ability while the Experimental Group increased only 4 units. This would result in an interpretation of a decrement of 4 units due to the treatment received by the Experimental Group. If a true treatment effect was actually present, it would be underestimated to the same degree. (Omitted in this reprinting is a 4-page section on Lord's [1960] and Porter's [1967] reliability-corrected covariance adjustments.)

BIASING PROCEDURES THAT COULD MAKE HEAD START LOOK GOOD

Selecting a control group from a generally more advantaged population has made Head Start look bad. Selecting a control from a generally less able population would make it look good. There are so many combinations of conditions that would produce this bias that we may be sure it has occurred in many studies. One could make Head Start voluntary, advertising its availability, then select as controls those non-Head Start children who eventually turn up at school from the same tenements and blocks as do the Head Start alumni. In this process, the control group would probably have mothers of lower contact with community information sources and of less concern for their child's school achievement. Or one could select as controls those who initially enrolled but who attended less than one fourth of the sessions. If we look to the probable biases in quasi-experimental evaluations of

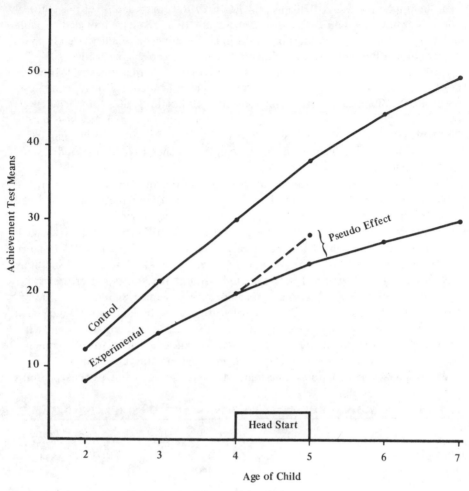

Figure 13.5   Pseudo effect generated by assuming the same growth rate in the Experimental Group as in a superior Control Group.

the "Sesame Street" preschooler's educational television program, they will no doubt be in this direction. In any given neighborhood, it will be the more competent homes that know of the program's existence, and make certain that their children get to see it.

SOCIAL SCIENCE'S UNREADINESS FOR APPLIED QUASI-EXPERIMENTAL EVALUATION

It is tragic that the social experiment evaluation most cited by presidents, most influential in governmental decision making, should have contained such a misleading bias. The technical and political background of this error needs discussion, particularly since it involves so much that is correct and forward looking, and has produced extremely important social experiments such as the New Jersey negative income tax experiment.

In an important essay, Williams and Evans (1969) have described the political processes leading to the massive Head Start evaluation, and have provided valuable guidelines for the proper political postures to be taken when, as must often happen, accurate evaluations show specific ameliorative programs to be ineffective.

There were political pressures from Congress for hardheaded evaluation of specific programs. These pressures can only be commended, and may in the long run make possible an experimenting society (Haworth, 1960; Campbell, 1969) which will do reality testing with exploratory modifications of its own structure. These program evaluation pressures are probably the most valuable part of a movement which also includes demands for more generalized "social indicators" and "data banks."

Within OEO the demand for evaluation led the Office of Planning, Research, and Evaluation to force evaluation of Head Start in spite of the reluctance of the Head Start administrators. Reluctance to expose operating programs to hardheaded evaluation is so common that, in the general case, a willingness to override such reluctance may be essential for social reality testing, even though in this instance the Head Start administrators were right, given the fact that the Head Start programs to be evaluated had been initiated without randomization or pretesting.

Commitment to reality testing on ameliorative programs should involve acceptance of the fact that some programs will turn out to be ineffective. When such outcomes are encountered, the political system should seek alternative approaches to solving the same problem, rather than abandon all remedial efforts. Williams and Evans do an outstanding job of clarification and advocacy on this point.

We academics are apt to assume that, where things go wrong in collaborations

TABLE 13.6　SUMMARY OF ANALYSES OF VARIANCE ON SIMULATED DATA

	Pretest	Posttest
Between Groups F	379.93	374.31
Within Groups MS	2.640	2.552
Within Groups df	998	998
Point Biserial r	.525	.522

TABLE 13.7　SUMMARY OF ANALYSES OF COVARIANCE ON SIMULATED DATA

	Type of Analysis	
	Usual	True Score
Adjusted Means		
Experimental Group	0.491	.991
Control Group	1.476	.976
Between Groups F	90.80	.01
Adjusted		
Within Groups MS	1.935	1.935
Within Groups df	997	997

between the political and scholarly communities, the failure comes from the political process, in the form of a failure to make use of our more than adequate wisdom. In this instance it was quite the reverse. As outlined in the preceding paragraphs, the political forces were positive, and if they survive or can be revived, are such as to make possible a reality-testing society. In this instance, the failure came from the inadequacies of the social science methodological community (including education, psychology, economics, and sociology) which as a population was not ready for this task. The one weakness in Williams and Evans' otherwise outstanding paper comes at this point. They state that ex post facto studies are a respected and widely used scientific procedure. While it would be hard to find any text since Chapin (1955) that has advocated them, most methodology texts are silent on the issue and condone comparable procedures. They cite "matching" as though it achieved its purpose. Warnings against matching as a substitute for randomization occur in a few texts, but probably 90% of social scientists teaching methodology at U.S. universities would approve the process. On using analysis of covariance to correct for pretreatment differences, the texts that treat the issue are either wrong or noncommital (that is, fail to specify the direction of bias), and probably 99% of experts who know of the procedure would make the error of recommending it. Note again that the competitive reanalysis of the Westinghouse-Ohio University data by Smith and Bissell (1970) repeats the original error in this regard. The prestige of complex multivariate statistics and their associated computer programs will perpetuate such mistakes for years to come, under such terms as dummy variable analysis, multiple covariate analysis of covariance, step-wise multiple regression, and the like. The deep-rooted seat of the bias is probably the unexplicit trust that, although the assumptions of a given statistic are technically not met, the effects of these departures will be unsystematic. The reverse is, in fact, true. The more one needs the "controls" and "adjustments" which these statistics seem to offer, the more biased are their outcomes.

THE CASE FOR TRUE EXPERIMENTS IN FUTURE EVALUATION OF COMPENSATORY EDUCATION

There are other possible quasi-experimental designs which avoid the biases here described although none are available for the data to which the Westinghouse-Ohio University study was limited. In a school system with good records of annual testings in the lower grades, a time series of such testings might be employed retrospectively (Campbell, 1970). Longitudinal studies which include some Head Start children offer another possibility (Campbell, 1969b). Looking to the future, by making explicit in quantified detail a policy of giving Head Start opportunity to the most needy, one could create Regression Discontinuity designs (Thistlethwaite and Campbell, 1960; Campbell, 1969a, 1969b) at the individual or school district level. Where highly similar pretests are available, where test-retest correlations are similar for experimentals and controls, and where the assumptions of homogeneous mean and variance growth are tenable, Lord's and Porter's common-factor covariance adjustments may be used with caution. But are there compelling reasons to limit ourselves to quasi-experimental designs when true experiments involving randomization would be so much more informative?

There are problems, of course, with randomization experiments. Randomization at the invitational level avoids the disappointment problem generated by randomly allocating eager applicants to the control condition. But it exaggerates the always present problem of experimental mortality inasmuch as not all those randomly invited accept the treatment. Using only those invited who accept as the experimental group produces a selection bias with favorable pseudo-effects. The unbiased solution of treating all those randomly assigned as though treated dilutes experimental effects, but is at present the recommended solution (Campbell and Stanley, 1963; 1966: 15-16). More sensitive and yet still unbiased procedures focusing on an upper edge of the experimental and control distributions rather than the whole are feasible (Campbell, 1965) and can be further developed. Randomization by neighborhoods or school districts rather than by individuals is an acceptable solution with superior external validity, but again *all* eligible children in the experimental areas must be compared with all eligible children in the control areas. While one can estimate what the magnitude of the effect would be if one could remove the dilution coming from including the untreated, the tests of significance must be made on the full samples created by randomization. These same strictures, however, apply to most quasi-experimental designs, and in particular to the very attractive Regression Discontinuity analysis.

Even though "true" experiments in the field setting are on these grounds more "quasi" than those in the laboratory, (and those in the laboratory more "quasi" than published reports and statistical treatments indicate), experiments with randomized assignment to treatments are greatly to be preferred where possible. We believe that any investigator fully attending to the presumptions he is making in using quasi-experimental designs will prefer the random assignment of children to treatments *where this is possible.*

Social ameliorative changes which are applied or made available to everyone do not readily permit the creation of control groups. These include across-the-board legal changes and television broadcasts. But those expensive remediations which are in short supply and which cannot be given everyone provide settings in which true experiments are readily possible. Once the decision makers in government and applied research are educated to their importance, they can become the standard evaluational procedure.

On the other hand, we must not create a political climate which demands that no ameliorative efforts be made unless they can be evaluated. There will be many things obviously worth doing which cannot be experimentally evaluated, and which should still be done. The shift to new math is an example. By making math achievement tests inappropriate it undermined the only convenient benchmark for its own evaluation. College education is another example, a boon for which we have almost no interpretable experimental or quasi-experimental evidence. (Since college education is given to those who need it least, the regression artifacts are biased to make it look effective.) We applied social methodologists should be alert to recognize such cases and not assume that every new program must be and can be evaluated.

On the other hand, where we can experiment and where the social costs of such experimentation are outweighed by the social value of reality testing, we should hold out for the least biased, most informative procedures.

There exist in administrators, researchers, legislators, and the general public "ethical" reluctances to random assignment. These center around a feeling that the control group is being deprived of a precious medicine it badly needs. But if it be recognized that the supposed boon is in fact in short supply, then it can be seen that the experiment has not increased the number so deprived, but has instead reassigned some of that deprivation so that the ethical value of knowing may be realized. Is randomization as the mode of such reassignment ethically defensible? It might represent an ethical cost (one nonetheless probably worth paying) if all the children in the nation had been rank ordered on need, and those most needy given the compensatory education up to the budgetary and staff limits of the program. But instead, the contrast is with a very haphazard and partially arbitrary process which contains unjust inversions of order of need far more extensive than a randomization experiment involving a few thousand children would entail. These unjust deprivations are normally not forced to our attention, and so do not trouble our ethical sensitivities as does the deprivation of the control group. But there is no genuine ethical contrast here.

Within randomization, there are some designs and stances that may ease any residual ethical burden. For example, the randomization could be limited to the boundary zone, at the least needy edge of those to be treated, and the most needy edge of the untreated. For this narrow band of children, all considered as essentially tied at the cutting point on a coarse grained eligibility score, random assignment to treatment and nontreatment could be justified as a tie-breaking process. We would learn about the effects of the program only for a narrow band of talent. We would wonder about its effectiveness for the most disadvantaged. But this would be better than nothing, and better than quasi-experimental information.

The funds set aside for evaulation are funds taken away from treatment. This cost-benefit trade-off decision has already been made when quasi-experimental evaluation has been budgeted, or when funds are committed to any form of budgeting and accounting. Taking these evaluational funds, one could use nine-tenths of them for providing experimental expansions of compensatory instruction, one-tenth for measurement of effects on the small experimental and control samples thus created. Here the ethical fucus could be on the lucky boon given to the experimentals. Since evaluation money would be used to expand treatment, the controls would not be deprived. In retrospect, we are sure that data from 400 children in such an experiment would be far more informative than those from the 4,000 tested by the best of quasi-experiments, to say nothing of an ex post facto study.

REFERENCES

Campbell, D. T. Invited therapy in an archival or institutional-records setting: with comments on the problem of turndowns. Duplicated memorandum, Northwestern University, August 1965. 13 pp.

–––. Reforms as experiments. *American Psychologist*, 1969, 24(4): 409-429. (a)

–––. Treatment-effect correlations and temporal attenuation of relationships in longitudinal studies. Duplicated memorandum, Northwestern University, December 1969. 15 pp. (b)

–––. Time-series of annual same-grade testings in the evaluation of compensatory educational experiments. Duplicated memorandum, Northwestern University, April 1970.

––– and K. N. Clayton. Avoiding regression effects in panel studies of communication impact. *Studies in public communication*, Department of Sociology, University of Chicago, 1961, no. 3, 99-118. Bobbs-Merrill Reprint No. S-353.

Campbell, D. T. and J. C. Stanley. Experimental and quasi-experimental designs for research on teaching. Pp. 171-246 in N. L. Gage (ed.) *Handbook of research on teaching*. Chicago: Rand McNally, 1963. Reprinted as *Experimental and quasi-experimental design for research*. Chicago: Rand McNally, 1966. Paper.

Chapin, F. S. *Experimental designs in sociological research*. Rev. ed.; New York: Harper, 1955.

Cicirelli, V., et al. *The impact of Head Start: An evaluation of the effects of Head Start on children's cognitive and affective development*. A report presented to the Office of Economic Opportunity pursuant to Contract B89-4536, June 1969. Westinghouse Learning Corporation, Ohio University. Distributed by: Clearinghouse for Federal Scientific and Technical Information, U.S. Department of Commerce, National Bureau of Standards, Institute for Applied Technology. PB 184 328.

Evans, S. H. and E. J. Anastasio. Misuse of analysis of covariance when treatment effect and covariate are confounded. *Psychological Bulletin*, 1968, 69: 225-234.

Haworth, L. The experimental society: Dewey and Jordan. *Ethics*, 1960, 71(1): 27-40.

Hovland, C. L., A. A. Lumsdaine and F. D. Sheffield. *Experiments on mass communication*. Princeton, N.J.: Princeton University Press, 1949.

Lord, F. M. Large-scale covariance analysis when the control variable is fallible. *Journal of the American Statistical Association*, 1960, 55: 307-321.

Lord, F. M. A paradox in the interpretation of group comparisons, *Psychological Bulletin*, 1967, 68, 304-305.

–––. Statistical adjustments when comparing preexisting groups. *Psychological Bulletin*, 1969, 72: 336-337.

McDill, E. L., M. S. McDill and J. Sprehe. *Strategies for success in compensatory education: An appraisal of evaluation research*. Baltimore: Johns Hopkins Press, 1969.

McNemar, Q. A critical examination of the University of Iowa studies of environmental influences upon the I.Q. *Psychological Bulletin*, 1940, 37: 63-92.

–––. *Psychological Statistics*. New York: Wiley, 1949; 4th ed., 1969.

Peters, C. C. and W. R. Van Voorhis. *Statistical procedures and their mathematical bases*. New York: McGraw Hill, 1940.

Porter, A. C. *The effects of using fallible variables in the analysis of covariance*. Ph.D. dissertation, University of Wisconsin, June 1967. University Microfilms, Ann Arbor, Mich., 1968.

–––. Comments on some current strategies to evaluate the effectiveness of compensatory education programs, and Comments on the Westinghouse-Ohio University study. Two memoranda prepared for Robert D. Hess for use at the Symposium on "The effectiveness of contemporary education programs in the early years: Reports from three national evaluations and longitudinal studies." Annual Meeting of the American Psychological Association, Washington, D.C., August 31, 1969.

Smith, A., E. Traganza and G. Harrison. Studies on the effectiveness of antidepressant drugs. *Psychopharmacology Bulletin*, 1969 (March): 1-53.

Smith, M. S. and J. S. Bissell. Report analysis: The impact of Head Start. *Harvard Educational Review*, 1970, 40(1): 51-104.

Thistlethwaite, D. L. and D. T. Campbell. Regression-discontinuity analysis: an alternative to the ex post facto experiment. *Journal of Educational Psychology*, 1960, 51: 309-317.

Thorndike, R. L. Regression fallacies in the matched groups experiment. *Psychometrika*, 1942, 7: 85-102.

Walker, H. M. and J. Lev. *Statistical inference*. New York: Holt, Rinehart & Winston, 1953.

Werts, C. E. and R. L. Linn. Analysing school effects: ancova with a fallible covariate. Research Bulletin #69-59, Educational Testing Service, July 1969. In press, *Educational and Psychological Measurement.*

Williams, W. and J. W. Evans. The politics of evaluation: the case of head start. *The Annals,* 1969, 385 (September): 118-132.

Winer, B. J. *Statistical principles in experimental design.* New York: McGraw-Hill, 1962.

REFERENCE UPDATE
Selected by Donald T. Campbell

Barnow, B. S., G. G. Cain, and A. S. Goldberger. Issues in the analysis of selectivity bias. In E. W. Stromsdorfer and G. Farkas (eds.) *Evaluation studies review annual* (Vol. 5). Beverly Hills, CA: Sage, 1980.

Boruch, R. F. and D. Rindskopf. On randomized experiments, approximation to experiments and data analysis. In L. Rutman (ed.) *Evaluation research methods: A basic guide.* Beverly Hills, CA: Sage, 1977.

Bryk, A. S. and H. I. Weisberg. Value-added analysis: A dynamic approach to the etimation of treatment effects. *Journal of Educational Statistics,* 1976, 1: 127-155.

Bryk, A. S. and H. I. Weisberg. Use of the nonequivalent control group design when subjects are growing. *Psychological Bulletin,* 1977, 84: 950-962.

Campbell, D. T. and R. F. Boruch. Making the case for randonmized assignment to treatments by considering the alternatives: Six ways in which quasi-experimental evaluations in compensatory education tend to underestimate effects. In C. A. Bennett and A. Lumsdaine (eds.) *Evaluation and experiments: Some critical issues in assessing social programs.* New York; Academic, 1975.

Cook, T. D. and D. T. Campbell. The design and conduct of quasi-experiments and true experiments in field settings. In m. D. Dunnette (ed.) *Handbook of industrial and organizatioal psychology.* Chicago: Rand McNally, 1976.

Director, S. M. Underadjustment bias in the evaluation of manpower training. *Evaluation Quarterly,* 1979, 3 (2); 190-218.

Games, P. A. Limitations of analysis of covariance on intact group quasi-experimental designs. *Journal of Experimental Education,* 1976, 44: 51-54.

Heckman, J. J. Sample selection bias as a specification error. *Econometrica,* 1979, 47 (1).

Kenny, A. A. A quasi-experimental approach to assessing treatment effects in the nonequivalent control group design. *Psychological Bulletin,* 1975, 82: 345-362.

Lord, F. M. A paradox in the interpretation of group comparisons. *Psychological Bulletin,* 1967, 68: 304-305.

McCleary, R., A. C. Gordon, D. McDowall, and M. D. Maltz. How a regression artifact can make any delinquency intervention program look effective. In L. Sechrest, S. G. West, M. A. Phillips, R. Redner, and W. Yeaton (eds.) *Evaluation studies review annual* (Vol. 4). Beverly Hills, CA: Sage, 1979.

Magidson, J. Toward a causal model approach for adjusting for pre-existing differences in the nonequivalent control group situation. *Evaluation Quarterly,* 1977, 1 (3): 399-420.

Maltz, M. D., A. C. Gordon, D. McDowall, and R. McCleary. An artifact in pretest-posttest designs: How it can mistakenly make delinquency programs look effective. *Evaluation Review,* 1980, 4 (2): 225-240.

Reichardt, C. S. The statistical analysis of data from the nonequivalent control group design. In T. D. Cook and D. T. Campbell (eds.) *Quasi-experimentaion: Design and analysis issues for field settings.* Boston: Houghton Mifflin, 1981.

Rubin, D. B. Estimating causal effects of treatments in randomized and nonrandomized studies. *Journal of Educational Psychology,* 1974, 66: 688-701.

Rubin, D. B. Assignment to treatment group on the basis of a covariate. *Journal of Educational Statistics,* 1977, 2: 1-26.

VII

COST-EFFECTIVENESS ANALYSIS AND
THE COMMUNICATION OF EVALUATION RESULTS

14

COST-EFFECTIVENESS ANALYSIS IN EVALUATION RESEARCH

HENRY M. LEVIN

Stanford University

I. INTRODUCTION

Costs and Public Policy Choices

The purpose of evaluation research is to obtain information that might be used to choose among alternative policies or programs for achieving social objectives. This decision orientation suggests that attempts to ascertain the impacts of the various approaches are not adequate in themselves to make such choices. Associated with any alternative is not only an impact or effect, but also a sacrifice or cost. The lower the cost for obtaining a given result, the greater will be the total impact of the social resources devoted to the problem. The focus of cost-effectiveness analysis in evaluation research is to determine that strategy or combination of strategies that maximizes the desired result for any particular resource or budget constraint.

In order to understand this concern more fully, it is necessary to consider the fact that government agencies and other institutions are faced with finite budgets and other resources for achieving their objectives.[1] Although each agency may have a relatively narrow set of goals, such as reducing crime, improving educational results, curbing pollution, improving nutrition, reducing infant mortality, and so on, there are presumably alternative methods for accomplishing these tasks. Traditionally, evaluation research has occupied itself only with comparing these alternatives with respect to their results. The costs of alternatives have not been considered. Yet, it is obvious that the less the cost of obtaining any particular set of

AUTHOR'S NOTE: This paper was prepared as a chapter for the *Handbook of Evaluation Research* being produced by The Society for the Psychological Study of Social Issues under the editorship of Marcia Guttentag. The author wishes to acknowledge the assistance of Linda Gunzel and Maureen McNulty in the preparation of the manuscript.

results, the greater will be the contribution of the program toward achieving agency goals because the limited resources will provide a greater impact.

In most respects, cost-effectiveness analysis is not a new form of evaluation research so much as it is one that attempts to integrate cost considerations into standard evaluation research designs. Because a major portion of the cost-effectiveness analysis is based upon the comparative effectiveness of the various alternatives, the approach presumes that such information will be provided by experimental or quasi-experimental research. This information on the probable differences in outcomes of particular strategies is then combined with data on the costs of implementing them in order to make cost-effectiveness comparisons. From these comparisons one can make tentative recommendations among alternatives on the basis of which approaches will maximize the desired outcomes for any particular level of resource use.

The vast majority of evaluation research endeavors fail to consider the cost component. This neglect appears to be largely attributable to the fact that much of the methodological basis for evaluation derives from the experimental sciences and particularly their applications in psychology. Because the preoccupation of such studies is with ascertaining whether there are "statistically significant" differences among experimental treatments and between experimental and control populations, this focus has also dominated much evaluation research. Questions of whether statistically significant differences in outcomes are socially significant, and cost analyses of such differences, have not been an important part of the evaluation agenda until quite recently.

Perhaps the willingness to nominate for policy consideration any program that shows statistically significant results in outcomes over alternatives derives from the fact that only too rarely can such differences be found. Under these circumstances, any differences are thought to be important and worthy of being used for policy recommendations by researchers. But such zeal may provide a very misleading answer once costs are taken into account. That is, the alternative that appears to yield better results in terms of comparative effectiveness may have costs that far outweigh its superiority in results.

This natural tendency to ignore costs is reflected by the following example. A study of computer-assisted instruction in mathematics found that children in grades 1-6 who had received such instruction showed greater gains on standardized tests than did students in matched control groups (Suppes and Morningstar, 1969a, 1969b). While this finding is certainly of interest to educational researchers and policy makers, it lacks a comparison of relative costs. Can the same gain in mathematics achievement be obtained for less cost by using a modification of the traditional mode of instruction?

The answer to that question is implied by other data collected for the experiment. It was found that one of the matched "control schools" using conventional instruction showed greater test score gains for grades 4 and 5 than did its computer-assisted counterpart. Further inquiry revealed that the teachers and administrators at the control school had instituted an additional twenty-five minutes per day of classroom instruction and practice in arithmetic for those two grades. The authors concluded tentatively "that twenty-five extra minutes of classroom drill can be more beneficial than five to eight minutes per day of computer-based drill" (Suppes and Morningstar, 1969b: 19).

While precise cost data are not readily available, estimates of comparative costs can be obtained. Because five hours per day of teacher instruction cost the schools in the sample about $350 per child for the year, an additional twenty-five minutes of such instruction had an added cost of about $35 per year. It appeared that the cost of a fully utilized and efficient system of computer-assisted instruction for five to eight minutes of drill and practice a day would be on the order of about $150 per year.[2] Thus, the computer-assisted alternative was about four times as costly as traditional instruction for achieving the same objective. Because the schools were already spending about $700 annually for each pupil, the computer-augmented approach would have required a 20% addition to the school budget in contrast with only a 5% increase for using conventional methods to increase mathematics performance of students.

In the world of public policy, the costs as well as the effects of alternative strategies must be considered in order to maximize the impact of the social resources devoted to the public good. The purpose of this exposition is to provide a framework for integrating costs into the evaluation framework in order to carry out a cost-effectiveness analysis of the various policy choices. Emphasis will be placed on the conceptual framework, methodology, and examples. As in most areas of evaluation, there is no standard set of applied rules that can be mastered to carry out cost-effectiveness comparisons. Rather there is a set of principles and considerations that must be combined with sensitivity, ingenuity, and intuition on the part of the analyst. Much of the focus of this description will be on the principles of their application, with the hope that these have some transferability to other policy evaluations under other circumstances and in other domains.

Cost-Effectiveness, Cost-Benefit, and Cost-Utility Analysis

Before proceeding with a review of the concepts and their implementations, it is useful to review the history of cost-effectiveness analysis and to compare it with its close relatives, cost-benefit and cost-utility analysis. The father of cost-effectiveness analysis is the more general cost-benefit analysis. The cost-benefit framework allows one to compare the costs and benefits to society of the various policy alternatives confronted. In its most refined form, the technique can be used to take account of such complexities as alternatives characterized by differences in the time allocation of benefits and costs and differences in who receives the benefits and who pays the costs (e.g., rich vs. poor or young vs. old).[4] Moreover, since there is an attempt to compare the monetary value of benefits with the monetary value of costs, the cost-benefit calculus enables the evaluator to use a common yardstick to assess the relative attractiveness of alternatives. Thus, by calculating the costs and benefits of policy alternatives in terms of monetary values, one can compare such dimensions as rates of return on investment, net differences between costs and benefits (net present values), and benefit-to-cost ratios. Of course no alternative would be undertaken whose costs exceeded benefits, and in general the ones that would be selected would be those that maximized the total social benefits relative to costs.

The earliest and perhaps the most imaginative use of cost-benefit analysis for public decision making has been in the evaluation of water resource projects. The Flood Control Act of 1936 required that the Corps of Army Engineers certify a project as feasible unless its total benefits exceeded its total costs. Accordingly, the last three decades have seen extensive development of techniques for measuring the benefits and costs of public investment in activities designed to improve navigation and flood control; to increase the output of hydroelectric power and water usable for agricultural, industrial, and domestic uses; and to expand and enhance the recreational potentiality of water resources (Eckstein, 1958; Krutilla and Eckstein, 1958).

In the application of cost-benefit analyses to water resource projects, most of the costs and benefits can be measured in monetary terms. For example, the costs of dredging and the construction of dams and other facilities, as well as costs of maintenance and operation, can generally be calculated directly from engineering data and cost experiences with similar projects. The monetary values of such benefits as hydroelectric power and water for agricultural, industrial, and domestic purposes can also be estimated by using the market prices of these outputs. The value of flood control can be assessed by deriving estimates of property destruction and loss of life that will be avoided by taming rampant waters. While recreational benefits are harder to determine, several techniques exist for calculating these (Clawson and Knetsch, 1966).

Given these measures of costs and benefits, proposed water resource projects with widely different purposes and in geographically dispersed locations can be ranked according to their net estimated contributions to social welfare (benefits minus costs) and other benefit-cost relationships. This information can be used to allocate the water-resource investment budget to that set of projects which maximize the net value of expected benefits.

A crucial assumption for performing benefit-cost analyses of alternatives is that the benefits or outcomes can be valued by their market prices or those of similar alternatives. Yet, the objectives of many, if not most, social programs often have no market counterpart. If a program is designed to improve the environment, how do we obtain a market price for the reduction of hydrocarbons and visible particles in the air or the reduction of pollution in water? While it is true that some of the benefits of such an action would be reflected in reduced medical costs and the added value of human lives saved, as well as in decreases in pollution-related deterioration of property, it is difficult to quantify the psychic benefits of clean air and water. How do we obtain a price for the aesthetics of open space or of conserving a rare species of bird or animal? What is the market price that will help us assess the benefits of increase in the self-concept, reading level, or music appreciation of a youngster? In each of these instances it is difficult to express outcomes in terms of their market values because a market does not exist for such services.[4]

In such situations the effectiveness of a strategy is expressed in terms of its actual physical or psychological outcome rather than its monetary value. That is, the monetary measures of resource costs are related to the effectiveness of a program in producing a particular impact. When the effectiveness of programs in achieving a particular goal (rather than their monetary values) is linked to costs, the approach is considered to be a cost-effectiveness rather than a cost-benefit analysis. For example, one might examine various alternatives for raising the literacy level of a population, for reducing hydrocarbons in the air, for reducing infant mortality, and so on. In this context, cost-effectiveness analysis enables us to examine the costs of alternative programs for achieving particular types of outcomes, but prevents us from comparing the costs directly with benefits. That is, the cost-effectiveness approach enables us to rank potential program choices according to the magnitudes of their effects relative to their costs, but we cannot ascertain whether a particular program is "worth it" in the sense that benefits exceed costs, because the latter are generally expressed in monetary units while the former are rendered in units of effectiveness for achieving a particular impact.

The cost-effectiveness method was developed primarily by military analysts in their evaluations of weapon systems. Because it is difficult to construct benefit-cost calculations for the horrors of war, the application of the cost-benefit framework to national defense was aimed at achieving particular "objectives" at minimal cost. Such objectives might include the destruction of enemy targets, effectiveness being assessed according to the portion of the specific target likely to be destroyed by various combinations of strategies such as manned bombers versus missiles (Hitch and McKean, 1960). It is probably safe to assert that its application to other social endeavors has not been extensive in part because social evaluators have been less conscious of the importance of costs in decision making than has the Pentagon.[5]

Despite the relatively underdeveloped status of cost-effectiveness analysis as an evaluation tool, it would seem to be a more appropriate approach to many types of evaluations than cost-benefit analysis. In particular, cost-effectiveness comparisons require only that the impacts of alternative strategies along with their respective costs be derived, while the cost-benefit framework requires that we put a monetary value on the impact. Because social experimentation enables us to obtain information on the impacts of alternative treatments or programs, data on effectiveness are easier to provide. That is, the results of policy-oriented experiments or quasi-experiments lend themselves naturally to cost-effectiveness comparisons. To the degree that the effects can also be translated later into monetary values, a cost-benefit framework can be applied at a second stage. Thus, the use of the cost-effectiveness approach does permit one to do a cost-benefit analysis as well, whenever the physical or psychological outcomes can be converted into monetary measures.

For example, a study of alternative population control strategies might evaluate contraceptive techniques and educational programs by their effect on birthrates. The measure of effectiveness for each option would be the reduction in birthrates, as compared with no change or an increase in birthrates among a similar population not participating in the experiment. In this hypothetical experiment, it would be possible to arrive at the levels of effectiveness in reducing birthrates of each combination and type of contraceptive technique and educational approach, and these levels could be compared with the relevant costs. From this information the potential choices could be ranked according to their cost-effectiveness ratios.

While this exercise would enable policy makers to choose among different approaches to reducing population growth, it would not permit them to compare the productivity of using resources for this purpose with that of applying them to improvements in health, education, transportation, or nutrition. Such a comparison would require that the benefits and costs of investing in any particular area be compared with those of other areas. To the degree that reductions in birthrates can be assessed in monetary terms, it is possible to convert cost-effectiveness data into cost-benefit information. Even if the ultimate cost-benefit calculations cannot be made because of inabilities to set a value on the benefits of a program, the cost-effectiveness rankings still represent a valuable basis for choosing among programs that have the same objective. In the presentation that follows, then, the emphasis will be on cost-effectiveness methodology, although it will be stressed that many of the issues are common to both cost-benefit and cost-effectiveness approaches.

Before proceeding to examine more extensively the meaning, methodology, and usefulness of cost-effectiveness analysis, it is useful to define one more related branch of evaluation, cost-utility analysis. While cost-benefit analysis enables a direct comparison of costs and benefits stated in monetary terms and cost-effectiveness analysis represents an attempt to evaluate directly the costs of alternative ways of achieving particular outcomes, cost-utility analysis incorporates the decision maker's subjective views in valuing the outcomes of alternative strategies (Fisher, 1964: 33-48).

In concept, cost-utility analysis relies more heavily upon qualitative factors and subjective judgments than do cost-benefit and cost-effectiveness analysis. As such, it is particularly useful where a complex set of outcomes is associated with each strategy, and they cannot be assessed by market values or other measures common to all of them (Lifson, 1968). Briefly, the decision maker assesses the results of alternative courses of action according to their perceived values of utilities to him. These utilities are then expressed with respect to the costs and the probabilities of obtaining the expected results. The decision maker sets a criterion for making choices, the most common of these being the maximization of expected utility subject to a budget constraint.

II. THE COST-EFFECTIVENESS TECHNIQUE

The use of cost-effectiveness analysis in evaluation can best be shown by constructing a simple illustration of its use. From this hypothetical example it is possible to grasp the added dimension that the approach provides for social decision making. Following this illustration we will attempt to describe the principles and procedures for considering and measuring costs and effects.

Assume that we are engaged in evaluating programs designed to reduce the rate of recidivism of convicts who are released from the state prison. For purposes of this exercise let us define the rate recidivism as that proportion of former prisoners who are arrested and convicted of criminal acts within five years of being released. The existing program is one that keeps a record of the addresses and employment circumstances of former prisoners, as well as requiring those who are released on parole to report periodically to their parole officers. Beyond these bookkeeping relationships there are no systematic attempts to provide either jobs or psychological counseling and assistance.

To reduce an apparently high rate of recidivism, the State Prison Authority wishes to consider a number of alternative programs for ex-prisoners. These include: (1) a job placement program, (2) a psychological services program, and (3) a program that combines both job placement and psychological services. With the assistance of evaluation experts, a major social experiment is initiated to determine the impacts of the three alternatives on the rate of recidivism. For a period of six months all of the released male prisoners who are returning to the major cities of the state are assigned randomly to one of four groups: (1) job placement, (2) psychological services, (3) combination of job placement and psychological services, or (4) normal existing arrangements for ex-prisoners.

After five and one-half years the experiment ends with the following results. The five-year rates of recidivism were 15% for those in the job placement program; 26% for those in the psychological services program; 12% for those in the combination program; and 37% for those ex-prisoners who received no special treatment. Based upon this appraisal it appears that all programs were more successful than the existing approach, but the combination treatment showed the best results, followed by the job placement program and the psychological services one. Under normal circumstances the evaluation might have ended here with the policy recommendation that the combination program be selected, but we wish to review the costs as well.

Table 14.1 shows a hypothetical cost-effectiveness comparison of the anti-recidivism programs for released prisoners. The three experimental treatments discussed above are compared with the results of the normal program. For simplicity we have assumed that exactly equal numbers—10,000 subjects—were assigned to each group. The five-year recidivism rates are shown, and beneath them in parentheses are noted the rankings of the results (1 is best). Based upon these rates we can calculate the number of persons who were not recidivous, who were not arrested and convicted of criminal acts within five years of their release from state prison.

Hypothetical total costs for each program are shown on the next line. It is assumed that the normal program is least expensive because it is essentially an "auditing" or "accounting" approach for maintaining information on the location and activities of each ex-prisoner. The job placement and psychological services programs are more costly, and the combination of them is the most expensive. It is assumed that some aspects of the combination program are duplicated in the separate ones, so that the cost of the combination approach is somewhat less than the combined total of the two separate components. When these costs are divided among the number of subjects in each group, it is clear that the "normal program" is the least expensive and the combination shows the highest average cost per subject.

But the average cost per subject tells us nothing about the cost for obtaining the

TABLE 14.1 COST-EFFECTIVENESS COMPARISON OF ANTI-RECIDIVISM PROGRAMS FOR RELEASED PRISONERS

	Treatment			
	Job Placement	Psychological Services	Combination of these	Normal Program
Experimental population	10,000	10,000	10,000	10,000
Five-year rate of recidivism	.15 (2)	.26 (3)	.12 (1)	.37 (4)
Number of persons not recidivous	8,500 (2)	7.400 (3)	8,800 (1)	6,300 (4)
Total cost	$10,000,000	$ 9,000,000	$16,000,000	$ 5,000,000
Average cost per subject	$1,000 (3)	$ 900 (2)	$1,600 (4)	$ 500 (1)
Average cost per nonrecidivous subject	$1,176 (2)	$1,216 (3)	$1,818 (4)	$ 794 (1)
Number of persons not recidivous in comparison with normal program	2,200 (2)	1,100 (3)	2,500 (1)	---
Additional cost beyond normal program	$ 5,000,000 (2)	$ 4,000,000 (1)	$11,000,000 (3)	---
Marginal cost per additional non-recidivous subject	$2,273 (1)	$3,636 (2)	$4,400 (3)	---

desired criterion, namely the reduction in recidivous subjects. The next line compares the average cost per nonrecidivous subject. According to this comparison, the "normal" program shows the lowest average cost per nonrecidivous subject, followed by the job placement program and the psychological services one, while the combination program seems to have the highest cost. But this comparison is not completely valid because the programs are being credited for subjects who probably would not have been recidivous even in the absence of the programs. For example, the "normal program" is merely a bookkeeping effort. While maintaining regular contact and information on the activities and whereabouts of released prisoners will have some effect on the likelihood of their returning to crime, it is likely that even in the absense of such a program a significant portion of the men would not be recidivous. Accordingly, using the total number of nonrecidivous subjects as a basis for calculations understates the cost of each "success", because it counts any nonrecidivous person as a credit to the program. This bias is most severe for the "normal program," but it is also evident for the other groups.

These preliminary calculations lead us to the final set of results in Table 14.1. If we assume that the "normal program" is required by law, then we do not have the opportunity to eliminate it. Assuming that each of the other treatments also provides for regular contact with the person and collection of the relevant information, the policy question is what cost (for each *additional* nonrecidivous person) is saved by one of the special treatments. In comparison with the "normal program," the job placement, psychological services, and combination programs enable an additional 2,200, 1,100, and 2,500 persons, respectively (out of 10,000 subjects), to avoid returning to crime and prison. As we noted from the recidivism rates, the combination program seems most successful, followed by job placement and psychological service programs.

But the additional costs beyond the normal program vary from treatment to treatment. While the job placement program cost an additional $5 million, the psychological services cost another $4 million, and the combination program had an added cost of $11 million in comparison with the standard approach. From these data we can calculate the marginal or additional cost for each additional nonrecidivous subject. This varies from $2,273 for the job placement program to $4,400 for the combination approach. In other words, it cost about half as much to reduce recidivism by one person via job placement as via the combination program. The psychological services program was about midway in cost per additional nonrecidivous subject.

In summary, although the experiment demonstrated that the combination program showed the most success in reducing recidivism, its higher cost would not be justified. Rather, job placement would appear to be the most promising approach from the cost-effectiveness vantage point. To illustrate the impact of choice of approach on the budget of the social agency that is administering the program, we can calculate that the cost of "saving" an additional 1,000 released prisoners from returning to prison is about $2.3 million under the job placement program, $3.6 million under the psychological services approach, and $4.4 million under the combination program.

This illustration brings out a number of points. First, often what appears to be the most "effective" program may not be the most *cost-effective*. In this instance the governmental cost for each additional nonrecidivous man would have been twice as high had the most "effective" treatment been used as a basis for program selection. Second, not only may effectiveness rankings differ from cost-effectiveness rankings, but the total social costs of making the wrong choice by not considering program costs may be substantial. Third, different measures of cost may provide different implications, as a comparison of the figures on average cost per subject, average cost per nonrecidivous subject, and marginal cost per additional nonrecidivous subject show. Therefore, it is imperative that the appropriate cost comparison be used in order to obtain appropriate results.

Finally, this particular example lends itself to a subsequent cost-benefit evaluation, since it is possible to assess in monetary terms many of the benefits of attenuating recidivism. The decrease in recidivism is equivalent to a concomitant reduction in crimes against property and people. These can be evaluated, in turn, according to the reduction in social costs associated with these crimes as reflected in decreases in property damage and the medical costs and lost earnings deriving from personal injury and death. Moreover, the increases in earnings and taxes from the employment of each additional nonrecidivous person can be estimated. Finally, the reduction in costs of the legal, penal, and police systems, as well as public assistance for dependents of the prisoner, associated with reduced crime can be calculated. All of these benefits taken together can be compared with the costs of reducing the recidivism rate to determine the value of such programs in comparison with other potential social investments.

While this illustration was used to demonstrate the usefulness of integrating the impacts of various alternatives with their costs, it did not focus on the derivation of cost data and their use, nor did it focus on the nature of the concept of effectiveness. In the next two sections we will address the measurement and application of costs, as well as some issues on measuring effects.

III. ASSESSING THE COSTS OF ALTERNATIVES

Before proceeding to a discussion of how to measure the costs of alternatives, it is important to set out the conceptual nature of costs. When one normally thinks of costs, he tends to focus on direct expenditures or what are often called accounting costs. That is, the costs of a particular action are commonly viewed as equivalent to the financial outlay associated with that activity. The concept of costs we will use is considerably broader. We define costs as representing that set of social sacrifices associated with any particular choice among social-policy alternatives.

The sacrifice or "opportunity cost" concept is based upon the economic notion of alternative uses of resources. When resources are used for one purpose, they cannot be used for other ends; therefore, the costs to society of choosing an alternative are the sacrifices implied by the "paths not taken." To the degree that these can be measured in monetary terms, we can calculate the costs associated with any alternative. In this sense the term *costs* refers to the monetary value of all the resources associated with any particular action, and their value is determined by their worth in the most productive alternative applications. Thus, the explicit expenditures associated with any particular course of action represent only a partial measure of the total costs.

A few examples of cost assessment are useful for delineating this principle. Using the criterion of costs as a sacrifice of other opportunities (or the value of foregone alternatives), we can examine the cost of a college education. It is obvious that a part of the cost of education is represented by direct expenditure on personnel, materials, and facilities. In addition, more subtle costs are imposed by the fact that individuals who enroll in colleges and universities are foregoing productive employment in the labor force. Not only does this represent a cost to them as individuals in the form of "lost" earnings, but it also represents a cost burden to society in terms of foregone production and tax contributions. Thus, the total cost of a college education includes not only the direct expenditures for education that normally come to mind, but also the implicit costs reflected in the earnings and production foregone by persons enrolling in colleges rather than working in the labor force (Schultz, 1960).

A second example is that of programs that use contributed imputs. For example, some educational and health endeavors draw heavily upon unpaid volunteers who contribute their time and energies. While such inputs will not be reflected in the budgeted costs of the programs, they represent resource costs nevertheless since they could be used for alternative endeavors. Accordingly, we normally impute a value to these contributed inputs in order to be fully aware of their hidden worth if the budget were to reflect the full burden of resource costs.

A final illustration of the divergence between accounting costs and true social costs is the value of client time. Many social endeavors require that the client take a considerable portion of his time to obtain services. The most poignant example probably appears in the health services. Some organizations require greater expenditure of patient time, in queuing and waiting for assistance, than do others. There is clearly a cost to the client or patient in terms of foregone work and other activities. For women the cost may be reflected in monetary outlays for child care, and for both men and women in the workforce there is a potential cost in the form of lost earnings. Even when there are no direct monetary costs due to waiting, there is a sacrifice of other alternatives that would have been undertaken during that time. To the degree that the evaluation of health service alternatives does not account for these costs, it will not reflect accurately the costs of the services.

As we will see below, a group of decision makers may rationally take into account only its own costs when making a choice among alternatives, but this does not mean that costs to other constituencies should be ignored in the overall evaluation. To the contrary, all costs should be reviewed for purposes of uncovering the true social sacrifice of resources associated with a given program and level of effectiveness. Beyond this an assessment can be made of who pays the costs. While the latter is of crucial importance for the decision maker considering a particular program, the former is necessary for overall social evaluations of cost-effectiveness comparisons.

There are two basic steps in determining the costs of particular alternatives. At the first stage it is necessary to determine the specific resources required and to place a monetary value on their use. The second step entails determining which of these costs must be taken into account by any particular decision maker and how he should construct the relevant cost comparison for the application he is concerned with. These phases will be addressed in turn.

Measuring Costs

The measurement of costs would be a relatively simple task if it were only a matter of scrutinizing accounting statements and selecting the appropriate numbers. Almost never is this the case. To the degree that the cost-effectiveness evaluations are based on social experiments, it is not likely that the collection of cost data was built-in to the evaluation design. When attempts have been made to collect such information, the data tend to be crude and incomplete in comparison with data collected on other aspects of the experiment. Moreover, even if rather precise cost data were derived for an experiment, it is not obvious that the same information could be used as a basis for a full-scale policy implementation. It is often difficult to separate the developmental costs of an experiment from the operating costs of a program; administrative costs of ongoing programs are likely to differ from their experimental counterparts; and the idiosyncracies of the experimental phase may not be duplicated in the routine of application.

In the case that cost-effectiveness comparisons will be based upon evaluations of actual programs rather than experiments, cost information may be easier to derive. Yet, as we noted above, the cost estimates may be incomplete because they are based upon expenditures rather than upon the cost of all resources that enter the program; and the classification of costs may be inappropriate for use in choosing among policy alternatives.

In the long run the best solution to these problems is to construct cost information systems as part of the social experiments and as an integral part of the social programs themselves. This procedure will enable the measurement and monitoring of costs on a continuous and relatively precise basis. It is hoped that an increasing amount of energy will be devoted to integrating cost information into experimental and program designs. Yet, until such information is collected routinely, cost-effectiveness comparisons will have to be made on the basis of ad hoc assessments. Fortunately, the conceptual basis for constructing a picture of costs is similar whether the effort is built into the program being evaluated or is designed as a separate endeavor. Accordingly, one overall approach can be used as a model for cost measurement.

The method of cost estimation advocated here will be denoted the "ingredients approach." The name derives from the focus on listing at the first step the ingredients or inputs required by the program, and assigning costs to them only after all of the ingredients are accounted for. While this priority may seem trivial at first, its importance stems from the attempt at an exhaustive listing of all of the resources utilized by a program. When one focuses immediately on costs, there is a tendency to omit from consideration those inputs that are not obvious or that do not enter budgets explicitly. The ingredients approach requires that the requisite inputs of all types required by a program be recognized for purposes of estimating program costs.

Accordingly, the first order of business is to write a description of the program and its components. From this summary one can attempt to list all of the ingredients that enter the program. Table 14.2 represents a hypothetical worksheet for estimating costs. In the right-hand column all of the program ingredients are listed by major category. These components include personnel, facilities or physical space, materials and equipment, other inputs, and the value of client time. The purpose of the ingredients column is to include exhaustively all of the elements required by the program in as detailed a breakdown as is necessary. Within each category are subcategories. Thus personnel can be divided into administrative personnel and then subdivided again into such specific titles as director, assistant director, secretary, clerical, and so on.

A separate category is set out for the value of client time and other client inputs.

TABLE 14.2 HYPOTHETICAL WORKSHEET FOR ESTIMATING COSTS

	Total Cost	Cost to Sponsor	Cost to Other Government Levels or Agencies	Contributed Private Inputs	Imposed Private Costs
Personnel					
Facilities					
Material and equipment					
Others (specify)					
Value of client time and other client inputs					
Total					
User charges		-( )			+( )
Other cash subsidies		-( )	+( )	+( )	
Net total					

As we asserted above, this resource is often neglected in cost calculations. Such an omission is equivalent to assuming that client time has a value of zero, and under such a presumption policy choices will be insensitive to the burden on the population receiving the services. One should list the number and types of man-days lost by the clients. For example, for an educational project one could provide the number of man-years of work foregone by a particular group of students. Health service programs might show the number of man-days of patient time associated with obtaining treatment, including travel and waiting time. In addition other client inputs should be accounted for in this section, for example, the transportation requirements to obtain services or the required purchase of some complementary ingredient. For example, educational programs often require the private purchase of books and materials, and many social projects have a transportation component.

Cost evaluation must consider these inputs in the total endeavor, whether the costs are borne privately or socially.

Given the list of ingredients, the next step is to estimate their costs. In the present case we will assume a one-year program. Multi-year program comparisons require certain analytical modifications that we will address in a later section. The cost of each ingredient is established either on the basis of cost experiences for that input or some other guideline.[6]

A major rule of cost estimation is to devote attention to any particular category according to the proportion of the total budget reflected by that component. Thus, if a category represents 50% of the total budget, the analyst should allocate around half of his energies to developing cost estimates for that classification. A category that represents only 5% of the total deserves no more than 5% of his attention. The reason for this principle is fairly obvious. Small percentage errors in estimating large categories can amount to large aggregate errors in cost measurement, while even large percentage errors in estimating trivial categories will have little effect on the total cost figure.

Because the personnel category typically accounts for 70 to 80% of the total budget, this component deserves the major share of attention in estimating costs. Fortunately, personnel costs can usually be appraised in a straightforward way from direct cost experience or from programs that use similar personnel capabilities. It is important to include not only salaries and wages, but also fringe benefits and other costs that employers must pay, such as contributions to health, life, and disability insurance plans, to pension plans, and to such payroll taxes as social security. These costs can be as high as one-third of salaries. The value of voluntary personnel is determined by what it would cost if such persons were paid for their services.

The costs of facilities is usually more difficult to estimate. In the simplest case, annual rental payments represent the cost. Where buildings are purchased or where the facilities used are part of a larger endeavor, the assessment of costs is more complicated. The "annual cost" of facilities that have been purchased is obtained by estimating the portion of the facilities used up (depreciated) in an annual period, as well as the opportunity cost of the investment in the sense that the investment could be obtaining social benefits in other uses. The "opportunity cost" aspect can be captured by applying an appropriate rate of interest to the net value of investment. The suitable interest rate depends upon a number of complicated factors, and the issues underlying the choice of rate have been hotly debated (Marglin, 1963; Baumol, 1968). Typically an interest rate of 5 to 10% is imputed.

The cost of depreciation is based conceptually on the fact that facilities have a limited life, so that in principle a portion of them are consumed by each year's use.[7] Thus, if a building has a 30-year life and lacks even salvage value at the end of that period, about one-thirtieth of that building is used up each year (assuming a constant annual depreciation.) In this instance the cost of depreciation would be calculated by taking one-thirtieth of the original cost of the building for each annual period. Added to this would be the opportunity cost of the investment which would be obtained by multiplying the chosen interest rate times the value of the building after present depreciation is accounted for.

To provide a simple example, assume that a project purchases a $900,000 building that has a 30-year life. Using the preceding methods of calculating the annual cost of that building, depreciation would be estimated at about $30,000 a year; and the opportunity cost of the investment would depend upon how much of the investment was depreciated. For example, if the building were 15 years old, we would calculate the opportunity cost for the sixteenth year on only $450,000, or half of the original cost of the building. At an interest rate of 5% that would amount to $22,500. (In the first year the estimated opportunity cost would be about $45,000; in the second year, $43,500; in the third year, $42,000; and so on.) In the sixteenth year, then, the cost of the facility would be $30,000 for depreciation plus $22,500 for the opportunity cost of the investment, with a total annual cost for that year of $52,500.

The measurement of facility costs may require fairly extensive computations if facilities are shared with other programs or are provided by a parent enterprise. In the former case the facilities and other resources may be shared by a number of activities of which only a particular one is the focus of the cost-effectiveness study. In the latter case the facilities may be inseparable in an accounting sense from the larger entity. An illustration of this phenomenon is the determination of the value of high-school facilities devoted to a school dropout program, or the value of the facilities used for an outpatient clinic located in a hospital.

There are several methods of estimating the costs of such facilities. If the total cost of shared facilities can be ascertained from the total rent or by estimating the depreciation and opportunity cost of investment of those that are owned, it is usually possible to prorate these costs among the individual programs. The basis for prorating costs should be some common denominator for all of the programs such as the proportion of the total space used by each program or some other appropriate guideline. This approach can also be used when facilities are provided by a parent enterprise such as a hospital, school, or community center. However, in some cases it is difficult to obtain the information required to prorate costs since this procedure requires data on other projects or on a parent organization that may not be participating in or cooperating with the evaluation. Under such circumstances, it is often preferable to use the alternative method of imputing a rental value equal to the annual rent for comparable facilities. As an illustration, assume that space of a comparable quality can be obtained in a similar location for about $2 per square foot per year. If the program that is being evaluated uses about 1,000 square feet, the imputed cost of facilities would be about $2,000 per annum.

In general, materials and equipment and other inputs can be costed on the basis of expenditures or on the basis of their market values if they have been contributed. The value of client time and other client inputs is based either on direct expenditures of clients where they are evident or on an assessment of the worth of client time. The former category may include client expenditures on books, materials, and other educational inputs in the case of schooling, or the privately borne costs of health programs, such as prescriptions and transportation. The latter category is meant to assess the loss of productive time from other activities, whether in the labor market or in the household. One rule of thumb that is often used to value client time is that of appraising it at its market value with respect to earnings foregone. In order to do this it is necessary to determine the age, racial, and sexual composition of the clientele. From these breakdowns it is possible to use Census data on earnings to determine opportunity cost (Becker, 1964.)

Treatment of Time in Cost Measurement

Where the program requires more than one year of operation to obtain effects, it is necessary to estimate the costs for each year. There is no problem if the costs do not vary from year to year; however, many multi-year programs required additional allocations in the initial period for training and other start-up costs. Other programs may entail higher costs in the later years. Merely to add annual costs for several years does not provide an appropriate basis for comparing multi-year programs whose costs have different time patterns. Programs that allocate the bulk of their costs in the earlier years are not directly comparable with those that allocate the bulk of their costs in later years because the former entail a higher opportunity cost by sacrificing resources earlier in time; thus those resources are withdrawn from alternative uses for a longer period than when they are used later in the program cycle.

As an illustration, let us consider two alternative programs that show total costs of $500,000 for a five-year period. Assume that program A spends $200,000 for the first year and $75,000 for each of the next four years. Assume that program B spends $50,000 for the first four years and $300,000 for the last year. While both programs expend $500,000 over a five-year period, the social burden is greater for program A.

One way of understanding this concept is to consider the projects as bank accounts with $500,000 in initial deposits. Since account A is drawn upon earlier than B, it will yield less interest, where the interest that is derived represents the productivity of investments of the bank. That is, when the money is spent on the program, it cannot be used for other productive endeavors which the bank would invest in. If we assume that the expenditure transactions that we noted for each year would be consummated on the first day of that year, bank account A (or program A) would accumulate about $43,500 in interest payments at a 5% rate of interest, compounded annually over the five-year period. Bank account B (or program B) would accumulate about $85,500 in interest over the same period.

In short, the expenditure pattern reflected in program A is more costly to society as reflected in foregone interest payments which in turn reflect the productivity of investment in alternative endeavors. (This is one of several places where the economic argument seems to cut corners. The money A spends is back in circulation doing its productive thing at year 1.) The earlier expenditure commitment of program A entails a greater social sacrifice of resources than that of program B even though both spend a total of $500,000 over a five-year period. To make the two comparable with respect to the time allocation, we calculate the present values of their expenditure streams by discounting future costs by a rate of interest that reflects their value in alternative endeavors. The formula for obtaining the present value of a stream of costs is:

$$\text{PVC} = \sum_{t=1}^{n} \frac{X_t}{(1 + i)^t}$$

where PVC represents the present value of a stream of costs; X_t denotes the cost for year t; n represents the final year in which costs are incurred; and i represents the appropriate rate of discount or interest. As we noted above, this rate of interest is supposed to reflect the rate of return to society of alternative uses of resources, but the selection of a particular rate depends upon a number of judgments (Baumol, 1968). Most studies utilize a rate of 5 to 10%; however, it is wise to select a number of rates within the appropriate range in order to ascertain the sensitivity of the result to the choice of discount rate.

Table 14.3 applies the present value approach to assessing costs of the two programs presented above. The first and third columns of the table show the allocation of annual costs over the five-year time span for the two alternatives. The second and fourth columns convert each of these annual "future" costs to present values by applying a 5% rate of interest or discount rate to the present value of cost formulation. Thus, the cost for each future year is shown according to its present

TABLE 14.3   CALCULATIONS OF PRESENT VALUE OF COST STREAMS
FOR TWO PROGRAMS

	Program A		Program B	
	(1) Annual Cost	(2) Present Value $\dfrac{X_t}{(1-i)}{}^t$	(3) Annual Cost	(4) Present Value $\dfrac{X_t}{(1-i)}{}^t$
Year 1	$200,000	$200,000	$ 50,000	$ 50,000
Year 2	75,000	71,429	50,000	46,619
Year 3	75,000	68,027	50,000	45,351
Year 4	75,000	64,789	50,000	43,193
Year 5	75,000	61,703	300,000	246,812
Total	$500,000	$465,948	$500,000	$432,975

value equivalent. Because we assumed that the costs in each year would be incurred on the first day of that year, the present value of the first-year costs is also the annual cost. Each subsequent year, however, is divided by the factor $(1 + i)^t$ where t is set to equal to 1 for the annual cost incurred in the second year, by virtue of the fact that it is allocated on the first day of the second year. When we add the separate present values in columns 2 and 4, we find that the total present value of costs for program A is about $466,000 while for program B it is only $433,000. If the programs showed equal effectiveness, program B would be a preferable policy choice because of its lower costs. In general, any comparison of programs characterized by different time patterns of costs will necessitate the conversion of the annualized costs into present values in order to make them comparable among programs.

Uncertainty and Cost Measurement

One other general aspect of cost measurement that should be considered is that of uncertainty. In some cases it may be extremely difficult to ascertain the costs of particular program ingredients. This is especially likely to be true in the assessment of programs, constructed on the basis of piecemeal experimental results, which have never been initiated as total programs. To the degree that the uncertainty applies to only a small fraction of the total ingredients (e.g., non-personnel inputs only), the total cost picture might not be affected appreciably by errors in estimating the costs of these inputs.

The usual treatment of uncertainty is to use the most comparable experience available as a basis for cost estimation. Such comparable data can be adjusted for idiosyncracies of the present application. Where the margins of error appear to be extremely large, it is preferable to suggest a reasonable upper boundary and a lower one. Different values can be used within this range to see to what degree the total cost estimates are sensitive to different assumptions. If total costs seem highly sensitive to the assumptions on which the cost estimates for particular components or ingredients are constructed, it is best to use several alternative assessments of costs in the final cost-effectiveness analysis to see if they affect the results. Normally a high and low value are estimated, and the midpoint or some other value within this range is selected as the most likely figure.[8]

Appropriate Cost Comparisons

As we noted in the illustration on criminal recidivism, cost comparisons are possible. Each is appropriate or inappropriate depending upon the questions one wishes to ask and who is asking the question. It is especially useful to review the allocation of costs among different social entities. From the point of view of society, the total cost of each program must be considered alongside its impact in order to make choices among programs. That is, the most efficient use of the society's resources is made when those programs are selected that show the greatest effects relative to the social sacrifice of resources that they entail. Certainly, an evaluator who is concerned with the largest social perspective will wish to consider the total social costs associated with each alternative.

A public agency may be much less concerned with total social costs than with its own cost burden. That is, a particular governmental unit will be interested primarily in maximizing the impact of its own resources. Its relevant cost comparison will be among the costs it incurs for each alternative, and there will be a tendency of the sponsoring agency to ignore costs borne by other entities.

The worksheet in Table 14.2 is designed to classify the costs among several of these entities including the sponsoring agency, other levels of government and government agencies, and the private sector. For reasons that will be explained, the private sector is divided into contributions and imposed private costs, especially those borne by clients. Because each of these groups may evaluate the "cost-effectiveness" of a program on the basis of its own costs (and benefits), such a classification is rather important for understanding policy choices and political support for particular programs that may appear to be inefficient when total costs and effects are reviewed.

Higher levels of government or other government agencies may contribute to a program by providing particular program ingredients or cash subsidies.[9] For example, some states provide the salaries for reading specialists used by local educational agencies. Another example of a contributed input is the surplus federal properties and equipment given by the federal government to other governmental agencies for public purposes. Cash subsidies are illustrated in public assistance monies used to support housing programs for low-income families. Other examples include the federal subsidies to local governments for acquisition of parks.

Private costs can be divided into contributed inputs and private cash contributions. The former include the value of time of volunteers (especially in hospitals, schools and libraries) and donated facilities, materials, and equipment. In addition, there is that large category of imposed private costs, the direct expenditures required of clients for obtaining the service. These represent a cash subsidy from the client to the sponsoring agency. Examples of user charges include the costs that clients must pay for health services, admissions fees to museums and other public institutions, and tuition and fees at public educational institutions.

To determine the net costs to these entities, both contributed inputs and cash subsidies must be taken into account. The various columns to the right of the Total Cost column enable the costs of ingredients to be allocated among the four classifications. Thus, the totals at the bottom of the columns represent the costs associated with the provisions of the ingredients in the program by each group. But, in addition to these there are cash subsidies to the sponsor from both government and private sources as we described above. Accordingly, at the bottom of the appropriate columns we must add or deduct the value of these cash subsidies to determine the net costs to each constituency.

This adjustment is implemented by adding user charges to the Imposed Private Costs and deducting this subsidy from the Cost to Sponsor. Likewise the case subsidies provided by other governmental levels and agencies and by private contributions should be added to the costs in those columns and should be deducted from the sponsor's costs. These transactions are symbolized by the parentheses with accompanying plus or minus signs. When these accounting transfers are made in the table, the results show the net total costs to each entity. After these adjustments it is obvious that the net cost to the sponsoring agency can be considerably less than the total cost of the program. If a program with relatively high cost-to-effectiveness ratios is more highly subsidized than one with relatively low cost-effectiveness, there is the risk that a sponsoring agency will select the program that is less appropriate from the perspective of the larger society. That is, the cost-effectiveness ratio *to the sponsoring agency* for any program is improved by a larger subsidy. The importance of this point is to illustrate the cause of possible divergence between agency optimization and the maximization of social objectives. Cost-effectiveness evaluation can play an important role in documenting the contradiction.

Other levels of government and private constituencies would opt rationally for programs that minimize the costs to their entity for any given level of program benefits. Thus, it is not difficult to see that each group, comparing its costs to the perceived effectiveness of particular programs, may calculate different priorities. These kinds of conflicts might even be more apparent if we were to analyze the distribution of the tax burden and benefits of particular programs (Gillespie, 1965). The former is generally beyond the scope of a cost-effectiveness analysis, and the latter will be reviewed in the later section on effectiveness.

Cost-effectiveness comparisons are made on the basis of cost compilations that might analyze costs in any one of several ways. The most common of these are: total costs for obtaining a given level of effectiveness, average costs per unit of effectiveness, and marginal costs for additional units of effectiveness.

The comparison of *total program costs* is most appropriate when we are confronted with alternatives of about equal effectiveness. For example, assume that we are confronted with three possible routes for a highway planned between two remote points. Each route has about the same distance, but they differ with respect to the types of construction and the types of property that will have to be condemned enroute. In that case the evaluator might simply wish to calculate the total cost of each alternative and select that choice which minimizes the total project costs.

When programs differ in terms of their effectiveness, it is usually advisable to compare the *average cost* per unit of effectiveness. For example, assume that we evaluate several approaches to decreasing infant mortality, including prenatal educational programs, different approaches to maternal prenatal services, and nutritional supplements. Every woman is assigned randomly to a treatment or to a control group, and the levels of infant mortality are calculated for the groups. The effectiveness of a program can then be stated in terms of the reductions per standard unit (e.g., 1,000 pregnancies) of aborted births and of infant mortality through the first year of life. The programs may show widely varying results and widely varying costs. Accordingly, dividing the reduction in infant mortalities associated with each treatment by the cost of the treatment yields the cost per standard reduction measure.

This average cost per unit of effectiveness has the very desirable quality of permitting cost-effectiveness comparisons among divergent programs with very different characteristics as long as the total costs of the programs are available and the outcomes of the programs are measured in the same effectiveness units. For example, using the concept of average cost per unit of effectiveness, it is possible to compare different remedial-reading programs in terms of the cost per additional point of reading score. Delinquency prevention programs can be evaluated according to their cost for reducing delinquency rates. Health programs can be contrasted on the basis of the cost per standardized reduction in the incidence of diseases.

While the average cost measure is extremely attractive because of its generalizability across widely divergent programs, it is characterized by one major problem. Such a criterion implies that the most efficient ranking of programs at one level of the output scale pertains also to other levels of output. In fact, often programs that show low average cost at modest levels of output will show relative high average costs at greater levels of output and vice-versa. A reason is that technologies vary according to their relative intensity of fixed costs. Fixed costs represent those basic ingredients that must be acquired in order to operate the program. They are invariant with respect to the level of output of the program to the degree that they must be obtained simply to offer *any* level of output, low or high. Accordingly, programs with large components of fixed costs will show relatively high average costs for low levels of output and low average costs for higher outputs.

As an illustration of fixed costs, consider a clinic designed to handle 400 patients per day. The program ingredients include the minimum physical facilities and specialized personnel necessary for operation. Even if only 100 patients a day are serviced, it is difficult to reduce these basic costs; but the average cost per patient will be about four times as high as at full capacity. Variable costs differ according to the number of patients serviced. For example, the number of X-rays, injections, and other patient services will be reduced with lower patient loads, but these costs are likely to be proportionate to patient load. That is, the average variable cost per patient is not strongly affected by scale of operation. If such a clinic were contrasted with a program that simply sent patients to community practitioners, it is possible that, for small numbers of patients, the cost per treatment would be lower for the latter alternative, but, for larger numbers of patients the "economies of scale" reflected in increasing utilization of the fixed overhead of the clinic would likely reduce the average cost of treatment below that for individual practitioners.

Figure 14.1 represents these cost relations. For relatively low numbers of patients it is possible to utilize individual practitioners at a relatively modest cost, but with larger numbers of patients the costs rise gradually because of the need to draw upon the more expensive practitioners in the community and also because the higher demand for practitioner services might stimulate higher prices. In contrast, the cost per patient treatment at the clinic would tend to be very high with few patients, but the cost per patient declines as the number of patients rises. Below about 200 patient treatments per day, the individual practitioner approach shows a lower cost per patient than the clinic, but beyond that level the clinic tends to be more cost-effective.

Comparisons of average cost per unit of effectiveness should be made only at

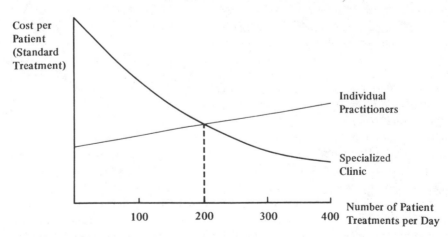

Figure 14.1 Hypothetical Average Cost Relationships for Individual Practitioners and a Specialized Clinic

that level of scale that is appropriate to the particular application being considered. Without taking the scale of a program into account, the results may be very misleading. For example, educational television and radio may be much less costly alternatives for teaching reading than their more traditional instructional counterparts for state and national educational systems with several hundred thousand students. But their high fixed costs make educational television and radio rather costly for teaching reading to student populations of a few thousand.

In some instances it is the additional cost or *marginal cost* per effectiveness unit that is the relevant measure of comparison. This is particularly true where average cost per unit of effectiveness changes according to the scale of program. Assume that the decision maker is faced with the choice of expanding existing programs or initiating another one. In such an event he may be less concerned about the average cost per unit of effectiveness than he is about the additional cost per effectiveness unit entailed in enlarging the existing alternatives or in creating a new program. The measurement of costs would address only those additional ingredients needed to expand the programs from their present levels, and these would be contrasted with the additional units of effectiveness that would result. This marginal-cost approach considers not all the program costs and effects, but only those at the margin. The same criterion can be used for program contraction where the decision maker wishes to choose that combination of programs that will ensure the largest reduction in the budget for a unit decrease in output.

Marginal cost-effectiveness comparisons are also appropriate when decision makers must allocate budget increases or decreases among competing programs (Schultz, 1969; Wildavsky, 1964; Rivlin, 1971). To maximize the impact of an increase, they will wish to allot additional funds to those programs that show the largest gains in output per unit of cost. Conversely, decreases in the budget should be spread among those programs that show the smallest loss of output for a given reduction in support. In these circumstances the analyst must review all potential programs according to how marginal increases or decreases in costs will affect the magnitudes of increases or decreases in output. In this analysis one need not consider all costs and effects, but only marginal costs and effects.

IV. MEASURING EFFECTIVENESS

Because most evaluation research tends to ignore cost analysis, we have devoted a substantial portion of this effort to the explanation of methods of measuring and analyzing costs. The existing approaches to social evaluation do have much to say about concepts and measures of effectiveness. Before evaluation studies proceed, they must select and operationalize a criterion. This criterion is the outcome or measure of effectiveness that is observed for all the alternative programs or strategies. We will not address the conceptualization and measurement of the criterion to the degree that we have reviewed the cost aspects. Nevertheless, three rather general issues are important to consider: (1) the time pattern of results, (2) measuring multiple outcomes, and (3) distributing effects among different populations.

The Time Pattern of Results

Just as the time allocation of costs may differ among programs, so may the time pattern of results. Consider two reading programs designed to bring "slow-readers" up to grade level in reading achievement. Program A emphasizes computer-assisted instruction and other technological aids, while Program B concentrates on small-group instruction and tutoring. Students are assigned randomly, and they remain with the program until they reach their grade equivalent in reading, at which time they are transferred to regular reading programs. At the end of five years it is observed that 80% of the children who were enrolled in program A reached this criterion compared with 70% of the children in program B. It is found that similar students who do not receive the special treatments do not obtain grade level reading proficiencies over the same period.

One possible way to carry out a cost-effectiveness comparison is to compare the total costs for the two programs with the total number of children brought up to grade level in reading within five years. This would yield the average cost—properly discounted to obtain its present value—for each program "success." But on further scrutiny we observe that the timing of "successes" varies as shown in Table 14.4. According to this presentation, program B shows relatively earlier successes than program A even though the results for program A surpass those of program B at the end of five years.

The earlier a student is able to read at grade level, the sooner he is able to benefit from regular instruction and to participate in standard reading activities for his age. If society places a premium on bringing students up to that level of proficiency quickly, it is clear that a comparison of the two programs should take the time pattern of impact into account. This adjustment can be made by weighing more heavily in calculations of effects the earlier successes than the later ones.

In the selection on measuring costs we presented a technique for doing this, the application of a discount rate to the stream of annual costs. The same approach can be used for making different time streams of effects more nearly comparable. That is, the additional number of children that are able to achieve at the appropriate reading level can be calculated for each of the five years, and the "present value" of this five-year pattern can be estimated by utilizing an appropriate discount rate much as the present value of costs was determined. The cost-effectiveness comparison of the two programs can then be based on present values of both costs and effects. In this example, the application of "present value" methodology would

TABLE 14.4 PROPORTION OF STUDENT COHORT WHOSE READING ACHIEVEMENT HAS REACHED THE MEAN ACHIEVEMENT AT THEIR GRADE LEVEL

	Program	
By End of Year	A	B
1	10	30
2	25	40
3	40	50
4	70	60
5	80	70

improve the relative standing of program B in comparison with using an approach that ignores the time pattern over which program outputs occur. In any endeavor where deferred outcomes are less preferable than present ones, it is wise to ensure that cost-effectiveness comparisons are based upon the appropriate adjustments.

Effectiveness Measures for Multiple Outcomes

Virtually all of the examples we have used envision the effectiveness of a program as a single output reflected by a single measure, but many social programs are characterized by broad aims that can be reflected in a large number of measurable (and unmeasurable) outcomes.[10] Educational programs that are designed to improve a child's achievement in one subject may also influence his performance in other subjects, as well as his attitudes (Levin, 1970b.) Delinquency prevention programs may not only decrease the amount of juvenile crime, but they may also increase the educational attainments, employability, and welfare of the young adults involved.

The focus on a single criterion measure of effectiveness ignores the other effects of programs. If the other impacts have no value, then there is no harm in omitting them. In all too many cases, however, the other effects are of some importance, and should be considered explicitly. When one considers more than one output, he is faced with the problem of how to integrate them in the cost-effectiveness framework.

Assume, for example, that we are asked to evaluate the effects of two instructional programs on *both* mathematics and reading scores. Table 14.5 shows two sets of hypothetical outcomes. In Case 1, Program A shows greater effectiveness per unit of cost than Program B for both reading and mathematics achievement. Accordingly, the evaluator would recommend the adoption of Program A. But in Case 2, Program A shows a superior effect relative to cost for reading, while Program B is more effective for mathematics. Which program is preferable from the cost-effectiveness vantage? It is obvious that there is no answer a priori. If Program A is chosen we will obtain higher reading scores, but will sacrifice 2 points of mathematics achievement. If Program B is chosen, mathematics scores will be higher, but reading scores will be less than optimal.

TABLE 14.5 HYPOTHETICAL TEST SCORE GAINS PER STUDENT FOR A GIVEN BUDGET INCREMENT TO EACH OF TWO PROGRAMS

	Case 1		Case 2	
	Reading	Mathematics	Reading	Mathematics
Program A	2	3	2	1
Program B	1	2	1	3

The only way we can obtain an unambiguous cost-effectiveness ranking between the two programs is to express the value of the outputs in common units. One of the advantages of cost-benefit analysis is that outputs are converted into monetary values. But it is often difficult to translate changes in attitudes, test scores, and improved health into monetary benefits. The alternative is to assign arbitrary weights to the outputs so that they can be aggregated into an effectiveness index. Because this requires an ethical or normative judgement that may not express the view of everyone concerned, it is best to use several alternative weighting schemes. This approach enables each person to use his own values in scrutinizing the results, and it permits the evaluator to see whether cost-effectiveness rankings of the programs change as output priorities change (Azzi and Cox, 1973; Weisbrod, 1968).

Table 14.6 shows hypothetical effectiveness ratings for the two educational programs represented in Case 2 of Table 14.5. The test score gains for a given budget increment are translated into an effectiveness index by applying weights. When reading scores are assigned a weight of 1 and mathematics scores are assigned a weight of 2, the composite effectiveness score for Program A is 4. The comparable weightings for Program B provide a composite score of 7. Given those weights, Program B is the more effective. If reading gains were valued three times as much as mathematics gains, Program A would show a value of 7 in contrast with a value of 6 for Program B.

To compare program effectiveness the higher rating for any set of weights is underlined and equal ratings are encircled. The display can be summarized by saying that only when the decision maker believes that reading gains are at least three times as important as mathematics gains will he choose Program A. Under other conditions he will either be indifferent to the two programs or choose B. This

**TABLE 14.6   EFFECTIVENESS RATINGS OF TWO EDUCATIONAL PROGRAMS
UNDER ALTERNATIVE WEIGHTING SCHEMES**

Case 2

Program A
Reading Weights

Mathematics Weights		1	2	3	4
	1	3	(5)	7	9
	2	4	6	8	(10)
	3	5	7	9	11
	4	6	8	10	12

Program B
Reading Weights

Mathematics Weights		1	2	3	4
	1	4	(5)	6	7
	2	7	8	9	(10)
	3	10	11	12	13
	4	13	14	15	16

approach forces the user to make an explicit ethical decision about the values of the outcomes and enables him to see the cost-effectiveness implications of his value choice. It also permits him to see how sensitive the rankings of the programs are to deviations from his weighting. The usual alternative is to ignore additional outcomes other than the particular one under scrutiny. That method places an implicit value of zero on other effects, and such a value judgment is (by default) not ordinarily obvious to the user of the evaluation findings. Accordingly, the explicit weighting scheme would seem to be a far superior approach for the multiple outcome program comparison.

Distribution of Effects Among Different Populations

A final aspect of the assessment of effectiveness is to evaluate who receives the benefits of the program. The use of a single effectiveness index for each outcome (e.g., the mean) assumes that the comparable programs have the same distribution of results across the population or that the distributions do not really matter (Azzi and Cox, 1973). The distribution of effects should be evaluated if a movement toward equality of outcomes is desirable. An example is found in education where there is a concern not only with the improvement in achievement test scores associated with a given approach, but also with the distribution of the scores (Block, 1971). In general, a program is considered to be more desirable the greater its ability to produce achievement gains and to reduce the variance in student achievement.

Assume a comparison of two instructional programs with equal average gains in student achievement. On closer scrutiny the first program has increased the test scores of all students by about the same amount, while the second has increased substantially the test scores of the top third of the student population with only modest or insignificant changes among the lower two-thirds. If we were to ignore the distribution of the results, we would rate the two programs equally effective. By attaching any positive value to the distributional consequences of the programs, we would prefer the first program over the second one for the same cost outlay.

Accordingly, when programs with equalization goals are evaluated, some attempt should be made to examine distributional changes as well as the average effect. This can be done in a number of ways (Jamison, et al., 1971). Perhaps the simplest way to measure distributional effect is to compare the change in the variance of the outcome, as well as the change in its level. Other distributional measures may be more appropriate depending upon the desired properties of the indicator (Atkinson, 1970). Given both a measure of change in outcome and its distribution, it is possible to obtain overall indices of effectiveness of programs by weighting the two according to decision priorities. This can be done by treating the measures as multiple outcomes and applying value weights to them in the manner suggested in the previous section. That is, the relative value of changes in the distribution and level of outcome can be assessed by setting out an analysis similar to that in Table 14.6.

Distributional concerns are important also when the production of benefits for one segment of the population is considered to have greater value than equal benefits for other segments. While this judgment is inherently an ethical one (as are all distributional considerations), it can be said that many programs express special concern for poor, aged, and minority populations. For example, consider housing rehabilitation programs that make use of low-cost loans and other subsidies. The effectiveness of such programs might be stated in terms of the number of housing units rehabilitated by such public endeavors. Then the approach that provides the greatest number of rehabilitations for a given cost would appear to be the most cost-effective. But what if the groups who are the primary beneficiaries of each program differ in composition? Under one program it is essentially middle- and upper-class persons who have purchased dilapidated buildings at highly subsidized interest rates; they refurbish the buildings to use as domiciles, or to rent and sell for profit. The other program has helped the poor, minorities, and the aged to form community corporations that systematically renovate the buildings for housing rentals to members of the communities.

If the total number of rehabilitated units were the only criterion of effectiveness, it is likely that the former program would be found to be more effective than the latter. To take the distribution of benefits into account, one can treat each distributional variable as an outcome of the program and weight the variables into the effectiveness index. In this case the proportion of direct recipients or participants who are classified as aged, minority, or poor would be ascertained, along with the number of housing units rehabilitated. These can be valued by alternative rating schemes into overall effectiveness ratings that can be compared with costs.

While the distributional aspects of social programs have been neglected in the past, to ignore them is to make distributional judgments nevertheless. Such an omission represents a tacit acceptance of the existing distribution of benefits of the programs that are being evaluated. Moreover, if the housing example is realistic and representative, a cost-effectiveness analysis that does not consider the distributional aspects of the results may be systematically biased in favor of the middle and upper classes.

V. ILLUSTRATIONS AND CONCLUSIONS

Now that the rationale and methodology for cost-effectiveness analysis of social programs have been presented, it may be useful to review studies that have utilized this analytical tool. The nuances of the technique are much better reflected in examples than in an abstract description of methods. The fact that cost-effectiveness analysis has not been widely employed for the analysis of social programs handicaps this endeavor; most of the applications have been in the area of military strategies and acquisition of weapon systems (Goldman, 1967; Quade, 1964). Cost-benefit approaches have typically been used for the evaluation of public policy in other areas, perhaps because economists prefer the wider comparability of cost-benefit results. Fortunately, many of the issues raised by cost-benefit techniques are pertinent to cost-effectiveness studies.

In recent years a number of survey articles, bibliographies, and volumes of readings have been published on the subject. The most comprehensive survey articles are those of Prest and Turvey (1965), and Musgrave (1969.) An excellent annotated bibliography is found in Hinrichs and Taylor (1969), and most of the other sources that are cited here offer extensive bibliographies. Among collections of readings on cost-benefit analysis, the most comprehensive are Dorfman (1965), Chase (1968), and Niskanen et al. (1973). These readings cover a wide variety of topics, including recreation, agricultural price supports, transportation, manpower training programs, nutrition, education, health, and methodological issues. Goldman (1967) presents a set of essays on cost-effectiveness analysis in decision making. While some of the issues treated are general, most of the papers concern the application of cost-effectiveness analysis to military decision-making.

Health Studies

Health programs represent a fertile area for cost-effectiveness and cost-benefit inquiries. Analyses in the health area have been especially varied with respect to subject and methodology. Provocative discussions of the problems in the economic evaluation of health endeavors and suggested directions for their solution are presented in Mushkin (1962) and Weisbrod (1961). The measurement of health is discussed in Hennes (1972).

Among studies of particular health topics, Maidlow and Berman (1972) attempted a benefit-cost analysis of alternative means of treating heroin addicts. A part of their evaluation was based upon the probability that former addicts would return to addiction. Attempts to estimate the costs of particular diseases are presented in Rice (1968) and tied to a general methodology. The costs of mental illness are estimated by Fein (1958), and the costs of syphilis, by Klarman (1965). These two works consider conceptual aspects of measurement.

The economics of preventing infectious kidney diseases is the focus of a study of Menz (1971). This inquiry evaluates the costs and results of a hypothetical program that would be differentiated by several different levels of intervention. Cost-effectiveness of periodic health examination strategies is explored by Forst (1973). The delivery of health services is explored in the work of Smith, Miller, and Golladay (1972), which used a cost-effectiveness framework to determine the optimal roles of paramedical personnel in the production of primary medical care.

Education and Manpower Training

Numerous cost-effectiveness and cost-benefit studies have been undertaken in the evaluation of educational and manpower training programs. In the area of elementary and secondary education, Corazzini (1968) and Hu, Lee, and Stromsdorfer (1971) have attempted to compare the costs and benefits of secondary vocational programs with general or comprehensive programs. Each of these explorations reports the conditions under which each of the alternatives might be considered superior. Levin (1970a) carried out a cost-effectiveness analysis of teacher selection where the measure of effectiveness was the increase in verbal acheivement of sixth graders. It was found that the use of more experienced teachers was five to ten times as costly as selecting teachers who showed higher verbal scores on a vocabulary test. Perl (1973) carried out a similar type of analysis for secondary schools. According to his results, the selection of more educated teachers would provide a considerably greater impact on student test scores per dollar of expenditure than reducing the average class size.

A study of the cost and performance of computer-assisted instruction for disadvantaged children (Jamison et al., 1971) deserves special mention. This investigation compared the test gains of children in three programs that utilized computer-assisted instruction (CAI) with those of children who received conventional instruction. Two of the programs focused on mathematics achievement, and the other concentrated on reading skills. In general, the students in the CAI programs outperformed their counterparts in the control groups. The authors also evaluated the distribution of the gains in test scores to see if gains were more (or less) variable in the CAI than in conventional instruction. The CAI students tended to show more nearly uniform gains than did their counterparts. Finally the relative costs of the CAI and conventional instruction were evaluated. The combination of experimental methodology with considerations of the distribution of results and costs makes this study an especially valuable reference.

Studies of dropouts (Weisbrod, 1965), preschool programs (Ribich, 1968: 83-97), and compensatory education expenditures for children from low-income backgrounds (Ribich, 1968: 83-97) have been evaluated with respect to the estimated increase in lifetime income associated with the effects of such programs. It has been found that in general, the costs of such programs exceed the benefits when income production is used as the criterion of success. Broader evaluations of education as a social investment have found relatively high returns in both the United States (Becker, 1964; Hanoch, 1967) and other countries (Psacharopoulos, 1973).

Manpower training programs have been evaluated by cost-benefit and cost-effectiveness techniques; an important and comprehensive review is found in Goldstein (1973). Ribich (1968: 34-50) compared a number of manpower training programs. In general, it appears that the benefits of such programs far exceed their cost. A comparison of particular approaches to "neighborhood youth corps" is presented in Somers and Stromsdorfer (1972). That evaluation included an analysis by race and sex of student of the effects of both in-school and summer youth corps programs with respect to a number of criteria including high-school graduation.

Other Studies

A wide variety of other subjects has been the focus of cost-effectiveness approaches. Douglas and Tweeten have suggested a method for calculating the cost of controlling crime. Empirical findings on the factors affecting the costs of local police services and fire services in the St. Louis metropolitan area are reviewed in Hirsch (1970: 170-171). A study of the effectiveness of correctional programs is found in Robinson and Smith (1971). Since no correctional program was found to be more effective than any other, it is likely that the least costly one would be preferred; but Robinson and Smith do not present the costs of the alternatives. Empirical analysis of the costs of different service levels of refuse collection at the municipal level is presented in Hirsch (1965).

A substantial number of studies have evaluated the provision of recreational services and facilities. A general review of the issues and methodology is found in Clawson and Knetsch (1966). Specific studies of interest include Mack and Myers (1965) and Krutilla and Cicchetti (1973). Highways and transportation have been the focus of numerous analyses. The evaluation of urban highway programs was undertaken in Mohring (1965) and Kain (1967). Navigation improvements are scrutinized in a cost-benefit framework by Haveman (1973). Cost-benefit studies of urban renewal by Rothenberg (1967) and of infant nutrition by Selowsky (1973) represent exceedingly provocative applications of these analytical tools to those areas.

Conclusion

The case for carrying out cost-effectiveness analyses of social alternatives is a strong one. Given limited resources to allocate among competing programs, evaluation for social choice must consider both the costs and the results of particular approaches. Yet this branch of inquiry, like most aspects of evaluation, is a relatively young one. The conceptualization and measurement of both costs and outcomes have not and probably cannot be routinized. Accordingly, the judgments of the evaluator in setting out decision rules and guidelines for estimating costs and effects represent a crucial variable in determining the outcome of the evaluation. The omission of particular cost components or program outcomes, the selection of a particularly high or low discount rate for future costs or results, and the method of estimation of costs of program ingredients all represent areas where different judgments may alter appreciably the cost-effectiveness ratings of alternatives (Williams, 1973). The preoccupation with means-ends relations at the expense of considering processes also represents a bias of the approach (Tribe, 1973).

The implications of the foregoing are that the cost-effectiveness analyst and the user of his results should feel obligated professionally to use the tool with wisdom and caution. In particular, the analyst is urged to make his assumptions about cost and output measurement as explicit as possible with a discussion of alternative assumptions and the likely effects that they would have on findings. Where feasible the calculations should by presented on the basis of alternative assumptions so that the reader can choose those that are consistent with his own understanding of the issue. The user should recognize the fact that the conclusions of such studies do not in themselves define a policy action. Rather they serve as useful—and, one would hope, potent—sources of information that must be combined with factors that have not been taken account of in the cost-effectiveness inquiry, in order to make public choices that are sensible, efficient, and equitable. In this context, cost-effectiveness analysis can be a powerful and productive ally.

NOTES

1. For an overview of public budgeting systems and analysis, see Lee and Johnson (1973.)

2. This estimate was calculated from data provided by Dean Jamison. The actual cost of the program that was used as the basis of the experiment was considerably higher because it was designed for research and development purposes rather than routine application.

3. It is not the purpose of this article to review the enormous theoretical and practical difficulties in deriving allocation decisions that will maximize social welfare. The classical treatment of the subject is found in Pigou (1951), and an excellent critique is Little (1957). Also see the important theoretical dilemma presented by Arrow (1951). The relationship between prices and costs on the one hand and value on the other is a rather complex one. In a capitalist society it is explained primarily by the theory of markets. A fundamental exposition can be found in Samuelson (1970), chaps. 20 and 22-25. The neoclassical treatment is found in Hicks (1946), chaps. 1-5. In recent years the realism of the theory has come under increasing criticism. See for example, Gintis (1972) and Galbraith (1970).

4. While it is possible to attempt to determine how much people would pay for such benefits, it is not clear that they could evaluate accurately the values of services that are highly diffusive and that they might not have experienced. There is also a moral problem in attempting to determine the value of a "social good" whose cost will be apportioned among recipients according to how highly they value it. See Musgrave (1959: 73-89).

5. It is not clear that the political variables that dominate the acquisition of weapons systems have been overcome by the analysts as is evidenced by the typical overruns on costs and underruns on performance of such recent purchases as the F111 and C5A aircraft. In this respect the cost-effectiveness studies of the Pentagon may be primarily academic in value.

6. No attempt is made here to explain basic accounting procedures. There are many readily available sources on this subject, for example, Anthony (1964), Horngren (1967), and Moore and Jaedicke (1967).

7. A discussion of the treatment of depreciation in cost accounting is found in Anthony (1964: 154-172).

8. The underestimation of costs is far more frequent than their overestimation. Certainly a part of this phenomenon is due to the tendency of analysts to be "optimistic" in their cost estimates of projects they favor. For some other reasons see Merewitz (1973).

9. One subsidy we have not mentioned is the set of government services, such as municipal police and fire protection, refuse collection, and so on, provided free of charge to government-sponsored programs. The value of this subsidy might be appropriately estimated from the foregone taxes.

10. The use of experimental techniques for the evaluation of broad-aim programs is beset with difficulties in both conceptualization and application. It has been suggested that a greater emphasis be put on the evaluation of process than end product (Weiss and Rein, 1972; Tribe, 1973).

REFERENCES

Anthony, R. N. *Management Accounting.* Homewood, Ill.: Irwin, 1964.

Arrow, Kenneth. *Social Choice and Individual Values.* New York: Wiley, 1951.

Atkinson, A. B. On the measurement of inequality. *Journal of Economic Theory,* 1970, 2: 221-224.

Azzi, Corry F. and James C. Cox. Equity and efficiency in program evaluation. *Quarterly Journal of Economics,* 1973, 495-502.

Baumol, W. J. On the social rate of discount. *American Economic Review,* 1968, 58: 788-802.

Becker, G. S. *Human Capital.* Princeton: Princeton University Press, 1964.

Block, J. H. *Mastery Learning.* New York: Holt, Rinehart and Winston, 1971.

Chase, Samuel B., Jr. (ed.) *Problems in Public Expenditure Analysis.* Washington, D.C.: Brookings Institution, 1968.

Chipman, J. S. The nature and meaning of equilibrium in economic theory. Pp. 35-64 in D. Martindale (ed.), *Functionalism in the Social Sciences: The Strength and Limits of Functionalism in Anthropology, Economics, Political Science, and Sociology.* Philadelphia: American Academy of Political and Social Science.

Clawson, Marian and Jack L. Knetsch. *Economics of Outdoor Recreation.* Baltimore: Johns Hopkins Press, 1966.

Corazżini, Arthur. The decision to invest in vocational education. *Journal of Human Resources,* 1968, 3: 82-120.

Dorfman, Robert (ed.) *Measuring Benefits of Government Investments.* Washington, D.C.: Brookings Institution, 1965.

Eckstein, Otto. *Water-Resource Development.* Cambridge: Harvard University Press, 1958.

Fein, Rashi. *Economics of Mental Illness.* New York: Basic Books, 1958.

Fishburn, C. *Decision and Value Theory.* New York: Wiley, 1964.

Fisher, G. H. The role of cost-utility analysis in program budgeting. In David Novick (ed.), *Program Budgeting.* Washington, D.C.: U.S. Government Printing Office, 1964.

Forst, B. E. An analysis of alternative periodic health examination strategies. Pp. 393-409 in Niskanen et al. (1973).

Galbraith, J. K. Economics as a system of belief. *American Economic Review,* 1970, 60: 469-478.

Gillespie, W. I. Effect of public expenditures on the distribution of income. Pp. 122-186 in R. A. Musgrave (ed.), *Essays in Fiscal Federalism.* Washington, D.C.: Brookings Institution, 1965.

Gintis, Herbert. Consumer behavior and the concept of soverignity. *American Economic Review,* 1972, 62: 267-278.

Goldman, T. A. (ed.) *Cost-Effectiveness Analysis.* New York: Praeger, 1967.

Goldstein, J. H. The effectiveness of manpower training programs: a review of research on the impact on the poor. Pp. 338-373 in Niskanen et al. (1973).

Hanoch, G. An economic analysis of earnings and schooling. *Journal of Human Resources,* 1967, 2: 310-329.

Haveman, R. H. The ex-post evaluation of navigation improvements. Pp. 249-276 in Niskanen et al. (1973).

Hennes, J. D. The measurement of health. *Medical Care Review,* 1972, 1268-1288.

Hicks, J. R. *Value and Capital.* 2nd ed. London: Oxford University Press, 1946.

Hinrichs, H. H. and G. M. Taylor. *Program Budgeting and Benefit-Cost Analysis.* Pacific Palisades: Goodyear, 1969.

Hirsch, Werner Z. Cost functions of an urban government service: refuse collection. *Review of Economics and Statistics,* 1965, 47: 87-92.

––––. *The Economics of State and Local Government.* New York: McGraw-Hill, 1970.

Hitch, C. J. and R. N. McKean. *The Economics of Defense in the Nuclear Age.* Cambridge: Harvard University Press, 1960.

Horngren, C. T. *Cost Accounting.* Englewood Cliffs, N.J.: Prentice-Hall, 1967.

Hu, Tei-wei, Maw Lin Lee and E. W. Stronsdorfer. Economic returns to vocational and comprehensive high school graduates, *Journal of Human Resources,* 1971, 25-50.

Jamison, Dean, D. Fletcher, Pratrick Suppes and Richard Atkinson. Cost and performance of computer-assisted instruction for education of disadvantaged children. Paper presented at the National Bureau of Economic Research Conference on Education as an Industry, Chicago, June 1971.

Kain, J. F. An analysis of metropolitan transportation systems. Pp. 155-187 in Thomas A. Goldman (ed.), *Cost-Effectiveness Analysis.* New York: Praeger, 1967.

Klarman, Herbert E. Syphilis control programs. Pp. 367-414 in Robert Dorfman (ed.), *Measuring Benefits of Government Investments.* Washington, D.C., 1965.

Krutilla, J. V. and Otto Eckstein. *Multiple Purpose River Development.* Baltimore: Johns Hopkins Press, 1958.

Krutilla, J. V. and C. J. Cicchetti. Evaluating benefits of environmental resources with special application to the Hells Canyon. Pp. 447-475 in Niskanen et al. (1973).

Lee, R. D., Jr., and R. W. Johnson. *Public Budgeting Systems.* Baltimore: University Park Press, 1973.

Levin, H. M. A cost-effectiveness analysis of teacher selection. *Journal of Human Resources,* 1970, 5: 24-33. (a)

––––. A new model of school effectiveness. Chap. 3 in *Do Teachers Make a Difference?* Washington, D.C.: U.S. Department of Health, Education, and Welfare, 1970. (b)

Lifson, Melvin W. Value Theory. Pp. 79-112 in J. Morley English (ed.), *Cost-Effectiveness—The Economic Evaluation of Engineered Systems.* New York: Wiley, 1968.

Little, I. M. D. *A Critique of Welfare Economics.* 2nd ed. London: Oxford University Press, 1957.

Mack, Ruth P. and Sumner Myers. Outdoor recreation. Pp. 71-116 in Robert Dorfman (ed.), *Measuring Benefits of Government Investments.* Washington, D.C.: Brookings Institution, 1965.

Maidlow, S. T. and Howard Berman. The economics of heroin treatment. *American Journal of Public Health,* 1972, 1397-1406.

Marglin, S. A. The social rate of discount and the optimal rate of investment. *Quarterly Journal of Economics,* 1963, 77: 95-112.

Menz, F. D. Economics of disease prevention: infectious kidney disease. *Inquiry,* 1971, 3-18.

Merewitz, Leonard. Cost Overruns in Public Works. Pp. 227-295 in Niskanen et al. (1973).

Mohring, Herbert. Urban highway investments. Pp. 231-291 in Robert Dorfman (ed.), *Measuring Benefits of Government Investments.* Washington, D.C.: Brookings Institution, 1965.

Moore, C. L. and R. K. Jaedicke. *Managerial Accounting.* Cincinnati: South-Western Publishing, 1967.

Morris, Douglas, and Luther Tweeten. The cost of controlling crime. *Annals of Regional Science of the Western Regional Science Association,* 1971, 5: 33-49.

Musgrave, R. A. Cost-benefit analysis and the theory of public finance. *Journal of Economic Literature,* 1969, 7: 797-806.

———. *The Theory of Public Finance.* New York: McGraw-Hill, 1959.

Musgrave, Richard A. and Peggy B. Musgrave. *Public Finance in Theory and Practice.* New York: McGraw-Hill, 1973.

Mushkin, Selma J. Health as an investment. *Journal of Political Economy,* 1962, 70: 129-142.

Niskanen, W. A., A. C. Harberger, R. H. Haveman, Ralph Turvey and Richard Seckhauser (eds.) *Benefit-Cost and Policy Analysis 1972.* Chicago: Aldine, 1973.

Perl, Lewis J. Family background, secondary school expenditure, and student ability. *Journal of Human Resources,* 1973, 6: 156-180.

Pigou, A. L. *A Study in Public Finance.* 3rd ed. London: Macmillan, 1951.

Prest, A. R. and R. Turvey. Cost-benefit analysis: a survey. *Economic Journal,* 1965, 75: 683-735.

Psacharopoulos, George. *Returns to Education.* San Francisco: Jossey-Bass, 1973.

Quade, E. S. *Analysis for Military Decisions.* Chicago: Rand McNally, 1964.

Ribich, Thomas. *Education and Poverty.* Washington, D.C.: Brookings Institution, 1968.

Rice, D. P. The Direct and Indirect Cost of Illness. Pp. 469-490 in *Federal Programs for the Development of Human Resources.* A compendium of papers submitted to the Subcommittee on Economic Progress, 1968.

Rivlin, Alice. *Systematic Thinking for Social Action.* Washington, D.C.: Brookings Institution, 1971.

Robinson, James and Gerald Smith. The effectiveness of correctional programs. *Journal of Research in Crime and Delinquency.* 1971, 17: 67-80.

Rothenberg, Jerome. *Economic Evaluation of Urban Renewal.* Washington, D.C.: Brookings Institution, 1967.

Samuelson, Paul A. *Economics.* 8th ed. New York: McGraw-Hill, 1970.

Schultz, Theodore W. Capital formation by education. *Journal of Political Economy,* 1960, 68: 571-583.

Schultze, Charles L. *The Politics and Economics of Public Spending.* Washington, D.C.: Brookings Institution, 1969.

Selowsky, Marcelo. An attempt to estimate rates of return to investment to infant nutrition. Pp. 410-428 in Niskanen et al. (1973).

Smith, K. R., Marianne Miller and F. L. Golladay. An analysis of the optimal of inputs in the production of medical services. *Journal of Human Resources,* 1972, 7: 208-225.

Somers, G. G. and E. W. Stromsdorfer. A cost-effectiveness analysis of in-school and summer neighborhood youth corps: nationwide analysis. *Journal of Human Resources,* 1972, 7: 446-459.

Suppes, Patric, and Mona Morningstar. Computer-assisted instruction. *Science,* 1969, 166: 343-350. (a)

———. Evaluation of three computer-assisted instruction programs. Psychology Series. Stanford, 1969. (b)

Tribe, L. H. Policy science: analysis or ideology? Pp. 3-47 in Niskanen et al. (1973).

Weisbrod, B. A. *Economics of Public Health.* Philadelphia: University of Pennsylvania Press, 1961.

———. Preventing high school dropouts. Pp. 117-148 in Robert Dorfman (ed.) *Measuring Benefits of Government Investments.* Washington, D.C.: Brookings Institution, 1965.

———. Income redistribution effects and benefit-cost analysis. Pp. 177-209 in Samuel B. Chase, Jr. (ed.), *Problems in Public Expenditures Analysis.* Washington, D.C.: Brookings Institution, 1968.

Weiss, R. S. and Martin Rein. The evaluation of broad-aim programs: difficulties in experimental design and an alternative. Pp. 236-249 in Carol H. Weiss (ed.), *Evaluating Action Programs.* Boston: Allyn and Bacon, 1972.

Wildavsky, Aaron. *The Politics of the Budgetary Process.* Boston: Little, Brown, 1964.

Williams, Alan. Cost-benefit analysis: bastard science? and/or insidious poison in the body politick? Pp. 48-74 in Niskanen et al. (1973).

REFERENCE UPDATE
Selected by Henry M. Levin

Abt, C. C. The public good, the private good and the evaluation of social programs: How inept government requirements increase costs and reduce effectiveness. *Evaluation Quarterly,* 1978, 2 (4).

Anderson, L. G. and R. F. Settle. *Benefit-cost analysis: A practical guide.* Lexington, MA; D. C. Heath, 1977.

Brier, S. S. and S. E. Feinberg. Recent econometric modeling of crime and punishment: Support for the deterrence hypothesis? *Evaluation Review,* 1980, 4 (2): 147-191.

Diggory, J. C. Calculation of some costs of suicide prevention using certain predictors of suicidal behavior. *Psychological Bulletin,* 1969, 71, (5): 373-386.

Doherty, N. and G. Crakes. Social progaram costs: Adjusting for research evaluation activities. *Evaluation Review,* 4 (4): 537-548.

Feldstein, M. The high cost of hospitals—and what to do about it. In T. D. Cook, M. L. D. Rosario, K. M. Hennigan, M. M. Mark, and W. M. K. Trochim (eds.) *Evaluation studies review annual* (Vol. 3). Beverly Hills, CA: Sage, 1978.

Haller, E. J. Cost analysis for educational program evaluation. In W. J. Popham (ed.) *Evaluation in education.* Washington, DC: American Educational Research Association, 1974.

Jamison, D. T., S. J. Klees, and S. J. Wells. *The costs of educational media.* Beverly Hills, CA: Sage, 1978.

Levin, H. M. Cost analysis. In N. L. Smith (ed.) *New techniques for evaluation.* Beverly Hills, CA: Sage, 1981.

Levin, H. M. and L. Woo. An evaluation of the costs of computer-assisted instruction. In E. House et al. (eds.) *Evaluation studies review annual* (Vol. 7). Beverly Hills, Ca: Sage, 1982.

Lumsden, K. and C. Ritchie. The open university: A survey and economic analysis. *Instructional Science,* 1975, 4 (3/4): 237-292.

Mayo, J., E. McAnany, and S. Klees. The Mexican telesecundaria: A cost-effectiveness analysis. *Instructional Science,* 4 (3/4): 197-236.

Mills, A. S., J. G. Massey, and H. M. Gregersen. Benefit-cost analysis of Voyageurs National Park. *Evaluation Review,* 1980, 4 (6): 715-738.

Mishan, E. J. *Cost-benefit analysis*. New York: Praeger, 1976.

Nagel, S. S. nonmonetary variables in benefit-cost evaluation. *Evaluation Review*, 1983, 7 (2): 37-64.

Rothenberg, J. Cost-benefit analysis: A methodological exposition. In M. Guttentag and E. Struening (eds.) *Handbook of evaluation research* (Vol. 2). Beverly Hills, CA: Sage, 1975.

Sassone, P. G. and W. A. Schaffer. *Cost-benefit analysis: A handbook*. New York: Academic, 1978.

Stokey, E. and M. Zechkauser. *A primer for policy analysis*. New York: Norton, 1978.

Thompson, M. S. *Benefit-cost analysis for program evaluation*. Beverly Hills, CA: Sage, 1980.

Thompson, M. S. and E. E. Fortess. Cost-effectiveness analysis in health program evaluation. *Evaluation Review*, 1980, 4 (4): 549-568.

Weinrott, M. R., R. R. Jones, and J. R. Howard. Cost-effectiveness of teaching family programs for delinquents: Results of a national evaluation. *Evaluation Review*, 1982, 6 (2); 173-201.

15

THE UTILIZATION OF EVALUATION

HOWARD R. DAVIS
and
SUSAN E. SALASIN

Appropriate utilization of evaluation can be a comfortable assumption if taken within the concepts of the cybernetic vision of the purposively guided society. In that vision a person at the helm reads the compass bearing, notes the degrees of departure from the desired course, and turns the wheel the required number of spokes to bring bearing into line with course. To carry further Campbell and Converse's analogy, the evaluator is, on more complex "vessels" of social programs, the navigator if not the helmsperson, who at least "must have a goal, current bearings, and contextual understanding of the forces about" (1972: 9). But can it be assumed, in the hurly-burly world of social program organizations, that feedback from the compas to the helm will lead to optimum fidelity between compass readings and wheel action?

CLEAR READINGS; OBSCURE ACTIONS

Evaluative data on an innovative furlough program adopted by a District of Columbia correctional institution indicate that barely 1% of inmates violate furlough in the program. Is the consequence community support for the innovation?

Within a federal applied research grant program, an evaluation of the utilization of project results indicates that only 11% are in use off the original site one year after project termination. Is corrective action quickly adopted?

Two evaluations of the Work Incentive (WIN) program of HEW indicate that the local welfare departments are not expanding the WIN program because to do so would demand substantial new funds. Is that barrier addressed?

A detailed study of the Emergency School Assistance Program showed that it has little immediate impact on attitudes about desegregation and the smoothness of the desegregation process. Are changes made to render the program more effective?

The impact of community mental health centers on the reduction of state hospital populations is examined. The evaluation finds that there are no great differences in resident rates between those catchment areas served by CMHC's and those which are not, when pre-CMHC data for each catchment area are statistically controlled. Do new policies and practices ensure a greater impact?

Actions on evaluation results vary as do evaluations themselves: sometimes its neglect; sometimes controversy; sometimes misuse. And sometimes disregard of invalid results is a warranted action. But sometimes—perhaps more commonly than we have an opportunity to see—consequent actions are precisely and effectively appropriate.

We will attempt to examine the winds and currents, the array of forces, impinging on evaluation utilization, consider an approach to predicting their influence on a given evaluation, and propose a guideline for use by evaluators who may wish to enhance even further their contributions to the destinies of the cause they serve.

OBSERVATIONS ON THE STATE OF EVALUATION UTILIZATION

Evaluation results do achieve appropriate utilization. Richardson (1972) offers one example. Evaluation of the National Defense Education Act loans to students who undertake a career in teaching suggested that this had not been a significant incentive. It was possible to conclude, with the concurrence of the Congress, that the feature should be eliminated, and it was. Lynn (1972) gives further illustrations of HEW utilization of evaluations of major programs, ranging from evaluations of the utilization of health care services to an array of educational assistance programs. Effective utilization of evaluation among federal agencies was reported by Riecker (1974) when those agencies participated in the evaluation. Beigel (1974) illustrates how local program self-evaluations can have meaningful impact on policies and practices. Both Weiss (1972) and Ciarlo (1974) stress that the evidence of effective utilization of evaluation becomes much clearer if one maintains observation over a sufficiently extended period.

Indeed, There May be Overutilization of Some Evaluation

Mushkin (1973) has called attention to numerous instances of well-known evaluations of major programs which were methodologically or conceptually unsound. In some instances decisions to terminate or reduce programs have been justified on the basis of those evaluations. It is a clear lesson that concern over utilization must emphasize *appropriate* use rather than just greater use.

Evaluators Sometimes Face the "Oppenheimer Risk"

Weiss (1973) has pointed out that evaluators who may be progressive in their orientations and dedicated to the growth and improvement of human services may find their work being used to justify sharply conservative predecisions resulting in cutback, rather than improvement, of social programs.

The Nature of Evaluations Determines Utilization to a Significant Extent

Summative evaluations, where the investigator is asking the question "Does this program work or not?" are quite similar to research enterprises. These may not have theoretical relevance; nevertheless, their utilization routes tend to follow those of other applied research results. Consequently, there may be less concern on the part of the evaluator about the adoption of the results within the host agency. In formative evaluations, where the evaluator is asking the question "How may this program be improved?" the payoff from the endeavor is entirely dependent upon the assimilation of the results within the agency in focus.

Compliance control evaluations would seem, on the surface, to lead toward more immediate utilization of results. When a site visit is made by a certifying body to check for compliance with standards, the incentive is quite great to bring things into shape. Similarly, if utilization review finds that practices are substandard and therefore third party payments are cut off, motivation to correct the practice should be high. The trouble with compliance control evaluation utilization is that it does not assure effective outcome in terms of consumer benefits. Furthermore, some people in service programs become highly skilled in compliant noncompliance. Utilization of the evaluation may be more apparent than real when it is mandated by authority.

The same may hold true with respect to evaluations carried out by supraordinate agencies without collaborative involvement of the people representing the program being evaluated. For a six-month period, clippings were made of news items on higher federal agency evaluations as they appeared in the *Washington Post*. With almost formula-like precision the paragraph just before the middle of the article was devoted to disparagement of the evaluation report by a spokesman for the evaluated agency. Again, there can be no question that a display of compliance must be exhibited in those circumstances. But from what is known about the ineffectiveness of most mandated organizational change, there is reason to wonder whether supra evaluations achieve the best utilization possible. It may be leading a horse to water.

Fuddling: A Never-Fail Response to Evaluation Feedback

President Kennedy once expressed his frustration over the fact that even Presidential Orders were so commonly fed into the "Federal Fuddle Factory" never to be heard of again, at least not in recognizable form. Fuddling is an ancient and revered skill as seen by many of us who consider ourselves accomplished bureaucrats. When addressing evaluation results, the skilled fudder would not deign to contest or criticize the report. She or he may feign cheerful assimilation of the implied recommendations, but try and prove it has not been done. One who loves the art may engage in protracted exchanges of requests for, and attempts at, clarification. Your mere everyday fuddler will assume a countenance of glassy obscurity if the subject of the evaluation comes up. We do not mean to treat this phenomenon too lightly. It quite probably amounts to a great loss of the potential benefits that could be realized from evaluation. On the other hand, the quality of so many evaluations in the past has been such as to render this happening a merciful one.

Evaluations of Evaluations: Too Rare

It is unfortunate that evaluations of evaluation utilization are rare. One study reported by Windle and Volkman (1973) provides some reason for optimism, at least insofar as utilization of self-evaluation in community mental health centers is concerned. Of 189 centers responding to their survey, 70% reported a total of 249 program changes resulting from evaluation activities. Eight percent of those changes led to the elimination or reduction of practices; 21% led to expansion; 31% led to the development of new practices; and 40% resulted in change of policies or practices. (136 centers failed to respond.) The most common type of evaluation activities was monitoring center service process; the next most common was measuring changes in clients, followed by assessing efficiency, evaluation by others, assessing incidents or prevalence of mental illness, evaluation of community attitudes, and client-involved assessment, in that order.

SIGNIFICANCE OF UTILIZATION IN THE EVALUATION FIELD

Growth of interest and faith in evaluation over the past few years has been unparalleled. As community advisory and control boards have pressed for accountability evaluations, requests for technical assistance in establishing evaluation within local facilities have climbed steeply.

At the federal level evaluation of programs almost invariably has been a requirement within enactments of social programs. For example, in the anticipated legislation on a new community mental health centers act not only would national-level evaluation continue to be required but each center would dedicate 2% of its grant funds to its own program evaluation.

For the past two years, surveys of the needs of community mental health centers reveal that program evaluation was the topic above all others, about which further information was needed.

When *Evaluation* magazine was launched in 1972, the anticipation was that the readership would amount to approximately 5,000 at the most. Two years later it has climbed to 30,000.

Training and orientation programs in evaluation have been subscribed to with enthusiasm. The Conference on Evaluation in Alcohol, Drug Abuse and Mental Health Programs held in April 1974 was planned for 400 participants. The Conference was expanded to include 750 with an additional 200 applicants turned down prior to the meeting because of space limitations.

New persons coming into the field seem to have little doubt about the potential of evaluation in contributing to the fulfillment of hopes and expectancies of the many beneficiaries of social programs. But neither do they seem to question the assumption that effective utilization can be taken for granted. At a national workshop held in Florida in spring of 1974, the group of new persons to the field of evaluation preferred not to have time consumed by a consideration of utilization techniques.

At the conference on evaluation referred to, Dr. Jack Zusman, co-organizer of the conference, announced his prediction that evaluation would turn out to be a current fad. If that proves true, one contributing factor may be a disenchantment among veteran evaluators, one growing out of evidence that appropriate utilization does not invariably follow evaluation.

Attkisson and coworkers (1973) visited more than 60 community mental health centers. They observed a generalized sentiment that "evaluation activities would not result in a net gain in program effectiveness. The consequences of this state of affairs is that managers are reluctant to invest resources necessary to effect a workable evaluation strategy, and evaluators often feel demoralized and unsupported in their roles" (Attkisson, 1973: 6).

Weiss (1973a) visited a sample of research evaluators originally for the purpose of discussing with them methodological problems in program evaluation. However, she found their frustration so great that they preferred to discuss their problems of personal relationships in their facilities rather than methodological ones. One interviewee expressed it this way: "[The project administrator] said, 'Educate me,' but he didn't sit still. He believed in research, he thought it should be done, but he had no understanding of how he should back it up or administer a combined service-research program. When I reported findings . . . he listened to me (I don't think he did more than glance at anything I'd written), but he didn't do anything about implementing the results" (Weiss, 1973a: 51).

An evaluator, who has been responsible for nearly $3 million worth of contract evaluations and who has engaged in intensive evaluation of his own, lamented to us recently that he was finding little professional satisfaction in his current work. His primary frustration stemmed from the futility of his efforts; there seemed to be so little response to the findings he supplied. As is the case with many evaluators, "Dr. A" came into the field of evaluation from research. He had gained wide respect through his many publications on the topic of personality development of a specific age group. His decision to dedicate himself to program evaluation was based upon the understandable belief that even more professional significance would be realized in that pursuit. But things turned out differently: his research studies bore theoretical relevance and accommodated his creative concepts; by contrast, his evaluation studies deal with largely ungeneralizable matters, directed by policy-makers rather than, by contrast, his own creativity. Results of his research studies were readily publishable; results of his evaluation studies seldom find open doors to publication. On reporting his research findings he received accolades from his colleagues; by contrast, on reporting evaluation studies he is apt to draw captious attacks on his methods. His research findings were used by other scientists; by contrast, he feels his evaluation findings rarely are used by anybody. In general, as he experiences it, the response to his dedicated endeavors has changed from approbation to opprobrium. Dr. A's laments describe contrasts experienced commonly by evaluators who have ventured away from the green fields of scientific discovery toward the jungle of organizational performance. It may be worth the hardships if the payoff in social significance of one's work is realized; without that, why live in the jungle?

A portion of the apparent demoralization among veteran evaluators may be attributed to the slow process of utilization of evaluation results. In the eyes of others, many of Dr. A's findgings are highly significant in guiding policies and practices. But for many months, his findings have been underground and waiting marriage with other determinants of change, only now reemerging in different costumes. Ciarlo (1974) reports that he, too, had reached the conclusion that evaluation results were generally ignored. But after continued close observation of the careers of his findings, he is learning that a time period of about nine months must pass before things begin to happen that can be traced to the evaluation effort. Even then decision-makers may not have conscious awareness of where the seeds of change were sown.

The findings of Windle and Volkman (1973), with respect to the report of high utilization rates from community mental health center evaluators, appears on the surface to be inconsistent with Attkisson's findings about demoralization among evaluators in centers. That suggests it may be important for evaluators to modify their expectations about both the timing and form of the utilization of their results. Also, perhaps better tracer evaluations of evaluation utilization itself would offer more reinforcement to evaluators.

A second suggestion is that evaluators might extend the range of their roles to encompass change consultation.

THE NEED FOR AN EVALUATOR/CHANGE CONSULTANT ROLE

Evaluation and planned change would seem to travel hand in hand. Yet it is mystifying to see how players in each group exclude the other. Very few persons straddle both specialties. This is reflected in the results of a little exercise we carried out recently: Among 600 references on evaluation, only 5% pertained to utilization, even under the broadest interpretation of that technology. But even worse, a review of 1,200 references on utilization contained only 2 1/2% which pertained to evaluation, again even in the broadest sense. It is as difficult to see how planned change can be carried out without evaluation as it is to understand how evaluation can realize its potential without consideration of planned change.

There are problems, to be sure, in asking the evaluator to extend her or his role in this direction. As Campbell (1973) has said, "academics continue to be reluctant to get involved in evaluation research." How much greater might be their reluctance to venture beyond that into the territory of utilitarianism! But Suchman (1962) wrote: "While this debate [relative to the evaluator becoming involved in action] may have a certain legitimacy in regard to nonevaluative research, it seems to us academic when it comes to evaluation studies." Buchanan and Wholey (1972) say it another way: "Evaluators, and critics of evaluation, must move from their present pre-occupation with evaluation as an end in itself and begin to think in terms of evaluation as part of policy planning and management systems."

We are not advocating that evaluators take up the cudgels to see that their own recommendations are adopted. There may, however, be some who feel that way. (At a program evaluation meeting in Colorado, one experienced, but perhaps frustrated, evaluator proposed that studies be undertaken only on the condition that the decision-makers agree beforehand to utilize the results as they emerged!). Guiding decision-makers in effective utilization of evaluation results would not seem to violate scientific values. Consideration of the determinants of utilization in designing evaluation hardly would create a value conflict at all. Even if evaluators were to extend their roles, significant benefits in the contributions of evaluators would be yielded.

Beyond the barrier of traditional value assumptions, others may loom in front of the evaluator considering change consultation:

(1) To employ a specific technique in deliberately bringing about change may be seen as just too Orwellian. Oh, if only the technique to be proposed were that effective! It may nudge the probability of desired change up a few percentage points, but "control" is hardly a threat. Further, anyone who institutes a new policy or practice must do the same; somehow we like to tell ourselves acceptance of change is a natural response to its goodness. The management of factors determining change must take place if it is to occur, even though employment of a technique may be denied. The overriding factor in most instances of change is power. What planned change techniques offer is an alignment of the other factors which will render the change more salutary concerned. (What comes to mind here is the state mental health director in the Midwest who announced he would fire a group of psychologists unless they stopped controlling people with those behavior modification techniques).

(2) Planned change is a poor second to power in modifying policies and practices. Power—of authority, of money, of whatever the "changee' must reckon with—is by far the most prominent instrument of change. Parents use it over children, teachers over students, employers over employees, the rich over the poor, and so on.

The change consultant may find her or his skills not altogether welcomed by some captains-of-the-ship who have been accustomed to a much quicker change model, the I-say-you-do one. But as Davis (1973) has described, change induced by power may have its problems, however underground and delayed they might be. But convincing decision-makers of this is often a difficult task. Furthermore, adopting change that specifically has been called for in evaluation results may restrict the decision-maker's degrees of freedom in responding to the multitude of persuaders within her or his organization.

(3) Planned change is hard! That was the Number One Principle listed by Fairweather and coworkers (1974) after what may be the most intensive experiment on planned change attempted so far in the human services field. There are no quick tricks in planned change. The reward of seeing desired consequences comes only after sustained effort, practice and belief in what one is about have been liberally injected into the process.

Fortunately, the reward of seeing evaluation results utilized in the service of program beneficiaries is great. Furthermore, despite the caveat about unconvinced decision-makers, the demand for consultants on planned change is growing from several quarters. The evaluator who encompasses such skills will quite surely experience an increased sense of service. The following descriptions may serve as examples of approaches to organizing the abundant information on planned change.

Five Research-Development-Dissemination-Utilization (RDDU) Models

Five models of the RDDU process have received notable attention in the literature. The first three to be described have been set forth by Havelock (1969), among others, and the last two by Sashkin, Morris, and Horst (1973), also among others.

(a) The first is the *research, development, and diffusion model.* This model assumes there is a relatively passive target audience of consumers which will accept an innovation if it is delivered through a suitable medium, in the right way, at the right time. It calls for a rational sequence of activities from research to development to packaging before dissenimantion takes place. It assumes large scale planning, and requires a division of labor and a separation of roles and functions. Evaluation is particularly emphasized in this model, in which there is a high initial development cost and which anticipates a high payoff in terms of the quantity and quality of long-range benefit through its capacity to reach a mass audience.

(b) The second is the *social interaction model,* which is more sensitive to the complex and intricate set of human relationships, substructures and processes that are involved in the dissemination phase, and which stresses the importance of face-to-face contacts. This model implies that a user can hold a variety of positions in the communication network, and that people tend to adopt and maintain attitudes and behavior which they perceive as normative for their psychological reference group. The size of the adopting group is basically irrelevant in this model, which follows essentially the process stages of knowledge and research diffusion, with appropriate influencing strategies used at each stage.

(c) Third is the *problem-solving model,* which starts with the user's needs as a beginning point for research, with diagnosis as an essential first step in the search for solutions. The outside helper, or change agent, in this model, is largely non-directive, mainly guiding the potential user through his own problem-solving processes and encouraging him to utilize internal resources. The model assumes that self-initiated and directed change has the firmest motivation and hence the best prospect for maintenance.

(d) In the fourth model, the *planned change model,* information is considered useful only if it leads to action, and is shared between the change agent and the client. The assumptive basis of this model is that change occurs through a consciously controlled sequential and continuous process of data generation, planning, and implementation. The changes made need to be stabilized and supported.

(e) The fifth model is the *action research model.* Although similar in some respects to the problem solving and planned change models, it is most distinctive in emphasizing the development of research within the organization. The type of research and its methodology are influenced by its concurrent conduct with the ongoing activity of the organization. The results of the research, while primarily intended for the organization itself, may prove useful to others and contribute to behavioral science itself. The model assumes the action research to be a continuous process of research, action, evaluation, and more research.

All five of the models may entail the use of a consultant. External data sources are used in the first two models. The problem-solving model uses internal data sources. The last two models employ both external and internal sources.

Training is not likely to be included in the first model, may well be included in the second, and is clearly included in the last three models.

Research activities are possible in the first and second models, but not necessarily included. Research by the client is a possible component of the problem-solving model. Planned change includes a limited form of research. The action reserach model includes several forms of research, including the evaluation of the change program, the evaluation of the change agent's functioning, and the study of the change process itself.

The Problem-Solving Dialogue Model. The *problem-solving dialogue model,* described in detail in Havelock and Lingwood (1973), builds on a problem-solving and a linkage approach to yield a highly comprehensive framework for analyzing a research development, dissemination, and utilization system.

Basically, the model may be described quite simply in terms of four components: (1) the client or *user system,* represented diagrammatically by a circle at the right; (2) the knowledge or research *resource system,* represented by a circle at the left; (3) a *need-processing system,* represennted by an arrow leading from the user system to the resource system; and (4) a *solution-processing system,* represented by an arrow leading from the resource system to the user system. The first two, it may be noted, are problem-solving systems; the last two represent the dialogue between the first two.

One may designate the system as a whole, with all the relationships among the subsystems depicted above, as the province of *macrosystem building.* The process is termed *microsystem building* when one considers actions in which many elements of the problem-solving dialogue are present simultaneously and are permitted to interact on a small scale.

Each of the components of the total dialogue system can be analyzed in great detail, according to one's purpose. Correspondingly, any real-life system can be described in terms of the dialogue system, elaborated to any degree or expressed in any appropriate manner. Research surveys may be made to cover designated provinces of the entire system, and sets of recommendations can be generated concerning chosen parts of the model.

This model has been used as the framework for studying four federal research dissemination agencies (Havelock and Lingwood, 1973), for charting eight "operational modes" reflecting various possible emphases by a research development, dissemination, and utilization agency, in examining resource linkage in educational innovations, and in determining the extent to which highway safety research communication may be considered as representing an effective system (Havelock and Markowitz, 1971).

The National Institute of Education Model. According to a National Institute of Education Task Force on Resources Planning and Analysis (National Institute of Education, 1973), the underlying model of the Institute calls for the coordinated operation of four subsystems: (1) a monitoring system; (2) an external research and development system; (3) a linkage and support system; and (4) an internal, problem-solving operating system. The last named is the school system, in which it is posited, a good deal of problem-solving activity occurs, aided and abetted by the other subsystems of the Institute. Hence the interest in "how and by whom problems get formulated in the first place" and "the organizational life of operating systems which will affect the possibility of implanting the solution to a problem" (NIE, 1973).

Some of the considerations affecting the program and plan of the National Institute of Education may be noted:

(1) The literature on social indicators provides a source for use in the monitoring system, as does multidisciplinary knowledge. Surveys of educational practice and R&D impact thereon represent the subject matter of the monitoring process.

(2) The tendency of R&D models to borrow from the "hard sciences" may not be suited to the needs of complex social situations. A concerted series of long-range and short-range programs and projects is necessary to the realization of the system's R&D mission.

(3) The building of the linkage and support system requires a consumer information strategy, an information dissemination strategy, and a product delivery strategy.

(4) In building problem-solving capacity in the operating system, it is necessary to provide support at the teacher level, the school level, the school district level, and the school/community level.

The model clearly encourages widespread involvement in the educational improvement process, emphasizes a problem-solving approach, and calls for well-supported, coordinated effort.

Miscellaneous Contributions to Model Building. It has been noted that the process of model building with respect to research utilization is in a fluid state. The literature abounds with many closely focused, as well as widely focused, sets of ideas that may prove helpful in carrying the process to a higher level of integration and to greater fruitfulness of conceptualization. Some of the additional notions regarding model building that have come to light in the preparation of the distillation are here presented.

1. Several writers sought to set down the types or categories of models.

    a. According to Chin (1961), there are two major categories of models the practitioner may use as a diagnostic tool for planning change: the *systems model* and the *developmental model.* Chin defines the major terms used in each type of model. For the systems model these include:

system; boundary; tension, stress, and conflict; equilibrium and steady state; and feedback. The terms defined in conjunction with the developmental model are: direction; identifiable state; form of progression; forces; and potentiality.

Chin raises five questions regarding the relationship of the change agent to the model:

(1) Does the the model account for stability and change?

(2) Where does the model locate the source of change?

(3) What does the model assume about the determination of goals and directions?

(4) Does the model provide levers for effecting change?

(5) How does the model place the change agent in the scheme of things?

Each model is examined in the light of these questions. Chin asserts that a third model for change is emerging, one that incorporates features from both the systems and developmental models. In this model, direct attention is paid to the induced forces producing change.

b. Bennis (1963) refers to three approaches to planned organizational change: (1) the *equilibrium model,* according to which the mechanism for change is tension release through anxiety reduction; (2) the *organic model,* in which the mechanism for change is power redistribution and conflict resolution; and (3) the *developmental model,* whereby the mechanism for change is the transformation of values.

All three approaches have a deep concern with applying social knowledge to create more viable social systems, a commitment to action, as well as a research role for the social scientist, and a belief that improved interpersonal and group relationships will ultimately lead to better organizational performance.

c. Hage and Aiken (1970) distinguish between the *"mechanical model"* and the *"organic model"* commonly referred to in the sociology of organizations in describing two "ideal" types of organizations manifesting, respectively, "static style" and "dynamic style."

2. A number of writers have presented models depicting particular aspects of the research development, dissemination, and utilization process.

a. Glaser and Ross (1971), for example, identify four models of *advocacy formation:* (1) the *fiat model;* (2) the *platonic* (rational appeal) *model;* (3) the *apostolic model;* and (4) the *conversion model.* Each is related to methods used to achieve advocacy.

Advocacy by fiat, or change by force of power, administrative regulation, or law, leads to change resulting from decisions of those in authority, as in military, hierarchical, and bureaucratic organizations.

The *platonic model* assumes that potential users can be persuaded through education and rational appeal to use particular research-based information or innovative procedures. As evidenced by both Fairweather (1973) and Glaser and Ross (1971), this approach apparently leads to intellectual adoption more than to behavioral modification.

The *apostolic model* attempts to stimulate conviction and motivation toward behavioral change through testimony and personal presentation and discussion in addition to written persuasion. Glaser and Ross (1971) found that many potential innovators appeared to appreciate intellectual stimulation afforded by such discussions, but the discussions did not necessarily dissipate the participants' doubts concerning implementation.

The *Conversion model* has a stronger emotional component, seemingly based on a more profound reordering of the conceptual frame of reference, with conversion facilitated by firsthand participation in an experience with a mutually reinforcing group of peers.

b.   Fairweather (1971) has developed a *model of experimental social innovation.* In his delineation of the attributes of social innovative experiments, he starts with the *definition* of a significant social problem whose basis includes engaging in naturalistic field observations (diagnosis) to describe the parameters of the problem in its actual community setting. The next step, *innovation,* creates and formulates different solutions as innovative subsystems. These subsystems then go through the process of *comparison,* whereby an experiment is designed to determine the efficacy of the different subsystems in solving the social problem. The innovative subsettings are implanted in appropriate social contexts so that they can be evaluated in their natural habitat. In the *evaluation* phase, the subsystems are continued in operation for several months or even years to allow for adequate outcome and process evaluation.

Throughout, participants in the subsystems are responsibly included, and a cross-disciplinary approach is employed, the social problem determing the fields and subject matter encompassed. Fairweather (1973) considers social innovative research to be the only humanitarian approach with social subsystems in which individuals function. While the model utilizes research in a natural setting, it follows the logical stages of (1) concern; (2) diagnosis; (3) formulation of alternatives; (4) implementation; and (5) evaluation.

c.   *Scientific communication as a system* is summarized by Menzel (1966) under five topical statements:

(1) Acts of scientific communication constitute a system.
(2) Several channels may act synergistically to bring about effective transmission of a message.
(3) Informal and unplanned communication plays a crucial role in the science information system.
(4) Scientists constitute publics.

(5) Science information systems serve multiple functions, including exhaustive search, reference, research stimulation, and scientist re-education.

d. Shannon's *information theory* is used by Dahling (1962) to illustrate the spread of an idea through an amazing number of disciplines, including: computer science, electronics, psychiatry, psychology, engineering, educational psychology, biology, physiology, radar, linguistics, biosociology, library work, optics, education, statistics, social science, and journalism, in the order enumerated.

A BRIEF INTRODUCTION TO INFORMATION
AND MODELS ON PLANNED CHANGE

Since 1955 the number of references dealing with planned change has grown from some 400 to over 20,000. Much of the literature consists of asserted notions. A large portion of the contributions are derived from observations and experiences. Some are research-based. Few are reports of experiments.

The proliferation of views staggers the imagination: There are the approaches of Lippitt, of Jenkins, of Jung, of Watson and Greiner, of Reuben, and Havelock, and Rogers, and Glaser. There are those labeled as theories of Zaltman-Duncan-Holbek, and of March and Simon, and of Burns and Stalker, and of Harvey and Mills, and of Wilson, and of Hage and Aiken. There are the processes of problem-solving; of research, development, and diffusion; of social interaction; of linkage; of reward structure; and of action research, and on to conflict theory and intervention theory.

For the reader sufficiently concerned, the following volumes may help provide order to the vast array of available information (all represent quite comprehensive overviews):

A Distillation of Principles on Research Utilization Volume I. DHEW Publication No. (HSM) 73-9148 GPO. $2.00.

An Annotated Bibliography on Research Utilization Volume II. DHEW Publication No. (HSM) 73-9149 GPO. $2.00.

A Manual on Research Utilization. DHEW Publication No. (HSM) 73-9147 GPO. $ .45.

Ronald G. Havelock and Mary C. Havelock, *Training for Change Agents* (Ann Arbor: University of Michigan, 1973).

Gerald Zaltman, Robert Duncan, and Jonny Holbek, *Innovations & Organizations* (New York: Wiley, 1973).

THE MOVE-OUT TIME

Fairweather has popularized for the change field the old military term "move-out time." It calls attention to the fact that in successful change inevitably action must occur. We face the same in this consideration of the Evaluator/Change Consultant role. Contemplation and review are necessary, but we have come to the point where we must answer the question "What plan is there for move-out?"

Already there is a mountain of proffered information, almost an endless number of dimensions along which to cut it, and an unending procession of advisors on how to cut it. But one hesitates to espouse a given single approach. There are three reasons we feel one comprehensive model is warranted at this time:

(1) No present "storage box" accommodates all available information. One phenomenon repeatedly confirmed in the dissemination field is that when information is purveyed in overwhelming amounts which often are inconsistent if not contradictory, absorption of the information is cut off. No one likes to have thirst quenched by a fire hose. The approach to be suggested in this section will allow cataloguing and retrieving of existing information and presumably subsequent knowledge. After rather extensive use to this time, no emerging information on change has failed to fit conceptually within the model.

(2) A model linked to familiar theory is needed for flexible and inventive application. Though the model to be presented underwent logical clustering of information during its evolution, its development unavoidably converged with a familiar model of human behavior.

(3) A working model is needed which meets the criteria of adequacy. The following criteria encompass those proposed by Chin (1961) and extended by such writers as McGuire (1970), McClelland (1968), and Shepard (1965):

(a) The model, above all, should be practical.
(b) The parts of the model should be manipulable.
(c) Economy of use should be a primary consideration.
(d) Ease of communication is important.
(e) The model should be comprehensive.
(f) Synergism—the force of factors working together—is important to consider.
(g) The model should lend itself to intervening in phases.
(h) Differential investment in working with the components of the model should be possible.
(i) The model should call attention to how the change process influences the rest of the system.
(j) The model should be flexible and versatile enough to apply to different organizational systems.
(k) The model should provide a basis for a subsequent evaluation of the effectiveness of change.
(l) The model should recognize the humanness of the participants involved.

Whether the model to be discussed here meets all of those criteria will remain open to debate; however, its design has been steered by them.

Much of the work on change focuses on the generation of sound information and its effective communication. This holds true for the many sophisticated technology transfer systems within federal agencies (NSF, 1973). Only one-fourth of one percent of the federal R&D dollar is dedicated to utilization, that is, transfer efforts that go beyond dissemination.

It would be a great boon indeed to mankind if effective action could be counted on as the direct consequence of communication of sound solutions to measured problems. Someone said recently that anyone who believes that having a problem pointed out to you, even backed by guidance on a solution that will evoke action to reduce that problem simply hasn't been married! The point was that in our daily lives we are richly blessed by "evaluators" and communicators of information on what we should do about those evaluations. The evaluation of the consequences of cigarette smoking, together with the solution to the problems discovered, may represent the best-disseminated information in the world. It is, of course, on the side of every pack of cigarettes. Yet the cigarette industry thrives. If the assumption we are talking about were valid, there would be no alcohol or drug abuse. Laws would not be broken. There would be no procrastination. Mental illness could be cured with advice. The puzzlement over why people who want to change and who know how to change cannot change represents a great human dilemma. It has been around a long time. Over 1,900 years ago, Saul of Tarsus, writing then as the apostle Paul (Romans 7:15) said, "For that which I do I allow not; for what I would do that do I not; but what I hate, that I do . . . But how to perform that which is good I find not."

Most of us can accept the reality of that dilemma at the individual level. But so often organizations are looked on as something ahuman. There are tables of organizations, functional statements, budget proposals, and systems designs. But are they? Brown (1973: 38) puts it this way: "Organization must be seen not as an abstract wall chart, but as a living reality, a structure of people with functions, capacities, interacting and tensing." Organization members " . . . have evolved as infinitely complex, distinct personalities, each with emotions, aspirations, intelligence, and incentives in unique combination" (1973: 10). Others (McGregor, 1960; Leavitt, 1965; Shepard, 1965; Marrow, 1972) have eloquently underscored that awareness.

The central characteristic of the model presented here is that it addresses the humans in organizations and social systems. It happens to espouse a behavioral model derived from learning theory, but any other concept of human performance probably would do well. The diverse backgrounds of evaluators from the social and behavioral sciences may very well lead them to adopt different conceptualizations of human performance. For instance, one of the commonly used techniques in organizational improvement is the Tavistock Group. Essentially it is a psychoanalytic model. A number of the approaches within the formal field of Organizational Development grow out of the Lewinian or Gestalt concepts.

If nothing further were stressed in terms of appropriate evaluation utilization, this would be enough; that is, assistance in appropriate utilization of evaluation findings addressing the human characteristics of persons involved would lead to significant gain in the field. This is particularly true in the human services area where so many evaluators have backgrounds of sophistication in addressing human characteristics.

In the form this particular model takes, there are three broad influencers to consider: (1) the motivation, drive, sensed *obligation* to "do something" about a matter; (2) availability of a selected course of action, an *idea* for achieving a solution; (3) consequences of implementing the idea for action. If the consequences are apt to bring displeasure, there will be *resistance* against choosing that particular idea. If the anticipated consequences are pleasurable—in the broad sense—the perceived *yield* will increase the likelihood of that idea as being used to reduce the problem state.

It is as simple as that. We hold that this basic paradigm is constant in its effect whether viewed at the laboratory or societal levels. Clearly, complexity advances with the level.

Three other concepts have strong influencing effects on the basic paradigm:

(1) The *values* of the individual, organization, or society. This encompasses not only attitudes and beliefs of the performing group but characteristics facilitating or limiting performance as well. For example, there is a vast body of knowledge on characteristics of organizations that render them likely to adopt any needed change, without specific regard to an evaluation finding or its selected solution. This might be the counterpart of personal styles and self-concept at the individual level.

(2) The capacity or *ability* to perform according to a selected idea. Organizational change commonly is dependent upon availability of funds, talents, manpower, time, space, and so forth.

(3) Prevailing *circumstances* and *timing*. The circumstance of a cocktail party makes chit-chat more likely. New legislation often directly influences changes within social programs at the front echelon.

Recently when this concept was discussed with a leading social worker in the field of community organization, she responded, "But this is a clinical concept; we have to deal with quite different elements in the community." Findings from the field of persuasion advise that, if you use terms and concepts alien to the background of another, you are apt to lose her or him. That may be a reason no single working model of change will be acceptable to all evaluators. The jargon and derivation of this model perhaps leans toward psychology. McCullough (1974) reports that in community mental health Ph.D.'s in psychology appear approximately five times more frequently than any other specific background category. But evaluators come from such diversified backgrounds that even that represents only two out of five, and in community mental health at that! This might serve as an illustration of how one's own *values* (characteristics) limit the selection of an *idea* to match an *obligation,* in this case to help reduce suboptimum utilization of evaluation! But we would hope specialists with other backgrounds would translate the human approach to change into their own jargon and concepts.

In reviewing actual instances of change according to the human action, we will select other than clinical examples partly as an offer of assurance that this model by no means has to be limited to that level.

Analyses of Change by the Human Action Model

Obligation. Motivation for change is not, of course, always problem-focused. Renewal, growth, the desire for change itself, or creative expression perhaps accounts for as much or more change than does problem identification. Lippitt (1971) advised, in fact, that problem-oriented change is seldom as effective as growth-oriented change. One might speculate that the reason for that might be found in the greater motivation, or obligation if you will, felt on the part of the growth-oriented innovator. But evaluation can enhance either source of motivation. Identification of fertile fields for invention as well as reinforcing confirmation of the effectiveness of positively motivated change seem to be essential contributions.

Not only should evaluation be seen as extending beyond problem identification; it may play a critical role in *reducing* what might otherwise be perceived as an obligation to change. As G. B. Shaw once said, "If it is not necessary to change then it is necessary not to change." A preoccupation here with processes of change does not imply that change is considered to be equated with goodness. Evaluation is an indispensable process in reaching that all-important decision on whether there is an obligation to change or an obligation not to change.

On Tuesday morning, October 16, 1962, the CIA presented an "evaluation" in the literal sense to the President of the United States. Photographs taken by U-2 aircraft had revealed areas of cleared foliage in Cuba. At first the clearings represented such a slight deviation from the base line photographs that the sense of obligation to take action was muted. But within hours the number of photographs taken would reach twenty-five miles if laid end-to-end! There no longer could be question of the threat to the life and dignity of the American people. The sense of obligation on the part of Congress and the people burgeoned after carefully planned visual presentation of evidence of the crisis through the news media (Kennedy, 1969).

More recently the Nation's unemployment rate jumped from 5.4% to 5.8% within one month. The wholesale index soared to a 46.8% annual increase. The Dow-Jones plunged 200 points for a twelve-year low of under 600. Prior to President Ford's message to the American people on inflation and recession, a national slogan was adopted by the Administration: "Inflation is our No. 1 enemy." With rapidly accelerating tempo, the news media carried stories on the gravity of the situation, especially with respect to inflation. In one day the Dow dived 28 points, conceivably a reflection of the effectiveness of the heightened awareness of the problem.

With more specific reference to a social program evaluation, an NIMH investigator reported his findings in late calendar 1973: Community mental health centers had not led to a reduction of public mental hospital residents as intended. He expressed disappointment over the inconspicuous display of assumed obligation to take action. His perplexity perhaps was not unusual among evaluators who become concerned over the lack of utilization of their findings. But a more penetrating look may explain why.

His evaluation was a controlled investigation of the relationship between the advent of a mental health center in a catchment area and the reduction of state hospital resident rates for that same catchment. But he received data from only 16 states, and most of those represented rural catchment areas. There was reason for questioning the generalizability of his findings. Also, there had been six other contracted evaluations which yielded ambiguous conclusions but offering illumination on how exceedingly difficult it was to measure validly such a causal relationship. One further in-house study had revealed a sizable difference between catchment areas with CMHC's and those without in terms of hospital resident rates. But that study did not control for pre-center rates.

On top of questions about the confidence in the data and conclusions themselves, there was the realization that all catchment areas had experienced a sharp reduction in hospital resident rates. From the standpoint of those who are expected to act on the evaluation findings, this problem loomed less large than myriad others demanding attention at the time.

This illustration also draws attention to the ethical dilemma of those involved both in producing evaluation findings and in utilizing the results. The evaluator felt conscience-bound to disseminate his findings broadly under a title well-planned to evoke alarm from those concerned with the CMHC program. His supervisor fully recognized his rights and even responsibility to make public the results of a tax-supported evaluation of a tax-supported program! But the supervisor also was concerned with clearing the report for publication because of the possibility of its being misleading. (The fact that admission rates in those catchment areas with CMHC's had been lowered was essentially lost in the report.) Outside pressure might well be evoked to place top priority on remedying this situation, not only at great cost but to the exclusion of other efforts considered to be of high priority. To withdraw resources from other priorities so that they might be reinvested in this pursuit would involve vast amounts of manpower and funds. The question was "Are the evaluation data and conclusions sufficiently cogent to warrant making a decision with such immense implications?" And should that decision be in effect turned over to possible sources that did not have responsibility for the full array of commitments of the CMHC program?

The supervisor took the risk of not clearing the report for publication in that form but did ask the evaluator to reconsider—not his data—but his conclusions and manner of expressing them. No whitewash occurred nor was it expected. The evaluator maintained his position on many points, and justifiably so. But others were re-expressed in words which, in one sense, would do a poorer job of increasing his sense of *obligation* but which also were less emotionally charged. The report, fine in most respects, was released and broad dissemination subsequently occurred.

Campbell (1974) has stated that any evaluators under his supervision would have full privilege of publishing their findings. And beyond doubt, the Freedom of Information Act eliminates any question about releasing evaluative data on federal programs. We also would hold that the evaluator has what amounts to a responsibility to present findings and conclusions as vividly as possible to decision-makers receiving the report. But it would seem to behoove the evaluator to proceed more circumspectly when it comes to amplifying the awareness of the *obligation* to act beyond those for whom the report is intended. In no way would this impair full presentation of data and objective interpretation of the findings. What we are saying is that, at the same time we are advocating that the evaluator take a role in stimulating motivation to take action on results, sensitive concern for the ethics involved must be maintained.

Decision-makers, too, must maintain the same concern. Who is to say that the initial report in this example was not simply threatening to the evaluator's supervisor? Could not any supervisor judge the conclusions of an evaluation report invalid and assume justification in squelching them? Ochberg (1973) has suggested that, once an evaluation report is written, the time has passed when a decision-maker can take a position objecting to either its tone or its dissemination. That decision should be agreed upon before the findings are available, trusting that the evaluator will not "go beyond her or his data" for the sake of intensifying motivation for utilization.

Sometimes informal evaluative "findings" influence both the magnitude and direction of *obligation*. The D.C. Correctional Agency which had attained a commendable goal of 1% furlough violations could have amplified that finding to the point where it would have evoked invigorated support for the innovation. But from over 1,000 inmates who had been on furlough, one committed rape and another was apprehended with a sawed-off machine gun in his possession as he was boarding a Metroliner while on furlough. Needless to say, the sensed *obligation* on the part of the authorities and the citizenry amplified in the opposite direction.

Sometimes the "unintentional side effects" having little to do with attainment of the front stage goal of a program (Scrivens, 1974) can overshadow other motivations to respond according to major evaluation findings. Head Start continues not only because the soundness of the negative findings are in question but because the side benefits are so meaningful and valued.

Evaluators, very likely, will wish to move cautiously in stimulating motivation to act on the basis of their findings alone. But in concert with decision-makers who are in positions of integrating the complex array of vectors impinging on their decisions, the evaluator can be a significantly helpful guide and consultant.

The most choice practice in ensuring that optimum motivation to act will follow the presentation of an evaluation report may be sound design of the evaluation plan from the outset. Methodological soundness is, of course, the focus of the entire Handbook. But building into the evaluation design steps to ensure an aim toward a relevant target should be considered no less vital. Levine and Williams (1971) offer suggestions for such steps. They amount to questions that the evaluator both poses and answers before the final design and launching of the evaluation:

1. What will be the purpose of this evaluation: compliance control, budget allocation, program improvement, evaluation capability-building?
2. For whom is the evaluation being carried out, and who are the people and the programs they represent who will be involved with implementing any utilization of the evaluation?
3. How might alternative results affect the decision?
4. Who will make the final decision, specifically what person or office?
5. How will the availability of results match the decision timetable?
6. Will results be read and understood and will there be a possibility of misinterpretation?
7. Can an evaluation-based decision actually be implemented in the subject program?

8. Why do the decision-makers really want the evaluation results?
9. How credible can this evaluation be?
10. What is the program in question, and to what problem is it addressed?
11. What do we actually know about this program at this point?
12. What do we *think* of the program; do we have biases?
13. What possible alternative actions can we consider in terms of recommendations?
14. What additional knowledge would we like to have and can we get it?

At NIMH the Office of Program Development and Analysis, which administers the 1% contract evaluation program for the Institute, asks similar questions of each staff member who proposes an evaluation for consideration. The procedure is giving promise of sharply upturning the quality of evaluations over those once based on "Wouldn't it be interesting if we knew such and such."

If evaluators have dealt skillfully with what we term Obligation in this model, appropriate utilization of results already should be at a high level of probability. But there are further determinants at play.

Idea. Knowing whether action is necessary is important; but it is a truism that, unless an effective idea can be selected for solving the problem, appropriate utilization of the evaluation can hardly occur.

At the time of the Cuban missile crisis, greatest effort went into debating the selection of action. General LeMay urged a military attack on the missile and aircraft installations. At the other extreme, Adlai Stevenson pleaded for abandonment of Jupiter sites in Turkey and Guantanamo. The President favored a quarantine with blockade. Heated debates continued night and day. Whether the blockade was actually the correct selection remained a matter of breath-holding suspense to the very end.

To help solve the Nation's inflation crisis, debate was formally planned to allow a testing of the implications of alternative ideas. Would a gasoline tax work and would it be acceptable? Would a surtax on incomes above $15,000 per year work and would it be accepted? An extensive array of other solution ideas were aired for consideration before the final selection was proposed.

To meet the need for greater service from CMHC's in reducing state hospital resident populations an array of proposals were made, some by the evaluator himself. Rehabilitation might become a sixth required service of CMHC grantees. The required policies on continuity of care might be extended to encompass all patients from a catchment area admitted to a mental hospital. Innovative approaches developed and tested by certain centers toward reducing or eliminating hospital admissions might be featured in the collaborative grant-supported magazine *Innovations*. Further research and development projects on effective practices to work with chronically ill might be stimulated. A top priority work group on community care alternatives might be established.

Each idea proposed was carefully considered from the standpoint of capacity to implement them, negative consequences, probable payoff, timeliness, and so on. As discussions of the possible solutions continued, partly as a result of the evaluator's gentle nudging, even the motivation to take action began to warm. Hope, feasibility, become stimulators of drive in themselves.

Some evaluators are urging strongly that the evaluation process formally encompass consideration of alternative decisions. The decision-theoretic approach (Guttentag, 1973) makes it explicit. Ciarlo (1974) specifically discusses decision alternatives as suggestions to users of reports. Though the number of trials of that method remain modest so far, there is early promise of exceedingly gratifying results.

There are three practices deemed advisable with respect to selecting ideas for solution:

1. Admit as large a pool of alternative proposals as can be accommodated initially.
2. Assess the suitability of proposals not only from the standpoint of the relevant determinants discussed in this model, but those of Glaser (1973: 436), known by the acronym CORRECT:
   a. *Credibility,* stemming from the soundness of evidence for its value or from its espousal by highly respected persons or institutions.
   b. *Observability,* or the opportunity for potential users to see a demonstration of the innovation or its results in operational practice.
   c. *Relevance* to coping with a persistent and sharply bothersome problem of concern to a large number of people (or to influential people).
   d. *Relative advantage* over existing practices (or yield, an incentive offer to change), that is, the conviction that the improvement will more than offset the considerable effort that may be involved in change.
   e. *Ease and understanding in installation* as contrasted to difficulty in putting it into operation or in transplanting it to different settings.
   f. *Compatibility* with potential users' previously established values, norms, procedures, and facilities.
   g. *Trialibility, divisibility, or reversibility,* which permits a pilot trial of the innovation one step at a time and does not call for an irreversible commitment by the system.
3. Persuasive communication should be planned for optimum effectiveness.

Conclusions from researches on communication indicate that the idea has a better chance of being accepted if: (1) the communicator identifies himself with his audience; (2) the presentation is pretested for readability, coherence, and understanding from the viewpoint of the audience for whom it is intended; (3) a factual report is made that people of prominence and influence agree, if indeed that is true; (4) positive reinforcement or benefits that can result are made clear, and any risks involved are surfaced and discussed; (5) logical and nonexaggerated emotional appeals are combined; (6) pictorial and other illustrative material are used where appropriate; (7) when objections are likely to arise they are taken account of at once; (8) the essential information is repeated, reiterated, and said again when practicable (Glaser, et al., 1966: Goldin, Margolin and Stotsky, 1969; Klein, 1968; Cohen, 1964).

Values. Decisions commonly are at least partly premade by individuals and organizations alike. Ideas proposed for adoption must match the range of considerable alternatives within the value system of those making decisions. This may serve as an example of what can happen: A member of a team of psychologists charged with serving a network of social agencies in Minnesota observed, during his testing, that many unmarried mothers were quite unfamiliar with contraceptive techniques. His solution was in the form of a rather nicely developed lecture and display of contraceptive devices. His demonstrations of the innovation were warmly accepted at Florence Crittendon and Lutheran Welfare homes, but then he tried it at Catholic Charities. His insensitivity to the values of the host agency led to what might be considered an abortion of his services there.

During the Cuban missile crisis, the values of the discussants of solutions were conspicuously reflected. Those who joined Le May and his proposal for attack were, for the most part, other military figures. Those siding with Stevenson's conciliatory position were primarily liberals. According to Robert Kennedy, the President and his close staff valued most the protection of lives, in both the United States and Cuba.

Solutions to the inflation crisis recognized the needs of industry and the political implications of a gasoline tax but also humanitarian concerns for the unemployed and those of low income.

In the case of evaluation findings about CMHC's and state hospitals, the values of the evaluator's supervisor quite likely played an unintentional role in the early resistance to dissemination of the findings. (This may be considered a fair statement because the senior author and the supervisor are the same person.) High-handed rule changes in the CMHC game at that late date were not seen as good form. The report as originally written conceivably could have been detrimental to the future of the community mental health movement. Indiscriminate emptying of state hospitals had never been accepted with high value. But planning for alleviation of the wretched conditions in communities faced by many discharged patients also was a high value, one to which the evaluator appealed in revising proposed solutions. Also appealed to was the value of the rights of an evaluator and the importance of utilization of such findings.

Characteristics of the organization and its members are also exceedingly important as determinants of change. The Organization Development field is almost totally dedicated to facilitating conditions that will allow an organization to become flexible and progressive. There are more references in the organizational change literature dealing with this element than with any other. The characteristics of the leader of the organization or of any of its components are critical. Five characteristics of the innovative leader drawn from researches are: She or he (1) advocates self-renewables of self and subordinates; (2) goal-oriented, not a stylist; (3) accepts risks; (4) rewards effectiveness; (5) and is an innovator herself or himself, as evidenced by past performance (Becker, 1970; Howard, 1967; Roberts and Larsen, 1971; Schmuck, 1968; Mackie and Christianson, 1967).

Fairweather (1974) has documented the critical importance of enthusiastic members of the organization who are willing to carry responsibility for seeing the change through. Innovative types have been studied by a number of researchers, just as have the leaders. They are bright, usually more so than the average employee; enjoy rather high respect and status among the staff members; are "authentic," that is, are people who seem to be comfortable in presenting themselves as they really are; are deviants from the rest of their group despite the respect most of them enjoy; are not particularly buddy-buddy with others, but are nevertheless comfortable, nonhostile, and independent; are "cosmopolite" in that their interests extend far beyond the local facilities, and they seize opportunities to attend national meetings and to talk with persons with broader variety of experiences; are persons who have had positive experience in the past with change; are either younger or older than most of the other staff members; are really not too successful in the organization to the point where they have much to lose by risking change; are secure and assume that their usefulness to the organization does not depend upon their being excessively conforming or compliant (Coleman, Katz and Menzel, 1966; Katz, 1961; McClelland, 1968; Rogers, 1962; Rogers and Shoemaker, 1971).

From the sociological perspective, Hage and Aiken (1970) have dealt extensively with many other organizational attributes as they influence readiness for change, such as the diversification of disciplines, the affluence of the supporting community, and so forth.

Unless the evaluator is prepared to invest heavy commitments of time in promoting the health of the organization, the most fruitful address of Values may be from the standpoint of (1) selecting Ideas likely to be adopted, and (2) anticipating the likelihood that change of a specific magnitude can be brought about successfully.

Ability. Resources necessary to bring about change, such as manpower, funds, level of employee ability, and freedom from competing demands, represent the most overlooked consideration in the change literature. Yet, in an experiment conducted by Glaser and Ross (1971), resources proved to be the primary barrier to adopting a weekend treatment plan in community mental health centers.

In consideration of the appropriate plan for responding to the build-up of Russian arms in Cuba, the President called for precise data on required ships, aircraft, and troops. It was even ascertained that the cost of American lives would amount to 25,000 if military action had to be used as a backup to a failure of the blockade.

President Ford's presentation of solutions to the inflation and the recession threat were followed by a precise statement of the costs: a family of four with an income of $20,000 would pay an additional tax of 12¢ a day. A work program for the unemployed would cost $5 million. The duration of the expenses would be one year.

In reviewing ideas for greater benefits for chronic mental patients, Institute decision-makers were faced with dwindling abilities to alter requirements of CMHC grantees. The program was slated for termination at that point. A new research and development grant emphasis to further study community alternatives to hospitalization would require $250,000 a year of "new money." A writer could be sent to programs in New York and Utah to prepare feature articles for *Innovations* magazine for $400 and an in-house task force on community alternatives could be established with ongoing operating funds. The evaluator could read his paper at an upcoming national meeting and submit it for publication with no funds other than those already committed.

In studying the utilization of the results of evaluation research projects, NIMH learned the inadvisability of funding innovative program trials the cost of which could never be met at the local level once federal funding terminated. Now all proposals for innovative program evaluations must estimate the basic cost of adopting the innovation if it does prove effective on evaluation.

Circumstances and Timing

More than human dignity will allow us to recognize, performance by both individuals and organizations is determined by the circumstances of the environment.

One of the best demonstrations of consummate skill in sensing appropriateness of timing and circumstances comes from history. In the early 1500s the priest, Martin Luther, had become concerned with the growing problem faced by poor people in purchasing indulgences, considered necessary at that time if one were to be cleansed of sins and thereby enter heaven. Instead of writing of his objections in a theoretical journal, he waited for the precise time to bring about change. As another priest, Tietzel, was moving through the local community selling indulgences, the resentment of the masses mounted. On the eve of All Saints Day it was the practice of the people in Germany to gather in the village squares to celebrate the driving-out of evil elements. At the height of the Halloween celebration, he marched to the church on the square in Wittenberg and nailed his 95 theses to the door. (A good change consultant would have recommended three which would have formed an acronym; but what did Luther know!) The move-out of his idea was launched rather more vigorously than he had anticipated. Another reformation was under way.

The Cuban missile crisis occurred on the heels of the cold war with Russia. Fears of communism remained great. The Bay of Pigs incident had been a recent stinging humiliation. The recollection in itself led to far more concerted planning on the missile crisis. The youthful spirited leadership thrived on challenge. If the buildup of installations had progressed more slowly, quite a different solution would have been chosen; namely, negotiations with Krushchev.

The advent of a new American president, confident and quite assured of congressional and citizen support, free from distracting stresses, almost surely influenced the direction of response to the inflation crisis. Political advisers urged delay of the implementation of action until after the forthcoming election out of their own sense of timing. Apparently, the rapidly mounting negative indicators of inflation and recession precluded such a consideration.

At the time the evaluation results on CMHCs in mental hospitals were reported, a multitude of demands for decisions on competing problems were pummeling the receivers of the report. Citizen backlash was mounting over what was seen as inappropriate return of some patients to inadequate community conditions. No great pressure was on to increase the rate of emptying mental hospitals. But as time went on general stresses on the decision-makers were reduced, and new legislation supporting community mental health was initiated. With it came the opportunity for building in new emphases on rehabilitative services, as advocated by nonfederal bodies. Over the next few months, motivation to take action on the evaluator's findings mounted steadily.

The wise change consultant often will advise delaying the implementation of an idea until events occur which will increase the probability of adoption. Some common events having that effect include the arrival of a new leader, a new budget cycle, crises, new legislation, the availability of exciting and challenging practice techniques, mounting dissatisfaction with conditions, and even seasonal variations.

Resistances

We have been using a rating scale to measure readiness for a specific change in a number of organizations. An outstanding revelation provided by several hundred responses is that resistance receives the most extreme rating in the negative direction. The seriousness of this finding is that it is seldom so visible on the surface when dealing with people in the change situation. Perhaps the sanctions of employment induce people to comply without ready expression of their reactions to that event. Such resistance, like icebergs floating on the sea, may well explain why so many changes revert back to former patterns. And as a matter of opinion, it seems too bad to us that employees so commonly have to bear the brunt of unilateral decisions to change: it is hard for them; it is bad for the organizations in the long run.

The likelihood of dire consequences if the wrong action were selected represented tremendous resistance to almost all ideas expressed during the thirteen days of the Cuban missile crisis. Beyond realistic fears, important figures strongly resisted the idea of anything except an aggressive response to Russia and Cuba—as a matter of dignity. Robert Kennedy reported that facilitating the expression of resistance was one of the most important steps taken during that crisis. He said that, by contrast, almost no resistance-based argument occurred when the Bay of Pigs incident was being considered. He attributed that costly mistake to the absence of free expression of resistances. One of Kennedy's most disappointing observations was that certain high-level cabinet members would express their resistances in peer discussions, only to conceal them and take the side of the President during discussions in his presence. Fear of expressing resistance is quite surely a great disservice to a leader.

When plans were in preparation for the anti-inflation campaign, great pains were taken to ensure that representatives of many factions had a chance to express their opinions during the Economic Summit meetings. From the evidence available, considerable care was exercised in ensuring that as many objections as possible were accommodated in selecting actions to be taken. Beyond that, the very fact that so many had the opportunity to be involved in the planning must have helped. Even with all the sensitive attention given to probable resistances to any solution adopted, notable objections continued. That illustrates a point to keep in mind about the change process: long after the move-out time, continual attention needs to be paid to resistances which may mount.

Resistances that seemed to arise in the face of evaluation results about the CMHC program and state mental hospitals were, it seems to us, quite understandable. To be confronted by one more problem at that point in time was not a welcome event in itself. To have an evaluator confront one with the assertion that a program to which there was great personal commitment had failed to achieve its objective was hardly "ego syntonic," particularly when there is other evidence to the contrary. The prospect of having possibly misleading information spread broadly was not inviting. The principle to learn from this is that, when an evaluator does feel she or he has negative data, the decision-maker might be asked to share the responsibility of making the interpretation. Of course, that runs the risk of unconscious underinterpretation. Fortunately, in the case at hand the evaluator was sufficiently patient and tactful to allow a smooth working-through of the initial resistances that were evoked.

It is often helpful for the change consultant to be able to anticipate typical sources of resistance. These commonly are among them:

Fear of economic loss.
Fears about personal security.
Fear of inability to learn readily the new skills required or to perform in a new role.
Fears about decreased personal convenience.
Fears about decreased job satisfaction.
Social fears (loss of status, separation from customary work associates).
Irritation with the manner of handling the change.
Cultural beliefs ("This will never work, it goes against what I have learned in the past, etc.").
Inertia.
Sense of present overcommitment.
Lack of interest.

There are numerous ways to address resistance. Perhaps the most important is to listen to its expression carefully to determine whether it is a front stage resistance that truly might call for a modification of plans. Discussion of anticipated problems among peers, with subsequent feedback in discussions with planners of the change, often helps. Trials of a new procedure may be advisable, with the understanding that an appraisal would be made collaboratively with the possibility of modification of the plan.

Persuasion may be used. Its success depends on the ability of the persuader to convince others that the rewards of the change counterbalance or outweigh the reasons for resistance.

Dispelling the fear that security is threatened might be carried out. This involves assuring a member of the organization that her or his position will not be eliminated in the process of change nor will the individual be called upon to perform new tasks that are beyond her or his capacity to master.

Developing a full understanding of the change is almost always a good idea. This includes why the change is needed, what is to be changed, how, by whom, when, what benefits can be expected, and what other outcomes can be anticipated. When there is a vacuum created by lack of understanding, it is filled by conjecture.

Often the change can be adroitly timed to coincide with growing feelings of dissatisfaction with the status quo. Speed often is important too; the longer the actual process of change takes, the greater the resistance.

The greater the extent of personal involvement in making decisions related to change, the less resistance there will be.

It is important to avoid implications of criticism. If those involved in the change process perceive it as criticism of what they have been doing, they will become resentful and defensive (Blum, Downing, 1964; Lippitt and Havelock, 1968; Mann and Neff, 1961; Watson and Glaser, 1965).

Yield

A significant reward that could be offered the American people for participating in anti-inflation measures was early leveling of inflation with subsequent benefits to each person. Even the wearing of WIN buttons was offered, deliberately or not, to provide the feeling of group acceptance and identification. Investment performance of industry was to be rewarded by tax benefits.

The putative failure of community mental health centers to reduce resident populations significantly faster than had occurred in catchment areas not served by centers was replaced by a consciousness of the challenge to do more for the chronically mentaly ill already in the community, as well as for those to follow. It became a positive exciting endeavor with the promise of intrinsic reward from seeing the growth of more appropriate community alternatives to hospitalization. Perhaps more could have been done, though it was hardly necessary. The advent of legislation for a new CMHC program provided a logical circumstance to address the evaluation findings directly. But the other ideas remained in force as well: dissemination of information about exemplary community programs for the chronically mentally ill, a special task force on community alternatives, and a somewhat extended research and development grant program on both mental hospital care and community alternatives. The improved state of affairs was, at the very least, in part the result of the evaluator's patient and persevering determination to ensure appropriate utilization of his evaluation results.

It would be difficult to think of any change experience at any level of organization in which the factors considered here have not played their roles as important influencers. Analysis in greater detail could be carried out for examples we have used, of course; but in reflecting on details not included here, we came to none that did not fit within the model of analysis.

The exercise also demonstrates the obvious; and that is, expertness in bringing about successful change does not require adherence to a prescribed schema; but the use of a guiding technique may well increase the frequency of successful change, simplify it, and reduce time and cost.

THE A VICTORY TECHNIQUE

There is a genuinely subjunctive mood underlying this description of the A VICTORY technique and outline. Appropriately seen, it is a vehicle to guide awareness and classification of the accumulating knowledge on planned change. Evaluation/change consultants may well design their own vehicles that would do as well or better; but as one way to get going, it represents a technique backed by as much diversified experience as any we know.

Before trying the A VICTORY technique in consultation practice, people commonly have asked, in essence, these three questions: (1) How much confidence can be placed in the usefulness of the A VICTORY technique? (2) Does A VICTORY call for a lock step approach to change? (3) Is it really necessary to address all the factors in planning for change?

As with other procedural checklists, A VICTORY sometimes has been looked on as a logical clustering of information at hand. One reviewer surmised that certain of the factors may have been chosen so that together they would spell a word! Actually, A VICTORY is a translation from a behavioral change model derived from learning theory As such, its seven factors are considered to encompass the necessary and sufficient determinants of program attainment. For those who may be interested, the matching behavioral model has been expressed as follows:

$$B = E_s + T + S_c + (P + H_s)(D \times C) - I$$

Behavior,	B	= PA,	Program Attainment.
Capacity,	C	= A,	Ability, or resources required.
Self-expectancy,	E_s	= V,	Values that give purpose, perceptions, characteristics.
Pattern,	P	= I,	Idea for proposed action steps.
Stimulus conditions,	S_c	= C,	Circumstances which prevail at the time.
Timing,	T	= T,	Timing.
Drive,	D	= O,	Obligation, the felt need or motivation.
Inhibitors,	I	= R,	Resistances as they are relevant to the desired change.
Habit strength,	H_s	= Y,	Yield, or the rewards that the anticipated change may bring about.

The content under each of the factors appearing in the outline to follow is based upon distillations of the entire literature on knowledge utilization and organizational change as deemed to pertain to human services. The generation of A VICTORY also has been dependent upon a series of conferences and experimental studies over the past ten years supported largely through NIMH in-house resources, contracts, and collaborative grants. Extensive help has been provided by consultants working in the field of change outside the topical area of mental health. The A VICTORY technique, in its several developing stages, has been applied in technical assistance and in research consultation and administration within the services program at NIMH. It also has had continual use as an internal management approach within that program.

Currently further collaborative studies are under way to examine the effectiveness and feasibility of using the A VICTORY technique: American Institutes for Research (community mental health centers and hospitals); Center for Dialog (community change); Human Interaction Research Institute (mental hospital change); Program Evaluation Resource Center (utilization of evaluation); and the MITRE Corporation (mission-oriented research process). With respect to the payoff from applying the A VICTORY technique, data from the collaborative projects are not yet developed to the point where sound conclusions can be drawn. There are verbal reports that its use seems to help in consulation, but often as a back-of-the-mind orientation. Within the PERC study, Kiresuk's Readiness-for-Change Scale derived from A VICTORY appears to offer valid discrimination among social agencies in the Minneapolis area. Ciarlo at Denver General did not find that the scale discriminated between three CMHCs that adopted his evaluation system and three that did not, following common exposure. Among five components within NIMH considering adoption of a new program evaluation system, a fourteen-item semantic differential-type rating on A VICTORY variables did match other criteria of adoption. In other applications A VICTORY has highlighted the intensity of often unspoken resistances to change. At HIRI Glaser and Berger report that the A VICTORY assessment among change processes in mental hospitals seems to be matching their other more exhaustive assessments of those processes.

One conclusion that seems to be emerging from use of A VICTORY in consulting on change is that the final outcome of the change process results in a different state of affairs from that intended at the outset. Change, mandated on the basis of authority, in contrast, generally seems to reflect a better fit between intention and outcome. From the standpoint of those in positions of program authority, this observation would speak against the use of planned change methods in utilizing evaluation results. On the other hand, one might propose that modifications in an original goal resulting from the participative approach and accommodation of other situations in the organizational milieu could lead to more effective utilization of evaluation in the long run.

There is one quantitative datum that may reflect the consequences of employing the A VICTORY technique: As it has been used in the consultation and management practices related to evaluative research in mental health services, the percentage of grant-funded projects which can report specific off-site utilization within one year after termination has grown from 11% in 1968 to 84% in 1974. This covers an investment of some $50 million. We do not suggest this has been a test of the A VICTORY technique by any means; numerous other factors have changed over those years, and the technique certainly has not been applied uniformly across all endeavors.

Perhaps the only conclusion we can draw at this point is that the A VICTORY technique seems to cause no harm and may at least offer the starting framework for planning the adoption of new policies or practices.

Does A VICTORY call for a lock step approach to change? As some people put it, "Would Michelangelo paint by numbers?" Though the factors in the A VICTORY outline give the impression of linear discreet steps, life does not work like that, as everyone knows. Whatever model of organizational behavior may be used, it would be more accurately depicted as a Venn diagram. If the factors were to be represented by circles, most of them indeed would overlap reflecting their interaction, rotation of position, and expansion or contraction. Without the sensitivity and skill of the change consultant, employing A VICTORY would be like playing a 1912 Wurlitzer automatic orchestra: the clarinet, marimba, tambourines, drums, and cymbals may all be there and play on cue, but something akin to cacophony comes out. As Morgan (1972) said: "Managing change effectively often requires more than technique and strategy. It calls for a new kind of thinking about change—as an element in planning, as a factor in all decisionmaking, and as a pervading force in practically all other aspects of management."

Is it really necessary to address all the factors in planning for change? In the assessment phase, preparatory to setting the change process in motion, it probably is necessary to consider all the factors. In many instances this could be done with a few moments of reflection based on what one already knows or senses about the total situation. But when the adoption of a new policy or practice is going to involve a number of people or when other parts of the system are going to be affected, the consultant may wish to extend the assessment all the way to the use of a measuring instrument.

In the actual plan for change, even of major proportions, concentrated attention may be required for only one or two of the factors. Efficient planning calls for application of the "Pareto Principle." Zilfredo Pareto (1848-1923) was an Italian sociologist and economist living in Switzerland who discovered and applied the idea that, in most situations, a few factors influence the outcome, while a great many others prove largely irrelevant and can have little effect on the situation no matter what one does about them. Pareto's statistical analysis revealed that 80% of the results come from 20% of the action in most endeavors. The trick is in discerning which 20% to invest! There lies the payoff from the assessment phase of the A VICTORY technique.

Before going further in considering applying such a technique as A VICTORY in planning the utilization of evaluation results, we need to consider what is perhaps the most critical element in this whole matter: the feelings of people involved in the change process—ultimate beneficiaries and program personnel, persons with decision-making power, and the evaluator/change consultant's own feelings. Even when social program change is occurring at the national level, many of us have a vague sense that something is happening. There are few feelings worse than the powerlessness stemming from cues that change is afoot but without awareness of the facts, particularly when people are on the receiving end of decisions within closed systems. Accordingly, asking as many people as feasible to participate in structured planning for change sounds defensible. But it must be done with sensitivity. On one occasion we presented a proposal for planning change to a large number of staff employees in a facility. As it happened at that time, their supporting budget was being considered for drastic reduction, and they knew it. In that context the proposal for change was seen as part of a plot to weed out unpopular functions and perhaps persons. Their response was most negative. Openly confronting those people with a request to participate in planning for change in that manner was not only insensitive but unkind under the circumstances. It is difficult to choose a path for appropriate participation: some people are made uneasy by lack of specification, but others are just as put off by overspecification smacking of manipulation. The only course to follow seems to be one of sensitive respect for the feelings and styles of consumers and employees alike. (The inadvisability of using a technique for manipulation hardly needs stressing here.)

As has been pointed out earlier, most decision-makers with sufficient power tend to be unconvinced that the more tedious, democratic, slow approach involved in planned change is worth it. They are too accustomed to seeing quick fidelity between their mandates and response from subordinates. To be sure, there are circumstances under which adoption of a solution by fiat makes much more sense than planned change. And, alas, it is still a matter of conjecture that participative change ultimately is more fruitful than mandated change, at least insofar as hard research results go. Further, decision-makers often have a multitude of pressures demanding action instead of contemplation. So at this level, too, the evaluator/ change consultant may have to perceive sensitively the feelings of people in power, keeping knowledge of change determinants in the back of his mind and demanding no commitment to a structured process. Still, effective help can be given without necessarily labeling the steps, as in working with an individual client or expressing love.

Again stressing Fairweather's (1974) primary conclusion that planned change is a consuming enterprise, we would urge change consultants to set their expectancies accordingly. Sometimes it simply will not be appropriate to invest sustained efforts in change; the process may give promise of occurring smoothly without guidance, time resources or role options may not be available, or even the desired change may not be that important. With respect to using a specific technique such as A VICTORY, it is understandable that many persons at the level of professional evaluator will develop their own unique approaches or even "wing it" as they go. For those persons we hope that A VICTORY will serve as a helpful reminder of factors influencing organizational change.

USE OF THE A VICTORY TECHNIQUE

The four steps in the use of the A VICTORY technique are: (1) Assessment, (2) Goal Definition, (3) Action, and (4) Follow-through.

(1) Assessment

For the purposes of this presentation, it will be assumed that the results of program evaluation are at hand. If the evaluation has been planned and conducted with an advanced eye on its ultimate utilization, the probability that the desired change will occur should be considerably higher than zero even at this point.

The assessment phase may be looked on as an evaluation in itself. However, in this case it is for the purpose of estimating the probability that the change will occur. It also has the purpose of guiding action plans toward enhancing the likelihood of change.

The qualitative assessment may be carried out by scanning the state of affairs as outlined below. The more affirmative the responses to the questions, the more likely that the desired change will occur. Those factors under which there may be a predominance of negative responses would become the ones to be addressed by Action steps. In some instances a negative assessment of specific factors might call for a change in the Program Goal or the Idea to be used. We would underscore the importance of this consideration: any change model should, in our opinion, generally *accommodate* rather than *manipulate* the views of persons involved.

OBLIGATION—Felt need to do something about a problem.

Has evaluation of needs been carried out and interpreted soundly?

Are there informal clues indicating needs for change: mistakes, vague or conflicting goals, lack of communication, poor decision-making, complaints, rumors, low morale?

Have forecasts been made about new needs?

Have individual needs of staff or employees been considered, especially those that might represent secondary or backstage motivations? If multiple needs exist throughout the system, has a priority ranking been made?

Following the determination of needs, have steps been taken to amplify awareness of those needs among staff and employees?

IDEA—Information relevant to taking steps to solve the problem.

Has vigorous effort been made to explore all sources of information toward finding the most suitable action to meet the obligation: work experiences, group discussions, literature retrieval, special publications?

Does proposed information meet the correct criteria: credibility, observability, relevance, relative advantage, ease of understanding, compatibility, and timing?

Has special attention been given to methods of communicating the information to all relevant persons?

Have persons concerned been given an opportunity to challenge the selection of the information, to simplify it, to elaborate it?

VALUES—Pre-decisions, beliefs, manners of operating, and characteristics of the program organization.

Has the organizational climate been assessed—open communication rather than one-way, supportive administration, mutual support among colleagues, participation in decision making, high morale, adequate time for reflection and testing new ideas?

Are the organizational goals clear and written down?

Is the organizational structure characterized by decentralized and distributed power?

Is the organization large enough to accommodate the kind of change being considered?

Is the organization reasonably affluent, secure, and "in good" with its benefactors?

Is the community served by the facility a reasonably supportive and liberal one?

Are social and physical distances among persons involved sufficiently close to enhance innovation?

Are social relationships of staff so open as to render likely individual initiative of innovators?

Has the tenure of chief decision-makers been reasonably short?

Has the organization had a history of successful innovations?

Are staff members rewarded for performance rather than status?

Is the top man at the organization a self-renewing, goal-oriented type of person himself?

With respect to the persons who may be involved with the change, are they either younger or older than most? Is their economic status reasonably adequate? Are they people with a personal sense of security in the facility? Are they the sort who attend meetings and mix with other professionals beyond the facility in which they work? Are they bright, authentic, not afraid to be deviants from the total group? Has consideration been given to the danger that supporters of the change are motivated by their own dissidence, indifference to the organization, disaffection, or resentment?

ABILITY—Capacities to carry out the solution: staff, funds, space, sanctions.

Have the funds necessary to support the change been identified?

Have sources of the needed funds been identified?

Has a prediction been made regarding manpower required to carry out and sustain the change?

Will special orientation or training in the new patterns of action be necessary?

Has the need for additional facilities been determined—office space, meeting rooms, parking, etc.?

Has there been a review of the product-losses that would occur; that is, if resources have to be taken from another part of the system, have the consequences of that withdrawal been given consideration?

CIRCUMSTANCES—Prevailing factors pressing for or detracting from certain actions.

Have fixed organizational characteristics—openness, attitude of leadership, clarity of goals—been assessed from the standpoint of the probability that any change can take place? Have restrictions on the nature of the change been judged vis-à-vis the organizational values?

Have characteristics of the catchment area or region served been considered in relation to the proposed change?

Are there changing organizational situations that would bear upon the success of the change—new budget periods, change in leadership, new mission for the facility?

TIMING—Synchrony with other significant events.

Has the time for predicted major changes in the organizational milieu been estimated?

Has the possible advent of new community concerns, legislative interest, and economical circumstances in the community been assessed from the standpoint of timing?

Are there impending crises relative to the proposed change with which the initiation of change might be timed?

Has the phasing of events in the personal lives of staff and employees been considered—holidays, for instance?

Has continual sensing of staff readiness for change been employed?

RESISTANCES—Both frontstage and backstage concerns for loss if specific action is taken.

Have plans been made to sense reactions to the proposed change?

Has the advisability of the proposed change been reconsidered in the light of any rational resistances that have been detected?

Has there been a sensitive exploration of the irrational resistances of staff—fear of loss of status or job security, misunderstanding, etc.?

Has thought been given to those who might be affected by the change, such as beneficiaries of the program, even though their support is not necessary to bring about the change?

YIELD—Felt rewards, benefits to program participants and consumers alike.

Have reasons for expecting the change to pay off been communicated to persons concerned?

Have direct, tangible rewards been planned for persons instrumental to the change?

Have indirect rewards been considered, such as better working conditions, opportunity for professional advancement, and for self-actualization?

Has direct and personal support from the top of the organization been planned?

Another approach to assessment currently under examination is by means of a quantitative instrument. Kiresuk (PERC) and Glaser and Berger (HIRI) are studying the feasibility of scales to appraise the positions of persons involved in change on each of the A VICTORY variables. Whether these scales will meet the standards of reliability and validity across varying change situations remains to be seen. In the meantime, the use of brief questionnaires tailored for the specific change situation is proving helpful. Though the interpretations must be viewed with caution, they do assist in confirming impressions gained through the more informal scanning approach.

The questionnaire that follows was sent to approximately 100 persons in a division at NIMH. Consideration was being given to the adoption of a new operational evaluation system. The questionnaire took the form of differential ratings on dimensions pertaining to the A VICTORY factors. (Only one was written for Circumstances and Timing; the same item on Yield appeared twice in different form to estimate rather consistency.) Responses were not identified with individuals but were for program components of origin.

Total scores for each of the program components matched precisely the overall ratings of adoption by the five respective components. That rating was based upon continuing open discussions and actual response after move-out, or adoption, time. Responses were consistently on the positive side on such dimensions as Idea, Obligation, Values, and Yield insofar as the program benefits were concerned. They were consistently negative on the side of Ability, Circumstances and Timing, Resistances, and Yield in terms of personal benefits. The persons to be involved with the change were saying, in effect, that the new system was clear, that they had no intention about rebelling against any instructions to adopt the system, that it was the thing to do, and finally that the program would benefit from such adoption. But at the same time they were saying that it was a time-consuming endeavor to maintain, perhaps one for which the payoff was not commensurate with the time and energy demanded. That particular point in time was a poor one to initiate such a system because cutbacks in funds and staff appeared to be so eminent at that point. Perhaps for that reason the proposed evaluation system was perceived as being potentially threatening and even detrimental to maintaining program performance. There was little chance of gaining personal benefits from the proposed system. Subsequent discussions with personnel precisely confirmed these impressions, gross as the assessment had been.

In consequence, the change process was allowed until environmental circumstances became more sanguine, the system was redesigned to require far fewer resources, participative planning was followed, and director-level staff gave individual reinforcement to persons engaged in maintaining the system. Administratively, from the short view, addressing the views of personnel meant that implementation of the system fell months behind schedule. And its final form differed from the initial plan. But from the long view, the modified plan proved to be both more effective and more efficient than the initial one would have been by all indications.

The pattern of responses to this brief questionnaire has reappeared in quite different situations in other parts of the country. What seems to be emerging as a general phenomenon is that employees of organizations accept the responsibility to comply manifestly with directives. That may be an assumed agreement one makes when joining an organization. Perhaps this is why unilateral planning by authorities is a common pattern. But people can manifest compliance without really doing things much differently. These exercises with the participant responses are demonstrating to us that the slower and more tedious process of planning for change may yield a different outcome, one from which all concerned benefit more. This is what writers in the management field—Marrow (1972), McGregor (1960), Brown (1973)—have been telling us for some time!

These items were drawn together for the specific case we have just discussed; however, the reader may find the example more illuminating by making imaginary ratings at any point along the line from the standpoint of one's own personal view on A VICTORY at this point. (The capitalized factor labels in parenthesis are added here for clarification. They do not appear on rating forms.)

(2) Goal Definition

As stressed by McGuire, the task of defining meaningful goals is one of the most important in effective program development. Exactly the same should be said about the importance of a clear goal in planned change. Without performance of this task the subsequent evaluation of the success of the change effort becomes extremely difficult. This is not to say that the unintentional side benefits of program change are to be ignored, nor is it to pretend that goal-irrelevant motivators play a big part in change—such as visibility for the launch, as White has described. But few changes produce optimum benefits without continuing readadjustments in the early stages. Those adjustments—as with all program improvements—can be rendered most beneficial if they are based upon evaluation of progress toward a prescribed goal.

An additional reason for defining a clear goal to be attained by the change in policies or practices is that desirable consequences are more likely to occur. We like to refer to this phenomenon as "target tropism." If you establish a clear expectation, people will tend to fulfill it. The validity of this assumption may be more experiential than experimental, though.

The reason for delaying goal definition until after an assessment of the probability of change perhaps is obvious: If the views of persons involved in the realities of the situation are taken into consideration in shaping the goal, the expectation it represents surely should have a greater chance of fulfillment. That sequence also represents the position that the planner of change should aspire to accommodate reality insofar as possible rather than manipulate it. To be sure, some adjustment in the actions of some people and in some conditions virtually has to be assumed. The farther down in the bucket the ping pong ball to be moved is, the greater the shifting of the other ping pong balls. But here is little wisdom in taking on windmills like Don Quixote unless it is essential for the good of the cause!

Questionnaire

Clarity of Idea (Idea)

Very clear	Obscure Unclear—but did not "succeed" in confusing

Time Investment (Ability)

Approach calls for negligible time investment	Approach calls for extravagant time investment

Fit with My Style (Values)

I strongly prefer a feel-as-you-go approach	I do prefer defined structure such as this approach entails

Willingness (Resistance)

I would be most reluctant to adopt this approach	I feel comfortable about adopting this approach

Benefits (Yield)

I think I'll feel personal benefits from this approach	I will gain no personal help from the approach

Appropriateness (Values)

Approach is just what our situation calls for	Approach is a poor fit with our program

Perceived Responsibility (Obligation)

Adoption appears to be optional	Adoption seems to be necessary

Importance (Yield)

Approach such as this is essential to good program payoff	Nothing to be gained from this endeavor

Soundness of Idea (Idea)

Seems invalid in basic concept and methods	Appears to be logical, based on solid material

Assessment (Resistance)

I anticipate no negative consequences to this approach	I see a number of negative consequences to this approach

Consequences (Yield)

Nothing to be gained by this approach	Approach will lead to greater program achievement

Felt Need (Obligation)

I feel strongly motivated to participate in this approach	I feel no need whatsoever to engage in this approach

Readiness of Implementation (Circumstances and Timing)

This is a poor time to adopt this approach	Things that are happening make it essential right now to adopt this approach

Required Skills (Ability)

Approach demands extensive orientation, practice, and skill	Approach seems simple to carry out

(3) Action

If the phases of the A VICTORY technique were to be followed in direct sequence, we now would be faced with taking action to shift conditions among critical factors to the extent necessary. But as is true in the individual helping relationship the assessment of the problem, the definition of the goal, and the action to improve determining conditions remain rather fluid and interchanging. The defined goal should remain intact for sufficiently long periods to lend itself to a measurement of whether things are proceeding as desired. A most important consideration in carrying out the action steps is the continual evaluation of how things are going. Change does not occur, of course, just at "move-out time," as

Fairweather terms it; rather, change progresses over time in the fashion of growth or root hairs of a plant. This process defies evaluation by most traditional methods. This may be another instance in which the decision-theoretic approach of Edwards (1965) and Guttentag (1973) would be of use, particularly in selecting specific plans for action.

The foregoing array of suggested actions could well evoke a response of weariness when confronted with what looks like an overwhelming burden, and most of us simply turn it off. But again we would like to emphasize that the list is cafeteria-like. Rarely would a change consultant find it necessary to employ the majority of the actions. Further, weariness is likely if the list is looked on as the result of someone's brainstorming session. Actually, the array represents a condensation of conclusions drawn from the body of literature and experiences on change. To be sure, many are based upon assertions derived out of authors' observations. But in those cases the conclusions will have been sufficiently frequent in their appearance in the literature to warrant.

OBLIGATION

Fight fire with fire, as it were; if true, indicate that a participative change at this time will preclude a coerced one later on.

If necessary, invoke the most common of all methods to stimulate motivation; namely, "normative sanction." The ultimate motivation for participating in change is to fulfill one's commitment to the job.

IDEA

Encourage participation in the selection of the action pattern, the solution, and the information about it. Encourage participants to challenge the information, to simplify it, to think of improvements.

Use available systems of retrieval, specialized journals, and digests.

Seek out expert consultants. If practicable, attend professional meetings and conferences in specific search of the needed information; take part in problem-solving exchange programs as they are developed.

Conduct discussion with key participants in change regarding treatment of the *information*—rendering it, prior to its communication to others, credible, observable, relevant to the *obligation* to change, manifestly superior in payoff to the present way of handling the problem, easily understood, and compatible with the agency's *value* systems.

Conduct a deliberate communication of the information or plan of action among all persons in groups concerned with the proposed change.

VALUES

Obtain consultation to help with objective review of the analysis already made of organizational values and characteristics, and also to help with feasible modifications.

Depending upon the change administrator's influence in the organization, in advance of specific attempts to bring about change, encourage top decision-makers to:

Advocate self-renewal of staff and employees.

Let it be known that experimenting persons have the right to make mistakes.

Create an atmosphere receptive to pilot experiments.

Encourage attendance at workshops, etc.

Arrange for rewards and recognition related to performance.

If there is top-level support for modifying the organization toward being more receptive to change in general, any of several techniques might be employed, usually through the assistance of a consultant:

Direct systemic alterations—bringing power systems (policy making, administration, socialization) into alignment with product systems (direct service and care to patients, community work).

Travistock group therapy—working through deeper interpersonal feelings about organizational social and working relationships.

Balancing the "managerial grid"—bringing about a *team* management system that is neither task-oriented (treating personnel as rented instruments) nor country club-oriented (treating personnel as though all stress were to be avoided).

Temporary systems —conducting a group session such as sensitivity training away from the usual work setting so that the usual barriers to close interpersonal relationships do not prevail; the purpose is to give staff self-understanding about their own roles in the organization.

Emerging needs monitoring—development of a standing group of personnel who carry the responsibility for continually advocating an orientation toward assessment of needs for change and stimulating their consideration.

In order to help adjust the fit of organizational values with a specific prospective change, the following might be employed:

Peer group discussion—participants in the change, without the presence of power figures from the organization, discuss their personal reactions to the change proposal and offer recommendations accordingly. (This approach also will be considered when dealing with *resistances* arising out of a clash between the *values* of the participants and requirements of the *information,* or action pattern; for instance, the values of professional mental health workers about new assignments of paraprofessional mental health workers within the organization.)

Mann systematic use of feedback—trial of the new approach followed by pre-arranged discussion sessions of relevant personnel about their experiences and appraisals of the trial vis-à-vis the organization.

Orientation sessions with benefactors and beneficiaries—early introduction to the planned change, when appropriate to pertinent representatives of the community, board, or other parts of the supra-system and with representatives of the client groups, including patients, their "significant others," and consultees.

Team piloting and specific change—early formation of key participants within the organization who will carry primary responsibility for bringing the change into actuality.

Legitimization of the change—arranging for the manifest endorsement and commitment of respected authorities.

ABILITY

Prepare specific budget for start-up costs and continuing costs.

Arrange inclusion of requests for funds in the organization's next periodic budget proposal.

Propose sources of immediate funds and discuss product-losses that would be involved, and how they might be covered. (If you use resources from A to start B, what happens to cover the losses of A?)

Explore grant mechanisms for start-up costs, using state and regional consultation.

Prepare manual or provide written references for participants if the information or pattern of action to be followed is sufficiently unfamiliar or complex.

Obtain an "action consultant" if available, a person thoroughly familiar with the *information* or action pattern who is also familiar with organizational problems and its employment.

Conduct a formal training program from the use of the *information*—conference, demonstration, study group, anticipatory rehearsal (dry run through the new practices followed by discussion).

Estimate specific facilities required and propose ways of arranging for them.

CIRCUMSTANCES

Review of earlier analysis—through group discussion or consultation, review of organizational characteristics in situations in a community conceivably influencing the proposed change.

Examine *circumstances* out of which the *information* grew—investigation, by visit if possible, of the attributes of the situation where a new action pattern was developed and tested. (Rarely are these adequately described in communications about new service methods.)

Assess the interaction of all factors influencing the change—consideration of how all of the A VICTORY factors might be brought into interaction more conducive to fulfilling the desired change.

TIMING

Review *timing* of *circumstances*—anticipation of changes and events that might influence the process of change.
Coordinate staff readiness with timing of circumstances.

Prepare for mustering of resources and support at move-out time.

RESISTANCES

Appraise resistances deemed to be rational—final consideration of whether the change should be modified or even abandoned.

Decide on advisability of fait accompli approach—bringing about change quickly and without working through resistances if the change is imperative and indeed nonnegotiable; it may be preferable not to evoke expressions of resistances about which nothing can be done.

Employ rational persuasion—intensification and broadening of communication approaches.

Use selective individual counseling—personal discussions with individuals who seem to have unique problems in reaction to the change.

Resolve complex resistances through group dynamics—utilization of some of the same techniques suggested for changing organizational values, such as Tavistock Therapy, T-groups, discussion at retreats, etc.

Use listening as a deliberate approach—allowing persons to express their resistances through the rare experience of being listened to.

Use advisory groups—involvement of representatives of participating factions.

Approach the change implementation slowly—introduction of elements of the change a few at a time, beginning, if possible, with the least disturbing.

Settle on partial change, if necessary and if better than nothing.

YIELD

Provide information on adequacy of the proposed pattern of action as a solution to the problem, by:

Special presentations, especially by a person who has employed the pattern.

Demonstration of the pattern and its yield, if practicable.

Visit to site where pattern has been employed.

Reward participants with timely feedback, attention, and interest.

Provide and *carry out* plan for specifically deserved rewards—pay incentive, new titles, professional opportunities, group recognition.

(4) Follow-through

Under ideal conditions the evaluator/change consultant's "contract," in whatever form of understanding, would retain that person's presence throughout the duration of the change process. In reality, alas, this is seldom so. Outside consultants may be long gone on other pursuits by the time the follow-through phase arrives. Even the inside consultant may find that resources and sanctions for working with the change process wane over time. This is particularly unfortunate because an almost invariable phenomenon of change occurs, namely, regression back to practices it was intended to supplant. A critical function in nurturing change, according to Jenkins (1962) is to ensure that a new condition is stabilized. The resistant forces tend to push almost all adjustments back to the former conditions. It may be more accurate to describe follow-through as a phase that should continue without interruption from the move-out point. Early disappointments are apt to snowball into counterproductive pressures before innovations have a chance to give people the experience of the expected yield.

Evaluation becomes a key element in the follow-through stage. So many things happen to people in organizational life that even if a change has brought about a better state of conditions, awareness of that improvement may not be all that conspicuous. If an evaluation of the attainments of the program proves positive, and if assessment of the unintended side benefits turns out likewise, the dissemination of this information can serve as an important reinforcer to stablize the change.

The primary purpose of evaluation in the follow-through phase, of course, is to signal any further needs for modification of actions. Thus, the feedback cycle is realized. But the task does not end at that point. The essence of growth and renewal, as identified by Gardner (1064), is continual evaluation. Havelock (1970) stresses that the cycle must be repeated for continued organizational improvement and renewal, with an accompanying increment in the organization's capacity. Campbell (1969) says it another way: The first cycle in the administration of systematic change is much like an experiment, with smoother operations a greater payoff likely with subsequent cycles and refinements. At first blush, the prospect of such ongoing cycles brings a picture of staggering resources that must be consumed. But each cycle in practice should require a lesser investment of time and effort, allowing attention to other problems as they are identified by evaluations.

In this chapter we have held that: (1) evaluation provides great hope for ultimate beneficiaries of social programs; (2) to fulfill that hope, effective utilization of evaluation is essential and that the very field of evaluation may be dependent upon evidence of such payoff; (3) the destinies of evaluation results are at least to some extent predictable and the careers of those results can be enhanced; (4) evaluators should consider extending their role to change consultation; (5) there is a vast body of information on change and models of conceptualization on which to base one's professional services; (6) utilization of evaluation may most effectively be achieved through the human approach to organizational change; and (7) the A VICTORY technique may at least represent a schema to consider in trying the evaluator change consultant role.

Finally, we must acknowledge that, if the A VICTORY technique is to be used in an attempt to increase the benefits from evaluation, one will be faced with a greater number of factors that must be addressed than in other approaches to change. But those factors are there whether or not the change consultant has invited them. If we do greet them, we can at least collaborate with them rather than having our evaluation results mastered by them.

Our final thought is about the great changes in history—how they could have been brought off so successfully without a change model to follow! Could it be that what we have described as the human action model, or the A VICTORY technique, is just an ordering of common sense? At the end of the Constitutional Convention, called in 1787 because the innovative solution to the problem of taxation-without-representation had struggled eleven years in adoption, Franklin walked to Washington's dais in Independence Hall where he had been presiding. Franklin sighed, "I didn't know until this day whether that carved sun-on-the-horizon on the back of your chair was rising or setting. Now I know it's rising." "Yes, Ben," said Washington, "it truly was A VICTORY."

REFERENCES

Attkisson, C. Clifford, et al., *A Working Model for Mental Health Program Evaluation.* Prepublication copy, November 1973.

Becker, Marshall H. Factors affecting diffusion of innovations among health professionals. *American Journal of Public Health.* 1970, 60 (2): 294-304.

Beigel. A. Evaluation on a shoestring. In Wm. A. Hargreaves et al. (eds.) *Resource Materials for Community Mental Health Program Evaluation.* San Francisco: NIMH, 1974.

Bennis. W. G. A new role for the behavioral sciences: Effecting organizational change. *Administrative Science Quarterly.* 1963, 8 (2): 125.

Blum, R. H. and J. J. Downing. Staff response to innovation in mental health service. *American Journal of Public Health.* 1964, 54: 1230-1240.

Brown, J. D. *The Human Nature of Organizations.* New York: Amacon, 1973. Pp. 10-38.

Buchanan, G. and J. Whaley. Federal level evaluation. *Evaluation,* 1972, 1 (1).

Campbell, A. and P. E. Converse. *The Human Meaning of Social Change.* New York: Russell Sage Foundation, 1972. P. 9.

Campbell, D. T. Experimentation revisited. *Evaluation,* 1973, 1 (3): 7-13.

———. Reforms as experiments. *American Psychologist,* 1969, 24: 409-429.

Chin, R. The utility of systems models and developmental models for practitioners. In W. G. Bennis, K. D. Benne, and R. Chin (eds.) *The Planning of Change.* 2d ed. New York: Holt, Rienhart & Winston, 1961. Pp. 297-312.

Ciarlo, J. Personal communication. August 1974.

Coheb, J. Factors of resistance to the resources of the behavioral sciences. *Journal of Legal Education,* 1959, 12: 67-70.

Coleman, J. S., E. Katz, and H. Mensel. *Medical Innovation: A Diffusion Study.* New York: Bobbs-Merrill, 1966.

Dahling, R. L. Shannon's information theory: The spread of an idea. In *Studies of Innovation and of Com munication to the Public. Studies in the Utilization of Behavioral Science.* Vol. 2. Stanford, Calif.: Institute for Communication Research. Stanford University, 1962. Pp. 117-140.

Davis, H. Innovation and change. In S. Feldman (ed.) *Administration in Mental Health.* New York: Charles C. Thomas, 1973.

Edwards, W. Tactical note on the relation between scientific and statistical hypotheses. *Psychological Bulletin,* 1965, 63(6): 400-402.

Fairweather, G. Experimental innovation defined. In H. H. Hornstein et al. (eds.) *Social Intervention: A Behavioral Science Approach.* New York: Free Press, 1971.

———. Innovation: A necessary but cosufficient condition for change. *Innovations,* 1973, 1: 25-27.

Fairweather, G. W., D. H. Sanders, and L. G. Tornatzky. *Creating Change in Mental Health Organizations.* New York: Pergamon, 1974.

Gardner, J. W. *Self Renewal: The Individual and the Innovative Society.* New York: Harper & Row, 1964.

Glaser, E. Knowledge transfer and institutional change. *Professional Psychology,* November 1973, Pp. 434-444.

Glaser, E. M. et al. *Utilization of Applicable Research and Demonstration Results.* Final report to Vocational Rehabilitation Administration, U.S. Department of Health, Education, and Welfare, Project RD-1263-G. Washington, D.C., 1966.

Glaser, E. M. and H. L. Ross. *Increasing the Utilization of Applied Research Results.* Final report to the National Institution of Mental Health, Grant no. 5 R12 MH 09250-02. Los Angeles, Calif.: Human Interaction Research Institute, 1971.

Goldin, G. J., K. N. Margolin, and B. A. Stotsky. The utilization of rehabilitation research: Concepts, principles and research. *Northeastern Studies in Vocational Rehabilitation,* no. 6, 1969.

Guttentag, M. Subjectivity and its use in evaluation research. *Evaluation,* 1973, 1 (2): 60-65.

Hage, J. and M. Aiken. *Social Change in Complex Organizations.* New York: Random House, 1970.

Havelock, R.G. *A Guide to Innovation in Education.* Ann Arbor: Center for Research on the Utilization of Scientific Knowledge, Institute for Social Research, University of Michigan, 1970.

———. *Planning for Innovation Through Dissemination and Utilization of Knowledge.* Ann Arbor: Center for Research on Utilization of Scientific Knowledge, Institute for Social Research, University of Michigan, 1969. Final report, Contract No. OEC-3-7-070038-2143, Office of Education, U.S. Department of Health, Education and Welfare.

Havelock, R. and M. Lingwood. *R & D Utilization and Functions: An Analytical Computation of Four Systems.* Ann Arbor: Institute for Social Research, University of Michigan, 1973.

Havelock, R. and E. Markowitz. *A National Problem-Solving System: Highway Safety Research and Decision-Makers.* Ann Arbor: University of Michigan, 1971.

Howard, E. How to be serious about innovating. *Nation's Schools,* April 1967, 79: 89-90, 130.

Jenkins, D. H. Force field analysis applied to a school situation. In W. G. Bennus, K. D. Benne, and R. Chin (eds.) *The Planning of Change: Readings in the Applied Behavioral Sciences.* New York: Holt, Rinehart & Winston, 1962. Pp. 238-244.

Katz, E. The social itinerary of technical change: Two studies on the diffusion of innovation. *Human Organization,* 1961, 20: 70-82.

Kennedy, R. F. *Thirteen Days.* New York: Norton, 1969.

Klein, H. D. *The Missouri Story, a Chronicle of Research Utilization and Program Planning.* Paper presented at the National Conference of Social Welfare, May 1968.

Leavitt, H. J. Applied organizational change in industry: Structural, technological and humanistic approaches. In J. G. March (ed.) *Handbook of Organizations.* Chicago: McNally, 1965.

Levine, R. A. and A. P. Williams Jr. *Making Evaluation Effective: A Guide.* Santa Monica, Calif.: Rand Corporation, 1971.

Lippitt, R. *Personal Communication.* Conference on change processes, Center for Research on the Utilization of Scientific Knowledge, 1971.

――― and R. Havelock. Needed research on research utilization. In *Research implications for educational diffusion.* East Lansing: Dept. of Education, Michigan State University, 1968.

Lynn, L. E., Jr. Notes from HEW. *Evaluation,* 1972, 1 (1): Pp. 24-28.

McClelland, W. A. The process of effecting change. Presidential address to the Division of Military Psychology, American Psychological Association, San Francisco, September 1968.

McCullough, P. *Training for evaluators—overview.* Supplemental material presented to the NIMH-sponsored conference on program evaluation in April 1974, Washington, D.C.

McGregor, D. *The Human Side of Enterprise.* New York: McGraw-Hill, 1960.

Mackie, R. R. and P. R. Christensen. *Translation and Application of Psychological Research.* Technical Report 716-1. Goleta, Calif.: Santa Barbara Research Park, Human Factors Research, Inc., 1967.

Maguire, L. M. *Observations and Analysis of the Literature on Change.* Philadelphia: Research for Better Schools, Inc., June 1970.

Mann, F. C. and F. W. Neff. *Managing Major Change in Organizations.* Ann Arbor, Mich.: Foundation for Research on Human Behavior, 1961.

Marrow, A. J. (ed.) *The Failure of Success.* New York: Amacon, 1972.

Menzel. H. A. Scientific communication: Five themes from social science research. *American Psychologist,* 1966, 21: 999-1004.

Morgan, J. S. *Managing Change.* New York: McGraw-Hill, 1972.

Mushkin, S. Evaluations: Use with caution. *Evaluation,* 1973, 1 (2): 31-35.

National Science Foundation. *Federal Technology Transfer.* Washington, D.C. 1973.

National Science Foundation. Knowledge into action: Improving the nation's use of the social sciences. Report of the Special Commission on the Social Sciences of the National Science Board. Report N S13 69-3. Washington, D.C.: U.S. Government Printing Office, 1969.

Ochberg, F. Personal communication. November 1973.

Richardson, E. R. Conversational contact. *Evaluation,* 1972, 1 (1).

Riecker, P. Prepublication document. 1974.

Roberts, A. O. H. and J. K. Larsen. *Effective Use of Mental Health Research Information.* Palo Alto, Calif.: American Institutes for Research, January 1971. Final report for National Institute of Mental Health, Grant no. 1 RO1 MH 15445.

Rogers, E. M. *Diffusion of Innovations.* New York: Free Press, 1962.

――― and F. F. Shoemaker. *Communication of Innovations: A Cross-cultural Approach.* New York: Free Press, 1971.

Sashkin, M., W. C. Morris, and L. Horst. A comparison of social and organizational change models. *Psychological Review,* 1973. 50 (6).

Schmuck, R. Social psychological factors in knowledge utilization. Pp. 143-173 in T. L. Eidell and J. M. Kitchel (eds.) *Knowledge Production and Utilization in Educational Administration.* Eugene: Center for the Advance Study of Educational Administration, University of Oregon, 1968.

Scrivens, M. Personal communication. August 1974.

Shepard, H. A. Changing interpersonal and interagency relationships in organizations. In J. C. March (ed.) *Handbook of Organizations.* Chicago: McNally, 1965.

Suchman, E. A. *Evaluation Research.* New York: Russell Sage Foundation, 1962. P. 162.

Tiffany, Donald W. and M. Phyllis. A source of problems between social science knowledge and practice. *Journal of Human Publications,* 1971, 19 (2).

Watson, G. and E. M. Glaser. What we have learned about planning for change. *Management Review,* 1965, 54 (11): 43-46.

Weiss, C. *Evaluation Research.* Englewood Cliffs. N.J.: Prentice-Hall, 1972.

―――. Between the cup and the lip. *Evaluation,* 1973, 1 (2). (a)

―――. Where politics and evaluation research meet. *Evaluation,* 1973, 1 (3): 37-45. (b)

Windle, C. and E. M. Volkman. *A Working Model for Mental Health Program Evaluation.* Prepublication copy, November, 1973.

REFERENCE UPDATE

Selected by Howard R. Davis and Susan E. Salasin

Alkin, M. C., R. Daillak, and P. White. *Using evaluations: Does evaluation make a difference?* Beverly Hills, CA: Sage, 1980.

Baggaley, A. R. Multivariate analysis: An introduction for consumers of behavioral research. *Evaluation Review*, 1981, 5 (1): 123-131.

Brown, R. D., L. A. Braskamp, and D. L. Newman. Evaluator credibility as a function of report style: Do jargon and data make a difference? *Evaluation Quarterly*, 1978, 2 (2): 331-342.

Ciarlo, J. A. (ed.) *Utilizing evaluation; Concepts and measurement techniques.* Beverly Hills, CA: Sage, 1981.

Datta, L. The impact of the Westinghouse/Ohio eavaluation of Project Head Start: An examination of the immediate and long-term effects and how they came about. In C. C. Abt (ed.) *The evaluation of social programs.* Beverly Hills, CA: Sage, 1976.

Denisto, O. L. Whether evaluation—Whether utilization. *Evaluation and Program Planning*, 1980, 3 (2): 91-94.

Guba, E. and Y. S. Lincoln. *Effective evaluation.* San Francisco: Jossey-Bass, 1981.

Leviton, L. S. and E. F. X. Hughes. Research on the utilization of evaluations: A review and synthesis. *Evaluation Review*, 1981, 5 (4): 525-548.

Patton, M. Q. *Utilization-focused evaluation.* Beverly Hills, CA: Sage, 1978.

Rice, R. F. Uses of social science information by federal bureaucrats: Knowledge for action versus knowledge for understanding. In C. H. Weiss (ed.) *Using social research in public policy making.* Lexington, MA: D. C. Heath, 1977.

Rich, R. F. The use of science in policy making: A comparative prospective on science policy. In D. Ashford (ed.) *Comparing public policies.* Beverly Hills, CA: Sage, 1978.

Stevens, W. F. and L. G. Tornatzky. The dissemination of evaluation: An experiment. *Evaluation Review*, 1980, 4 (3): 339-354.

Thompson, P. A., R. D. Brown, and J. Furgason. Jargon and data do make a difference: The impact of report styles on lay and professional evaluation audiences. *Evaluation Review*, 5 (1): 269-279.

Weeks, E. C. *Factors affecting the utilization of evaluation findigs in administrative decision-making.* Unpublished doctoral dissertation, University of California, Irvine, 1979. (a)

Weeks, E. C. Factors affecting the utilization of evaluation at the local level: An empirical test. In H. C. Schulberg and J. M. Jerrell (eds.) *The evaluator and management.* Beverly Hills, CA: Sage, 1979. (b)

Weiss, C. H. The challenge of social research to decision making. In C. H. Weiss (ed.) *Using social research in public policy making.* Lexington, MA: D. C. Heath, 1977.

Weiss, C. H. Knowledge creep and decision accretion. *Knowledge: Creation, Diffusion, Utilization*, 1980, 1 (3): 381-404.

AUTHOR INDEX

SUBJECT INDEX

A VICTORY, 410-423; see also change
action, analytic and enumerative, 95
administrators: experimental, definition of, 114;
trapped, in social reform experimentation,
131-133; trapped, defined, 111
advocacy, types of models, 393-394
alcohol safety action programs, 144
alcoholics, treatment of, 248
alternatives, cost of assessing, 354-366
analysis: change by human action model, 398-
406; cost-effectiveness in e.r., 345-374;
methods of, 255-256; statistical, 201; of variance, in multiple regression, 302-305
analysts, military, and cost-effectiveness, 349
analytic action, as strategy in e.r., 95
analytic studies: contrasted with enumerative
studies, 95-96; examples of, 102-104; possible
mistakes in, 97-98
analytical survey, 189
artificial conditions, 11
assessment, subjective, 238-240

Bayesian techniques, 148
benefit-to-cost ratio, 164-167
British breathalyser crackdown, 121-122
bureaucratic model of society: client-center-
edness of, 72; place of equality and justice in,
72

Career Education project, 177
catchment area, 209, 210, 213-215, 217, 218-219,
223-224; community resources, 215; description of, 218; environment and mortality,
epidemiology, ethnicity, family structure,
physical environment, poverty, social class,
215; sociocultural factors and facility use,
215, 223
causal analysis, schistosomiasis, 193-195
cause or causality, 200
change: A VICTORY technique, 410-423; as
basis for construction of measures, 240-242;
change by Human Action model, 398-406;
assessment and, 413-418; circumstances and
timing in, 406-407; follow-through and, 422-
423; goal definition and, 418-420; models of
planned, 395; necessary resources for, 405;

residual scores, 244; resistance to, 407-409;
scores, 243-247; study of in e.r., 232-267;
timing as a factor, 406-407
coding: contrast, 305; dummy variable, 302-304
common-factor covariance, 324
communication, scientific as a system, 394-395
community health centers, 384
community medicine and mental health, 213-214
community mental health evaluation centers,
388
components, temporal, 248
concept of environment, source of disease, 191
concept of immunity, host, 192-193
concept, source, 191
concepts, organizing principles, 190
Conference on Evaluation in Alcohol, Drug
Abuse and Mental Health Programs of April
1974, 286
Congress; "social indicators" and "data" banks,
107
Connecticut Crackdown, 111-117
control group experiments, randomized, as in
social control programs, 130-131
control series design, in experimental social
reform, 117-121
controlled experiments, impact of experimenter's beliefs and values on, 66-67
cost measurement and uncertainty, 361-362
cost-benefit analysis: comparison with cost-
utility and cost-effectiveness analysis, 347 -
351
cost effectiveness: maximum use of resources,
345; analysis in e.r., 345-374; and public
policy choices, 345-347; military analysts'
development, 349; example of, 350-354; "present value" method, 367; review of studies,
372-373; time pattern of results, 367-368; use
of evaluation of experiments and quasi-
experiments, 349
cost-utility: compared to cost-benefit and cost-
effectiveness analysis, 347-350; defined, 350
cost: appropriateness, 362-366; definition, 354;
measurement of, 355-360
COVARAN, 265-267
covariance, 283
criteria, useful in selecting programs for evaluation, 38-39

433

ABOUT THE EDITORS

ELMER L. STRUENING is Director of the Epidemiology of Mental Disorders Research Department, Psychiatric Institute, New York State Office of Mental Health, and Associate Professor in the Division of Epidemiology, School of Public Health, Columbia University. He serves on the faculty of the Psychiatric Epidemiology Training Program and as Director of the Community Support System Evaluation Research Program at Psychiatric Institute.

MARILYNN B. BREWER is Professor of Psychology and Director of the Institute for Social Science Research at the University of California, Los Angeles. She received her Ph.D. from Northwestern University in social psychology and has been a member of the faculty of Loyola University of Chicago and University of California, Santa Barbara. She is coauthor of *Principles of Research in Social Psychology* and has authored numerous books and articles in the areas of research methodology, social cognition, and intergroup relations. She has been elected president of the Society for the Psychological Study of Social Issues and of the Western Psychological Association.

ABOUT THE AUTHORS

DONALD T. CAMPBELL is University Professor of Social Relations and Psychology at Lehigh University (Bethlehem, Pennsylvania). He is best known for his work with Donald W. Fiske on the multitrait-multimethod matrix approach to test validity, and with Julian C. Stanley and Thomas D. Cook on quasi-experimental design. He is Past President of the American Psychological Association, and a member of the National Academy of Sciences. He has received Distinguished Scientific Contribution Awards from the American Psychological Association and the American Educational Research Association, the Kurt Lewin Award of the Society for the Psychological Study of Social Issues, and the first Myrdal Prize in Science of the Evaluation Research Society.

JACOB COHEN is Professor of Psychology and Coordinator of the Quantitative Psychology Program of New York University's Graduate Psychology Department. He previously worked extensively with the Veterans Administration, his research interests including practice and research in clinical psychology and later quantitative research methodology in the behavioral sciences. In addition to many articles and chapters in books, he has authored an introductory statistics text, and a handbook entitled *Statistical Power Analysis for the Behavioral Sciences* (1977, Academic Press). In collaboration with Patricia Cohen, he is coauthor of *Multiple Regression/Correlational Analysis for the Behavioral Sciences,* 2nd ed. (1983, Lawrence Erlbaum Associates).

HOWARD R. DAVIS is Chief of the Mental Health Services Development Branch of the National Institute of Mental Health. Among his primary professional interests is the promotion of utilization of scientific knowledge in bringing about organizational change, a topic about which he has written extensively. He holds B.A., MSW, and Ph.D. degrees, and he taught, practiced, and consulted in psychology before joining the staff of NIMH in 1963.

W. EDWARDS DEMING is a consultant in statistical studies. He is the author of several books on statistical methods and has written over 150 articles on the subject. He worked in Japan for more than a decade, beginning in 1950, and contributed to the revolution in the quality of most Japanese-manufactured products, causing the Cabinet of Japan to award to him in 1960 the Emperor's Medal of the Sacred Treasure. Japanese manufacturers have created the annual Deming Prize in his honor. He has lectured in many universities all over the world, and currently holds the position of Professor of Statistics at New York University.

HERBERT W. EBER is currently President of the Psychological Resources Associates, of Atlanta, Georgia. He received his Ph.D. from the University of North Carolina with a major in clinical psychology. He is the author of several personality tests, "A Personality Test for Persons of Limited Reading Skills," and "IPAT Tests on Tape." He has also authored a textbook, *Samples of Scientific Psychology.* He is coauthor, with Raymond Cattell, of the 1963 revisions of the *16 Personality Factor Questionnaire.* His major areas of research concern personality testing and methodology.

WARD EDWARDS is Director of the Social Science Research Institute, Professor of Psychology, and Professor of Industrial and Systems Engineering at the University of Southern California. He was previously associate director of the Highway Safety Research Institute and head of the Engineering Psychology Laboratory at the University of Michigan. He received his Ph.D. from Harvard University. He is a consultant to numerous American organizations, both governmental and private. He has published widely in professional journals, including the *Journal of Experimental Psychology, American Journal of Psychology,* and *Psychological Review.* His recent research has focused on two areas: validation and simplification of multiattribute utility measurement, and use of utility measurement as a tool to understand and help to deal with social opposition to new and potentially risky technologies.

ALBERT ERLEBACHER received his Ph.D. in psychology at the University of Wisconsin, and now teaches at Northwestern University in the Department of Psychology, His areas of interest are statistics and experimental design.

LEE GUREL is Chief of Research in Mental Health and Behavioral Sciences at the Veterans Administration Medical Center, Washington, D.C., and was formerly Director of the Office of Member Services and Manpower of the American Psychiatric Association. He received his Ph.D. in 1952 from Purdue University and is author or coauthor of over 100 publications in a wide range of subject areas. He is a past president of the Division of Psychologists in Public Service of the American Psychological Association and a past president of the District of Columbia Psychological Association.

MARCIA GUTTENTAG was, at the time of publication of the *Handbook of Evaluation Research* (Vols. 1 and 2), President of the Division of Personality and Social Psychology of the American Psychological Association. She was a developmental social psychologist at the Harvard University Graduate School of Education, and had also served as Professor of Psychology at the Graduate Center, CUNY, and Director of the Harlem Research Center. She also served as evaluation consultant to UNESCO, the Office of Child Development, the National Institute of Mental Health, and other federal agencies. She was chairwoman of the Task Force on the Evaluation of Training in Community Mental Health, for the National Institute of Mental Health, and coauthor of the *Evaluation of Training* and many chapters and articles on evaluation.

HENRY M. LEVIN is Professor in the School of Education and Department of Economics and the Director of the Institute for Research on Educational Finance and Governance at Stanford University. He is a former Fellow at the Center for Advanced Study in the Behavioral Sciences. Prior to his arrival at Stanford in 1968, he was a Research Associate in the Economic Studies Division of the Brookings Institution. He has also served on the faculties of Rutgers and New York Universities. He has been consultant to many state and federal agencies on issues in public finance, the economics of education, and cost-effectiveness analysis, and he is currently a consultant to the World Bank. He is the author of over 100 scholarly articles and the author or coauthor of 8 books. He was the President of the Evaluation Research Society in 1982.

JUM C. NUNNALLY was, at the time of publication of the *Handbook of Evaluation Research* (Vols. 1 and 2), Professor of Psychology at Vanderbilt University. He received his Ph.D. at the University of Chicago, after which he worked with the American Institute for Research, performing studies of personality characteristics and abilities relating to successful performance of naval officers. He also served on the faculty of the University of Illinois at the Institute of Communications Research and in the Department of Psychology, where his work involved studies of public attitudes and psychometric theory.

SUSAN E. SALASIN is Chief of the Research Diffusion and Utilization Section, Mental Health Services Development Branch of the National Institute of Mental Health. Among her professional responsibilities, she also serves as Editorial Director for *Evaluation,* an experimental publication designed to further the adoption of program evaluation in human services organizations. Her primary professional interest is in program evaluation and knowledge utilization as a means of stimulating, facilitating, and guiding organizational change.

GIDEON SJOBERG is Professor of Sociology at the University of Texas at Austin. He is the author of *The Preindustrial City* (1960) and coauthor (with Roger Nett) of *A Methodology for Social Research.* In addition, he has written numerous articles and chapters in books on a wide variety of topics. He is currently completing a book (with Ted P. Vaughan) on *A Sociology of Morals* and is also studying the impact of bureaucracy on modern social life.

KURT SNAPPER received his Ph.D. in psychology from the University of Michigan, where his major field of research was psychological decision theory. He has authored several papers on decision-theoretic approaches to evaluation research and social indicators. Currently he is Senior Research Scientist at the Social Research Group, George Washington University.

M. SUSSER is Gertrude H. Sergievsky Professor of Epidemiology and Director of the Sergievsky Center at Columbia University. He is the author of *Causal Thinking in the Health Sciences: Concepts and Strategies in Epidemiology* (1973, Oxford University Press) and *Community Psychiatry: Epidemiologic and Social Themes* (1968, Random House). He is coauthor (with Z. Stein, G. Saenger, and F. Marolla) of *Famine and Human Development: Studies of the Dutch Hunger Winter 1944/5* (1975, Oxford University Press); (with D. Rush and Z. Stein) of *Diet in Pregnancy: A Randomized Controlled Trial of Nutritional Supplementation* (1980, Alan Liss); and (with W. Watson) of *Sociology in Medicine* (1971, 1962, Oxford University Press). He is author or editor of a series of reports under the blanket title of *Reports on the Mental Health Services in the City of Salford*

(England), published from 1959 to 1965. He has authored or coauthored many scholarly and professional articles and monographs, both in the United States and abroad.

CAROL H. WEISS is Senior Lecturer and Senior Research Associate at the Harvard University Graduate School of Education. She is the author of *Social Science Research and Decision-Making* (Columbia University Press, 1980), *Evaluation Research: Methods of Assessing Program Effectiveness* (Prentice-Hall, 1972), and other books on evaluation research and the utilization of research in policymaking. She has published many articles in such journals as *Evaluation Review, Policy Analysis, New Directions in Program Evaluation, Journal of Higher Education, American Sociological Review,* and *Public Administration Review.* She serves on the editorial boards of *Society, American Behavioral Scientist, Policy Studies Journal,* and *Knowledge: Creation, Diffusion, Utilization,* among others. The winner of the Evaluation Research Society's Myrdal Award for Science in 1980, she is President of the Policy Studies Organization (1983-1984) and was the first Congressional Fellow of the American Sociological Association (1983).

92